SARASIN & PARTNERS

TOP 3000 CHARITIES 2016

We are delighted to be sponsoring the 2016 edition of the Top 3000 Charities Guide again, which is an essential reference tool for trustees and executives alike.

2015 provided longer-term investors with a bumpy ride. However, the end result for a typical well-diversified, multi asset charity portfolio is likely to have been about +3.5% after costs. Given that inflation has been close to zero during 2015, this effectively means a 'real' return, give or take, of 3.5%.

When we look back a little further over the past five years, long-term portfolios should have produced returns of a little less than 6.5% per annum net of costs. With inflation of c.2%, this means 'real' expendable returns of about 4% per annum.

The 1 and the 5 year number are very much in keeping with the historic results achieved by UK charities and in-line with what we have suggested was likely over the period ahead.

Looking ahead, when combined with very low levels of current and projected inflation, extremely high debt levels and rather worrying demographic trends now would seem to be an opportune moment to conduct a reappraisal of how much economic growth we might expect in the future. Our initial findings suggest returns will be lower, as will inflation, resulting in similar sustainable spending levels.

However, we suspect there are three specific themes investors will need to prepare for in 2016: first, income management against a backdrop of dividend cuts, second geopolitics against a backdrop of US Presidential elections and waning US hegemony and third, the management of sterling exposure against the backdrop of a possible Brexit.

On balance we feel that 2016 is likely to be another year of steady if rather dull economic progress and small positive investment returns. However, as with 2015, we would be surprised if investment markets don't get 'spooked' by at least one or a combination of the events mentioned above. We are sure that the Top 3,000 Charities Guide will offer readers guidance and advice as to how to navigate these choppy waters.

Richard Maitland Partner, Head of Charities

Charity Financials
Wilmington Insight

Charity Financials
6-14 Underwood Street
London
N1 7JQ
Tel: 020 7566 8201
Fax: 020 7608 1163
www.charityfinancials.com
@Charityfins

EDITOR
Daniel Holland

DATA DEVELOPMENT MANAGER
Mark Pincher

ADVERTISING SALES MANAGER
Marcus Levi (020 7549 2548)

SENIOR SALES EXECUTIVE
Shane Ryan (020 7549 2588)

MARKETING MANAGER
Rachael Hampton

CUSTOMER SERVICES
Emily Martin

PUBLISHING SERVICES
Jacqueline Hobbs

INFORMATION TECHNOLOGY
Stephen Grainge

PRODUCTION MANAGER
Susan Sixtensson

PUBLISHER
Tanya Noronha

Contents

Charity Focus

Contents

Tailoring bespoke portfolios for over 350 charities*.

Our skill and expertise in managing charities'
investments is renowned and could be why we are one
of the largest fund managers in the sector.

Our committment to charity investing is second to none.
We are constantly investing in research and trustee
training to further improve our offering. To find out
more call John Handford on the number below.

+44 (0)20 7038 7000.
www.sarasinandpartners.com

SARASIN
& PARTNERS

Committed to charity investment.

SARASIN
& PARTNERS

A 'signal' from Paris

And why shareholders must be active in their response to climate change

Natasha Landell-Mills, Head of Stewardship, Sarasin & Partners LLP

"Do we have a signal? …We have a horn, we have a horn from a very large ship that has already changed the course of its direction, and if we can't see this we are either deaf to the horn, or blind to the ship, … but we do have a major transition here already in place."
Christiana Figueres, Executive Secretary, United Nations Framework Convention on Climate Change, 27th October 2015

Political negotiations dealing with climate change have typically been viewed as 'noise' by financial markets: repeated promises that will have minimal impact to the more powerful forces driving demand for fossil fuels ever upward. This has been a broadly sensible investment strategy, until now.

The conclusion of the UN-sponsored meeting on climate change in Paris in December represents a watershed in the long-running effort by climate scientists to get politicians to act for the long-term benefit of the planet.

While the broad outlines of the deal announced in Paris could have been foreseen from the preparatory talks, it still reflects a new determination amongst global leaders to confront climate change. Paris has shifted the debate from whether the world should act to contain damaging climate change, to how fast action should be taken, and who should bear the costs.

In brief, the Paris deal is a clear signal for the transformation of our energy sector.

What did world leaders agree?
There are three particularly significant components of the deal agreed in Paris.

First, a unified statement from almost 200 countries affirming that they are committed not just to containing global warming to 2°C, but setting an even tougher aspirational target of 1.5°C.

Second, the first agreement where developing countries – which include

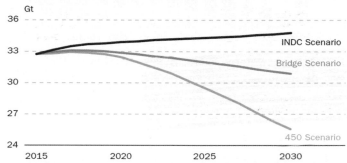

Global energy-related CO2 emissions by IEA scenario

Source: IEA, 2015, "World Energy Outlook special report: Energy and Climate Change"

Note: 450 Scenario is the IEA's scenario associated with achieving a 2°C target; the Bridge scenario includes short-term measures to keep the 2°C target alive, INDC scenario is the projected emissions given national level commitments.

some of the largest emitters like China and India – signed up to action to contain emissions. This ensured that the US (the world's second largest emitter after China) remained at the table.

Thirdly, because the commitments made by individual countries fall short of the 2°C goal (see chart above), the agreement included a regular five-yearly review to create space for countries to ratchet up their commitments so that the political targets may be met.

A roadmap for decarbonisation
A review of statements from fossil fuel companies (which stand to lose out most from decarbonisation) following Paris, might leave one thinking nothing has changed. But these sentiments are underpinned by a hope for continued political inertia; the fact is that governments are resolved to act.

There is already evidence of a transformation well underway. For the first time, power consumption in the UK and US seems to have become disconnected from GDP growth (power consumption has not risen as GDP has recovered). And the substitution away

from fossil fuels in the power and transport sectors is continuing to gather steam. In 2014, for instance, about 45% of the world's new power capacity came from renewables.

Taken together, these shifts have contributed to the IEA's finding that, for the first time on record, energy-related CO2 emissions did not rise in 2014, despite global economic growth.

The transformation of our energy system will have to accelerate if we are to meet the 2°C target. Currently, about 80% of global energy consumption comes from fossil fuels.

This will need to fall to zero in the second half of this century (unless carbon capture technologies can be rolled out on a large scale). The largest reductions in emissions will have to come from the power and transport sectors, which account for approximately 40% and 25% of emissions respectively.

Consider the power sector. According to the International Energy Agency (IEA), renewables are expected to account for over a quarter of power generation by

Global renewables-based power capacity additions by type and share of total capacity additions

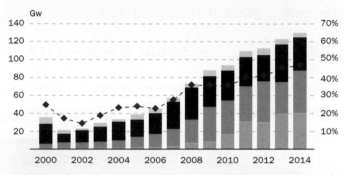

■ Other renewables ■ Hydro ■ Wind ■ Solar PV
◆ Share of total additions (right axis)

Source: IEA, 2015, "World Energy Outlook special report: Energy and Climate Change"

2020. In terms of growth, renewables will account for about two-thirds of net addition to power capacity over the next 5 years, and wind and solar power alone will account for nearly half the global power capacity increase.

Turning to transport – the largest consumer of oil – the IEA sets out how decarbonisation could be achieved. They estimate that over 50% of light duty vehicle sales by 2050 will need to be electric or plug-in hybrid electric vehicles (EVs and PHEVs), which are in turn drawing power from cleaner forms of energy.

Denial cannot be a long-term strategy for fossil fuel companies

The IEA projections do not sit well with coal, oil and gas majors' forecasts. There is minimal commentary in listed fossil fuel extraction companies' annual reports about how they rationalise the disconnect between their strategic ambitions for growth and the global commitments to phase out fossil fuel use. Their claim that political promises are unlikely to be met is no longer a convincing risk management strategy, and leaves companies (and their shareholders) poorly prepared for the future.

This failure of companies to assess and communicate their climate risks to shareholders has attracted the attention of securities regulators. The New York Attorney General announced in November that he was investigating the

largest listed US coal producer Peabody Energy and the oil and gas major ExxonMobil for their failure to disclose their climate risks properly. Peabody settled within days.

The problem for shareholders

The disconnect between companies' strategies and political commitments to control climate change poses problems for shareholders for two reasons.

On the one hand, if the oil and gas companies are right and their strategic plans are achieved then this could mean the world has failed to contain climate change, thereby imposing an unknowable, but potentially devastatingly high, human cost.

On the other hand, if the oil and gas companies are wrong about their long-term forecasts, then shareholders' capital is likely being misallocated. Further investment in the development of reserves that may never be extracted due to falling demand could result in major asset impairments – or capital destruction – down the road. This is the problem of 'stranded assets'. The fact that impairments happen in the future only kicks the can down the road, and permits the wrong decisions to be made today. In the end, shareholders will bear the pain.

Take, for instance, the Royal Dutch Shell takeover offer for BG Group, which is predicated on a $70/bbl oil price (later reduced to 'mid-60s') to break even. It

is far from clear that oil (or gas) prices will revert to the long-term average, as Shell's Board argues. If political momentum accelerates action to reduce consumption of fossil fuels, long-term oil and gas demand and prices will likely fall below their expectations.

Shell's shareholders must hope the Board is applying tough stress tests for scenarios that take account of the deal reached in Paris, rather than risking massive destruction of shareholder capital.

This is the moment for shareholders to be active

For all fossil fuel dependent companies, shareholders would benefit from Boards that proactively assess the long-term risks facing the business from climate change, and set out how these risks are to be managed.

The large fossil fuel companies have an important role to play in ensuring a smooth transition to a low-carbon future. Yet, history tells us that companies faced with disruptive threats too often look the other way. Take railroad companies faced with the rise of the automobile; or Kodak faced with digital photography; or established taxi companies faced with Uber.

Shareholders, meanwhile, may be better positioned to see threats, and have an interest in encouraging change. They also have powerful tools to get across their views, from regular engagements, to voting directors off boards, to proposing shareholder resolutions, and ultimately to selling the shares.

But the existence of levers to pressure Boards to act does not necessarily mean shareholders (and the asset managers to whom this power is often delegated) will use them. We have seen how accountability at several of the largest banks broke down during the financial crisis, and the devastating impacts this had for shareholders and society.

It is vital that when it comes to climate risks we do not make the same mistakes. Shareholders have an important responsibility to hold executives and

Boards to account. They should take their signal from Paris.

Natasha Landell-Mills, Head of Stewardship, Sarasin & Partners LLP

Crowe Clark Whitehill™

Charities: reporting on Solvency and Liquidity Risks

Naziar Hashemi, not for profit partner, Crowe Clark Whitehill LLP

Richard Bowen, not for profit director, Crowe Clark Whitehill LLP

In the uncertain economic conditions of the past few years there has necessarily been a greater emphasis across the charity sector on financial monitoring and, in particular, on ensuring that the going concern assumption in the preparation of period end accounts continues to be valid. This has perhaps been heightened by recent high profile cases of charities with financial problems such as Kids Company.

In 2012 the Sharman Inquiry, which was established by the Financial Reporting Council (FRC), published a report on Going Concern and Liquidity Risks. In response to this report, in September 2014, the FRC updated the UK Corporate Governance Code.

In October 2015 the FRC issued for consultation draft guidance on the Going Concern Basis of Accounting and Reporting on Solvency and Liquidity Risks for companies that do not apply the UK Corporate Governance Code. Whilst this guidance refers to "directors" and "companies", the report makes it clear that it is designed to relate to all other entities preparing accounts under the going concern basis and it will therefore be applicable to charities and charity trustees. Once published in its final form, the guidance will replace the current guidance which was issued in 2009.

Solvency and Liquidity Risk guidance

The draft guidance defines Solvency Risk as "the risk that a company will be unable to meet its liabilities in full" and Liquidity Risk as "the risk that a company will be unable to meet its liabilities as they fall due". Although compliance with the new guidance is not proposed to be mandatory, it is anticipated that it will become best practice for all entities other than those that are small. Trustees of larger charities will therefore be expected to follow the guidance.

"Consideration of funding streams, the timing of cash flows and the risk of extensive pre-financing needs to be carefully monitored"

The tenor of the guidance is to encourage directors to think broadly about risk and uncertainties including a focus on solvency and liquidity. It also aims to improve reporting on the going concern basis of accounting by linking this reporting with the material uncertainties and principal risks. Importantly the guidance encourages directors to take a broader longer term view and go beyond the specific requirements in accounting standards.

Reporting considerations for Charities

The draft guidance links well with SORP 2015 which requires charities' trustees in their annual report to disclose uncertainties about the charity's ability to continue as a going concern and explain the nature of these uncertainties. SORP 2015 also requires the trustees to disclose the principal risks and uncertainties facing the charity and an explanation of how the charity manages these including a brief explanation about those factors that support the conclusion that the charity is a going concern. Furthermore, where there are no material uncertainties about the charity's ability to continue, this should be stated. The draft guidance for the first time explicitly states that "Directors should consider threats to solvency and liquidity as part of their assessment of risks and uncertainties faced by the company".

The information on risks and uncertainties will also need to link in with the required disclosures on the amount of the charity's reserves and why they are held or, if no reserves are held, the reasons for this. There is additionally the requirement to compare the amount of reserves held with the charity's reserves policy and explain, where relevant, what steps the trustees are taking to bring the amount of reserves the charity holds into line with the level of reserves identified by the trustees as being appropriate.

Whilst the draft guidance notes that the period of assessment will ultimately be a matter of judgement for the directors and will depend on the facts and circumstances of the company, it goes on to state that *"except in rare circumstances it should be significantly longer than 12 months from the approval of the financial statements"*.

It is perhaps worth noting that a recent report reviewing some major UK companies' reporting found that, in tackling the new Corporate Code provisions on risk, internal control and viability, the majority of UK companies were for the long term viability statement considering a three year look out period.

Risk factors to consider

The draft guidance sets out some of the factors which directors should consider as part of their assessment process but also explains that it is the directors that need to determine the relevance of these factors considering the size, complexity and the particular circumstances of the organisation, its industry and the general economic conditions. The factors suggested are:

- Forecasts and budgets
- Timing of cash flows
- Sensitivity analysis
- Products, services and markets
- Financial and operational risk management
- Borrowing facilities
- Contingent liabilities
- Subsidiary companies

In addition there may be charity-specific issues to consider including ensuring that there are no breaches of trust with respect to any restricted income or endowed funds and that the charity is able to meet its obligations in relation to these funds. Trustees may be held liable for a breach of trust if they apply restricted funds for purposes outside of the relevant restriction.

The Charity Commission in their guidance 'Managing financial difficulties & insolvency in charities' (CC12) explain:

"It is important for planning purposes that the trustees are aware of the ways in which their charity's assets and resources can be used. Some funds can be used for all of a charity's purposes and some have restrictions on use placed on them by their donors.

An understanding of the nature of the separate funds of a charity is crucial to the understanding of its financial position. Such considerations must be taken into account when analysing and assessing the solvency of a charity.

It is a breach of trust to use endowment or restricted funds for purposes other than those for which they were given by the donor."

Many charities rely on unpredictable income streams such as donations or legacies much of which is under pressure. Increasingly, grants and other funding are being based on payment related to results with cash being received after expenditure has been incurred by the charity. This can put pressure on the charity's available liquid resources and increase the

liquidity risks. The variability in available funding may also lead to charities having to dip into their unrestricted funds to maintain their current provision of services or to invest in future income generation.

"A good report will have a clear thread of reporting between the charity's objectives and activities, achievements and performance and its plans for future periods"

There have been of late some high profile cases of charities going into liquidation. For example, in their report on its operational compliance case into BeatBullying, the regulator says the charity, which went into liquidation, had no reserves and was "quickly affected by the cancellation of anticipated funding". More recently the Charity Commission has started a statutory inquiry into Kids Company. At Kids Company, free reserves were very low which coupled with the fundamental risks arising from its demand led business model led to its collapse at the first hint of reputational trouble.

There is no one size fits all yardstick for charity reserves, but to set an effective reserves policy trustees must link reserves with the risk management and forecasting process and consider the charity's operating realities.

There is much that charities can do to avoid a solvency or liquidity crisis. As with most businesses the key focus should be on careful cash management. Good management information is vital and it is important to reassess how a charity identifies what is key to its financial management and records and reports on what matters. Consideration of funding streams, the timing of cash flows and the risk of extensive pre-financing needs to be carefully monitored. Additionally there should be regular reviews of the overall risks facing the charity as well

as a regular review of its reserves and reserves policy.

Trustee reporting
A good Trustees' Report provides a clear linking of the aims, objectives, achievements and performance explanations within the Trustees' report to the financial statements. A good report will have a clear thread of reporting between the charity's objectives and activities, achievements and performance and its plans for future periods. It should also include information about the resources the charity needs if it to be able to achieve its goals.

The FRC draft guidance reiterates this point by stating that *"Directors should consider the placement of disclosures with a view to facilitating the effective communication of that information"*. It discusses grouping of similar or related disclosures to reduce duplication and enable linkage and the use of cross references.

The draft guidance refers to signposting as *"a means by which a user's attention can be drawn to complementary information that is related to a matter disclosed in a component of the annual report"*. Although a charity must continue to meet its legal and regulatory disclosure requirements in the various parts of its annual report and financial statements, the use of signposting to link this information may be a way in which Trustees can improve their overall reporting.

We have for some time seen trends towards better clearer reporting by companies and charities alike. There continues to be a movement towards linking the various strands of reporting by charities and towards linking the narrative with the numbers as a means of explaining what the charity has done with the resources entrusted to it. The improved reporting on the solvency and liquidity position of a charity will perhaps become an important part of this narrative.

Naziar Hashemi, not for profit partner and Richard Bowen, not for profit director – Crowe Clark Whitehill LLP

An introduction to the Top 3000 charities in the UK

Daniel Holland, Editor, Charity Financials

Who are the top 3,000 charities?

The Top 3,000 charities is an accurate listing of the largest charities in the UK based on an aggregate of their income, expenditure and funds as recorded in their latest available financial statements.

All entrants in the 2016 edition have either generated at least £3.815 million of income, have spent over £3.692 million during the year, or have assets worth at least £8.936 million. When compared to last years edition of the book we can see that the income threshold has increased by £182,000, the expenditure threshold has increased by £185,000 and the net assets threshold has increased by £443,000.

What percentage of total financial activity is represented?

In financial terms the population covers total incoming resources worth £43.966 billion, which represents 69.2% of all income for all charities registered in England and Wales. Similarly expenditure of £42.783 billion represents 64.7% of the aggregate total.

> ### the population covers total incoming resources worth £43.966 billion, which represents 69.2% of all income for all charities registered in England and Wales

Breakdown of charities by size

The charities making up the top 3,000 vary considerably in financial terms. Figure 1 illustrates the variation of the figures over the past three years. The number of charities with income over £100 million continued its year on year growth, rising by 2 to 65. The number of organisations that generated over £50 million in income also saw an increase, rising by 2.8% during the year to 147. 44.5% of the population have income less than £5 million, in sharp contrast, only 4.9% have income over £50 million, up from 4.8% in last years edition.

The value of net assets has also shown growth once again. The number of charities experiencing growth has risen in all of the net asset bands shown in Figure 1, with the largest percentage growth of 6% being for those with net assets in excess of £50 million. Similar to the income statistics, the financial disparity can be seen across the population with 6.8% having net assets worth over £100 million whilst 38.6% have net assets worth less than £10 million.

Figure 1: The number of charities by income and fund values

Income	2014 ed.	2015 ed.	2016 ed.	% change	Funds	2014 ed.	2015ed.	2016ed.	% change
>£100m	59	63	65	3.2	>£300m	35	50	52	4.0
>£50m	133	143	147	2.8	>£100m	161	197	206	4.6
>£10m	763	857	895	4.4	>£50m	344	400	424	6.0
>£5m	1,431	1,596	1,665	4.3	>£20m	853	976	1,016	4.1
>£3m	2,041	2,103	2,122	0.9	>£10m	1,614	1,774	1,843	3.9

Growth trends

The Growth Trends table on page 1.36 shows that 62% of charities experienced an increase in their income. This equates to 1,860 charities, a decrease from last years 1,980. The table also shows that 76% of charities experienced a rise in total fund values.

Income and expenditure breakdowns

The aggregate values of the top 3,000 charities according to the structure of the 2005 SORP (Statement of Recommended Practice) are laid out in Figure 2. This shows that over 34% of income generated is voluntary and just under half comes from charitable activities and government funded income in the form of contracts.

During the year investment management costs have increased by £69 million, which is reflective of the £237 million growth in investment income. A total of £36.9 billion was spent on conducting charitable activities, which is representative of 86.3% of total expenditure.

over 34% of income generated is voluntary and just under half comes from charitable activities

The charity tables

The Top 3,000 Charities presents several tables which rank charities by a range of criteria. The Legacy Tends table on page 1.14 shows that Cancer Research UK once again received the most legacy income of £169 million, a growth of 8% on what they received last year, which is significantly more than the RNLI in second place with £113 million.

The Investment Income Trends table on page 1.24 shows that The Wellcome Trust generated the most investment income with £341 million, a growth of 14% on last year, whilst The Church Commissioners for England remained in second place received £138 million.

The Charity Employment Trends table on page 1.32 shows that Save the Children International's workforce once again increased, rising to 14,156 from last years 11,061. Marie Stopes International who are now in second place increased their staff numbers by 1,560, now employing a total of 10,306 members of staff. There are a total of twelve charities that employ over 5,000 people.

Daniel Holland
Editor
Charity Financials

Figure 2: **Aggregate Income & Expenditure and year on year change**

SORP headings	2016 ed.	2015 ed.	% 2016 ed.	% 2015 ed.	% change
voluntary income	£14,973m	£14,142m	34.1%	33.2%	5.9%
investment income	£2,879m	£2,642m	6.5%	6.2%	9.0%
other activities for generating funds	£4,037m	£3,826m	9.2%	9.0%	5.5%
charitable activities	£21,108m	£20,746m	48.0%	48.7%	1.7%
other income	£970m	£1,207m	2.2%	2.8%	-19.6%
Total income	£43,967m	£42,563m	100.0%	100.0%	3.3%
voluntary costs	£1,661m	£1,542m	3.9%	3.8%	7.7%
investment costs	£551m	£482m	1.3%	1.2%	14.3%
other activities for generating funds	£2,994m	£2,806m	7.0%	6.9%	6.7%
charitable expenditure	£36,923m	£35,221m	86.3%	86.4%	4.8%
governance	£397m	£392m	0.9%	1.0%	1.3%
other costs	£255m	£337m	0.6%	0.8%	-24.3%
Total expenditure	£42,781m	£40,780m	100.0%	100.0%	4.9%

Charity Trends

Definitions

Year-ends and accounting periods

The columns headed this year and last year relate to the latest and preceding accounting periods respectively. Any non 12 month accounting periods have been annualised for the purposes of calculating statistics.

Growth

Growth in source of income and total income is calculated by taking the average percentage change in the source of income and total income for the latest three years.

Where sufficient information to calculate a three year average is not available this has been noted, eg 20%[2] under the column Growth indicates a two year average.

Expenditure

(1) Growth

The percentage change in total expenditure between the current and preceding year.

(2) Expressed as a percentage of income.

Total expenditure divided by total income for the latest year.

Expenditure cover in months

(1) Total Funds

Calculated by dividing total funds by the latest year's total expenditure

(2) Unrestricted Funds

For the purposes of calculating cover on unrestricted funds, total expenditure has been reduced by expenditure from restricted funds where appropriate.

Employment costs

This represents total employee remuneration (including social security, pension contributions and other employment costs).

Average cost per employee

Total employment costs divided by the average number of employees during the year.

Increase in average cost per employee

Calculated by taking the percentage change in average cost per employee between the current and preceding year.

Direct Expenditure

Included within this heading are grants awarded and other expenditure incurred in accordance with the charity's aims.

Indirect Expenditure

Included within this heading are fundraising and publicity costs, administration costs and other expenditure not forming part of the direct charitable expenditure of the charity.

Legacy Trends - The Top 150 Charities (1-50)

	Charity	Period	Legacy Income		Growth (3 year average)		Legacies as % of Income	
			This Year	Last Year	Legacy Income	Total Income	This Year	Last Year
1	Cancer Research UK	31-Mar-15	£169m	£163m	8%	9%	27%	25%
2	Royal National Lifeboat Institution	31-Dec-14	£113m	£118m	5%	3%	59%	62%
3	RSPCA	31-Dec-14	£63.7m	£62.0m	6%	3%	51%	51%
4	Macmillan Cancer Support	31-Dec-14	£62.0m	£59.2m	7%	15%	28%	31%
5	British Heart Foundation	31-Mar-15	£60.8m	£55.5m	5%	5%	21%	20%
6	National Trust	28-Feb-15	£50.5m	£45.9m	5%	4%	10%	10%
7	PDSA	31-Dec-14	£44.2m	£40.6m	5%	2%	44%	42%
8	Salvation Army Trust	31-Mar-15	£43.9m	£47.9m	3%	6%	23%	24%
9	Guide Dogs for the Blind Association	31-Dec-14	£34.9m	£33.7m	2%	16%	35%	45%
10	Royal National Institute of Blind People	31-Mar-15	£34.0m	£40.8m	(1)%	1%	30%	34%
11	RSPB	31-Mar-15	£30.6m	£30.4m	4%	4%	23%	24%
12	Age UK	31-Mar-15	£27.8m	£22.1m	7%	1%	16%	13%
13	Marie Curie Cancer Care	31-Mar-15	£26.2m	£26.4m	5%	4%	17%	17%
14	Cats Protection	31-Dec-14	£24.2m	£25.3m	8%	8%	53%	58%
15	Dogs Trust	31-Dec-14	£24.2m	£20.1m	10%	9%	29%	26%
16	British Red Cross Society	31-Dec-14	£22.2m	£21.8m	4%	7%	8%	10%
17	Great Ormond St Hosp Children's Charity	31-Mar-15	£22.0m	£11.5m	31%	7%	27%	15%
18	Arthritis Research UK	31-Mar-15	£21.2m	£18.4m	13%	5%	53%	51%
19	NSPCC	31-Mar-15	£20.9m	£20.9m	1%	~	16%	17%
20	Donkey Sanctuary	31-Dec-14	£20.8m	£20.0m	8%	12%	64%	65%
21	Blue Cross	31-Dec-14	£17.5m	£14.3m	8%	6%	52%	49%
22	Alzheimer's Society	31-Mar-15	£16.9m	£14.7m	11%	9%	19%	18%
23	Crisis	30-Jun-15	£16.6m	£13.9m	25%	6%	64%	59%
24	Barnardo's	31-Mar-15	£16.3m	£18.6m	3%	7%	5%	7%
25	Save the Children	31-Dec-14	£16.2m	£18.3m	~	5%	4%	5%
26	Royal British Legion	30-Sep-14	£16.0m	£12.6m	14%	(1)%	12%	10%
27	SHELTER	31-Mar-15	£13.9m	£3.72m	85%	10%	20%	6%
28	Oxfam GB	31-Mar-15	£13.8m	£14.1m	(1)%	1%	3%	4%
29	Woodland Trust	31-Dec-14	£13.1m	£9.02m	21%	12%	34%	27%
30	Parkinson's UK	31-Dec-14	£12.7m	£8.32m	13%	12%	42%	34%
31	Diabetes UK	31-Dec-14	£12.5m	£11.5m	3%	14%	30%	30%
32	Stroke Association	31-Mar-15	£11.7m	£8.94m	26%	7%	31%	27%
33	Blind Veterans UK	31-Mar-15	£11.7m	£11.3m	6%	2%	43%	42%
34	Yorkshire Cancer Research	31-Mar-15	£11.6m	£2.97m	89%	79%	65%	58%
35	Multiple Sclerosis Society	31-Dec-14	£10.7m	£9.20m	1%	(3)%	41%	38%
36	Royal Air Force Benevolent Fund	31-Dec-14	£10.7m	£7.92m	16%	7%	49%	41%
37	Battersea Dogs & Cats Home	31-Dec-14	£10.4m	£8.85m	(2)%	24%	31%	39%
38	Christian Aid	31-Mar-15	£9.32m	£12.9m	11%	2%	9%	12%
39	WWF UK	30-Jun-15	£9.07m	£11.7m	(2)%	(1)%	14%	19%
40	John Black Charitable Foundation	31-Mar-15	£8.65m	£10.4m	-	-	81%	72%
41	Brooke Hospital for Animals	31-Mar-15	£8.20m	£7.89m	6%	1%	47%	45%
42	Help for Heroes	30-Sep-14	£8.12m	£3.37m	65%	(7)%	22%	10%
43	Action on Hearing Loss	31-Mar-15	£8.05m	£7.73m	(4)%	1%	22%	16%
44	Sightsavers International	31-Dec-14	£7.26m	£9.71m	(1)%	6%	4%	5%
45	Leonard Cheshire Disability	31-Mar-15	£7.24m	£4.53m	10%	1%	4%	3%
46	Medecins sans Frontieres (UK)	31-Dec-14	£6.58m	£10.4m	75%	21%	15%	29%
47	Royal Star & Garter Home, The	31-Dec-14	£6.38m	£7.46m	(11)%	106%	9%	47%
48	Bloodwise	31-Mar-15	£6.24m	£6.81m	(2)%	2%	30%	31%
49	Royal Mencap Society	31-Mar-15	£6.20m	£6.21m	5%	(1)%	3%	3%
50	Gurkha Welfare Trust	30-Jun-15	£6.15m	£5.69m	23%	34%	23%	38%

Legacy Trends - The Top 150 Charities (51-100)

	Charity	Period	Legacy Income		Growth (3 year average)		Legacies as % of Income	
			This Year	Last Year	Legacy Income	Total Income	This Year	Last Year
51	Jewish Care	31-Mar-15	£5.88m	£4.49m	23%	2%	12%	8%
52	Christie Charitable Fund, The	31-Mar-14	£5.83m	£4.36m	5%	6%	39%	33%
53	Redwings Horse Sanctuary	31-Dec-14	£5.78m	£5.30m	10%	6%	61%	51%
54	SSPCA	31-Dec-14	£5.71m	£6.22m	(8)%	(1)%	40%	45%
55	Royal Marsden Cancer Campaign	31-Mar-15	£5.53m	£4.05m	37%	30%	24%	26%
56	Motor Neurone Disease Association	31-Jan-15	£5.53m	£5.70m	21%	27%	22%	34%
57	Hearing Dogs for Deaf People	31-Mar-15	£5.50m	£5.25m	22%	14%	65%	63%
58	Amnesty International UK Section	31-Dec-14	£5.43m	£3.54m	28%	8%	33%	25%
59	Wood Green Animal Shelters	31-Mar-15	£5.36m	£4.26m	11%	6%	53%	47%
60	St Christopher's Hospice	31-Mar-15	£5.35m	£5.07m	5%	2%	27%	26%
61	Children's Society	31-Mar-15	£5.34m	£7.02m	(6)%	4%	11%	14%
62	Children's Hospice South West	31-Mar-15	£5.33m	£3.27m	47%	19%	31%	28%
63	UNICEF-UK	31-Dec-14	£5.09m	£4.43m	9%	4%	5%	6%
64	Institute of Cancer Research	31-Jul-15	£5.08m	£4.58m	51%	15%	4%	4%
65	Sue Ryder	31-Mar-15	£4.93m	£5.14m	(2)%	7%	5%	6%
66	Alzheimer's Research UK	31-Aug-14	£4.83m	£3.80m	32%	20%	34%	34%
67	WaterAid	31-Mar-15	£4.69m	£5.61m	34%	14%	6%	8%
68	Art Fund	31-Dec-14	£4.65m	£1.87m	74%	59%	19%	18%
69	St Joseph's Hospice, Hackney	31-Mar-15	£4.60m	£2.67m	-	-	30%	20%
70	Scope	31-Mar-15	£4.50m	£4.90m	2%	(1)%	4%	5%
71	International Fund for Animal Welfare	30-Jun-14	£4.25m	£5.53m	(2)%	(5)%	22%	26%
72	National Trust for Scotland	28-Feb-15	£4.16m	£4.72m	(24)%	(4)%	9%	10%
73	CLIC Sargent Cancer Care for Children	31-Mar-15	£4.11m	£2.56m	11%	6%	16%	10%
74	World Society for the Protection of Animals	31-Dec-14	£4.03m	£3.91m	13%	7%	12%	14%
75	Greenpeace Environmental Trust	31-Dec-14	£3.89m	£2.36m	21%	12%	73%	66%
76	World Horse Welfare	31-Dec-14	£3.89m	£5.10m	1%	4%	51%	61%
77	Action for Children	31-Mar-15	£3.85m	£5.14m	(8)%	(4)%	2%	3%
78	Asthma UK	30-Sep-14	£3.83m	£2.52m	20%	8%	41%	33%
79	Norwood	31-Mar-15	£3.81m	£2.97m	72%	(3)%	11%	8%
80	Imperial College Healthcare Charity	31-Mar-15	£3.80m	£1.66m	1,060%	21%	56%	38%
81	Cinnamon Trust	31-Mar-15	£3.79m	£2.68m	24%	18%	83%	70%
82	London City Mission	31-Dec-14	£3.74m	£2.57m	50%	33%	29%	28%
83	Brit.YearlyMtngofTheReligiousSocietyofFriends	31-Dec-14	£3.72m	£5.05m	13%	3%	33%	42%
84	St Michael's Hospice	31-Mar-15	£3.69m	£1.11m	121%	35%	41%	13%
85	St Ann's Hospice	31-Mar-15	£3.59m	£3.10m	46%	9%	29%	26%
86	Erskine	30-Sep-14	£3.44m	£5.36m	(13)%	(2)%	15%	22%
87	Midlands Air Ambulance Charity	31-Mar-15	£3.42m	£5.06m	54%	~	38%	47%
88	Cambridge Foundation	31-Jul-11	£3.41m	£3.34m	91%	4%	7%	8%
89	Medical Research Foundation	31-Mar-15	£3.38m	£1.78m	52%	34%	65%	31%
90	Princess Alice Hospice	31-Mar-15	£3.37m	£3.06m	3%	8%	22%	21%
91	Kidney Research UK	31-Mar-15	£3.32m	£2.22m	24%	7%	36%	27%
92	Helen & Douglas House	31-Mar-15	£3.23m	£1.16m	71%	9%	27%	11%
93	St Catherine's Hospice Limited	31-Mar-15	£3.22m	£6.16m	101%	14%	30%	46%
94	Rowcroft House Foundation Limited	31-Mar-15	£3.21m	£1.81m	26%	9%	38%	25%
95	Society for Protection of Animals Abroad	31-Dec-14	£3.13m	£2.72m	14%	11%	47%	46%
96	Tearfund	31-Mar-15	£3.08m	£3.21m	(9)%	(4)%	5%	5%
97	Moorfields Eye Hospital Special Trustees	31-Mar-15	£3.05m	£0.99m	50%	22%	86%	66%
98	Thames Hospicecare	31-Mar-15	£3.00m	£0.53m	358%	30%	37%	10%
99	Samaritans	31-Mar-15	£3.00m	£1.92m	19%	5%	23%	15%
100	St Barnabas Hospices (Sussex) Ltd	31-Mar-15	£2.91m	£4.14m	1%	5%	20%	27%

Legacy Trends - The Top 150 Charities (101-150)

	Charity	Period	Legacy Income		Growth (3 year average)		Legacies as % of Income	
			This Year	Last Year	Legacy Income	Total Income	This Year	Last Year
101	ABF The Soldiers Charity	31-Mar-15	£2.91m	£2.09m	1%	10%	14%	14%
102	Weizmann Institute Foundation	30-Sep-14	£2.85m	£0.75m	83%	20%	48%	24%
103	Children's Hospice Association Scotland	31-Mar-15	£2.82m	£1.88m	29%	8%	28%	22%
104	Methodist Homes	31-Mar-15	£2.82m	£2.70m	4%	6%	2%	2%
105	Royal Air Forces Association	31-Dec-14	£2.80m	£2.28m	19%	5%	28%	26%
106	Musicians Benevolent Fund	31-Dec-14	£2.78m	£1.84m	~	~	55%	45%
107	SSAFA	31-Dec-14	£2.75m	£2.52m	8%	5%	5%	4%
108	Camphill Village Trust Limited	31-Mar-15	£2.59m	£3.03m	5%	(10)%	13%	15%
109	Leeds Teaching Hospitals Charitable Fdn	31-Mar-15	£2.58m	£1.04m	172%	17%	39%	21%
110	Hope House Children's Hospices	31-Dec-14	£2.54m	£2.49m	32%	7%	33%	33%
111	Mission Aviation Fellowship UK	31-Dec-14	£2.48m	£2.39m	4%	2%	20%	20%
112	Yorkshire Air Ambulance	31-Mar-15	£2.47m	£1.49m	41%	20%	33%	23%
113	Fdn&Friends of RoyalBotanicGardens, Kew	31-Mar-15	£2.42m	£1.55m	133%	42%	8%	10%
114	Injured Jockeys Fund	31-Mar-15	£2.39m	£1.40m	44%	26%	36%	25%
115	Churches Conservation Trust	31-Mar-15	£2.39m	£0.60m	450%	29%	18%	7%
116	Bransby Horses	31-Dec-14	£2.35m	£1.99m	~	2%	57%	53%
117	Great North Air Ambulance Service	31-Mar-15	£2.33m	£1.52m	19%	1%	30%	20%
118	Watch Tower Bible Tract Society Britain	31-Aug-14	£2.32m	£1.65m	16%	16%	5%	5%
119	Dorothy House Foundation Ltd	31-Mar-15	£2.29m	£1.66m	40%	11%	21%	16%
120	Chartered Accountants' Benevolent Assoc	31-Dec-14	£2.29m	£1.98m	470%	31%	47%	48%
121	Trinity Hospice & Palliative Care Services	31-Mar-15	£2.27m	£2.28m	25%	12%	26%	24%
122	Mercy Ships - UK	31-Dec-14	£2.26m	£0.57m	167%	16%	35%	12%
123	MIND	31-Mar-15	£2.21m	£1.73m	7%	8%	6%	5%
124	East Anglia's Children's Hospices	31-Mar-15	£2.21m	£1.31m	37%	5%	21%	13%
125	Arthritis Care	31-Dec-14	£2.18m	£3.81m	9%	(1)%	49%	64%
126	Kent, Surrey & Sussex Air Ambulance Trust	31-Mar-15	£2.18m	£1.30m	31%	12%	20%	14%
127	St Wilfrid's Hospice (Eastbourne)	31-Mar-15	£2.16m	£1.59m	(5)%	1%	39%	28%
128	Welsh Air Ambulance Charitable Trust	31-Jul-14	£2.15m	£0.70m	88%	15%	25%	10%
129	Sense - National Deafblind & Rubella Assoc	31-Mar-15	£2.12m	£2.31m	(1)%	2%	3%	3%
130	Compassion in World Farming	31-Mar-15	£2.10m	£1.87m	14%	(2)%	34%	29%
131	Douglas Macmillan Hospice	31-Mar-15	£2.09m	£1.17m	49%	11%	18%	11%
132	Christ's Hospital Foundation	31-Aug-14	£2.09m	£0.46m	82%	9%	9%	2%
133	Wessex Children's Hospice Trust	31-Mar-15	£2.07m	£1.22m	27%	13%	24%	17%
134	ActionAid	31-Dec-14	£2.06m	£1.64m	(1)%	~	3%	3%
135	Addenbrooke's Charitable Trust	31-Mar-15	£2.06m	£1.06m	50%	11%	22%	12%
136	Pilgrims Hospices in East Kent	31-Mar-15	£2.05m	£2.32m	(4)%	3%	16%	18%
137	St Francis Hospice	31-Mar-15	£2.05m	£2.21m	(1)%	4%	19%	20%
138	ORBIS Charitable Trust	31-Dec-14	£2.00m	£0.82m	47%	17%	35%	17%
139	Chest Heart & Stroke Scotland	31-Mar-15	£1.98m	£2.38m	(13)%	1%	25%	30%
140	Society of St Columban for Foreign Missions	31-Mar-15	£1.96m	£1.41m	2%	1%	44%	32%
141	National Osteoporosis Society	31-Dec-14	£1.96m	£1.52m	23%	17%	40%	45%
142	Rowans Hospice	31-Mar-15	£1.94m	£2.21m	21%	13%	27%	32%
143	Air Ambulance Service	31-Dec-14	£1.93m	£1.85m	57%	32%	16%	17%
144	North London Hospice	31-Mar-15	£1.93m	£1.16m	24%	9%	20%	13%
145	Sobell House Hospice Charity Limited	31-Mar-15	£1.91m	£1.29m	65%	17%	42%	31%
146	St John Ambulance	31-Dec-14	£1.90m	£1.60m	21%	5%	2%	2%
147	Leprosy Mission England	31-Dec-14	£1.89m	£2.08m	11%	6%	30%	32%
148	Ex-Services Mental Welfare Society	31-Mar-15	£1.86m	£1.70m	6%	(1)%	12%	10%
149	Pallant House Gallery	31-Mar-15	£1.84m	£0.02m	4,177%	43%	45%	1%
150	Gideons International British Isles	31-Dec-14	£1.84m	£0.48m	85%	13%	41%	16%

Aggregate Income, Expenditure and Funds

	2015	2014	2013	2012	2011
legacies	£1,872m	£1,836m	£1,670m	£1,573m	£1,588m
public grants	£2,163m	£2,094m	£2,205m	£2,376m	£2,830m
lottery, arts council	£337m	£344m	£503m	£277m	£315m
gifts in kind	£497m	£530m	£466m	£403m	£336m
donations	£10,104m	£9,338m	£8,501m	£7,565m	£7,058m
donated goods	£406m	£457m	£453m	£439m	£391m
other trading	£2,450m	£2,248m	£2,068m	£1,983m	£1,894m
other inc generating	£1,181m	£1,121m	£1,057m	£900m	£839m
interest, dividends, rent	£2,879m	£2,642m	£2,448m	£2,281m	£2,169m
charitable activities	£21,108m	£20,746m	£19,734m	£18,958m	£19,505m
other income	£970m	£1,207m	£482m	£675m	£604m
TOTAL INCOME	**£43,966m**	**£42,563m**	**£39,586m**	**£37,429m**	**£37,529m**
voluntary costs	£1,661m	£1,542m	£1,438m	£1,378m	£1,307m
cost generating fnds	£2,994m	£2,806m	£2,727m	£2,687m	£2,590m
investment costs	£551m	£482m	£314m	£272m	£281m
grant expenditure	£7,566m	£6,861m	£6,916m	£6,261m	£5,677m
direct charitable exp	£29,357m	£28,360m	£26,119m	£25,434m	£25,814m
governance	£397m	£392m	£382m	£391m	£391m
other costs	£255m	£337m	£226m	£202m	£249m
TOTAL EXPENDITURE	**£42,783m**	**£40,779m**	**£38,121m**	**£36,626m**	**£36,309m**
land & buildings	£35,218m	£32,631m	£27,784m	£25,864m	£24,477m
other fixed assets	£6,796m	£6,445m	£5,234m	£4,705m	£4,678m
fxd investments	£101,851m	£94,644m	£82,981m	£74,695m	£72,274m
stocks, debtors	£6,848m	£6,654m	£5,833m	£5,293m	£5,112m
cur investments	£3,328m	£2,204m	£2,042m	£2,202m	£2,305m
cash deposits	£14,290m	£16,362m	£15,433m	£15,801m	£15,188m
creditors	£16,916m	£15,697m	£14,662m	£13,922m	£14,227m
borrowings	£7,152m	£7,093m	£6,712m	£7,819m	£6,662m
pension liability	£3,502m	£2,696m	£2,656m	£2,248m	£1,929m
endowment funds	£46,481m	£43,296m	£34,349m	£29,667m	£28,436m
other restricted funds	£21,042m	£20,122m	£17,303m	£15,805m	£15,027m
unrestricted funds	£76,039m	£71,990m	£65,502m	£60,712m	£59,103m
pension fund	£(2,785)m	£(1,954)m	£(1,878)m	£(1,611)m	£(1,336)m
TOTAL FUNDS	**£140,777m**	**£133,454m**	**£115,275m**	**£104,573m**	**£101,230m**
GAINS, REVALUATIONS	**£6,217m**	**£11,516m**	**£8,050m**	**£2,242m**	**£5,274m**

Analysis of Income Statistics

Source	Aggregate Amount				Percentage number of charities with income from the particular source		Importance of the source to the charities concerned, expressing income from the particular source as a percentage of their total income					
	2015		2014				Upper Quartile		Median		Lower Quartile	
legacies	£1,872m	4%	£1,836m	4%	25%	26%	19%	17%	7%	7%	2%	1%
public grants	£2,163m	5%	£2,094m	5%	11%	11%	26%	25%	10%	10%	2%	2%
lottery, arts council	£337m	1%	£344m	1%	4%	4%	21%	25%	8%	11%	1%	2%
gifts in kind	£497m	1%	£530m	1%	6%	6%	6%	5%	2%	2%	1%	1%
donations	£10,104m	23%	£9,338m	22%	71%	71%	50%	50%	16%	16%	3%	2%
donated goods	£406m	1%	£457m	1%	2%	2%	26%	24%	13%	14%	5%	4%
other trading	£2,450m	6%	£2,248m	5%	29%	28%	23%	24%	9%	8%	2%	2%
other inc generating	£1,181m	3%	£1,121m	3%	31%	31%	13%	13%	4%	4%	1%	1%
interest, divids, rent	£2,879m	7%	£2,642m	6%	94%	94%	40%	40%	3%	3%	~	~
charitable activities	£21,108m	48%	£20,746m	49%	66%	67%	93%	93%	62%	61%	19%	20%
other income	£970m	2%	£1,207m	3%	37%	35%	4%	4%	1%	1%	~	~
Total	**£43,966m**	**100%**	**£42,562m**	**100%**								

NOTES

1 A total of 3,000 charities are covered, being those falling within the top 2,000 by income, expenditure, or funds.

2 The figures are based on an aggregation of each charity's latest available annual report adjusted in accordance with How the Guide is Compiled. The income amounts are based on an aggregation of all charities' income and include an element of double counting re inter charity grant making and Arts Council grants.

Voluntary Income Trends - The Top 100 Charities (1-50)

Charity	Period	Voluntary Income (excluding legacies)		Growth (3 year average)		As % of Total Income	
		This Year	Last Year	Voluntary Income	Total Income	This Year	Last Year
1 Save the Children International	31-Dec-14	£694m	£527m	136%	136%	100%	100%
2 Arts Council England	31-Mar-15	£449m	£461m	5%	6%	96%	97%
3 Charities Aid Foundation	30-Apr-15	£430m	£381m	6%	6%	92%	91%
4 Save the Children	31-Dec-14	£341m	£313m	5%	5%	92%	91%
5 Oasis Charitable Trust	31-Aug-14	£262m	£154m	58%	57%	96%	96%
6 Cancer Research UK	31-Mar-15	£262m	£237m	7%	9%	41%	36%
7 Tate	31-Mar-15	£171m	£136m	36%	26%	77%	76%
8 Sightsavers International	31-Dec-14	£165m	£181m	5%	6%	88%	90%
9 British Council	31-Mar-15	£157m	£165m	-	10%	16%	19%
10 Motability	31-Mar-15	£152m	£1.49m	3,372%	174%	84%	5%
11 Macmillan Cancer Support	31-Dec-14	£152m	£127m	20%	15%	70%	67%
12 British Red Cross Society	31-Dec-14	£118m	£106m	4%	7%	45%	47%
13 Oxfam GB	31-Mar-15	£111m	£104m	(1)%	1%	28%	27%
14 NSPCC	31-Mar-15	£89.0m	£89.7m	(2)%	~	66%	71%
15 UNICEF-UK	31-Dec-14	£84.9m	£72.2m	3%	4%	91%	91%
16 British Film Institute	31-Mar-15	£82.0m	£76.8m	(16)%	(14)%	83%	82%
17 Christian Aid	31-Mar-15	£79.1m	£78.1m	(1)%	2%	79%	75%
18 Islamic Relief Worldwide	31-Dec-14	£78.8m	£57.6m	16%	7%	79%	63%
19 Intl Planned Parenthood Federation	31-Dec-14	£78.7m	£80.0m	~	~	97%	97%
20 Victoria and Albert Museum	31-Mar-15	£76.0m	£54.3m	14%	12%	75%	67%
21 Comic Relief	31-Jul-14	£73.0m	£96.4m	(7)%	(8)%	87%	84%
22 RSPB	31-Mar-15	£72.3m	£67.8m	3%	4%	54%	53%
23 Voluntary Service Overseas	31-Mar-15	£72.3m	£64.8m	10%	11%	94%	94%
24 British Museum	31-Mar-15	£70.8m	£88.2m	2%	5%	60%	61%
25 World Vision UK	30-Sep-14	£70.6m	£65.9m	2%	2%	98%	99%
26 Salvation Army Trust	31-Mar-15	£66.8m	£66.8m	4%	6%	34%	34%
27 Royal British Legion	30-Sep-14	£66.3m	£63.0m	1%	(1)%	50%	51%
28 Marie Curie Cancer Care	31-Mar-15	£66.0m	£64.7m	7%	4%	42%	42%
29 Stewardship Services (UKET) Ltd	30-Sep-14	£63.2m	£59.8m	6%	6%	95%	95%
30 Gatsby Charitable Foundation	05-Apr-15	£62.4m	£48.3m	41%	22%	82%	75%
31 Amnesty International Limited	31-Dec-14	£61.4m	£58.4m	19%	19%	100%	99%
32 Salvation Army International Trust	31-Mar-15	£60.0m	£34.6m	30%	28%	88%	84%
33 Royal National Lifeboat Institution	31-Dec-14	£58.0m	£51.7m	4%	3%	31%	27%
34 Catholic Agency for Overseas Development	31-Mar-15	£55.7m	£50.9m	12%	(2)%	99%	99%
35 Royal Opera House Covent Garden	31-Aug-14	£54.6m	£50.5m	5%	5%	43%	44%
36 Dogs Trust	31-Dec-14	£53.8m	£49.7m	9%	9%	64%	65%
37 Natural History Museum	31-Mar-15	£53.3m	£47.7m	3%	3%	65%	63%
38 Tearfund	31-Mar-15	£53.3m	£53.5m	(6)%	(4)%	86%	90%
39 British Heart Foundation	31-Mar-15	£53.2m	£46.8m	10%	5%	18%	17%
40 Church of Scot Uninc. Councils Cttees	31-Dec-14	£50.9m	£52.2m	1%	(2)%	46%	44%
41 Science Museum Group	31-Mar-15	£50.3m	£52.1m	(14)%	(10)%	69%	66%
42 BBC Children in Need	30-Jun-14	£50.2m	£43.1m	13%	12%	90%	91%
43 WaterAid	31-Mar-15	£50.1m	£44.5m	10%	14%	60%	60%
44 Racing Foundation, The	31-Dec-14	£49.9m	£9.00m	-	-	98%	95%
45 Great Ormond St Hosp Children's Charity	31-Mar-15	£48.7m	£48.3m	2%	7%	60%	65%
46 WWF UK	30-Jun-15	£47.6m	£45.6m	(1)%	(1)%	75%	72%
47 Stoller Charitable Trust	05-Apr-14	£47.3m	£0.09m	16,734%	8,076%	100%	48%
48 ActionAid	31-Dec-14	£46.5m	£46.2m	(1)%	~	74%	73%
49 Cambridge Foundation	31-Jul-11	£46.4m	£37.0m	3%	4%	93%	92%
50 Royal National Theatre	31-Mar-15	£45.4m	£47.6m	15%	17%	33%	38%

Voluntary Income Trends - The Top 100 Charities (51-100)

Charity	Period	Voluntary Income (excluding legacies)		Growth (3 year average)		As % of Total Income	
		This Year	Last Year	Voluntary Income	Total Income	This Year	Last Year
51 Southampton Row Trust Limited	30-Apr-15	£45.3m	£35.2m	32%	31%	99%	99%
52 Elim Foursquare Gospel Alliance	30-Sep-14	£44.7m	£43.8m	1%	3%	65%	66%
53 RSPCA	31-Dec-14	£43.6m	£43.4m	(2)%	3%	35%	36%
54 Church of Jesus Christ of Latter Day Saints	31-Dec-14	£42.1m	£47.0m	(2)%	(2)%	96%	97%
55 Tate Foundation	31-Mar-15	£41.7m	£35.9m	28%	27%	99%	99%
56 Guide Dogs for the Blind Association	31-Dec-14	£41.0m	£32.5m	22%	16%	41%	43%
57 Canal & River Trust	31-Mar-15	£40.6m	£40.2m	-	-	22%	25%
58 Royal Botanic Gardens, Kew	31-Mar-15	£40.4m	£42.2m	6%	6%	71%	71%
59 Disasters Emergency Committee	31-Mar-15	£40.3m	£69.8m	303%	290%	99%	100%
60 Jisc	31-Jul-15	£39.2m	£58.4m	-	235%	28%	36%
61 Allchurches Trust	31-Dec-14	£38.7m	£54.7m	(4)%	(12)%	96%	98%
62 Prince's Trust	31-Mar-15	£37.3m	£33.9m	12%	6%	57%	56%
63 Queen Elizabeth Diamond Jubilee Trust	30-Jun-14	£36.0m	£22.2m	-	-	100%	99%
64 Alzheimer's Society	31-Mar-15	£35.3m	£30.3m	8%	9%	39%	37%
65 England and Wales Cricket Trust	31-Jan-15	£35.1m	£14.0m	105%	94%	99%	98%
66 Imperial War Museum	31-Mar-15	£34.8m	£41.3m	15%	13%	61%	70%
67 Thalidomide Trust	30-Sep-14	£34.6m	£17.2m	35%	30%	88%	82%
68 Muslim Aid	31-Dec-14	£34.6m	£26.6m	4%	4%	100%	100%
69 Medecins sans Frontieres (UK)	31-Dec-14	£34.5m	£23.2m	23%	21%	78%	64%
70 Watch Tower Bible Tract Society Britain	31-Aug-14	£33.2m	£15.4m	43%	16%	74%	50%
71 Arts Council of Wales, The	31-Mar-15	£32.8m	£35.1m	(3)%	(3)%	99%	98%
72 National Gallery	31-Mar-15	£32.7m	£45.6m	(33)%	(29)%	78%	88%
73 Compassion UK	30-Jun-14	£32.1m	£28.3m	10%	10%	100%	100%
74 Plan International UK	30-Jun-15	£31.2m	£31.9m	(12)%	15%	39%	50%
75 Football Foundation	31-May-15	£31.1m	£30.0m	6%	7%	95%	96%
76 CAMFED International	31-Dec-14	£31.0m	£31.1m	35%	35%	99%	99%
77 Westminster RC Diocesan Trust	31-Dec-14	£30.8m	£27.9m	7%	11%	61%	63%
78 Royal National Institute of Blind People	31-Mar-15	£30.7m	£30.9m	2%	1%	27%	26%
79 Focus Learning Trust	31-Jul-14	£28.6m	£27.6m	132%	130%	89%	89%
80 Gerald Ronson Foundation, The	31-Dec-14	£28.4m	£1.02m	944%	641%	98%	70%
81 World Society for the Protection of Animals	31-Dec-14	£27.8m	£23.9m	3%	7%	81%	86%
82 Age UK	31-Mar-15	£27.6m	£24.1m	2%	1%	16%	14%
83 Forster Foundation CIO, The	31-Jan-15	£27.4m	-	-	-	100%	-
84 National Museums Scotland	31-Mar-15	£27.1m	£27.2m	(1)%	3%	80%	84%
85 London Diocesan Fund	31-Dec-14	£27.0m	£27.1m	2%	4%	73%	77%
86 HALO Trust	31-Mar-15	£26.5m	£24.1m	5%	5%	100%	100%
87 Fdn&Friends of RoyalBotanicGardens, Kew	31-Mar-15	£26.2m	£14.1m	44%	42%	91%	89%
88 Amanat Charitable Trust	30-Nov-14	£26.2m	£17.5m	25%	25%	96%	94%
89 SHELTER	31-Mar-15	£26.1m	£24.9m	7%	10%	37%	43%
90 Ahmadiyya Muslim Jamaat International	31-Dec-14	£26.1m	£25.0m	6%	6%	100%	100%
91 Aga Khan Foundation (United Kingdom)	31-Dec-14	£25.9m	£15.6m	34%	33%	100%	99%
92 South Bank Centre	31-Mar-14	£25.8m	£27.3m	~	3%	53%	54%
93 Clyde Gateway URC	31-Mar-15	£25.7m	£48.1m	16%	20%	69%	98%
94 Barnardo's	31-Mar-15	£25.2m	£25.1m	(4)%	7%	9%	9%
95 Christian Vision	31-Dec-14	£24.6m	£11.4m	17,870%	49%	64%	48%
96 Beamish Museum Limited	31-Jan-15	£24.4m	£0.71m	1,128%	114%	74%	9%
97 PDSA	31-Dec-14	£24.3m	£23.8m	4%	2%	24%	25%
98 Prostate Cancer UK	31-Mar-15	£23.8m	£30.7m	4%	3%	99%	99%
99 Diabetes UK	31-Dec-14	£22.6m	£21.2m	30%	14%	54%	54%
100 Goldman Sachs Gives (UK)	30-Jun-14	£22.6m	£18.4m	(2)%	(2)%	97%	96%

Additional Statistics on The Top 100 Charities

| Charity | Period | Fundraising costs As % of Total Vol. Inc. | | Management, Admin costs | | | |
| | | | | As % of Total Exp. | | As % of Total Inc. | |
		This Year	Last Year	This Year	Last Year	This Year	Last Year
1 Save the Children International	31-Dec-14	~	-	1%	1%	1%	1%
2 Arts Council England	31-Mar-15	-	-	~	~	~	~
3 Cancer Research UK	31-Mar-15	24%	22%	~	~	~	~
4 Charities Aid Foundation	30-Apr-15	-	-	~	~	~	~
5 Save the Children	31-Dec-14	9%	10%	~	~	~	~
6 Oasis Charitable Trust	31-Aug-14	2%	2%	~	~	~	~
7 Macmillan Cancer Support	31-Dec-14	32%	31%	~	1%	1%	~
8 Sightsavers International	31-Dec-14	8%	5%	1%	~	1%	~
9 Royal National Lifeboat Institution	31-Dec-14	16%	15%	~	~	~	~
10 Tate	31-Mar-15	2%	2%	1%	1%	~	~
11 British Council	31-Mar-15	-	-	1%	1%	1%	1%
12 Motability	31-Mar-15	1%	51%	1%	1%	~	1%
13 British Red Cross Society	31-Dec-14	35%	39%	1%	1%	1%	1%
14 Oxfam GB	31-Mar-15	19%	22%	~	~	~	~
15 British Heart Foundation	31-Mar-15	27%	27%	~	~	~	~
16 Salvation Army Trust	31-Mar-15	9%	8%	~	~	~	~
17 NSPCC	31-Mar-15	21%	21%	1%	1%	~	1%
18 RSPCA	31-Dec-14	19%	18%	1%	1%	1%	1%
19 RSPB	31-Mar-15	15%	16%	~	~	~	~
20 Marie Curie Cancer Care	31-Mar-15	47%	48%	~	~	~	~
21 UNICEF-UK	31-Dec-14	29%	29%	1%	1%	1%	1%
22 Christian Aid	31-Mar-15	16%	15%	1%	1%	1%	1%
23 Royal British Legion	30-Sep-14	19%	18%	1%	1%	1%	1%
24 British Film Institute	31-Mar-15	1%	2%	~	~	~	~
25 Intl Planned Parenthood Federation	31-Dec-14	4%	3%	2%	2%	2%	2%
26 Islamic Relief Worldwide	31-Dec-14	11%	14%	2%	2%	2%	2%
27 Dogs Trust	31-Dec-14	30%	30%	~	~	~	~
28 Victoria and Albert Museum	31-Mar-15	5%	7%	~	~	~	~
29 Guide Dogs for the Blind Association	31-Dec-14	41%	41%	1%	2%	1%	2%
30 Comic Relief	31-Jul-14	22%	12%	~	~	~	~
31 Voluntary Service Overseas	31-Mar-15	11%	10%	1%	3%	1%	3%
32 World Vision UK	30-Sep-14	15%	16%	1%	1%	1%	1%
33 British Museum	31-Mar-15	2%	1%	~	~	~	~
34 National Trust	28-Feb-15	4%	4%	~	~	~	~
35 Great Ormond St Hosp Children's Charity	31-Mar-15	26%	32%	4%	1%	2%	1%
36 PDSA	31-Dec-14	17%	16%	~	~	~	~
37 Royal National Institute of Blind People	31-Mar-15	32%	22%	1%	1%	1%	1%
38 Stewardship Services (UKET) Ltd	30-Sep-14	-	-	~	~	~	~
39 Gatsby Charitable Foundation	05-Apr-15	-	-	~	~	~	~
40 Amnesty International Limited	31-Dec-14	-	-	2%	2%	2%	2%
41 Salvation Army International Trust	31-Mar-15	-	-	4%	3%	2%	3%
42 WWF UK	30-Jun-15	25%	26%	1%	2%	1%	1%
43 Tearfund	31-Mar-15	10%	9%	~	~	~	~
44 Catholic Agency for Overseas Development	31-Mar-15	11%	11%	1%	1%	1%	1%
45 Age UK	31-Mar-15	12%	10%	~	~	~	~
46 WaterAid	31-Mar-15	30%	32%	1%	1%	1%	1%
47 Royal Opera House Covent Garden	31-Aug-14	9%	7%	~	~	~	~
48 Natural History Museum	31-Mar-15	21%	24%	1%	~	1%	1%
49 Alzheimer's Society	31-Mar-15	28%	28%	~	~	~	~
50 Church of Scot Uninc. Councils Cttees	31-Dec-14	1%	1%	1%	1%	1%	1%

by Voluntary Income - (1-50)

| Direct Charitable Expenditure | | | | Total Expenditure (this year) | | Expenditure Cover in Months (this year) | | (last year) | |
| As % of Total Exp. | | As % of Total Inc. | | | | | | | |
This Year	Last Year	This Year	Last Year	Growth	As % of Total Income	Total Funds	Unrestricted Funds	Total Funds	Unrestricted Funds
99%	98%	99%	98%	32%	100%	~	-	~	-
100%	100%	99%	99%	(2)%	99%	4	~	4	~
70%	70%	67%	57%	12%	95%	7	6	7	6
100%	100%	96%	97%	10%	96%	28	1	29	2
88%	86%	83%	78%	13%	94%	4	~	4	~
97%	97%	56%	71%	35%	58%	26	~	24	~
68%	67%	69%	64%	22%	101%	4	2	4	3
92%	95%	91%	95%	(8)%	99%	1	1	1	~
77%	77%	64%	62%	3%	83%	53	5	52	7
67%	71%	33%	43%	(1)%	48%	155	1	134	1
99%	99%	99%	101%	11%	100%	5	4	5	4
97%	94%	31%	92%	104%	32%	26	(2)	3	(2)
70%	67%	69%	68%	11%	98%	6	4	7	5
77%	74%	74%	69%	6%	97%	2	~	2	~
40%	46%	39%	52%	(8)%	100%	~	(1)	(1)	(2)
65%	66%	60%	56%	7%	92%	37	9	38	8
76%	79%	72%	78%	2%	95%	8	5	8	5
82%	83%	78%	80%	2%	95%	17	5	17	5
73%	73%	71%	73%	1%	96%	9	(5)	11	(2)
64%	64%	68%	68%	~	106%	8	3	8	3
69%	70%	69%	69%	18%	99%	1	~	1	~
84%	85%	79%	83%	(6)%	94%	4	2	4	2
74%	78%	64%	77%	(6)%	86%	32	13	29	12
98%	99%	83%	127%	(30)%	85%	4	(4)	3	(1)
94%	93%	103%	91%	10%	109%	11	1	13	1
85%	87%	79%	91%	(4)%	93%	6	1	5	1
68%	66%	67%	62%	17%	99%	19	19	22	22
78%	77%	54%	69%	(2)%	70%	84	~	74	~
60%	62%	56%	70%	10%	93%	12	7	12	6
84%	90%	106%	99%	(15)%	127%	13	2	13	1
88%	87%	84%	86%	8%	95%	3	1	3	1
84%	84%	83%	89%	~	98%	3	1	2	1
87%	89%	77%	69%	(6)%	89%	82	2	73	3
87%	87%	88%	88%	7%	101%	28	(2)	28	(3)
46%	83%	21%	132%	(68)%	47%	81	15	21	2
67%	65%	70%	66%	6%	104%	9	4	12	6
81%	86%	84%	87%	(2)%	104%	11	4	11	3
100%	100%	89%	85%	10%	89%	18	1	18	2
72%	75%	44%	59%	(8)%	61%	99	-	82	-
94%	95%	80%	86%	(1)%	85%	5	1	4	~
94%	95%	57%	81%	19%	60%	50	7	46	6
75%	73%	72%	72%	(2)%	97%	10	3	9	3
90%	91%	93%	96%	3%	103%	4	1	5	1
88%	88%	84%	88%	4%	96%	8	2	7	2
50%	49%	48%	47%	6%	97%	2	2	2	2
78%	77%	72%	75%	7%	92%	5	2	4	2
85%	85%	82%	85%	8%	97%	20	(1)	22	(1)
70%	72%	71%	77%	2%	100%	72	1	71	~
82%	82%	84%	74%	24%	102%	6	4	7	5
97%	84%	99%	94%	(16)%	102%	18	(1)	16	~

Additional Statistics on The Top 100 Charities

Charity	Period	Fundraisng costs As % of Total Vol. Inc.		Management, Admin costs As % of Total Exp.		As % of Total Inc.	
		This Year	Last Year	This Year	Last Year	This Year	Last Year
51 BBC Children in Need	30-Jun-14	9%	9%	6%	5%	5%	6%
52 Science Museum Group	31-Mar-15	5%	4%	1%	1%	1%	1%
53 Racing Foundation, The	31-Dec-14	-	-	1%	2%	~	~
54 Cambridge Foundation	31-Jul-11	~	~	~	~	~	~
55 ActionAid	31-Dec-14	15%	19%	~	~	~	~
56 Stoller Charitable Trust	05-Apr-14	-	-	3%	2%	~	7%
57 Elim Foursquare Gospel Alliance	30-Sep-14	1%	1%	2%	2%	1%	1%
58 Royal National Theatre	31-Mar-15	4%	3%	~	~	~	~
59 Southampton Row Trust Limited	30-Apr-15	-	-	~	~	~	~
60 Church of Jesus Christ of Latter Day Saints	31-Dec-14	-	-	~	~	~	~
61 Tate Foundation	31-Mar-15	3%	3%	~	~	~	~
62 Barnardo's	31-Mar-15	33%	28%	1%	1%	1%	1%
63 Medecins sans Frontieres (UK)	31-Dec-14	9%	7%	~	~	~	~
64 Canal & River Trust	31-Mar-15	7%	5%	1%	1%	1%	1%
65 Royal Botanic Gardens, Kew	31-Mar-15	-	-	~	~	~	~
66 Disasters Emergency Committee	31-Mar-15	10%	5%	~	~	~	~
67 SHELTER	31-Mar-15	23%	36%	~	~	~	~
68 Jisc	31-Jul-15	-	-	1%	1%	1%	1%
69 Allchurches Trust	31-Dec-14	-	-	2%	2%	~	~
70 Prince's Trust	31-Mar-15	17%	20%	~	1%	~	1%
71 Queen Elizabeth Diamond Jubilee Trust	30-Jun-14	-	-	1%	4%	~	~
72 Watch Tower Bible Tract Society Britain	31-Aug-14	-	-	~	~	~	~
73 Diabetes UK	31-Dec-14	20%	19%	1%	1%	1%	1%
74 England and Wales Cricket Trust	31-Jan-15	-	-	1%	1%	~	~
75 Imperial War Museum	31-Mar-15	12%	7%	1%	1%	1%	1%
76 Cats Protection	31-Dec-14	21%	13%	~	~	~	~
77 Thalidomide Trust	30-Sep-14	-	-	1%	1%	1%	1%
78 Muslim Aid	31-Dec-14	7%	7%	~	~	~	~
79 National Gallery	31-Mar-15	4%	2%	1%	1%	1%	1%
80 Arts Council of Wales, The	31-Mar-15	-	-	~	~	~	~
81 Compassion UK	30-Jun-14	10%	12%	1%	1%	1%	1%
82 Plan International UK	30-Jun-15	16%	16%	~	~	~	~
83 World Society for the Protection of Animals	31-Dec-14	20%	12%	3%	5%	3%	5%
84 Westminster RC Diocesan Trust	31-Dec-14	-	-	~	~	~	~
85 Football Foundation	31-May-15	-	-	1%	1%	1%	1%
86 CAMFED International	31-Dec-14	3%	3%	1%	1%	1%	1%
87 Donkey Sanctuary	31-Dec-14	17%	15%	1%	1%	1%	1%
88 Fdn&Friends of RoyalBotanicGardens, Kew	31-Mar-15	7%	13%	1%	1%	~	1%
89 Focus Learning Trust	31-Jul-14	-	-	~	~	~	~
90 Gerald Ronson Foundation, The	31-Dec-14	-	-	13%	9%	~	6%
91 Woodland Trust	31-Dec-14	16%	21%	~	1%	~	1%
92 Parkinson's UK	31-Dec-14	21%	23%	2%	1%	1%	2%
93 Forster Foundation CIO, The	31-Jan-15	-	-	16%	-	~	-
94 National Museums Scotland	31-Mar-15	2%	2%	1%	1%	1%	1%
95 London Diocesan Fund	31-Dec-14	-	-	1%	1%	1%	1%
96 HALO Trust	31-Mar-15	-	-	1%	~	1%	~
97 Battersea Dogs & Cats Home	31-Dec-14	52%	48%	~	~	~	~
98 Amanat Charitable Trust	30-Nov-14	1%	1%	~	~	~	~
99 Blue Cross	31-Dec-14	42%	45%	1%	1%	1%	1%
100 Ahmadiyya Muslim Jamaat International	31-Dec-14	-	-	~	~	~	~

by Voluntary Income - (51-100)

Direct Charitable Expenditure				Total Expenditure (this year)		Expenditure Cover in Months (this year)		(last year)	
As % of Total Exp.		As % of Total Inc.							
This Year	Last Year	This Year	Last Year	Growth	As % of Total Income	Total Funds	Unrestricted Funds	Total Funds	Unrestricted Funds
83%	87%	70%	92%	(8)%	84%	13	-	10	-
77%	78%	82%	80%	(4)%	106%	61	~	58	~
86%	86%	2%	7%	72%	3%	732	98	463	166
100%	100%	97%	104%	15%	97%	1	~	1	~
88%	84%	89%	76%	10%	101%	3	1	3	1
94%	90%	3%	268%	161%	3%	409	409	110	110
93%	92%	83%	84%	1%	90%	26	(4)	26	(3)
78%	88%	71%	73%	21%	91%	8	~	8	~
100%	95%	98%	93%	29%	99%	11	~	13	~
100%	100%	103%	98%	(3)%	104%	69	66	69	66
97%	98%	93%	138%	(21)%	96%	8	2	6	1
77%	78%	76%	76%	5%	99%	1	(1)	1	~
90%	93%	78%	88%	13%	87%	3	3	2	2
79%	79%	76%	76%	10%	96%	46	2	46	1
89%	89%	85%	85%	(5)%	95%	34	29	30	26
90%	95%	92%	103%	(45)%	102%	1	~	1	~
66%	62%	57%	65%	~	86%	6	4	4	2
99%	99%	92%	84%	(5)%	93%	11	8	9	7
97%	97%	25%	18%	1%	26%	487	18	480	2
83%	83%	80%	86%	(1)%	96%	8	6	7	5
94%	27%	20%	1%	564%	21%	77	20	219	119
78%	99%	77%	102%	39%	98%	10	8	14	7
73%	74%	64%	64%	8%	87%	7	4	6	4
99%	99%	36%	55%	63%	37%	51	51	50	50
80%	82%	75%	66%	12%	93%	46	(1)	50	(1)
64%	72%	55%	59%	9%	85%	25	3	25	3
98%	98%	163%	145%	108%	166%	28	25	60	58
92%	92%	83%	92%	18%	90%	7	2	6	2
95%	96%	82%	61%	9%	86%	193	1	197	1
100%	99%	101%	103%	(9)%	101%	1	~	1	1
89%	88%	85%	87%	10%	96%	1	1	~	~
86%	85%	76%	85%	12%	89%	3	1	2	1
79%	84%	81%	87%	21%	101%	4	3	5	3
98%	98%	75%	83%	4%	76%	58	4	55	3
97%	97%	99%	92%	12%	102%	5	5	6	6
96%	96%	85%	96%	(12)%	89%	5	2	3	1
78%	80%	71%	71%	7%	91%	26	16	27	17
84%	83%	43%	74%	4%	51%	31	7	20	1
100%	100%	98%	100%	2%	99%	~	~	~	~
87%	91%	3%	59%	11%	4%	461	461	149	149
81%	77%	62%	62%	10%	77%	54	7	56	6
76%	79%	71%	91%	1%	93%	6	6	5	5
84%	-	~	-	-	~	2,749	2,749	-	-
90%	91%	82%	86%	~	90%	63	1	59	1
95%	94%	104%	101%	6%	108%	121	1	123	1
99%	100%	102%	105%	8%	104%	3	3	3	3
52%	58%	47%	61%	27%	91%	25	8	31	10
98%	97%	78%	81%	41%	80%	10	4	11	4
67%	67%	70%	72%	10%	104%	22	22	25	24
100%	100%	99%	89%	15%	99%	5	4	6	5

Investment Income Trends - The Top 200 Charities by

Charity	Period	Investment Income		Growth (3 Year Average)		As % of Total Income	
		This Year	Last Year	Investment Income	Total Income	This Year	Last Year
Wellcome Trust	30-Sep-15	£341m	£299m	16%	22%	78%	88%
Church Commissioners for England	31-Dec-14	£138m	£139m	(2)%	(2)%	98%	100%
Children's Investment Fund Foundation	31-Aug-14	£111m	£96.6m	52%	31%	97%	96%
City Bridge Trust, The	31-Mar-15	£87.7m	£36.8m	42%	39%	95%	90%
Leverhulme Trust	31-Dec-14	£78.8m	£73.9m	6%	6%	100%	100%
Garfield Weston Foundation	05-Apr-15	£56.6m	£51.8m	10%	10%	100%	100%
Canal & River Trust	31-Mar-15	£46.4m	£41.9m	-	-	26%	26%
National Trust	28-Feb-15	£27.1m	£26.9m	(4)%	4%	5%	6%
M R Gross Charities Limited	31-Mar-15	£23.5m	£5.11m	119%	68%	92%	62%
Robertson Trust	05-Apr-15	£20.2m	£18.4m	12%	14%	99%	99%
Lloyd's Register Foundation	30-Jun-15	£19.5m	£12.0m	-	-	100%	100%
ACT Foundation	31-Mar-15	£19.4m	£17.9m	8%	8%	100%	100%
Wolfson Foundation	05-Apr-15	£18.3m	£19.8m	(9)%	(9)%	100%	100%
Charities Aid Foundation	30-Apr-15	£17.4m	£19.4m	(3)%	6%	4%	5%
Representative Body of the Church in Wales	31-Dec-14	£17.2m	£17.1m	(1)%	~	90%	87%
CBHA	31-Mar-15	£17.0m	£10.7m	6,751%	29%	91%	86%
Health Foundation, The	31-Dec-14	£17.0m	£14.3m	~	~	99%	99%
Teresa Rosenbaum Golden Charitable Trust	31-Mar-15	£16.3m	£19.9m	266%	241%	96%	97%
Paul Hamlyn Foundation	31-Mar-15	£16.2m	£17.8m	6%	5%	99%	99%
Helping Foundation, The	30-Dec-14	£15.7m	£12.4m	27%	44%	54%	35%
Guy's & St Thomas' Charity	31-Mar-15	£14.1m	£12.7m	17%	13%	80%	82%
Christian Vision	31-Dec-14	£13.7m	£12.2m	8%	49%	36%	51%
A W Charitable Trust	30-Jun-14	£12.5m	£13.5m	17%	31%	98%	99%
Arthritis Research UK	31-Mar-15	£12.2m	£10.4m	175%	5%	31%	29%
Society of Jesus	30-Sep-14	£11.5m	£12.6m	~	(8)%	37%	49%
Henry Smith Charity	31-Dec-14	£11.3m	£10.4m	(3)%	(2)%	98%	98%
Save the Children	31-Dec-14	£10.9m	£9.57m	5%	5%	3%	3%
Framework Housing Association	31-Mar-15	£10.8m	£9.86m	13%	5%	38%	35%
Barts and The London Charity	31-Mar-15	£10.6m	£9.14m	5%	(1)%	80%	73%
Whitgift Foundation	31-Aug-14	£10.5m	£11.2m	(2)%	5%	20%	23%
Dulwich Estate	31-Mar-15	£9.47m	£9.77m	2%	2%	98%	98%
National Trust for Scotland	28-Feb-15	£9.35m	£8.85m	1%	(4)%	20%	18%
Joseph Rowntree Foundation	31-Dec-14	£9.06m	£8.44m	5%	6%	96%	97%
Charles Wolfson Charitable Trust	05-Apr-15	£8.30m	£8.67m	2%	2%	100%	100%
Benesco Charity	05-Apr-15	£8.14m	£8.55m	2%	2%	100%	100%
Christ's Hospital Foundation	31-Aug-14	£8.11m	£7.80m	~	9%	37%	41%
John Lyon's Charity	31-Mar-15	£7.99m	£7.24m	7%	7%	100%	100%
Thompson Family Charitable Trust	31-Jan-15	£7.94m	£6.71m	13%	13%	100%	100%
Letchworth Garden City Heritage Foundation	30-Sep-14	£7.92m	£7.82m	-	-	81%	79%
4 Charity Foundation	31-Mar-15	£7.76m	£7.03m	4%	4%	99%	100%
Moondance Foundation	30-Nov-14	£7.74m	£5.87m	70%	3%	28%	16%
Milton Keynes Parks Trust Ltd	31-Mar-15	£7.69m	£7.21m	12%	(12)%	80%	75%
Gatsby Charitable Foundation	05-Apr-15	£7.17m	£9.56m	(19)%	22%	9%	15%
Trust for London	31-Dec-14	£7.16m	£8.08m	(2)%	3%	78%	89%
Linbury Trust	05-Apr-15	£7.16m	£6.91m	5%	9%	88%	79%
Morden College	31-Mar-15	£7.12m	£7.73m	~	~	68%	71%
FIA Foundation for Automobile & Society	31-Dec-14	£7.05m	£6.65m	10%	5%	94%	90%
Shlomo Memorial Fund	30-Sep-14	£6.74m	£7.29m	(1)%	9%	75%	97%
Rothschild Foundation	28-Feb-15	£6.69m	£6.32m	85%	(22)%	24%	21%
Esmée Fairbairn Foundation	31-Dec-14	£6.57m	£8.95m	(18)%	(18)%	100%	100%

Investment Income - (1-50)

Investment Inc As % of Investments		Funds Analysis this year		last year		Expenditure cover (in Months) this year		last year	
This Year	Last Year	Restricted	Unrestricted	Restricted	Unrestricted	Total Funds	Unrestricted Funds	Total Funds	Unrestricted Funds
2%	2%	-	£16,907m	-	£16,737m	170	170	231	231
2%	2%	£6,740m	-	£6,125m	-	297	-	285	-
4%	4%	£2,622m	-	£2,446m	-	228	-	297	-
7%	4%	£631m	£510m	£578m	£446m	329	147	313	136
3%	3%	£2,051m	£93.0m	£1,929m	£98.4m	303	13.2	449	21.8
1%	~	£10,730m	£123m	£10,426m	£120m	2,205	25.0	2,321	26.4
7%	7%	£635m	£24.9m	£579m	£17.1m	45.9	1.73	45.6	1.31
3%	3%	£1,227m	£(77.0)m	£1,194m	£(108)m	27.6	(1.85)	27.9	(2.76)
829%	70%	£7.05m	£51.4m	£7.05m	£12.0m	102	89.3	31.8	20.1
7%	5%	£242m	£20.4m	£333m	£18.2m	164	12.7	245	12.7
7%	5%	£234m	£16.2m	£223m	£10.7m	191	12.4	149	6.82
14%	14%	£2.07m	£78.3m	£(13.6)m	£77.1m	59.7	58.2	53.5	65.0
2%	3%	£729m	-	£702m	-	267	-	257	-
1%	1%	£1,000m	£53.0m	£947m	£51.5m	28.2	1.42	29.4	1.52
3%	4%	£251m	£356m	£251m	£340m	362	212	345	198
448%	370%	-	£34.2m	-	£30.1m	28.9	28.9	43.9	43.9
2%	2%	£832m	-	£782m	£4.27m	256	-	294	1.59
46%	55%	£28.9m	£6.40m	£28.9m	£7.30m	136	24.6	154	31.0
2%	3%	£660m	-	£600m	-	302	-	271	-
8%	6%	-	£116m	-	£105m	106	106	116	116
2%	2%	£603m	£13.6m	£519m	£15.5m	198	4.37	148	4.27
5%	5%	£273m	-	£231m	-	192	-	178	-
6%	7%	£4.25m	£112m	£3.61m	£102m	149	144	163	157
8%	7%	£117m	£44.6m	£101m	£47.1m	54.5	15.0	53.0	16.8
3%	4%	£474m	£4.03m	£452m	£6.25m	196	1.65	135	1.83
1%	1%	£833m	£6.00m	£778m	£7.52m	254	1.81	232	2.22
10%	9%	£104m	£4.49m	£90.9m	£2.89m	3.72	0.15	3.64	0.11
126%	140%	£15.3m	£5.73m	£14.6m	£6.00m	8.95	2.43	9.17	2.67
3%	3%	£259m	£95.6m	£230m	£78.0m	296	79.8	289	73.4
6%	6%	£232m	£0.33m	£228m	-	53.3	0.08	53.6	-
11%	14%	£263m	-	£236m	-	204	-	286	-
5%	5%	£207m	£21.0m	£195m	£21.0m	55.6	5.13	55.7	5.42
3%	3%	-	£320m	-	£316m	374	374	378	378
35%	101%	£188m	£32.0m	£160m	£31.2m	300	43.7	308	50.4
33%	374%	£178m	£30.6m	£150m	£30.3m	282	41.4	293	49.3
2%	3%	-	£343m	-	£314m	143	143	139	139
2%	2%	£341m	-	£307m	-	441	-	426	-
7%	7%	-	£114m	-	£105m	334	334	359	359
60%	55%	£132m	£(0.92)m	£129m	£(0.40)m	127	(0.89)	113	(0.35)
8%	8%	£14.9m	£12.7m	£4.91m	£10.6m	57.5	26.5	31.2	21.3
8%	7%	-	£99.7m	-	£78.8m	225	225	190	190
6%	6%	£91.9m	£3.79m	£85.3m	£4.07m	118	4.69	105	4.77
1%	2%	£384m	-	£347m	-	98.8	-	82.4	-
3%	4%	£292m	£0.20m	£267m	£0.12m	224	0.16	215	0.10
5%	4%	£140m	-	£153m	-	209	-	210	-
4%	5%	£195m	£19.9m	£183m	£18.6m	269	24.8	268	24.8
2%	2%	£50.7m	£254m	£43.6m	£263m	199	166	184	158
1,283%	612%	£28.8m	£21.0m	£26.9m	£18.6m	80.2	33.8	103	42.0
1%	2%	£7.46m	£516m	£7.76m	£448m	333	329	244	240
1%	1%	-	£837m	-	£802m	236	236	244	244

Investment Income Trends - The Top 200 Charities by

Charity	Period	Investment Income		Growth (3 Year Average)		As % of Total Income	
		This Year	Last Year	Investment Income	Total Income	This Year	Last Year
Tudor Trust	31-Mar-15	£6.55m	£6.90m	(11)%	(11)%	100%	100%
Gannochy Trust	31-May-15	£6.41m	£6.12m	3%	3%	100%	100%
Shulem B. Association Ltd	30-Sep-14	£6.38m	£5.98m	5%	(1)%	55%	41%
Local Trust	31-Mar-15	£6.35m	£5.32m	1,317%	(48)%	100%	100%
Big Local Trust	31-Mar-15	£6.35m	£5.32m	-	-	100%	100%
National Fund	05-Apr-15	£6.27m	£4.63m	(11)%	(11)%	100%	100%
Corporation of Trinity House	31-Mar-15	£6.24m	£5.94m	6%	6%	73%	74%
Church of Scotland General Trustees	31-Dec-14	£6.11m	£5.94m	1%	5%	28%	34%
Delapage Ltd	31-Mar-14	£6.11m	£6.62m			39%	41%
Collegiate Charitable Foundation, The	31-Aug-14	£6.10m	£5.75m	4%	4%	99%	100%
St Monica Trust	31-Dec-14	£6.04m	£6.12m	1%	6%	23%	25%
Cancer Research UK	31-Mar-15	£6.00m	£1.90m	59%	9%	1%	~
London Diocesan Fund	31-Dec-14	£6.00m	£5.60m	5%	4%	16%	16%
Methodist Church In Great Britain, The	31-Aug-14	£5.95m	£5.04m	23%	(1)%	14%	11%
Oasis Charitable Trust	31-Aug-14	£5.93m	£4.21m	843%	57%	2%	3%
Salvation Army Trust	31-Mar-15	£5.89m	£5.19m	1%	6%	3%	3%
Newmarston Limited Group	28-Feb-15	£5.75m	£7.54m	(2)%	39%	40%	43%
Shetland Charitable Trust	31-Mar-15	£5.72m	£5.75m	(2)%	(1)%	55%	55%
Nuffield Foundation	31-Dec-14	£5.72m	£4.47m	10%	61%	89%	26%
Babraham Institute	31-Mar-15	£5.44m	£6.95m	8%	10%	12%	12%
Exilarch's Foundation	31-Dec-14	£5.44m	£5.41m	~	(6)%	82%	100%
Independent Age	31-Dec-14	£5.41m	£5.40m	1%	(17)%	67%	66%
Historic Royal Palaces	31-Mar-15	£5.38m	£3.61m	6%	10%	6%	5%
Waterloo Foundation, The	31-Dec-14	£5.34m	£5.03m	5%	38%	64%	44%
Somerset House Trust	31-Mar-15	£5.24m	£3.63m	18%	11%	41%	33%
RSPCA	31-Dec-14	£5.18m	£3.00m	27%	3%	4%	2%
Council for World Mission	31-Dec-14	£5.16m	£4.57m	7%	6%	94%	88%
Liverpool Roman Catholic Archdiocesan	31-Dec-14	£5.14m	£4.86m	10%	(4)%	14%	12%
Greenham Common Community Trust	31-Mar-15	£5.02m	£4.61m	4%	10%	60%	66%
Gilmoor Benevolent Fund Limited	31-Mar-15	£4.98m	£4.72m	1%	52%	34%	82%
Royal Albert Hall	31-Dec-14	£4.92m	£5.37m	2%	10%	18%	21%
Millennium Awards Trust, The	31-Mar-15	£4.90m	£3.99m	7%	7%	100%	100%
Foundation for Social Entrepreneurs	31-Mar-15	£4.90m	£3.99m	7%	13%	38%	31%
Motability Tenth Anniversary Trust, The	31-Mar-15	£4.81m	£4.38m	23%	444%	100%	8%
Royal Society, The	31-Mar-15	£4.74m	£4.55m	5%	2%	6%	6%
Royal British Legion	30-Sep-14	£4.72m	£4.61m	(1)%	(1)%	4%	4%
Land Restoration Trust	31-Mar-15	£4.71m	£4.21m	76%	68%	42%	18%
Becht Family Charitable Trust, The	03-Oct-14	£4.69m	£4.39m	8%	8%	100%	100%
Salvation Army Officers Pension Fund	31-Mar-15	£4.55m	£4.55m	8%	11%	28%	35%
St John's Hospital	31-Dec-14	£4.50m	£4.47m	(1)%	1%	81%	87%
Gosling Foundation Limited	31-Mar-15	£4.45m	£4.45m	(1)%	85%	100%	23%
Monument Trust	05-Apr-15	£4.42m	£4.44m	(13)%	(19)%	98%	100%
Thames Reach	31-Mar-14	£4.42m	£4.19m	(10)%	(13)%	27%	27%
Thomas Pocklington Trust	31-Mar-15	£4.42m	£4.25m	4%	(3)%	52%	50%
Zochonis Charitable Trust	05-Apr-15	£4.40m	£4.38m	10%	145%	100%	17%
Westminster RC Diocesan Trust	31-Dec-14	£4.38m	£4.87m	8%	11%	9%	11%
Millennium Point Trust	31-Mar-15	£4.34m	£4.24m	2%	2%	77%	77%
Rhodes Trust	30-Jun-14	£4.31m	£3.93m	6%	50%	20%	33%
Eranda Foundation	05-Apr-15	£4.26m	£3.97m	3%	3%	100%	100%
Thalidomide Trust	30-Sep-14	£4.22m	£3.74m	6%	30%	11%	18%

Investment Income - (51-100)

This Year	Last Year	Restricted (this year)	Unrestricted (this year)	Restricted (last year)	Unrestricted (last year)	Total Funds (this year)	Unrestricted Funds (this year)	Total Funds (last year)	Unrestricted Funds (last year)
3%	3%	-	£243m	-	£232m	154	154	129	129
4%	4%	£167m	£8.45m	£155m	£9.13m	539	26.0	465	25.8
10%	12%	£42.9m	£10.3m	£30.5m	£10.1m	79.5	15.4	46.5	11.6
3%	3%	£207m	-	£205m	-	152	-	231	-
4%	4%	-	£207m	-	£205m	152	152	231	231
1%	1%	£444m	-	£403m	-	8,609	-	7,191	-
3%	3%	£238m	£1.03m	£201m	£0.59m	350	1.50	296	0.87
3%	4%	£684m	£6.04m	£663m	£5.69m	476	4.17	449	3.81
42%	62%	-	£45.3m	-	£40.9m	84.4	84.4	61.0	61.0
21,028%	16,420%	~	£0.34m	-	£0.33m	0.68	0.67	0.66	0.66
3%	3%	£222m	£14.4m	£219m	£14.3m	106	6.48	115	7.06
2%	1%	£55.0m	£282m	£35.8m	£278m	6.71	5.62	6.96	6.16
5%	5%	£398m	£2.80m	£384m	£2.50m	121	0.84	123	0.80
4%	3%	£125m	£50.3m	£115m	£45.7m	53.3	15.3	38.4	10.9
18%	20%	£328m	£5.35m	£226m	£3.08m	25.5	0.41	23.7	0.32
2%	2%	£422m	£134m	£417m	£115m	37.4	9.02	38.3	8.29
7%	9%	-	£48.6m	-	£40.7m	102	102	98.8	98.8
3%	3%	£251m	£(4.89)m	£232m	£(2.55)m	209	(4.15)	189	(2.10)
2%	2%	£286m	£4.17m	£257m	£3.98m	318	4.56	101	1.54
6%	13%	£114m	£33.5m	£107m	£28.7m	38.8	8.84	42.8	9.04
7%	7%	£64.3m	£1.58m	£59.0m	£0.78m	125	3.02	111	1.45
4%	3%	£139m	£10.4m	£148m	£3.25m	179	12.5	305	6.54
15%	11%	£4.35m	£35.9m	£2.11m	£36.2m	5.72	5.10	6.01	5.68
5%	5%	-	£115m	-	£111m	161	161	174	174
105%	77%	£(0.19)m	£86.9m	£(0.21)m	£87.9m	74.9	75.1	76.9	77.1
5%	3%	£113m	£52.5m	£117m	£45.5m	16.6	5.26	16.7	4.65
4%	3%	£17.6m	£126m	£10.9m	£134m	182	160	224	207
4%	4%	£89.4m	£81.7m	£87.8m	£79.2m	50.0	23.9	48.4	23.0
9%	8%	£43.7m	£8.53m	£43.2m	£8.70m	72.1	11.8	85.1	14.3
5%	6%	£19.7m	£93.3m	£13.7m	£85.2m	224	185	324	279
18%	20%	£30.6m	£3.04m	£27.3m	£1.05m	18.2	1.65	16.9	0.63
4%	3%	£124m	£3.41m	£120m	£2.62m	265	7.11	337	7.20
4%	3%	£128m	£4.58m	£125m	£3.59m	111	3.84	121	3.38
2%	2%	£190m	£2.65m	£178m	£2.85m	462	6.34	396	6.24
2%	2%	£181m	£84.2m	£167m	£86.8m	44.6	14.2	43.4	14.9
2%	2%	£177m	£127m	£178m	£123m	31.7	13.2	29.5	12.0
4%	4%	£117m	£8.29m	£106m	£6.61m	264	17.4	213	12.5
2%	3%	-	£194m	£0.65m	£161m	(12,372)	(12,372)	1,192	1,187
3%	3%	-	£176m	-	£152m	253	253	213	213
4%	5%	£94.7m	£17.6m	£89.0m	£16.0m	302	47.5	299	45.7
4%	5%	£78.6m	£22.1m	£77.3m	£19.5m	666	146	214	43.0
3%	3%	£102m	-	£138m	-	25.0	-	45.7	-
75%	72%	£10.0m	£0.63m	£9.93m	£0.59m	7.83	0.47	8.11	0.46
3%	3%	£163m	£3.38m	£154m	£3.65m	217	4.40	188	4.35
2%	2%	£194m	£1.88m	£198m	£1.77m	549	5.26	614	5.44
5%	6%	£173m	£12.6m	£162m	£9.18m	57.9	3.93	55.3	2.97
9%	9%	£43.6m	£1.62m	£43.5m	£1.81m	95.3	3.42	340	13.6
3%	3%	£145m	£7.02m	£129m	£7.25m	151	6.95	148	7.88
4%	4%	£92.6m	£4.11m	£88.1m	£4.63m	225	9.53	257	12.8
3%	2%	£13.2m	£137m	£4.74m	£152m	27.7	25.3	60.2	58.4

Investment Income Trends - The Top 200 Charities by

Charity	Period	Investment Income		Growth 3 Year Average		As % of Total Income	
		This Year	Last Year	Investment Income	Total Income	This Year	Last Year
Bernard Sunley Charitable Foundation	31-Mar-15	£4.19m	£3.79m	9%	9%	100%	100%
Ernest Cook Trust	31-Mar-15	£4.11m	£3.93m	8%	7%	97%	98%
Reuben Foundation	31-Dec-14	£4.11m	£3.82m	7%	8%	98%	99%
Papworth Trust	31-Mar-15	£4.04m	£3.98m	-	3%	18%	18%
Shell Foundation	31-Dec-14	£4.02m	£3.36m	7%	36%	20%	22%
Social Investment Business Foundation	31-Mar-15	£4.00m	£4.54m	(10)%	(2)%	28%	27%
British Heart Foundation	31-Mar-15	£4.00m	£4.30m	(14)%	5%	1%	2%
LankellyChase Foundation, The	31-Mar-15	£3.99m	£3.81m	(2)%	(4)%	96%	99%
Church of Scot Uninc. Councils Cttees	31-Dec-14	£3.98m	£5.98m	(9)%	(2)%	4%	5%
Comic Relief	31-Jul-14	£3.91m	£6.09m	(16)%	(8)%	5%	5%
Chevras Tsedokoh Limited	30-Sep-14	£3.86m	£3.98m	(1)%	(1)%	100%	100%
Education Endowment Foundation, The	31-Mar-15	£3.82m	£5.30m	(4)%	(53)%	62%	68%
Clothworkers' Foundation	31-Dec-14	£3.78m	£3.31m	14%	165%	62%	10%
Oxford Diocesan Board Finance	31-Dec-14	£3.72m	£3.57m	14%	5%	14%	15%
John Ellerman Foundation	31-Mar-15	£3.69m	£2.31m	34%	34%	100%	100%
Refuge	31-Mar-15	£3.69m	£3.67m	2%	~	36%	33%
Dulverton Trust	31-Mar-15	£3.65m	£3.54m	4%	4%	100%	100%
Blind Veterans UK	31-Mar-15	£3.65m	£3.81m	7%	2%	13%	14%
University College London Hospitals Charity	31-Mar-15	£3.64m	£3.09m	18%	37%	22%	19%
Goldsmiths' Company Charity	31-Mar-15	£3.58m	£3.52m	(7)%	(13)%	97%	99%
Rufford Foundation, The	05-Apr-15	£3.58m	£3.66m	71%	286%	100%	100%
Cambridge Commonwealth Trust	31-Jul-13	£3.55m	£3.48m	12%	3%	49%	55%
LGS General Charitable Trust	31-Aug-15	£3.50m	£3.50m	23%	18%	91%	100%
29th May 1961 Charitable Trust	05-Apr-15	£3.41m	£3.42m	3%	4%	97%	100%
Anchor Trust	31-Mar-15	£3.35m	£2.73m	7%	~	1%	1%
Dunhill Medical Trust	31-Mar-15	£3.34m	£3.17m	3%	(28)%	100%	100%
Rochester Bridge Trust	31-Mar-15	£3.26m	£3.35m	11%	12%	100%	96%
Khodorkovsky Foundation	31-Dec-14	£3.25m	£3.10m	8%	8%	100%	100%
Kennedy Trust for Rheumatology Research	30-Sep-14	£3.24m	£2.55m	29%	18%	9%	9%
Corporation of the Sons of the Clergy	31-Dec-14	£3.24m	£3.21m	2%	7%	80%	87%
S F Foundation	31-Jan-15	£3.21m	£4.38m	1%	9%	46%	63%
Stratford Upon Avon Town Trust	31-Dec-14	£3.19m	£3.28m	(1)%	(2)%	99%	96%
Royal Society of Chemistry	31-Dec-14	£3.14m	£3.47m	(5)%	6%	6%	7%
Cecil Alan Pilkington Trust Fund	31-Mar-15	£3.10m	£3.25m	4%	4%	87%	88%
Barnardo's	31-Mar-15	£3.08m	£3.86m	(6)%	7%	1%	1%
P F Charitable Trust	31-Mar-15	£3.06m	£3.20m	7%	7%	100%	100%
Nesta	31-Mar-15	£3.02m	£3.44m	-	-	19%	22%
Jerusalem Trust	05-Apr-15	£3.02m	£2.59m	9%	7%	100%	100%
Dame Alice Owen's Foundation	31-Dec-14	£3.01m	£2.85m	10%	15%	100%	71%
Roman Catholic Diocese of Southwark	31-Dec-14	£3.01m	£2.88m	5%	3%	10%	10%
Harpur Trust, The	30-Jun-14	£2.96m	£2.49m	5%	2%	5%	5%
Hertford British Hospital, Paris	31-Dec-14	£2.94m	£3.14m	6%	2%	75%	76%
Burghley House Preservation Trust	31-Jan-15	£2.94m	£2.65m	4%	2%	37%	35%
Maudsley Charity	31-Mar-14	£2.91m	£2.84m	4%	29%	73%	47%
Sir Jules Thorn Charitable Trust	31-Dec-14	£2.91m	£2.44m	7%	7%	100%	100%
Campden Charities Trustee	31-Mar-15	£2.90m	£2.92m	4%	4%	98%	98%
Birmingham Diocesan Trust	31-Dec-14	£2.90m	£2.80m	4%	1%	14%	12%
Sutton's Hospital in Charterhouse	25-Mar-15	£2.89m	£2.34m	10%	14%	67%	63%
Institute of Our Lady of Mercy, The	31-Dec-14	£2.88m	£2.87m	~	(19)%	20%	21%
YMCA Watford & District Branch	31-Mar-15	£2.88m	£2.80m	16%	22%	33%	31%

Investment Income - (101-150)

Investment Inc As % of Investments		Funds Analysis this year		last year		Expenditure cover (in Months) this year		last year	
This Year	Last Year	Restricted	Unrestricted	Restricted	Unrestricted	Total Funds	Unrestricted Funds	Total Funds	Unrestricted Funds
4%	4%	£103m	-	£98.6m	-	351	-	347	-
3%	3%	£128m	£4.38m	£125m	£4.38m	345	11.4	348	11.8
11%	11%	-	£79.3m	£2.50m	£74.8m	174	174	549	531
40%	45%	£19.8m	£5.54m	£18.6m	£6.06m	13.6	2.98	13.0	3.20
1%	1%	£300m	£10.9m	£280m	£7.86m	166	5.81	143	3.89
7%	6%	£73.9m	£1.87m	£133m	£1.89m	12.4	0.31	78.0	1.09
1%	2%	£15.6m	£(21.6)m	£12.8m	£(43.4)m	(0.25)	(0.90)	(1.17)	(1.66)
3%	3%	-	£140m	-	£130m	294	294	281	281
3%	4%	£179m	£(9.09)m	£178m	£(1.94)m	18.3	(0.98)	15.9	(0.17)
2%	2%	£92.4m	£21.1m	£130m	£7.65m	12.7	2.36	13.1	0.73
10%	10%	-	£17.1m	-	£17.8m	125	125	123	123
3%	4%	£1.74m	£111m	£2.01m	£113m	96.2	94.7	124	122
3%	3%	£147m	£0.50m	£132m	£1.09m	268	0.90	251	2.06
3%	3%	£379m	£7.67m	£353m	£6.61m	198	3.93	184	3.39
3%	2%	-	£135m	£1.30m	£123m	287	287	339	335
62%	71%	£2.81m	£2.02m	£2.61m	£2.23m	5.69	2.38	5.87	2.70
5%	4%	-	£91.4m	-	£88.4m	317	317	261	261
3%	3%	£66.1m	£87.4m	£62.4m	£87.2m	61.1	34.8	62.0	36.1
3%	2%	£36.5m	£75.5m	£10.2m	£93.1m	74.4	50.1	61.4	55.3
3%	3%	£118m	£1.59m	£107m	£1.26m	371	4.95	298	3.47
3%	4%	-	£103m	-	£100m	283	283	274	274
4%	4%	£4.60m	£94.1m	£4.28m	£80.8m	161	154	169	161
1,025%	1,137%	£0.11m	£0.05m	£0.11m	£0.03m	0.47	0.14	0.44	0.10
1%	3%	£110m	£2.20m	£108m	£1.88m	278	5.47	216	3.64
11%	4%	£250m	-	£249m	-	11.3	-	11.7	-
3%	3%	-	£125m	-	£114m	322	322	351	351
4%	4%	£90.9m	£3.08m	£85.5m	£3.53m	513	16.8	460	18.2
1%	1%	£320m	-	£307m	-	451	-	418	-
1%	1%	£39.8m	£172m	£44.0m	£142m	104	84.7	72.0	55.0
4%	4%	£1.54m	£87.6m	£1.43m	£84.7m	328	322	362	356
9%	12%	-	£28.6m	-	£25.2m	90.0	90.0	66.2	66.2
6%	6%	£51.1m	£2.85m	£50.0m	£3.35m	176	9.33	142	8.90
3%	3%	£28.6m	£49.1m	£26.9m	£70.1m	16.9	10.7	24.5	17.7
4%	4%	£86.3m	-	£83.9m	-	302	-	298	-
4%	5%	£32.6m	£(14.4)m	£30.1m	£(8.79)m	0.75	(0.59)	0.92	(0.38)
3%	3%	£110m	£2.37m	£102m	£2.06m	488	10.3	423	8.40
1%	1%	£390m	£3.19m	£362m	£1.39m	147	1.19	153	0.59
3%	3%	£93.6m	£(0.17)m	£88.7m	£(0.88)m	280	(0.51)	234	(2.35)
4%	3%	£80.2m	£1.54m	£80.8m	£1.14m	259	4.90	450	6.27
7%	7%	£71.4m	£10.1m	£71.2m	£8.09m	33.9	4.21	30.8	3.14
3%	3%	£122m	£8.09m	£113m	£6.82m	33.0	2.05	30.2	1.72
9%	9%	-	£26.6m	-	£29.7m	142	142	151	151
6%	5%	£55.4m	£4.28m	£52.3m	£3.72m	96.8	6.95	93.0	6.18
3%	3%	£116m	£0.48m	£100m	£0.46m	173	0.72	186	0.85
2%	2%	£112m	-	£109m	-	356	-	96.2	-
2%	2%	£143m	£0.28m	£126m	£0.69m	512	0.98	444	2.44
4%	4%	£58.2m	£57.5m	£58.2m	£55.2m	66.4	33.0	65.2	31.7
4%	4%	£71.6m	£0.05m	£67.3m	£1.19m	129	0.09	188	3.26
4%	4%	£19.2m	£170m	£19.7m	£165m	121	109	125	111
76%	75%	-	£5.58m	-	£5.49m	7.79	7.79	7.25	7.25

Investment Income Trends - The Top 200 Charities by

Charity	Period	Investment Income		Growth 3 Year Average		As % of Total Income	
		This Year	Last Year	Investment Income	Total Income	This Year	Last Year
CHK Charities Limited	31-Jan-15	£2.87m	£2.78m	9%	10%	100%	100%
Royal Navy and Royal Marines Charity	31-Dec-14	£2.82m	£2.80m	6%	(3)%	21%	25%
Mayfair Charities	31-Mar-15	£2.81m	£2.72m	(2)%	(24)%	67%	64%
Lincoln Diocesan Trust Board Finance Ltd	31-Dec-14	£2.80m	£2.91m	~	1%	26%	24%
Drapers Charities Pooling Scheme	31-Jul-14	£2.77m	£2.68m	15%	(17)%	72%	88%
Barnwood House Trust	31-Dec-14	£2.76m	£3.01m	17%	10%	84%	86%
Carnegie Trust for Universities Scotland	30-Sep-14	£2.74m	£2.67m	7%	5%	95%	98%
Joseph Rank Trust, The	31-Dec-14	£2.73m	£2.62m	3%	3%	100%	100%
Westway Trust	31-Mar-15	£2.72m	£2.58m	2%	3%	33%	33%
Royal Commission for the 1851 Exhibition	31-Dec-14	£2.71m	£2.34m	5%	5%	100%	100%
Army Central Fund, The	30-Jun-15	£2.71m	£2.63m	6%	20%	99%	90%
NGT Foundation	31-Mar-15	£2.69m	£2.83m	(3)%	(3)%	100%	100%
Salvation Army International Trust	31-Mar-15	£2.69m	£2.56m	16%	28%	4%	6%
Beit Trust	31-Dec-14	£2.68m	£2.45m	5%	5%	100%	100%
Consumers' Association	30-Jun-15	£2.66m	£2.41m	36%	8%	3%	3%
Peter Harrison Foundation	31-May-14	£2.64m	£2.35m	67%	(25)%	100%	100%
Royal Masonic Trust For Girls and Boys	31-Mar-15	£2.59m	£1.57m	29%	26%	29%	29%
Stewardship Services (UKET) Ltd	30-Sep-14	£2.57m	£2.61m	4%	6%	4%	4%
Kusuma Trust UK	31-Mar-15	£2.57m	£2.75m	(8)%	(8)%	100%	100%
Royal Brompton Hospital Charity	31-Mar-15	£2.56m	£2.76m	~	11%	33%	40%
Ely Diocesan Board of Finance, The	31-Dec-14	£2.56m	£2.33m	7%	5%	28%	26%
Headley Trust	05-Apr-15	£2.55m	£2.24m	7%	4%	100%	100%
Barrow Cadbury Trust	31-Mar-15	£2.54m	£2.60m	~	~	98%	93%
Richmond Charities' Almshouses	31-Dec-14	£2.54m	£2.30m	6%	7%	84%	83%
Royal National Lifeboat Institution	31-Dec-14	£2.50m	£3.40m	(20)%	3%	1%	2%
Edward James Foundation Limited	30-Sep-14	£2.49m	£2.25m	6%	22%	26%	12%
Royal College of Surgeons	30-Jun-15	£2.48m	£2.34m	6%	7%	8%	8%
February Foundation, The	28-Feb-15	£2.48m	£1.86m	53%	(1)%	20%	11%
Poor Servants of the Mother of God	31-Mar-15	£2.47m	£2.55m	2%	2%	16%	17%
Foyle Foundation	31-Dec-14	£2.47m	£3.00m	(7)%	(20)%	96%	100%
British Academy	31-Mar-15	£2.45m	£1.99m	28%	4%	7%	6%
Sir Thomas White's Charity	30-Sep-14	£2.43m	£2.03m	7%	7%	99%	98%
NHS Gtr Glasgow & Clyde Endowments	31-Mar-12	£2.39m	£1.97m	-	-	22%	20%
Said Foundation	31-Aug-14	£2.38m	£1.66m	22%	15%	50%	48%
Park Charitable Trust, The	31-Mar-14	£2.35m	£2.71m	126%	66%	100%	91%
Cranstoun Drug Services	31-Mar-15	£2.33m	£0.02m	4,034%	13%	21%	~
Keswick Foundation	31-Dec-14	£2.32m	£2.14m	6%	6%	99%	99%
Royal Literary Fund	05-Apr-15	£2.32m	£1.81m	5%	4%	89%	81%
General Medical Council	31-Dec-14	£2.32m	£1.30m	18%	(2)%	2%	1%
Great Ormond St Hosp Children's Charity	31-Mar-15	£2.32m	£2.66m	(11)%	7%	3%	4%
E P A Cephalosporin Fund	05-Apr-15	£2.31m	£1.65m	13%	13%	100%	100%
Guild Estate Endowment	31-Dec-14	£2.30m	£2.28m	(1)%	(1)%	100%	100%
Claude and Sofia Marion Foundation, The	31-Dec-14	£2.29m	£0.77m	512%	11%	68%	34%
John James Bristol Foundation	30-Sep-14	£2.29m	£1.64m	19%	19%	100%	100%
Institution of Engineering and Technology	31-Dec-14	£2.29m	£4.07m	4%	(2)%	4%	7%
Action Housing & Support Limited	31-Mar-15	£2.29m	£1.89m	23%	~	37%	30%
Dolphin Square Charitable Foundation, The	31-Mar-15	£2.27m	£3.04m	(5)%	241%	21%	10%
Chalfords Limited	31-Dec-14	£2.26m	£2.04m	(2)%	4%	72%	72%
Talbot Village Trust	31-Dec-14	£2.24m	£2.09m	8%	7%	100%	97%
Franciscan Missionaries Charitable Trust	31-Dec-14	£2.23m	£2.16m	1%	17%	29%	47%

Investment Income - (151-200)

Investment Inc As % of Investments		Funds Analysis				Expenditure cover (in Months)			
		this year		last year		this year		last year	
This Year	Last Year	Restricted	Unrestricted	Restricted	Unrestricted	Total Funds	Unrestricted Funds	Total Funds	Unrestricted Funds
3%	3%	£96.3m	£3.11m	£89.1m	£3.11m	415	13.0	394	13.3
4%	4%	£67.0m	£14.4m	£63.3m	£13.6m	88.5	15.7	87.8	15.5
2%	3%	£7.14m	£104m	£5.91m	£93.2m	229	215	185	174
3%	3%	£168m	£0.85m	£166m	£2.06m	142	0.72	156	1.91
4%	4%	£77.6m	£3.28m	£73.9m	£2.48m	494	20.0	468	15.2
3%	4%	£0.77m	£84.4m	£0.74m	£80.6m	356	353	367	363
4%	4%	£72.2m	£1.48m	£68.5m	£2.16m	294	5.93	322	9.86
3%	3%	£17.8m	£71.9m	£16.8m	£66.1m	373	299	377	301
8%	9%	£45.3m	£0.59m	£38.6m	£0.37m	70.2	0.90	60.5	0.58
3%	3%	-	£94.2m	-	£83.0m	422	422	407	407
5%	5%	£0.20m	£59.4m	£0.26m	£56.7m	291	290	173	172
5%	6%	£45.0m	£5.63m	£37.5m	£5.03m	196	21.8	167	19.7
3%	3%	£147m	£24.6m	£117m	£17.2m	49.7	7.12	46.1	5.91
3%	3%	-	£94.3m	-	£93.0m	457	457	443	443
5%	6%	-	£52.9m	-	£49.5m	6.44	6.44	6.31	6.31
6%	5%	£45.2m	£0.78m	£45.2m	£0.07m	183	3.09	55.9	0.09
2%	1%	£23.0m	£143m	£20.3m	£136m	157	135	181	158
3%	3%	£81.0m	£7.32m	£73.3m	£6.81m	17.9	1.48	17.9	1.52
1%	1%	£304m	£2.73m	£277m	£2.03m	1,327	11.8	1,283	9.34
2%	3%	£20.3m	£86.1m	£15.8m	£78.1m	165	133	158	132
7%	6%	£110m	£5.80m	£105m	£4.93m	158	7.89	152	6.82
3%	3%	£73.6m	£0.15m	£72.0m	£0.23m	140	0.29	147	0.46
3%	3%	£86.1m	-	£80.2m	-	212	-	198	-
17%	17%	£107m	£5.37m	£90.6m	£4.85m	496	23.7	465	23.6
1%	1%	£628m	£67.0m	£579m	£83.1m	52.9	5.10	51.9	6.52
6%	5%	£64.6m	£(0.87)m	£62.7m	£(0.33)m	80.5	(1.10)	79.3	(0.41)
3%	3%	£56.4m	£24.9m	£77.4m	-	30.6	9.39	31.7	-
4%	4%	£53.5m	£2.59m	£45.2m	£0.88m	843	38.9	547	10.5
3%	3%	£78.7m	£31.5m	£71.0m	£30.7m	98.7	28.2	87.3	26.4
3%	4%	£21.3m	£60.7m	£16.3m	£60.2m	135	100	135	107
14%	13%	£17.8m	£0.20m	£16.4m	£0.20m	6.55	0.07	6.29	0.08
4%	4%	£57.2m	-	£55.2m	-	319	-	288	-
4%	3%	£56.1m	£23.4m	£54.1m	£25.0m	100	29.5	84.9	26.9
3%	3%	£58.8m	-	£55.2m	-	148	-	112	-
47%	9%	-	£1.98m	-	£1.10m	5.41	5.41	4.53	4.53
83%	1%	£1.75m	£2.10m	£1.71m	£2.15m	4.19	2.28	4.29	2.39
2%	3%	£102m	£0.21m	£82.9m	£0.13m	542	1.12	336	0.54
2%	1%	£145m	£3.17m	£134m	£3.66m	362	7.75	415	11.0
9%	5%	-	£68.2m	-	£64.9m	8.10	8.10	8.49	8.49
1%	1%	£206m	£48.2m	£185m	£23.4m	80.5	15.3	21.1	2.37
3%	2%	£70.1m	£0.61m	£68.1m	£0.54m	202	1.74	917	7.20
6%	6%	£36.1m	£0.13m	£35.7m	£0.12m	191	0.68	187	0.60
8%	3%	-	£29.2m	-	£27.0m	584	584	452	452
4%	3%	£60.6m	£1.95m	£57.7m	£1.98m	323	10.1	527	17.5
2%	3%	£68.7m	£77.2m	£69.4m	£67.8m	34.2	18.1	28.1	13.9
257%	170%	£0.34m	£(0.18)m	£0.30m	£1.24m	0.35	(0.38)	3.10	2.49
7%	7%	-	£149m	-	£140m	873	873	1,108	1,108
6%	7%	-	£29.4m	-	£18.9m	99.1	99.1	37.7	37.7
7%	7%	£35.7m	£6.97m	£35.7m	£6.25m	305	49.8	284	42.3
3%	3%	£67.5m	£15.5m	£62.5m	£15.6m	226	42.1	214	42.6

Charity Employment Trends - The Top 100 Charities

Charity	Period	Number of Employees		Employment Costs		Average Cost per Employee	
		This Year	Last Year	This Year	Last Year	This Year	Last Year
Save the Children International	31-Dec-14	14,156	11,061	£173m	£123m	£12,251	£11,130
Marie Stopes International	31-Dec-14	10,306	8,746	£99.7m	£93.1m	£9,670	£10,641
Nuffield Health	31-Dec-14	10,136	9,806	£247m	£221m	£24,349	£22,578
British Council	31-Mar-15	8,708	8,045	£340m	£326m	£39,091	£40,547
Royal Mencap Society	31-Mar-15	8,586	8,287	£142m	£150m	£16,571	£18,154
Barnardo's	31-Mar-15	8,381	8,254	£162m	£156m	£19,332	£18,937
Anchor Trust	31-Mar-15	7,850	8,445	£122m	£125m	£15,553	£14,827
Methodist Homes	31-Mar-15	6,207	6,048	£104m	£101m	£16,824	£16,730
National Trust	28-Feb-15	5,899	5,572	£195m	£185m	£32,976	£33,177
Action for Children	31-Mar-15	5,363	4,709	£110m	£117m	£20,442	£24,764
Academies Enterprise Trust	31-Aug-15	5,280	6,149	£196m	£215m	£37,055	£34,915
Community Integrated Care	31-Mar-15	5,178	5,041	£81.6m	£77.3m	£15,751	£15,337
Orders St John Care Trust	31-Mar-15	4,766	4,952	£73.8m	£70.9m	£15,487	£14,321
Leonard Cheshire Disability	31-Mar-15	4,692	4,861	£103m	£106m	£21,999	£21,841
Marie Curie Cancer Care	31-Mar-15	4,409	4,352	£94.9m	£92.1m	£21,530	£21,158
Cancer Research UK	31-Mar-15	3,964	3,798	£132m	£126m	£33,199	£33,228
United Learning Trust	31-Aug-15	3,698	3,302	£147m	£128m	£39,727	£38,802
Scope	31-Mar-15	3,555	3,589	£65.6m	£66.1m	£18,444	£18,416
United Response	31-Mar-15	3,465	3,368	£60.6m	£60.2m	£17,500	£17,867
National Autistic Society	31-Mar-15	3,421	3,610	£65.4m	£67.0m	£19,110	£18,550
British Red Cross Society	31-Dec-14	3,358	3,200	£88.5m	£83.3m	£26,355	£26,031
St Andrew's Healthcare	31-Mar-15	3,275	3,188	£129m	£123m	£39,267	£38,645
Sense - National Deafblind & Rubella Assoc	31-Mar-15	3,258	3,287	£57.1m	£57.5m	£17,528	£17,507
Sue Ryder	31-Mar-15	3,240	2,240	£54.2m	£52.5m	£16,744	£23,455
Fusion Lifestyle	31-Dec-14	3,200	3,108	£37.5m	£33.9m	£11,726	£10,918
Ormiston Trust	31-Aug-14	3,098	2,698	£109m	£87.7m	£35,251	£32,514
Oasis Community Learning	31-Aug-15	2,990	2,609	£118m	£105m	£39,451	£40,058
Salvation Army Trust	31-Mar-15	2,882	2,889	£74.4m	£69.5m	£25,817	£24,063
Save the Children	31-Dec-14	2,856	3,551	£54.5m	£51.9m	£19,075	£14,602
International Medical Corps (UK)	30-Jun-14	2,743	1,968	£12.5m	£12.6m	£4,573	£6,407
Turning Point	31-Mar-15	2,729	2,575	£70.8m	£68.6m	£25,955	£26,646
British Heart Foundation	31-Mar-15	2,709	2,617	£67.1m	£64.0m	£24,769	£24,455
Oasis Charitable Trust	31-Aug-14	2,682	1,951	£107m	£74.7m	£39,806	£38,290
Thera Trust	31-Mar-15	2,663	2,312	£45.7m	£40.6m	£17,159	£17,567
HF Trust Limited	31-Mar-15	2,634	2,430	£53.6m	£52.0m	£20,344	£21,381
Richmond Fellowship Scotland	31-Mar-13	2,528	2,482	£50.7m	£48.9m	£20,071	£19,695
Royal National Institute of Blind People	31-Mar-15	2,471	2,490	£63.1m	£64.4m	£25,522	£25,873
Church of Scot Uninc. Councils Cttees	31-Dec-14	2,421	2,513	£78.1m	£99.1m	£32,275	£39,452
Salvation Army Social Work Trust	31-Mar-14	2,412	2,592	£54.1m	£54.5m	£22,434	£21,024
Crime Reduction Initiatives	31-Mar-15	2,374	2,128	£96.0m	£83.2m	£40,447	£39,094
Alzheimer's Society	31-Mar-15	2,355	2,182	£48.5m	£42.1m	£20,586	£19,311
Culture and Sport Glasgow	31-Mar-15	2,215	2,256	£70.1m	£68.6m	£31,660	£30,389
RSPB	31-Mar-15	2,195	2,217	£56.3m	£55.9m	£25,666	£25,200
Alternative Futures Group Ltd	31-Mar-15	2,187	1,947	£50.3m	£45.9m	£23,014	£23,554
Brandon Trust	31-Mar-15	2,064	2,045	£34.6m	£36.3m	£16,778	£17,737
Wellcome Trust	30-Sep-15	2,057	1,733	£128m	£102m	£62,421	£58,973
Gatsby Charitable Foundation	05-Apr-15	2,033	1,425	£4.73m	£4.87m	£2,325	£3,418
Oxfam GB	31-Mar-15	2,011	1,959	£113m	£108m	£56,042	£55,334
Quarriers	31-Mar-15	1,999	2,001	£29.9m	£30.6m	£14,943	£15,283
Autism Initiatives UK	31-Mar-15	1,951	2,036	£32.7m	£34.6m	£16,780	£16,974

by Number of Employees - (1-50)

Increase in Average Cost per Employee		Employment cost as % of Total Expenditure		Expenditure Classification
This Year	Last Year	This Year	Last Year	
10%	109%	25%	23%	International activities
(9)%	(17)%	44%	46%	Social services and relief
8%	10%	35%	32%	Health and medical
(4)%	(2)%	35%	37%	International activities
(9)%	2%	76%	79%	Health and medical
2%	2%	56%	56%	Social services and relief
5%	5%	46%	49%	Social services and relief
1%	(11)%	60%	60%	Social services and relief
(1)%	15%	39%	40%	Conservation and protection
(17)%	1%	69%	69%	Social services and relief
6%	18%	61%	64%	Education, training and research
3%	1%	79%	77%	Social services and relief
8%	(33)%	78%	73%	Social services and relief
1%	~	66%	69%	Health and medical
2%	3%	58%	56%	Health and medical
~	(2)%	22%	23%	Health and medical
2%	34%	65%	67%	Education, training and research
~	(21)%	63%	64%	Health and medical
(2)%	1%	79%	78%	Health and medical
3%	(21)%	70%	71%	Health and medical
1%	2%	34%	36%	Social services and relief
2%	4%	72%	73%	Health and medical
~	2%	70%	70%	Health and medical
(29)%	2%	58%	58%	Health and medical
7%	6%	51%	51%	Culture, sport and recreation
8%	(12)%	70%	70%	Philanthropic intermediation
(2)%	11%	68%	69%	Education, training and research
7%	~	42%	42%	Religion
31%	(26)%	16%	17%	International activities
(29)%	(8)%	20%	26%	International activities
(3)%	~	71%	73%	Social services and relief
1%	3%	23%	20%	Health and medical
4%	(25)%	68%	64%	Religion
(2)%	~	86%	87%	Health and medical
(5)%	3%	72%	73%	Health and medical
2%	-	86%	85%	Health and medical
(1)%	(1)%	53%	53%	Health and medical
(18)%	40%	70%	75%	Religion
7%	11%	50%	53%	Social services and relief
3%	7%	69%	72%	Civil rights, citizenship, and law and order
7%	8%	52%	56%	Health and medical
4%	(2)%	54%	54%	Culture, sport and recreation
2%	4%	44%	44%	Conservation and protection
(2)%	(6)%	85%	85%	Health and medical
(5)%	(6)%	76%	78%	Health and medical
6%	(10)%	11%	12%	Health and medical
(32)%	(97)%	10%	10%	Philanthropic intermediation
1%	4%	29%	30%	International activities
(2)%	(2)%	72%	71%	Social services and relief
(1)%	4%	77%	77%	Health and medical

Charity Employment Trends - The Top 100 Charities

Charity	Period	Number of Employees		Employment Costs		Average Cost per Employee	
		This Year	Last Year	This Year	Last Year	This Year	Last Year
Elim Foursquare Gospel Alliance	30-Sep-14	1,920	1,685	£26.1m	£24.8m	£13,601	£14,700
MacIntyre Care	31-Mar-15	1,847	2,109	£33.8m	£34.2m	£18,298	£16,206
Age UK	31-Mar-15	1,846	1,934	£50.0m	£49.9m	£27,059	£25,779
Cornerstone Community Care	31-Mar-15	1,844	1,682	£30.0m	£27.0m	£16,258	£16,061
Shaw Trust	31-Mar-15	1,831	1,617	£42.5m	£43.7m	£23,189	£27,001
NSPCC	31-Mar-15	1,830	1,810	£71.8m	£70.8m	£39,251	£39,117
MERLIN	31-Dec-14	1,782	3,623	£10.0m	£22.9m	£5,624	£6,315
Royal National Lifeboat Institution	31-Dec-14	1,763	1,670	£63.3m	£59.1m	£35,905	£35,389
St John Ambulance	31-Dec-14	1,729	1,682	£46.9m	£46.3m	£27,126	£27,527
Disabilities Trust	31-May-14	1,699	1,606	£33.6m	£30.7m	£19,753	£19,093
Heritage Care	31-Mar-15	1,699	1,698	£29.9m	£29.8m	£17,586	£17,543
PDSA	31-Dec-14	1,694	1,682	£53.7m	£50.5m	£31,694	£30,039
St Mungo Community Housing Association	31-Mar-15	1,668	1,219	£47.3m	£35.1m	£28,337	£28,800
Avante Partnership	31-Mar-15	1,665	1,795	£20.9m	£22.0m	£12,575	£12,279
Royal Masonic Benevolent Institution	31-Mar-15	1,653	1,506	£24.2m	£23.1m	£14,652	£15,332
RSPCA	31-Dec-14	1,624	1,616	£49.7m	£48.8m	£30,600	£30,212
Canal & River Trust	31-Mar-15	1,604	1,555	£58.3m	£55.0m	£36,347	£35,370
Abbeyfield Society	30-Mar-15	1,585	1,596	£25.1m	£23.9m	£15,839	£15,002
Affinity Trust	30-Sep-14	1,515	1,230	£32.7m	£30.4m	£21,589	£24,678
British Library	31-Mar-15	1,495	1,591	£59.4m	£61.6m	£39,730	£38,720
ExtraCare Charitable Trust	31-Mar-15	1,477	1,849	£27.4m	£27.6m	£18,533	£14,920
Macmillan Cancer Support	31-Dec-14	1,474	1,305	£57.9m	£50.5m	£39,281	£38,689
CITB-ConstructionSkills	31-Dec-14	1,457	1,438	£77.5m	£61.5m	£53,180	£42,779
AQA Education	30-Sep-14	1,425	1,471	£57.7m	£59.2m	£40,477	£40,226
CFBT Education Trust	31-Aug-14	1,419	3,360	£64.2m	£91.3m	£45,217	£27,162
St Anne's Community Services	31-Mar-15	1,358	1,324	£35.0m	£34.6m	£25,747	£26,127
Victim Support	31-Mar-15	1,354	1,257	£39.6m	£36.0m	£29,275	£28,634
Pre-school Learning Alliance	31-Mar-15	1,345	1,383	£26.0m	£26.8m	£19,323	£19,382
4Children	31-Mar-15	1,253	1,216	£18.3m	£16.8m	£14,626	£13,846
Tate	31-Mar-15	1,252	1,243	£40.7m	£38.9m	£32,510	£31,281
Guide Dogs for the Blind Association	31-Dec-14	1,240	1,158	£47.7m	£42.9m	£38,468	£37,047
Turning Point Scotland	31-Mar-15	1,232	1,210	£22.4m	£21.6m	£18,169	£17,882
Livability	31-Mar-15	1,220	1,250	£28.8m	£30.8m	£23,639	£24,617
Choice Support	31-Mar-15	1,216	1,324	£30.6m	£29.5m	£25,178	£22,271
Allchurches Trust	31-Dec-14	1,216	1,237	£75.9m	£72.2m	£62,432	£58,388
Richmond Fellowship	31-Mar-15	1,207	1,141	£27.5m	£26.4m	£22,756	£23,172
Care South	31-Mar-15	1,207	1,218	£21.3m	£20.7m	£17,616	£16,958
Royal National Theatre	31-Mar-15	1,198	1,134	£46.9m	£46.9m	£39,149	£41,358
Foundation for Credit Counselling	31-Dec-14	1,187	1,099	£29.9m	£27.6m	£25,177	£25,096
Royal Voluntary Service	29-Mar-15	1,183	1,262	£23.8m	£23.5m	£20,117	£18,648
YHA (England and Wales)	28-Feb-15	1,174	1,228	£18.9m	£17.8m	£16,072	£14,514
Tearfund	31-Mar-15	1,171	1,139	£21.8m	£21.4m	£18,655	£18,786
Addaction	31-Mar-15	1,143	1,144	£39.3m	£37.8m	£34,402	£33,040
City and Guilds of London Institute	31-Aug-14	1,140	1,199	£61.7m	£55.0m	£54,092	£45,842
Milestones Trust	31-Mar-15	1,139	1,108	£19.8m	£19.6m	£17,390	£17,654
Mytime Active	31-Mar-15	1,137	1,454	£16.1m	£17.4m	£14,187	£11,965
Royal British Legion	30-Sep-14	1,135	1,130	£35.4m	£34.6m	£31,183	£30,619
Fremantle Trust	31-Mar-15	1,125	1,058	£31.9m	£29.5m	£28,367	£27,894
Salvation Army Officers Pension Fund	31-Mar-15	1,122	1,135	-	-	-	-
Sheffield City Trust	31-Mar-15	1,121	1,334	£17.0m	£16.6m	£15,184	£12,475

by Number of Employees - (51-100)

Increase in Average Cost per Employee		Employment cost as % of Total Expenditure		Expenditure Classification
This Year	Last Year	This Year	Last Year	
(7)%	19%	43%	41%	Religion
13%	(4)%	74%	75%	Health and medical
5%	(4)%	29%	31%	Social services and relief
1%	13%	83%	83%	Health and medical
(14)%	(13)%	40%	41%	Health and medical
~	(2)%	56%	57%	Social services and relief
(11)%	15%	37%	37%	International activities
1%	1%	40%	39%	Health and medical
(1)%	2%	48%	48%	Health and medical
3%	1%	72%	70%	Health and medical
~	~	81%	80%	Social services and relief
6%	1%	52%	52%	Conservation and protection
(2)%	~	66%	66%	Housing and community affairs
2%	4%	72%	76%	Social services and relief
(4)%	2%	58%	57%	Social services and relief
1%	(5)%	42%	42%	Conservation and protection
3%	33%	34%	35%	Conservation and protection
6%	5%	59%	52%	Social services and relief
(13)%	(3)%	88%	88%	Health and medical
3%	5%	50%	45%	Culture, sport and recreation
24%	(12)%	50%	44%	Social services and relief
2%	1%	26%	28%	Health and medical
24%	1%	26%	23%	Education, training and research
1%	2%	37%	38%	Business and professional
66%	(11)%	50%	60%	Education, training and research
(1)%	1%	85%	85%	Housing and community affairs
2%	3%	73%	72%	Civil rights, citizenship, and law and order
~	3%	73%	75%	Social services and relief
6%	(8)%	57%	66%	Social services and relief
4%	(1)%	38%	36%	Culture, sport and recreation
4%	2%	51%	50%	Health and medical
2%	(4)%	83%	83%	Social services and relief
(4)%	3%	74%	75%	Health and medical
13%	(20)%	88%	89%	Housing and community affairs
7%	-	727%	702%	Religion
(2)%	(14)%	59%	69%	Health and medical
4%	(1)%	62%	62%	Social services and relief
(5)%	4%	37%	45%	Culture, sport and recreation
~	8%	71%	67%	Civil rights, citizenship, and law and order
8%	39%	32%	29%	Social services and relief
11%	(8)%	40%	41%	Culture, sport and recreation
(1)%	19%	34%	34%	International activities
4%	6%	64%	67%	Health and medical
18%	(3)%	50%	50%	Education, training and research
(2)%	(4)%	73%	73%	Health and medical
19%	(9)%	53%	53%	Culture, sport and recreation
2%	(2)%	31%	28%	Social services and relief
2%	3%	72%	74%	Health and medical
-	-	-	-	Social services and relief
22%	21%	31%	11%	Social services and relief

Growth Trends

	Upper Quartile		Median		Lower Quartile	
EXPENDITURE expressed as						
a percentage of income	107%	(105%)	98%	(98%)	89%	(89%)
INCOME GROWTH (all)	**13%**		**3%**		**(4)%**	
62% of Charities increased their						
INCOME over the previous year by:	23%		10%		4%	
and 38% experienced a reduction of:	20%		8%		3%	
EXPENDITURE GROWTH (all)	**13%**		**4%**		**(3)%**	
67% of charities increased their						
EXPENDITURE by:	20%		9%		4%	
and 33% reduced theirs by:	16%		7%		3%	
FUNDS GROWTH (all)	**11%**		**4%**		-	
74% of Charities had an						
increase in their funds of:	15%		7%		3%	
and 26% declined by	19%		6%		2%	
NET ASSET COVER						
for expenditure						
(expressed in months)	**166**	(169)	**28**	(27)	**6**	(7)
Excluding land, buildings	**61**	(60)	**10**	(10)	**2**	(2)
Excluding land, buildings and investments	**9**	(15)	**3**	(6)	**(1)**	(1)

Highest Paid Directors' Pay (£)

	Top 100 Charities by income		Top 100-500 Charities by income		Top 500-1000 Charities by income		Top 1000-1500 Charities by income	
	this year	last year	this year	last year	this year	last year	this year	last year
Highest	£785,000	£855,000	£385,000	£325,000	£505,000	£515,000	£305,000	£248,627
Upper	£205,000	£195,000	£145,000	£145,000	£125,000	£115,000	£105,000	£105,000
Median	£155,000	£147,500	£115,000	£105,000	£95,000	£95,000	£85,000	£85,000
Lower	£135,000	£135,000	£95,000	£95,000	£75,000	£75,000	£75,000	£75,000
Lowest	£85,000	£75,000	£65,000	£63,241	£55,000	£62,500	£10,000	£10,000
Average	£193,141	£196,473	£123,923	£121,299	£107,575	£105,084	£94,963	£94,159

Charity Auditor Profiles

The Auditor Profile section of *Top 3000 Charities* describes the full range of services offered to charities by each firm. This information, together with contact names and expertise, will help charities to select the right firm.

Buzzacott
CHARTERED ACCOUNTANTS

Buzzacott LLP
130 Wood Street
London EC2V 6DL
Tel: +44 (0)20 7556 1200
Email: charities@buzzacott.co.uk
Web: buzzacott.co.uk

Why Buzzacott?

At Buzzacott we define ourselves by the needs of our clients. These needs range from those of nuns to those of hedge fund managers. The relationships we build are both personal and enduring. They are founded on continuity of personnel, ease of access and a depth of specialist knowledge, which leads the industry in certain key areas.

An experienced team

Our Charity and Not-for-Profit team is wholly specialist. Each of the 80 strong team work full time with charity and not-for-profit sector clients. We work with over 350 not-for-profit organisations, including faith-based charities, educational establishments, welfare, healthcare and environmental charities, youth and arts organisations and international development charities. We also maintain a regular dialogue with regulators, representative and umbrella bodies.

Comprehensive support

We offer training for trustees and strategic advice to management, as well as a comprehensive tax, accounting and audit service, bespoke to your needs. We will design or review internal controls and advise on risk and financial management, so critical for this sector. We also advise on grants management systems through our IT consultancy team and offer a range of payroll and HR consultancy services.

Making your life easier

Buzzacott do all this from a background of specialist experience and technical knowledge which inform our recommendations and ensure they take full account of legislation. Our focus is to make the difficult job our clients do as easy as possible.

Get in touch

If you would like to find out more about how we could work together, please e-mail charities@buzzacott.co.uk or call +44 (0)20 7556 1200 and we will be happy to discuss your needs.

Deloitte.

Deloitte LLP
2 New Street Square
London, EC4A 3BZ
Tel: 020 7936 3000
Fax: 020 7583 1198
Email: rmotazedi@deloitte.co.uk
Web: www.deloitte.co.uk

Background

Deloitte LLP is a member firm of Deloitte Touche Tohmatsu, a leading professional services organisation, whose member firms deliver world class audit, tax, consulting and corporate finance services, with around 225,000 people in more than 150 countries.

Our Dedicated Group

We are a leading provider of business advisory services to Charities and Not For Profit organisations of all sizes and act for many of the top 100 charities. The group is staffed by professionals with wide ranging expertise who have experience and commitment to the voluntary sector. The group is represented throughout the country in 17 offices and has 18 Partners, 40 Managers and over 300 professional staff, all of whom receive regular training. As a sign of our commitment to the sector, we offer special rates for our charity clients.

We are members of and work closely with CFG, NCVO and the Charity Tax Group.

Our Services

We do more than act as auditors. We believe in adding value in many ways. We are proactive and work as trusted advisors to many charities. Members of our Charities and Not For Profit Group are active in the sector – writing, lecturing, attending conferences – and have extensive experience across a wide range of issues that affect charities.

We believe that providing services to a charity requires an appreciation of the special factors affecting voluntary organisations in general and the specific charity in particular. Our specialist group enables us to concentrate our experience and coordinate our approach to provide a reliable and cost effective service.

We regularly publish articles, newsletters and technical updates. These include:

PULSE quarterly newsletter
Surveying Trustee's Annual report
Restructuring Charities and Not for profit orgnaisations

Contact

For further information about our value added service contact Reza Motazedi, Head of Charities and Not For Profit on 020 7007 7646, or email rmotazedi@deloitte.co.uk

haysmacintyre
chartered accountants & tax advisers

haysmacintyre
26 Red Lion Square
London
WC1R 4AG
Tel: 020 7969 5500
Fax: 020 7969 5600
Email: mjessa@haysmacintyre.com
Web: www.haysmacintyre.com
Twitter: @haysmacintyre
LinkedIn: www.linkedin.com/company/haysmacintyre

About haysmacintyre

We are a leading mid-tier firm of Chartered Accountants and tax advisers in central London, providing advice to charities and not for profit organisations across the UK and internationally.

We help our clients solve problems, grasp opportunities and achieve their goals.

As a mid-tier firm we're large enough to provide a wide range of services, yet small enough to offer a personal, responsive approach. We spend time getting to know our clients so we can tailor our services and they can benefit from the support of someone who can give them accurate and appropriate advice.

haysmacintyre is a founding member of MSI Global Alliance (MSI), an international alliance of independent legal and accounting firms, with 250 members in more than 100 countries.

Charity expertise

haysmacintyre's leading charities and not for profit team provides high quality compliance, taxation and advisory services to over 600 UK and international organisations.

Representing 40% of our annual fees, our specialist team has in-depth knowledge of the sector and is one of the largest in the UK, allowing us to deliver a proactive, comprehensive and cost effective service. As a client, you will benefit from advisers who understand the specific challenges you face, as well as maximising your impact, improving your value and planning effectively for the future.

As part of our commitment to the sector we also provide regular conferences, seminars and publications.
Please find full details on our website www.haysmacintyre.com/events and www.haysmacintyre.com/publications.

haysmacintyre is proud to have been ranked in the top four firms for "Charity Expertise" for nine consecutive years in the annual *Charity Finance* Audit Survey. haysmacintyre was also a finalist for Best Employer 2015 and named Mid-Tier Firm of the Year 2014 at The British Accountancy Awards.

Services to charities

There is an increasing level of pressure on charities due to the constant pace of change in the sector. We provide a wide range of services including:

● Business outsourcing ● Company Secretarial ● Employment tax
● External audit and assurance services ● Financial due diligence
● Financial governance ● Gift Aid ● Internal audit
● International grant certification ● IT services – cloud based, security, infrastructure and application reviews ● Risk management ● Tax planning and group structuring ● Trustee and Board training ● VAT

M A Z A R S

AUDIT * TAX * ADVISORY

Mazars LLP
Tower Bridge House
St Katharine's Way
London
E1W 1DD
Tel: 020 7063 4000
Fax: 020 7063 4001

Who are we?	Mazars LLP is the UK firm of Mazars, an international business advisory and accountancy group providing independent advice to charities. Mazars aims to help its clients by providing quality professional services in a personal style.
Our commitment to the sector	We act for 100 charities in the 'Top 3000 charities' category with a combined income of approximately £783m. The firm has been involved with the charity sector for over 100 years.

We host seminars, respond to sector consultation and are involved with organisations such as the Charity Finance Group, the Association of Chief Executives of Voluntary Organisations, Charity Law Association and Charity Tax Group.

Mazars recently published the Board Charter for Charities which forms part of the legacy material of the former Lord Mayor of London, Fiona Woolf. |
| **Our National Charity Sector Group** | We provide audit (internal and external), tax, VAT and advisory services to over 600 charity clients through our dedicated Charity Sector Group. |
| **What does it mean for you as a voluntary organisation?** | Our approach is based on understanding clients, the charity sector and the changing regulatory framework. We add value by challenging and bringing creative solutions and practical advice. |

Our services

- strategic consulting
- business planning
- corporate governance
- mergers
- collaborative working
- financial management

- financial reporting
- audit & assurance
- trustee training
- BPI consultancy
- tax planning
- employment taxes

- direct taxes
- indirect taxes
- IT consultancy
- financial planning
- investment management

How to contact us

Our charity specialists may be contacted about the following:

London and South East	Nicola Wakefield	nicola.wakefield@mazars.co.uk	020 8661 1826 (Head of CSG)
	Paul Gibson	paul.gibson@mazars.co.uk	020 7063 4000
Northern	Janine Fox	janine.fox@mazars.co.uk	0161 831 1125
Midlands	Ian Holder	ian.holder@mazars.co.uk	0121 232 9500
	Kate Angus	kate.angus@mazars.co.uk	0121 232 9500
South	Richard Bott	richard.bott@mazars.co.uk	0117 973 4481
West	David I'Anson	david.i'anson@mazars.co.uk	01202 680 777
	Tracy Satherley	tracey.satherley@mazars.co.uk	0117 317 1520
Chilterns	Stephen Brown	stephen.brown@mazars.co.uk	01908 257 129
	Anita Wanless	anita.wanless@mazars.co.uk	01865 257 238
Scotland	John McLeod	john.mcleod@mazars.co.uk	0131 313 7924
VAT	Robin Simpson	robin.simpson@mazars.co.uk	0113 387 8835
Direct Tax	Phil Waller	phil.waller@mazars.co.uk	0121 232 9500

Discover the difference

PKF Cooper Parry
No. 8 Calthorpe Road,
Edgbaston,
Birmingham B15 1QT
Tel: 0121 456 4456

PKF Cooper Parry
Sky View, Argosy Road,
East Midlands Airport,
Castle Donington DE74 2SA
Tel: 01332 411163

Email: simona@pkfcooperparry.com
Web: www.pkfcooperparry.com
Independent member of PKF International

About PKF Cooper Parry

PKF Cooper Parry is the largest independent firm of Chartered Accountants and business advisers in the Midlands and was recently announced in The Sunday Times 100 Best Small Companies to work for 2016.

We are a team of 350 passionate people, delivering a broad spectrum of professional business services, up-to-the minute technical expertise and personal advice to charities and voluntary organisations, businesses and individuals across the Midlands, UK and Internationally.

As a member of the 11th largest global network, PKF International, we can support our clients to expand across 150 countries and 5 continents, allowing us to provide a truly global approach to our offering.

Our Not for Profit team

Our dedicated not-for-profit team services over 100 charities. Our team is made up of 2 partners and 3 managers all having a passion for the sector. In addition several of the partners act as trustees of local charities and not-for-profit organisations.

Our services

Our service range includes:

- audit and compliance;
- independent examination;
- grant audits;
- governance reviews;
- risk assessment and mitigation;
- charities SORP advice;
- VAT and taxation advice;
- payroll
- IT Solutions and Support

Our experience

An essential part of the service offered by PKF Cooper Parry is a commitment to provide a personal attentive service that is partner-led.

Our approach to working with clients is very much tailored towards your organisation's structure, systems and operations.

Our clients are in all the major areas of the sector including grant-making foundations, religious institutions, private and academy schools, as well as bodies involved in health, social services, the arts and housing.

Further information

To find out more please contact Simon Atkins on simona@pkfcooperparry.com or call 0121 456 4456.

Chartered Accountants & Professional Business Advisers

Shipley LLP
10 Orange Street, Haymarket
London WC2H 7DQ
Tel: 020 7312 0000
Email: enquiries@shipleys.com
Web: www.shipleys.com

About us

We are a medium-sized firm of Chartered Accountants and Professional Business Advisers, ranked in the top 60 of UK practices by Accountancy Age. We have offices in London and Godalming, Surrey and employ around 100 members of staff.

We are also a member of AGN International, a global association of independent accounting and advisory businesses.

Our experience

Our clients include local and large national charities as well as others in the not-for-profit sector such as educational and sporting organisations and collection agencies.

We work with all types of charities at all stages of their development. Our team is experienced in dealing with the complex challenges and changing legislative requirements that face the sector and this allows them to deliver the most appropriate independent advice.

Our charity team

The two leading members of the team consist of the Managing Principal of Shipleys, Simon Robinson, who holds the Diploma in Charity Accounting (DCHA), and Sarah Leek who specialising in the audit of charities, not-for-profits and pension schemes.

Services for charities

Our services for charities includes:

- Audit and compliance
- Accounting systems
- Management accounting
- Corporate governance
- VAT planning and compliance
- Tax planning
- Payroll

Get in touch

If you are interested in finding out more about us, please contact Simon Robinson at simon.robinson@shipleys.com or Sarah Leek at sarah.leek@shipleys.com. You can also contact them on 020 7312 0000.

Simon Robinson   Sarah Leek

At Sarasin & Partners, we realise that one size doesn't fit all.

Designing an investment strategy to suit each client's needs is central to our philosophy. Tailored benchmarks enable trustees to measure performance against their own objectives. Strategic support is on-going as each charity's circumstances evolve.

If you would like to discuss how to tailor a bespoke investment policy that meets your charity's particular requirements, please call John Handford on the number below.

+44 (0)20 7038 7000.
www.sarasinandpartners.com

SARASIN
& PARTNERS

Committed to charity investment.

Top Investment Managers
(Ranked by the total number of clients in the Top 3000 Charities)

	Top 100 Clients	Value of Clients Invs & Cash	Top 500 Clients	Value of Clients Invs & Cash	Top 1000 Clients	Value of Clients Invs & Cash	Top 3000 Clients	Value of Top 3000 Invs & Cash
Cazenove Charities	28	£3,386m	90	£5,163m	155	£6,100m	190	£6,417m
Sarasin & Partners LLP	23	£1,943m	81	£3,939m	131	£4,556m	149	£4,672m
CCLA Investment Management Limited	9	£840m	47	£1,509m	86	£1,867m	135	£2,133m
Rathbone Investment Management Ltd	4	£306m	35	£1,190m	88	£1,712m	132	£1,969m
Investec Wealth & Investment	5	£11,105m	32	£11,715m	88	£12,401m	129	£12,616m
BlackRock	16	£1,012m	56	£2,046m	80	£2,287m	90	£2,321m
Brewin Dolphin	2	£218m	19	£945m	48	£1,231m	85	£1,412m
Ruffer LLP	13	£576m	49	£1,311m	71	£1,476m	84	£1,541m
Newton Investment Management Limited	11	£1,576m	45	£2,474m	66	£2,674m	75	£2,714m
Barclays Wealth and Investment Management	0	-	16	£436m	35	£607m	62	£739m
Quilter Cheviot	1	£32m	15	£393m	41	£662m	53	£723m
Smith & Williamson Investment Management Ltd	3	£139m	20	£561m	42	£808m	49	£859m
Charles Stanley & Co. Limited	1	£19m	12	£297m	30	£501m	40	£539m
J.P. Morgan	6	£616m	18	£906m	25	£963m	26	£967m
UBS Wealth Management	2	£226m	11	£507m	18	£580m	25	£618m
Royal London Asset Management	7	£238m	13	£308m	19	£355m	24	£375m
JM Finn & Co	1	£11m	6	£235m	17	£341m	24	£382m
HSBC Global Asset Management (UK) Ltd	1	£31m	11	£381m	17	£452m	23	£478m
Waverton Investment Management	2	£63m	12	£276m	19	£380m	22	£400m
Veritas Asset Management(UK) Ltd	6	£359m	16	£520m	21	£554m	22	£561m

Note: (1) Investments, cash and property of clients with joint fund managers have been allocated evenly to each fund manager

Analysis of Investment Managers by cash, investments and property of top 3000 clients
(Ranked by the total cash, investments and property of clients in the Top 3000 Charities)

	Total Cash of Top 3000 clients	Total Investments of Top 3000 Clients	Total Property of Top 3000 Clients	Total Value of Top 3000 Clients cash, inv and prop	Total Investment Income of Top 3000 Clients
Investec Wealth & Investment	£306m	£12,160m	£150m	£12,616m	£107m
Cazenove Charities	£718m	£4,714m	£985m	£6,417m	£182m
Sarasin & Partners LLP	£641m	£3,395m	£636m	£4,672m	£158m
Newton Investment Management Limited	£338m	£2,287m	£89m	£2,714m	£81m
Cambridge Associates Limited	£66m	£2,207m	£148m	£2,421m	£40m
BlackRock	£258m	£1,988m	£76m	£2,321m	£60m
CCLA Investment Management Limited	£322m	£1,426m	£385m	£2,133m	£78m
Rathbone Investment Management Ltd	£218m	£1,506m	£244m	£1,969m	£56m
Ruffer LLP	£172m	£1,226m	£143m	£1,541m	£46m
Brewin Dolphin	£164m	£927m	£321m	£1,412m	£51m
Partners Capital LLP	£77m	£921m	£295m	£1,294m	£26m
J.P. Morgan	£87m	£851m	£28m	£967m	£17m
Smith & Williamson Investment Management Ltd	£220m	£560m	£79m	£859m	£22m
Troy Asset Management Limited	£261m	£574m	£24m	£858m	£18m
Goldman Sachs International Limited	£52m	£689m	£15m	£756m	£12m
Barclays Wealth and Investment Management	£182m	£441m	£115m	£739m	£22m
Quilter Cheviot	£134m	£563m	£26m	£723m	£22m
UBS Wealth Management	£99m	£518m	£1m	£618m	£19m
PIMCO Europe Ltd.	£16m	£589m	£6m	£611m	£21m
Capital International Limited	£15m	£553m	£6m	£573m	£20m

Note: (1) Investments, cash and property of clients with joint fund managers have been allocated evenly to each fund manager
*   (2) Investment property has been included in property, rental income has been included in investment income.*

Investment Management Groups

The Investment Management Groups section of *The Top 3000 Charities* describes the full range of services offered to charities by each management group. This information, together with details of funds under management, investment philosophy and contact names, will help charities to make the right investment management choices.

BLACKROCK®

BlackRock
12 Throgmorton Avenue
London
EC2N 2DL
Tel: 020 7743 3000
Web: www.blackrock.co.uk/charities

About BlackRock	BlackRock has been investing on behalf of charities and endowments for over thirty years and today manages approximately £3 billion for over 3,000 UK charities*. Our dedicated team aims to give every charity the support they need to flourish, seeking to bring clients the best of BlackRock. We combine a global investment team with an unparalleled risk management system to deliver solutions using the full spectrum of assets. Solutions include the ability to offer ethical screening to suit a charity's requirements, as well as a number of ethically focused funds.

Our Investment Offering

- Six tax efficient Common Investment Funds tailored for charities
- Access to BlackRock's comprehensive range of pooled funds
- Active and passive solutions, including iShares® ETFs
- A number of ethically focused funds
- A rigorous corporate governance and responsible investment programme
- Individual portfolio management for charities with sizeable accounts

Contact Us:

Mike Marsham
Head of Family Offices,
Charities and Endowments
Tel: 020 7743 5770
mike.marsham@blackrock.com

Candida de Silva
Tel: 020 7743 1084
candida.desilva@blackrock.com

Luke Twyman
Tel: 020 7743 1415
luke.twyman@blackrock.com

*Source: BlackRock, as at 30/09/2015
Authorised and regulated by the Financial Conduct Authority

C Hoare & Co
37 Fleet Street
London EC4P 4DQ
Tel: 020 7353 4522
Web: www.hoaresbank.co.uk
Email: CharitiesTeam@hoaresbank.co.uk

About C Hoare & Co	C. Hoare & Co. is the UK's oldest family-owned bank, established by Richard Hoare in 1672. The eight Partners continue to own and direct it with unlimited liability. This stable family ownership enables us to maintain good risk management and avoid the temptation to chase rapid growth over the short term. The bank has one of the strongest balance sheets across its industry peers.

Providing discretionary portfolio management services to more than 300 charities is a key part of our thriving investment business. In addition, our specialist Charities Team offers trustees access to a wealth of in-house expertise in banking, lending, cash administration and foreign exchange. We have a longstanding connection to the sector through the bank's history of philanthropy and the Hoare family's own charitable trust, which is also actively involved in social impact investing.

Our Approach to Investment Management

We combine investments across asset classes, creating bespoke portfolios for our customers. In addition to core components such as equities, bonds, alternative assets and cash, we aim to enhance returns by gaining exposure to investment themes that we believe have strong potential. These diverse sources of returns, together with rigorous due diligence and a commitment to ensuring liquidity and transparency, have served our customers well in both rising and falling markets.

We construct portfolios to achieve each charity's long-term objectives with due consideration to volatility. Our process involves a continuous analysis of markets and funds along with checks and controls to ensure portfolios are aligned with their objectives, within a risk-controlled framework. Each stage requires different skills and personal qualities. Separating these areas allows our professionals to focus on their area of expertise.

Fund Selection

We do not run our own funds and this allows us to select the best fund managers in each sector purely on merit. We invest with managers who have particular strengths or biases that we believe are best suited to the market conditions as identified by our Strategy Team. Our process allows us complete objectivity in both asset allocation and fund selection. We are just as happy to invest in passive funds as we are in active funds, if doing so is in the customer's best interest. We incorporate CIFs (Common Investment Funds) into charity portfolios only where they meet our strict fund selection criteria.

Conclusion

A strong and consistent performance track record is backed by our outstanding level of customer service. Our clean fee structure helps ensure that our interests are aligned with those of our customers. Our longevity and historic family ownership are very appealing to charities, many of which are long-established themselves and hoping to exist in perpetuity.

Contact

Simon Barker
Head of Charities
020 7353 4522
simon.barker@hoaresbank.co.uk

Alex Bolland
Senior Portfolio Manager
Charities Team
020 7353 4522
alex.bolland@hoaresbank.co.uk

Robert Inglis
Senior Portfolio Manager
Charities Team
020 7353 4522
robert.inglis@hoaresbank.co.uk

CAZENOVE
CAPITAL MANAGEMENT

Charity Investment from 👑 **Schroders**

Cazenove Capital Management
12 Moorgate
London
EC2R 6DA
Tel: 020 7658 3636
Web: www.cazenovecharities.com

Achieving your charity's investment objectives takes time and thought

We understand that the demands on charities are constantly changing and that meeting charitable objectives can be challenging. Cazenove Charities' team of twenty seven specialists is dedicated to providing our clients with wide-ranging investment support. We have worked with charities for over 80 years.

Our investment proposition targets the needs of charities and we are fortunate to be able to offer a broad range of services, backed by the resource and strong investment performance of a leading global investment group.

Charity Times, Charity Investment Manager of the Year 2015

"Leadership over many years through various forums, sponsorships and policy development"

Our services:

- Investment support for charities of all sizes and purpose

- A suite of Common Investment Funds, covering a range of asset classes, including the Charity Multi-Asset Fund

- Each of our clients is provided with a dedicated account team of three people

- Tailored investment portfolios, including those designed for long term inflation protection

- Comprehensive reports, online access, a regular training programme and regular events for charities

- Responsible investment specialists who ensure environmental, social and governance policies are at the heart of our process

Contact us:

Giles Neville
Head of Charities

020 7658 6975
giles.neville@cazenovecapital.com

Kate Rogers
Head of Policy, Charities

020 7658 2480
kate.rogers@cazenovecapital.com

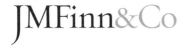

JM Finn & Co
4 Coleman Street
London
EC2R 5TA
Tel: 020 7600 1660
Email: mark.powell@jmfinn.com
Web: www.jmfinn.com

A tailored approach

We offer a high quality, personalised investment management service that aims to meet the individual demands of charities and their trustees. Designed to help guide our clients through the increasingly complex investment world, our tailored approach draws on traditional client service values in a world where individual investment manager discretion is often replaced by a process-driven response.

Long term investing

Many of our clients have a longer term time horizon and a generally conservative attitude to investment, with a variety of investment goals; from preserving capital for future generations to providing an income for retirement or just funding a dream.

Individual accountability

By placing an investment manager as the primary point of contact for all our relationships, we can ensure that each client receives a personal level of service, as your manager will be responsible for managing your portfolio as well as the relationship. Our tailored approach allows for increased flexibility which can be useful if your, or your charity's, specific circumstances change.

Trust

We understand that to engage a discretionary portfolio manager there needs to be a high level of trust and therefore we seek to become one of your trusted advisers. To determine how we are doing on this score across our existing clients, we asked them in a survey which confirmed a high degree of trust and confidence in both the individual investment manager and JM Finn & Co.

Whatever your charity's goal, while our advice is deemed to be restricted under FCA rules as we do not provide advice on all financial products, such as pensions and life assurance, we instil impartiality and accountability across the firm, which combine to provide the trustees with the level of personal service you might expect of someone entrusted to look after your investments.

Contact

Mark Powell
Tel: 020 7600 1660
Email: mark.powell@jmfinn.com

M&G Investments
M&G Charities Department
PO Box 9038
Chelmsford
CM99 2XF
Charity Helpline: 0800 917 4472
Email: charities@mandg.co.uk
Web: www.mandg.co.uk/charities

About M&G

M&G launched the UK's first Unit Trust and has continued to launch ground-breaking products ever since, introducing one of the UK's first specialist equity[1] funds for charities in 1960, the first pure corporate bond[2] fund in 1994 and, in 2010, an innovative corporate bond fund focused on inflation-linked credit. Our experience, expertise and innovation has earned us a reputation as a leader in equities, fixed interest and multi asset investing. Currently, funds under management total over £247bn of which nearly £1.4bn relates to charities.

Services offered to charities

M&G has been involved with the investment management of charitable funds for over 55 years and is one of the UK's largest and most experienced managers of such funds. M&G offers two specialist pooled funds for charities: Charifund and Charibond. Alternatively, we are happy to discuss investment opportunities for charities within our extensive range of OEIC funds covering all key asset classes[3] , where appropriate.

Charifund

The Equities Investment Fund for Charities (Charifund) was launched in 1960 and is a suitable investment for the equity portion of charitable funds. It's designed to provide a high and growing income for charities, while at the same time protecting their capital from the erosive effect of inflation.

The fund is a charity, ensuring that charities investing in Charifund obtain the benefits of an investment in a unit trust, such as low charges and a wide spread of investments - whilst qualifying for the same tax treatment as other UK equity charitable funds.

Charibond

The Charibond Charities Fixed Interest Common Investment Fund (Charibond) was launched in 1976 as an actively managed fixed interest fund. It invests in deposits, UK Government bonds (Gilts) and other sterling denominated fixed income securities.

Charibond is designed to produce a high income while preserving capital[4] values. It is available to all charities registered in the UK allowed to invest in common investment funds.

Contact us

For further information on our investment services for charities, please call Richard Macey (020 7548 3731) or James Potter (020 7548 3882) directly, or contact us via the details listed above.

Please remember that past performance is not a guide to future performance. The value of stockmarket investments will fluctuate, which will cause fund prices to fall as well as rise and you may not get back the original amount you invested.

[1]Equities: Shares of ownership in a company. [2]Corporate bonds: Fixed income securities issued by a company. [3]Asset Class: Category of assets, such as cash, company shares, fixed income securities. [4]Capital: Refers to the financial assets, or resources, that a company has to fund its business operations. Source of statistics: M&G FUM statistics as at 30.09.15. Source of charities FUM statistics: M&G statistics as at 30.09.15. This Financial Promotion is issued by M&G Securities Limited which has been appointed as the fund manager for Charibond, and as sub-manager and agent by Charities Investment Managers Limited which is the manager of Charifund. M&G Securities Limited is registered in England No. 90776 and Charities Investment Managers Limited is registered in England No. 638485. The registered office of both is Laurence Pountney Hill, London EC4R 0HH. M&G Securities Limited provides investment products. M&G Securities Limited and Charities Investment Managers Limited are authorised and regulated by the Financial Conduct Authority in the UK. Charibond's charity registered number is 271815, and Charifund's charity registered number is 249958.

 **MAYFAIR CAPITAL**

The Property Income Trust for Charities (PITCH)

Mayfair Capital Investment Management Ltd.
2 Cavendish Square
London
W1G 0PU
Tel: 020 7495 1929
Web: www.mayfaircapital.co.uk

Why invest in PITCH?	• PITCH has a good track record on delivering its investment objective. It is designed specifically for charity investors with tax efficiency (no SDLT payable on property acquisitions)
	• The current size of PITCH gives us the ability to deliver alpha through careful stock selection and asset management, whilst still providing asset diversification.
	• The Fund offers a target yield to investors of 6%, whilst at least maintaining capital value in real terms.
	• Income is distributed monthly without the deduction of tax.
	• Ethical and environmental principles lie at the heart of our investment process.
	• Fund fees are competitive with the market with the overall Fund's TER c. 0.65% on GAV / 0.76% on NAV.

Why Mayfair Capital Investment Management?	• Ability to unlock value – at Mayfair Capital we implement our research informed, market-aware expertise to unlock value and deliver fund performance in excess of client benchmarks/objectives.
	• We place clients first – putting clients first is our priority with a high degree of integrity in managing our clients' equity.
	• An experienced management team – the team possesses a wealth of experience; each have spent 25-30 years in real estate.
	• A socially responsible investor – we apply environment and ethical sensitivity in the management of our business and funds. PITCH has adopted formal ethical and environmental policies.
	• We focus on delivering income - we possess superior transaction skills with a broad contact base across the property industry.
	• An independent business – as an owner managed business Mayfair Capital's future is directly linked to the quality of our decision making and integrity in managing our clients' equity.

Contact   For more information on the Property Income Trust for Charities: www.pitch-fund.co.uk

James Thornton
Fund Director
020 7291 6662
jthornton@mayfaircapital.co.uk

James Lloyd
Marketing Director
020 7291 6664
jlloyd@mayfaircapital.co.uk

Simon Martindale
Fund Manager
020 7291 6668
smartindale@mayfaircapital.co.uk

PARTNERS CAPITAL

Partners Capital LLP
5 Young Street
London W8 5EH
Tel: +44 (0) 20 7938 5200
Fax: +44 (0) 20 7938 5201
Website: www.partners-cap.com

About Partners Capital	Partners Capital is a leading Outsourced Investment Office based in London, Boston, New York City, Hong Kong and Singapore serving charities, endowments, foundations, pensions and high net-worth families globally.

The firm was founded in 2001 by investment professionals seeking an independent and conflict free adviser to provide portfolio construction advice and rigorous analysis of investment opportunities. From its initial focus as the "money managers to the money managers", Partners Capital has grown to over $17 billion in assets under management and has become an adviser to endowments and foundations as well as prominent family offices and successful entrepreneurs across the U.S., U.K., Europe and Asia. Charitable endowments have become a large proportion of the institutional client base, which now includes Oxford and Cambridge Colleges, and many of the most highly respected museum and charitable foundations located around the world. |
| **Investment Philosophy** | Partners Capital deploys an investment philosophy that embraces many of the powerful diversification benefits of the "endowment model" of investing, but with a more dynamic approach to asset allocation. This seeks to clearly delineate between performance derived from market factors and that of the skills of individual managers. This has been enhanced by our years of experience in constructing bespoke client portfolios in a challenging array of market environments. We have built upon and refined our investment strategy embracing more rigorous risk budgeting and improving capabilities in tactical asset allocation and manager selection. Unique to our evolved strategy is acute risk control at the overall portfolio level, based on constant monitoring of look-through manager market risk exposures. We are committed to constructing and managing diversified, all-asset-class portfolios with a particular focus on Private Markets, in addition to Liquid Market Strategies. |
| **Investment Service** | Our mission is to deliver the most advanced proven institutional investment strategy to our individual and institutional clients. We provide wholly independent advice on asset allocation and access to what we believe to be best-of-breed asset managers across all asset classes and geographic markets. This access is strongly enhanced by the quality of our community of shareholders and clients, most of whom are veteran investors themselves in specialist sectors around the world.

We create tailored investment portfolios depending on a client's risk profile, time horizon, liquidity constraints, tax domicile and investment objectives. Client portfolios are constructed of either direct investments in underlying investment funds or using Partners Capital pooled vehicles. We also offer single asset class mandates, particularly in private equity and private debt. |

Contact Details

John Collis
Partner
john.collis@partners-cap.com
+44 20 7938 5249

Nick Rider
Principal
nick.rider@partners-cap.com
+44 20 7938 5280

Kelly Shek
Principal
kelly.shek@partners-cap.com
+44 20 7938 5296

QUILTER CHEVIOT
INVESTMENT MANAGEMENT

**Quilter Cheviot
One Kingsway
London
WC2B 6AN
Tel: +44 (0)20 7150 4005
Fax: +44 (0)20 7845 6155
Web: www.quiltercheviot.com**

Background

Quilter Cheviot is owned by Old Mutual Group, and is a stand-alone business within the Old Mutual Wealth division. Quilter Cheviot manages assets in excess of £16.9 billion*, focusing on providing and managing bespoke investment portfolios for charities, trusts, pension funds and private clients, centred upon an award-winning investment process. The management of charity portfolios is very much within our core competence, led by our London based dedicated Charities team, who in turn are aided by and support, as appropriate, our regional charity specialists.

Services for charities

We provide investment services to an established and growing number of charities and manage £1.4bn** on behalf of charities making us one of the leading charity managers in the sector. The annual Charity Finance Survey positions us within the top fifteen charity fund managers in the UK and in 2013 we were recognised at the Charity Times Awards for our investment services.

Many of our investment managers are also trustees of charities. We therefore understand the challenges and dilemmas that come with this responsibility. We believe it is crucial that Trustees have direct access to the investment manager and immediate team, thereby avoiding the use of relationship managers. Our investment philosophy is to ensure that our process is entirely open and understood. This works on the principle that the best returns are achieved when our firm and the charity work as a team. We offer comprehensive reporting, efficient administration and most importantly, a competitive and transparent fee. In addition, we are delighted to provide bespoke investment forums and trustee investment training which is tailored to a charity's specific requirements.

*30 September 2015
**30 June 2015

Contacts

William Reid
Head of Charities
William.reid@quiltercheviot.com
020 7150 4193

Howard Jenner
Investment Director
Howard.jenner@quiltercheviot.com
020 7150 4167

Gemma Woodward
Executive Director
gemma.woodward@quiltercheviot.com
020 7150 4320

Royal London Asset Management
55 Gracechurch Street
London
EC3V 0RL
Tel: +44 (0) 207 506 6570
Fax: +44 (0) 207 506 6796
Please contact: Philip Clifford, Sales Director
Email: philip.clifford@rlam.co.uk
www.rlam.co.uk

Company profile

Royal London Asset Management (RLAM) is one of the UK's leading fund management companies for the charity sector. Our experienced team of investment specialists manages over £83 billion of assets (at 30/09/15), including £2.4 billion on behalf of 150 charities. We pride ourselves on the breadth and quality of the investment options we offer. As an independently managed company with the Royal London Group, which was established in 1861, we benefit from the strong backing of the UK's largest mutual life and pensions provider, while retaining the external perspective of a commercial fund management business.

Our approach

We wholeheartedly believe in adding value though active fund management and are widely recognised for the wealth of experience we bring to managing our clients' funds. Our focus is firmly set on achieving the best possible returns in a risk controlled manner for the charities who entrust us with their assets. Investing assets on behalf of charities requires an appreciation of this sector as well as expert knowledge of our own sector. Our success is based on truly understanding the investment objectives of the charities we manage assets for and using our in-depth market knowledge to exploit the market opportunities that will help us meet these requirements. We believe that the experience and skills of our fund management team set us apart, giving us an edge in a highly competitive market. Quite simply, by exploring parts of the market that others often overlook, our fund managers are able to add value to your portfolios.

Areas of expertise

In an environment of lower returns, pressure on charities is increasing. Your focus is on your charitable activity; ours is on helping you meet your specific investment goals. We have extensive experience of investing in fixed income, cash, equities and property, and have demonstrated superior performance over the longer term. This experience extends to combining asset classes to construct multi-asset portfolios, designed to meet clients' specific needs. Some of our charity clients additionally have specific ethical and sustainable requirements and we can offer both segregated mandates as well as pooled funds to cater to these needs.

At RLAM we can work with you to construct a dynamic portfolio according to your specific requirements. We offer capital growth opportunities, absolute return, inflation matching, cash plus solutions, and income matching, utilising our wide range of short dated bond funds.

Responsible investment

At RLAM we believe clients should not have to make a choice between performance and responsible investment considerations. We offer a range of ethical and sustainable solutions and can evidence that this style of investment, can outperform the market, producing strong and steady returns. RLAM is a signatory to the UNPRI (United Nations Principles for Responsible Investment) and was an early signatory to the UK Stewardship Code.

Issued by Royal London Asset Management January 2016. Information correct at that date unless otherwise stated. Royal London Asset Management Limited, registered in England and Wales number 2244297; Royal London Unit Trust Managers Limited, registered in England and Wales number 2372439. RLUM Limited, registered in England and Wales number 2369965. All of these companies are authorised and regulated by the Financial Conduct Authority. All of these companies are subsidiaries of The Royal London Mutual Insurance Society Limited, registered in England and Wales number 99064. Registered Office: 55 Gracechurch Street, London, EC3V 0RL. The marketing brand also includes Royal London Asset Management Bond Funds Plc, an umbrella company with segregated liability between sub-funds, authorised and regulated by the Central Bank of Ireland, registered in Ireland number 364259. Registered office: 70 Sir John Rogerson's Quay, Dublin 2, Ireland. Ref: 1185-PRO-12/2015-CH

Ruffer LLP
80 Victoria Street
London
SW1E 5JL
Tel: 020 7963 8100

Key points	● 20 year track record ● Segregated portfolios ● Dedicated fund manager ● Common investment fund ● £18 billion under management at 31 December 2015
Background	At Ruffer, we have a distinctive approach to investing and currently manage over £2 billion for a diverse range of charity clients.
Absolute return investment philosophy	Our focus is on delivering consistent positive returns, regardless of how the financial markets perform. Instead of following benchmarks, Ruffer simply aims not to lose money on a 12 month rolling basis and to deliver a return greater than the return on cash. In our view, benchmarking against market-weighted indices has the unintended consequence of moving the management of market risk from investment managers (where it belongs) to the trustees. We believe this is wrong and work to protect and grow the value of charities' assets throughout the market cycle.
Segregated portfolios, dedicated fund managers	Ruffer prides itself on offering a service to its clients rather than a product. Clients usually have their own segregated portfolio with a designated investment manager. Portfolios are constructed by each client's manager, who tailors the portfolio to specific needs such as income or ethical restrictions. Segregated management also ensures that each portfolio is fully transparent.
Common Investment Fund	A Common Investment Fund is also managed within the Ruffer Group.
Ownership	Ruffer LLP is a privately-owned investment management firm. The Limited Liability Partnership arrangement aligns the interests of its members with those of its clients in seeking to achieve long term, sustainable investment returns.
Contact	For further information please contact Christopher Querée or Trevor Bradley.

Ruffer LLP is authorised and regulated by the Financial Conduct Authority.

Sarasin & Partners LLP
Juxon House
100 St Paul's Churchyard
London EC4M 8BU
Tel: +44 (0)20 7038 7000
Fax: +44 (0)20 7038 6864
Web: www.sarasinandpartners.com

Charity Services Overview	Sarasin & Partners manages investments of £5.3 billion* for around 370 charities, representing over 39% of the firm's total Assets under Management. We also manage investments for UK private clients, pension funds, and other institutions with total funds under management of £13.4 billion*

Underpinning our personalised service is the philosophy that we provide investment strategies to suit any charity's specific needs. Our particular expertise is determining and reviewing the appropriate mix of asset classes suitable to meet the circumstances of each charity.

We are well known for our commitment to education having trained over 3,800 trustees. The reference for this training is our Compendium of Investment – written to support charities planning their investment policy in conjunction with their chosen manager. |
| **Services and Products** | In our management of charitable funds we are used to balancing the conflicting needs of charities for both current income and future capital growth and to working within the powers laid down by individual charities' trust deeds.

How we could help you
- By providing a stable team of experienced, careful people who will give you a genuinely personal service
- By contributing proven specialist charity sector expertise to the planning of the most appropriate investment policy for you
- By using our innovative Alpha Common Investment Funds to create a strategic asset mix that best suits your investment objectives
- By delivering good long-term investment performance based on the disciplined application of a clearly-defined investment process. Over the past 10 years, charities who have followed our Endowment Model have achieved a total return of more than 18% ahead of the WM Charity Peer Group on a like-for-like, gross of fees and charges comparison**
- By providing first class administration with regular reports of unusual depth and clarity
- By offering publications, seminars, events and training courses that help in keeping abreast of developments in charity finance and provide opportunities for the exchange of information with fellow charity trustees and officers |
| **Contact** | John Handford on 020 7038 7000 or email: john.handford@sarasin.co.uk |

Richard Maitland
Head of Charities

John Handford
Head of Charity Marketing

Guy Monson
Chief Investment Officer

*As at 31st December 2015.
** Source: Sarasin & Partners LLP, Lipper and The WM Company (supplied quarterly by the WM Company) as at 31.12.15. The most recent WM data is an estimate.
Please note that the value of shares and the income from them can fall as well as rise and you may not get back the amount originally invested. This can be as a result of market movements and also of variations in the exchange rates between currencies.

Sarasin & Partners LLP is a limited liability partnership registered in England and Wales with registered number OC329859 and is authorised and regulated by the Financial Conduct Authority.

THE TOP LEGAL ADVISERS BY NUMBER OF CHARITY CLIENTS

Bates Wells Braithwaite (London)	1/272
Stone King LLP	2/218
Wilsons Solicitors LLP	3/161
Anthony Collins Solicitors LLP	4/129
Freeths LLP (Trading as Henmans Freeth)	5/128
Farrer & Co LLP	6/127
Bircham Dyson Bell LLP	7/107
Russell-Cooke	8/104
Withers LLP	9/ 73
Hempsons	10/ 61
DWF LLP	11/ 58
Blake Morgan	12/ 56
Charles Russell Speechlys LLP	13/ 53
Veale Wasbrough Vizards	14/ 46
Bond Dickinson LLP	15/ 45
Wrigleys Solicitors LLP	16/ 37
Trowers & Hamlins LLP	17/ 32
Mills & Reeve LLP	18/ 29
Pothecary Witham Weld	19/ 28
Burness Paull LLP	20/ 25

Charity Legal Advisers

The Legal Advisers section of *The Top 3000 Charities* describes the full range of services offered to charities by each firm. This information, together with the profiles which follow will help charities to select the right firm.

Bates Wells Braithwaite

Bates Wells Braithwaite
10 Queen Street Place
London
EC4R 1BE
Tel: 020 7551 7777
Fax: 020 7551 7800
Web: www.bwbllp.com

The Firm	Bates Wells Braithwaite (BWB) advises significantly more charity clients in the top 3,000 than any other law firm and is described by Legal 500 as delivering "an exceptional level of service". Based in the City of London, BWB is a full service law firm ranked as first tier for charity law by both Legal 500 and Chambers UK. BWB is the first UK law firm to become a Certified B Corporation.
The Charity & Social Enterprise Team	The Charity and Social Enterprise team of 33 lawyers (including 11 partners) is the largest in the country and includes many expert practitioners. Chambers UK says "their expertise in charity is second to none". The Real Estate, Dispute Resolution, Employment and Public & Regulatory law teams undertake an equal amount of work for clients in this sector.

Services

BWB provides a full range of legal and advisory services to charities, including:

- registration and advice on charitable status;
- charity tribunal proceedings;
- constitutional reviews and reorganisations;
- mergers and takeovers;
- Charity Commission inquiries;
- fundraising agreements and schemes;
- investment including social finance;
- political activities and campaigning;
- tax planning, financing and VAT;
- intellectual property, data protection and information law;
- governance; and
- legacies and probate disputes

BWB's Impact and Advisory division helps clients to plan, measure and develop impact, in addition to creating and realising value through strategic projects.

BWB is at the heart of policy and legislative changes and advise on cutting edge social economy issues for charities including:

- commercial/corporate services for public interest organisations;
- trading and business ventures;
- social finance and innovative investment models

BWB has also recently launched Get Legal, an online tool allowing charities to create customised legal documents at affordable rates.

Contact

Julian Blake
Joint Head of Charity & Social Enterprise Team
Tel: 020 7551 7746
Email: j.blake@bwbllp.com

Philip Kirkpatrick
Joint Head of Charity & Social Enterprise Team
Tel: 020 7551 7762
Email: p.kirkpatrick@bwbllp.com

CharlesRussell Speechlys

Charles Russell Speechlys LLP
5 Fleet Place
London
EC4M 7RD
Tel: +44 (0)20 7203 5000
Fax: +44 (0)20 7203 0200
Email: mike.scott@crsblaw.com
Web: www.charlesrussellspeechlys.com

Our Charities and Not-For-Profit Group

At Charles Russell Speechlys we have one of the largest charity and not-for-profit practices in the country. The group spans the entire firm, sharing expertise, knowledge and resources to provide our clients with the support and advice they need to help them respond to the challenges they face. With strength in depth, we bring expertise from the firm's very broad general practice, both in the UK and internationally.

We act for a diverse range of charities and not-for-profit organisations. Our clients include household names, national and international charities, family charitable trusts, foundations, schools and professional and governing bodies.

We have particular knowledge of and involvement in the arts, environment, healthcare, museums and heritage, higher education, military, philanthropy, religious organisations, schools and sport. We have been consistently ranked as one of the top legal advisers to charities by Charity Finance Magazine and the Chambers and Legal 500 directories.

Your needs

We advise clients on a diverse range of legal issues including:

- Establishment and incorporation
- Charity law including Charities Acts 2006 and 2011
- Governance and Trustees' powers and responsibilities
- Charity Commission schemes, orders and investigations
- Constitutional amendment, group restructuring, mergers and joint venture
- Companies Act 2006
- Legacies: administration and disputes
- Litigation and other dispute resolution
- Commercial law including trading activities, outsourcing, fundraising, franchising and licensing
- Administration of charitable trusts
- Intellectual property rights, information technology and data protection
- Philanthropy advice
- Property, planning and construction
- Social enterprise
- Reputation management
- Taxation
- Employment and pensions
- Common investment funds, social impact investing and FCA authorisation and regulation.

Benefits that we bring to you

- **Extensive experience** working with charities meaning the advice you will receive will be practical and relevant as well as technically correct
- **Breadth of expertise and resource** across a range of relevant services
- **Flexibility** assisted by our regional offices in the coverage, delivery and cost of our services
- **Excellent value for money** via competitive fees and a genuine commitment to provide added value wherever we can
- **Friendly and approachable lawyers** who will be committed to providing you with the best possible service at all times, working as one team with your staff and other professional advisers
- **A range of added value services including**: Bespoke training, seminars (including our popular trustee training programme), legal updates, service reviews, use of our meeting rooms and extranets

Contact

Michael Scott
Tel: +44(0)20 7203 5069
mike.scott@crsblaw.com

"They perform outstandingly. I have absolute confidence when they speak categorically that it is watertight."
Chambers UK, 2016

HUNTERS
INCORPORATING
MAY, MAY & MERRIMANS

Hunters incorporating May, May & Merrimans
9 New Square
Lincoln's Inn
London, WC2A 3QN
Tel: 020 7412 0050
Fax: 020 7412 0049
Email: paa@hunters-solicitors.co.uk
Web: www.hunters-solicitors.co.uk

The firm

Hunters has a substantial and well established background as a trusted adviser in all aspects of charity work, having provided a broad range of charities with advice from its offices in Lincoln's Inn for 300 years.

On 1st April 2015 Hunters merged with Private Client firm May, May & Merrimans. By joining forces, the firm has created one of the largest private client departments in the country, with the expertise and resources to maintain the highest standards.

The Firm's successful merger with a niche firm of Vernor-Miles & Noble in April 2011 greatly strengthened the Charities Department at Hunters, introducing a substantial portfolio of charity clients particularly in the religious sector.

The Charities Department further expanded with the appointment of Dominik Opalinski as a Partner in April 2012. Dominik, has extensive experience in advising a broad range of charities and not-for-profit organisations (including schools), particularly in relation to governance, risk management (including safeguarding), social enterprises and collaborative ventures. Dominik was the architect of the unique national scheme approved by the Cabinet, the Scottish Executive and Northern Ireland office for the benefit of emergency service personnel and their families on whose behalf he also successfully lobbied for an amendment to the Charities Bill 2005 with the support of leading members of the House of Lords amongst others.

The firm's Charities Department has developed a reputation for providing proactive and pragmatic advice with a commercial steer to a broad range of national and international charities ranging from those in the licensed trade to medical, religious and emergency services charities.

Hunters has a particular knowledge of medical and health charities, emergency and rescue services, schools and religious orders. It also acts for a number of trade and professional charities. Hunters maintains its highly individual and partner-led approach which is tailored to the needs of particular clients in the work involved.

Specialist skills

The closely integrated nature of the firm ensures that each department's specialist knowledge can be harnessed and tailored to the clients requirements and advantage.

Hunters is ranked in the Legal 500 2015. The group's Head of Department Paul Almy is described as *"experienced and highly skilled"* and Partner Dominik Opalinski is known as being *"accessible and relentless in achieving his objective"*.

The group is also recommended in Chambers 2016 as *"client-focused, and take the time to understand clients"*. Paul Almy is highlighted in particular.

Further information

To find out more about the firm and how we may be able to help you, please telephone 020 7412 0050 or visit our website www.hunters-solicitors.co.uk

SK STONE KING

Stone King LLP
Boundary House
91 Charterhouse Street
London
EC1M 6HR
Tel: 020 7796 1007
Fax: 020 7796 1017
Email: info@stoneking.co.uk
Website: www.stoneking.co.uk
for other offices please see contact details below

Our Charity Law Practice	Charity and Social Enterprise legal services are at the heart of Stone King.
	We endeavour to deliver wisdom, protection, value and service with every piece of work we undertake on behalf of our clients.
	Our commitment to providing the highest quality client care is at the core of our ethos. It informs our firm's strategic development and our investment in recruiting and developing the people best suited to help our clients.
	We appreciate the need for all of our clients to procure legal advice effectively and are committed to providing a prompt, efficient and value-for-money service.
Charity and Social Enterprise Team	Recognised as a leading practice in the UK by Chambers and Legal 500, we act for hundreds of voluntary and not for profit organisations ranging across a broad spectrum of sizes and aims. Fielding one of the largest specialist legal teams nationally of over 50 lawyers, we provide a comprehensive and tailored service to meet all of our clients' needs. Many of our lawyers are recognised as leaders in the charity legal field.
Our specialist services	We provide advice on a broad range of legal and practical issues including:

- Formation and registration of new charities and social enterprise organisations
- Charity Commission investigations, review visits and Interim Manager appointments
- Charity mergers and incorporations
- Duties and liabilities of trustees, trustee training
- Governance and compliance issues
- Modernising and restructuring charity constitutions
- Fundraising, corporate sponsorship, legacies and legacy disputes
- Grant and funding issues
- Employment matters including TUPE, HR procedures and policies
- Establishing trading subsidiaries, commercial agreements
- Property acquisition, lease, disposal and construction matters
- Intellectual property, data protection and privacy law
- Dual registration and international cross-border issues

Please contact us	Head of Charity & Social Enterprise Sector – Jonathan Burchfield (jrb@stoneking.co.uk)

13 Queen Square
Bath
BA1 2HJ
Tel: 01225 337599
Fax: 01225 335437

Thirty Station Road
Cambridge
CB1 2RE
Tel: 01223 351000
Fax: 01223 314027

Wilsons
Solicitors

4 Lincoln's Inn Fields
London WC2A 3AA
Tel: 020 7998 0420
Fax: 020 7242 7661

Wilsons Solicitors LLP
Alexandra House
St Johns Street
Salisbury, Wiltshire SP1 2SB
Tel: 01722 412 412
Fax: 01722 411 500
Web: www.wilsonslaw.com
Email: gillian.fletcher@wilsonslaw.com

Our firm	Wilsons have one of the UK's largest and most senior specialist teams of charity lawyers advising on all areas of a charity's legal needs. We operate seamlessly between our Salisbury and London offices and act for over 550 of the nation's leading charities across a wide diversity of sectors. The firm's clients include RNLI, RSPCA, Guide Dogs for the Blind and PDSA and we act for special interest charitable sectors including independent schools, academies, care providers and armed forces charities. With 28 partners and a total staff of 155 Wilsons provides top quality advice and unbeatable rates.

Our services

- Constitutional and governance reviews
- Charity Commission regulation
- Trustee powers and duties
- Identification/management of conflicts of interest
- Trustee appointments, retirements and removals
- Mergers and incorporation

- Fundraising and trading laws
- Legacy administration
- Contested wills and probate
- Statutory wills
- Commercial law
- Property
- Employment law

Charities and education team

Key members in the team:

Gillian Fletcher (T: 020 7998 0422 E: gillian.fletcher@wilsonslaw.com) is the director of charity law and governance and advises on a wide range of charity law issues including the establishment of new charities, breaches of trust and governance issues. She has extensive experience in charity litigation and the use of the Charity Commission's regulatory powers.

Peter Jeffreys (T: 01722 427 758 E: peter.jeffreys@wilsonslaw.com) is a partner and specialises in legacy administration, probate and administration of estates for charities and charity law generally. He regularly acts for charities in the Court of Protection in statutory will applications and is highly regarded as a lecturer on wills, probate and related matters.

Fiona Campbell-White (T: 020 7998 0425 E: fiona.campbell-white@wilsonslaw.com) is a partner who has particular experience in acting for charities on a wide variety of general contentious matters (from governance issues to contract/tort disputes), with her more recent focus being on legacy disputes.

Judith Beddow (T: 01722 427 740 E: judith.beddow@wilsonslaw.com) is head of our commercial property team and carries out a significant amount of work for charities including property work for schools and community buildings using grant money.

Geraldine White (T: 01722 427 657 E: geraldine.white@wilsonslaw.com) is a partner in our employment department and she specialises in providing contentious and non-contentious employment law advice including drafting and advising on contracts of employment, service agreements and company policies; acting in employment tribunal and high court proceedings; and advising on general HR matters including disciplinary, grievance and dismissal procedures.

WRIGLEYS
— SOLICITORS —

**19 Cookridge Street
Leeds
LS2 3AG
Tel: 0113 244 6100**

**Wrigleys Solicitors LLP
3rd Floor, Fountain
Precinct, Balm Green
Sheffield S1 2JA
Tel: 0114 267 5588**

**Email: malcolm.lynch@wrigleys.co.uk
Web: www.wrigleys.co.uk**

Type of organisation	Wrigleys is a specialist law firm with a dedicated Charities and Social Economy team of over 20 lawyers who advise many hundreds of charities and organisations in the voluntary, community and social enterprise sectors. Wrigleys Solicitors was established in 1996 as a niche practice for private and charity clients. Now with over 185 staff, the firm's focus remains on charity and social economy clients, private clients, pensions clients and property advice.
Services to Charities	Our services & expertise include: • Governance & structures • Trading • Social investment & charity bond issues • Fundraising & commercial participators • Operations & contracts • Social enterprise • Employment & HR • Property • Public & third sector pensions • Mergers & restructuring • Community care • Charities administration Wrigleys Solicitors LLP is authorised and regulated by the Financial Conduct Authority to give advice on financial promotions
Our clients	Our clients cover a wide range of charitable activities and Wrigleys supports the sector through our membership of Acevo, Charity Finance Group and Charity Tax Reform Group. Members of the Charity Team are all members of the Charity Law Association and participate in its work. The *Legal 500* guide considers Wrigleys a top tier leading charity law firm and the *Chambers & Partners Guide to the Legal Profession* has given the firm a national ranking. **"They are experienced, knowledgeable, and always support us at short notice."** **"Incredibly willing to help us, and a great understanding of how charities work on a practical level."** ***Client comments from Chambers & Partners 2016***

Contacts

Malcolm Lynch
malcolm.lynch@wrigleys.co.uk
Tel: 0113 204 5724

Chris Billington
chris.billington@wrigleys.co.uk
Tel: 0113 204 5734

Sylvie Nunn
sylvie.nunn@wrigleys.co.uk
Tel: 0113 204 5726

Elizabeth Wilson
elizabeth.wilson@wrigleys.co.uk
Tel: 0113 204 5721

Sue Greaves
sue.greaves@wrigleys.co.uk
Tel: 0114 267 5625

Dr John McMullen
john.mcmullen@wrigleys.co.uk
Tel: 0113 204 5706

Berkeley Applegate & Webb
Lowcroft, Church Road,
Wombourne
West Midlands
WV5 9EZ
Tel: 01902 324194
Email: customerservice@onsiteinsurance.co.uk
Web: www.onsiteinsurance.co.uk

About Berkeley Applegate & Webb

Our insurance broking business dates its origin to 1966 when Alan Webb left his employment with the Provincial Insurance Company and opened the office of Alan J Webb & Co in Brierley Hill in the West Midlands.

The family run business provided insurance to local people and businesses in addition to Mr Webb's particular expertise in providing services to churches and charities.

The business incorporated as Berkeley Applegate Webb & Co (Midlands) Limited, in January 1969 and, in 1975, moved to its present home in the South Staffordshire village of Wombourne. Mr Webb served as managing director until retirement January 1990 when he was succeeded by the current MD, Steve Hester, who continues to adhere to the principles with which Mr Webb started the business. The company continues to be focussed on the requirements of churches, charities and Community Interest Companies as well as an additional specialism of construction insurance.

Berkeley Applegate & Webb and Onsite Insurance are trading styles
of Berkeley Applegate Webb & Co (Midlands) Limited
which is authorised and regulated by the Financial Conduct Authority.

Our service

We are independent insurance brokers with no ties to any insurance provider. We provide independent and impartial insurance advice.

Our rural location and efficient procedures result in lower operating costs which enable us to offer an efficient and cost-effective service to meet the requirements and budgets of small and medium sized charities.

Your Contacts

Steve Hester
Managing Director

Jenny Middleton
Office Manager

customerservice@onsiteinsurance.co.uk

Telephone 01902 324194

THE TOP CHARITY BANKS BY NUMBER OF CHARITY CLIENTS

Barclays	1/687
NatWest	2/627
Lloyds Bank Corporate Markets	3/389
HSBC Bank PLC	4/374
Royal Bank of Scotland Group plc, The	5/352
Bank of Scotland Corporate	6/155
The Co-operative Bank plc	7/147
CAF Bank Ltd	8/142
Coutts & Co	9/116
Clydesdale Bank PLC	10/ 59
Santander UK PLC	11/ 46
C Hoare & Co	12/ 45
Allied Irish Bank (GB)	13/ 41
Unity Trust Bank PLC	14/ 40
Triodos Bank	15/ 28
CCLA	16/ 27
Scottish Widows Bank PLC	17/ 27
Yorkshire Bank PLC	18/ 23
Child & Co	19/ 20
Handelsbanken	20/ 16

the fundraiser

Lead by example

Make sure your team know where they are going. Read The Fundraiser blog for the latest charity sector insight and advice

Case studies - find out what other large charities are doing

How to guides - practical fundraising and charity management advice

Interviews - charity leaders share their experiences

Trends and research - what is happening in the voluntary sector

Opinion and debates - fundraising experts discuss current issues

In depth articles and analysis - we research the latest fundraising innovations to keep you ahead of the curve

The essential resource for every charity. Expert, online, and free.

www.the-fundraiser.co.uk

Brought to you by Charity Choice; helping charities for over 25 years

CharityChoice

HERE'S TO THOSE WHO CHANGED THE WORLD

THE DONKEY SANCTUARY

Dr Elisabeth Svendsen MBE Founder of The Donkey Sanctuary
(by Mike Hollist)

WHAT WILL YOUR LEGACY BE?

Help protect and care for abused donkeys by remembering us in your will.

To receive a copy of our Leaving a Legacy guide 'Your questions answered' or to speak directly with our **Legacy Team** please contact **01395 578222**
marie.wilson@thedonkeysanctuary.org.uk

RETURN FORM TO:

THE DONKEY SANCTUARY
Legacy Department (TC),
Sidmouth, Devon, EX10 0NU.

A charity registered with the Charity Commission for England and Wales No. 264818

Name: Mr/Mrs/Miss

Address

Postcode

Email

www.thedonkeysanctuary.org.uk/legacy

0014_14_DS

Looking for a charity?

Charity Choice is the UK's most popular charity directory. We help people to help charities — whether by donations, event fundraising, legacy gifts, volunteering, or simply finding the charity that is the right match for them.

CharityChoice

www.charitychoice.co.uk

THE

PROFESSIONAL

ADVISERS SECTION

AUDITORS AND THEIR CHARITY CLIENTS

A C MOLE & SONS, Stafford House, Blackbrook Park Avenue, Taunton, Somerset, TA1 2PX. Tel: 01823 624450. Fax: 01823 444533. E-mail: christineglover@acmole.co.uk. Charity specialists: I Pinder.

1610 Limited	7.2
Tone Leisure (Taunton Deane) Limited	7.683

A J BROWN, 91 Front Street, Acomb, York, North Yorkshire, YO24 3BU.

New Kadampa Tradition	7.458

A R RAYMOND & CO LTD, 67 London Road, St Leonards-on-Sea, East Sussex, TN37 6AR. Tel: 01424 424653.

Magdalen Lasher Charity	7.406

A9 PARTNERSHIP LTD, 47 Commercial Road, Lerwick, Shetland, ZE1 0NJ. Tel: 01595 696424. Fax: 01595 694296. E-mail: lerwick@a9partnership.co.uk. Internet: www.a9partnership.co.uk. Charity specialists: P C Hetherington (Director).

Shetland Amenity Trust	7.604

ABACUS PARTNERS LLP, Unit A, Abbott's Wharf, 93 Stainsby Road, London, E14 6JL. Tel: 020 75385042. Fax: 020 7538 9655. E-mail: nur@abacusllp.co.uk.

APASENTH	7.34
East London Mosque Trust Ltd, The	7.221

ACKLANDS LIMITED, 4 Hillside, Cotham Hill, Bristol, BS6 6JP. Tel: 0117 923 7788. E-mail: support@acklands.co.uk. Internet: www.acklands.co.uk.

Stoneleigh Abbey Limited	7.660

ADDITIONS ACCOUNTANTS LTD, 7 Queen Avenue, Liverpool, Merseyside, L2 4TZ. Tel: 0151 236 4554. Fax: 0151 236 3554. Internet: www.additionsgroup.com.

Options for Supported Living	7.482

ADS ACCOUNTANCY LIMITED, 7 Faraday Court, First Avenue, Burton-on-Trent, Staffordshire, DE14 2WX. Tel: 01530 813220. Internet: www.ads-accountancy.co.uk.

Consolidated Charity of Burton upn Trent	7.177

ADVANTAGE ACCOUNTANCY & ADVISORY LLP, 38 Cathedral Road, Cardiff, CF11 9LL. Tel: 02922 331169. E-mail: info@adv-accountancy.co.uk. Internet: www.adv-accountancy.co.uk.

St David's Foundation Hospice Care	7.642

AHMED & CO, Ferrari House (2nd Floor), 102 College Road, Harrow, Middlesex, HA1 1ES.

Harrow Central Mosque and Islamic Centre	7.303

ALBERT GOODMAN, Mary Street House, Mary Street, Taunton, Somerset, TA1 3NW. Tel: 01823 286096. Fax: 01823 257319. E-mail: ag@albertgoodman.co.uk. Internet: www.albertgoodman.co.uk. Charity specialists: P Hake.

Dorset & Somerset Air Ambulance Charity	7.208
Fairfield Charitable Trust	7.246
Somerset Redstone Trust	7.627

ALBURY ASSOCIATES LIMITED, 1 Olympic Way, Wembley, London, HA9 0NP.

Shree Swaminarayan Sidhant Sajivan Mandal	7.606

ALEXANDER SLOAN, 1 Atholl Place, Edinburgh, EH3 8HP. Tel: 0131 225 8282. Fax: 0131 225 6889. Internet: www.alexandersloan.co.uk. Charity specialists: Isabell Grey.

East Lothian Housing Association	7.222
Garvald Edinburgh	7.269

ALEXANDER SLOAN, 38 Cadagon Street, Glasgow, G2 7HF. Tel: 0141 204 8989. Fax: 0141 248 9931. E-mail: info@alexandersloan.co.uk. Internet: www.alexandersloan.co.uk. Charity specialists: Allan Cunningham. Allison Devine. M Mulholland.

Baird Trust	7.54

ALLCHURCH BAILEY, 93 High Street, Evesham, Worcestershire, WR11 4DU. Tel: 01386 765888. Fax: 01386 765926. E-mail: general@allchurchbailey.co.uk. Internet: www.allchurchbailey.co.uk.

John Martin's Charity	7.360

ALLEN TULLY AND CO, 19 Palace Square, London, SE19 2LT. Tel: 020 8303 1333.

Order of Hermit Friars of St Augustine	7.483

ALLIOTTS, Imperial House, 15 Kingsway, London, WC2B 6UN. Tel: 020 7240 9971. Fax: 020 7240 9692. E-mail: london@alliotts.com. Internet: www.alliotts.com. Charity specialists: Nigel J Armstrong. Stephen Meredith. Ian Davies. Jackie Withey.

Seamen's Hospital Society	7.595

ALLIOTTS, Friary Court, 13-21 High Street, Guildford, Surrey, GU1 3DL. Tel: 01483 533119. Fax: 01483 537339. E-mail: guildford@alliotts.com. Internet: www.alliotts.com. Charity specialists: Stephen Meredith. Richard D E Hopes. Chris Cairns.

London Marathon Charitable Trust Limited	7.399
Police Dependants' Trust Limited, The	7.507

ALLOTTS, Sidings Court, Lakeside, Doncaster, South Yorkshire, DN4 5NU. Tel: 01302 349218. Fax: 01302 321739. E-mail: donc@Allotts.co.uk. Internet: www.allotts.co.uk.

Doncaster Deaf Trust	7.205

ALLOTTS BUSINESS SERVICES LTD, The Old Grammar School, 13 Moorgate Road, Rotherham, South Yorkshire, S60 2EN. Tel: 01709 828 400. Fax: 01709 829 807. E-mail: info@allotts.co.uk. Internet: www.allotts.co.uk. Charity specialists: M Garrison. Liz Yates. Mrs J N Saunders (Director).

Groundwork Wakefield Limited	7.290

ANDERSON ANDERSON & BROWN LLP, 9 Queens Road, Aberdeen, Grampian, AB15 4YL. Tel: 0122 462 5111. Fax: 0122 462 6007. E-mail: charities@aab.co.uk. Internet: www.aab.co.uk.

Aberdeen Endowments Trust	7.5

ANDERSON BARROWCLIFF LLP, Waterloo House, Teesdale South, Thornaby-on-Tees, Stockton-on-Tees, TS17 6SA. Tel: 01642 660 300. Fax: 01642 660 301. E-mail: theteam@anderson-barrowcliff.co.uk. Internet: www.anderson-barrowcliff.co.uk.

Middlesbrough Diocesan Trust	7.425
Tees Valley Community Foundation	7.671

ANDORRAN LTD, 6 Manor Park Business Centre, Mackenzie Way, Cheltenham, Gloucestershire, GL51 9TX. Tel: 01242 244856. Fax: 01242 245275. Internet: www.andorran.co.uk.

Gloucestershire Everyman Theatre	7.278

ANDREWS AND PALMER LTD, 32 The Square, Gillingham, Dorset, SP8 4AR.

W F Southall Trust	7.710

APPLEBY & WOOD, 40 The Lock Building, 72 High Street, London, E15 2QB. Tel: 020 8534 0383. Fax: 020 8519 6571. E-mail: Appleby.Wood@btinternet.com. Charity specialists: R Oswald.

Catholic Institute for International Relations	7.119
Solaraid	7.626
Vision Redbridge Culture & Leisure	7.707

APSLEYS, 21 Bampton Street, Tiverton, Devon, EX16 6AA. Tel: 01884 257725. Fax: 01884 256724. Internet: www.apsleys.com. Charity specialists: D Wicks.

Tiverton Almhouse Charity	7.681
Viscount Amory's Charitable Trust	7.707

ARMSTRONG WATSON, Fairview House, Victoria Place, Carlisle, Cumbria, CA1 1HP. Tel: 01228 690200. Fax: 01228 690201. E-mail: lyn.carroll@armstrongwatson.co.uk. Internet: www.armstrongwatson.co.uk. Charity specialists: A Johnston (Senior Partner).

Cumbrian Community Foundation	7.189
Five Lamps Organisation	7.255

ARMSTRONGS, 1 & 2 Mercia Village, Torwood Close, Westwood Business Park, Coventry, Warwickshire, CV4 8HX. Tel: 02476 715 111. Fax: 02476 712 344. E-mail: info@armstrongs-accountancy.co.uk. Internet: www.armstrongs-accountancy.co.uk.

Penderels Trust	7.495

ARNOLD HILL & CO, Craven House, 16 Northumberland Avenue, London, WC2N 5AP. Tel: 020 7306 9100. Fax: 020 7306 9120. Internet: www.arnoldhill.co.uk.

Padwa Charitable Foundation, The	7.489

ARRAM BERLYN GARDNER, 30 City Road, London, EC1Y 2AB. Tel: 020 7330 0000. Fax: 020 7330 0001. E-mail: abg@abggroup.co.uk.

Internet: www.abggroup.co.uk.
Charity specialists: Julie Piper (Partner). Paul Berlyn (Partner). Gary Jackson (Senior Partner).

Pears Family Charitable Foundation, The	7.495
Teresa Rosenbaum Golden Charitable Trust	7.673

ARTHUR GAIT & COMPANY, 18 Gold Tops, Newport, Newport, Gwent, NP20 5WJ. Tel: 01633 262 352. Fax: 01633 250 478. E-mail: admin@arthurgait.co.uk. Internet: www.arthurgait.co.uk.

Monmouth Diocesan Board of Finance	7.431
Monmouth Diocesan Trust	7.432

ASPENS, Suite F9, Waterside Centre, North Street, Lewes, East Sussex, BN7 2PE. Tel: 01273 480699. Fax: 01273 478808. E-mail: enquiries@aspensaccountants.co.uk. Internet: www.aspensaccountants.co.uk.

Connection at St Martin's	7.176

ATKINS FERRIE, Lakeside Offices, The Old Cattle Market, Coronation Park, Helston, Cornwall, TR13 OSR. Tel: 01326 572600. Fax: 01326 563629. E-mail: info@atkinsferrie.co.uk. Internet: www.atkinsferrie.co.uk. Charity specialists: A Ferrie.

Spectrum	7.632

ATKINSON FINCH & CO, Central Chambers, 45-47 Albert Street, Rugby, Warwickshire, CV21 2SG. Tel: 01788 543164. Fax: 01788 546278. E-mail: reception@atkinsonfinchandco.co.uk. Internet: www.atkinsonfinchandco.co.uk. Charity specialists: S Bolton.

British Assoc Counselling & Psychotherapy	7.92

AUDIT SCOTLAND, 110 George Street, Edinburgh, EH2 4LH. Tel: 0845 146 1010. Fax: 0845 146 1009. E-mail: info@audit-scotland.gov.uk. Internet: www.audit-scotland.gov.uk.

Royal Botanic Garden Edinburgh	7.553

B D & M LIMTED, 20 St. Martinsfield, Martinstown, Dorchester, Dorset, DT2 9JU. Tel: 01305 889464.

Peacock Charitable Trust	7.495

B OLSBERG & CO, Enterprise House, 3 Middleton Road, Manchester, Lancashire, M8 5DT. Tel: 0161 660 3492.

A W Charitable Trust	7.4
Newmarston Limited Group	7.461

BACHA & BACHA, Steamhouse, 555 White Hart Lane, London, N17 7RP. Tel: 020 8881 8686. Internet: /www.bachaglobal.com.

Tottenham Grammar School Foundation	7.683

BAINES JEWITT, 43 Yarm Lane, Stockton-on-Tees, TS18 3EA. Tel: 01642 673601. Fax: 01642 617528. Internet: www.bainesjewitt.co.uk.

Goshen Trust	7.282

BAKER CHAPMAN & BUSSEY, 3 North Hill, Colchester, Essex, CO1 1DZ. Tel: 01206 715000. Fax: 01206 715010. Charity specialists: A Taylor.

St Helena Hospice	7.644

BALDWIN MCCRANOR, Clifford House, 38-44 Binley Road, Coventry, Warwickshire, CV3 1JA.

Midland Sports Centre for the Disabled	7.426

BANKS & CO, 1 Carnegie Road, Newbury, Berkshire, RG14 5DJ. Tel: 01635 47337. Fax: 01635 32180. E-mail: office@banksco.co.uk. Internet: www.banksco.co.uk.

Brampton Trust	7.84

BARLOW ANDREWS LLP, Carlyle House, 78 Chorley New Road, Bolton, Lancashire, BL1 4BY. Tel: 01204 527 451. Fax: 01204 364 573. E-mail: dak@barlow-andrews.co.uk. Internet: www.barlowandrews.co.uk.

Brookvale	7.101
Burton Family Charitable Trust, The	7.105
Zochonis Charitable Trust	7.752

BARNETT & TURNER LLP, Cromwell House, 68 West Gate, Mansfield, Nottinghamshire, NG18 1RR. Tel: 01623 659659. Fax: 01623 420844. Internet: www.barnettandturner.co.uk.

Brunts Charity	7.102

BATES WESTON, The Mills, Canal Street, Derby, Derbyshire, DE1 2RJ. Tel: 01332 365855. Fax: 01332 291294. E-mail: waynet@batesweston.co.uk. Internet: www.batesweston.co.uk.

General Conference of the New Church	7.270

BDO LLP, 55 Baker Street, London, W1U 7EU. Tel: 020 7486 5888. Fax: 020 7487 3686. Internet: www.bdo.co.uk. Charity specialists: Ian Mathieson.

Abbeyfield Society	7.5
Academy of Medical Sciences	7.8
Art Fund	7.40
Barristers' Benevolent Association	7.59
BEN-Motor & Allied Trades Benevolent Fund	7.64
British Academy	7.91
British Refugee Council	7.98
British Safety Council	7.98
Certified Accountants Educational Trust	7.125
Charity of Walter Stanley	7.130
Chartered Institute of Environmental Health	7.133
Chartered Institute of Purchasing & Supply	7.134
College of Occupational Therapists	7.160
Design Council	7.199
Dogs Trust	7.203
Dominican Sisters Congregation Newcastle	7.204
Dulwich Estate	7.214
Edward Cadbury Charitable Trust	7.228
Field Lane Foundation	7.253
Foundation for Social Entrepreneurs	7.259
Frances Augustus Newman Foundation	7.262
Girlguiding UK	7.274
Hamps & Isle of Wight Air Ambulance	7.298
Hampshire Autistic Society	7.298
Institute for Fiscal Studies	7.332
Institute of Grocery Distribution	7.335
Institution of Civil Engineers	7.338
Livability	7.391
London City Mission	7.397
Metropolitan Support Trust	7.424
Millennium Awards Trust, The	7.427
Muscular Dystrophy Campaign	7.439
National Council Voluntary Organisations	7.444
Philharmonia	7.500
Portsmouth Diocesan Board Of Finance	7.509
Royal Academy of Engineering	7.549
Royal Society for Prevention Accidents	7.571
RUSI	7.575
Samaritans	7.585
Shakespeare Globe Trust	7.599
South London YMCA	7.629
Teenage Cancer Trust	7.671
Tommy's, the baby charity	7.682
Trident Reach the People Charity	7.686
Trusthouse Charitable Foundation	7.690
Y Care International	7.743
YMCA England	7.745
YMCA Fairthorne Group	7.745
YMCA London South West	7.746

BDO LLP, Citypoint, 65 Haymarket Terrace, Edinburgh, EH12 5HD. Tel: 0131 347 0347. Fax: 0131 347 0330. E-mail: info@bdo.co.uk. Internet: www.bdo.co.uk. Charity specialists: Kerry Anderson. Martin J Gill. M Hepburn. C Scott. Barbara Southern.

Aberlour Child Care Trust	7.6
Age Scotland	7.17
Alzheimer Scotland - Action on Dementia	7.28
Capital City Partnership Limited	7.113

Chest Heart & Stroke Scotland	7.137
Edinburgh Leisure	7.225
Moredun Foundation, The	7.433
Moredun Research Institute	7.434
Royal Blind	7.553
SCVO	7.592
Scottish War Blinded	7.593
Support for Ordinary Living	7.664
Thistle Foundation	7.677
Voluntary Action Fund	7.709

BDO LLP, 2 City Place, Beehive Ring Road, Gatwick, Surrey, RH6 OPA. Tel: 01293 591000. Fax: 01293 591001. Charity specialists: Don Bawtree.

Action Against Hunger (UK)	7.9
Addaction	7.13
Ambika Paul Foundation	7.29
Amnesty International UK Section	7.30
Archbishops' Council	7.37
Arthritis Research UK	7.40
Barnardo's	7.57
Blue Cross	7.76
BMS World Mission	7.77
Book Aid International	7.79
British Pregnancy Advisory Service	7.97
BSS	7.102
Carers Trust	7.114
CFBT Education Trust	7.125
Challenge Network	7.126
Chartered Management Institute	7.135
Childhood First	7.140
Christian Vision	7.146
Church Army	7.147
City and Guilds of London Institute	7.152
David Elaine Potter Charitable Foundation	7.194
David & Ruth Lewis Family Charitable Trust	7.194
Debra	7.196
Dyslexia Action	7.217
East of England Agricultural Society	7.223
Ed & TrainingTst of Chartered Insurance Inst	7.227
Essex Community Foundation	7.240
Ex-Services Mental Welfare Society	7.243
FitzRoy Support	7.255
Geological Society of London	7.272
Goodenough College	7.281
Groundwork UK	7.290
Help for Heroes	7.308
Hintze Family Charitable Foundation, The	7.313
Hospital of St John and St Elizabeth	7.321
Inst of Marine Engineering, Science & Tech	7.335
Institute of Physics	7.336
Institute of Psychoanalysis	7.337
Institution of Chemical Engineers	7.337
Institution of Structural Engineers	7.339
International Fund for Animal Welfare	7.342
Jack Petchey Foundation	7.349
Kathleen & Michael Connolly Foundation UK	7.366
Landmark Trust	7.378
Letchworth Garden City Heritage Foundation	7.386
Museum of London Archaeology	7.440
NACRO	7.442
Nat Centre for Young People with Epilepsy	7.443
National Film and Television School	7.445
National Foundation for Youth Music	7.446
Nesta	7.456
Newlife Foundation for Disabled Children	7.461
Nuffield Foundation	7.474
Nuffield Trst for Res.&Pol.Studies in Health	7.475
Outward Housing	7.486
Overseas Bishoprics Fund	7.486
PDSA	7.494
Regent's University London	7.530
Roddick Foundation, The	7.542
RSPCA	7.572
Salvation Army International Trust	7.584
Scout Association	7.594
Sisters of Charity of St Paul	7.613
Social Investment Business Foundation	7.620
Starlight Children's Foundation	7.656
Staying First	7.657
Stewardship Services (UKET) Ltd	7.658
Sue Ryder	7.663
Tearfund	7.670
Treloar Trust	7.685
Voluntary Service Overseas	7.709
Whiteley Homes Trust	7.725

WomanCare Global 7.736

BDO LLP, 4 Atlantic Quay, 70 York Street, Glasgow, G2 8JX. Tel: 0141 248 3761. Fax: 0141 248 1653. E-mail: info@bdo.co.uk. Internet: www.bdo.co.uk.
Charity specialists: M Gill. Andrew McNamara. C Scott. Sarah Steele.

NHS Gtr Glasgow & Clyde Endowments 7.462
Richmond Fellowship Scotland 7.537
YMCA Glasgow 7.745

BDO LLP, Pannell House, Park Street, Guildford, Surrey, GU1 4HN. Tel: 01483 564646. Fax: 01483 578880. Internet: www.bdo.co.uk.
Charity specialists: Richard Faulkner.

Richmond Church Charity Estates 7.537
Richmond Parish Lands Charity 7.538

BDO LLP, 1 Bridgewater Place, Leeds, West Yorkshire, LS11 5RU. Tel: 01132 443 839. Fax: 01132 041 200. E-mail: PKF@UK.PKF.Com. Internet: www.bdo.co.uk.

Doncaster Culture and Leisure Trust 7.204
Yorkshire Sculpture Park 7.749

BDO LLP, Pannell House, 159 Charles Street, Leicester, Leicestershire, LE1 1LD. Tel: 0116 250 4400. Fax: 0116 285 4651. Internet: www.bdo.co.uk.
Charity specialists: Nish Bathia. Roger Merchant.

Building and Social Housing Foundation 7.103
Gideons International British Isles 7.274
LOROS 7.384
National Space Science Centre 7.453

BDO LLP, St Hugh's, 23 Newport, Lincoln, Lincolnshire, LN1 3DN. Tel: 01522 531441. Fax: 01522 510185. Internet: www.bdo.co.uk.
Charity specialists: Roger Merchant.

St Barnabas Hospice Lincolnshire Trust 7.638

BDO LLP, 5 Temple Square, Temple Street, Liverpool, Merseyside, L2 5RH. Tel: 0151 237 4500. Fax: 0151 237 4545. E-mail: info@bdo.co.uk. Internet: www.bdo.co.uk.
Charity specialists: Brian G Ricketts. Mark Sykes.

BDO LLP, 3 Hardman Street, Spinningfields, Manchester, Greater Manchester, M3 3AT. Tel: 01618 177 500. Internet: www.bdo.co.uk.
Charity specialists: F J Cooke. D Bancroft. Mark Sykes.

Community Integrated Care 7.164
Furniture Resource Centre 7.266
Lifeline Project 7.388
Manchester Diocesan Board of Finance 7.408
Threshold Housing Project 7.680

BDO LLP, Cedar House, 105 Carrow Road, Norwich, Norfolk, NR1 1HP. Tel: 01603 615914. Fax: 01603 756950. E-mail: info@bdo.co.uk. Internet: www.bdo.co.uk.
Charity specialists: Nick Buxton.

Christian Blind Mission (United Kingdom) 7.145
Dulwich Picture Gallery 7.215
River Farm Foundation 7.539

BDO LLP, Regent House, Clinton Avenue, Nottingham, Nottinghamshire, NG5 1AZ. Tel: 0115 960 8171. Fax: 0115 960 3665. Internet: www.bdo.co.uk.
Charity specialists: Roger Merchant.

Congregational Federation 7.176
Lady Hind Trust 7.377
Nottingham YMCA 7.473
WCS Care Group Limited 7.717

BDWM, The Granary, Grange Lane, Lower Broadheath, Worcester, Worcestershire, WR2 6RW.

Worcester Consolidated Municipal Charity 7.738

BEAK KEMMENOE, 1-3 Manor Road, Chatham, Kent, ME4 6AE. Tel: 01634 830100. Fax: 01634 814080. E-mail: accountants@beakkemmenoe.co.uk. Internet: www.bkca.co.uk.

Larkfield With Hill Park Autistic Trust Limited 7.380

BEAVIS MORGAN, 82 St John Street, London, EC1M 4JN.

Hospice of Hope Romania Limited 7.319

BEEVER AND STRUTHERS, 15 Bunhill Row, London, EC1Y 8LP. Tel: 020 8902 0809. Fax: 020 8902 2722. E-mail: james.lambden@beeverstruthers.co.uk. Internet: www.beeverstruthers.co.uk.

Langley House Trust 7.379
Southside Partnership 7.631

BEEVER AND STRUTHERS, Central Buildings, Richmond Terrace, Blackburn, Aberdeenshire, BB1 7AP. Tel: 01254 686 600. Fax: 01254 682 483. Internet: www.beeverstruthers.co.uk.

Pilling Trust Fund, The 7.504
Training 2000 7.685

BEEVER AND STRUTHERS, St George's House, 215-219 Chester Road, Manchester, Greater Manchester, M15 4JE. Tel: 0161 832 4901. Fax: 0161 835 3668. E-mail: maria.hallows@beeverstruthers.co.uk. Internet: www.beeverstruthers.co.uk.

BEGBIES CHARTERED ACCOUNTANTS, 9 Bonhill Street, London, EC2A4DJ. Tel: 020 7628 5801. Internet: www.begbiesaccountants.co.uk.
Charity specialists: Catherine Dee. Daniel Valentine.

Newby Trust 7.459
Triangle Trust 1949 Fund 7.686

BERG KAPROW LEWIS LLP, 35 Ballards Lane, Finchley, London, N3 1XW. Tel: 020 8922 9222. Fax: 020 8922 9223. E-mail: brian.wolkind@bkl.co.uk. Internet: www.bkl.co.uk.
Charity specialists: Brian J Wolkind. Russell Smith. Sum Wong.

Hill Foundation, The 7.312

BESSLER HENDRIE, Albury Mill, Mill Lane, Chilworth, Guildford, Surrey, GU4 8RU.

Actors' Benevolent Fund 7.13

BEVAN & BUCKLAND, Langdon House, Langdon Road, Swansea Waterfront, Swansea, SA1 8QY. Tel: 01792 410100. Fax: 01792 648105. E-mail: mail@bevanbuckland.co.uk. Internet: www.bevanbuckland.co.uk.

Welsh Air Ambulance Charitable Trust 7.718

BFCA LTD, Beaumont Business Centres, 80 Coleman Street, London, EC2R 5BJ. Tel: 0207 489 6481. Internet: www.bfca.eu.

Harbour Foundation 7.301

BFCD CHARTERED ACCOUNTANTS, 1 Castlewood Avenue, Rathmines, Dublin. Tel: 00 353 1 497 0935. Fax: 00 353 1 496 0061. E-mail: info@bfcd.ie. Internet: www.bfcd.ie.
Charity specialists: R Butler.

Catholic Foreign Missions 7.119

BHP CHARTERED ACCOUNTANTS, 2 Rutland Park, Sheffield, South Yorkshire, S10 2PD. Tel: 0114 266 7171. Fax: 0114 266 9846. E-mail: jane.marshall@bhp.co.uk. Internet: www.bhp.co.uk.

Our specialist team of 30 professionals acts for over 250 charities and not for profit organisations. Clients include incorporated entities, trusts, academies and social enterprises, as well as large organisations with complex structures and funds.

Members of BHP's charity team hold the ICAEW Diploma in Charity Accounting (DChA), demonstrating BHP's high level of competence in charity accounting and financial management which makes a real difference to organisations in the charity sector. Many members of the team are also charity trustees and school governors with a deep understanding of the challenges faced by charity trustees.

For more information visit www.bhp.co.uk/charities

Charity specialists: Jane Marshall (Head of Charities and Not for Profit). Philip Allsop (Partner). Simon Buchan (Head of VAT). Rachelle Rowbottom (Charity Tax Specialist).

Action Housing & Support Limited 7.10
Bluebell Wood Children's Hospice 7.77
Hospital of Gilbert, Earl of Shrewsbury 7.320
International Water Association 7.345
Magna Trust 7.407
Retreat York, The 7.534
Rotherham Hospice Trust 7.546
SheffCare 7.600
Sheffield Church Burgesses Trust 7.600
Sheffield Hospitals Trust & Related Charities 7.602
Skill Force Development 7.617
St Luke's Hospice 7.647
Wilf Ward Family Trust 7.728

BHP CHARTERED ACCOUNTANTS, 57-59 Saltergate, Chesterfield, Derbyshire, S40 1UL. Tel: 01246 232121. Fax: 01246 201359. E-mail: jane.marshall@bhp.co.uk. Internet: www.bhp.co.uk.
Charity specialists: Jane Marshall (Head of Charities and Not for Profit). Simon Buchan (Head of VAT). Rachelle Rowbottom (Charity Tax Specialist).

Ashgate Hospice 7.43

BHP CHARTERED ACCOUNTANTS, First Floor, Mayesbrook House, Lawnswood Business Park, Redvers Close, Leeds, West Yorkshire, LS16 6QY. Tel: 0113 274 3496. Fax: 0113 274 3486. E-mail: mike.jackson@bhp.co.uk. Internet: www.bhp.co.uk.
Charity specialists: Mike Jackson (Partner). Jane Marshall (Head of Charities and Not for Profit). Simon Buchan (Head of VAT). Rachelle Rowbottom (Charity Tax Specialist).

Sports Coach UK 7.633

BHP CHARTERED ACCOUNTANTS, Bathurst House, 86 Micklegate, York, North Yorkshire, YO1 6LQ. Tel: 01904 628551. Fax: 01904 623533. E-mail: guy.ward@bhp.co.uk. Internet: www.bhp.co.uk.

Charity specialists: Jane Marshall (Head of Charities and Not for Profit). Guy Ward (Partner). Simon Buchan (Head of VAT). Rachelle Rowbottom (Charity Tax Specialist).

Allen Lane Foundation	7.26
Compass	7.168
Lady Elizabeth Hastings' Charities	7.376
York Archaeological Trust	7.747

BHP CLOUGH & COMPANY, New Chartford House, Centurion Way, Cleckheaton, West Yorkshire, BD19 3QB. Tel: 01274 876333. Fax: 01274 876334.
E-mail: lesley.kendrew@bhpclough.co.uk.
Internet: www.bhp.co.uk.
Charity specialists: Lesley Kendrew (Partner). Jane Marshall (Head of Charities and Not for Profit). Simon Buchan (Head of VAT). Rachelle Rowbottom (Charity Tax Specialist).

L'Arche	7.375

BIRD SIMPSON & CO, 144 Nethergate, Dundee, DD1 4EB. Tel: 01382 227841. Fax: 01382 202622. E-mail: admin@birdsimpson.co.uk.
Internet: www.birdsimpson.co.uk.
Charity specialists: I P Garland. N S Young.

Gowrie Care Limited	7.283
Northern Housing Company	7.470

BISHOP FLEMING, 16 Queen Square, Bristol, BS1 4NT. Tel: 0117 9100 250. Fax: 0117 9100 251. E-mail: jscaife@bishopfleming.co.uk.
Internet: www.bishopfleming.co.uk.
Charity specialists: Joe Scaife (Head of Charity and Not-for-profit Group, Bristol). Dave Brown - specialist area: VAT. Tim Borton - specialist area: Charities, Education and Not-for-Profit, Exeter. Pam Tuckett - specialist area: Charities and Not-for-profit, Plymouth. Will Hanbury - specialist area: Charities, Torquay. David Savill - specialist area: Housing Associations.

Bristol Drugs Project	7.90
Children's Hospice South West	7.141
Clifton Suspension Bridge Trust	7.156
Congregation of La Retraite Trustees	7.171
Dorothy House Foundation Ltd	7.208
Longfield	7.401
Prospect Foundation	7.516
Skills for Health Limited	7.617

BISHOP FLEMING, Stratus House, Emperor Way, Exeter Business Park, Exeter, Devon, EX1 3QS. Tel: 01392 448800. Fax: 01392 448899.
E-mail: tborton@bishopfleming.co.uk.
Internet: www.bishopfleming.co.uk.
Charity specialists: Tim Borton (Partner). Dave Brown (Director of VAT Services). Will Hanbury. Alison Oliver. David Savill (Partner). Joe Scaife. Pam Tuckett.

EDP - Drug and Alcohol Services	7.226
Exeter Diocesan Board of Finance, The	7.244
Hospiscare	7.320
Les Filles de la Croix	7.386
Mare and Foal Sanctuary	7.409
Robert Owen Communities	7.541
Steel Charitable Trust	7.657
United Reformed Church (South Western)	7.696

BISHOP FLEMING, Cobourg House, Mayflower Street, Plymouth, Devon, PL1 1LG. Tel: 01752 262611. Fax: 01752 667882.
E-mail: ptuckett@bishopfleming.co.uk.
Internet: www.bishopfleming.co.uk.

China Fleet Trust	7.143
Marine Biological Association United Kingdom	7.411

BISHOP FLEMING, 50 The Terrace, Torquay, Devon, TQ1 1DD. Tel: 01803 291100. Fax: 01803 293092.
E-mail: torquay@bishopfleming.co.uk.
Internet: www.bishopfleming.co.uk.

Dartmouth Trust	7.193
Rowcroft House Foundation Limited	7.548

BISHOP FLEMING, Chy Nyverow, Newham Road, Truro, Cornwall, TR1 2DP. Tel: 01872 275651. Fax: 01872 222996.
E-mail: truro@bishopfleming.co.uk.
Internet: www.bishopfleming.co.uk.

National Maritime Museum Cornwall Trust	7.449

BISHOP FLEMING RABJOHNS, 1-3 College Yard, Worcester, Worcestershire, WR1 2LB. Tel: 01905 723 100. Fax: 01905 723 279. E-mail: awood@bishopflemingrabjohns.co.uk.
Internet: www.bishopflemingrabjohns.co.uk.
Charity specialists: R G Shaw (Business & Tax Adviser, VAT Consultant) - specialist area: Charities & VAT.

Malvern Theatres Trust Ltd	7.408

BISHOP SIMMONS, Mitre House, School Road, Bedworth, Warwickshire, CV12 9JB. Tel: 024 7631 4404. Fax: 024 7631 9660.

Nicholas Chamberlaine School Foundation	7.462

BLICK ROTHENBERG LLP, 16 Great Queen Street, Covent Garden, London, WC2B 5AH. Tel: 020 7486 0111. Fax: 020 7935 6852. E-mail: email@blickrothenberg.com.
Internet: www.blickrothenberg.com.

Maurice & Vivienne Wohl Philanthropic Fdn	7.417
Maurice Wohl Charitable Foundation	7.417
Phillips & Rubens Charitable Trust	7.501

BLUE SPIRE SOUTH LLP, Cawley Priory, South Pallant, Chichester, West Sussex, PO19 1SY. Tel: 01243 781234. Fax: 01243 791770.
Internet: www.bluespiregroup.com.

Clara E Burgess Charity	7.155
Jesus House	7.353
John R Murray Charitable Trust	7.360
Muriel Jones Foundation, The	7.439
Royal Navy & Royal Marines Children's Fund	7.568
Royal Sailors' Rests	7.570

BOOTH AINSWORTH LLP, Alpha House, 4 Greek Street, Stockport, Greater Manchester, SK3 8AB. Tel: 0161 474 0200. Fax: 0161 474 0660. Internet: www.boothainsworth.co.uk.

Sisters of St Joseph Province	7.615
Stockport Sports Trust	7.659

BOURNE & CO, 3 Charnwood Street, Derby, Derbyshire, DE1 2GY. Tel: 01332 340159. Fax: 01332 292705.
Charity specialists: N Gale.

Liversage Trust	7.393

BOURNER BULLOCK, Sovereign House, 212-224 Shaftesbury Avenue, London, WC2H 8HQ. Tel: 020 7240 5821. Fax: 020 7240 5827. E-mail: bb@bournerbullock.co.uk.
Internet: www.bournerbullock.co.uk.
Charity specialists: S Fleming. D Wheeler.

Elton John Aids Foundation	7.231
Emmanuel Community Charitable Trust Ltd	7.232

BOWKER ORFORD & CO, 15-19 Cavendish Place, London, W1G 0DD. Tel: 020 7636 6391. Fax: 020 7580 3909.
E-mail: mail@bowkerorford.com.
Internet: www.bowkerorford.com.

Jordan Charitable Foundation	7.362

BRAIDWOOD & COMPANY, Willow Grange, The Street, Betchworth, Surrey, RH3 7DJ. Tel: 01737 843 034. Fax: 01737 844 266.
Charity specialists: Mrs C E Braidwood (Partner).

Sino-British Fellowship Trust	7.609

BRANSTON ADAMS, Suite 2, Victoria House, South Street, Farnham, Surrey, GU9 7QU.

Truemark Trust	7.687

BREBNERS, The Quadrangle, 180 Wardour Street, London, W1V 3AA. Tel: 020 7734 2244. Fax: 020 7287 5315.

E-mail: partners@brebners.com.
Internet: www.brebner.co.uk.
Charity specialists: J Ebdon.

BFI Trust	7.68

BRENNAN NEIL & LEONARD, 32 Brenkley Way, Blezard Business Park, Tyne and Wear, NE13 6DS. Tel: 0191 236 8007. Fax: 0191 236 4484. Internet: www.bnlaccountants.co.uk.

Education & Services for People with Autism	7.226

BRIGHT GRAHAME MURRAY, 131 Edgware Road, London, W2 2AP. Tel: 020 7402 7444. Fax: 020 7402 8444. E-mail: post@bgm.co.uk.
Internet: www.bgm.co.uk.

Joe and Rosa Frenkel Charitable Trust, The	7.356

BRINDLEY MILLEN LIMITED, 167 Turners Hill, Cheshunt, Hertfordshire, EN8 9BH. Tel: 01992 631133. Fax: 01992 640204.
Internet: www.brindleymillen.com.

Philip King Charitable Trust	7.501

BRONSENS, 6 Langdale Court, Witney, Oxfordshire, OX28 6FG. Tel: 01993 776593.

Edward Penley Abraham Research Fund	7.228
Guy Newton Research Fund	7.293
Ruskin Mill Trust	7.578

BROOMFIELD & ALEXANDER, Ty Derw,, Lime Tree Court, Cardiff Gate Business Park, Cardiff, CF23 8AB. Tel: 02920 549939. Fax: 02920 739430. Internet: www.broomfield.co.uk.

Drive	7.212
Llamau Limited	7.394
Order St John Priory for Wales	7.483
Tenovus	7.673

BROOMFIELD & ALEXANDER, Waters Lane Chambers, Waters Lane, Newport, NP20 1LA. Tel: 01633 265828. Fax: 01633 221 457.
Internet: www.broomfield.co.uk.

Chapter (Cardiff)	7.127
Gotal Housing Trust	7.280
Llandaff Diocesan Board Finance	7.394
Royal Welsh Agricultural Society Limited	7.575
Wallich Clifford Community	7.712

BSG VALENTINE, Lynton House, 7-12 Tavistock Square, London, WC1H 9BQ. Tel: 020 7393 1111. Fax: 020 7393 1122. E-mail: info@bsgvalentine.com.
Internet: www.bsgvalentine.com.

Percy Bilton Charity	7.497

BTP ASSOCIATES LTD, Orbit Business Centre, Rhydycar Business Park, Merthyr Tydfil, CF48 1DL. Tel: 0800 0439351. Fax: 01685 382323. E-mail: btp@btpassoc.co.uk.
Internet: www.btpassoc.co.uk.

Workers' Educational Assoc South Wales Ltd	7.739

BURGESS HODGSON & CO, Camburgh House, 27 New Dover Road, Canterbury, Kent, CT1 3DN. Tel: 01227 454627. Fax: 01227 452967. Internet: www.burgess-hodgson.co.uk.
Charity specialists: P Clark.

Apostolic Church, The	7.35
Society of St Pius X	7.623

BURMAN & CO, Brunswick House, Birmingham Road, Redditch, Worcestershire, B97 6DY. Tel: 01527 69667. Fax: 01527 584191.
Charity specialists: D Burman.

St Giles Hospice	7.643

BURTON SWEET, Pembroke House, 15 Pembroke House, Clifton, Bristol, BS8 3BA. Tel: 0117 914 2057. Fax: 0117 973 3781. E-mail: ed.marsh@burton-sweet.co.uk.
Internet: www.burton-sweet.co.uk.

Bristol Benevolent Institution	7.89
International Aid Trust	7.340
Mr Willats' Charity	7.437
St Mary Redcliffe Vestry	7.650

BURTON SWEET, Cooper House, Lower Charlton Estate, Shepton Mallet, Somerset, BA4 5QE.

Western Community Leisure	7.722

Buzzacott

CHARTERED ACCOUNTANTS

BUZZACOTT LLP, 130 Wood Street, London, EC2V 6DL. Tel: 020 7556 1200.
E-mail: charities@buzzacott.co.uk.
Internet: www.buzzacott.co.uk.

> "The professionalism, attention to detail and expertise which is provided is exceptional and their empathy and understanding of our way of life and the services we offer, is very reassuring."
> Quote from recent client survey
>
> For more information see our profile in the colour section

Charity specialists: Catherine Biscoe (Audit and Finance). Edward Finch (Audit and Finance). Amanda Francis (Audit and Finance). Katharine Patel (Audit and Finance). Avnish Savjani (Audit and Finance). Kimberly Bradshaw (HR Consultancy). David Fardell (IT Consultancy). Luke Savvas (Direct Taxation).

A Team Foundation	7.4
Action Medical Research	7.11
Albert Hunt Trust	7.23
Almeida Theatre Company	7.27
Aquaterra Leisure	7.36
Architectural Association Incorporated	7.38
Army Cadet Force Association	7.39
Band Trust	7.55
Barbara Ward Children's Foundation	7.56
Bill Brown's Charitable Settlement 1989	7.70
Borrow Foundation, The	7.81
British Association for Adoption & Fostering	7.92
British Home & Hospital for Incurables	7.94
Burberry Foundation, The	7.104
Butterfly Conservation	7.106
C Alma Baker Trust	7.106
Carpenters' Company Charitable Trust	7.117
Central Foundation Schools of London	7.122
Charity for Roman Catholic Congregation	7.128
Marist Sisters	7.130
Community of St Mary the Virgin	7.166
Good Shepherd Sisters	7.171
Congregation of Sisters of Jesus & Mary	7.172
Cong of the Daughters of the Cross of Liege	7.173
Daughters of the Holy Ghost	7.173
Congregation of the Little Sisters of the Poor	7.174
Congregation of Servants of Mary(London)	7.174
Congregation of the Sisters of Nazareth Trust	7.174
Cong. of the Sisters of Nazareth Generalate	7.175
Congregation of the Sisters of St Anne	7.175
Congregation of the Sisters of St Martha	7.175
Coram	7.179
Corporation of Trinity House	7.181
Cyclists' Touring Club	7.190
Denys Eyre Bower Bequest, The	7.197
DHL UK Foundation	7.200
Douai Abbey	7.209
Dr Edwards Bishop King's Fulham Charity	7.211
Ealing Community Transport	7.218
English Dominican Congregation Ch Fund	7.235
February Foundation, The	7.250
Federation London Youth Clubs	7.250
Foundling Museum	7.261
Franciscan Missionaries Charitable Trust	7.263
Girls Friendly Soc in England & Wales	7.275
Grocers' Charity	7.289
Hackney Joint Estate Charity	7.295
Handmaids of the Sacred Heart of Jesus	7.300
HCT Group	7.304

Healthcare Management Trust, The	7.306
Healthcare Quality Improvement Partnership	7.306
Institute of the Franciscan Missionaries	7.337
International Medical Corps (UK)	7.343
International Rescue Committee UK	7.344
Juvenile Diabetes Research Foundation	7.365
Kidney Research UK	7.371
King Edward VII's Hospital Sister Agnes	7.372
Leathersellers Company Charitable Fund	7.381
London Catalyst	7.397
London Community Foundation	7.397
Lumos Foundation	7.404
Mary Ward Settlement	7.415
Med Col of St Bartholomew's Hospital	7.419
Mental Health Foundation	7.421
Missio	7.429
Mount Saint Bernard Abbey	7.436
National Skills Academy For Social Care	7.452
Nazareth Care Charitable Trust	7.455
Nightingale Hammerson	7.463
Notre Dame de France Trust	7.472
Order of Friars Minor	7.482
Order of Friars Minor (Capuchin) Province	7.482
PayPal Giving Fund UK	7.494
People's Health Trust	7.497
PohWER	7.506
PACEY	7.515
Queen Mary's Roehampton Trust	7.520
Queen's Nursing Institute	7.520
Religious Sisters of Charity	7.531
Richard Reeve's Foundation	7.536
Riders for Health	7.538
Rothermere Foundation	7.546
Royal Astronomical Society	7.552
Royal Institute International Affairs	7.562
Royal Marsden Cancer Campaign	7.564
Rustington Convalescent Home Carpenters Co	7.578
S L G Charitable Trust	7.578
SistersoftheSacred Hearts of Jesus & Mary	7.580
Salesians of Don Bosco UK	7.582
Samuel Sebba Charitable Trust	7.586
Sheppard Trust	7.604
Simon Gibson Charitable Trust	7.609
Sisters Hospitallers of the Sacred Heart	7.613
Sisters of Charity of St Vincent de Paul	7.613
Sisters Notre Dame Namur	7.614
Sisters of St Joseph of Annecy	7.614
Sisters of St Joseph of Peace	7.615
Sisters of the Holy Cross	7.615
Sisters Holy Family Bordeaux	7.616
Presentation Sisters	7.616
Social Care Institute for Excellence	7.620
Society ofthe Holy Child Jesus Eur.Province	7.624
Society of the Sacred Heart	7.624
South of England Foundation	7.629
St Albans Diocesan Board Finance	7.635
St Joseph's Hospice, Hackney	7.646
St Luke's Parochial Trust	7.648
St Margaret's Convent (Uckfield)	7.648
Stone Family Foundation, The	7.660
Stroke Association	7.662
Summerfield Charitable Trust	7.664
Suva Foundation Limited, The	7.666
Tellus Mater Foundation Ltd	7.672
Tony Blair Governance Initiative	7.683
St Benedict's Abbey Ealing	7.688
Little Company of Mary	7.688
University College London Hospitals Charity	7.700
Westminster Almshouses Foundation	7.722
Westminster RC Diocesan Trust	7.723
Will Trust of Gerald Segelman Deceased, The	7.729
Yale University Press London	7.744
Young Foundation, The	7.750
Youth United Foundation	7.751

BWMACFARLANE, Castle Chambers, Castle Street, Liverpool, Merseyside, L2 9SH.
Tel: 0151 236 1494. Fax: 0151 236 1095.
E-mail: enquiries@bwm.co.uk.
Internet: www.bwm.co.uk.

Catholic Blind Institute	7.119
Eleanor Rathbone Charitable Trust [The]	7.229
John Moores Foundation	7.360
Liverpool Diocesan Board of Finance, The	7.392
Liverpool Merchants Guild	7.393
National Youth Advocacy Service	7.454
Oblates of Mary Immaculate	7.478

Roy Castle Lung Cancer Foundation	7.548
Royal School for Blind Liverpool	7.570
West Lancashire Freemasons' Charity	7.720

CALCUTT MATTHEWS, 19 North Street, Ashford, Kent, TN24 8LF. Tel: 01233 623300.
Fax: 01233 623400. E-mail: enquiries@calcutt-m.co.uk. Internet: www.calcutt-m.co.uk.
Charity specialists: N Hume. Rosanna Manser.

International Bible Students Association	7.341
Watch Tower Bible Tract Society Britain	7.714

CAMPBELL DALLAS LLP, 4 Atholl Crescent, Perth, Perth and Kinross, PH1 5NG. Tel: 01738 441 888. Fax: 01738 441 666.
E-mail: neil.morrison@campbelldallas.co.uk.
Internet: www.campbelldallas.co.uk.

Live Active Leisure Limited	7.392
North Ayrshire Leisure	7.465

CAMPBELL DALLAS LLP, Titanium 1, King's Inch Place, Renfrew, Strathclyde, PA4 8WF. Tel: 0141 886 6644. Fax: 0141 886 2773.
E-mail: glasgow@campbelldallas.co.uk.
Internet: www.campbelldallas.co.uk.

Health and Social Care Alliance, The	7.305

CANSDALES, Chartered Accountants, Bourbon Court, Nightingales Corner, Little Chalfont, Buckinghamshire, HP7 9QS. Tel: 01494 765428. Fax: 01494 763911.
E-mail: jamesf@cansdales.co.uk.
Internet: www.cansdales.co.uk.
Charity specialists: J Foskett (Partner).

PROSPECTS	7.516

CARPENTER BOX, Amelia House, Crescent Road, Worthing, West Sussex, BN11 1QR. Tel: 01903 234094. Fax: 01903 209591.
E-mail: accounts@carpenterbox.com.
Internet: www.carpenterbox.com.

Queen Alexandra Hospital Home	7.519

CARSTON, First Floor, Tudor House, 16 Cathedral, Cardiff, CF11 9LJ. Tel: 0292 023 3223. Fax: 0292 038 7476.
E-mail: philippa@carstonaccountants.co.uk.
Internet: www.carstonaccountants.co.uk.

Waterloo Foundation, The	7.715

CARTER BACKER WINTER, 66 Prescot Street, London, E1 8HG. Tel: 020 7309 3800. Fax: 020 7309 3801. E-mail: info@cbw.co.uk.
Internet: www.cbw.co.uk.
Charity specialists: P Winter.

BFHU	7.93
Campden Charities Trustee	7.110
Safe Haven London	7.581
Sri Guru Singh Sabha	7.635

CARTWRIGHTS, Regency House, 33 Wood Street, Barnet, Hertfordshire, EN5 4BE. Tel: 020 8441 1731. Fax: 020 8441 2456.
E-mail: reception@cartwrights-ca.co.uk.
Internet: www.cartwrights-ca.co.uk.

Drug Safety Research Trust, The	7.212

CBHC LLP, Riverside House, 1-5 Como Street, Romford, Essex, RM7 7DN. Tel: 01708 333300. Fax: 01708 333311.
E-mail: enquiries@cbhc.uk.com.
Internet: www.cbhc.uk.com.
Charity specialists: M R W Spencer. D M Belbin. A J Everard (Managing Partner).

Norwood and Newton Settlement	7.472
St Lukes Hospice	7.647

CHADWICK & COMPANY, Capital House, 272 Manchester Road, Droylsden, Manchester, Greater Manchester, M43 6PW. Tel: 0161 370 9600. Fax: 0161 301 5445.
E-mail: info@chadwickandco.co.uk.
Internet: www.chadwickandco.co.uk.

Tameside Sports Trust	7.668

CHAMPION ACCOUNTANTS, 54 Caunce Street, Blackpool, Lancashire, FY1 3LJ. Tel: 01253 621 512. Fax: 01253 752 576. E-mail: blackpool@championgroup.co.uk. Internet: www.championgroup.co.uk.

Fylde Coast YMCA	7.267

CHAMPION ACCOUNTANTS, 2nd Floor, Refuge House, 33-37 Watergate Row, Chester, Cheshire, CH1 2LE. Tel: 01244 312351. Fax: 01244 404440. E-mail: chester@champion-accounts.co.uk. Internet: www.champion-accounts.co.uk.

Claire House Appeal	7.155

CHAMPION ACCOUNTANTS, 1 Worsley Court, High Street, Worsley, Manchester, Greater Manchester, M28 3NJ. Tel: 0161 703 2500. Fax: 0161 703 8212. E-mail: info@championgroup.co.uk. Internet: www.championgroup.co.uk.

Francis House Family Trust	7.263

CHAMPION ACCOUNTANTS, 71-73 Hoghton Street, Southport, Merseyside, PR9 0PR. Tel: 01704 535 687. Fax: 01704 500 855. E-mail: southport@championgroup.co.uk. Internet: www.championgroup.co.uk.

Queenscourt Hospice	7.521

CHATER ALLAN, 4a Newmarket Road, Cambridge, Cambridgeshire, CB5 8DT. Tel: 01223 354233. Fax: 01223 460702. E-mail: graham.day@chaterallan.co.uk. Internet: www.chaterallen.co.uk.

Ely Diocesan Board of Finance, The	7.231
Racing Welfare	7.523
Voiceability Advocacy	7.708
Windhorse Trust, The	7.732

CHAVEREYS, Mall House, Faversham, Kent, ME13 8JL. Tel: 01795 594495. Fax: 01795 594499. E-mail: richard.hopper@chavereys.co.uk. Internet: www.chavereys.co.uk.

Godinton House Preservation Trust	7.279

CHD ASSOCIATES LLP, Eden Point, Three Acres Lane, Cheadle, Cheshire, SK8 6RL.

Steinberg Family Charitable Trust, The	7.657

CHEETHAM & CO, Homelea House, Faith Avenue, Quarriers Village, Bridge of Weir, Renfrewshire, PA11 3TF. Tel: 01505 615 646. Fax: 01505 615 060. E-mail: djc@cheethamandco.co.uk. Internet: www.cheethamandco.co.uk.

Scottish Autism	7.591

CHIENE + TAIT LLP, 61 Dublin Street, Edinburgh, EH3 6NL. Tel: 0131 558 5800 / 020 3178 6825. Fax: 0131 558 5899. E-mail: charities@chiene.co.uk. Internet: www.chiene.co.uk. Charity specialists: K McDowell (Partner & Head of Charities & Education Group). J M Chittleburgh (Partner & Head of Social Housing Group).

Action Group Ltd	7.10
Ark Housing Association	7.39
Carnegie UK Trust	7.116
Cattanach Charitable Trust	7.120
Community Lifestyles Limited	7.164
Festival City Theatres Trust	7.251
Hopetoun House Preservation Trust	7.317
Maggie Keswick Jencks Cancer Trust	7.406
National Galleries of Scotland Foundation	7.447
Pitlochry Festival Theatre	7.504
Rosslyn Chapel Trust	7.545
Royal College of Physicians of Edinburgh	7.557
St Columba's Hospice	7.641
Viewpoint Housing Association	7.705

CHITTENDEN HORLEY, 456 Chester Road, Old Trafford, Manchester, Greater Manchester, M16 9HD. Tel: 0161 888 2340. Fax: 0845 280 1673. E-mail: info@chltd.co. Internet: www.chcl.org.uk.

Greater Manchester Arts Centre	7.286

CITROEN WELLS, Devonshire House, 1 Devonshire Street, London, W1W 5DR. Tel: 020 7304 2000. Fax: 020 7304 2020. Internet: www.citroenwells.co.uk. Charity specialists: J W Prevezer.

Balcombe Charitable Trust	7.54
Bishop Radford Trust, The	7.73
Dawat-e-Hadiyah Trust (United Kingdom)	7.195
Maria Assumpta Trust	7.410
Religious of the Assumption	7.531

CK AUDIT, No. 4 Castle Court 2, Castlegate Way, Dudley, West Midlands, DY1 4RH. Tel: 01384 245200. Fax: 01384 245250. E-mail: enquiry@ckca.co.uk. Internet: www.ckca.co.uk.

Black Country Living Museum Trust	7.74
Sandwell Community Caring Trust	7.586

CLARITY, 2 Lancaster Close, Weston Heights, Stevenage, Hertfordshire, SG1 4RX. Tel: 07779 833797. E-mail: cbush.clarity@btinternet.com.

Equity Charitable Trust	7.238

CLARK BROWNSCOMBE, 8 The Drive, Hove, Sussex, BN3 3JT. Tel: 01273 739277. Fax: 01273 725346. Internet: www.clarkbrownscombe.accessweb.co.uk.

Grace Eyre Foundation	7.283
Reta Lila Howard Foundation	7.533
Reta Lila Weston Tst for Medical Research	7.533

CLARK BROWNSCOMBE, 2 St.Andrews Place, Lewes, East Sussex, BN7 1UP. Tel: 01273 476311. Fax: 01273 486606. E-mail: admin@cblewes.co.uk. Internet: www.clarkbrownscombe.accessweb.co.uk. Charity specialists: R Scrivins.

Glyndebourne Arts Trust	7.278
Glyndebourne Productions Limited	7.279

CLARKE NICKLIN, Clarke Nicklin Group, Clarke Nicklin House, Brooks Drive, Cheadle Royal Business Park, Cheadle, Cheshire, SK8 3TD. Tel: 0161 495 4700. Internet: www.clarkenicklin.co.uk.

Manchester & District Home for Lost Dogs	7.408

CLARKSON & COMPANY, Centre of Excellence, Hope Park, Trevor Foster Way, Bradford, West Yorkshire, BD5 8HH. Tel: 01274 224315. Fax: 01274 737111. E-mail: info@clarkson.uk.com. Internet: www.clarksonandcompany.co.uk.

Christians Against Poverty	7.146

CLAY SHAW BUTLER, 24 Lammas Street, Carmarthen, Carmarthenshire, SA31 3AL. Tel: 01267 228 500. Fax: 01267 228 510. E-mail: info@clayshawbutler.com. Internet: www.clayshawbutler.com.

Cerebra	7.125
National Botanic Garden Wales	7.443

CLB COOPERS, Ship Canal House, 98 King Street, Manchester, Greater Manchester, M2 4WU. Tel: 0161 245 1000. E-mail: manchester@clbcoopers.co.uk. Internet: www.clbcoopers.co.uk. Charity specialists: B Goldenfield.

GreaterManchester AccessibleTransport	7.286

CLIVE OWEN LLP, 140 Coniscliffe Road, Darlington, County Durham, DL3 7RT. Tel: 01325 349700. Fax: 01325 383475. E-mail: chris.beaumont@cliveowen.com.

Internet: www.cliveowen.com. **Charity specialists:** C Beaumont (Partner). T Luckett. Mary McArthur.

Shears Foundation	7.600

COBB BURGIN & CO, 129a Middleton Boulevard, Woollaton Park, Nottingham, Nottinghamshire, NG8 1FW. Tel: 0115 9283900. Fax: 0115 9280694.

Crossroads Care East Midlands	7.222

COBLEY DESBOROUGH, Artisans' House, 7 Queensbridge, Northampton, Northamptonshire, NN4 7BF. Tel: 01604 823560. E-mail: enquiries@cobdes.co.uk. Internet: www.cobdes.co.uk.

New Testament Church of God	7.458

COCKE VELLACOTT & HILL, Unit 3 Dock Offices, Surrey Quays Road, Surrey Quays, London, SE16 2XU. Tel: 020 7394 1717. Fax: 020 7740 1673. E-mail: colinbrailey@c-v-h.co.uk. Internet: www.cockevellacottandhill.co.uk www.cockevellacottandhill.co.uk. Charity specialists: C W Brailey (Partner). K Panayi (Manager).

Sisters of the Finding of Jesus	7.175
Eiris Foundation	7.229

COHEN ARNOLD, New Burlington House, 1075 Finchley Road, London, NW11 0PU. Tel: 020 8731 0777. Fax: 020 8731 0778. E-mail: davidgoldberg@cohenarnold.com. Internet: www.cohenarnold.com. Charity specialists: D Birns.

4 Charity Foundation	7.3
Achisomoch Aid Co	7.8
Chalfords Limited	7.126
Charitworth	7.128
Chevras Tsedokoh Limited	7.138
Donating Charity	7.204
Extonglen Limited	7.245
Frankgiving Limited	7.263
Gilmoor Benevolent Fund Limited	7.274
Hurdale Charity	7.325
Keren Association	7.369
Kisharon	7.375
Lonia Ltd	7.402
M R Gross Charities Limited	7.405
Mayfair Charities	7.417
Rachel Charitable Trust	7.522
Raphael Freshwater Memorial Association Ltd	7.526
S F Foundation	7.578
Shlomo Memorial Fund	7.605
Shulem B. Association Ltd	7.607
Tagmarsh Charity Limited	7.667
United Talmudical Associates	7.698
Wiseheights	7.733

COLLARDS, 2 High Street, Kingston-upon-Thames, Surrey, KT1 1EY. Tel: 020 8247 4480. Fax: 020 8247 4481. Internet: www.collardpartners.com.

BPR Trust	7.83

COMPASS ACCOUNTANTS LIMITED, The Tanneries, East Street, Titchfield, Hampshire, PO14 4AR. Tel: 01329 844145. Fax: 01329 844148. E-mail: contact@compassaccountants.co.uk. Internet: www.compassaccountants.co.uk. Charity specialists: Jeff Walton.

HMS Victory Preservation Company, The	7.314
Mary Rose Trust	7.414

CONDIES, 10 Abbey Park Place, Dunfermline, Fife, KY12 7NZ. Tel: 01383 721421. Fax: 01383 729865. E-mail: info@condie.co.uk. Internet: www.condie.co.uk.

Dynamic Earth Charitable Trust	7.217

CONSILIUM AUDIT LIMITED, 169 West George Street, Glasgow, G2 2LB.

Glasgow Association for Mental Health 7.275

COULTHARDS MACKENZIE, 9 Risborough Street, London, SE1 0HF. Tel: 0203 267 1000. Fax: 0207 922 1261. E-mail: london@coulthards.co.uk. Internet: www.coulthards.co.uk. Charity specialists: M Church.

Clare Milne Trust	7.155
Royal College of Pathologists	7.557

COWAN & PARTNERS, 60 Constitution Street, Leith, Edinburgh, EH6 6RR. Tel: 0131 554 0724. Fax: 0131 553 2267. E-mail: john.kennedy@cowanandpartners.co.uk. Internet: www.cowanandpartners.co.uk.

Royal Yacht Britannia Trust 7.575

COWGILL HOLLOWAY, 42-44 Chorley New Road, Bolton, Lancashire, BL1 4AP. Tel: 01204 414243. Fax: 01204 414244. Internet: www.cowgills.co.uk.

Amanat Charitable Trust 7.28

COX COSTELLO & HORNE, Langwood House, 63-81 High Street, Rickmansworth, Hertfordshire, WD3 1EQ. Tel: 01923 771977. Fax: 01923 771988.

E Hayes Dashwood Foundation	7.218
Holstein UK	7.315

CRANE & PARTNERS, Leonard House, 5-7 Newman Road, Bromley, Kent, BR1 1RJ. Tel: 020 8464 0131. Fax: 020 8464 6018. Internet: www.craneandpartners.com. Charity specialists: Richard E Lane.

Bolton Community Leisure Limited 7.78

CRAWFORD SEDGWICK & CO, 38 Hill Street, Belfast, County Antrim, BT1 2LB. Tel: 028 9032 1731. Fax: 028 9024 7521. Charity specialists: J Sedgwick.

Cedar Foundation 7.122

CREASEYS GROUP LIMITED, Level 1, Brockbourne House, 77 Mount Ephraim, Tunbridge Wells, Kent, TN4 8BS. Tel: 01892 546546. Fax: 01892 511232. E-mail: roger.ward@creaseys.co.uk. Internet: www.creaseys.co.uk.

CRITCHLEYS LLP, Greyfriars Court, Paradise Square, Oxford, Oxfordshire, OX1 1BE. Tel: 01865 261100. Fax: 01865 261201. E-mail: marketing@critchleys.co.uk. Internet: www.critchleys.co.uk. Charity specialists: R M Kirtland - specialist area: Charities Audit. Frances T Kidd (Marketing Manager).

British Horse Society	7.94
Conservation Education & Research Trust	7.177
E P A Cephalosporin Fund	7.218
H D H Wills 1965 Charitable Trust	7.294
Helen & Douglas House	7.307
Khodorkovsky Foundation	7.370
Michael Uren Foundation, The	7.425
Mulberry Bush Organisation Limited, The	7.438
New College Development Fund	7.457
Nominet Charitable Trust	7.463
Open Society Foundation	7.481
Oxford Diocesan Board Finance	7.487
Quaker International Educational Trust	7.518
Society Salutation Mary Virgin Ltd	7.624
Soll (Vale)	7.627
Tolkien Trust	7.682

CROMBIES, 34 Waterloo Road, Wolverhampton, West Midlands, WV1 4DG. Tel: 01902 773 993. Internet: www.crom.co.uk.

County Air Ambulance Trust 7.183

Crowe Clark Whitehill™

CROWE CLARK WHITEHILL LLP, St Bride's House, 10 Salisbury Square, London, EC4Y 8EH. Tel: 020 7842 7100. Fax: 020 7583 1720. E-mail: nonprofits@crowecw.co.uk. Internet: www.croweclarkwhitehill.co.uk.

Crowe Clark Whitehill is the leading provider of audit and related services to the charity sector. Specialists in our dedicated not for profit unit offer a broad range of services, tailored to the unique needs of charities. Our worldwide network, Crowe Horwath International, operates in over 100 countries worldwide.

To subscribe to our technical briefings, please email nonprofits@crowecw.co.uk.

Charity specialists: P Framjee (Head of Not for Profit, Audit & Advisory Partner) - specialist area: Charities and NGOs. A J Pianca (Audit and Advisory Partner) - specialist area: charities & education. T M Allison (Audit and Advisory Partner) - specialist area: charities & education. N Hashemi (Audit and Advisory Partner) - specialist area: Charities and NGOs. M E Hicks (Audit and Advisory Partner) - specialist area: charities & education. N May (Audit and Advisory Partner) - specialist area: Charities, NGOs and Education. A Manning (Risk and Assurance Partner) - specialist area: internal audit, risk and governance. S Ball (Employment Taxation Partner) - specialist area: employment taxation. P Fay (Tax Partner) - specialist area: tax. L Field (Tax Partner) - specialist area: tax. A Blackburn (VAT Partner) - specialist area: VAT. R Warne (VAT Partner) - specialist area: VAT. R G Dawes (Technical Director).

Academies Enterprise Trust	7.7
ACORD	7.8
Afghanaid	7.15
Alan Babette Sainsbury Charitable Fund	7.22
Alzheimer's Society	7.28
Amnesty International Limited	7.30
Ashden Charitable Trust	7.43
Association of Commonwealth Universities	7.47
Avante Partnership	7.51
Backstage Trust	7.53
Benenden Hospital Trust	7.65
Big Local Trust	7.70
BirdLife International	7.70
Blind Veterans UK	7.76
Breakthrough Breast Cancer	7.86
Breast Cancer Care	7.86
British Academy of Film & Television Arts	7.91
British Editorial Society Bone Joint Surgery	7.92
BLESMA	7.95
Brooke Hospital for Animals	7.101
Business in the Community	7.105
Campaign to Protect Rural England	7.110
Catholic Agency for Overseas Development	7.118
Centre for Eng. & Manufacturing Excellence	7.124
Charles Hayward Foundation	7.131
Chartered Institute for Securities &Investment	7.132
Chartered Inst of Personnel & Development	7.134
Children with Cancer UK	7.142
Christ's Hospital Foundation	7.144
Christian Aid	7.145
CIPFA	7.151
Citizens Advice	7.152
Civil Service Benevolent Fund, The	7.154
Climate Group, The	7.157
Compassion in World Farming	7.168
Council for Awards in Care,Health&Education	7.182

Council for World Mission	7.182
Depaul International	7.197
Depaul UK	7.197
Design Museum	7.199
Dolphin Square Charitable Foundation, The	7.203
Douglas Haig Memorial Homes	7.209
EveryChild	7.243
Fairley House School	7.246
Fairtrade Foundation	7.247
FARM-Africa	7.248
Gatsby Charitable Foundation	7.270
General Medical Council	7.271
Glass House Trust	7.276
Grand Charity, The	7.284
GVEP International	7.293
Haig Housing Trust	7.296
Harpur Trust, The	7.302
Headley Trust	7.305
Health Foundation, The	7.305
Health Poverty Action	7.305
Henry Smith Charity	7.309
Indigo Trust	7.331
Institute for Government	7.333
Institute of Development Studies	7.334
Intl Agency for the Prevention of Blindness	7.340
International HIV/AIDS Alliance	7.342
International House Trust	7.343
Intl Institute for Environment&Development	7.343
International Inst for Strategic Studies	7.343
Islamic Relief Worldwide	7.347
J J Charitable Trust	7.349
Jerusalem Trust	7.352
John Coates Charitable Trust	7.357
John James Bristol Foundation	7.359
Kay Kendall Leukaemia Fund	7.366
King's Fund, The	7.373
Local Trust	7.396
London Philharmonic Orchestra	7.400
Marine Society & Sea Cadets	7.411
Marine Stewardship Council	7.411
Mark Benevolent Fund, The	7.411
Mark Leonard Trust	7.412
Medical Research Foundation	7.419
MERLIN	7.423
MIND	7.428
Monument Trust	7.432
Multiple Sclerosis Society	7.438
National Autistic Society	7.442
National Children's Bureau	7.444
Oasis Charitable Trust	7.477
Oasis Community Learning	7.477
ORBIS Charitable Trust	7.482
Parkinson's UK	7.491
Place2Be	7.504
Practical Action	7.512
Pre-school Learning Alliance	7.512
Queen Elizabeth Diamond Jubilee Trust	7.519
Ramblers Association	7.525
Relief International UK	7.531
Rethink Mental Illness	7.534
Roundhouse Trust	7.547
Royal Albert Hall	7.551
Royal Ballet School	7.552
Royal Ballet School Endowment Fund	7.553
Royal College of Anaesthetists	7.555
Royal College of Physicians of London	7.557
Royal College of Surgeons	7.558
Royal Hospital for Neuro-disability	7.562
Royal Mencap Society	7.566
Royal National Lifeboat Institution	7.567
RSPB	7.572
Royal Star & Garter Home, The	7.574
Sainsbury Centre Endowment Fund	7.582
Sainsbury Laboratory	7.582
Serpentine Trust	7.597
Sightsavers International	7.608
Sir Jules Thorn Charitable Trust	7.612
Society for Protection of Animals Abroad	7.621
Society of Petroleum Engineers Europe	7.623
Sparks Charity	7.632
Staples Trust	7.656
Tedworth Charitable Trust	7.671
Terrence Higgins Trust	7.673
Three Guineas Trust	7.679
True Colours Trust	7.687
Trust for London	7.688
United Synagogue	7.698
Victim Support	7.704

Abingdon 7.144
ꞏiety 7.148
Arts and Leisure Trust 7.168
ꞏurs of Paris 7.172
7.189
ꞏeaf People 7.306
ꞏhip Evangelical Students 7.341
7.388
ꞏn Hospital Trust 7.459
ꞏsic Therapy Centre 7.464
ꞏjudicator for Higher Ed. 7.478
ꞏtion 7.515
7.535
ꞏech Eng Central Trust 7.559
ꞏent Trust 7.568
ꞏg Christian Knowledge 7.620

73 Park Lane, Croydon,
Tel: 020 8686 8876.
32.
ꞏeburke.co.uk.
ꞏeburke.co.uk.

ꞏnthe Charity Trust 7.495

, Greenbox, Westonhall
Bromsgrove, Worcestershire,
7 558539.

E-mail: curo.info@curoca.co.uk.
Internet: www.curoca.co.uk.

Shri Venkateswara (Balaji) Temple of UK 7.607

DAFFERNS, One Eastwood, Harry Weston Road, Binley Business Park, Coventry, West Midlands, CV3 2UB. Tel: 024 7622 1046. Fax: 024 7663 1702. E-mail: hub@dafferns.com.
Internet: www.dafferns.com.

Alan Edward Higgs Charity 7.22
Bond's Hospital Estate Charity 7.79
Coventry Freemen's Charity 7.184
General Charity (Coventry) 7.270
Jones 1986 Charitable Trust 7.362
Sir Thomas White's Charity 7.612
Smallpeice Trust 7.618

DAINS, 15 Colmore Row, Birmingham, West Midlands, B3 2BH. Tel: 0121 200 7900. Fax: 0845 555 8811. E-mail: birmingham@dains.com. Internet: www.dains.com.

Belgrade Theatre Trust (Coventry) 7.64
Lichfield Diocesan Board Of Education, The 7.387
Lichfield Diocesan Board Of Finance 7.387
Steps to Work (Walsall) Limited 7.657

DAINS, St Johns Court, Wiltell Road, Lichfield, Staffordshire, WS14 9DS. Tel: 01543 263484. Internet: www.dains.com.

St John's Hospital Lichfield 7.645

DAVID OWEN & CO, 17 Market Place, Devizes, Wiltshire, SN10 1BA. Tel: 01380 722211. Fax: 01380 729524.
Charity specialists: M Buckland.

Fulmer Charitable Trust 7.266

DAVIES TRACEY, Swan House, Westpoint Road, Teesdale Business Park, Stockton-on-Tees, TS17 6BP. Tel: 01642 606 003. Fax: 01642 606 004. Internet: www.daviestracey.co.uk.

Butterwick 7.106

DE CLARON LTD, 3a, The Vale, London, NW11 8SB. Tel: 020 8201 8407. Internet: www.claron.com.

Ezer V'Hatzalah Ltd 7.245

7.527
Royal Air Force Charitable Trust, The 7.550
Royal Corps Signals Benevolent Fund 7.559
Royal National College for the Blind 7.566
St Christopher's School (Bristol) 7.640
Thomson Media Foundation, The 7.678
Three Counties Agricultural Society 7.679
United Christian Broadcasters 7.695
Wyggeston's Hospital 7.743

CROWE CLARK WHITEHILL LLP, 10 Palace Avenue, Maidstone, Kent, ME15 6NF. Tel: 01622 767676. Fax: 01622 769020. E-mail: ian.weekes@crowecw.co.uk. Internet: www.croweclarkwhitehill.co.uk. Charity specialists: I Weekes.

Brighton Dome and Festival Limited 7.88
East Malling Research 7.222
Fast Malling Trust, The 7.222
Heart of Kent Hospice, The 7.307
Kent, Surrey & Sussex Air Ambulance Trust 7.369
Leeds Castle Foundation 7.381
William Brake Charitable Trust 7.730
Worth Abbey 7.742

CROWE CLARK WHITEHILL LLP, 3rd Floor, The Lexicon, Mount Street, Manchester, Greater Manchester, M2 5NT. Tel: 0161 214 7500. Fax: 0161 214 7501. E-mail: vicky.szulist@crowecw.co.uk. Internet: www.croweclarkwhitehill.co.uk. Charity specialists: V Szulist. M Jayson. S McLean. R Durrant. L Jones.

Booth Charities 7.79
Borough Care Services 7.80
Chetham's Hospital School and Library 7.138
Guy Pilkington Memorial Home Limited 7.293
King David Schools (Manchester) 7.371
Pharmacist Support 7.500
Turning Point 7.691
WIEGO Ltd 7.736

CROWE CLARK WHITEHILL LLP, Black Country House, Rounds Green Road, Oldbury, West Midlands, B69 2DG. Tel: 0121 543 1900. Fax: 0121 552 0787. E-mail: helen.drew@crowecw.co.uk. Internet: www.croweclarkwhitehill.co.uk. Charity specialists: K Brown. H Drew.

Colonel W H Whitbread Charitable Trust 7.161
Myton Hospices, The 7.441
Old Swinford Hospital 7.479

CROWE CLARK WHITEHILL LLP, Aquis House, 49-51 Blagrave St, Reading, Berkshire, RG1 1PL. Tel: 0118 959 7222. Fax: 0118 958 4640. E-mail: alastair.lyon@crowecw.co.uk. Internet: www.croweclarkwhitehill.co.uk. Charity specialists: J Joyce. A Lyon.

ACT Foundation 7.9

Deloitte.

DELOITTE LLP, 2 New Street Square, London, EC4A 3BZ. Tel: 020 7936 3000. Fax: 020 7583 1198.
Internet: www2.deloitte.com/uk/en/pages/charities-and-not-for-profit.

Charity specialists: Reza Motazedi (National Head of Charities and Not For Profit). Sue Barratt. Mark Hill. David Hall. Jayne Rowe. Charlotte Morris. Jane Curran. Sarah Shillingford. Helen George.

Alexandra Palace and Park 7.24
Allchurches Trust 7.25
Bloodwise 7.76
British Motor Industry Heritage Trust 7.96
British Red Cross Society 7.98
Choice Support 7.143
Church Commissioners for England 7.147
David Hockney Foundation (UK) Limited 7.194
Earl Haig Fund Scotland 7.219
England and Wales Cricket Trust 7.234
Get Kids Going 7.273
Guide Dogs for the Blind Association 7.291
Int. Baccalaureate Org (UK) 7.340
Islamia Schools Trust 7.346
Lloyd's Register Foundation 7.395
London Symphony Orchestra 7.401
Motability 7.435
Motability Tenth Anniversary Trust, The 7.435
National Memorial Arboretum Company Ltd 7.450
NSPCC 7.452
Premier League Charitable Fund 7.513
RCN Foundation 7.528
Royal Academy of Dance 7.549
Royal British Legion 7.554
Duke & Duchess of Cambridge & Prince Harry 7.560
Santander UK Foundation Limited 7.587
Save the Children 7.588
Waqf Al-Birr Educational Trust 7.714
Westminster Foundation 7.723
Yusuf Islam Foundation 7.751

DELOITTE LLP, 19 Bedford Street, Belfast, County Antrim, BT2 7EJ. Tel: 028 9032 2861. Fax: 028 9023 4786.
Internet: www.deloitte.co.uk.
Charity specialists: Shana Fagan - specialist area: Assurance and Advisory.

RBS PeopleCharity, The 7.527

DELOITTE LLP, Four Brindleyplace, Birmingham, West Midlands, B1 2HZ. Tel: 0121 632 6000. Fax: 0121 695 5678.
Internet: www.deloitte.co.uk.
Charity specialists: Jonathan Dodworth. Sarah Anderson.

Birmingham Royal Ballet 7.73

DELOITTE LLP, 3 Rivergate, Temple Quay, Bristol, BS1 6GD. Tel: 0117 921 1622. Fax: 0117 929 2801. Internet: www.deloitte.com. Charity specialists: Mark Hill. Laurence Hedditch. Ian Howse. Clare Edge. Michelle Hopton.

Bristol Charities	7.89
St John's Hospital	7.645
St Monica Trust	7.651

DELOITTE LLP, City House, 126-130 Hills Road, Cambridge, Cambridgeshire, CB2 1RY. Tel: 01223 460222. Fax: 01223 350839. Internet: www.deloitte.co.uk. Charity specialists: Richard Crane. Stuart Henderson. Matthew Hall.

Hult International Business School	7.324
R. Ormonde Shuttleworth Remembrance Trust	7.536
Sobell Foundation	7.619
Traffic International	7.684

DELOITTE LLP, 5 Callaghan Square, Cardiff, CF10 5BT. Tel: 029 2046 0000. Fax: 029 2026 4444. Internet: www.deloitte.co.uk. Charity specialists: Mark Hill. Laurence Hedditch. Ian Howse. Clare Edge.

Welsh National Opera	7.718
WJEC CBAC	7.734

DELOITTE LLP, Deloitte & Touche House, Earlsfort Terrace, Dublin. Tel: 00 353 1417 2200. Fax: 00 353 1417 2300. Internet: www.deloitte.co.uk. Charity specialists: Jackie Henry.

GOAL (International)	7.279

DELOITTE LLP, Lomond House, 9 George Square, Glasgow, G2 1QQ. Tel: 0141 204 2800. Fax: 0141 314 5893. Internet: www.deloitte.co.uk. Charity specialists: Susan Forrester.

Quarriers	7.519

DELOITTE LLP, 1 City Square, Leeds, West Yorkshire, LS1 2AL. Tel: 0113 243 9021. Fax: 0113 244 5580. Internet: www.deloitte.co.uk. Charity specialists: Matthew Hughes. Sarah Anderson.

Caring for Life	7.115
Congregational & General Charitable Trust	7.176
Family Fund, The	7.247
LGS General Charitable Trust	7.387
St Gemma's Hospice Leeds	7.643
York Museums Trust	7.748

DELOITTE LLP, PO Box 500, 2 Hardman Street, Manchester, Greater Manchester, M60 2AT. Tel: 0161 832 3555. Fax: 0161 829 3800. Internet: www.deloitte.co.uk. Charity specialists: Anthony Farnworth. Sarah Anderson.

Alliance Family Foundation	7.26
David Lewis Centre	7.194
Euro Charity Trust	7.241
Lowry Centre Trust	7.403
Making Space	7.407
Mines Advisory Group	7.429
Morgan Foundation	7.434
St Ann's Hospice	7.637
Together Trust	7.681

DELOITTE LLP, Gainsborough House, 34-40 Grey Street, Newcastle upon Tyne, Tyne and Wear, NE1 6AE. Tel: 0191 261 4111. Fax: 0191 232 7665. Internet: www.deloitte.co.uk. Charity specialists: Paul Williamson (Partner in charge of Charities). Sarah Anderson.

Central Manchester Univ Hosp NHS Trust	7.123

DELOITTE LLP, 1 Woodborough Road, Nottingham, Nottinghamshire, NG1 3FG. Tel: 0115 950 0511. Fax: 0115 959 0060. Internet: www.deloitte.co.uk. Charity specialists: Mark Doleman.

Christian Conference Trust	7.145

DELOITTE LLP, Abbots House, Abbey St, Reading, Berkshire, RG1 3BD. Tel: 0118 950 8141. Fax: 0118 950 8101. Internet: www.deloitte.co.uk. Charity specialists: Susan Barratt. Andy Hornby.

English National Opera	7.235
Fdn&Friends of RoyalBotanicGardens, Kew	7.259
Francis Crick Insitute Limited, The	7.262
Royal Society, The	7.573

DELOITTE LLP, Mountbatten House, 1 Grosvenor Square, Southampton, Hampshire, SO15 2BZ. Tel: 023 8033 4124. Fax: 023 8033 0948. Internet: www.deloitte.co.uk. Charity specialists: Toby Wright.

Bournemouth Symphony Orchestra	7.82

DELOITTE LLP, 3 Victoria Square, Victoria Street, St Albans, Hertfordshire, AL1 3TF. Tel: 01727 839 000. Fax: 01727 831 111. Internet: www.deloitte.co.uk. Charity specialists: Heather Bygrave. Craig Wisdom.

Imperial College Healthcare Charity	7.329
National Gallery Trust	7.447
NGT Foundation	7.461
Royal Brompton Hospital Charity	7.555
Trustees of the London Clinic Limited	7.689

DEREK ROTHERA & CO, Units 15 & 16, 7 Wenlock Road, London, N1 7SL. Tel: 020 7226 1199. Fax: 020 7226 9446. E-mail: rothera&co@rothera.demon.co.uk.

Eric & Salome Estorick Foundation	7.238

DEXTER AND SHARPE, Rollestone House, Bridge Street, Horncastle, Lincolnshire, LN9 5HZ. Tel: 01507 526 071. Fax: 01507 524 423. E-mail: info@dextorsharpe.co.uk. Internet: www.dextorsharpe.demon.co.uk.

Bourne United Charities	7.81

DIXON WILSON, 22 Chancery Lane, London, WC2A 1LS. Tel: 020 7680 8100. Fax: 020 7680 8101. E-mail: joannaboatfield@dixonwilson.co.uk. Internet: www.dixonwilson.com.

DODD & CO, Fifteen Rosehill, Montgomery Way, Rosehill Estate, Carlisle, Cumbria, CA1 2RW. Tel: 01228 530 913. Fax: 01228 515 485. E-mail: carlisle@doddaccountants.co.uk. Internet: www.doddaccountants.co.uk.

Carlisle Diocesan Board of Finance	7.116
Rokpa Trust	7.543

DONALD REID & CO, Prince Albert House, 20 King Street, Maidenhead, Berkshire, SL6 1DT. Tel: 01628 760000. Fax: 01628 760001. E-mail: info@donaldreid.co.uk. Internet: www.donaldreid.co.uk.

Spoore, Merry & Rixman Foundation, The	7.633

DOUGLAS HOME & CO, 47-49 The Square, Kelso, Borders, TD5 7HW. Tel: 01573 225082. Fax: 01573 226442. Internet: www.douglashomeandco.co.uk. Charity specialists: A Drummond.

Abbotsford Trust	7.5

DTE BUSINESS ADVISORY SERVICES LIMITED, Park House, 26 North End Road, London, NW11 7PT. Tel: 0161 767 1200. Fax: 0161 767 1212. E-mail: payroll@dtegroup.com. Internet: www.dtepayroll.com.

Old Vic Theatre Trust 2000	7.479

DUNCAN SHEARD GLASS, 43 Castle Street, Castle Chambers, Liverpool, Merseyside, L2 9TL. Tel: 0151 243 1200. Fax: 0151 236 1430. E-mail: liverpool@dsg.uk.com. Internet: www.dsg.uk.com.

Autism Initiatives UK	7.49
Cecil Pilkington Charitable Trust	7.122

Port Sunlight Village Trust [The]	7.509

DUNKLEY'S, Woodlands Grange, Woodlands Lane, Bradley Stoke, Bristol, BS32 4JY. Tel: 01454 619900. Fax: 01454 619911. E-mail: advice@dunkleys.co. Internet: www.dunkleys.co.

Perseverance Trust	7.498

DUTTON MOORE, Aldgate House, 1-4 Market Place, Hull, HU1 1RS. Tel: 01482 326617. Fax: 01482 329863. Charity specialists: J Gilleard.

Beverley Consolidated Charity	7.68
Humberside Engineering Training Assoc	7.325
Preston Rd Neigbourhood Development Co.	7.513

DYKE YAXLEY, 8 Hollinswood Court, Stafford Park 1, Telford, Shropshire, TF3 3DE. Tel: 01952 216100. Fax: 01743 235794. E-mail: info@dykeyaxley.co.uk. Internet: www.dykeyaxley.co.uk.

Katharine House Hospice	7.366

EDWARD THOMAS PEIRSON & SONS, 21 The Point, Rockingham Road, Market Harborough, Leicestershire, LE16 7NU. Tel: 01858 464400. Fax: 01858 434167. E-mail: info@etpeirson.co.uk.

Market Harborough & the Bowdens Charity	7.412

EDWARDS & KEEPING, Unity Chambers, 34 High East Street, Dorchester, Dorset, DT1 1HA. Tel: 01305 251333. Fax: 01305 251465. Internet: www.edwardsandkeeping.co.uk. Charity specialists: R J A Edwards.

Elizabeth and Prince Zaiger Trust	7.230
Home Devenish	7.315

EDWARDS PEARSON & WHITE, 8 Jury Street, Warwick, Warwickshire, CV34 4EW. Tel: 01926 494312. Fax: 01926 401600.

Coventry and Warwickshire Mind	7.183

EDWIN SMITH , 32 Queens Road, Reading, Berkshire, RG1 4AU. Tel: 0118 958 1956. Fax: 0118 950 9602. E-mail: edwinsmith@btinternet.com. Charity specialists: P Nixon.

Kingwood Trust	7.373

ELLIOT WOOLFE & ROSE, Equity House, 128-136 High Street, Edgware, Middlesex, HA8 7TT. Tel: 020 8952 0707. Fax: 020 8952 2332. Internet: www.ewr.co.uk.

Al-Khair Foundation	7.21

ELLIS ATKINS & CO, 1 Paper Mews, 330 High Street, Dorking, Surrey, RH4 2TU. Tel: 01306 886 681. Fax: 01306 889 897. E-mail: info@ellisatkins.co.uk. Internet: www.ellisatkins.co.uk.

Institute of Biomedical Science	7.333

ELMAN WALL, 5-7 John Prince's Street, London, W1G 0JN. Tel: 020 7493 9595. Fax: 020 7493 8585. E-mail: jonw@elmanwall.co.uk. Internet: www.elmanwall.co.uk. Charity specialists: R Elman.

Mike Gooley Trailfinder Charity	7.427

ELSON GEAVES, Unit 2, 446 Commercial Road, Aviation Business Park, Christchurch, Dorset, BH23 6NW. Tel: 01202 581999. Fax: 01202 590022. E-mail: info@elsongeaves.com. Internet: www.elsonaccountants.com.

Encompass (Dorset)	7.233

ENSORS, Anglia House, 285 Milton Road, Cambridge, Cambridgeshire, CB4 1XQ. Tel: 01223 420721. Fax: 01223 424516. Internet: www.ensors.co.uk.

Age UK Hertfordshire	7.17

ENSORS, Warwick House, Ermine Business Park, Huntingdon, Cambridgeshire, PE29 6XY. Tel: 01480 417800. Fax: 01480 417801. Internet: www.ensors.co.uk.

Varrier Jones Foundation	7.703

ENSORS, Cardinal House, 46 St Nicholas Street, Ipswich, Suffolk, IP1 1TT. Tel: 01473 220022. Fax: 01473 220033. E-mail: ips@ensors.co.uk. Internet: www.ensors.co.uk. Charity specialists: Helen S Rumsey. I C Brookman.

Age UK Suffolk	7.19
Ormiston Trust	7.484
St Edmundsbury & Ipswich Diocesan Bd of Fin	7.642
Suffolk Foundation, The	7.663

ERNST & YOUNG LLP, 1 More London Place, London, SE1 2AF. Tel: 020 7951 2000. Fax: 020 7951 1345. Internet: www.ey.com/UK.

Absolute Return for Kids (ARK)	7.7
BBC Media Action	7.61
Dr Mortimer & Theresa Sackler Fdtn	7.211
GarfieldWestonTrustforWestminsterAbbey	7.269
RMCC (Ronald McDonald House Charities)	7.540
Sackler Trust, The	7.579

ERNST & YOUNG LLP, Bedford House, 16 Bedford Street, Belfast, County Antrim, BT2 7DT. Tel: 028 9024 6525. Fax: 028 9024 0920. Internet: www.ey.com/UK. Charity specialists: W Forde.

Extern Organisation	7.244
Northern Ireland Assoc for Mental Health	7.470

ERNST & YOUNG LLP, 10 George Street, Edinburgh, EH2 2DZ. Tel: 0131 777 20000. Fax: 0131 777 2001. Internet: www.ey.com/UK. Charity specialists: Nancy McFadzean (Senior Manager). A Melville.

R S Macdonald Charitable Trust	7.522
Royal Highland Agricultural Soc Scotland	7.561

ERNST & YOUNG LLP, George House, 50 George Square, Glasgow, G2 1RR. Tel: 0141 552 3456. Fax: 0141 553 1812. Internet: www.ey.com/UK. Charity specialists: J A Bishop.

Inverness Leisure Limited	7.345
R&A Foundation, The	7.521
Scottish Association for Mental Health	7.591

ERNST & YOUNG LLP, Barony House, Stoneyfiled Business Park, Stonyfield, Inverness, Highland, IV2 7PA. Tel: 01463 667000. Fax: 01463 667001. Internet: www.ey.com/UK.

High Life Highland	7.311

ERNST & YOUNG LLP, P O Box 3, Lowgate House, Kingston upon Hull, HU1 1JJ. Tel: 01482 325531. Fax: 01482 320284. Internet: www.ey.com/UK.

EMIH	7.232

ERNST & YOUNG LLP, 1 Bridgewater Place, Water Lane, Leeds, West Yorkshire, LS11 5QR. Tel: 0113 298 2200. Fax: 0113 298 2201. Internet: www.ey.com/UK. Charity specialists: Joanna Bradbourne.

Asda Foundation Limited	7.42
Veolia Environmental Trust, The	7.704

ERNST & YOUNG LLP, 400 Capability Green, Luton, Bedfordshire, LU1 3AE. Tel: 01582 643000. Fax: 01582 643001. Internet: www.ey.com/UK. Charity specialists: R King. N Arthur.

Buckinghamshire Hospitals NHS Trust	7.103

ERNST & YOUNG LLP, City Gate, St James Boulevard, Newcastle upon Tyne, Tyne and Wear, NE1 4JD. Tel: 0191 247 2500.

Fax: 0191 247 2601. E-mail: cmulley@uk.ey.com. Internet: www.ey.com/UK.

African Agricultural Technology Foundation	7.16
Alnwick Garden Trust	7.27
Baltic Flour Mills Visual Arts Trust	7.55
Diocese of Hexham and Newcastle	7.201
Rathbone Training	7.526
RC Diocese of Hexham & Newcastle	7.543
Sir John Priestman Charity Trust	7.611
University of Newcastle DevelopmentTrust	7.701

ERNST & YOUNG LLP, Apex Plaza, Reading, Berkshire, RG1 1YE. Tel: 0118 950 0611. Fax: 0118 950 7744. Internet: www.ey.com/UK. Charity specialists: Jill Perry.

Brighton & Sussex Univ Hospitals NHS Trust	7.88
Oxford Radcliffe Hospitals Charitable Fund	7.488

F W BERRINGER & CO, Lygon House, 50 London Road, Bromley, Kent, BR1 3RA. Tel: 020 8290 1113. Fax: 020 8460 8562. E-mail: info@fwberringer.co.uk. Internet: www.fwberringer.co.uk. Charity specialists: J Corney.

FAIRHURST, Douglas Bank House, Wigan Lane, Wigan, Lancashire, WN1 2TB. Tel: 01942 241103. Fax: 01942 825689. E-mail: jad@fairhurstaccountants.com. Internet: www.fairhurstaccountants.com.

Eric Wright Trust	7.238

FELTON PUMPHREY, 12 Sheet Street, Windsor, Berkshire, SL4 1BG. Tel: 01753 840111. Fax: 01753 850028. E-mail: Windsor@fpca.co.uk. Internet: www.fpca.co.uk. Charity specialists: R Rhodes.

Community of St John Baptist General	7.165
European Assoc for Cardio Thoracic Surgery	7.241

FENLEYS, 1st Floor, 168 High Street, Watford, Hertfordshire, WD17 2EG. Tel: 01923 238211. Fax: 01923 817491. E-mail: info@fenleys.co.uk. Internet: www.fenleys.co.uk. Charity specialists: S Fyles.

Hannah Susan Samuel Victor Greig Fund	7.300

FIANDER TOVELL LLP, Stag Gates House, 63/64 The Avenue, Southampton, Hampshire, SO17 1XS. Tel: 023 8033 2733. Fax: 023 8033 9543. E-mail: paulmeacher@fiandertovell.co.uk. Internet: www.fiandertovell.co.uk. Charity specialists: Mary Wallbank.

FINEGAN GIBSON, Highbridge House, 23-25 High Street, Belfast, County Antrim, BT1 2AA. Tel: 028 9032 5822. Fax: 028 9023 5822. E-mail: cd@fgibson.co.uk. Internet: www.fgibson.co.uk. Charity specialists: C Dolan. P Dolan. D Gibson.

Bryson Charitable Group	7.102
Northern Ireland Hospice	7.470

FIRTH PARISH, 1 Airport West, Lancaster Way, Yeadon, Leeds, West Yorkshire, LS19 7ZA. Tel: 0113 387 9060. Fax: 0113 387 9061. E-mail: info@firth-parish.com. Internet: www.firth-parish.com.

Community Foundation for Calderdale	7.162

FISH PARTNERSHIP LLP, The Mill House, Boundary Road, Loudwater, High Wycombe, Buckinghamshire, HP10 9QN. Tel: 01628 527956. Fax: 01628 810385. E-mail: post@fishpartnership.co.uk. Internet: www.fishpartnership.co.uk.

Ramakrishna Vedanta Centre	7.524

FITCH CHARTERED ACCOUNTANTS, 27-29 Gordon Street, Belfast, County Antrim, BT1 2LG. Tel: 028 9032 2047. Fax: 028 9032

3798. E-mail: office@fitch.tv. Internet: www.fitch.tv. Charity specialists: M Fitch (Managing Director).

Ulster Independent Clinic	7.693

FLETCHER & PARTNERS, Crown Chambers, Bridge Street, Salisbury, Wiltshire, SP1 2LZ. Tel: 01722 327801. Fax: 01722 323839. E-mail: james.fletcher@fletchpart.co.uk. Internet: www.fletchpart.co.uk. Charity specialists: J Fletcher. M F Tompsett.

Game & Wildlife Conservation Trust	7.268
Salisbury City Almshouse and Welfare	7.583
Stanley Picker Trust, The	7.655

FMCB, Hathaway House, Popes Drive, Finchley, London, N3 1QF. Tel: 020 8346 6446. Internet: FMCB.

Dollond Charitable Trust	7.203

FORREST BURLINSON, Owl Lane, Dewsbury, Wakefield, West Yorkshire, WF12 7RQ. Tel: 01924 465 851. Fax: 01924 457 001. E-mail: info@forrestburlinson.co.uk. Internet: www.forrestburlinson.co.uk.

Community of the Resurrection	7.167

FORRESTER BOYD, 26 South St Mary's Gate, Grimsby, North East Lincolnshire, DN31 1LW. Tel: 01472 350601. Fax: 01472 241748. E-mail: info@forrester-boyd.co.uk. Internet: www.forrester-boyd.co.uk. Charity specialists: J G Adams.

Goodwin Development Trust Limited	7.282

FORRESTER BOYD, 66-68 Oswald Road, Scunthorpe, North Lincolnshire, DN15 7PG. Tel: 01724 863105. Fax: 01724 281325. E-mail: scunthorpe@forrester-boyd.co.uk. Internet: www.forrester-boyd.co.uk.

Jerry Green Dog Rescue	7.352

FOX EVANS, Abbey House, Manor Road, Coventry, West Midlands, CV1 2FW. Tel: 024 7625 7317. Internet: www.foxevans.co.uk.

29th May 1961 Charitable Trust	7.2

FOXLEY KINGHAM, Prospero House, 46-48 Rothesay Road, Luton, Bedfordshire, LU1 1QZ. Tel: 01582 540 800. Fax: 01582 480 901. E-mail: accountants@fkca.co.uk. Internet: www.fkca.co.uk.

Active Luton	7.12
Baily Thomas Charitable Fund, The	7.54
Radcliffe Trust, The	7.523
Society of the Helpers of the Holy Souls	7.624

FPM, FPM House, 3 Downshire Road, Newry, County Down, BT34 1ED. Tel: 028 3026 1010. Fax: 028 3026 2345. E-mail: fpm@fpmca.com. Internet: www.fpmca.com.

Action Cancer	7.9

FRAME KENNEDY, Metropolitan House, 31-33 High Street, Inverness, Highland, IV1 1HT. Tel: 01463 239100. Fax: 01463 225339. E-mail: enquiries@fkfhighland.co.uk. Internet: www.fkfhighland.co.uk.

Abernethy Trust	7.6

FRANCIS CLARK LLP, Vantage Point, Woodwater Park, Pynes Hill, Exeter, Devon, EX2 5FD. Tel: 01392 667000. Fax: 01392 667001. E-mail: mpn@francisclark.co.uk. Internet: www.francisclark.co.uk. Charity specialists: M Hill - specialist area: Charity Advise.

AIM Foundation	7.20
Cornwall Care	7.180
Devon Air Ambulance Trust	7.200
Eden Trust	7.224
National Marine Aquarium	7.449
Plymouth Marine Laboratory	7.506
South West Lakes Trust	7.630
St Loye's Foundation	7.646

Westbank Community Health and Care 7.721

FRANCIS CLARK LLP, North Quay House, Sutton Harbour, Plymouth, Devon, PL4 0RA. Tel: 01752 301010. Fax: 01752 312430. E-mail: mail@francisclark.co.uk. Internet: www.francisclark.co.uk. Charity specialists: M Hill - specialist area: Charity Advice.

St Luke's Hospice Plymouth 7.648

FRANCIS CLARK LLP, Blackbrook Business Park, Blackbrook Gate 1, Taunton, Somerset, TA1 2PX. Tel: 01823 275925. Fax: 01823 240169. E-mail: mail@francisclark.co.uk. Internet: www.francisclark.co.uk.

Viridor Credits Environmental Company 7.706

FRANCIS CLARK LLP, Sigma House, Oak View Close, Edginswell Park, Torquay, Devon, TQ2 7FF. Tel: 01803 320100. Fax: 01803 320101. E-mail: mail@francisclark.co.uk. Internet: www.francisclark.co.uk. Charity specialists: P Cliff. C Hicks. M Hill - specialist area: Charity Advice.

Buckfast Abbey Trust	7.103
Exeter Royal Academy for Deaf Education	7.244
Plymouth Diocesan Trust	7.505
Plymouth Secular Clergy Fund	7.506
Shared Lives South West	7.599
South West Environmental Parks Limited	7.630
St Cecilia's Abbey Ryde Isle of Wight	7.639
Whitley Wildlife Conservation Trust, The	7.726

FRANCIS CLARK LLP, Lowin House, Tregolls Road, Truro, Cornwall, TR1 2NA. Tel: 01872 276477. Fax: 01872 222783. E-mail: mail@francisclark.co.uk. Internet: www.francisclark.co.uk. Charity specialists: L M Bennett (Manager) - specialist area: Charity Taxation.

Cornwall Hospice Care 7.180

FRANCIS GRAY, 32 Queens Road, Aberystwyth, Ceredigion, SY23 2HN. Tel: 01970 625 754. E-mail: office@francisgray.co.uk. Internet: www.francisgray.co.uk.

James Pantyfedwen Foundation 7.350

FRENCH DUNCAN LLP, 56 Palmersion Place, Edinburgh, EH12 5AY. Tel: 0131 225 6366. Fax: 0131 220 1041. Internet: www.frenchduncan.co.uk.

Harmeny Education Trust 7.302

FRENCH DUNCAN LLP, Macfarlane Gray House, Castlecraig Business Park, Springbank Road, Stirling, FK7 7WT. Tel: 01786 451745. Fax: 01786 472528. Internet: www.frenchduncan.co.uk.

Keep Scotland Beautiful 7.367

FSPG, 21 Bedford Square, London, WC1B 3HH. Tel: 020 7637 4444. Fax: 020 7323 2857. E-mail: fspg@compuserve.com. Charity specialists: H Stern.

Magen David Adom UK 7.406

GALBRAITH PRITCHARDS, 20 Barns Street, Ayr, South Ayrshire, KA7 1XA. Tel: 01292 264 631. Fax: 01292 610 045. E-mail: rwilson@gpca.co.uk. Internet: www.gpca.co.uk.

Irvine Bay Urban Regeneration Company 7.346

GALLAGHER PARTNERSHIP LLP, PO Box 698, 2nd Floor, Titchfield House, 69-85 Tabernacle Street, London, EC2A 4RR. Tel: 020 7490 7774. Fax: 020 7490 5354. E-mail: partners@gallaghers.co.uk. Internet: www.gallaghers.co.uk. Charity specialists: M Palmer.

Prism The Gift Fund	7.515
Retired Greyhound Trust	7.534

GANE JACKSON SCOTT, 144 High Street, Epping, Essex, CM16 4AS. Tel: 01992 574 224. Fax: 01992 560 587. E-mail: gjs@ganejackson.co.uk. Internet: www.ganejacksonscott.co.uk.

Grange Farm Centre Trust 7.284

GARBUTT & ELLIOTT, Arabesque House, Monks Cross Drive, Huntington, York, North Yorkshire, YO32 9GW. Tel: 01904 464100. Fax: 01904 464111. E-mail: info@garbutt-elliott.co.uk. Internet: www.garbutt-elliott.co.uk.

Harrogate District Hospice Care	7.303
Human Relief Foundation	7.324
St Leonard's Hospice York	7.646
Yorkshire Agricultural Society	7.748

GARTON GRAHAM & CO, 56 Grammar School Yard, Hull, East Riding of Yorkshire, HU1 2NB. Tel: 01482 213555. Fax: 01482 329005. Charity specialists: D W Graham.

Hull Truck Theatre Company 7.323

GARY SARGEANT & CO, 5 White Oak Square, London Road, Swanley, Kent, BR8 7AG. Tel: 01322 614 681. Fax: 01322 613 290. E-mail: info@gary-sargeant.co.uk. Internet: www.gary-sargeant.co.uk.

Community of Our Lady of Fidelity 7.165

GEENS, 68 Liverpool Road, Stoke-on-Trent, ST4 1BG. Tel: 01782 847952. Fax: 01782 744357. E-mail: info@geens.co.uk. Internet: www.geens.co.uk. Charity specialists: S J Arcure. C B V France.

Douglas Macmillan Hospice 7.209

GEOGHEGANS, 6 St Colme Street, Edinburgh, EH3 6AD. Tel: 0131 225 4681. Fax: 0131 220 1132. E-mail: mike.crerar@geoghegans.co.uk. Internet: www.geoghegans.co.uk. Charity specialists: Andrew Pass (Associate, Charities Unit).

Edina Trust	7.224
Kirkhouse Trust	7.374
RSABI	7.576
Scottish Wildlife Trust	7.593

GEORGE ARTHUR, York House, 4 Wigmores South, Welywn Garden City, Hertfordshire, AL8 6PL. Tel: 01707 324 163. Fax: 01707 375 516. E-mail: mail@georgearthur.co.uk. Internet: www.georgearthur.co.uk.

Sir Malcolm Stewart Bart Gen. Trust 7.612

GEORGE HAY, St George's House, George Street, Huntingdon, Cambridgeshire, PE29 3GH. Tel: 01480 426500. Fax: 01480 426501. E-mail: huntingdon@georgehay.co.uk. Internet: www.georgehay.co.uk. Charity specialists: Toni Hunter.

Huntingdon Freemen's Trust 7.325

GEORGE HAY & COMPANY, 83 Cambridge Street, Pimlico, London, SW1V 4PS. Tel: 020 7630 0582. Fax: 020 7630 1502. Internet: www.georgehay.com. Charity specialists: N Christie.

Metropolitan City Police Orphans Fund	7.424
Police Rehabilitation Centre	7.507

GERALD EDELMAN , 25 Harley Street, London, W1G 9BR. Tel: 020 7299 1400. Fax: 020 7631 0917. Charity specialists: Patricia Norris.

Kennedy Leigh Charitable Trust	7.368
Reuben Foundation	7.534
Rose Foundation	7.545
Trumros	7.687

GIBBONS MANNINGTON & PHIPPS, 82 High Street, Tenterden, Kent, TN30 6JG. Tel: 01580 765171. Fax: 01580 764634. E-mail: info@gmpaccountants.co.uk. Internet: gmpaccountants.co.uk.

St Michael's Hospice Hastings 7.651

GIBSON BOOTH LTD, 12 Victoria Road, Barnsley, South Yorkshire, S70 2BB. Tel: 01226 213131. Fax: 01226 213141. E-mail: enquiries@gibsonbooth.co.uk. Internet: www.gibsonbooth.co.uk.

Barnsley Premier Leisure 7.58

GIBSON BOOTH, New Court, Abbey Road, North Shepley, Huddersfield, West Yorkshire, HD8 8BJ. Tel: 01484 600234. Fax: 01484 607871. E-mail: info@gibson-booth.co.uk. Internet: www.gibsonbooth.co.uk.

David and Claudia Harding Foundation, The 7.193

GIBSON MCKERRELL BROWN LLP, 14 Rutland Square, Edinburgh, EH1 2BD. Tel: 0131 228 8319. Fax: 0131 228 3700. E-mail: jcordery@g-m-b.co.uk. Internet: www.gibsonmckerrellbrown.co.uk.

Miss Agnes H Hunter's Trust 7.429

GILBERT ALLEN & CO, Churchdown Chambers, Bordyke, Tonbridge, Kent, TN9 1NR. Tel: 01732 770100. Fax: 01732 369300. Charity specialists: J Duncan.

Michael Bishop Foundation	7.425
National Gardens Scheme Charitable Trust	7.447

GLOVER STANBURY & CO, 27 Bridgeland Street, Bideford, Devon, EX39 2PZ. Tel: 01237 471881. Fax: 01237 470133. E-mail: info@GloverStanbury.co. Internet: www.GloverStanbury.co.uk. Charity specialists: M Chance.

Bideford Bridge Trust 7.69

GOLDBLATT MCGUIGAN, Alfred House, 9 Alfred Street, Belfast, County Antrim, BT2 8EQ. Tel: 028 9031 1113. Fax: 028 9031 0777. Internet: www.goldblattmcguigan.com.

Action Mental Health	7.11
Camphill Communities Trust	7.110
Simon Community Northern Ireland	7.609

GOLDWINS, 75 Maygrove Road, West Hampstead, London, NW6 2EG. Tel: 020 7372 6494.

Aspinall Foundation, The	7.44
Radha Soami Satsang Beas British Isles	7.523

Goodman Jones

GOODMAN JONES LLP, 29-30 Fitzroy Square, London, W1T 6LQ. Tel: 020 7388 2444. Fax: 020 7388 6736.
E-mail: charities@goodmanjones.com.
Internet: www.goodmanjones.com/charities.

We help charities by providing advice, support, and the reassurance that all your financial and compliance aspects are well-managed, allowing you to focus on your important work.

As charity specialists, we give advice that is based on our in-depth knowledge and understanding of the complexities of the requirements for charities, and tailor our advice to the specific needs of each organisation.

By keeping up to date with the ever-changing, ever-demanding requirements in the sector, our dedicated charity team is able to keep our advice cost-effective by having solutions at our fingertips.

In addition to core accounts audit/examination, and tax compliance services, we provide a wide range of business and organisational support services, including VAT advice, gift aid, management accounts, payroll, governance, and charity trading.

We pride ourselves on our accessibility, and the level of attention and personal service our clients receive.

Charity specialists: Julian Flitter. Martin Bailey.
Punchdrunk   7.518

GRAHAM JONES, 16-20 South Street, Hythe, Hampshire, SO45 6EB. Tel: 02380 847048. Fax: 02380 879048. E-mail: mail@gjca.co.uk. Internet: www.gjca.co.uk.

Dibden Allotments Fund   7.201

GRANT THORNTON UK LLP, 30 Finsbury Square, London, EC2P 2YU. Tel: 020 7184 4300. Fax: 020 7184 4301. Internet: www.grant-thornton.co.uk.

Young Enterprise   7.750

GRANT THORNTON UK LLP, Grant Thornton House, Melton Street, London, NW1 2EP. Tel: 020 7383 5100. Fax: 020 7383 4715. Internet: www.grant-thornton.co.uk. Charity specialists: Carol Rudge (Head of Not for Profit).

Action for Children	7.10
Associated Board Royal Schools Music	7.45
Association of Accounting Technicians	7.46
Asthma UK	7.47
Canal & River Trust	7.111
CARE International UK	7.114
Chartered Institute Building	7.132
Diabetes UK	7.200
Disabilities Trust	7.201
Fusion Lifestyle	7.266
Gloucestershire Care Partnership	7.278
Hertford British Hospital, Paris	7.310
ifs School of Finance	7.328
Institute of Cancer Research	7.334
London Diocesan Board for Schools	7.398

Museum of London	7.440
NHS Confederation	7.462
Norwood	7.472
Orders St John Care Trust	7.483
Orthopaedic Research UK	7.484
Oxfordshire Care Partnership, The	7.488
Pirbright Institute	7.504
Royal Horticultural Society	7.561
Royal Opera House Covent Garden	7.569
Royal Opera House Endowment Fund 2000	7.569
Royal Opera House Foundation	7.569
Royal Society of Medicine	7.573
Shottermill Rec. Ground & Swimming Pool	7.606
Smile Train UK, The	7.619
St George's Hospital Charity	7.643
St John Ambulance	7.644
Tate Foundation	7.669
Tate Members	7.669
Teach First	7.670
UFI Charitable Trust	7.692
United Bible Societies Association, The	7.695
World Society for the Protection of Animals	7.741

GRANT THORNTON UK LLP, Colmore Plaza, 20 Colmore Circus, Birmingham, West Midlands, B4 6AT. Tel: 0121 212 4000. Fax: 0121 212 4014. Internet: www.grant-thornton.co.uk. Charity specialists: Kyla Bellingall (Regional Head - Central).

Church of Jesus Christ of Latter Day Saints	7.149
Farmland Reserve UK Limited	7.249
Services Sound Vision Corporation	7.598

GRANT THORNTON UK LLP, Hartwell House, 55-61 Victoria Street, Bristol, BS1 6FT. Tel: 0117 305 7600. Fax: 0117 305 7784.

Ernest Cook Trust	7.239
North Bristol NHS Trust Charitable Funds	7.465
Royal United Hospital Bath NHS Trust Ch Fd	7.574

GRANT THORNTON UK LLP, 11-13 Penhill Road, Cardiff, CF11 9UP. Tel: 029 2023 5591. Fax: 029 2038 3803. Internet: www.grant-thornton.co.uk. Charity specialists: Sally McKinley (Regional Head - South).

Above and Beyond	7.7
Elim Foursquare Gospel Alliance	7.230
Wales Council for Voluntary Action	7.711

GRANT THORNTON UK LLP, The Explorer Building, Fleming Way, Crawley, West Sussex, RH10 9GT. Tel: 0870 381 7000. Fax: 0870 381 7005. Internet: www.grant-thornton.co.uk. Charity specialists: E Walsh. T Lewin.

Nuffield Health   7.474

GRANT THORNTON UK LLP, The Explorer Building, Fleming Way, Manor Royal, Gatwick, Surrey, RH10 9GT. Tel: 0870 381 7000. Fax: 0870 381 7005. Internet: www.grant-thornton.co.uk.

SSAFA   7.626

GRANT THORNTON UK LLP, 95 Bothwell Street, Glasgow, G2 7JZ. Tel: 0141 223 0000. Fax: 0141 223 0001. Internet: www.grant-thornton.co.uk. Charity specialists: Diana Penny (Regional Head - Scotland and NI).

Archdiocese of Glasgow, The	7.37
Brothers of Charity Services (Scotland)	7.101
Dunard Fund	7.215
Dundee Student Villages	7.215
Mungo Foundation, The	7.439
National Theatre of Scotland	7.453
Scottish Catholic International Aid Fund	7.591
Scottish Sports Council Trust Company	7.593
Scottish Youth Hostels Association	7.594
Sportscotland	7.634

GRANT THORNTON UK LLP, No 1 Whitehall Riverside, Whitehall Road, Leeds, West Yorkshire, LS1 4BN. Tel: 0113 245 5514. Fax: 0113 246 5055. Internet: www.grant-

thornton.co.uk.
Charity specialists: Graham Nunns (Regional Head - North).

Autism Plus Limited	7.50
B G Campbell Trust Fund	7.53
Catholic Care (Diocese of Leeds)	7.119
Children's Food Trust, The	7.140
Coal Industry Social Welfare Organisation	7.158
Community Foundation for Leeds	7.163
Community Links (Northern)	7.164
Community of the Holy Cross	7.166
Conservation Volunteers, The	7.177
Edith Murphy Foundation	7.226
Higher Education Academy, The	7.311
Leeds Teaching Hospitals Charitable Fdn	7.382
Leeds Theatre Trust	7.382
Leicester Diocesan Board Finance	7.383
Leics Independent Educational Trust	7.384
North York Moors Historical Railway	7.468
Northern College for Residential Adult Ed	7.470
Samworth Foundation	7.586
Sheffield Futures	7.601
Skills for Justice	7.618
South Yorkshire Community Foundation	7.631
St Andrew's Hospice	7.636
St Anne's Community Services	7.637
Wakefield Diocesan Board Finance	7.710
YHA (England and Wales)	7.744

GRANT THORNTON UK LLP, 4 Hardman Square, Manchester, Greater Manchester, M3 3EB. Tel: 0161 953 6900. Fax: 0161 953 6901. Internet: www.grant-thornton.co.uk. Charity specialists: Joanne Love (Regional Head - North West).

Congregation of the Brothers of Charity	7.172
Higher Education Careers Services Unit	7.311
IVCC	7.348
Lord Leverhulme's Charitable Trust	7.402
Manchester Sport and Leisure Trust	7.408
Newground Together	7.460
Northern Ballet Theatre	7.469
P H Holt Foundation	7.489
Rochdale Boroughwide Cultural Trust	7.541
Wigan Leisure and Cultural Trust	7.727

GRANT THORNTON UK LLP, Grant Thornton House, 202 Silbury Boulevard, Milton Keynes, Buckinghamshire, MK9 1LW. Tel: 01908 660666. Fax: 01908 690180. Internet: www.grant-thornton.co.uk. Charity specialists: Steve Robinson (Regional Head - Central & East).

Ability Housing Association	7.7
Anguish's Educational Foundation	7.33
Babraham Institute	7.53
Biochemical Society	7.70
Chartered Accountants' Benevolent Assoc	7.132
Forum Trust Limited	7.258
Genome Analysis Centre, The	7.271
ICAEW Foundation & Educational Charities	7.327
Institute of Food Research	7.335
John Innes Centre	7.358
John Innes Foundation	7.358
Milton Keynes Community Foundation	7.428
Nat Institute of Agricultural Botany Trust	7.448
NIAB	7.462
Norfolk Community Foundation	7.464
Norwich Consolidated Charities	7.471
Norwich Town Close Estate Charity	7.472
Paul Bassham Charitable Trust	7.493
West London YMCA	7.721

GRANT THORNTON UK LLP, Elgin House, Billing Road, Northampton, Northamptonshire, NN1 5AU. Tel: 01604 623800. Fax: 01604 230486. Internet: www.grant-thornton.co.uk. Charity specialists: Steve Robinson.

Northampton Theatres Trust	7.468
Northamptonshire Arts Management Trust	7.469
United Learning Trust	7.696

GRANT THORNTON UK LLP, 3140 Rowan Place, John Smith Drive, Oxford Business Park South, Oxford, Oxfordshire, OX4 2WB. Tel: 01865 799899. Fax: 01865 724420.

Internet: www.grant-thornton.co.uk.
Charity specialists: Mahmood Ramji (Regional Head - South).

Beit Trust	7.63
Earth Trust	7.220
FIA Foundation for Automobile & Society	7.252
Hospital of St Cross Foundation	7.321
Picker Institute Europe	7.502
Univ Old Members' Trust, The	7.699

GREAVES WEST & AYRE, 1-3 Sandgate, Berwick-upon-Tweed, Northumberland, TD15 1EW. Tel: 01289 306688. Fax: 01289 307189. E-mail: reception@gwayre.co.uk. Internet: www.greaveswestayre.co.uk. Charity specialists: A J Patterson. J H Coats. S W Allister. A N Ayre. P B Ayre. R H Dagleish. C M Frame.

Congregation of the Ursulines of Jesus	7.176

GRIFFIN STONE MOSCROP & CO, 21-27 Lamb's Conduit Street, London, WC1N 3GS. Tel: 020 7935 3793. Fax: 020 7486 1282. E-mail: mail@gsmaccountants.co.uk. Internet: www.gsmaccountants.co.uk.

Barnabas Fund	7.57
Mr & Mrs J A Pye's Charitable Settlement	7.437

GRIFFINS, Griffins Court, 24-32 London Road, Newbury, Berkshire, RG14 1JX. Tel: 01635 265 265. Fax: 01635 265 266. E-mail: info@griffins.co.uk. Internet: www.griffins.co.uk. Charity specialists: T Boothby.

Colefax Charitable Trust	7.159
Donnington Hospital Trust	7.207

HAINES WATTS, New Derwent House, 69 - 73 Theobalds Road, London, WC1X 8TA. Tel: 020 7025 4650. Fax: 020 7025 4666. E-mail: london@hwca.com. Internet: www.hwca.com.

HAINES WATTS, Hyland Mews, 21 High Street, Clifton, Bristol, BS8 2YF. Tel: 0117 974 2569. Fax: 0117 970 6152. E-mail: bristol@hwca.com. Internet: www.hwca.com.

J A Clark Charitable Trust	7.348

HAINES WATTS, 7 Neptune Court, Vanguard Way, Cardiff, CF24 5PJ. Tel: 02920 300101. Fax: 02920 300108. E-mail: adhill@hwca.co.uk. Internet: www.hwca.com.

Cardiff RC Archdiocesan Trust	7.37
Cartrefi Cymru	7.117
Innovate Trust	7.332
Mirus-Wales	7.429
Perthyn	7.498

HAINES WATTS, 71 Francis Road, Edgbaston, Birmingham, B16 8SP. Tel: 0121 456 1613. Fax: 0121 456 1614. E-mail: birmingham@hwca.com. Internet: www.hwca.com.

Birmingham MIND	7.71
Birmingham Dogs Home	7.72
Midlands Air Ambulance Charity	7.426
Vincent Wildlife Trust	7.706

HAINES WATTS, Hamilton Office Park, 31 High View Close, Leicester, Leicestershire, LE4 9LJ. Tel: 0116 276 2761. Fax: 0116 274 3001. Internet: www.hwca.com.

HAINES WATTS, 1st Floor, Northern Assurance Buildings, Albert Square, 9-21 Princess Street, Manchester, Greater Manchester, M2 4DN. Tel: 0161 932 6413. Fax: 0161 834 2230. Internet: www.hwca.com.

Francis C Scott Charitable Trust	7.262

HAINES WATTS, Floor 11, Cale Cross House, Newcastle upon Tyne, Tyne and Wear, NE1 6SU. Tel: 0845 673 3337. Fax: 0845 673 3338. Internet: www.hwca.com.

Auckland Castle Trust, The	7.48
Blyth Valley Arts and Leisure Ltd	7.77
Changing Lives	7.127
Groundwork North East	7.289
Lempriere Pringle Charitable Trust, The	7.384
NCFE	7.455
North Country Leisure	7.465
St Mary Magdalene & Holy Jesus Trust	7.649
Zurbaran Trust, The	7.752

HAINES WATTS, Old Station House, Station Approach, Newport Street, Swindon, Wiltshire, SN1 3DU. Tel: 01793 533838. Fax: 01793 434930. Internet: www.hwca.com.

Archange Lebrun Trust Limited	7.37
Duchesne Trust	7.212
National Youth Agency	7.454

HALL LIFFORD HALL, Greyfriars Lodge, 5 Greyfriars, Waterford, Dublin.

ESCRS Limited	7.242

HALLIDAYS ACCOUNTANTS LLP, Riverside House, Kings Reach Business Park, Yew Street, Stockport, Cheshire, SK4 2HD. Tel: 0161 476 8276. Fax: 0161 476 8277. E-mail: clientservices@hallidays.co.uk. Internet: www.hallidays.co.uk. Charity specialists: Anna Bennett (Partner).

Pure Innovations Limited	7.518

HARDCASTLE BURTON, 166 Northwood Way, Northwood, Middlesex, HA6 1RB.

Life Opportunities Trust	7.388

HARDIE CALDWELL LLP, Citypoint 2, 25 Tyndrum Street, Glasgow, G4 0JY. Tel: 0141 331 9600. Fax: 0141 331 9601. E-mail: mhopper@hardiecaldwell.co.uk. Internet: www.hardiecaldwell.co.uk. Charity specialists: Marion Hopper.

Active Stirling Limited	7.13
C-Change Scotland	7.107
Citizens Theatre Ltd	7.152
Hansel Foundation	7.301
St Andrew's Hospice (Lanarkshire)	7.637
Yorkhill Children's Charity	7.748

HARRIS BASSETT LIMITED, 5 New Mill Court, Phoenix Way, Enterprise Park, Swansea, SA7 9FG. Tel: 01792 772627. Fax: 01792 772826. E-mail: info@harrisbassett.co.uk. Internet: www.harrisbassett.co.uk.

Hafal	7.296

HARRISON BEALE & OWEN, Highdown House, 11 Highdown Road, Leamington Spa, Warwickshire, CV31 1XT. Tel: 01926 422292. Fax: 01926 456999. E-mail: info@hboltd.co.uk. Internet: www.hboltd.co.uk. Charity specialists: P Horgan.

Castel Froma	7.117
Johnson Association, The	7.361

HARRISON HOLT, High Park, Kirkbymoorside, York, YO62 7HS. Tel: 01751 430 100. E-mail: philipholt@harrisonholt.co.uk. Internet: harrisonholt.co.uk.

Elizabeth Frankland Moore & Star Fdn	7.230

HARTLEY FOWLER, Tuition House, 4th Floor, 27-37 St George's Road, Wimbledon, London, SW19 4EU. Tel: 020 8946 1212. Fax: 020 8947 0998. E-mail: hfldn@pavilion.co.uk. Internet: www.hartleyfowler.com. Charity specialists: R Morris. M A Fowler.

Groundwork London	7.289

HARTLEY FOWLER, 44 Springfield Road, Horsham, Sussex, RH12 2PD. Tel: 01403 254322. Fax: 01403 266498. Internet: www.hartleyfowler.com. Charity specialists: I Gilchrist.

Assoc of Anaesthetists of GB & Ireland	7.46

HAS ACCOUNTANTS, Prince Albert House, 2b Mather Avenue, Prestwich, Greater Manchester, M25 0LA.

Asser Bishvil Foundation	7.45
Helping Foundation, The	7.308
Park Charitable Trust, The	7.491

HASLERS, Old Station Road, Loughton, Essex, IG10 4PL. Tel: 020 8418 3333. Fax: 020 8418 3334. E-mail: advice@haslers.com. Internet: www.haslers.com.

Virunga Foundation	7.707

HAWSONS, Pegasus House, 463a Glossop Road, Sheffield, South Yorkshire, S10 2QD. Tel: 0114 266 7141. Fax: 0114 266 1456. E-mail: email@hawsons.co.uk. Internet: www.hawsons.co.uk.

City of Sheffield Theatre Trust	7.154
Sheffield Diocesan Board of Finance	7.601
Sheffield Media and Exhibition Centre	7.602
Sheffield Theatres Crucible Trust	7.602
Sheffield Theatres Trust	7.602

haysmacintyre
chartered accountants & tax advisers

HAYSMACINTYRE, 26 Red Lion Square, London, WC1R 4AG. Tel: 020 7969 5500. Fax: 020 7969 5600. E-mail: marketing@haysmacintyre.com. Internet: www.haysmacintyre.com.

> haysmacintyre's leading charities and Not for Profit team provides high quality compliance, taxation and advisory services to over 600 UK and international organisations. Our specialist team is one of the largest in the country, allowing us to deliver a proactive, comprehensive and cost effective service.

Charity specialists: Jeremy Beard (Head of Professional Institutes, Membership Bodies). Anna Bennett (Partner). Kathryn Burton (Partner) - specialist area: Charities. Sam Coutinho (Partner) - specialist area: Schools. Adam Halsey (Partner, Head of Faith Charities). Murtaza Jessa (Partner, Head of General Charities). Phil Salmon (VAT Partner). David Sewell (Partner, Head of Schools). Bernie Watson (Partner) - specialist area: Charities. Richard Weaver (Partner, Head of Charities and Not for Profit). Tracey Young (Partner) - specialist area: Schools.

Alexian Brothers of Province of Sacred Heart	7.24
Alliance of Sector Skills Councils	7.26
Anna Freud Centre	7.33
Apollo Foundation, The	7.35
Arundel and Brighton Diocesan Trust	7.42
Aston-Mansfield Charitable Trust	7.47
Bath Wells Diocesan Board Finance	7.60
Berks, Bucks & Oxon Wildlife Trust	7.66
Bernard Sunley Charitable Foundation	7.66
Bernie Grant Centre Partnership	7.67
Book Trust	7.79
Brain Research Trust	7.84
Breast Cancer Campaign	7.86
Brentwood Roman Catholic Diocesan Trust	7.87
Sisters of Charity of Jesus and Mary	7.94
British Sports Trust	7.99

Burdett Trust for Nursing	7.104
Cabrini Children's Society	7.107
CAMFED International	7.110
Canterbury Cathedral Trust Fund	7.112
Canterbury Diocesan Board of Finance	7.112
Catholic Apostolic Church	7.118
Caudwell Children	7.120
Chance to Shine Foundation Ltd	7.126
CILIP	7.133
Chartered Quality Institute	7.135
Chelmsford Diocesan Board Finance	7.136
Chichester Diocesan Fd Bd Finance	7.138
Clifton Diocesan Trust	7.156
Clothworkers' Foundation	7.157
Common Purpose Charitable Trust	7.162
Faithful Companions of Jesus	7.166
Compton Hospice	7.169
Congregation of the Jesus Charitable Trust	7.171
Congregation of La Sainte Union	7.171
Congregation of the Daughters of Wisdom	7.173
Cranstoun Drug Services	7.184
Cripplegate Foundation	7.186
Croydon Almshouse Charities	7.187
Cutty Sark Trust	7.189
Cystic Fibrosis Trust	7.190
Dacorum Sports Trust	7.191
Daughters Mary Joseph English Province	7.193
Demelza House Children's Hospice	7.196
Earl Fitzwilliam Charitable Trust	7.218
Edmund Rice Bicentennial Trust Ltd	7.226
Ellenor Lions Hospices	7.231
Elrahma Charity Trust	7.231
Energy Institute	7.233
Engineering UK	7.234
English Speaking Union Commonwealth	7.236
English Stage Company Ltd	7.236
Family Action	7.247
Fitzwilliam Wentworth Amenity Trust	7.255
Forest Young Men's Christian Association	7.257
French Huguenot Church Ldn Charitable Trust	7.265
Friends of the Earth Trust	7.265
General Optical Council	7.271
Gloucester Diocesan Board Finance	7.278
Grace & Compassion Benedictines	7.283
Gray's Inn Scholarships Trust	7.284
Greenham Common Community Trust	7.286
Greenwich & Bexley Comm. Hospice Ltd	7.287
Guildford Diocesan Board of Finance	7.292
Gurkha Welfare Trust	7.292
Hammersmith United Charities	7.297
HCPT - The Pilgrimage Trust	7.304
Hospice St Francis Berkhamsted Limited	7.319
HSF Health Plan	7.323
Ian Mactaggart Trust	7.327
In Kind Direct	7.330
Inc Council of Law Reporting England Wales	7.330
Institute for War Peace Reporting Limited	7.333
Institute of Daughters of Mary Help	7.334
Ironbridge Gorge Museum Trust Limited	7.346
Jewish Care	7.354
JTL	7.364
Keychange Charity	7.370
Leadership Foundation for Higher Education	7.381
Legacy Trust UK	7.383
Leprosy Mission International	7.385
London Academy of Music and Dramatic Art	7.397
London Diocesan Fund	7.398
London Oratory Charity	7.400
Lord's Taverners	7.403
Mactaggart Third Fund	7.406
Make-A-Wish Foundation (UK)	7.407
Marr-Munning Trust	7.412
Mayflower Theatre Trust	7.417
Moorfields Eye Hospital Special Trustees	7.433
Mothers' Union	7.435
Motor Neurone Disease Association	7.435
Musicians Benevolent Fund	7.440
National Fed'n of Women's Institutes	7.445
National Osteoporosis Society	7.451
National Society for Epilepsy	7.452
Nene Park Trust	7.456
Northampton RC Diocesan Trust	7.468
NUMAST Welfare Funds	7.475
NYU in London	7.476
Officers Association	7.478
Outlook Care	7.485
Outward Bound Trust	7.485
Overseas Development Institute	7.486

Peace Hospice Care	7.494
People 1st	7.496
People Potential Possibilities	7.496
Perennial	7.498
Physiological Society, The	7.502
Poor Servants of the Mother of God	7.508
Portsmouth RC Diocesan Trustees	7.510
Postal Heritage Trust	7.510
Prison Advice & Care Trust (PACT)	7.515
Racing Foundation, The	7.523
Rainbow Trust Children's Charity	7.524
Rambert Trust	7.525
Rehabilitation for Addicted Prisoners	7.530
Rennie Grove Hospice Care	7.531
Restless Development	7.533
ReVitalise Respite Holidays	7.535
Rochester Bridge Trust	7.541
Roch. Diocesan Society & Bd of Fin	7.542
Roman Catholic Diocese of East Anglia	7.543
Roman Catholic Diocese of Southwark	7.544
Royal Aeronautical Society	7.550
Royal Air Force Club	7.551
Royal Alfred Seafarers' Society	7.552
Royal British Legion Poppy Factory Limited	7.554
Royal College of Emergency Medicine, The	7.555
Royal Institution of Naval Architects	7.563
Royal London Society for the Blind	7.564
Royal Scottish Corporation	7.570
Royal Society of Arts	7.571
Saferworld	7.581
SEMTA	7.589
Science, Tech, Eng & Mathematics Network	7.590
Seckford Foundation	7.595
SeeAbility	7.596
Severn Hospice	7.598
Sir Harold Hood Charitable Trust	7.610
Sisters of the Holy Family	7.616
Sisters of the Sacred Heart of Mary UK	7.616
Skills Active UK	7.617
Society for Assistance of Ladies	7.621
S Lon Ch Fund&Sthwk Diocesan Bd Fin	7.629
Spurgeons	7.635
St Francis Hospice	7.642
St Giles Trust	7.644
St Wilfrid's Hospice (South Coast)	7.655
Thinkaction	7.676
Thrombosis Research Institute	7.680
Together: Working for Wellbeing	7.682
Tree of Hope	7.685
Franciscan Sisters Minoress	7.689
Tuixen Foundation, The	7.690
UK Sailing Academy	7.693
Union Sisters Mercy Great Britain	7.695
United Jewish Israel Appeal	7.696
USPG	7.702
V&A Foundation, The	7.702
Victory Services Association Ltd	7.705
Wates Foundation	7.715
YMCA Watford & District Branch	7.716
Weavers Company Benevolent Fund	7.717
Westminster Society	7.723
Whitgift Foundation	7.726
Winchester Diocesan Board of Finance	7.732
Wine & Spirit Education Trust Ltd	7.732
Woodland Trust	7.737
Diocese of Worcester	7.738
World Federation - Muslim Communities	7.740
YMCA Downslink Group	7.745

HAZLEWOODS LLP, Windsor House, Bayshill Road, Cheltenham, Gloucestershire, GL50 3AT. Tel: 01242 237661. Fax: 01242 584263. E-mail: sl@hazlewoods.co.uk. Internet: www.hazlewoods.co.uk.

Cheltenham Festival	7.137
Novalis Trust	7.474
Nuffield Trust for Forces of the Crown	7.475

HAZLEWOODS LLP, Windsor House, Barnett Way, Barnwood, Gloucester, Gloucestershire, GL4 3RT. Tel: 01452 634800. Fax: 01452 371900. Internet: www.hazlewoods.co.uk.

Barnwood House Trust	7.58
Gloucester Charities Trust	7.277

HB ACCOUNTANTS, Amwell House, 19 Amwell Street, Hoddesdon, Hertfordshire, EN11 8TS. Tel: 01992 444466. Fax: 01992 447476. E-mail: directors@hbaccountants.co.uk. Internet: www.hbaccountants.co.uk. Charity specialists: Keith Grover.

St Olave, St Thomas and St John United	7.653

HEDLEY DUNK, Trinity House, 3 Bullace Lane, Dartford, Kent, DA1 1BB. Tel: 01322 221157. Fax: 01322 274215. E-mail: info@hedleydunk.co.uk. Internet: www.hedleydunk.co.uk.

Sisters of Mercy, Gravesend	7.614

HENDERSON & CO, 73 Union Street, Greenock, Inverclyde, PA16 8BG. Tel: 01475 720202. Fax: 01475 720203. E-mail: info@hen.co.uk. Internet: www.hen.co.uk.

Greenock Arts Guild Limited	7.287

HENDERSON LOGGIE, 48 Queen's Road, Aberdeen, Aberdeenshire, AB15 4YE. Tel: 01224 322 100. Fax: 01224 327 911. E-mail: charities@hendersonloggie.co.uk. Internet: www.hendersonloggie.co.uk.

Aberdeen Foyer	7.6

HENDERSON LOGGIE, The Vision Building, 20 Greenmarket, Dundee, DD1 4QB. Tel: 01382 200055. Fax: 01382 200764. E-mail: charities@hendersonloggie.co.uk. Internet: www.hendersonloggie.co.uk. Charity specialists: Fiona Bullions (Director of Accounting Services).

Dundee Repertory Theatre	7.215
Fife Cultural Trust	7.253
Fife Sports & Leisure Trust Ltd	7.253
St Andrews Links Trust	7.637
Worldwide Cancer Research	7.742

HENDERSON LOGGIE, 34 Melville Street, Edinburgh, EH3 7HA. Tel: 0131 226 0200. Fax: 0131 220 3269. E-mail: charities@hendersonloggie.co.uk. Internet: www.hendersonloggie.co.uk. Charity specialists: Jandy Stevenson.

Capability Scotland	7.113
Carnegie Trust for Universities Scotland	7.116
Edinburgh International Festival Society	7.225
Foundation Scotland	7.260
Global Alliance For Livestock Vet Med.	7.277
Mercy Corps Scotland	7.422
Postcode Global Trust	7.511
Postcode Green Trust	7.511
Postcode Heroes Trust	7.511
RCAHMS	7.527
Royal Zoological Society of Scotland	7.576
SSPCA	7.592
Scottish Veterans Garden City Association Inc	7.593
Victim Support Scotland	7.704

HEW TITTENSOR, Fourwinds, Wengeo Lane, Ware, Hertfordshire, SG12 0EH. Tel: 01920 460896. Internet: www.tittensorandco.co.uk.

Marie Louise Von Motesiczky Charitable Trust	7.410

HEWITT WARIN LTD, Harlow Enterprise Hub, Edinburgh Way, Harlow, Essex, CM20 2NQ. Tel: 01279 311485. Internet: www.hewittwarin.com.

Church Growth Trust	7.147
Finchley Charities	7.254

HEYWOOD SHEPERD, 1 Park Street, Macclesfield, Cheshire, SK11 6SR. Tel: 01625 427459. Fax: 01625 511276. E-mail: info@heywoodshepard.co.uk. Charity specialists: N A Kennington.

East Cheshire Hospice	7.220

HICKS & CO, 53 Lampton Road, Hounslow, Middlesex, TW3 1LY. Tel: 020 8572 0931. Fax: 020 8577 6100. E-mail: enquiries@hicksandco.co.uk. Internet: www.hicksandco.co.uk.

Charity of Elizabeth Jane Jones, The   7.129

HIGSON & CO, White House, Wollaton Street, Nottingham, Nottinghamshire, NG1 5GF. Tel: 0115 947 5662. E-mail: gjs@higson-accountants.co.uk. Internet: www.higson-accountants.co.uk.

Notts Roman Catholic Diocesan Trustees   7.473

HILL WOOLDRIDGE AND CO, 107 Hindes Road, Harrow, Middlesex, HA1 1RU. Tel: 020 8427 1944. Fax: 020 8863 2081. E-mail: info@hillwooldridge.co.uk. Internet: www.hillwooldridge.co.uk.

Federation European Biochemical Societies   7.250

HILLIER HOPKINS LLP, Dukes Court, 32 Duke Street, St James's, London, SW1Y 6DF. Tel: 020 7930 7797. Fax: 020 7004 7149. E-mail: info@hhllp.co.uk. Internet: www.hillierhopkins.co.uk.

Africa Centre Limited   7.15

HILLIER HOPKINS LLP, 2a Alton House Office Park, Gatehouse Way, Aylesbury, Buckinghamshire, HP19 8YF. Tel: 01296 484831. Fax: 01296 437157. E-mail: info@hhllp.co.uk. Internet: www.hillierhopkins.co.uk.

Thomas Hickman's Charity   7.677
William Harding's Charity   7.730

HILLIER HOPKINS LLP, Radius House, 51 Clarendon Road, Watford, Hertfordshire, WD17 1HP. Tel: 01923 232938. Fax: 01923 817159. E-mail: info@hhllp.co.uk. Internet: www.hillierhopkins.co.uk.

FamilyLives   7.248
Peter Stebbings Memorial Charity   7.500
Robert McAlpine Foundation   7.540

HOLDSTOCK NICHOLLS TRAIN & CO, 593 Anlaby Road, Hull, East Riding of Yorkshire, HU3 6ST. Tel: 01482 504 114. Fax: 01482 561 738. E-mail: mikeh@hnt.co.uk. Internet: www.hnt.co.uk.

Hull Trinity House Charities   7.323

HOLLIS AND CO LIMITED, 35 Wilkinson Street, Sheffield, South Yorkshire, S10 2GB. Tel: 0114 281 6166. Internet: www.hollisco.co.uk.

Evan Cornish Foundation   7.242

HOLMES PEAT THORPE, Unit F21 Basepoint Business & Innovation Centre, 110 Butterfield, Great Marlings, Luton, Bedfordshire, LU2 8DL. Tel: 01582 434 311. Fax: 01582 434 319. E-mail: info@hptluton.co.uk. Internet: www.hpt-luton.com.

Stowe House Preservation Trust   7.661

HOUGHTON STONE, The Conifers, Filton Road, Hambrook, Bristol, BS16 1QG. Tel: 0117 957 9000. E-mail: info@houghtonstone.co.uk. Internet: www.houghtonstone.co.uk.

ASDAN   7.42

HOWARD WORTH, Drake House, Gadbrook Park, Northwich, Cheshire, CW9 7RA. Tel: 01606 369000. Fax: 01606 369010. E-mail: northwich@howardworth.co.uk. Internet: www.howardworth.co.uk.

St Luke's (Cheshire) Hospice   7.647

HPCA LTD, Station House, Connaught Road, Brookwood, Woking, Surrey, GU24 0ER. Tel: 01483 485444. Fax: 01483 522000.

St Peter's Home and Sisterhood   7.653
Woking Homes   7.734

HPH ACCOUNTANTS, 21 Victoria Avenue, Harrogate, North Yorkshire, HG1 5RD. Tel: 01423 520 623. Fax: 01423 520 629. Internet: www.hphonline.co.uk.

Charles Elsie Sykes Trust   7.131

HPH ACCOUNTANTS, 54 Bootham, York, North Yorkshire, YO30 7XZ. Tel: 01904 611164. Fax: 01904 611596. Internet: www.hphonline.co.uk. Charity specialists: R W Woolley - specialist area: Charity & Not for Profit Sector.

Wilberforce Trust   7.728
York Conservation Trust   7.747

HW FISHER & COMPANY, Acre House, 11-15 William Road, London, NW1 3ER. Tel: 020 7388 7000. Fax: 020 7380 4900. E-mail: charity@hwfisher.co.uk. Internet: www.hwfisher.co.uk. Charity specialists: Andy Rich. Sailesh Mehta. Neal Gilmore. Daryl Haines. Jonathan Lachmann.

Adolescent and Children's Trust, The   7.14
Asfari Foundation, The   7.43
Borough Market (Southwark)   7.80
Church Communities UK   7.147
Clore Duffield Foundation   7.157
Estate Charity of William Hatcliffe   7.241
Frank Jackson Foundation, The   7.263
Gerald Ronson Foundation, The   7.273
Greenhouse Schools Project Limited   7.286
Jean Shanks Foundation   7.352
JW3 Trust Limited   7.365
King Fahad Academy Limited   7.372
Langdon Community   7.378
Langdon Foundation   7.379
Oxford Group   7.488
Pilgrim Trust   7.503
Policy Exchange Ltd   7.507
SignHealth   7.608
Sir Robert Geffery's Almhouse Trust   7.612
Soho Theatre Company   7.625
TRAID   7.674

HYSONS, 14 London Street, Andover, Hampshire, SP10 2PA. Tel: 01264 323791. Fax: 01264 332426. E-mail: info@hysons.co.uk. Internet: www.hysons.co.uk.

Army Dependants' Trust, The   7.39

INDEPENDENT AUDITORS LLP, Emstrey House (North), Shrewsbury Business Park, Shrewsbury, Shropshire, SY2 6LG. Tel: 01743 562007. Fax: 01743 264404. E-mail: jon@indaud.co.uk. Internet: www.indaud.co.uk. Charity specialists: John Dale.

C B and H H Taylor 1984 Trust   7.107
Oakdale Trust   7.476
William Adlington Cadbury Charitable Trust   7.729

IOANNOU & CO, 767 High Road, London, N12 8LQ. Tel: 020 8343 5730.

Fetal Medicine Foundation   7.252

IZOD BASSETT, Chartered Accountants and Statutory Auditors, 105 High Street, Needham Market, Ipswich, Suffolk, IP6 8DQ. Tel: 01449 722 211. Fax: 01449 723 471. E-mail: chris@izodbassett.co.uk.

Felix Thornley Cobold Agricultural Trust   7.251

J L WINDER & CO, 125 Ramsden Square, Barrow-in-Furness, Cumbria, LA14 1XA. Tel: 01229 820390.

Sir John Fisher Foundation   7.611

J W SMITH & CO LTD, 17a Yorkersgate, Malton, North Yorkshire, YO17 7AA.

Avocet Trust   7.52
Town Trust or Lords Estate   7.684

JACOB CAVENAGH & SKEET, 5 Robin Hood Lane, Sutton, Surrey, SM1 2SW. Tel: 020 8643 1166. Fax: 020 8643 3467. E-mail: jcs@jcssutton.co.uk. Internet: www.jcssutton.co.uk.

Christ Embassy   7.144
Congregation of the Passion Jesus Christ   7.174
Ernest Luff Homes   7.239
Hyde Park Place Estate Charity   7.326

Memralife Group   7.420
Mission Care   7.430
Pilgrim Homes   7.502
Pilgrims' Friend Society   7.503
Premier Christian Media Trust   7.512
Ruach Inspirational Church of God   7.576
Servants Fellowship International   7.598

JAMES COWPER LLP, Mill House, Overbridge Square, Hambridge Lane, Newbury, Berkshire, RG14 5UX. Tel: 01635 35255. Fax: 01635 40500. E-mail: mfarwell@jamescowper.co.uk. Internet: www.jamescowper.co.uk. Charity specialists: Mike Farwell.

Arundel Castle Trustees   7.42
Berkshire Maestros   7.66
Fire Fighters Charity   7.254
Mary Hare School   7.414

JAMES COWPER LLP, 2 Chawley Park, Cumnor Hill, Oxford, Oxfordshire, OX2 9GG. Tel: 01865 861166. Fax: 01865 200501. E-mail: mfarwell@jamescowper.co.uk. Internet: www.jamescowper.co.uk.

Children's Links   7.141

JAMES COWPER LLP, 3 Wesley Gate, Queen's Road, Reading, Berkshire, RG1 4AP. Tel: 0118 959 0261. Fax: 0118 939 3385. E-mail: apeal@jamescowper.co.uk. Internet: www.jamescowper.co.uk. Charity specialists: Alex Peal.

Bromley Trust   7.100
Earley Charity   7.219
Oxford Diocesan Council For Social Work   7.487
Thames Valley Air Ambulance   7.675

JAMES S ANDERSON & CO, Pentland Estate, Loanhead, Edinburgh, EH20 9QH. Tel: 0131 440 1373. Fax: 0131 440 1015. Charity specialists: J Anderson.

Blair Drummond Camphill Trust Limited   7.74

JAMES SCOTT, Sadler House, 14/16 Sadler Street, Middleton, Greater Manchester, M24 5UJ. Tel: 0161 653 2274. Fax: 0161 643 0450. Internet: www.jamesscott.com.

Stoller Charitable Trust   7.659

JAMESONS, 92 Station Road, Clacton-on-Sea, Essex, CO15 1SG. Tel: 01255 220044. Fax: 01255 220999. E-mail: info@jamesons.net. Internet: www.thejamesonspartnership.co.uk.

Clacton Family Trust   7.154

JEFFREY ALTMAN & CO, Wayman House, 141 Wickham Road, Shirley, Croydon, Surrey, CR0 8TE. Tel: 020 8654 6700. Fax: 020 8654 5700. E-mail: jeffaltco@aol.com. Charity specialists: J Altman.

Kent Autistic Trust   7.368

JOHN DI MAMBRO & CO, 16 Muir Street, Hamilton, Hamilton, Lanarkshire, ML3 6EP. Tel: 01698 421 538.

Cora Foundation   7.179
Good Shepherd Centre Bishopton, The   7.281
St Mary's Kenmure   7.650

JOHN W HINKS & CO, 19 Highfield Road, Edgbaston, Birmingham, West Midlands, B15 3BH. Tel: 0121 456 0190. Fax: 0121 456 0191. E-mail: info@jwhinks.co.uk. Internet: www.jwhinks.co.uk.

Leprosy Mission England   7.385

JOHN YELLAND & COMPANY, 22 Sansome Walk, Worcester, Worcestershire, WR1 1LS. Tel: 01905 612822. Fax: 01905 23157. Charity specialists: J A Yelland.

Bransford Trust, The   7.85
St Richard's Hospice Foundation   7.654

JOHNSTON CARMICHAEL, Bishop's Court, 29 Albyn Place, Aberdeen, Grampian, AB10 1YL.
E-mail: jean.main@jcca.co.uk.
Internet: www.jcca.co.uk.
Charity specialists: Donna Harper (Partner). I Roy (Partner).

Inspire (Partnership Through Life) Ltd	7.332
James Hutton Institute, The	7.350
Sport Aberdeen	7.633

JOHNSTON CARMICHAEL, Nevis House, Beechwood Park, Inverness, Highland, IV2 3BW.
Tel: 01463 224 848. Fax: 01463 710 624.
Internet: www.jcca.co.uk.

Millennium Link Trust	7.427
Scottish Association for Marine Science	7.590

JOLLIFFE CORK, 33 George Street, Wakefield, West Yorkshire, WF1 1LX. Tel: 01924 376045. Fax: 01924 290522.
E-mail: wakefield@jolliffecork.co.uk.
Internet: www.jolliffecork.co.uk.
Charity specialists: A Perkin. Claire L Lawton.

United Reformed Church (Yorkshire) Trust	7.697
Wakefield Hospice	7.711

JONES AVENS, Piper House, Dukes Court, Bognor Road, Chichester, West Sussex, PO19 8FX. Tel: 0124 378 9031. Fax: 0124 353 2212. E-mail: mail@jonesavens.co.uk.
Internet: www.jonesavens.co.uk.
Charity specialists: N Lacey.

Edward James Foundation Limited	7.228
Pallant House Gallery	7.490
Stansted Park Foundation	7.656

JONES AVENS, 53 Kent Road, Southsea, Portsmouth, Hampshire, PO5 3HU. Tel: 023 9282 0726. Fax: 023 9229 1224.
Internet: www.jonesavens.co.uk.
Charity specialists: T Millett.

Rowans Hospice	7.547

JONES HARRIS, 17 St Peter's Place, Fleetwood, Lancashire, FY7 6EB. Tel: 01253 874 255. Fax: 01253 770 533. Internet: www.jones-harris.co.uk.

Lancaster Foundation	7.377

JOSEPH MILLER & CO, Floor A, Milburn House, Dean Street, Newcastle upon Tyne, Tyne and Wear, NE1 1LE. Tel: 0191 232 8065. Fax: 0191 222 1554. E-mail: advice@joseph-miller.co.uk. Internet: www.joseph-miller.co.uk.

Barbour Foundation, The	7.56
Joseph Strong Frazer Trust	7.363
W A Handley Charity Trust	7.710

JRW GROUP, THE, 19 Buccleuch Street, Hawick, Borders, TD9 0HL. Tel: 01450 372267. Fax: 01450 373591.
E-mail: abiggar@jrwca.com.
Internet: www.jrwca.com.

Borders Sport & Leisure Trust	7.80

JWPCREERS LLP, Genesis 5, Church Lane, Heslington, York, North Yorkshire, YO10 5DQ. Tel: 01904 717260. Fax: 01904 438913.
E-mail: se@jwpcreers.co.uk.
Internet: www.jwpcreers.co.uk.
Charity specialists: D E Dorman.

Chapter of Order of the Holy Paraclete	7.128
Normanby Charitable Trust	7.465
York Citizens Theatre Trust	7.747
York Minster Fund	7.748

KAY JOHNSON GEE LLP, Griffin Court, 201 Chapel Street, Manchester, Greater Manchester, M3 5EQ. Tel: 0161 832 6221. Fax: 0161 834 8479.
E-mail: mike.garrett@kayjohnsongee.com.
Internet: www.kayjohnsongee.com.

Onside Youth Zones	7.480

KEELINGS LIMITED, Broad House, 1 The Broadway, Old Hatfield, Hertfordshire, AL9 5BG. Tel: 01707 258844. Fax: 01707 258811.
E-mail: enquiries@keelings.co.uk.
Internet: www.keelings.co.uk.
Charity specialists: R Ali. E Pritchard.

Jesus Hospital Charity in Chipping Barnet	7.353

KEENS SHAY KEENS, Sovereign Court, 230 Upper Fifth Street, Milton Keynes, Buckinghamshire, MK9 2HR. Tel: 01908 674 484. Fax: 01908 690 371.
E-mail: ksk@keens.co.uk.
Internet: www.keens.co.uk.

Old Possum's Practical Trust	7.479

KEITH VAUDREY & CO, First Floor, 15 Young Street, London, W8 5EH. Tel: 020 7795 6535. Fax: 020 7937 6433.
E-mail: KeithVaud@aol.com.
Internet: www.kvcharteredaccountants.co.uk.
Charity specialists: G J H Keith - specialist area: Religious Charities. J I Boroucki.

Carmelite Charitable Trust	7.116
Charity Roman Union Order St Ursula	7.130
Little Way Association	7.391
Missionaries of Africa (The White Fathers)	7.431
Sons of the Sacred Heart of Jesus, The	7.627
St Joseph's Society for Foreign Missions	7.646

KELSALL STEELE LTD, Woodlands Court, Truro Business Park, Threemilestone, Truro, Cornwall, TR4 9NH. Tel: 01872 271655. Fax: 01872 277206. E-mail: enquiries@kelsallsteele.co.uk.
Internet: www.kelsallsteele.co.uk.

Cinnamon Trust	7.150

KEN TAIT & CO, 18 Avon Street, Hamilton, Lanark, Strathclyde, ML3 7JW.

Marchig Animal Welfare Trust	7.409

KENDALL WADLEY, 21 St Owen Street, Hereford, Herefordshire, HR1 2JB. Tel: 01432 356 462. Fax: 01432 356 419.
E-mail: hereford@kwca.co.uk.
Internet: www.kwca.co.uk.

E F Bulmer Benevolent Fund	7.217

KENNETH EASBY LTD, Oak House, Market Place, Bedale, North Yorkshire, DL8 1AQ. Tel: 01677 422188. Fax: 01677 428941.
E-mail: info@kennetheasby.co.uk.
Internet: www.kennetheasby.co.uk.

G M Morrison Charitable Trust	7.268

KEYMER HASLAM & CO, 4-6 Church Road, Burgess Hill, West Sussex, RH15 9AE. Tel: 01444 247871. Fax: 01444 871071.
Internet: www.keymerhaslam.co.uk.
Charity specialists: P Dickinson.

St Peter & St James Charitable Trust	7.653

KING & TAYLOR, Joynes House, New Road, Gravesend, Kent, DA11 0AT. Tel: 01474 569777. Fax: 01474 355623.
Internet: www.kingandtaylor.co.uk.
Charity specialists: R Hiscock.

Siri Guru Nanak Darbar (Sikh Temple)	7.613

KING LOOSE & CO, St John's House, 5 South Parade, Summertown, Oxford, Oxfordshire, OX2 7JL.

Charity of Thomas Dawson	7.130

KINGS MILL PARTNERSHIP, 75 Park Lane, Croydon, Surrey, CR9 1XS. Tel: 020 8686 7942. Fax: 020 8667 0909.
E-mail: charities@kingsmill.co.uk.
Internet: www.kingsmill.co.uk.

KINGSCOTT DIX LIMITED, Goodridge Court, Goodridge Avenue, Gloucester, Gloucestershire, GL2 5EN. Tel: 01452 520 251.
E-mail: kdg@kingscott-dix.co.uk.
Internet: www.kingscott-dix.co.uk.

Reed Foundation, The	7.529

KINGSTON SMITH LLP, Devonshire House, 60 Goswell Road, London, EC1M 7AD. Tel: 020 7566 4000. Fax: 020 7566 4010.
E-mail: nbrooks@kingstonsmith.co.uk.
Internet: www.kingstonsmith.co.uk.
Charity specialists: Nick Brooks (Head of Not For Profit Sector). Neil Finlayson. James Cross. Sandra de Lord. Martin Burchmore. Anjali Kothari. Jonathan Seymour (Hayes). Keith Halstead (Redhill). Brian Pope (Romford). David Benton (Romford). David Goodridge (St Albans). David Montgomery (Redhill). Gordon Follows (St Albans). Cliff Ireton (West end).

A M Qattan Foundation	7.3
Addenbrooke's Charitable Trust	7.13
Aid to the Church in Need (UK)	7.20
All Saints Educational Trust	7.25
Architectural Heritage Fund	7.38
Art Services Grants Ltd	7.40
Association for Project Management	7.46
Battersea Dogs & Cats Home	7.60
Bletchley Park Trust	7.76
British Museum Friends	7.96
British Museum Trust Limited, The	7.97
British Union of Seventh-Day Adventists	7.99
Cancer Recovery Foundation UK	7.112
Catch22	7.118
Catholic Trust for England and Wales	7.120
Centre for Economic Policy Research	7.123
Centre for Effective Dispute Resolution	7.124
Charles Skey Charitable Trust	7.131
Chelsea & Westminster Health Charity	7.136
Children's Trust	7.142
Crime Reduction Initiatives	7.186
D&AD	7.191
Diabetes Research & Wellness Foundation	7.200
Drinkaware Trust, The	7.212
Elizabeth Finn Care	7.230
Essex Wildlife Trust	7.240
Fair Share Trust	7.246
Fleming Wyfold Art Foundation	7.256
Friends Royal Academy	7.265
Global Partners (UK)	7.277
Gosling Sports Park	7.282
Great Britain Sasakawa Foundation	7.284
Greenwich Royal Naval College Foundation	7.288
Guy's & St Thomas' Charity	7.293
Hampstead Wells & Campden Trust	7.299
Honourable Artillery Company	7.316
Honourable Society Middle Temple Trust	7.316
Horniman Public Museum and Public Park	7.318
Imperial War Museum	7.329
International Alert	7.340
International Students House	7.345
Jagclif Charitable Trust	7.350
John Black Charitable Foundation	7.357
John Ellerman Foundation	7.358
Joseph Rank Trust, The	7.363
Kathleen Hannay Memorial Charity	7.366
Kennedy Trust for Rheumatology Research	7.368
King's College Hospital Charity	7.372
Leeds Diocesan Trust	7.382
Lennox Wyfold Foundation	7.384
LEPRA	7.385
Lister Institute of Preventive Medicine	7.391
Locality (UK)	7.396
London Mathematical Society	7.400
Luton Cultural Services Trust	7.404
MacIntyre Care	7.405
Maudsley Charity	7.416
MCCH Society	7.418
Medical Foundation for Victims of Torture	7.419
Methodist Central Hall Westminster	7.423
Mission Aviation Fellowship UK	7.430
Mountview Academy of Theatre Arts	7.436
National Childbirth Trust	7.444
National Deaf Children's Society	7.444
NFER	7.446
Netherhall Educational Association	7.457
North England Seventh-Day Adventists	7.466
North London Hospice	7.467
P F Charitable Trust	7.489
Parmiter's School Foundation	7.492
Peter Harrison Foundation	7.499
PLUS (Providence Linc United Services)	7.505
Queen Elizabeth's Fndtn For Disabled People	7.520

Raleigh International Trust	7.524
Rank Foundation Limited	7.525
Rank Prize Fund	7.525
RedR UK	7.528
Refuge	7.529
Rich Mix Cultural Foundation	7.535
Royal Academy of Arts	7.548
Royal Academy Trust	7.549
Royal Air Force Benevolent Fund	7.550
Royal College of Paediatrics	7.556
Royal Commission for the 1851 Exhibition	7.558
Royal Free Hampstead Charitable Trust	7.560
Royal Literary Fund	7.563
Royal Naval Ben. Society for Officers	7.567
Royal Navy and Royal Marines Charity	7.568
Royal Philharmonic Orchestra	7.569
Royal Society Musicians Great Britain	7.573
RSAS AgeCare	7.576
S O V A	7.579
Sadler's Wells Trust	7.580
Said Foundation	7.581
Sequoia Trust, The	7.597
Sigrid Rausing Trust	7.608
Society of Antiquaries of London	7.621
Society of Jesus	7.622
South England Seventh-Day Adventists	7.628
St Clare West Essex Hospice Care Trust	7.640
St Vincent de Paul Society	7.655
UK Community Foundations	7.692
Union Jack Club, The	7.694
United Response	7.697
Universities UK	7.700
Vibrance	7.704
Westway Trust	7.724
Whitechapel Gallery	7.725
Womankind (Worldwide)	7.736
World Villages for Children	7.741
YWCA Central Club	7.751

KIRBY ROOKYARD & CO, 1 Castle Court, St Peters Street, Colchester, Essex, CO1 1EW. Tel: 01206 562133. Fax: 01206 763340. E-mail: mail@kirbyrookyard.co.uk. Charity specialists: G L Rookyard.

Acorn Villages	7.8

KLSA LLP, Klaco House, 28-30 St. John's Square, London, EC1M 4DN. Tel: 0207 490 5525. Fax: 0207 490 4876. E-mail: enquiries@klsa.net. Internet: www.klsa.net.

Shri Vallabh Nidhi - UK	7.607

KNIGHT GOODHEAD LTD, 7 Bournemouth Road, Chandlers Ford, Eastleigh, Hampshire, SO53 3DA. Tel: 023 8026 2480. Fax: 023 8026 2484. E-mail: chris@knightgoodhead.co.uk. Internet: www.knightgoodhead.co.uk.

Sheiling Trust	7.603

KNILL JAMES, One Bell Lane, Lewes, East Sussex, BN7 1JU. Tel: 01273 480480. Fax: 01273 476941. E-mail: charities@knilljames.co.uk. Internet: www.knilljames.co.uk. Charity specialists: Sue Foster. Kevin Powell. Mark Filsell.

Sussex Community Foundation	7.665

KNOX CROPPER, 8/9 Well Court, London, EC4M 9DN. Tel: 020 7332 6400. Fax: 020 7248 9225. E-mail: kc@knoxcropper.co.uk. Internet: www.knoxcropper.co.uk. Charity specialists: D Wilson.

BAC	7.60
Fight For Sight	7.254
Housing Pathways Trust	7.322
Moravian Church	7.433
Mrs E M Bates Trust	7.437
National Heart & Lung Inst. Foundation, The	7.448
Resolution Trust, The	7.532
Royal Masonic Benevolent Institution	7.565
Royal Medical Benevolent Fund	7.565
Salvation Army Officers Pension Fund	7.584
Salvation Army Social Work Trust	7.584
Salvation Army Trust	7.584

St Andrew Holborn Charity	7.636
St Andrew Holborn Church Foundation	7.636

KPH AUDIT & ASSURANCE SERVICES LTD, 255 Poulton Road, Wallasey, Wirral, Merseyside, CH44 4BT. Tel: 0151 638 8550. Fax: 0151 638 8550. E-mail: tracey@kphaccountants.co.uk. Internet: www.kbhaccountants.co.uk.

Austin Hope Pilkington Trust	7.49
Becht Family Charitable Trust, The	7.63
Pilkington Charities Fund	7.503

KPMG LLP, Canary Wharf, 15 Canada Square, London, E14 5GL. Tel: 020 7311 1000. Internet: www.kpmg.co.uk.

Apax Foundation, The	7.34
Barts and The London Charity	7.59
IMechE Benevolent Fund	7.65
BHP Billiton	7.68
Cats Protection	7.120
CBHA	7.121
Charities Aid Foundation	7.128
Children's Investment Fund Foundation	7.141
Children's Society	7.142
Esmée Fairbairn Foundation	7.240
Goldsmiths' Company Charity	7.281
Institution of Mechanical Engineers	7.338
IFFIM Co	7.341
Intl Planned Parenthood Federation	7.344
John Laing Charitable Trust	7.359
Malaria Consortium	7.407
Medecins sans Frontieres (UK)	7.418
Peabody Trust	7.494
Potanin Foundation	7.511
Queen's Trust, The	7.521
Quintin Hogg Trust	7.521
Royal Collection Trust	7.555
Save the Children International	7.588
Seafarers UK	7.594
Southampton Row Trust Limited	7.631
Trinity College London	7.686
Trust Thamesmead	7.689
Weston Provident Fund	7.724

KPMG LLP, PO BOX 695, 8 Salisbury Square, London, EC4Y 8BB. Tel: 020 7311 1000. Fax: 020 7311 3311. Internet: www.kpmg.co.uk. Charity specialists: S Braid. Ms M Fallon.

Aga Khan Foundation (United Kingdom)	7.16
Daiwa Anglo Japanese Foundation	7.192
EMMS Nazareth	7.233
English National Ballet	7.235
Goldsmiths Centre, The	7.280
Impetus Private Equity Foundation	7.330
Prince of Wales's Charitable Fndtn	7.514
Prudential Staff Charitable Trust	7.517
Thailand Border Consortium	7.674
Virgin Unite	7.706

KPMG LLP, 37 Albyn Place, Aberdeen, Grampian, AB10 1JB. Tel: 01224 591000. Fax: 01224 590909. Internet: www.kpmg.co.uk. Charity specialists: R Clark. G Macrae. B Hutcheson.

Rowett Research Institute	7.548
Shetland Recreational Trust	7.605
University of Aberdeen Development Trust	7.700

KPMG LLP, Stokes House, 17-25 College Square East, Belfast, Northern Ireland, BT1 6HD. Tel: 028 9024 3377. Fax: 028 9089 3893. Internet: www.kpmg.co.uk. Charity specialists: D Wilkinson.

KPMG LLP, One Snowhill, Snow Hill Queensway, Birmingham, West Midlands, B4 6GH. Tel: 0121 232 3000. Fax: 0121 232 3500. Internet: www.kpmg.co.uk. Charity specialists: C Graham. Karen Hanlan. J Gone - specialist area: NHS Trusts.

Education and Training Foundation	7.227
Enable Care & Home Support	7.233
Glasgow Student Villages Limited	7.276
Goodman Foundation, The	7.281

KPMG LLP, 100 Temple Street, Bristol, BS1 6AG. Tel: 0117 905 4000. Fax: 0117 905 4001. E-mail: andrew.pitt@kpmg.co.uk. Internet: www.kpmg.co.uk.

BCS, The Chartered Institute for IT	7.61
BRUNELCARE	7.102
Salisbury District Hospital Charitable Fund	7.583

KPMG LLP, Botanic House, 100 Hills Road, Cambridge, Cambridgeshire, CB2 1AR. Tel: 01223 366692. Fax: 01223 460701. Internet: www.kpmg.co.uk.

Papworth Trust	7.490

KPMG LLP, Britannia Quay, 3 Assembly Square, Cardiff, CF10 4AX. Tel: 029 2046 8000. Fax: 029 2046 8200. Internet: www.kpmg.co.uk. Charity specialists: D A Bowen. G Lloyd.

Jane Hodge Foundation	7.351
Moondance Foundation	7.432
Wales Millennium Centre	7.711

KPMG LLP, 1 Forest Gate, Brighton Road, Crawley, West Sussex, RH11 9PT. Tel: 01293 652000. Fax: 01293 652100. Internet: www.kpmg.co.uk. Charity specialists: Ms M Fallon.

Age UK	7.17
BBC Children in Need	7.61
Circle Care and Support Limited	7.151
Comic Relief	7.162
London Transport Museum	7.401
Marie Curie Cancer Care	7.410
World Cancer Research Fund (WCRF UK)	7.739

KPMG LLP, 1 Stokes Place, St Stephen's Green, Dublin. Tel: 00 353 708 1000. Fax: 00 353 708 1122. Internet: www.kpmg.ie. Charity specialists: Nicky Kilroy.

Concern Worldwide (UK)	7.170

KPMG LLP, Saltire Court, 20 Castle Terrace, Edinburgh, EH1 2EG. Tel: 0131 222 2000. Fax: 0131 527 6666. E-mail: vivienne.hodgson@kpmg.co.uk. Internet: www.kpmg.co.uk. Charity specialists: G Macrae. D Watt.

Children's Hospice Association Scotland	7.141
Edinburgh Military Tattoo (Charities) Ltd	7.225

KPMG LLP, 191 West George Street, Glasgow, G2 2LJ. Tel: 0141 226 5511. Fax: 0141 204 1584. Internet: www.kpmg.co.uk. Charity specialists: C Denholm.

Glasgow Science Centre Limited	7.275
Glasgow Science Centre Charitable Trust	7.276
HALO Trust	7.297
North Lanarkshire Leisure Ltd	7.467
Shetland Charitable Trust	7.604
South Lanarkshire Leisure Ltd	7.629

KPMG LLP, 6 Lower Brook Street, Ipswich, Suffolk, IP4 1AP. Tel: 01473 233499. Fax: 01473 230131. Internet: www.kpmg.co.uk. Charity specialists: T Ingram.

Transforming Education in Norfolk	7.685

KPMG LLP, 1 The Embankment, Neville Street, Leeds, West Yorkshire, LS1 4DW. Tel: 0113 231 3000. Fax: 0113 231 3200. Internet: www.kpmg.co.uk. Charity specialists: M Harding.

Bradford Diocesan Board of Finance, The	7.83
Coalfields Regeneration Trust	7.158
Donisthorpe Hall	7.205
Hollybank Trust	7.315
Joseph Rowntree Foundation	7.363
Liz and Terry Bramall Charitable Trust, The	7.394
Opera North	7.481
Ripon Diocesan Board of Finance	7.539
Sheffield City Trust	7.601
Skills for Care	7.617
Unipol Student Homes	7.695
Yorkshire Air Ambulance	7.749

KPMG LLP, 8 Princes Parade, Liverpool, Merseyside, L3 1QH. Tel: 0151 473 5100. Fax: 0151 473 5200.
Internet: www.kpmg.co.uk.
Charity specialists: J Sandford.

North of England Zoological Society	7.467

KPMG LLP, St James' Square, Manchester, Greater Manchester, M2 6DS. Tel: 0161 838 4000. Fax: 0161 838 4040.
Internet: www.kpmg.co.uk.
Charity specialists: J Sandford. T Rees.

Co-operative Community Inv Foundation	7.158
Hallé Concerts Society	7.297
League Football Education	7.381
UK Biobank Ltd	7.692

KPMG LLP, Quayside House, 110 Quayside, Newcastle upon Tyne, Tyne and Wear, NE1 3DX. Tel: 0191 401 3700. Fax: 0191 401 3750. Internet: www.kpmg.co.uk.
Charity specialists: M Thompson.

Angel Foundation	7.32
County Durham Community Foundation	7.183
Durham Aged Mineworkers' Homes Assoc	7.216
Greggs Foundation	7.288
Railway Housing Association and Benefit Fund	7.524

KPMG LLP, St Nicholas House, Park Row, Nottingham, Nottinghamshire, NG1 6FQ. Tel: 0115 935 3535. Fax: 0115 935 3500. Internet: www.kpmg.co.uk.
Charity specialists: I Chisholm.

Nottingham University Hospitals General Fund	7.473

KPMG LLP, Plym House, 3 Longbridge Road, Marsh Mills, Plymouth, Devon, PL6 8RT. Tel: 01752 632100. Fax: 01752 632110. Internet: www.kpmg.co.uk.
Charity specialists: R Hubble.

Chichester Festival Theatre	7.139
Donkey Sanctuary	7.206
Shelterbox	7.603
Theatre Royal (Plymouth)	7.676

KPMG LLP, Edward VII Quay, Navigation Way, Preston, Lancashire, PR2 2YF. Tel: 01772 722822. Fax: 01772 736777.
Internet: www.kpmg.co.uk.
Charity specialists: S Dunn.

Blackburn Diocesan Board Finance Limited	7.74
Chelsea F C Foundation Limited	7.137
Football League (Community) Limited, The	7.257
Wordsworth Trust	7.738

KPMG LLP, Arlington Business Park, Theale, Reading, Berkshire, RG7 4SD. Tel: 0118 964 2000. Fax: 0118 964 2222.
E-mail: christopher.wilson@kpmg.co.uk.
Internet: www.kpmg.co.uk.
Charity specialists: C Wilson.

Anchor Trust	7.31
Outreach 3 Way	7.485
Places for People Scotland Care & Support Ltd	7.505

KPMG LLP, South Coast Office, Dukes Keep, Southampton, Hampshire, SO14 3EX. Tel: 02380 202000. Fax: 02380 202001.
Internet: www.kpmg.co.uk.
Charity specialists: A Cory-Wright.

KPMG LLP, 58 Clarendon Road, Watford, Hertfordshire, WD17 1DE. Tel: 01923 214000. Fax: 01923 2145000.
Internet: www.kpmg.co.uk.
Charity specialists: Janet Brandreth. Tania Potter.

BRE Trust	7.85

KRESTON REEVES, Montague Place, Quayside, Chatham, ME4 4QU. Tel: 01634 899800. Fax: 01634 899801.
E-mail: enquiries@krestonreeves.com.
Internet: www.krestonreeves.com.

Kreston Reeves is one of the major accountancy and financial service firms in London and the South East and employ over 300 staff including 39 partners based in London, Kent and Gatwick. The firm acts as adviser for a wide range of Charities and not for profit organisations, offering a comprehensive range of services from audit and accountancy, VAT and tax advice to financial planning, risk assessment, advice on governance, merges and trading for profit. Its long involvement in the sector has enabled the firm to develop the specialist expertise charities increasingly require.

Charity specialists: Susan Robinson. Peter Manser. Peter Hudson. Stephen Tanner. Sam Rouse. James Peach. Rupert Moyle. Peter Barton. Alun Edwards. Zoe O'Brien.

Kent Community Foundation	7.369
Kent Wildlife Trust	7.369
R.Watts&Rochester CityAlmshouseCharities	7.536
Royal Engineers Association	7.559

KRESTON REEVES, 37 St Margaret's Street, Canterbury, Kent, CT1 2TU. Tel: 01227 768231. Fax: 01227 458383.
E-mail: enquiries@krestonreeves.com.
Internet: www.krestonreeves.com.
Charity specialists: Susan Robinson. Peter Manser. Sam Rouse. Alun Edwards. Rupert Moyle. Rob Sellers.

CHK Charities Limited	7.143
Ernest Kleinwort Charitable Trust	7.239
Howletts Wild Animal Trust, The	7.322
IES London	7.328
Martha Trust	7.413

KRESTON REEVES, Griffin House, 135 High Street, Crawley, West Sussex, RH10 1DQ. Tel: 01293 776152. Fax: 01293 855138.
E-mail: enquiries@krestonreeves.com.
Internet: www.krestonreeves.com.
Charity specialists: James Peach. Susan Robinson. Rupert Moyle. Daryl Nicholson.

Batchworth Trust	7.60
Hinrichsen Foundation	7.313

KRESTON REEVES, Third Floor, 24 Chiswell Street, London, EC1Y 4YX. Tel: 020 7382 1820. Fax: 020 7382 1821.
E-mail: enquiries@krestonreeves.com.
Internet: www.krestonreeves.com.
Charity specialists: Peter Hudson. Stephen Tanner. Susan Robinson. Rupert Moyle. Zoe O'Brien.

Groundwork South Trust Limited, The	7.290

KTS OWENS THOMAS LTD, The Counting House, Celtic Gateway, Cardiff, CF11 0SN. Tel: 02920 829000. E-mail: 3da@ktsowensthomas.com.
Internet: www.ktsowensthomas.com.

Community Foundation Wales	7.163
National Waterfront Museum Swansea	7.454
Ty Hafan	7.692

LAMBERT CHAPMAN LLP, 3 Warners Mill, Silks Way, Braintree, Essex, CM7 3GB. Tel: 01376 326266. Fax: 01376 552221.
E-mail: nick@lambert-chapman.co.uk.
Internet: www.lambert-chapman.co.uk.
Charity specialists: J Smith-Daye.

Missionary Franciscan Sisters	7.544

LAMONT PRIDMORE, 136, Highgate, Kendal, Cumbria, LA9 4HW. Tel: 01539 732377.
Internet: www.lamontpridmore.co.uk.

Brathay Trust	7.85

LANDAU MORLEY LLP, York House, Empire Way, Wembley, Middlesex, HA9 0FQ. Tel: 020 8903 5122. Fax: 020 8782 1666.
E-mail: plk@landaumorley.co.uk.
Internet: www.landaumorley.co.uk.
Charity specialists: P L Kutner.

Archie Sherman Charitable Trust	7.38
Federation of Synagogues	7.251
Jewish Secondary Schools Movement	7.355
Neil Kreitman Foundation	7.456
UOHC Foundation	7.701

LANG BENNETT, The Old Carriage Works, Moresk Road, Truro, Cornwall, TR1 1DG. Tel: 01872 272047. Fax: 01872 223297.
Internet: www.lang-bennetts.co.uk.

Tempus Leisure Limited	7.672

LANGDOWNS DFK, Fleming Court, Leigh Road, Eastleigh, Southampton, SO50 9PD. Tel: 023 8061 3000. Fax: 023 8064 9700.
E-mail: eastleigh@langdowns.co.uk.
Internet: www.langdowns.co.uk.

Wessex Archaeology Ltd	7.719

LARKING GOWEN, Unit 1, Claydon Business Park, Great Blakenham, Ipswich, Suffolk, IP6 0NL. Tel: 01473 833411. Fax: 01473 833314. E-mail: charities@larking-gowen.co.uk.
Internet: www.larking-gowen.co.uk.

Suffolk Wildlife Trust	7.664

LARKING GOWEN, King Street House, 15 Upper King Street, Norwich, Norfolk, NR3 1RB. Tel: 01603 624181. Fax: 01603 667800.
E-mail: lg@larking-gowen.co.uk.
Internet: www.larking-gowen.co.uk.

Constance Travis Charitable Trust	7.178
Great Hospital, Norwich	7.285
Hymns Ancient and Modern	7.326
Morley Agricultural Foundation, The	7.434
Redwings Horse Sanctuary	7.528
Sloane Robinson Foundation	7.618
Theatre Royal (Norwich) Trust	7.676
Walsingham College Trust Association	7.713

LEACH & CO, Ashley House, 136 Tolworth Broadway, Surbiton, Surrey, KT6 7LA. Tel: 020 83398850.
Charity specialists: M Boundy.

English Province of our Lady of Charity	7.235

LEONARD JONES & CO, 1 Printing House Yard, London, E2 7PR.

Will Charitable Trust	7.729
Will Woodlands	7.729

LEROY REID & CO, 299 Northborough Road, Norbury, London, SW16 4TR. Tel: 020 8679 4459. Fax: 020 8765 0827.
Charity specialists: Leroy Reid.

Church of Pentecost - UK, The	7.149

LEWIS GOLDEN & CO, 40 Queen Anne Street, London, W1G 9EL. Tel: 020 7580 7313. Fax: 020 7580 2179.
Internet: www.lewisgolden.com.
Charity specialists: N W Benson.

Gosling Foundation Limited	7.282
Hobson Charity Limited	7.314
Joseph Levy Charitable Foundation	7.362

LIEBERMAN & CO, 2L Cara House, 339 Seven Sisters Road, London, N15 6RD. Tel: 020 8800 9296. Fax: 020 8800 2849.

Melow Charitable Trust	7.420

LISHMAN SIDWELL CAMPBELL & PRICE, John Aislabie Wing, Eva Lett House, 1 South Crescent, Ripon, North Yorkshire, HG4 1SN.

Harewood House Trust	7.302

LITTLE & CO, 45 Park Road, Gloucester, Gloucestershire, GL1 1LP. Tel: 01452 308 966. Fax: 01452 302 195.
Internet: www.littglos.co.uk.

Country Houses Foundation	7.182

LIVESEY SPOTTISWOOD, 17 George Street, St Helens, Merseyside, WA10 1DB. Tel: 01744 730901. Fax: 01744 451813.
E-mail: info@LSonline.co.uk.
Internet: www.lsonline.co.uk.

Cecil Alan Pilkington Trust Fund	7.121
Willowbrook Hospice	7.731

LLYR JAMES, 25 Bridge Street, Carmarthen, Carmarthenshire, SA31 3JS. Tel: 01267 237754. Fax: 01267 238418.
Charity specialists: L James.

Welsh Books Council	7.718

LOGAN & BREWERTON, Astral House, Granville Way, Bicester, Oxfordshire, OX26 4JT. Tel: 01869 326520. Fax: 01608 642287.
E-mail: advice@astral-lbh.co.uk.
Internet: www.astral-lbh.co.uk.

Style Acre	7.663

LONSDALE & MARSH, Orleans House, Edmund Street, Liverpool, Merseyside, L3 9NG. Tel: 0151 236 8211. Fax: 0151 236 4485.
E-mail: liverpool@lonsdales.co.uk.
Internet: www.lonsdales.co.uk.

Woodlands Hospice Charitable Trust Limited	7.737

LOPIAN GROSS BARNETT & CO, 6th Floor, Cardinal House, 20 St Mary's Parsonage, Manchester, Greater Manchester, M3 2LG. Tel: 0161 832 8721. Fax: 0161 835 3085.
E-mail: mail@lopiangb.co.uk.
Internet: www.lopiangb.co.uk.

Samjo Limited	7.585

LOVEWELL BLAKE LLP, Bankside 300, Peachman Way, Broadland Business Park, Norwich, Norfolk, NR7 0LB. Tel: 01603 663300. Fax: 01603 692238.
E-mail: mpx@lovewell-blake.co.uk.
Internet: www.lovewell-blake.co.uk.

All Hallows Healthcare Trust	7.25
Break	7.86
British Trust for Ornithology	7.99
Community All Hallows Ditchingham Norfolk	7.165
East Anglian Air Ambulance	7.220
Geoffrey Watling Charity, The	7.272
Norfolk Wildlife Trust	7.464
Norwich Diocesan Board of Finance, The	7.471
Petans	7.499

LUBBOCK FINE, Paternoster House, 65 St Paul's Churchyard, London, EC4M 8AB. Tel: 020 7490 7766. Fax: 020 7490 5102.
E-mail: enquiries@lubbockfine.co.uk.
Internet: www.lubbockfine.co.uk.

Community Security Trust	7.167
Oshwal Association of the UK	7.485
Tavistock Inst of Medical Psychology	7.670

LUCKMANS DUCKETT PARKER, Victoria House, 44-45 Queens Road, Coventry, West Midlands, CV1 3EH. Tel: 024 7662 7200. Fax: 024 7622 5050. E-mail: partners@luckmans.com.
Internet: www.luckmans.com.

Addington Fund, The	7.14
Swanswell Charitable Trust	7.667

LUCRAFT HODGSON & DAWES LLP, 2/4 Ash Lane, Rustington, West Sussex, BN16 3BZ. Tel: 01903 772244. Fax: 01903 771071.
Internet: www.lucrafts.co.uk.

Martlets Hospice Limited	7.413

M+A PARTNERS, 7 The Close, Norwich, Norfolk, NR1 4DJ. Tel: 01603 227600. Fax: 01603 227610.
E-mail: enquiries@mapartners.co.uk.
Internet: www.mapartners.co.uk.

Lind Trust	7.390

M AKRAM & CO, 413 Lea Bridge Road, London, E10 7EA. Tel: 020 8558 8620. Fax: 020 8923 2816. E-mail: advisor@makramco.com.

Palestinians Relief and Development Fund	7.489

M R SALVAGE LIMITED, 7-8 Eghams Court, Boston Drive, Bourne End, Buckinghamshire, SL8 5YS. Tel: 01628 522773. Fax: 01628 810406. E-mail: meyrickf@mrsalavage.co.uk.
Internet: www.mrsalvage.co.uk.

Teikyo Foundation UK	7.672

M.D. COXEY & CO LTD, 25 Grosvenor Road, Wrexham, LL11 1BT. Tel: 01978 355477. Fax: 01978 358020.
E-mail: admin@mdcoxey.com.
Internet: www.mdcoxey.com.

Wrexham (Parochial) Educational Fdn	7.742

MCBRIDES, Nexus House, 2 Cray Road, Sidcup, Kent, DA14 5DA. Tel: 020 8309 0011. Fax: 020 8309 7879.
E-mail: info@mcbridesllp.com.
Internet: www.mcbridesllp.com.
Charity specialists: Gavin Barclay.

John Roan Foundation	7.360
John Townsend Trust, The	7.361

MCCABE FORD WILLIAMS, Bank Chambers, 1 Central Avenue, Sittingbourne, Kent, ME10 4AE. Tel: 01795 479111. Fax: 01795 428810. E-mail: clair.rayner@mfw.co.uk.
Internet: www.mfw.co.uk.

Active Life Ltd	7.12
Halo Leisure Services Limited	7.297
Hertsmere Leisure	7.310
Mytime Active	7.441
Wave Leisure Trust Limited	7.716

MCEWAN WALLACE, 68 Argyle Street, Birkenhead, Merseyside, CH41 6AF. Tel: 0151 647 6681. Fax: 0151 666 2115.
E-mail: enquiries@mcwallace.co.uk.
Internet: www.mcwallace.co.uk.

Imagine Independence	7.328
West Kirby Residential School	7.720
Wirral Hospice St John's	7.733

MACILVIN MOORE REVERES LLP, 7 St Johns Road, Harrow, Middlesex, HA1 2EY. Tel: 0208 863 1234. Fax: 0208 863 1123.
E-mail: info@mmrca.co.uk.
Internet: www.mmrca.co.uk.

Intl Society for Krishna Consciousness	7.344

MACKENZIE FIELD, Hyde House, The Hyde, Edgware Road, London, NW9 6LA.

Dontchev Foundation	7.207

MACKENZIE KERR, Redwood, 19 Culduthel Road, Inverness, Highland, IV2 4AA. Tel: 01463 235353. Fax: 01463 235171.
Internet: www.mackenziekerr.com.
Charity specialists: J Fraser. K Ross. Fiona Ross.

Highland Hospice	7.312

MCLACHLAN + TIFFIN, Clifton House, Craigard Road, Crieff, Perth and Kinross, PH7 4BN. Tel: 0131 228 5526.
E-mail: mclachlan@tiffins.com.
Internet: www.tiffin.co.uk.
Charity specialists: J E McLachlan.

Room to Read	7.545

MCLINTOCKS, 2 Hillards Court, Chester Business Park, Chester, Cheshire, CH4 9PX. Tel: 01244 680 780. Fax: 01244 680 968.
E-mail: info@mclintocks.net.
Internet: www.mclintocks.net.

Cheshire Residential Homes	7.137

MALTHOUSE & CO, America House, Rumford Court, Rumford Place, Liverpool, Merseyside, L3 9DD. Tel: 0151 284 2000. Fax: 0151 284 2200. Internet: www.malthouse.com.
Charity specialists: J Malthouse.

Nugent Care	7.475

MARK J REES LLP, Granville Hall, Granville Road, Leicester, Leicestershire, LE1 7RU. Tel: 0116 254 9018. Fax: 0116 254 8308.
E-mail: enquiries@markjrees.co.uk.
Internet: www.markjrees.co.uk.

Kelmarsh Trust	7.367

MARSH AND MOSS, The Gables, Bishop Meadow Road, Loughborough, Leicestershire, LE11 5RE. Tel: 01509 212668. Fax: 01509 210570.
E-mail: enquiries@marshandmoss.co.uk.
Internet: www.marshandmoss.co.uk.
Charity specialists: M Shannon - specialist area: Charity Audit.

Rosminian Sisters Providence	7.545

MARTIN AND COMPANY, 25 St Thomas Street, Winchester, Hampshire, SO23 9HJ. Tel: 01962 844300. E-mail: info@martin-company.co.uk.
Internet: www.martinandcompany.co.uk.

Hilden Charitable Fund	7.312
Royal Agricultural Benevolent Institution	7.550

MARTIN & HELLER, 5 North End Road, London, NW11 7RJ. Tel: 020 8455 6789. Fax: 020 8455 2277.

Moreshet Hatorah Ltd	7.434
Society of Friends of the Torah Limited	7.622

MARTLET PARTNERSHIP LLP, Martlet House, E1 Yeoman Gate, Yeoman Way, Worthing, Sussex, BN13 3QZ. Tel: 01903 600555. Fax: 01903 600828. E-mail: info@martletpartnership.com.
Internet: ww.martletpartnership.com.

Sir Edward Lewis Foundation	7.610

MAXWELL & CO, The Granary, Hones Yard, 1 Waverley Lane, Farnham, Surrey, GU9 8BB.

Seedbed Christian Community Trust	7.596
St Luke Centre Management Company	7.647

MAYNARD HEADY LLP, 40-42 High Street, Maldon, Essex, CM9 5PN.

L M Kendon Settlement	7.376

AUDIT * TAX * ADVISORY

**MAZARS LLP, Tower Bridge House, St Katharine's Way, London, E1W 1DD. Tel: 020 7063 4000. Fax: 020 7063 4001.
E-mail: nicola.wakefield@mazars.co.uk - audit; stuart.law@mazars.co.uk - payroll.
Internet: www.mazars.co.uk.**

Mazars is committed to the charity sector and through years of experience understands the value and forces – political, competitive, commercial and regulatory – which are shaping it.

By keeping abreast of such issues we are able to deliver independent advice to our 600 plus clients. We act as a sounding board and provide a source of support. Where relevant we challenge constructively.

Our London region centre of excellence for the provision of services to our charity clients is based in our Sutton office.

For more information see our profile in the front colour section.

Charity specialists: Nicola J Wakefield (Head of Charity Sector Group, Partner). Paul H Gibson (National Senior Manager).

Alpha International	7.27
Rugby Football Foundation	7.577

**MAZARS LLP, 45 Church Street, Birmingham, West Midlands, B3 2RT. Tel: 0121 232 9500. Fax: 0121 232 9501.
E-mail: ian.holder@mazars.co.uk.
Internet: mazars.co.uk.
Charity specialists:** Ian G M Holder (Partner). Kate Angus (Senior Manager).

Birmingham Children's Hospital Charities	7.71
Birmingham Repertory Theatre	7.72
Children s Family Trust	7.140
Framework Housing Association	7.262
King Henry VIII Endowed Trust Warwick	7.372
Performances Birmingham Ltd	7.498
Royal Life Saving Society UK	7.563
Severn Trent Water Charitable Trust Fund	7.598
Shakespeare Birthplace Trust	7.599
St Basil's	7.638
St Mary's Hospice	7.650
Sunfield Children's Homes Limited	7.664
Universities & Colleges Christian F'ship	7.699
University Hospital Birmingham Charities	7.700
YMCA Black Country Group	7.744

**MAZARS LLP, 37 Frederick Place, Brighton, Brighton & Hove, BN1 4EA. Tel: 01273 206788. Fax: 01273 820901.
E-mail: nicola.wakefield@mazars.co.uk.
Internet: mazars.co.uk.
Charity specialists:** Nicola J Wakefield (Head of Charity Sector Group, Partner). Cara Bushell (Manager).

Tomorrow's People Trust	7.682

MAZARS LLP, Clifton Down House, Beaufort Buildings, Bristol, BS8 4AN. Tel: 0117 973 4481. Fax: 0117 974 5203.

E-mail: richard.bott@mazars.co.uk.
Internet: mazars.co.uk.
Charity specialists: Richard Bott. Tracy Satherley (Senior Manager). Jon Marchant.

Action on Addiction	7.11
Bristol Diocesan Board Finance Ltd	7.89
Bristol Old Vic and Theatre Royal Trust Ltd	7.90
CharteredInstitute of Logistics&Transport UK	7.133
Echoes of Service	7.223
Eveson Charitable Trust	7.243
Freeways	7.264
Freeways Trust	7.264
George Muller Charitable Trust [The]	7.273
Mercy Ships - UK	7.423
Salisbury Diocesan Board of Education	7.583
Salisbury Diocesan Board Finance	7.583
SS Great Britain Trust	7.635
St Peter's Hospice	7.654
Stewards Company	7.658
Wallscourt Foundation	7.712
Weston Hospicecare	7.723
Wildfowl and Wetlands Trust	7.728

**MAZARS LLP, 90 St Vincent Street, Glasgow, G2 5UB. Tel: 0141 226 4924. Fax: 0141 204 1338. E-mail: peter.jibson@mazars.co.uk.
Internet: mazars.co.uk.
Charity specialists:** Peter Jibson (Partner).

British Journal of Anaesthesia, The	7.95
St Margaret's Hospice (Clydebank)	7.649

**MAZARS LLP, Mazars House, Gelderd Road, Leeds, West Yorkshire, LS27 7JN. Tel: 0113 204 9797. Fax: 0113 387 8760.
E-mail: alastair.smith@mazars.co.uk.
Internet: mazars.co.uk.**

York Diocesan Board Finance Ltd	7.747
Yorkshire Cancer Research	7.749

**MAZARS LLP, The Lexicon, Mount Street, Manchester, Greater Manchester, M2 5NT. Tel: 0161 831 1100. Fax: 0161 831 1101.
E-mail: janine.fox@mazars.co.uk.
Internet: mazars.co.uk.
Charity specialists:** Janine Fox (Director).

Addiction Dependency Solutions	7.14
After Adoption	7.16
Alder Hey Children's Charity, The	7.23
Bluecoat, The	7.77
LHASA	7.387
Newton Dee Camphill Community Ltd	7.461
Operation Mobilisation	7.481
Samaritan's Purse International	7.585
Seashell Trust	7.595
Southwell Diocesan Board Finance	7.631
Congregation of Christian Brothers	7.688
W O Street Charitable Foundation	7.710
Wirral Autistic Society	7.733

**MAZARS LLP, The Pinnacle, 160 Midsummer Boulevard, Milton Keynes, Buckinghamshire, MK9 1FF. Tel: 01908 664466. Fax: 01908 257101. E-mail: stephen.brown@mazars.co.uk.
Internet: mazars.co.uk.
Charity specialists:** Steve Brown (Partner). Anita Wanless (Senior Manager). Emma Grose (Manager).

D D McPhail Charitable Settlement	7.191
Hospice of Our Lady & St John	7.319
Ibbett Trust	7.327
Opportunity International United Kingdom	7.481
Peterborough Diocesan Board Finance	7.500
Solicitors Benevolent Association	7.626

**MAZARS LLP, Cartwright House, Tottle Road, Nottingham, Nottinghamshire, NG2 1RT. Tel: 0115 943 5363. Fax: 0115 943 5300.
E-mail: ian.holder@mazars.co.uk.
Internet: mazars.co.uk.**

Derby Diocesan Board Finance Ltd	7.198
Djanogly Learning Trust	7.202

**MAZARS LLP, 8 New Fields, 2 Stinsford Road - Nuffield, Poole, Dorset, BH17 0NF. Tel: 01202 680777. Fax: 01202 682671.
E-mail: david.i'anson@mazars.co.uk.**

Internet: mazars.co.uk.
Charity specialists: David I'Anson. Nigel Ballard. Lianne Treichel.

Borough of Havant Sport & Leisure Trust	7.81
Julia's House	7.364
Marwell Wildlife	7.414
National Motor Museum Trust Ltd	7.450
Royal Natl Mission to Deep Sea Fishermen	7.567
Royal Navy Submarine Museum	7.568
Tank Museum, The	7.669
Weldmar Hospicecare Trust	7.717

**MAZARS LLP, Times House, Throwley Way, Sutton, Surrey, SM1 4JQ. Tel: 020 8661 1826. Fax: 020 8643 5058.
E-mail: nicola.wakefield@mazars.co.uk.
Internet: mazars.co.uk.
Charity specialists:** Nicola J Wakefield (Head of Charity Sector Group, Partner). Alistair J Fraser (Partner). Paul H Gibson (Senior Manager). Katherine Peacock (Manager). Michael Gibson (Manager). Tarryn Gilbert (Manager).

Bader International Study Centre	7.54
Benevolent Fund Institution of Civil Engineers	7.65
Brit.YearlyMtngofTheReligiousSocietyofFriends	7.90
British School of Osteopathy	7.98
CAYSH	7.121
Chapter 1	7.127
Church Urban Fund	7.150
Churches Conservation Trust	7.150
City Gateway	7.153
COLET	7.154
Crimestoppers Trust	7.186
Foyle Foundation	7.261
Friends of the Elderly	7.265
Future Leaders Charitable Trust Ltd	7.267
Hampton Fuel Allotment Charity	7.300
Homeless Link	7.316
Institute of Fundraising	7.335
Kennedy Memorial Fund	7.368
L H A London Limited	7.376
Living Streets (The Pedestrians' Association)	7.394
Mission Aviation Fellowship International	7.430
Princess Alice Hospice	7.514
Royal Foundation of St Katharine, The	7.560
Royal National Children's Foundation	7.566
Shooting Star CHASE	7.605
St Barnabas Hospices (Sussex) Ltd	7.638
St Christopher's Hospice	7.640
TLC Care Attendant Service	7.681
UK Youth	7.693
United Reformed Church	7.696
Vocational Training Charitable Trust	7.708

MELINEK FINE LLP, Foframe House, 35-37 Brent Street, London, NW4 2EF. Tel: 0203 411 2001. Internet: www.melinckfine.com.

B E Perl Charitable Trust	7.53
David Tannen Charitable Trust	7.195
Huntingdon Foundation Limited	7.325

**MENZIES LLP, Lynton House, 7-12 Tavistock Square, London, WC1H 9LT. Tel: 020 7387 5868. Fax: 020 7388 3978.
E-mail: london@menzies.co.uk.
Internet: www.menzies.co.uk.
Charity specialists:** R Watson.

CDP Worldwide	7.121
Compassion UK	7.169

**MENZIES LLP, Blackwater Valley, Victoria House, 50-58 Victoria Road, Farnborough, Hampshire, GU14 7PG. Tel: +44 (0)1252 541244. Fax: +44 (0)1252 524000.
E-mail: blackwatervalley@menzies.co.uk.**

Brain Tumour Charity	7.84

**MENZIES LLP, Leatherhead, Ashcombe House, 5 The Crescent, Leatherhead, Surrey, KT22 8DY. Tel: +44 (0)1372 226300. Fax: +44 (0)1372 360053.
E-mail: leatherhead@menzies.co.uk.
Internet: www.menzies.co.uk.**

London Grid for Learning Trust	7.399
New Victoria Hospital Limited, The	7.458
Surrey Wildlife Trust	7.665

Victoria Foundation, The   7.705

MERALI'S CHARTERED ACCOUNTANTS, Scottish Provident House, 76-80 College Road, Harrow, Middlesex, HA1 1BX. Tel: 020 8861 3040. Fax: 020 8861 3078.

Al-Khoei Benevolent Foundation   7.21

MERCER & HOLE, Gloucester House, 72 London Road, St Albans, Hertfordshire, AL1 1NS. Tel: 01727 869141. Fax: 01727 869149. E-mail: stalbans@mercerhole.co.uk. Internet: www.mercerhole.co.uk. Charity specialists: Wendy Bambrick. G Farnes. Louise Giles. M Reed. P Webster. E M Wood.

Beatrice Laing Trust   7.62
Christopher Laing Foundation   7.146
Church Lands Charity   7.148
Kirby Laing Foundation   7.374
Maurice Hilda Laing Charitable Trust   7.416
Sheepdrove Trust, The   7.600
Tompkins Foundation   7.683

MERCER LEWIN, 41 Cornmarket Street, Oxford, Oxfordshire, OX1 3HA. Tel: 01865-724 139.

Oxford Trust, The   7.488

MESTON REID & CO, 12 Carden Place, Aberdeen, Grampian, AB10 1UR. Tel: 01224 625554. Fax: 01224 626089. Internet: www.mestonreid.com.

Camphill Rudolf Steiner Estates   7.111
Camphill Rudolf Steiner Schools   7.111

METHERELL GARD LTD, Burn View, Bude, Cornwall, EX23 8BX. Tel: 01288 352381. Fax: 01288 355962. E-mail: bude@mgard.co.uk. Internet: www.mgard.co.uk.

Blanchminster Trust   7.75

MHA MACINTYRE HUDSON, New Bridge Street, 30-34 New Bridge Street, London, EC4V 6BJ. Tel: +44 (0)20 7429 4100. Fax: +44 (0)20 7248 8939. E-mail: charities@mhllp.co.uk. Internet: www.macintyrehudson.co.uk. Charity specialists: James Gransby. Stuart Manning. Colin Mills. Robert Nelson. Sunder Singh. Sally Knight. Elaine Olson-Williams. Bianca Silva. Simon Erskine. Peter Gotham. Chris Harris. Rakesh Shaunak. Helen Blundell.

African Medical & Research Foundation UK   7.16
Bankers Benevolent Fund, The   7.55
Beaverbrook Foundation   7.63
Blenheim CDP   7.75
Chatham Maritime Trust   7.136
Creative Foundation Limited - Group, The   7.185
Cremation Society of Great Britain, The   7.185
Cruse Bereavement Care   7.187
Daughters of Jesus, The   7.193
Essex & Herts Air Ambulance Trust   7.240
Florence Nightingale Aid Sickness Trust   7.256
Institute of Brewing & Distilling   7.334
Nineveh Charitable Trust   7.463
NorthamptonshireMusic&PerformingArtsTst   7.469
Pilgrims Hospices in East Kent   7.503
Prostate Cancer UK   7.517
Refugee Action   7.529
Richmond Charities' Almshouses   7.537
S4E Limited   7.579
Shumei Eiko   7.608
St Catherine's Hospice Limited   7.639
Stock Exchange Benevolent Fund   7.659
United St Saviour's Charities   7.698
Walthamstow&Chingford Almshouse Charity   7.713
Woking & Sam Beare Hospices   7.735

MICHAEL DUFTY PARTNERSHIP LTD, The Counting House, 59-61 Charlotte Street, St Paul's Square, Birmingham, West Midlands, B3 1PX. Tel: 0121 233 0222. Fax: 0121 233 0504. E-mail: info@mdponline.com. Internet: www.mdponline.com.

George Cadbury Fund B Account   7.272

MICHAEL GEORGE & CO, Dawes Court House, Dawes Court, High Street, Esher, Surrey, KT10 9QD. Tel: 01372 469939. Fax: 01372 467724. E-mail: info@michael-george-accountants.co.uk. Internet: www.michael-george-accountants.co.uk.

CongregationDominicanSistersofMaltaTrst   7.173

MICHAEL KAY & COMPANY, 2 Water Court, Water Street, Birmingham, West Midlands, B3 1HP. Tel: 0121 236 0060. Fax: 0121 236 4800. E-mail: info@michaelkaycompany.co.uk. Internet: www.michaelkaycompany.co.uk.

Autism West Midlands   7.50

MILSTED LANGDON LLP, Motivo House, Alvington, Yeovil, Somerset, BA20 2FG. Tel: 01823 445566. Fax: 01823 445555. E-mail: advice@milsted-langdon.co.uk. Internet: www.milsted-langdon.co.uk.

H B Allen Charitable Trust   7.294

MITCHELL CHARLESWORTH, 24 Nicholas Street, Chester, Cheshire, CH1 2AU. Tel: 01244 323051. Fax: 01244 344535. Internet: www.mitchellcharlesworth.co.uk.

Hospice of the Good Shepherd Ltd   7.320

MITCHELL CHARLESWORTH, 5 Temple Square, Temple Street, Liverpool, Merseyside, L2 5RH. Tel: 0151 255 2300. Fax: 0151 255 2301. Internet: www.mitchellcharlesworth.co.uk. Charity specialists: P Griffiths.

Parkhaven Trust   7.491

MITCHELL CHARLESWORTH, Centurion House, 129 Deansgate, Manchester, Greater Manchester, M3 3WR. Tel: 0161 817 6100. Fax: 0161 817 6101. E-mail: paul.both@mitchellcharlesworth.co.uk. Internet: www.mitchellcharlesworth.co.uk. Charity specialists: P Booth (Partner).

Groundwork Oldham and Rochdale   7.290
Trafford Community Leisure Trust   7.684

MMG ARCHBOLD, Chapelshade House, 78-84 Bell Street, Dundee, DD1 1RQ. Tel: 01382 322004. Fax: 01382 224292. Internet: www.mmgca.co.uk.

Tayside NHS Board Endowment Fund   7.670

MONAHANS, 38-42 Newport Street, Swindon, Wiltshire, SN1 3DR. Tel: 01793 818300. Fax: 01793 818301. E-mail: marketing@monahans.co.uk. Internet: www.monahans.co.uk. Charity specialists: Linda Boss.

British & Foreign Bible Society   7.91
Joffe Charitable Trust   7.356
White Horse Care Trust, The   7.725

MONAHANS, Clarks Mill, Stallard Street, Trowbridge, Wiltshire, BA14 8HH. Tel: 01225 785520. Fax: 01225 785521. E-mail: trowbridge@monahans.co.uk. Internet: www.monahans.co.uk.

Chippenham Borough Lands Charity   7.143
Comm. Foundation for Wiltshire & Swindon   7.163
Developing Health and Independence   7.199
Mathematics in Education and Industry   7.416
Wiltshire Wildlife Trust   7.731

MOORE AND SMALLEY, Fylde House, Skyways Commercial Campus, Amy Johnson Way, Blackpool, Lancashire, FY4 3RS. Tel: 01253 404404. Fax: 01772 259441. E-mail: info@mooreandsmalley.co.uk. Internet: www.mooreandsmalley.co.uk.

Jah-Jireh Charity Homes   7.350

MOORE AND SMALLEY, Richard House, Winckley Square, Preston, Lancashire, PR1 3HP. Tel: 01772 821021. Fax: 01772 259441. E-mail: info@mooreandsmalley.co.uk. Internet: www.mooreandsmalley.co.uk.

Charity specialists: P R Metcalf (Partner, Charity Trusts) - specialist area: Audit, Charity and Not for Profit Orgs.

Bolton Hospice   7.78
Child Action Northwest   7.139
East Lancashire Hospice   7.221
Imagine Act and Suceed   7.328
Institute of the Blessed Virgin Mary   7.337
Integrate (Preston and Chorley)   7.339
Lancashire Wildlife Trust   7.377
St Catherine's Hospice (Lancashire)   7.639
Trinity Hospice & Palliative Care Services 7.686

MOORE AND SMALLEY, Priory Close, St Mary's Gate, Lancaster, Lancashire, LA1 1XB. Tel: 01524 62801. Fax: 01772 259441. E-mail: info@mooreandsmalley.co.uk. Internet: www.mooreandsmalley.co.uk.

Brian Mercer Charitable Trust   7.87
Lancaster Roman Catholic Diocesan Trust   7.378

MOORE STEPHENS LLP, 150 Aldersgate Street, London, EC1A 4AB. Tel: 020 7334 9191. Fax: 020 7248 3408. Internet: www.moorestephens.co.uk. Charity specialists: M Barber. T T Cripps - specialist area: Private Client Charities.

ABF The Soldiers Charity   7.6
Ashley Family Foundation, The   7.44
Aston Student Villages   7.47
British & Foreign School Society, The   7.91
Centre 404   7.123
Chartered Inst of Building Services Engineers 7.134
Chicken Shed Theatre Trust, The   7.139
Cinema and Television Benevolent Fund   7.150
City Bridge Trust, The   7.153
Corporation of the Sons of the Clergy   7.181
Electrical Safety Council   7.229
Epping Forest   7.237
European Renal Association   7.242
Fairfield (Croydon)   7.246
Foundation for Liver Research   7.259
Greensleeves Homes Trust   7.287
Hampstead Heath   7.299
Hestia Housing and Support   7.310
ITF Seafarers Trust   7.348
John Marshall's Charity   7.359
London Housing Foundation   7.399
London Library   7.399
Muslim Aid   7.440
National Fund   7.446
OMF International (UK)   7.480
Passage 2000   7.492
PRS For Music Members Benevolent Fund   7.517
Royal College of General Practitioners   7.556
Royal Town Planning Institute   7.574
Saddlers' Company Charitable Fund   7.580
Savitri Waney Charitable Trust   7.588
Schroder Charity Trust   7.589
Schroder Foundation, The   7.589
Scripture Union   7.594
St Luke's Hospice (Harrow & Brent)   7.648
St Olave's & St Saviour's Schools Foundation 7.652
Thames Reach   7.675
Twin   7.691

MOORE STEPHENS LLP, 30 Gay Street, Bath, Bath & North East Somerset, BA1 2PA. Tel: 01225 486100. Fax: 01225 448198. E-mail: bath@moorestephens.co.uk. Internet: www.moorestephens.co.uk. Charity specialists: Mark Burnett. Sue Carter.

American Museum in Britain   7.29
Circadian Trust   7.151
Holburne Museum   7.314

MOORE STEPHENS LLP, Donegall House, 7 Donegall Square North, Belfast, County Antrim, BT1 5GB. Tel: 028 9032 9481. Fax: 028 9043 9185. Internet: www.moorestephens.co.uk.

Community Foundation for N Ireland   7.163
Praxis Care Group   7.512

MOORE STEPHENS LLP, Beaufort House, 94-96 Newhall Street, Birmingham, West Midlands, B3 1PB. Tel: 0121 233 2557.
E-mail: guy.smith@moorestephens.com.
Internet: www.moorestephens.co.uk.

Birmingham Museums Trust	7.72
Foundation of Lady Katherine Leveson, The	7.260
Islamic Help	7.347
KIDS	7.371
Lantra	7.379
West Midlands Special Needs Transport	7.721

MOORE STEPHENS LLP, City Gates, 2-4 Southgate, Chichester, West Sussex, PO19 8DJ. Tel: 01243 531 600. Fax: 01243 520 637.
Internet: www.moorestephens.co.uk.

Portsmouth Naval Base Property Trust	7.510

MOORE STEPHENS LLP, Oakley House, Headway Business Park, 3 Saxon Way West, Corby, Northamptonshire, NN18 9EZ. Tel: 01536 461900. Fax: 01536 461100.
Internet: www.moorestephens.co.uk.

Northamptonshire Assoc of Youth Clubs	7.469

MOORE STEPHENS LLP, Priory House, Pilgrims Court, Sydenham Road, Guildford, Surrey, GU1 3RX. Tel: 01483 538881. Fax: 01483 537331. Internet: www.moorestephens.co.uk.

Chain of Hope	7.126
Jerwood Charitable Foundation	7.353

MOORE STEPHENS LLP, Kings House, 40 Billing Road, Northampton, Northamptonshire, NN1 5BA. Tel: 01604 638 361. Fax: 01604 232 086. Internet: www.moorestephens.co.uk.

Analytical Chemistry Trust Fund	7.31
Caribbean Biodiversity Fund	7.115
Lamport Hall Preservation Trust	7.377
Maud Elkington Charitable Trust	7.416
Wycliffe UK Ltd	7.743

MOORE STEPHENS LLP, Prospect House, 58 Queens Road, Reading, Berkshire, RG1 4RP. Tel: 0118 952 4700.
Internet: www.moorestephens.co.uk.

Benesco Charity	7.65
Charles Wolfson Charitable Trust	7.131
Microbiology Society	7.425
Thornton-Smith and Plevins Trust	7.679
Whale Dolphin Conservation Society	7.724

MOORE STEPHENS LLP, 12 Alma Square, Scarborough, North Yorkshire, YO11 1JU. Tel: 01723 360361. Fax: 01273 500564. Internet: www.moorestephens.co.uk. Charity specialists: C Tate.

St Catherine's Hospice Trust	7.639

MOORE STEPHENS (SOUTH) LLP, 33 The Clarendon Centre, Salisbury Business Park, Dairy Meadow Lane, Salisbury, SP1 2TJ. Tel: 01722 335182. Fax: 01722 412154. Internet: www.moorestephens.co.uk.

Army Central Fund, The	7.39
Royal Logistic Corps Association Trust	7.564

MORACLE, Lee Valley Technopark, Ashley Road, London, N17 9LN. Tel: 0208 880 4195. Fax: 0208 801 0891.
Internet: www.moracleandco.com.

World Mission Agency	7.741

MORRIS & YOUNG, 6 Atholl Crescent, Perth, Perth and Kinross, PH1 5JN. Tel: 01738 626257. Fax: 01738 630845.
E-mail: sandyfyfe@morrisandyoung.co.uk.
Internet: www.morrisandyoung.co.uk.
Charity specialists: Sandy Fyfe.

Gannochy Trust	7.268

MORRIS CROCKER, Station House, North Street, Havant, Hampshire, PO9 1QU. Tel: 023 9248 4356. Fax: 023 9249 8163.
E-mail: pu@morriscrocker.co.uk.
Internet: www.morriscrocker.co.uk.

Rifles Benevolent Trust, The	7.538
United Reformed Church Wessex Trust Ltd	7.697
You Trust	7.750

MUIR & ADDY, Muir Building, 427 Holywood Road, Belfast, County Antrim, BT4 2LT. Tel: 028 9076 8775. Fax: 028 9076 0631.
E-mail: info@muiraddy.co.uk.
Internet: www.muiraddy.co.uk.

Disability Action	7.201

MURAS BAKER JONES, Regent House, Bath Avenue, Wolverhampton, West Midlands, WV1 4EG. Tel: 01902 393 000. Fax: 01902 393 010. E-mail: oliver.ross@muras.co.uk.
Internet: www.muras.co.uk.
Charity specialists: Ms D J Baker. T P Brueton. O Ross.

People in Action	7.496
Wolverhampton Grand Theatre (1982)	7.735

MYERS CLARK, Iveco House, Station Road, Watford, Hertfordshire, WD17 1DL. Tel: 01923 224411. Fax: 01923 235303.
E-mail: paulw@myersclark.co.uk.
Internet: www.myersclark.co.uk.

Dame Alice Owen's Foundation	7.192
John Apthorp Charity, The	7.356
Ofenheim Charitable Trust	7.478

MYRUS SMITH, Norman House, 8 Burnell Road, Sutton, Surrey, SM1 4BW. Tel: 020 8661 1625. Fax: 020 8643 3446.
E-mail: mail@myrussmith.co.uk.
Internet: www.myrussmith.co.uk.
Charity specialists: K Fisher.

Alliance House Foundation	7.26

NAIRNE SON & GREEN, 477 Chester Road, Manchester, Greater Manchester, M16 9HF. Tel: 0161 872 1701. Fax: 0161 876 4752.

Salford Diocesan Trust	7.582
Diocese of Shrewsbury Trust	7.607
Society of African Missions	7.621

NASIR MAHMUD, Falcon House, 257 Burlington Road, New Malden, Surrey, KT3 4NE.

Al-Shirkatul Islamiyyah	7.22

NATIONAL AUDIT OFFICE, 157-197 Buckingham Palace Road, London, SW1W 9SP. Tel: 020 7798 7000. Fax: 020 7798 7070.
E-mail: enquiries@nao.gsi.gov.uk.
Internet: www.nao.org.uk.
Charity specialists: D Corner (Director of Corporate Policy).

Arts Council England	7.41
Board of Trustees for the Royal Armouries	7.78
British Council	7.92
British Film Institute	7.93
British Library	7.95
British Museum	7.97
CITB-ConstructionSkills	7.151
Engineering Construction Training Board	7.234
Geffrye Museum	7.270
Historic Royal Palaces	7.314
National Army Museum	7.442
National Gallery	7.447
National Maritime Museum	7.449
National Museum of Royal Navy, The	7.450
Nat Museums & Galleries on Merseyside	7.450
National Portrait Gallery	7.451
Natural History Museum	7.455
Nursing & Midwifery Council	7.476
Royal Air Force Museum	7.551
Royal Botanic Gardens, Kew	7.554
Science Museum Group	7.590
Sports Council Trust Company	7.634
Tate	7.669
Victoria and Albert Museum	7.705
Wallace Collection	7.712

NAYLOR WINTERSGILL, Carlton House, Grammar School Street, Bradford, West Yorkshire, BD1 4NS. Tel: 01274 733184.

Fax: 01274 393702.
E-mail: accountants@naylorwintersgill.co.uk.
Internet: www.naylorwintersgill.co.uk.

Abbeyfield Ilkley Society	7.4
Bradford Trident Ltd	7.83

NELSON GILMOUR SMITH, 47 Cadzow Street, Hamilton, Lanarkshire, ML3 6ED. Tel: 01698 284888.
Internet: www.nelsongilmoursmith.co.uk.

VAMW Care	7.703

NEVILL, HOVEY & CO, Southgate Close, Launceston, Cornwall, PL15 9DU. Tel: 01566 772109.

Gerald Palmer Eling Trust Company	7.273

NEWBY CASTLEMAN, West Walk Building, 110 Regent Road, Leicester, Leicestershire, LE1 7LT. Tel: 0116 254 9262. Fax: 0116 247 0021. E-mail: sdc@newbyc.co.uk.
Internet: www.newbycastleman.co.uk.
Charity specialists: S D Castleman.

Cope Children's Trust	7.179

NEWTON & GARNER, Building 2, 30 Friern Park, North Finchley, London, N12 9DA. Tel: 020 8445 5272. Fax: 020 8446 7427. Internet: www.newtonandgarner.co.uk.

Hadley Trust	7.296

NICHOLSONS, 1st Floor, Bridge House, 25 Fiddlebridge Lane, Hatfield, Hertfordshire, AL10 0SP. Tel: 01707 630 887. Fax: 01707 630 899. E-mail: Gillian@nicholsons.biz.

Isabel Hospice	7.346

NICHOLSONS, Newland House, The Point, Lincoln, Lincolnshire, LN6 3QN. Tel: 0845 2766555. Fax: 0845 2766559.
E-mail: emma@nicholsonsca.co.uk.
Internet: www.nicholsonsca.co.uk.

NICKLIN LLP, Church Court, Stourbridge Road, Halesowen, West Midlands, B63 3TT. Tel: 0121 550 9916. Fax: 0121 550 9390.

Mary Stevens Hospice	7.415

NIREN BLAKE, Brook Point, 1412 High Road, London, N20 9BH. Tel: 020 8492 0770.

Kabbalah Centre	7.365

NORMAN COX & ASHBY, Grosvenor Lodge, 72 Grosvenor Road, Tunbridge Wells, Kent, TN1 2AZ. Tel: 01892 522 551. Fax: 01892 522 553. E-mail: chartac@nca72.co.uk.
Internet: www.normancoxandashby.co.uk.
Charity specialists: Mark Gower-Smith.

SMB Charitable Trust	7.619

NUNN HAYWARD, Sterling House, 20 Station Road, Gerrards Cross, Buckinghamshire, SL9 8EL. Tel: 01753 888211. Fax: 01753 889669. E-mail: mail@nunn-hayward.com.
Internet: www.nunn-hayward.com.

Paul Strickland Scanner Centre	7.493

NYMAN LIBSON PAUL, Regina House, 124 Finchley Road, London, NW3 5JS. Tel: 0207 433 2400. Fax: 0207 433 2401.
E-mail: mail@nymanlibsonpaul.co.uk.
Internet: www.nymanlibsonpaul.co.uk.
Charity specialists: R J Paul. P G Taiano - specialist area: Entertainment Industry.

Hampstead Theatre	7.299
Hampstead Theatre Foundation	7.299
Jewish Joint Burial Society	7.354
Polonsky Foundation, The	7.508
Regent's Park Theatre Limited	7.530

O'BRIEN & PARTNERS, Highdale House, 7 Centre Court, Treforest Industrial Estate, Pontypridd, Rhondda Cynon Taff, CF37 5YR. Tel: 01443 841184. Fax: 01443 842284.
Internet: www.obrienandpartners.co.uk.

Kaleidoscope Project Limited   7.365

**OLD MILL AUDIT LLP, 4 Challeymead Business
Park, Melksham, Wiltshire, SN12 8BU.
Tel: 01225 701210. Fax: 01225 709817.
E-mail: marketing@oldmillgroup.co.uk.
Internet: www.oldmillgroup.co.uk.**
Royal Bath and West of England Society   7.553

**OLD MILL AUDIT LLP, Bishopbrook House,
Cathedral Avenue, Wells, Somerset, BA5 1FD.
Tel: 01749 343366. Fax: 01749 344986.
E-mail: wells@oldmillgroup.co.uk.
Internet: www.oldmillgroup.co.uk.**
Downside Abbey General Trust   7.210
South Street Green Room Foundation   7.630

**OWAIN BEBB A'I GWMNI, 32 Y Maes,
Caernarfon, Gwynedd, LL55 2NN. Tel: 01286
675916. Fax: 01286 677634.
Internet: www.owainbebb.net.**
Anheddau Cyf   7.33

**P S J ALEXANDER & CO, 1 Doughty Street,
London, WC1N 2PH. Tel: 020 7404 5466.
Fax: 020 7242 6801.**
Akshar Educational Trust   7.21
Sarjudas Foundation   7.587

**PALMERS, 28 Chipstead Station Parade,
Chipstead, Coulsdon, Surrey, CR5 3TF.**
Medlock Charitable Trust   7.420

**PARKER CAVENDISH, 28 Church Road,
Stanmore, Middlesex, HA7 4XR. Tel: 020 8954
2727. Fax: 020 8954 8058.
E-mail: ParkerCavendish@Compuserve.com.
Charity specialists:** M Lock.
Robert Luff Foundation Limited   7.540

**PARKHURST HILL, Plym House, 3 Longbridge
Road, Marsh Mills, Plymouth, Devon, PL6 8LT.
Tel: 01752 666601. Fax: 01752 666612.
E-mail: info@parkhurst-hill.co.uk.
Internet: www.parkhurst-hill.co.uk.**
Dame Hannah Rogers Trust   7.192

**PAUL HOWLEY & CO, 42 Pitt Street, Barnsley,
South Yorkshire, S70 1BB. Tel: 01226 205 154.
Fax: 01226 734 973.
Internet: www.paulhowley.com.**
Barnsley Hospice Appeal   7.58

**PAWLEY & MALYON, 15 Bedford Square,
London, WC1B 3JA. Tel: 020 7462 9020.
Fax: 020 7462 9040.
E-mail: paul.neville@pawley-malyon.com.
Internet: www.pawley-malyon.com.**
Derek Butler Trust, The   7.198

**PEM, Salisbury House, Station Road,
Cambridge, Cambridgeshire, CB1 2LA.
Tel: 01223 728222. Fax: 01223 461424.
E-mail: jcoplowe@pem.co.uk.
Internet: www.pem.co.uk.**

PEM are a leading provider of audit and
advisory services to the charity and not
for profit sector. With over 140 years of
experience our clients are in good
company - we're accountants for two
thirds of the Cambridge University
Colleges, science research institutions,
academies and independent schools.

We understand that the ever-changing
legal and regulatory environment of this
sector requires proactive advisers. Our
dedicated team are on hand to provide
specialist advice tailored to your
organisation's specific requirements.

Charity specialists: Paul Chapman. Laragh Jeanroy.
Judith Coplowe.
Association for Cultural Exchange Ltd   7.46
Cambridge Arts Theatre Trust Ltd, The   7.108
Cambridge Crystallographic Data Centre   7.108
Cambridge Union Society, The   7.109
Company of Biologists Limited   7.168
Countryside Restoration Trust   7.182
Evelyn Trust   7.242
Fauna & Flora International   7.249
Foundation of Edward Storey   7.260
Girton Town Charity   7.275
Harris (Belmont) Charity   7.303
Henry Moore Foundation   7.309
Mrs L D Rope Third Charitable Settlement   7.438
Ogden Trust   7.479
Ormiston Families   7.484
Sir Halley Stewart Trust   7.610
SOS Children's Villages UK   7.628
Sports Aid Trust   7.633
Talisman Charitable Trust   7.668

**PITT GODDEN AND TAYLOR, Brunel House,
George Street, Gloucester, Gloucestershire,
GL1 1BZ. Tel: 01452 308153. Fax: 01452
309859. E-mail: mike.godden@pg-t.co.uk.
Internet: www.pittgoddentaylor.co.uk.
Charity specialists:** M Godden.
Sylvanus Lysons Charity   7.667
Trustees of the Bernadine Sisters Charity   7.689

**PJE, First Floor, Storws Fawr, Drury Lane,
Aberaeron, Ceredigion, SA46 0BP. Tel: 01545
571000. Fax: 08709 223296.
E-mail: info@pje.co.uk. Internet: www.pje.co.uk.**
Mudiad Meithrin   7.438

PJE, 4 Clifton Road, Clifton, Bristol, BS8 1AG.
Andrew Anderson Trust   7.31

**PJE, 23 College Street, Lampeter, Ceredigion,
SA48 7DY. Tel: 01570 423773. Fax: 08709
223296. E-mail: info@pje.co.uk.
Internet: www.pje.co.uk.**
Urdd Gobaith Cymru   7.701

PKF Cooper Parry
Discover the difference

**PKF COOPER PARRY, Sky View, Argosy Road,
East Midlands Airport, Castle Donington, East
Midlands, DE74 2SA. Tel: 01332 411163.
E-mail: simona@pkfcooperparry.com.
Internet: www.pkfcooperparry.com.**

PKF Cooper Parry is the largest
independent firm of Chartered
Accountants and business advisers in
the Midlands and was recently
announced in The Sunday Times 100
Best Small Companies to work for 2016.

We are a team of 350 passionate
people, delivering a broad spectrum of
professional business services, up-to-the
minute technical expertise and personal
advice to charities, voluntary
organisations, businesses and
individuals across the Midlands, UK and
Internationally.

How can we help

Our dedicated not-for-profit team
services over 100 charities. Our team is
made up of 2 partners and 3 managers
all having a passion for the sector. In
addition several of the partners act as
trustees of local charities and not-for-
profit organisations.

Our service range includes:
• audit and compliance;
• independent examination;
• grant audits;
• governance reviews;
• risk assessment and mitigation;
• charities SORP advice;
• VAT and taxation advice;
• payroll
• IT Solutions and Support
For further information please contact
Simon Atkins,
simona@pkfcooperparry.com

Charity specialists: Simon Atkins.
1893 Derby RSD Company   7.2
Air Ambulance Service   7.20
Baron Davenport's Charity   7.58
BID Services   7.69
Camden Society   7.109
G J W Turner Trust   7.268
Harborne Parish Lands Charity   7.301
Midland Mencap   7.426
Midlands Arts Centre   7.426
Millennium Point Trust   7.428
Murray Hall Community Trust   7.439
Portland College   7.509
Royal School for the Deaf Derby   7.570
St Martin's Trust   7.649
Thera Trust   7.676
Westhill Endowment   7.722
Woodbrooke Quaker Study Centre   7.737
Worcestershire YMCA Limited   7.738

PKF COOPER PARRY, No.8 Calthorpe Road, Edgbaston, Birmingham, West Midlands, B15 1QT. Tel: 0121 456 4456.
E-mail: simona@pkfcooperparry.com.
Internet: www.pkfcooperparry.com.

PKF LITTLEJOHN LLP, 1 Westferry Circus, Canary Wharf, London, E14 4HD. Tel: 020 7516 2200. Fax: 020 7516 2400.
E-mail: smorrison@pkf-littlejohn.com.
Internet: www.pkf-littlejohn.com.
Charity specialists: Sarah Morrison.

Conciliation Resources	7.170
East End Community Foundation	7.221
Harrow Development Trust	7.303
Hedley Foundation Limited	7.307
Jewish Community Secondary School Trust	7.354
John Horseman Trust, The	7.358
John Lyon's Charity	7.359
Medical Research Council Technology	7.419
Royal Hospital Chelsea Appeal Ltd	7.561

PLUMMER PARSONS, 18 Hyde Gardens, Eastbourne, East Sussex, BN21 4PT. Tel: 01323 641200. Fax: 01323 641767.
E-mail: Eastbourne@plummer-parsons.co.uk.
Internet: www.plummer-parsons.co.uk.
Charity specialists: J Marshall.

Charity of the Congregation of Our Lady	7.129

PM+M SOLUTIONS FOR BUSINESS LLP, Greenbank Technology Park, Challenge Way, Blackburn, Lancashire, BB1 5QB. Tel: 01254 679131. Fax: 01254 681759.
E-mail: blackburn@pmm.co.uk.
Internet: www.pmm.co.uk.

Hospice Care for Burnley and Pendle	7.318

PRENTIS & CO, 115c Milton Road, Cambridge, Cambridgeshire, CB4 1XE. Tel: 01223 352024. Fax: 01223 364317.
Charity specialists: N A Prentis.

British Medical Association Scholarship	7.96
Imperial Society of Teachers of Dancing	7.329
Needham Research Institute	7.456

PRICE & COMPANY, 30-32 Gildredge Road, Eastbourne, East Sussex, BN21 4SH. Tel: 01323 639661. Fax: 01323 738198.
E-mail: advice@price.co.uk.
Internet: www.price.co.uk.
Charity specialists: Tim Firth.

Catherine Cookson Charitable Trust	7.118
St Wilfrid's Hospice (Eastbourne)	7.655

PRICE BAILEY, 7th Floor Dashwood House, 69 Old Broad Street, London, EC2M 1QS. Tel: 020 7065 2660.
E-mail: helena.wilkinson@pricebailey.co.uk.
Internet: www.pricebailey.co.uk.
Charity specialists: Daren Moore. Richard Vass. Gary Miller. Helena Wilkinson.

Mission to Seafarers	7.430
Westminster Drug Project	7.722

PRICE BAILEY, Causeway House, 1 Dane Street, Bishop's Stortford, Hertfordshire, CM23 3BT. Tel: 0800 434 6460. Fax: 01279 755417.
E-mail: helena.wilkinson@pricebailey.co.uk.
Internet: www.pricebailey.co.uk.
Charity specialists: Mr D Moore. Richard Vass. Gary Miller. Helena Wilkinson.

Allan Nesta Ferguson Charitable Trust	7.25
Harlow Health Centres Trust Ltd	7.302

PRICE BAILEY, Tennyson House, Cambridge Business Park, Cambridge, Cambridgeshire, CB4 0WZ. Tel: 01223 565035.
E-mail: helena.wilkinson@pricebailey.co.uk.
Internet: www.pricebailey.co.uk.
Charity specialists: Gary Miller. Mr D Moore. Richard Vass. Helena Wilkinson.

East Anglia's Children's Hospices	7.220
Wood Green Animal Shelters	7.736

PRICE BAILEY, Richmond House, Broad Street, Ely, Cambridgeshire, CB7 4AH. Tel: 01353 662892. Fax: 01353 666873.
E-mail: helena.wilkinson@pricebailey.co.uk.
Internet: www.pricebailey.co.uk.
Charity specialists: Richard Vass. Gary Miller. Helena Wilkinson.

Thomas Parsons Charity	7.677

PRICE BAILEY, 20 Central Avenue, St Andrews Business Park, Thorpe St Andrew, Norwich, Norfolk, NR7 0HR. Tel: 01603 709330. Fax: 01603 709331.
E-mail: helena.wilkinson@pricebailey.co.uk.
Internet: www.pricebailey.co.uk.
Charity specialists: Gary Miller. Mr D Moore. Richard Rass. Helena Wilkinson.

Thursford Collection, The	7.680

PRICEWATERHOUSECOOPERS LLP, 7 More London, London, SE1 2RT. Tel: 020 7583 5000. Fax: 020 7804 1003.
E-mail: liz.m.hazell@uk.pwc.com.
Internet: www.pwc.co.uk/eng/industries/charities.html.
Charity specialists: Ian Oakley-Smith (Head of Charity Sector Team). Amanda Berridge. Claire Eustace. Clive Everest. Jill Halford. Liz Hazell. David P Hurst. Keith Lawson. Kevin Lowe. Amanda Lyons. Antony Timmins. Fiona Westwood. David Wildey. Andrew Woolf.

Action for Blind People	7.10
Action on Hearing Loss	7.11
Atlantic Charitable Trust	7.48
British Heart Foundation	7.93
Cancer Research UK	7.112
Charity of Sir Richard Whittington	7.129
Church of England Pensions Board	7.148
Duke of Edinburgh's Award Intl Foundation	7.214
Duke of Edinburgh's Award	7.214
Earl of Northampton's Charity	7.219
Fidelity UK Foundation	7.252
Goldman Sachs Gives (UK)	7.280
Great Ormond St Hosp Children's Charity	7.285
Keswick Foundation	7.370
Leonard Cheshire Disability	7.385
Leverhulme Trade Charities Trust	7.386
Lloyds Foundation for England and Wales	7.395
LTA Trust, The	7.404
Macmillan Cancer Support	7.405
Mercers' Charitable Foundation	7.422
Paul Hamlyn Foundation	7.493
Plan International UK	7.505
Prince's Trust	7.514
Royal British Legion Industries Ltd	7.554
Royal National Institute of Blind People	7.566
Royal National Theatre	7.567
Scope	7.590
Somerset House Trust	7.627
South Bank Centre	7.628
Tennis Foundation	7.672
Thomson Reuters Foundation	7.678
University of Notre Dame (USA) in England	7.701
Vodafone Foundation, The	7.708
Wellcome Trust	7.718

PRICEWATERHOUSECOOPERS LLP, 1 Embankment Place, London, WC2N 6RH. Tel: 020 7583 5000. Fax: 020 7212 4652.
Internet: www.pwc.com.

Corporation of the Church House	7.180
Football Foundation	7.256
Independent Age	7.331
Leverhulme Trust	7.386
Marie Stopes International	7.410
Shell Foundation	7.603
WaterAid	7.715
Weizmann Institute Foundation	7.717

PRICEWATERHOUSECOOPERS LLP, Waterfront Plaza, 8 Laganbank Road, Belfast, County Antrim, BT1 3LR. Tel: 028 9024 5454. Fax: 028 9041 5600.
E-mail: martin.h.pitt@uk.pwc.com.
Internet: www.pwc.com.
Charity specialists: Martin Pitt.

Exceed Worldwide	7.243

PRICEWATERHOUSECOOPERS LLP, Cornwall Court, 19 Cornwall Street, Birmingham, West Midlands, B3 2DT. Tel: 0121 265 5000. Fax: 0121 265 5050.
E-mail: rachel.heald@uk.pwc.com.
Internet: www.pwc.com.
Charity specialists: Rachel Heald. Neil Philpott. Chris Hibbs.

Leicester Theatre Trust	7.383
Sears Group Trust	7.595
St Andrew's Healthcare	7.636

PRICEWATERHOUSECOOPERS LLP, 31 Great George Street, Bristol, BS1 5QD. Tel: 0117 930 7068. Fax: 0117 929 0519.
E-mail: fiona.westwood@uk.pwc.com.
Internet: www.pwc.com.
Charity specialists: Fiona Westwood. Mark Birtles. Martin Corbett. Paul Dalton. Steph Mustoe. Natalie Tarr.

Andrews Charitable Trust	7.32
At-Bristol Ltd	7.48
Bristol, Clifton, & West of England Zoo	7.89
Dutch Oak Tree Foundation	7.216
ICAN	7.327
James Tudor Foundation, The	7.351
National Trust	7.454
Quartet Community Foundation	7.519
Shaw Trust	7.599
Sustrans	7.666
Zurich Community (UK) Trust	7.753

PRICEWATERHOUSECOOPERS LLP, Abacus House, Castle Park, Cambridge, Cambridgeshire, CB3 0AN. Tel: 01223 460055. Fax: 01223 552300.
E-mail: adrian.james.bennett@uk.pwc.com.
Internet: www.pwc.com.
Charity specialists: Adrian Bennett. Hayley Clark. Liz Hazell.

Bell Educational Trust Ltd	7.64
Cambridge Commonwealth Trust	7.108
Cambridge Foundation	7.109
Forest Trust, The	7.257
Thalidomide Trust	7.674

PRICEWATERHOUSECOOPERS LLP, One Kingsway, Cardiff, CF10 3PW. Tel: 029 2023 7000. Fax: 029 2080 2400.
E-mail: kevin.a.williams@uk.pwc.com.
Internet: www.pwc.com.
Charity specialists: Kevin Williams.

Presbyterian Church of Wales	7.513
Representative Body of the Church in Wales	7.532
St James's Place Foundation	7.644

PRICEWATERHOUSECOOPERS LLP, One Spencer Dock, North Wall Quay, Dublin. Tel: 00353 1 6789999. Fax: 00353 1 7048600.
E-mail: teresa.harrington@ie.pwc.com.
Internet: www.pwcglobal.com.
Charity specialists: Teresa Harrington. Aisling Fitzgerald. Richard Sammon.

Chaseley Trust	7.135
Momentum Scotland	7.431

PRICEWATERHOUSECOOPERS LLP, Erskine House, 68-73 Queen Street, Edinburgh, EH2 4NH. Tel: 0131 226 4488. Fax: 0131 260 4008. E-mail: lindsey.paterson@uk.pwc.com.
Internet: www.pwc.com.
Charity specialists: Kenny Wilson. Gerard Seenan. Lindsey Paterson. Caroline Macefield. Magnus Aitken. Sarah Caldwell. Allan McGrath.

National Museums Scotland	7.451

PRICEWATERHOUSECOOPERS LLP, 141 Bothwell Street, Glasgow, G2 7EQ. Tel: 0141 355 4000. Fax: 0141 355 4005.
E-mail: lindsey.paterson@uk.pwc.com.
Internet: www.pwc.com.
Charity specialists: Gillian Collin. Lindsey Paterson. Kenny Wilson.

Beatson Institute for Cancer Research	7.62
Church of Scotland General Trustees	7.149
Church of Scot Uninc. Councils Cttees	7.149
Culture and Sport Glasgow	7.188
Loretto Care	7.403
Mary's Meals	7.415
National Galleries of Scotland	7.446
National Library of Scotland	7.448
Sense Scotland	7.597
VSA	7.709

PRICEWATERHOUSECOOPERS LLP, 2 Humber Quays, Wellington Street, Hull, HU1 2BN. Tel: 0148 222 4111. Fax: 0148 258 4120. E-mail: jeremy.thomlinson@uk.pwc.com. Internet: www.pwc.com. Charity specialists: Jeremy Thomlinson. Anthony Blackwell.

Sir James Reckitt Charity, The	7.611

PRICEWATERHOUSECOOPERS LLP, Benson House, 33 Wellington Street, Leeds, West Yorkshire, LS1 4JP. Tel: 0113 289 4000. Fax: 0113 289 4460. E-mail: anthony.blackwell@uk.pwc.com. Internet: www.pwc.com. Charity specialists: Anthony Blackwell.

Doncaster & Bassetlaw Hospitals Trust	7.204
Institute of Our Lady of Mercy, The	7.336
Sense - National Deafblind & Rubella Assoc	7.597

PRICEWATERHOUSECOOPERS LLP, 8 Princes Parade, St Nicholas Place, Liverpool, Merseyside, L3 1QJ. Tel: 0151 227 4242. Fax: 0151 227 4575. E-mail: rachel.mcilwraith@uk.pwc.com; nick.boden@uk.pwc.com. Internet: www.pwc.com. Charity specialists: Rachel Mcilwraith. Nick Boden.

Consumers' Association	7.178

PRICEWATERHOUSECOOPERS LLP, 101 Barbirolli Square, Lower Moseley Street, Manchester, Greater Manchester, M2 3PW. Tel: 0161 245 2000. Fax: 0161 245 2904. E-mail: ian.c.marsden@uk.pwc.com; nick.boden@uk.pwc.com. Internet: www.pwc.com. Charity specialists: Ian Marsden. Nick Boden. Claire Duce.

AQA Education	7.35
Christie Charitable Fund, The	7.146
Cogent SSC Limited	7.159
Royal Exchange Theatre Company	7.560

PRICEWATERHOUSECOOPERS LLP, Exchange House, Central Business Exchange, Midsummer Boulevard, Milton Keynes, Buckinghamshire, MK9 2DF. Tel: 01908 353000. Fax: 01908 353141. E-mail: stephen.eames@uk.pwc.com. Internet: www.pwc.com. Charity specialists: S Eames.

Milton Keynes Parks Trust Ltd	7.428

PRICEWATERHOUSECOOPERS LLP, 89 Sandyford Road, Newcastle upon Tyne, Tyne and Wear, NE1 8HW. Tel: 0191 232 8493. Fax: 0191 261 9490. E-mail: nicola.wright@uk.pwc.com. Internet: www.pwc.com. Charity specialists: Steve Simpson. Nicola Wright.

Comm Fdn (Tyne&Wear&Northumberland)	7.164
Foundation of Light	7.260
National Energy Action	7.445
Newcastle Healthcare Charity	7.459
Newcastle Theatre Royal Trust	7.460
Newcastle upon Tyne Hospitals NHS Charity	7.460
St Cuthberts Care	7.641
William Leech Charity	7.730
William Leech Charity Trust	7.730
William Leech Foundation Trust	7.731

PRICEWATERHOUSECOOPERS LLP, Princess Court, 23 Princess Street, Plymouth, Devon, PL1 2EX. Tel: 01752 267441. Fax: 01752 673514.

E-mail: heather.c.ancient@uk.pwc.com. Internet: www.pwc.com. Charity specialists: Heather Ancient.

Dartington Hall Trust, The	7.192

PRICEWATERHOUSECOOPERS LLP, 9 Greyfriars Road, Reading, Berkshire, RG1 1JG. Tel: 0118 959 7111. Fax: 0118 960 7700. E-mail: keith.evans@uk.pwc.com. Internet: www.pwc.com. Charity specialists: Keith Evans.

Jisc	7.355

PRICEWATERHOUSECOOPERS LLP, 1 East Parade, Sheffield, South Yorkshire, S1 2ET. Tel: 0114 272 9141. Fax: 0114 275 2573. Internet: www.pwcglobal.com.

Sheffield Galleries and Museums Trust	7.601

PRICEWATERHOUSECOOPERS LLP, 3 Ocean Way, Southampton, Hampshire, SO14 3JT. Tel: 023 8083 5164. E-mail: ian.wishart@uk.pwc.com. Internet: www.pwc.com.

Care South	7.114
Enham	7.236

PRICEWATERHOUSECOOPERS LLP, 10 Bricket Road, St Albans, Hertfordshire, AL1 3JX. Tel: 0172 784 4155. Fax: 0172 789 2333. E-mail: andrew.latham@uk.pwc.com. Internet: www.pwc.com. Charity specialists: Andrew Latham.

Ashridge (Bonar Law Memorial) Trust	7.44
Oxfam GB	7.486
Tesco Charity Trust	7.674

PRICEWATERHOUSECOOPERS LLP, The Atrium, 1 Harefield Road, Uxbridge, Middlesex, UB8 1EX. Tel: 01895 522000. Internet: www.pwc.com.

Laureus Sport for Good Foundation	7.380

PRINCECROFT WILLIS LIMITED, Towngate House, 2-8 Parkstone Road, Poole, Dorset, BH15 2PW. Tel: 01202 663600. Fax: 01202 663601. E-mail: nick.love@princecroftwillis.co.uk. Internet: www.princecroftwillis.co.uk. Charity specialists: Bill Law. N Love. J Smuland. Claire Walt.

Bournemouth Young Men's Christian Assoc	7.82
Diverse Abilities Plus Limited	7.202
Talbot Village Trust	7.668

PURCELLS, 4 Quex Road, London, NW6 4PJ. Tel: 020 7328 3272. Fax: 020 7328 2140. Internet: www.purcells.co.uk.

Entindale	7.237

QUINTAS PARTNERS, Heron House, Blackpool Park, Blackpool, Cork. Tel: +353 21 4641400. Fax: +353 21 4220055. E-mail: info@quintas.ie. Internet: www.quintas.ie.

Society of Mary Reparatrice	7.622

R A CLEMENT ASSOCIATES, 5 Argyll Square, Oban, Argyll and Bute, PA34 4AZ. Tel: 01631 562643. Fax: 01631 566043. E-mail: mail@raclement.co.uk. Internet: www.raclement.co.uk. Charity specialists: Duncan J Grout. Fiona McGlynn (Charity & Audit Partner). Shona F Wardrop (Charity Team Leader).

West Highland College UHI	7.720

R E JONES & CO, 132 Burnt Ash Road, Lee, London, SE12 8PU. Tel: 020 8318 1417. Fax: 020 8463 0340. E-mail: enquiries@rejonesandco.co.uk. Internet: www.rejonesandco.co.uk.

Amateurs Trust, The	7.29
EBM Charitable Trust	7.223
Enid Linder Foundation	7.236

Sandra Charitable Trust	7.586

R P SMITH & CO, 28 St Thomas's Road, Chorley, Lancashire, PR7 1HX.

Bootstrap Company (Blackburn)	7.80

RAFFINGERS STUART, 19-20 Bourne Court, Southend Road, Woodford Green, Essex, IG8 8HD. Tel: 020 8551 7200. Fax: 020-8551 0912. E-mail: info@raffingers-stuart.co.uk. Internet: www.raffingers-stuart.co.uk.

Bright Red Dot Foundation	7.88
Chabad Lubavitch UK	7.125

RANDALL & PAYNE, Chargrove House, Shurdington Road, Cheltenham, Gloucestershire, GL51 4GA. Tel: 01242 548600. Fax: 01242 548605. Internet: www.randall-payne.co.uk.

National Benevolent Charity, The	7.443

RAWLINSON & HUNTER, Eighth Floor, 6 New Street Square, New Fetter Lane, London, EC4A 3AQ. Tel: 020 7842 2000. Fax: 020 7842 2080. E-mail: mail@rawlinson-hunter.com. Internet: www.rawlinson-hunter.com.

Eighty Eight Foundation, The	7.228
Forster Foundation CIO, The	7.257
Ingram Trust	7.331
Rufford Foundation, The	7.577
Sterling Charity, The	7.658

RAWLINSONS, Ruthlyn House, 90 Lincoln Road, Peterborough, PE1 2SP. Tel: 01733 568321. Fax: 01733 341358. E-mail: mark.jacksons@rawlinsons.co.uk. Internet: www.rawlinsons.co.uk. Charity specialists: A Cox.

British Gas Energy Trust	7.93
Vivacity Culture & Leisure	7.708

RAYNER ESSEX LLP, Tavistock House South, Tavistock Square, London, WC1H 9LG.

Clydpride	7.158

RDP NEWMANS LLP, Lynwood House, 373/375 Station Road, Harrow, Middlesex, HA1 2AW. Tel: 020 8357 2727. Fax: 020 8357 2027. Internet: www.rdpnewmans.com.

Ahavat Shalom Charity Fund	7.19

REED SMITH, Copia House, Great Cliffe Court, Great Cliffe Road, Barnsley, South Yorkshire, S75 3SP.

Wentworth Castle & Stainborough Park Trust	7.719

REES POLLOCK, 35 New Bridge Street, London, EC4V 6BW. Tel: 020 7778 7200. Fax: 020 7329 6408. Internet: www.reespollock.co.uk.

Claude and Sofia Marion Foundation, The	7.155

REESRUSSELL LLP, 37 Market Square, Witney, Oxfordshire, OX28 6RE.

Betel of Britain	7.67
Ditchley Foundation, The	7.202
Guiting Manor Amenity Trust	7.292
Lifeline Community Projects	7.388

RIBCHESTERS, 67 Sadler Street, Durham, County Durham, DH1 3NP. Tel: 0191 384 8581. Fax: 0191 383 0193. E-mail: office@ribchesters.co.uk. Internet: www.ribchesters.co.uk. Charity specialists: D Holloway.

Developing Initiatives, Support in Community	7.199

RICHARD PLACE DOBSON, 1-7 Station Road, Crawley, West Sussex, RH10 1HT. Tel: 01293 521191. Fax: 01293 614422. E-mail: darren@placedobson.co.uk. Internet: www.placedobson.co.uk.

RICHARDS SANDY PARTNERSHIP, THE,
Thorneloe House, 25 Barbourne Road,
Worcester, Worcestershire, WR1 1RU.

Ombersley Conservation Trust	7.480

RICKARD KEEN LLP, 9 Nelson St, Southend-on-
Sea, Essex, SS1 1EH. Tel: 01702 347771.
Fax: 01702 330951.
Internet: www.rickardkeen.com.

Prospects Learning Foundation Limited	7.517

ROBINSON REED LAYTON, Peat House,
Newham Road, Truro, Cornwall, TR1 2DP.
Tel: 01872 276116. Fax: 01872 222172.
E-mail: post@rrlcornwall.co.uk.
Internet: www.rrlcornwall.co.uk.

Hall for Cornwall Trust	7.296
Truro Diocesan Board Finance Ltd	7.687

ROBINSON RICE, 93 Banks Road, West Kirby,
Wirral, CH48 0RB. Tel: 0151 625 6647.
Internet: www.rra.uk.com.

Arch Initiatives	7.36

ROBSON LAIDLER LLP, Fernwood House,
Fernwood Road, Jesmond, Tyne and Wear,
NE2 1TJ. Tel: 0191 281 8191. Fax: 0191 281
6279. Internet: www.robson-laider.co.uk.

Beamish Museum Limited	7.62

RODNEY PITTS, 4 Fairways, 1240 Warwick
Road, Knowle, Solihull, West Midlands,
B93 9LL. Tel: 01564 779971. Fax: 01564
770499. Internet: www.rodneypitts.com.

Henry Barber Trust	7.308

ROFFE SWAYNE, Ashcombe Court, Woolsack
Way, Godalming, Surrey, GU7 1LQ. Tel: 01483
416232. Fax: 01483 426617.
E-mail: tkelly@roffeswayne.com.
Internet: www.roffeswayne.com.
Charity specialists: J Cleaver. J Fisher.

Anglo-Omani Society, The	7.32
Ian Karten Charitable Trust	7.326
Meath Epilepsy Trust	7.418
Watts Gallery	7.716

ROGERS SPENCER, Newstead House, Pelham
Road, Nottingham, Nottinghamshire, NG5 1AP.
Tel: 0115 960 8412. Fax: 0115 969 1878.
Internet: www.rogers-spencers.co.uk.

Bridge Estate	7.87

ROSTRONS, Yare House, 62-64 Thorpe Road,
Norwich, Norfolk, NR1 1RY. Tel: 01603
619166. Fax: 01603 619167.
E-mail: advice@rostron.com.
Internet: www.rostron.com.

Benjamin Foundation, The	7.66

ROTHMANS LLP, Chilworth Point, 1 Chilworth
Road, Southampton, Hampshire, SO16 7JQ.
Tel: 023 8021 1088.
Internet: www.rothmansllp.com.

FARA Foundation	7.248

ROUSE PARTNERS LLP, 55 Station Road,
Beaconsfield, Buckinghamshire, HP9 1QL.
Tel: 01494 675321. Fax: 01494 672290.
E-mail: info@rousepartners.co.uk.
Internet: www.rousepartners.co.uk.
Charity specialists: G Gaffney.

Dawliffe Hall Educational Foundation	7.195

ROWLAND HALL, 44-54 Orsett Road, Grays,
Essex, RM17 5ED. Tel: 01375 373828.
Fax: 01375 391375.
E-mail: rsnoxall@rowlandhall.co.uk.
Internet: www.rowlandhall.co.uk.

William Palmer College Educational Trust	7.731

ROWLANDS, Rowlands House, Portobello Road,
Birtley, Chester-le-Street, County Durham,
DH3 2RY. Tel: 0191 4112468.
Internet: www.rowlandsaccountants.co.uk.

Ballinger Charitable Trust	7.55

ROY PINNOCK & CO, 68 London Road, St
Albans, Hertfordshire, AL1 1NG. Tel: 01727
840361. Fax: 01727 840831.
E-mail: pinnockco@btinternet.com.
Internet: www.pinnockco.co.uk.

Royal Entomological Society of London	7.559

ROYCE PEELING GREEN, The Copper Room,
Deva Centre, Trinity Way, Manchester, Greater
Manchester, M3 7BG. Tel: 0161 608 0000.
Fax: 0161 608 0001. E-mail: info@rpg.co.uk.
Internet: www.rpg.co.uk.
Charity specialists: C Poston.

Federation of Jewish Services	7.250

RPG CROUCH CHAPMAN LLP, 62 Wilson Street,
London, EC2A 2BU. Tel: 020 7782 0007.
Fax: 020 7782 0939.
E-mail: admin@rpgcrouchchapman.co.uk.
Internet: www.rpgcrouchchapman.co.uk.
Charity specialists: K J Chapman. N M Heath.

JNF Charitable Trust	7.355
KKL Executor and Trustee Company Ltd	7.375
Moor House School	7.432

RSM, National Office, 25 Farringdon Street,
London, EC4A 4AB. Tel: 020 3201 8000.
Fax: 020 3201 8001.
E-mail: nick.sladden@rsmuk.com.
Internet: www.rsmuk.com.

Abbeycroft Leisure	7.4
Abbeyfield Kent Society, The	7.5
Acorns Children's Hospice Trust	7.9
Ahmadiyya Muslim Jamaat International	7.19
Aimwell Charitable Trust	7.20
Aldeburgh Music	7.23
Alternative Futures Group Ltd	7.27
Alzheimer's Research UK	7.28
Animal Health Trust	7.33
Anthony Nolan	7.34
Aspire Sports and Cultural Trust	7.45
Autism Sussex Ltd	7.50
Avenues East	7.51
Avenues London	7.51
Avenues South East	7.51
Avenues Trust Group, The	7.52
Beatson Oncology Centre Fund	7.63
bet365 Foundation	7.67
Birmingham Diocesan Board Finance	7.71
Birmingham Diocesan Trust	7.71
Birmingham Hippodrome Theatre Trust Ltd	7.72
Blatchington Court Trust	7.75
Box Moor Trust	7.82
Brandon Trust	7.84
Bristol Music Trust	7.90
Britten-Pears Foundation	7.100
Broadening Choices for Older People	7.100
Canterbury Oast Trust	7.113
Carr-Gomm Scotland	7.117
Centrepoint	7.124
Chartered Institute of Arbitrators	7.132
Chartered Institute of Taxation	7.134
Childwick Trust	7.142
Christadelphian Care Homes	7.144
Citizens Advice Scotland	7.152
City of Birmingham Symphony Orchestra	7.153
Community Options	7.167
Cottage and Rural Enterprises Limited	7.181
Coventry Diocesan Board of Finance	7.184
Creative and Cultural Industries Limited	7.184
Creative Skillset - Skillset Sector Skills Council	7.185
Culture Coventry	7.188
D'Oyly Carte Charitable Trust	7.191
Denville Hall	7.197
Dominican Council	7.203
Douglas Turner Trust	7.210
Dudley and W Midlands Zoological Society	7.213
Edinburgh Festival Fringe Society Ltd	7.225
Education Endowment Foundation, The	7.227
ExtraCare Charitable Trust	7.245
Farmington Trust	7.249
Focus Learning Trust	7.256
Fostering Network	7.258

George Gibson Almshouses Foundation	7.272
Gwyneth Forrester Trust	7.294
Hanover (Scotland) Housing Association	7.301
Haynes International Motor Museum	7.304
Healthcare Financial Management Association	7.306
Heritage Care	7.310
HF Trust Limited	7.311
Hillsong Church London	7.313
Homeless International	7.316
Horder Healthcare	7.317
Hospice in the Weald	7.319
Ian Askew Charitable Trust	7.326
Injured Jockeys Fund	7.331
Inspiring Scotland	7.332
Institute of Advanced Motorists	7.333
Institute of Materials, Minerals & Mining	7.336
Institute of Occupational Medicine	7.336
Institution of Engineering and Technology	7.338
Inst. of Occupational Safety & Health	7.339
Insurance Charities	7.339
International Centre for Life Trust	7.341
Jamie Oliver Food Foundation	7.351
Journalists' Charity	7.364
Keep Britain Tidy	7.367
Kings Place Music Foundation	7.373
Kingsway International Christian Centre	7.373
Land Restoration Trust	7.378
Lawes Agricultural Trust	7.380
Legal Education Foundation, The	7.383
LIONHEART	7.391
Liverpool Charity and Voluntary Services	7.392
Louis Baylis Charitable Trust	7.403
Margaret Blackwood Housing Association	7.409
Mary Kinross Charitable Trust	7.414
Mental Health Concern	7.421
Mental Health Matters	7.421
Methodist Church In Great Britain, The	7.423
Methodist Homes	7.424
Morden College	7.433
NABS	7.441
National Centre for Social Research	7.443
NEBOSH	7.445
National Trust for Scotland	7.453
Newham Training and Education Centre	7.460
North East Autism Society	7.466
North Music Trust	7.467
Panacea Society	7.490
Paul Mellon Centre for Studies British Art	7.493
Pickering & Ferens Homes	7.502
Porchlight	7.509
Printing Charity, The	7.514
Raystede Centre for Animal Welfare	7.527
Relate	7.530
Retail Trust	7.533
Roffey Park Institute	7.542
Rothamsted Research Ltd	7.546
Rothschild Archive Ltd	7.546
Royal Air Forces Association	7.551
Royal College of Psychiatrists	7.558
Royal Geographical Society	7.561
Royal Institution of Great Britain	7.562
Royal Shakespeare Company	7.571
Royal Society of Chemistry	7.572
Royal Society of Edinburgh	7.572
Royal Voluntary Service	7.575
Sandwell Leisure Trust	7.587
Savoy Educational Trust	7.588
Secular Clergy Common Fund	7.596
Society of Chemical Industry	7.622
Society of St Columban for Foreign Missions	7.623
Soil Association	7.625
Soka Gakkai International UK	7.625
Spiritualists National Union	7.632
Springboard Sunderland Trust	7.634
St Elizabeth Hospice (Suffolk)	7.642
St John of God Hospitaller Services Ltd	7.645
St Margaret's Somerset Hospice	7.649
St Michael's Hospice (North Hampshire)	7.651
St Nicholas Hospice Care	7.652
St Oswald's Hospice	7.653
Stonyhurst Charitable Fund	7.660
Structural Genomics Consortium	7.662
Suffolk Agricultural Association	7.663
Sutton Coldfield Municipal Charities	7.666
Sutton's Hospital in Charterhouse	7.666

Teesside Hospice Care Foundation	7.671
Thompson Family Charitable Trust	7.678
Twycross Zoo	7.691
UCKG HelpCentre	7.699
UCAS	7.699
Volant Charitable Trust	7.709
WCMC 2000	7.716
Wigmore Hall Trust	7.727
Wise Group	7.733
World Horse Welfare	7.740
Youth Sport Trust	7.751
Zoological Society of London	7.752

RSM, Vantage, Victoria Street, Basingstoke, Hampshire, RG21 3BT. Tel: 01256 312312. E-mail: basingstoke@rsmuk.com. Internet: www.rsmuk.com. Charity specialists: K Barwick. C Cairns.

Andrew Lloyd Webber Foundation, The	7.31
Anglo-European College of Chiropractic	7.32
Hope and Homes for Children	7.317
Loddon School Company	7.396

RSM, Ground Floor, 33-35 Cathedral Road, Cardiff, CF11 9HB. Tel: 02920 642200. Fax: 02920 642201. E-mail: cardiff@rsmuk.com. Internet: www.rsmuk.com.

National Library of Wales, The	7.449

RSM, Highfield Court, Tollgate, Chandlers Ford, Hampshire, SO53 3TY. Tel: 023 8064 6464. Fax: 023 8064 6666. E-mail: southampton@rsmuk.com. Internet: www.rsmuk.com. Charity specialists: K Edwards.

Find A Future	7.254
Valley Leisure	7.702

RSM, Highfield Court, Tollgate, Chandler's Ford, Eastleigh, Hampshire, SO53 3TY. Tel: 023 8064 6464. Internet: www.rsmuk.com.

Anvil Trust Ltd	7.34

RSM, First Floor, Quay 2, 139 Fountainbridge, Edinburgh, EH3 9QG. Tel: 0131 659 8300. Fax: 0131 221 8821. Internet: www.rsmuk.com.

Bield Housing Association	7.69

RSM, 2 Wellington Place, Leeds, West Yorkshire, LS1 4AP. Tel: 0113 244 5451. Fax: 0113 242 6308. E-mail: leeds.wellingtonplace@rsmuk.com. Internet: www.rsmuk.com. Charity specialists: Dr K G Chrystie - specialist area: Commercial.

APS	7.35
Foundation	7.258
Foundation for Credit Counselling	7.259
Martin House	7.413
N Police Convalescent & Treatment Centre	7.471
St George's Police Children Trust	7.643

RSM, Rivermead House, 7 Lewis Court, Grove Park, Leicester, Leicestershire, LE19 1SD. Tel: 0116 282 0550. Fax: 0116 282 0551. Internet: www.rsmuk.com. Charity specialists: Ian Monk. Katherine Allen.

Age UK Leicestershire & Rutland	7.18

RSM, The Poynt, 45 Wollaton Street, Nottingham, Nottinghamshire, NG1 5FW. Tel: 0115 948 9400. Fax: 0115 948 9401. E-mail: nottingham@rsmuk.com. Internet: www.rsmuk.com. Charity specialists: D J Parish (Audit Director).

Ashorne Hill Management College	7.44
British Psychological Society	7.97
Muslim Hands	7.441
National Institute of Adult Education	7.448

RSM, 88-96 Market Street West, Preston, Lancashire, PR1 2EU. Tel: 01772 202 655. Fax: 01772 202 631. Internet: www.rsmuk.com.

Birtenshaw	7.73
Derian House Children's Hospice	7.198
Sisters of the Cross and Passion	7.615

RSM, Unit 15, Aquarium, 1 - 7 King Street, Reading, Berkshire, RG1 2AN. Tel: 0118 953 0350. Fax: 0118 953 0351. E-mail: reading@rsmuk.com. Internet: www.rsmuk.com.

Butchers & Drovers Charitable Inst	7.105
Slough Community Leisure	7.618
Thames Hospicecare	7.675
Walk the Walk Worldwide	7.712

RSM, Tenon House, Ferryboat Lane, Sunderland, Tyne and Wear, SR5 3JN. Tel: 0191 511 5000. Fax: 0191 511 5001. E-mail: sunderland@rsmuk.com. Internet: www.rsmuk.com. Charity specialists: I Corner.

Sherburn House Charity	7.604

RUSSELL BRENNAN KEANE BUSINESS ADVISORS, Chartered Accountants & Registered Auditor, 96 Lower Baggot Street, Dublin 2, Dublin.

Teresa Ball International Solidarity Fund	7.673

RUSSELL NEW, The Courtyard, Shoreham Road, Upper Beeding, Steyning, West Sussex, BN44 3TN. Tel: 01903 816699. Fax: 01903 816622. E-mail: info@russellnew.com. Internet: www.russellnew.com. Charity specialists: Dawn James.

Guild Care	7.291
Masonic Samaritan Fund	7.415
Royal Masonic Hospital Charity	7.565

RYECROFT GLENTON, 32 Portland Terrace, Newcastle upon Tyne, Tyne and Wear, NE2 1QP. Tel: 0191 281 1292. Fax: 0191 212 0075. E-mail: charities@ryecroft-glenton.co.uk. Internet: www.ryecroft-glenton.co.uk. Charity specialists: D Anderson.

Lord Crewe's Charity	7.402
Percy Hedley Foundation	7.497
Sir James Knott Trust	7.610
Vardy Foundation	7.703

S SYEDAIN & CO, Heron House, 2nd Floor, 109 Wembley Hill Road, Wembley, Middlesex, HA9 8DA. Tel: 020 8903 5593.

Edhi International Foundation UK	7.224

SADOFSKYS CHARTERED ACCOUNTANTS, Princes House, Wright Street, Hull, East Riding of Yorkshire, HU2 8HX. Tel: 01482 228488. Fax: 01482 228489.

Joseph & Annie Cattle Trust	7.362

Saffery Champness
CHARTERED ACCOUNTANTS

SAFFERY CHAMPNESS, 71 Queen Victoria Street, London, EC4V 4BE. Tel: 0207 841 4000. Fax: 0207 841 4100. E-mail: charities@saffery.com. Internet: www.saffery.com.

Saffery Champness is a Top 20 firm of chartered accountants with a 160-year history. This gives it a strong culture and long-term focus that makes the firm unlike other accounting practices.

Saffery Champness' national Not-for-Profit Team operates from offices in London, Bournemouth, Bristol, Edinburgh, Harrogate, High Wycombe, and Peterborough. The firm advises over 300 charities and other not-for-profit entities in the UK on tax, VAT and accounting issues, and provides a risk-based audit for many. Clients range from new start-up charities to centuries-old livery companies, from clubs and membership organisations to social enterprises and service delivery charities, from grantgivers and endowed foundations to theatres and cultural organisations.

Charity specialists: Liz Hazell (Head of Not-for-Profit Practice). Cara Turtington. John Shuffrey. Alison Hone (VAT). Mark McGarry (Tax). Russell Moore (VAT).

4Children	7.3
Architects Benevolent Society	7.38
Bible & Gospel Trust	7.69
Brook Young People	7.101
Burghley House Preservation Trust	7.104
Chatsworth House Trust	7.136
Chief Fire Officers Association, The	7.139
Colyer-Fergusson Charitable Trust	7.161
Contemporary Dance Trust	7.178
De Haan Charitable Trust	7.195
Donmar Warehouse Projects	7.207
Dorothy Kerin Trust	7.208
Dowager Countess Eleanor Peel Trust	7.210
Drapers' Charitable Fund	7.211
Drapers Charities Pooling Scheme	7.211
Duchy of Lancaster Benevolent Fund	7.213
Duchy of Lancaster Jubilee Trust	7.213
Duke of Devonshire's Charitable Trust	7.213
Dyers Company Charitable Trust	7.217
Englefield Charitable Trust	7.234
Eranda Foundation	7.238
Fishmongers' Company's Charitable Trust	7.255
Foundation Trust Network, The	7.261
Future of Russia Foundation	7.267
Gilbert Trust for the Arts	7.274
Grace Trust, The	7.283
Grenadier Guards Charity, The	7.288
Haberdashers' Benevolent Foundation, The	7.295
Haberdashers' Educational Foundation	7.295
Hackney Empire	7.295
Hughes Travel Trust	7.323
Lawrence Atwell's Charity	7.380
Linbury Trust	7.389
Lyric Hammersmith	7.404
Merchant Taylors' Consolidated Charities	7.422
National Rifle Association	7.451
Patrick & Helena Frost Foundation, The	7.492
RAC Foundation for Motoring	7.522
Rothschild Foundation (Hanadiv) Europe	7.547

Rothschild Foundation	7.547
Royal Academy of Dramatic Art	7.549
Royal Artillery Charitable Fund, The	7.552
Royal Society of Wildlife Trusts	7.573
Royal Trinity Hospice	7.574
Ruddock Foundation for the Arts	7.577
Sir Andrew Judd Foundation	7.609
Stonewall Equality Ltd	7.660
Thomas Howell's Trust	7.677
Variety the Children's Charity	7.703

SAFFERY CHAMPNESS, Midland House, 2 Poole Road, Bournemouth, Dorset, BH2 5QY. Tel: 01202 204 744. Fax: 01202 204 745. Internet: www.saffery.com. Charity specialists: David Macey. Nick Fernyhough.

Autistic Wessex	7.50
Sailors Society	7.581
Valentine Charitable Trust, The	7.702

SAFFERY CHAMPNESS, St Catherine's Court, Berkeley Place, Clifton, Bristol, BS8 1BQ. Tel: 0117 915 1617. Fax: 0117 915 1618. Internet: www.saffery.com. Charity specialists: Michael Strong.

Hispanic Luso Brazilian Council	7.313
Watershed Arts Trust Limited	7.715

SAFFERY CHAMPNESS, Edinburgh Quay, 133 Fountainbridge, Edinburgh, EH3 9BA. Tel: 0131 221 2777. Fax: 0131 221 2778. Internet: www.saffery.com. Charity specialists: Kenneth McDowell. Max Floydd. Jamie Younger.

Buccleuch Living Heritage Trust, The	7.103
Crerar Hotels Trust, The	7.185
Dovecot Foundation	7.210

SAFFERY CHAMPNESS, Mitre House, North Park Road, Harrogate, North Yorkshire, HG1 5RX. Tel: 01423 568012. Fax: 01423 501798. Internet: www.saffery.com. Charity specialists: Alison Robinson.

Ampleforth Abbey Trust	7.30
Yorkshire Wildlife Trust	7.749

SAFFERY CHAMPNESS, Fox House, 26 Temple End, High Wycombe, Buckinghamshire, HP13 5DR. Tel: 01494 464 666. Fax: 01494 459 618. Internet: www.saffery.com. Charity specialists: Karen Bartlett.

College Estate Endowment Charity, The	7.160
Guild Estate Endowment	7.291
Horse Trust	7.318
Stratford Upon Avon Town Trust	7.661

SAFFERY CHAMPNESS, Unex House, Bourges Boulevard, Peterborough, PE1 1NG. Tel: 01733 353 300. Fax: 01733 353 301. Internet: www.saffery.com. Charity specialists: Jane Hill.

Wildlife Trust BCNP, The	7.728

SAGARS ACCOUNTANTS LTD, Gresham House, 5-7 St Paul's Street, Leeds, West Yorkshire, LS1 2JG. Tel: 0113 297 6789. Fax: 0113 297 6790. E-mail: s.seaman@sagars.co.uk. Internet: www.sagars.co.uk. Charity specialists: C Jones.

Leeds Grand Theatre and Opera House	7.382

SAGE & COMPANY, 102 Bowen Court, St Asaph Business Park, St Asaph, Denbighshire, LL17 0JE. Tel: 01745 586360. Fax: 01745 586370. E-mail: info@sageco.co.uk. Internet: www.sageco.co.uk.

St Asaph Diocesan Board of Finance	7.638

SAINT & CO, 26 High Street, Annan, Dumfries and Galloway, DG12 6AJ. Tel: 01461 202732. Fax: 01461 201212. E-mail: annan@saint.co.uk. Internet: www.saint.co.uk.

Holywood Trust	7.315

SAMPSON WEST, Mitre House, 12-14 Mitre Street, London, EC3A 5BU. Tel: 020 7404 5040. Fax: 020 7404 5977. E-mail: finance@sampsonwest.co.uk. Internet: www.sampsonwest.co.uk.

John Armitage Charitable Trust	7.357

SANDERS & ASSOCIATES, 100 Ashmill Street, London, NW1 6RA. Tel: 020 7569 7160. Fax: 020 7224 9762. Internet: www.sandersandassociates.co.uk.

Congregation of Our Lady of Sion	7.172

SAYER VINCENT, 8 Angel Gate, City Road, London, EC1V 2SJ. Tel: 020 7841 6360. Fax: 0870 458 7455. E-mail: svinfo@sayervincent.co.uk. Internet: www.sayervincent.co.uk.

ActionAid	7.12
Affinity Trust	7.15
AKO Foundation	7.21
Alcohol Research UK	7.23
Ambitious about Autism	7.29
Aquarius Action Projects	7.36
Arthritis Care	7.40
Article 19 Research & Information Centre	7.41
Baring Foundation	7.57
Barrow Cadbury Trust	7.59
Bishopsgate Foundation	7.73
Brendoncare Foundation	7.87
British Institute of Innkeeping	7.94
British Lung Foundation	7.96
Buttle Trust	7.106
Camphill Village Trust Limited	7.111
Carers UK	7.115
College of Estate Management	7.160
College Optometrists	7.160
Community Links Trust	7.165
Community of St Mary at the Cross	7.166
Compton Verney	7.169
Concern Universal	7.170
Contact a Family	7.178
Crisis	7.186
CSV	7.187
Disasters Emergency Committee	7.202
Earl Mountbatten Hospice	7.219
Edge Foundation	7.224
Equinox Care	7.237
Father Hudson's Society	7.249
Fellowship of School of Economic Science	7.251
Forum for the Future, The	7.258
Fremantle Trust	7.264
Friends Provident Charitable Foundation	7.266
Greenpeace Environmental Trust	7.287
Havens Christian Hospice	7.304
HelpAge International	7.308
Hospice UK	7.320
Institution of Eng Technology Ben Fund	7.338
Intl Network for Availability Of Scientific Pub	7.344
Joseph Rowntree Charitable Trust	7.363
Keech Hospice Care	7.367
LankellyChase Foundation, The	7.379
London Early Years Foundation, The	7.398
Medical Aid for Palestinians	7.418
Money Advice Trust	7.431
Movember Europe	7.436
North Devon Hospice	7.466
Oakhaven Trust	7.476
Phyllis Tuckwell Memorial Hospice	7.501
Pony Club	7.508
Responsible Gambling Trust	7.532
Richard Cloudesley's Charity	7.536
RoyalCol.of Obstetricians & Gynaecologists	7.556
Royal College of Ophthalmologists	7.556
Royal College of Radiologists	7.558
Royal Institute of British Architects	7.562
Send a Cow	7.596
SHELTER	7.603
SHP	7.606
Sir John Cass's Foundation	7.611
Solace Women's Aid	7.625
St Michael's Hospice	7.651
Three C's Support	7.679
Thurrock Community Leisure	7.680
Toynbee Hall	7.684

Tudor Trust	7.690
UNICEF-UK	7.694
Vista	7.707
Walsingham	7.713
Wessex Children's Hospice Trust	7.719
Whizz-Kidz	7.726
YWCA England & Wales	7.752

SAYER VINCENT, King's House, Orchard Street, Bristol, BS1 5EH. Tel: 0117 905 5002. Fax: 0117 905 5386. E-mail: svinfo@sayervincent.co.uk. Internet: www.sayervincent.co.uk.

British Small Animal Veterinary Assoc	7.99
Meningitis Now	7.421

SAYERS BUTTERWORTH LLP, 3rd Floor, 12 Gough Square, London, EC4A 3DW. Tel: 020 7936 1910. Fax: 020 7936 4161. E-mail: mwright@sayersb.co.uk. Internet: www.sayersb.co.uk. Charity specialists: M Wright.

Africa Educational Trust	7.15
Belvedere Trust	7.64
Roger Raymond Charitable Trust	7.542

SB&P LLP, 2-8 Oriel Road, Bootle, Merseyside, L20 7EP. Tel: 0151 922 4272. Fax: 0151 922 6780. E-mail: info@sb-p.co.uk. Internet: www.sb-p.co.uk.

Sacred Heart Fathers Trust	7.579

SCOTT VEVERS, 65 East Street, Bridport, Dorset, DT6 3LB. Internet: www.scottvevers.co.uk.

Alice Ellen Cooper-Dean Charitable Fndtn	7.24

SCOTT-MONCRIEFF, Exchange Place 3, Semple Street, Edinburgh, EH3 8BL. Tel: 0131 473 3500. Fax: 0131 473 3535. E-mail: gillian.donald@scott-moncrieff.com. Internet: www.scott-moncrieff.com.

Bethany Christian Trust	7.67
Centre for the Moving Image	7.124
Changeworks	7.127
Children 1st	7.140
Culture NL Limited	7.189
Eden Court Highlands	7.223
ELCAP	7.229
Enjoy East Lothian	7.237
Free Church of Scotland	7.264
General Teaching Council For Scotland	7.271
Horsecross Arts Ltd	7.318
Johnson & Johnson Corporate Citizenship Trust	7.361
MacRobert Trust	7.405
Medical Research Scotland	7.420
Mount Stuart Trust, The	7.436
Penumbra	7.496
Robertson Trust	7.541
Scottish Chamber Orchestra	7.592
Social Investment Scotland	7.620
West Lothian Leisure	7.721

SCOTT-MONCRIEFF, 25 Bothwell Street, Glasgow, G2 6NL. Tel: 0141 567 4500. Fax: 0141 567 4535. E-mail: gillian.donald@scott-moncrieff.com. Internet: www.scott-moncrieff.com.

City of Glasgow College Foundation	7.153
Clyde Gateway URC	7.157
Community Safety Glasgow	7.167
Erskine	7.239
Partners for Inclusion	7.492
Riverside Inverclyde	7.539
Royal Scottish National Orchestra	7.571
Scottish Ballet	7.591
Scottish Opera	7.592
Talbot Association Limited	7.668
Turning Point Scotland	7.691

SCRUTTON BLAND, Sanderson House, Museum Street, Ipswich, Suffolk, IP1 1HE. Tel: 01473 259201. Fax: 01473 231643. E-mail: mail@scruttonbland.co.uk. Internet: www.scruttonbland.co.uk.

Lord Belstead Charitable Trust, The	7.402

SHAIK & CO. LTD, 1145 Oldham Road, Newton Heath, Manchester, Greater Manchester, M40 2FU. Tel: 0161 683 5591.

UK Islamic Mission   7.693

SHAW GIBBS, 264 Banbury Road, Summertown, Oxford, Oxfordshire, OX2 7DY. Tel: 01865 292200. Fax: 01865 292201. E-mail: gibbs.ox@dial.pipex.com. Internet: www.edmundgibbs.com. Charity specialists: S R Knowles.

Open Doors with Brother Andrew   7.480

SHEARS & PARTNERS, 88 Edgware Way, Edgware, Middlesex, HA8 8JS. Tel: 020 8238 2888.

Joshua Trust Group, The   7.364

SHEEN STICKLAND LLP, 7 East Pallant, Chichester, West Sussex, PO19 1TR. Tel: 01243 781255. Fax: 01243 788049. E-mail: chichester@sheen-stickland.co.uk. Internet: www.sheen-stickland.co.uk. Charity specialists: Trevor James - specialist area: Charities/Litigation Support. P Wright - specialist area: Charities/ Business Advice.

Bulldog Trust   7.104
F Glenister Woodger Trust, The   7.245
Hampshire & Isle of Wight Wildlife Trust   7.298
Hospital of the Blessed Mary   7.321
Merchant Navy Welfare Board   7.422
Shipwrecked Mariners' Society   7.605
Solent Mind   7.626

SHIPLEYS LLP, 10 Orange Street, Haymarket, London, WC2H 7DQ. Tel: 020 7312 0000. Fax: 020 7312 0022. E-mail: leeks@shipleys.com. Internet: www.shipleys.com.

London's Air Ambulance Ltd   7.400
River and Rowing Museum Foundation   7.539

SIMMONS GAINSFORD LLP, 52 New Town, Uckfield, East Sussex, TN22 5DE. Tel: 01825 746888. Fax: 01825 746899. E-mail: solutions@simmonsgainsford.co.uk. Internet: www.simmonsgainsford.co.uk.

Gurdjieff Society Limited, The   7.292

SIMMONS GAINSFORD LLP, 7/10 Chandos Street, Cavendish Square, London, W1M 9DQ. Tel: 020 7447 9000. Fax: 020 7447 9001. Internet: www.simmonsgainsford.co.uk. Charity specialists: M Pizer.

J Isaacs Charitable Trust   7.348

SIMPSON WREFORD & PARTNERS, Suffolk House, George Street, Croydon, Surrey, CR0 0YN. Tel: 020 8681 5500. Fax: 020 8681 8926. E-mail: info@simpsonwreford.com. Internet: www.simpsonwreford.com. Charity specialists: Nick Hunwick.

Lloyd's Benevolent Fund   7.395

SINCLAIR SCOTT, 3 Wellington Square, Ayr, South Ayrshire, KA7 1EN.

Great Steward of Scotland's Dumfries Hse Tst 7.285

SLATER JOHNSTONE, 3 Thimble Lane, Knowle, Solihull, West Midlands, B93 0LY. Tel: 01564 770089. Charity specialists: F Slater.

Central England Quakers (CEQ)   7.122
Polden Puckham Charitable Foundation   7.506

SMAILES GOLDIE, Regent's Court, Princess Street, Hull, HU2 8BA. Tel: 01482 326916. Fax: 01482 215009. E-mail: service@smailesgoldie.co.uk. Charity specialists: M Sharpley.

Burton Constable Foundation   7.105
North Humberside Hospice Project   7.466

SMITH & WILLIAMSON, 25 Moorgate, London, EC2R 6AY. Tel: 020 7131 8305. Fax: 020 7131 4001. E-mail: info@smith.williamson.co.uk. Internet: www.smith.williamson.co.uk.

Broadway Homelessness and Support   7.100
Central Young Men's Christian Association   7.123
Chatham Historic Dockyard Trust   7.135
Northampton County Council on Addiction   7.183
Croftlands Trust   7.187
Dulverton Trust   7.214
Eurocentres UK   7.241
FOUNDATION66   7.261
Housing for Women   7.322
J Paul Getty Jnr General Charitable Trust   7.349
London Cyrenians Housing   7.398
Parham Park Trust (1984)   7.491
Phoenix House   7.501
Richmond Fellowship   7.537
Rumi Foundation, The   7.577
Society of St James   7.623
St John's Winchester Charity   7.645
St Mungo Community Housing Association   7.652
Surrey Community Development Trust   7.665
Theatre Royal Bath Ltd   7.675
Thomas Pocklington Trust   7.678
Underwood Trust   7.694
YMCA Training   7.746

SMITH & WILLIAMSON, Portwall Place, Portwall Lane, Bristol, BS1 6NA. Tel: 0117 376 2229. Fax: 0117 376 2002. E-mail: matthew.maneely@smith.williamson.co.uk. Internet: www.smith.williamson.co.uk. Charity specialists: S Butt. M Maneely.

Eduserv   7.227

SMITH & WILLIAMSON, 1 Bishops Wharf, Walnut Tree Close, Guildford, Surrey, GU1 4RA. Tel: 01483 407104. Fax: 01483 407101. E-mail: adrian.wild@smith.williamson.co.uk. Internet: www.smith.williamson.co.uk. Charity specialists: Adrian Wild.

Rikkyo School in England Trust   7.538
Titsey Foundation   7.681

SMITH & WILLIAMSON, Old Library Chambers, 21 Chipper Lane, Salisbury, Wiltshire, SP1 1BG. Tel: 01722 434821. Fax: 01722 434801. E-mail: peter.treadgold@smith.williamson.co.uk. Internet: www.smith.williamson.co.uk. Charity specialists: P Treadgold.

Basil Samuel Charitable Trust   7.59

SMITH & WILLIAMSON, Imperial House, 18-21 Kings Park Road, Southampton, Hampshire, SO15 2AT. Tel: 023 8082 7600. Fax: 023 8082 7601. E-mail: julie.mutton@smith.williamson.co.uk. Internet: www.smith.williamson.co.uk.

Alabaré Christian Care Centres   7.22
Dorset Wildlife Trust   7.209

SMITH COOPER, Livery Place, 35 Livery Street, Colmore Business District, Birmingham, West Midlands, B3 2PB. Tel: 0121 236 6789. Internet: www.smithcooper.co.uk.

Church of God of Prophecy Trust   7.148
Witton Lodge Community Association   7.734

SMITH COOPER, 2 Lace Market Square, Nottingham, Nottinghamshire, NG1 1PB. Tel: 0115 945 4300. Fax: 0115 945 4305. Internet: www.smithcooper.co.uk.

Autism East Midlands   7.49

SMITH HODGE & BAXTER, Thorpe House, 93 Headlands, Kettering, Northamptonshire, NN15 6BL. Tel: 01536 514871. Fax: 01536 460575. E-mail: info@smith-hodge.co.uk. Internet: www.smith-hodge.co.uk.

Wicksteed Charitable Trust   7.727

SMITH PEARMAN, Hurst House, High Street, Ripley, Surrey, GU23 6AY. Tel: 01483 225457. Fax: 01483 211023.

E-mail: keith@smithpearman.com.
Internet: www.smithpearman.com.
Charity specialists: K Hardy. T Hardy.

St Clement Danes Holborn Estate Charity   7.641

SOBELL RHODES, Monument House, 215 Marsh Road, Pinner, Middlesex, HA5 5NE. Tel: 020 8866 2151.

Jewish Museum London   7.354

SOMERBYS, 30 Nelson Street, Leicester, Leicestershire, LE1 7BA. Tel: 0116 279 5700. Fax: 0116 279 5799. E-mail: advice@somerbys.co.uk. Internet: www.somerbys.co.uk.

Nat Soc CoE for Promoting Religious Ed   7.452
Ulverscroft Foundation   7.694

SPENCER FELLOWS & CO, 169 New London Road, Chelmsford, Essex, CM2 0AE. Tel: 01245 266831. Fax: 01245 492945. Internet: www.spencerfellows.co.uk. Charity specialists: R Harman.

Farleigh Hospice   7.248

SPENSER WILSON & CO, Equitable House, 55 Pellon Lane, Halifax, West Yorkshire, HX1 5SP. Tel: 01422 331001. Fax: 01422 365070. E-mail: enquiries@spenserwilson.co.uk. Internet: www.spenserwilson.co.uk.

Constance Green Foundation   7.177

SPOFFORTHS, One Jubilee Street, Brighton, Brighton & Hove, BN1 1GE. Tel: 01273 811 000. Fax: 01273 811 001. E-mail: brighton@spofforths.co.uk. Internet: www.spofforths.co.uk.

New England Company   7.457

SPOFFORTHS, 9 Donnington Park, 85 Birdham Road, Chichester, West Sussex, PO20 7AJ. Tel: 01243 787 627. Fax: 01243 532 757. E-mail: chichester@spofforths.co.uk. Internet: www.spofforths.co.uk.

Pargiter Trust   7.490
Royal Masonic Trust For Girls and Boys   7.565

SPOFFORTHS, Springfield House, Springfield Road, Horsham, West Sussex, RH12 2RG. Tel: 01403 253282. Fax: 01403 250926. E-mail: horsham@spofforths.co.uk. Internet: www.spofforths.co.uk. Charity specialists: P Lansberry.

Camelia Botnar Foundation   7.109
Marcela Trust, The   7.409

SPOFFORTHS, A2 Yeoman Gate, Yeoman Way, Worthing, West Sussex, BN13 3QZ. Tel: 01903 828 728. Fax: 01903 828 729. E-mail: worthing@spofforths.co.uk. Internet: www.spofforths.co.uk.

Bowerman Charitable Trust   7.82
Order St Augustine Mercy Jesus   7.483

STATUTORY AUDITORS LLP, Suite 2.9 Central House, 1 Ballards Lane, London, N3 1LQ. Tel: 020 7684 3434. Fax: 020 7100 0303. E-mail: info@statutoryauditors.co.uk. Internet: www.statutoryauditors.co.uk.

Brahma Kumaris World Spiritual UniversityUK 7.83

STEPHEN MICHAEL ASSOCIATES, 1st Floor, 3 More London Riverside, London, SE1 2RE. Tel: 020 7252 5567. Internet: www.stephenmichael.co.uk.

Redeemed Christian Church of God   7.528

STEPHENSON COATES, West 2, Asama Court, Newcastle upon Tyne, Tyne and Wear, NE4 7YD. Tel: 0191 256 7766. Fax: 0191 256 7676. E-mail: john@stephensoncoates.co.uk. Internet: www.stephensoncoates.co.uk. Charity specialists: J Stephenson.

JGW Patterson Foundation, The   7.355

STEPHENSON SMART & CO, Stephenson House, 15 Church Walk, Peterborough, PE1 2TP. Tel: 01733 343275. Fax: 01733 557157. E-mail: enquiries@stephensonsmart.com. Internet: www.stephensonsmart.com. Charity specialists: P Evans.

YMCA Norfolk	7.746

STEWART & COMPANY, Knoll House, Knoll Road, Camberley, Surrey, GU15 3SY. Tel: 01276 61203. Fax: 01276 25450. Charity specialists: P Stewart.

GroceryAid	7.289

STREETS LLP, Tower House, Lucy Tower Street, Lincoln, Lincolnshire, LN1 1XW. Tel: 0845 880 0320. Fax: 0845 880 0321. E-mail: info@streetsweb.co.uk. Internet: www.streetsweb.co.uk. Charity specialists: R Anderson.

Age UK Lincoln	7.18
Grimsthorpe and Drummond Castle Trust	7.288
Hospital of the Holy & Undivided Trinity	7.322
Lincoln Diocesan Trust Board Finance Ltd	7.389
Lincolnshire Agricultural Society	7.389

STYLES & CO, Heather House, 473 Warrington Road, Warrington, Cheshire, WA3 5QU. Tel: 01925 761 600. Fax: 01925 761 601. E-mail: mail@stylesandco.co.uk. Internet: www.stylesandco.co.uk.

St Rocco's Hospice	7.654
Wigan & Leigh Hospice	7.727

SUGARWHITE ASSOCIATES, 5 Windus Road, London, N16 6UT. Tel: 020 8880 8910.

Lolev Charitable Trust, The	7.396
Rontades Limited	7.544

SUMMERS MORGAN, Sheraton House, Lower Rd, Chorleywood, Rickmansworth, Hertfordshire, WD3 5LH. Tel: 01923 284212.

John Booth Charitable Foundation, The	7.357
New Wine Trust	7.458

TAIT WALKER CHARTERED ACCOUNTANTS, Bulman House, Regent Centre, Gosforth, Newcastle upon Tyne, Tyne and Wear, NE3 3LS. Tel: 0191 285 0321. Fax: 0191 284 9117. Internet: www.taitwalker.co.uk. Charity specialists: Simon Brown.

1989 Willan Charitable Trust	7.2
Age UK North Tyneside	7.18
Age UK Northumberland	7.18
Azure Charitable Enterprises	7.52
NECA	7.455
NETA Training Trust	7.457

TAYLORCOCKS, 3 Acorn Business Centre, Northarbour Road, Cosham, Portsmouth, Hampshire, PO6 3TH.

Bournemouth Healthcare Trust, The	7.81
Colt Foundation	7.161

TEAM AUDIT LLP, 161 College Street, St Helens, Merseyside, WA10 1TY.

Wrexham Diocesan Trust	7.742

THOMAS & YOUNG, 240-244 Stratford Road, Shirley, Solihull, West Midlands, B90 3AE.

Warwickshire Wildlife Trust	7.714

THOMAS BARRIE & CO LLP, Atlantic House, 1a Cadogan Street, Glasgow, G2 6QE. Tel: 0141 221 2257. Fax: 0141 221 1785. E-mail: contact@thomasbarrie.co.uk. Internet: www.thomasbarrie.co.uk. Charity specialists: P G Greig.

Christian Schools (Scotland)	7.145

THOMAS WESTCOTT, 26-28 Southernhay East, Exeter, Devon, EX1 1NS. Tel: 0139 228 8555. Fax: 0139 228 8556.

E-mail: exeter@thomaswestcott.co.uk. Internet: www.thomaswestcott.co.uk. Charity specialists: Sarah Watts.

Heathcoat Trust	7.307
Norman Family Charitable Trust	7.464
WESC Foundation	7.719

THOMPSON JENNER LLP, 28 Alexandra Terrace, Exmouth, Devon, EX8 1BD. Tel: 01395 279521. Fax: 01395 272384. E-mail: exmouth@tjllp.com. Internet: www.thompson-jenner.co.uk. Charity specialists: N Curtis.

South West Grid for Learning Trust	7.630

THORNE LANCASTER PARKER, Aldwych House, 81 Aldwych, London, WC2B 4HN. Tel: 020 7404 2161. Fax: 020 7831 2261. E-mail: nfo@tlpaccountants.co.uk. Internet: www.tlpaccountants.co.uk.

RMIG Endowment Trust	7.540

THORNE WIDGERY, 33 Bridge Street, Hereford, Herefordshire, HR4 9DQ. Tel: 01432 276393. Internet: www.thornewidgery.co.uk.

Hereford Diocesan Board Finance	7.309

THORNTON SPRINGER LLP, 67 Westow Street, London, SE19 3RW. Tel: 020 8771 8661. Fax: 020 8771 4623. E-mail: ts@thorntonspringer.co.uk. Internet: www.thorntonspringer.co.uk.

United Ref. Church Southern Prov. Trust ltd	7.697

TIDY BOND, 8a Hythe Street, Dartford, Kent, DA1 1BX.

Oasis Care and Training Agency (OCTA)	7.477

TLL ACCOUNTANTS, 7-9 Station Road, Hesketh Bank, Preston, Lancashire, PR4 6SN. Tel: 01772 812163. Fax: 01772 814411. E-mail: pbuck@tllaccountants.com. Internet: www.tllaccountants.com.

Age UK Lancashire	7.17
North West Air Ambulance	7.468
Oaklea Trust, The	7.477

TOMKINSON TEAL AND CO, Hanover Court, 5 Queen Street, Lichfield, Staffordshire, WS13 6QD. Tel: 01543 255612. Fax: 01543 415461.

Jaffray Care Society	7.349

TRANTER LOWE, 23 Tan Bank, Wellington, Telford, Shropshire, TF1 1HJ. Tel: 01952 244215. Fax: 01952 245371.

Science Museum Foundation	7.589

TREE ACCOUNTANCY LTD, 3 Kelvin Street, Manchester, Greater Manchester, M4 1ET. Tel: 0161 220 2920. Fax: 0161 220 2921. E-mail: hello@treeaccountancy.co.uk. Internet: www.treeaccountancy.co.uk.

Bauer Radio's Cash for Kids Charities	7.61

TRY LUNN & CO CHARTERED ACCOUNTANTS, Roland House, Princes Dock Street, Hull, HU1 2LD. Tel: 01482 325765.

Deflog V Q Trust Limited, The	7.196

TUDOR JOHN, Nightingale House, 46-48 East Street, Epsom, Surrey, KT17 1HQ. Tel: 01372 742323. Fax: 01372 745697. Internet: www.tudorjohn.co.uk. Charity specialists: D C S Nelson.

Artists' General Benevolent Institution	7.41
Barnes Workhouse Fund	7.57

T.W.TASKER F.C.A, 52A Station Road, Ashington, Northumberland, NE63 9UJ. Tel: 01670 852 342. Fax: 01670 522 282.

Coquet Trust, The	7.179

Charity specialists: Subarna Banerjee (National head of UHY charity & NFP group, partner). Colin Wright (Audit partner). Mark Giddens (Tax partner). Elizabeth Mitchell (Audit manager). Jodie Mulley (Tax manager).

Garfield Weston Foundation	7.269
Wolfson Family Charitable Trust	7.735
Wolfson Foundation	7.735

UHY HACKER YOUNG, St John's Chambers, Love Street, Chester, Cheshire, CH1 1QN. Tel: 01244 320532. Fax: 01244 505930. E-mail: chester@uhy-uk.com. Internet: www.uhy-uk.com. Charity specialists: John Ierston (Charity specialist partner). Nick Jenkins (Charity specialist partner).

Mrs D M France-Hayhurst Charitable Trust	7.437

UHY HACKER YOUNG, St James Building, 79 Oxford Street, Manchester, Greater Manchester, M1 6HT. Tel: 0161 236 6936. Fax: 0161 228 0117. E-mail: manchester@uhy-uk.com. Internet: www.uhy-uk.com. Charity specialists: David Symonds (Charity specialist partner).

StreetGames UK	7.662

UHY HACKER YOUNG, 22 The Ropewalk, Nottingham, Nottinghamshire, NG1 5DT. Tel: 0115 959 0900. Fax: 0115 947 0628. E-mail: j.warsop@uhy-uk.com. Internet: www.uhy-uk.com. Charity specialists: M Madin. J Warsop.

Nottingham Playhouse Trust Ltd	7.473

UHY HACKER YOUNG, Thames House, Roman Square, Sittingbourne, Kent, ME10 4BJ. Tel: 01795 475363. Internet: www.uhy-uk.com.

Ashdown Medway Accomodation Trust	7.43

UNW LLP, Citygate, St James' Boulevard, Newcastle upon Tyne, Tyne and Wear, NE1 4JE. Tel: 0191 243 6000. Internet: www.unw.co.uk. Charity specialists: Joanna Gray.

Durham Diocesan Board of Finance, The	7.216
Great North Air Ambulance Service	7.285
Newcastle Diocesan Board Finance	7.459
Northern Rock Foundation	7.471
Reece Foundation, The	7.529

VARSANI JOSEPH LTD, 18 The Broadway, East Lane, Wembley, Middlesex, HA9 8JU. Tel: 020 8904 2241. Fax: 020 8904 3766. Internet: www.varsani.com.

Shree Kutch Satsang Swaminarayan Temple	7.606

VENITT & GREAVES, 115 Craven Park Road, London, N15 6BL. Tel: 020 8802 4782.

Yesamach Levav	7.744

VOISEY & CO, 8 Winmarleigh Street, Warrington, Cheshire, WA1 1JW. Tel: 01925 650703. Fax: 01925 415295. E-mail: info@voisey.u-net.com.

Lady Hewleys Charity	7.376

W H PRIOR & SON, Railway Court, Doncaster, South Yorkshire, DN4 5FB. Tel: 01302 349271. Fax: 01302 322197. E-mail: whp@whprior.co.uk. Internet: www.whprior.co.uk. Charity specialists: A Prior.

Roman Catholic Diocese Hallam Trust	7.543

W J MATTHEWS & SON, 11-15 Bridge Street, Caernarfon, Gwynedd, LL55 1AB. Tel: 01286 673 555. Fax: 01286 678 733.

Isle of Anglesey Charitable Trust, The	7.347

WAGSTAFFS CHARTERED ACCOUNTANTS, Richmond House, Walkern Road, Stevenage, Hertfordshire, SG1 3QP. Tel: 01438 740074. Fax: 01438 741075. Internet: www.wags.co.uk.

Stevenage Leisure	7.658

WALES AUDIT OFFICE, 24 Cathedral Road, Cardiff, CF11 9LJ. Tel: 029 2026 2550. Fax: 029 2039 7070. Internet: www.audit-commission.gov.uk.

Amgueddfa Cymru	7.30
Arts Council of Wales, The	7.41
Cardiff and Vale Health Charity	7.113
Rhondda Cynon Taff Welsh Church Fund	7.535
Sports Council for Wales Trust	7.634

WALLWORK NELSON & JOHNSON, Chandler House, 7 Ferry Road Office Park, Riversway, Preston, Lancashire, PR2 2YH. Tel: 01772 430000. Fax: 01772 430012. E-mail: mail@wnj.co.uk. Internet: www.wnj.co.uk. Charity specialists: P Woodburn.

Caritas Care	7.115
Compton Verney Collection Settlement	7.169
Compton Verney Fund	7.170
Peter Moores Charitable Trust	7.499

WALTER HUNTER & CO, 24 Bridge Street, Newport, Gwent, NP20 4SF. Tel: 01633 265323. Fax: 01633 258431. E-mail: enquiries@walterhunter.co.uk. Internet: www.walterhunter.co.uk.

Gwent Assoc of Voluntary Organisation	7.294

WALTONS CLARK WHITEHILL LIMITED, Maritime House, Harbour Walk, The Marina, Hartlepool, Cleveland, TS24 0UX. Tel: 01429 234414. Fax: 01429 231263. E-mail: heather.odriscoll@waltonscw.co.uk. Internet: www.waltonscw.co.uk. Charity specialists: Louise Baker.

TTE Technical Training Group, The	7.690

WARREN & CO, Meadhaven, Church Lane, Bristol, BS48 3QF. Tel: 01275 464444. Fax: 01275 464444. Charity specialists: Ms L J Warren.

Milestones Trust	7.427

WATLING & HIRST, Cawley Place, 15 Cawley Road, Chichester, West Sussex, PO19 1UZ. Tel: 01243 783 818. Fax: 01243 531 939. E-mail: info@watlingandhirst.com. Internet: www.watlingandhirst.com.

Aldingbourne Trust	7.24

WATSON BUCKLE, York House, Cottingley Business Park, Bradford, West Yorkshire, BD16 1PE. Tel: 01274 516 700. Fax: 01274 516 755. Internet: www.watsonbuckle.co.uk.

Collegiate Charitable Foundation, The	7.161
Martin Foundation, The	7.413

WBV LIMITED, 33 Heathfield, Swansea, Dyfed, SA1 6HD.

St David's Diocesan Board of Finance	7.641

WELLERS, 1 Vincent Square, London, SW1P 2PN. Tel: 020 7630 6665. Fax: 020 7630 1977. E-mail: info.london@wellersaccountants.co.uk. Internet: www.wellersaccountants.co.uk.

Global Charities	7.277

WELLERS, 8 King Edward Street, Oxford, Oxfordshire, OX1 4HL. Tel: 01865 723131. Fax: 01865 726583. Internet: www.wellersaccountants.com.

Blenheim Foundation, The	7.75
Nuffield Oxford Hospitals Fund	7.474

WELSH WALKER CA, 179A Dalrymple Street, Greenock, Strathclyde, PA15 1BX. Tel: 01475 722233. Fax: 01475 888086. E-mail: info@welshwalker.co.uk. Internet: www.welshwalker.co.uk.

Inverclyde Leisure	7.345

WENN TOWNSEND, 5 Gosditch Street, Cirencester, Gloucester, Gloucestershire, GL7 2AG. Tel: 01285 659778. Fax: 01285 641265. Internet: www.wenntownsend.co.uk.

Cotswold Archaeological Trust	7.181

WENN TOWNSEND, 30 St Giles, Oxford, Oxfordshire, OX1 3LE. Tel: 01865 559900. Fax: 01865 310019. E-mail: information@wenntownsend.co.uk. Internet: www.wenntownsend.co.uk. Charity specialists: Graham Cole. Deborah Pluck.

Culham St Gabriel's Trust	7.188
Doris Field Charitable Trust	7.207
Dorneywood Trust, The	7.208
God's House in Ewelme	7.279
Guideposts Trust	7.291
Islamic Trust	7.347
Oxford Archaeological Unit Ltd	7.487
Oxford Centre Hebrew & Jewish Studies	7.487
Response Organisation	7.532
Sobell House Hospice Charity Limited	7.619
St Michael's and All Saints Charity	7.650

WHEAWILL & SUDWORTH, P O Box B30, 35 Westgate, Huddersfield, West Yorkshire, HD1 1PA. Tel: 01484 423691. Fax: 01484 518803. Internet: www.wheawills.co.uk. Charity specialists: D Butterworth.

Bridgewood Trust	7.88
Kirklees Active Leisure	7.374
Kirkwood Hospice	7.374

WHITEHEAD & HOWARTH, 327 Clifton Drive, Lytham St Annes, Lytham, Lancashire, FY8 1HN. Tel: 01253 725111. Fax: 01253 723631. E-mail: info@w-and-h.com. Internet: www.whaccountants.co.uk. Charity specialists: P Gibbons.

Ormerod Home Trust Limited	7.484

WHITELAW WELLS, 9 Ainslie Place, Edinburgh, EH3 6AT. Tel: 0131 226 5822. Fax: 0131 240 5498. E-mail: mail@whitelawwells.co.uk. Internet: www.whitelawwells.co.uk. Charity specialists: D A Main - specialist area: Charities and Tax.

Souter Charitable Trust	7.628

WHITING & PARTNERS, Norfolk House, Hamlin Way, King's Lynn, Norfolk, PE30 4NG. Tel: 01553 774745. Fax: 01553 775180. Internet: www.whitingandpartners.co.uk.

Starling Family Charitable Trust, The	7.656

WHITNALLS, Cotton House, Old Hall Street, Liverpool, Merseyside, L3 9TX. Tel: 0151 236 5028. Fax: 0151 236 2124. Internet: www.whitnalls.co.uk.

Sisters of Mercy-St Anthony's Convent	7.614

Whittingham Riddell

chartered accountants

**WHITTINGHAM RIDDELL LLP, Belmont House, Shrewbury Business Park, Shrewsbury, Shropshire, SY2 6LG. Tel: 01743 273 273. Fax: 01743 273 274.
Internet: www.whittinghamriddell.co.uk.**

Whittingham Riddell has a specialist team operating from offices in England and Wales which is dedicated to advising charities of all sizes; providing general accounting, taxation and governance advice and support. Our services also include year-end Statutory Audit, Independent Examinations and Assistance with Annual Return Completion and Submission.

Our extensive portfolio has enabled us to develop an in-depth knowledge of the accounting and broader issues consistent with this specialist sector. Our charities team offers a proactive service to our clients, which extends beyond the specifics of any engagement. In addition, we host an annual technical update seminar, publish newsletters and e-bulletins and deliver bespoke presentations and training workshops to suit the specific requirements of our clients.

Beacon Centre for the Blind	7.62
Bethphage Mission (Great Britain)	7.68
Derwen College	7.198
Field Studies Council	7.253
Garsington Opera	7.269
Hope House Children's Hospices	7.317
Weston Park Foundation	7.724
Wheler Foundation, The	7.725
Whitley Animal Protection Trust	7.726

**WHITTINGHAM RIDDELL LLP, Hafren House, 5 St. Giles Business Park, Newtown, Powys, SY16 3AJ. Tel: 01686 626230. Fax: 01686 621116.
Internet: www.whittinghamriddell.co.uk.**

Ymddiriedolaeth Clough Williams-Ellis Fdn	7.746

**WHITTLE & CO, Century House South, North Station Road, Colchester, Essex, CO1 1RE. Tel: 01206 762200. Fax: 01206 762210.
E-mail: mail@whittles.co.uk.
Internet: www.whittles.co.uk.
Charity specialists:** T Moriarty. Rachel Skells. R Ward. P Whittle.

Autism Anglia	7.49
Colchester Catalyst Charity	7.159
Special Air Service Regimental Association	7.632

**WILDER COE, 233-237 Marylebone Road, London, NW1 5QT. Tel: 020 7724 6060. Fax: 020 7724 6070.
E-mail: info@wildercoe.co.uk.
Internet: www.wildercoe.co.uk.**

Delapage Ltd	7.196

WILDIN & CO, King's Building, Lydney, Gloucestershire, GL15 5HE.

Hand in Hand International	7.300

WILKINS KENNEDY LLP, Bridge House, London Bridge, London, SE1 9QR. Tel: 020 7403 1877. Fax: 020 7403 1605.

**E-mail: charities@wilkinskennedy.com.
Internet: www.wilkinskennedy.com.
Charity specialists:** John Howard (Head of Not-for-Profit Group). Michelle Wilkes (Partner).

Baptist Union Corporation	7.56
Baptist Union of Great Britain	7.56
Intl Foundation for Aids to Navigation	7.342
Jean Sainsbury Animal Welfare Trust	7.352
R L Glasspool Charity Trust	7.522
Sangha Tri-National Trust Fund Ltd	7.587
Young Vic Company Limited	7.750

**WILKINS KENNEDY LLP, Greytown House, 221-227 High Street, Orpington, Kent, BR6 0NZ. Tel: 01689 827505. Fax: 01689 831478.
E-mail: charities@wilkinskennedy.com.
Internet: www.wilkinskennedy.com.**

Augustinians of the Assumption	7.48
Caldecott Foundation Limited	7.108
Embrace the Middle East	7.232
Family Fed for World Peace & Unification	7.247
JCA Charitable Foundation	7.351
London School for the Performing Arts	7.401
Ranyard Charitable Trust	7.526
St Saviour's Medical Charity	7.654
Strode Pk Foundation for Disabled People	7.662

**WILKINS KENNEDY LLP, Templars House, Lulworth Close, Chandlers Ford, Eastleigh, Hampshire, SO53 3TL. Tel: 023 8024 7070. Fax: 023 8024 7071.
Internet: www.wilkinskennedy.com.**

Poole Arts Trust	7.508

**WILKINS KENNEDY LLP, Mount Manor House, 16 The Mount, Guildford, Surrey, GU2 4HN. Tel: 01483 306 318. Fax: 01483 565 384.
Internet: www.wilkinskennedy.com.**

A S Charitable Trust	7.3

**WILKINS KENNEDY LLP, Athenia House, 10-14 Andover Road, Winchester, Hampshire, SO23 7BS. Tel: 01962 852 263. Fax: 01962 841 197.
E-mail: winchester@wilkinskennedy.com.
Internet: www.wilkinskennedy.com.**

Trustees of Congregattion of Most Holy Redeemer	7.544

**WILLIAM DUNCAN & CO, 30 Miller Road, Ayr, Strathclyde, KA7 2AY. Tel: 01292 265 071. Fax: 01292 610 246.
Charity specialists:** J Wallace. S J Bargh.

Ayrshire Hospice	7.52

WILLIAM FORTUNE & SON, Collingwood House, Hartlepool, Cleveland, TS24 7EN.

Hospital of God at Greatham	7.321

**WILLIAMS DENTON, 13 Trinity Square, Llandudno, Conwy, LL30 2RB. Tel: 01492 877478. Fax: 01492 874880.
E-mail: llandudno@williamsdenton.co.uk.
Internet: www.williamsdenton.co.uk.**

Cyngor Alcohol Information Service Limit	7.190
Ffestiniog & Welsh Highland Railways Trust	7.252

**WILLIAMS GILES, 12 Conqueror Court, Sittingbourne, Kent, ME10 5BH. Tel: 01795 478044. Fax: 01795 427757.
E-mail: admin@williamsgiles.co.uk.
Internet: www.williamsgiles.co.uk.**

Supported Fostering Services Charitable Trust	7.665

WILLIAMS ROSS, 4 Ynys Bridge Court, Gwaelod-y-Garth, Cardiff, CF15 9SS.

G C Gibson Charitable Trust	7.267

**WILLIAMSON & DUNN, 3 West Craibstone Street, Aberdeen, Grampian, AB11 6YW. Tel: 01224 581288. Fax: 01224 583948.
Internet: www.williamsonanddunn.com.
Charity specialists:** G Pye.

Cornerstone Community Care	7.180

WILLIAMSON MORTON THORNTON LLP, 45 Grosvenor Road, St Albans, Hertfordshire, AL1 3AW. Tel: +44 (0)1727 838255. Fax: +44 (0)1727 861052.

Dunhill Medical Trust	7.216

WILSON HENRY LLP, 145 Edge Lane, Liverpool, Merseyside, L7 2PF.

Royal Liverpool Philharmonic Society	7.563

**WILSON WRIGHT LLP, Thavies Inn House, 3-4 Holborn Circus, London, EC1N 2HA. Tel: 020 7832 0444. Fax: 020 7832 0400.
E-mail: kevin.maddison@wilsonwright.co.uk.
Internet: www.wilsonwright.com.**

Exilarch's Foundation	7.244
Imperial College Trust	7.329
Jewish Blind & Disabled	7.353

**WISE & CO, Wey Court West, Union Road, Farnham, Surrey, GU9 7PT. Tel: 01252 711 244. Fax: 01252 737 221.
E-mail: info@wiseandco.co.uk.
Internet: www.wiseandco.co.uk.
Charity specialists:** Mark Dickinson. Treena Turner. Amanda Thomas. Ghislaine Tradgett. Yvonne Harman. Liz McGrath. Elise Pullen.

Active Nation UK Ltd	7.12
Boltini Trust, The	7.78
British Kidney Patient Association	7.95

WM AUDIT LLP, Rauter House, 1 Sybron Way, Crowborough, Sussex, TN6 3DZ.

Peter Lang Children's Trust Limited	7.499

**WMT CHARTERED ACCOUNTANTS, Second Floor, 45 Grosvenor Road, St Albans, Hertfordshire, AL1 3AW. Tel: 0800 158 5829.
E-mail: info@wmtllp.com.
Internet: www.wmtllp.com.**

Emmott Foundation Ltd	7.232
National Assoc for Colitis and Crohn's	7.442

**WOODWARD HALE, 38 Dollar Street, Cirencester, Gloucestershire, GL7 2AN. Tel: 01285 659341. Fax: 01285 885511.
Charity specialists:** V Cowling

Blagrave Trust, The	7.74

**WRIGHT VIGAR LTD, 15 Newland, Lincoln, Lincolnshire, LN1 1XG. Tel: 01522 531341. Fax: 01522 546286.
E-mail: action@wrightvigar.co.uk.
Internet: www.wrightvigar.co.uk.**

Lincolnshire Wildlife Trust	7.390
Linkage Community Trust	7.390

**WRIGLEY PARTINGTON, Sterling House, 501 Middleton Road, Chadderton, Oldham, Greater Manchester, OL9 9LY. Tel: 0161 622 0222. Fax: 0161 627 5446.
Internet: www.wrigleypartington.co.uk.**

Positive Steps	7.510

**WYLIE & BISSET LLP, 168 Bath Street, Glasgow, G2 4TP. Tel: 0141 566 7000. Fax: 0141 566 7001. E-mail: jenny.simpson@wyliebisset.com.
Internet: www.wyliebisset.com.
Charity specialists:** Jenny Simpson.

East Kilbride District Eng Grp Training Assoc	7.221
Glasgow Simon Community	7.276
INCLUDEM	7.330
Jobs & Business Glasgow	7.356
Kibble Education and Care Centre	7.371
Prince and Princess of Wales Hospice	7.513
Queen's Cross Workspace	7.520
Royal Col. Physicians & Surgeons Glasgow	7.557
Sacro	7.580
Strathcarron Hospice	7.661
West Dunbartonshire Leisure Trust	7.720

BANKS AND THEIR CHARITY CLIENTS

ADAM & COMPANY PLC, 22 King Street, London, SW1Y 6QY. Tel: 020 7839 4615. Fax: 020 7839 5994. Internet: www.adambank.com.

Newby Trust (J)	7.459

ADAM & COMPANY PLC, 22 Charlotte Square, Edinburgh, EH2 4DF. Tel: 0131 225 8484. Fax: 0131 225 5136. E-mail: AIM@adambank.com. Internet: www.adambank.com. Charity specialists: Laura Thomson (Marketing Assistant).

Comic Relief (J)	7.162
Crerar Hotels Trust, The	7.185
Dunard Fund	7.215
Hopetoun House Preservation Trust	7.317
Lancaster Foundation	7.377

AHLI UNITED BANK, 35 Portman Square, London, W1H 6LR. Tel: 020 7487 6500. Internet: www.ahliunited.com.

Harrow Central Mosque and Islamic Centre (J)	7.303

AL RAYAN BANK, 44 Hans Crescent, Knightsbridge, London, SW1X 0LX. Tel: 020 3713 8747. Internet: www.alrayanbank.co.uk.

Human Relief Foundation (J)	7.324

ALLIED IRISH BANK, Bankcentre, Ballsbridge, Dublin. Internet: www.aib.ie.

Cinema and Television Benevolent Fund (J)	7.150
Edmund Rice Bicentennial Trust Ltd	7.226
ESCRS Limited (J)	7.242
South Bank Centre (J)	7.628

ALLIED IRISH BANK (GB), Bankcentre, Belmont Road, Uxbridge, Middlesex, UB8 1SA. Tel: (01895) 272222. Fax: (01895) 619303. Internet: www.aibgb.co.uk.

Africa Educational Trust (J)	7.15
Brothers of Charity Services (Scotland) (J)	7.101
Charity of Elizabeth Jane Jones, The (J)	7.129
Congregation of the Brothers of Charity (J)	7.172
Congregation of the Sisters of St Anne (J)	7.175
Eden Trust	7.224
Fremantle Trust	7.264
Good Shepherd Centre Bishopton, The (J)	7.281
Haberdashers' Benevolent Foundation, The (J)	7.295
Haberdashers' Educational Foundation (J)	7.295
Honourable Artillery Company (J)	7.316
Institute of Grocery Distribution (J)	7.335
International House Trust	7.343
JGW Patterson Foundation, The	7.355
John Moores Foundation	7.360
Johnson Association, The	7.361
L H A London Limited (J)	7.376
Larkfield With Hill Park Autistic Trust Limited	7.380
Little Way Association (J)	7.391
Methodist Homes (J)	7.424
Milestones Trust (J)	7.427
Nottingham YMCA	7.473
Peter Lang Children's Trust Limited (J)	7.499
Rontades Limited (J)	7.544
Royal Academy of Dramatic Art	7.549
Sacred Heart Fathers Trust	7.579
Scottish Catholic International Aid Fund (J)	7.591
Sightsavers International (J)	7.608
Sisters of St Joseph of Peace (J)	7.615
Society of St Columban for Foreign Missions	7.623
St Luke's Hospice (Harrow & Brent)	7.648

St Olave's & St Saviour's Schools Foundation	7.652
Teresa Ball International Solidarity Fund (J)	7.673
St Benedict's Abbey Ealing (J)	7.688
United Christian Broadcasters (J)	7.695
WCS Care Group Limited (J)	7.717
Whiteley Homes Trust (J)	7.725
World Vision UK (J)	7.741
YMCA Fairthorne Group	7.745
YMCA Glasgow (J)	7.745
Young Vic Company Limited	7.750

AMC BANK LIMITED, Charlton Place, Charlton Road, Andover, Hampshire, SP10 1RE. Tel: 01264 360560. Internet: www.amconline.co.uk.

Ymddiriedolaeth Clough Williams-Ellis Fdn (J)	7.746

BANCO BILBAO VIZCAYA, 108 Cannon Street, London, EC4N 6EU. Tel: 020 7623 3060. Fax: 020 7648 7610.

Sisters Hospitallers of the Sacred Heart (J)	7.613

BANK OF INDIA, 293 Harrow Road, Wembley, Middlesex, HA0 4TL.

Shree Kutch Satsang Swaminarayan Temple (J)	7.606
Shri Venkateswara (Balaji) Temple of UK (J)	7.607

BANK LEUMI (UK) PLC, 20 Stratford Place, London, W1C 1BG. Tel: 020 7907 8000. Fax: 020 7907 8001.

BFHU	7.93
Weizmann Institute Foundation (J)	7.717

BANK OF AMERICA, 5 Canada Sq, London, E14 5AQ. Tel: 0207 174 4000.

BHP Billiton	7.68

BANK OF BARODA, 32 City Road, London, EC1Y 2BD. Tel: 020 7457 1515. Fax: 020 7457 1523. E-mail: ce.uk@bankofbaroda.com. Internet: www.bankofbarodauk.com.

Shri Venkateswara (Balaji) Temple of UK (J)	7.607

BANK OF IRELAND, Bow Bells House, 1 Bread Street, London, EC4M 9BE. Tel: 020 3201 6000. Internet: www.bank-of-ireland.com.

Camphill Communities Trust	7.110
Concern Worldwide (UK) (J)	7.170
Congregation of the Sisters of St Martha (J)	7.175
Croydon Almshouse Charities	7.187
Extern Organisation	7.244
Netherhall Educational Association (J)	7.457
Order St Augustine Mercy Jesus (J)	7.483
Praxis Care Group	7.512
Safe Haven London	7.581
Sisters of St Joseph Province (J)	7.615
Sisters of the Cross and Passion (J)	7.615
Union Sisters Mercy Great Britain	7.695

BANK OF NEW YORK EUROPE LTD, One Canada Square, London, E14 5AL.

Rothschild Foundation (Hanadiv) Europe (J)	7.547
Thomas Hickman's Charity (J)	7.677
William Harding's Charity (J)	7.730

BANK OF SCOTLAND CORPORATE, PO Box 5, The Mound, Edinburgh, EH1 1YZ. Tel: 0870 600 5000. Internet: www.bankofscotland.co.uk/corporate.

Abbotsford Trust	7.5

Aberdeen Endowments Trust (J)	7.5
Action Group Ltd	7.10
Active Luton (J)	7.12
Affinity Trust (J)	7.15
Age Scotland	7.17
Age UK Suffolk	7.19
Alice Ellen Cooper-Dean Charitable Fndtn (J)	7.24
Alliance of Sector Skills Councils (J)	7.26
Alzheimer's Research UK (J)	7.28
Alzheimer Scotland - Action on Dementia	7.28
Association for Project Management	7.46
Aston Student Villages	7.47
Ayrshire Hospice	7.52
Baird Trust	7.54
Bauer Radio's Cash for Kids Charities	7.61
Benesco Charity	7.65
Bethany Christian Trust	7.67
Bible & Gospel Trust (J)	7.69
Birmingham Diocesan Board Finance	7.71
Booth Charities (J)	7.79
Bradford Diocesan Board of Finance, The (J)	7.83
Bridgewood Trust (J)	7.88
British Journal of Anaesthesia, The (J)	7.95
British Lung Foundation (J)	7.96
British Museum Friends (J)	7.96
Caldecott Foundation Limited (J)	7.108
Capital City Partnership Limited	7.113
Chalfords Limited	7.126
Changeworks (J)	7.127
Charles Wolfson Charitable Trust	7.131
Chartered Institute for Securities &Investment	7.132
CILIP (J)	7.133
Chest Heart & Stroke Scotland (J)	7.137
Children 1st	7.140
Children's Hospice Association Scotland	7.141
Christian Vision (J)	7.146
Church of Scot Uninc. Councils Cttees (J)	7.149
Citizens Advice Scotland (J)	7.152
Citizens Theatre Ltd	7.152
City of Glasgow College Foundation (J)	7.153
CLC International (UK) (J)	7.156
Clothworkers' Foundation	7.157
Cogent SSC Limited	7.159
Coventry Diocesan Board of Finance	7.184
Cripplegate Foundation (J)	7.186
Donisthorpe Hall	7.205
Dovecot Foundation	7.210
Dundee Repertory Theatre	7.215
Dundee Student Villages	7.215
East Kilbride District Eng Grp Training Assoc	7.221
East Lothian Housing Association (J)	7.222
Eden Court Highlands	7.223
Enjoy East Lothian	7.237
ESCRS Limited (J)	7.242
Fair Share Trust (J)	7.246
Festival City Theatres Trust	7.251
Focus Learning Trust	7.256
Fdn&Friends of RoyalBotanicGardens, Kew (J)	7.259
Free Church of Scotland (J)	7.264
G J W Turner Trust	7.268
G M Morrison Charitable Trust	7.268
Glasgow Association for Mental Health	7.275
Glasgow Student Villages Limited	7.276
Greenock Arts Guild Limited	7.287
Greenwich Royal Naval College Foundation (J)	7.288
Grimsthorpe and Drummond Castle Trust	7.288
Grocers' Charity	7.289
Henry Barber Trust (J)	7.308
Henry Smith Charity	7.309
Highland Hospice	7.312
Horsecross Arts Ltd	7.318

Ian Karten Charitable Trust	7.326
Inspiring Scotland (J)	7.332
Institute of Occupational Medicine	7.336
Inverclyde Leisure	7.345
Jobs & Business Glasgow	7.356
Kathleen Hannay Memorial Charity	7.366
Keep Scotland Beautiful	7.367
Kirby Laing Foundation	7.374
Kirkhouse Trust	7.374
Langley House Trust	7.379
Leeds Castle Foundation (J)	7.381
Lennox Wyfold Foundation	7.384
MacRobert Trust	7.405
Maggie Keswick Jencks Cancer Trust (J)	7.406
Maurice Hilda Laing Charitable Trust (J)	7.416
Medecins sans Frontieres (UK)	7.418
Mercy Corps Scotland (J)	7.422
Mercy Ships - UK	7.423
Miss Agnes H Hunter's Trust	7.429
Moredun Foundation, The	7.433
Moredun Research Institute	7.434
Motability (J)	7.435
Mountview Academy of Theatre Arts (J)	7.436
National Assoc for Colitis and Crohn's (J)	7.442
National Galleries of Scotland (J)	7.446
National Galleries of Scotland Foundation	7.447
National Institute of Adult Education	7.448
National Library of Scotland (J)	7.448
New England Company	7.457
Newham Training and Education Centre	7.460
Oakhaven Trust (J)	7.476
P F Charitable Trust (J)	7.489
Penumbra	7.496
Perthyn (J)	7.498
Pitlochry Festival Theatre	7.504
PACEY (J)	7.515
Quarriers (J)	7.519
Quartet Community Foundation	7.519
R S Macdonald Charitable Trust	7.522
Responsible Gambling Trust	7.532
Robertson Trust	7.541
Royal British Legion Poppy Factory Limited (J)	7.554
Royal College of Physicians of Edinburgh	7.557
Royal London Society for the Blind (J)	7.564
Royal Marsden Cancer Campaign (J)	7.564
Royal Philharmonic Orchestra (J)	7.569
Royal Scottish National Orchestra	7.571
Royal Society of Edinburgh	7.572
Royal Society of Medicine (J)	7.573
RSABI	7.576
S L G Charitable Trust	7.578
Sacro	7.580
Sailors Society (J)	7.581
Samaritans (J)	7.585
Scottish Association for Marine Science	7.590
Scottish Association for Mental Health	7.591
Scottish Catholic International Aid Fund (J)	7.591
SSPCA (J)	7.592
Scottish Sports Council Trust Company	7.593
Sense Scotland	7.597
Shears Foundation	7.600
Shetland Charitable Trust	7.604
Sisters of St Joseph of Peace (J)	7.615
Social Investment Scotland	7.620
Souter Charitable Trust	7.628
South of England Foundation	7.629
St James's Place Foundation (J)	7.644
St Margaret's Hospice (Clydebank)	7.649
Starlight Children's Foundation (J)	7.656
Steel Charitable Trust (J)	7.657
Stock Exchange Benevolent Fund	7.659
Surrey Wildlife Trust	7.665
Thera Trust (J)	7.676
Turning Point Scotland	7.691
University of Aberdeen Development Trust	7.700
Volant Charitable Trust	7.709
VSA	7.709
West Lothian Leisure (J)	7.721
Weston Provident Fund	7.724
Workers' Educational Association (J)	7.739
Worth Abbey (J)	7.742
YMCA Glasgow (J)	7.745
Yorkhill Children's Charity	7.748

BANQUE POPULAIRE, 2 rue de la Halle, 65100 Lourdes.

HCPT - The Pilgrimage Trust (J)	7.304

BARCLAYS, One Churchill Place, Canary Wharf, London, E14 5HP. Tel: 020 7441 2000.
Internet: www.barclays.com/corporatebanking.
Charity specialists: David McHattie.

4 Charity Foundation (J)	7.3
Abbeyfield Ilkley Society	7.4
Abbeyfield Society	7.5
Ability Housing Association (J)	7.7
Achisomoch Aid Co	7.8
Action for Blind People (J)	7.10
Addenbrooke's Charitable Trust	7.13
Adviza	7.14
Affinity Trust (J)	7.15
Afghanaid (J)	7.15
African Medical & Research Foundation UK (J)	7.16
Age UK	7.17
Age UK Hertfordshire	7.17
Age UK Leicestershire & Rutland	7.18
Age UK North Tyneside	7.18
Ahavat Shalom Charity Fund	7.19
Air Ambulance Service	7.20
Aldeburgh Music	7.23
Alder Hey Children's Charity, The	7.23
Alexandra Palace and Park (J)	7.24
Alice Ellen Cooper-Dean Charitable Fndtn (J)	7.24
All Hallows Healthcare Trust	7.25
Alliance of Sector Skills Councils (J)	7.26
Alnwick Garden Trust	7.27
Alzheimer's Research UK (J)	7.28
Ampleforth Abbey Trust	7.30
Angel Foundation	7.32
Anglo-Omani Society, The	7.32
Anguish's Educational Foundation	7.33
Anna Freud Centre	7.33
Anthony Nolan	7.34
Anvil Trust Ltd	7.34
APS	7.35
Cardiff RC Archdiocesan Trust	7.37
Archie Sherman Charitable Trust	7.38
Architectural Heritage Fund	7.38
Article 19 Research & Information Centre (J)	7.41
Ashgate Hospice	7.43
Aspinall Foundation, The	7.44
Associated Board Royal Schools Music (J)	7.45
At-Bristol Ltd	7.48
Auckland Castle Trust, The	7.48
Avante Partnership	7.51
Avenues East	7.51
Avenues London	7.51
Avenues South East	7.51
Avenues Trust Group, The	7.52
Barbour Foundation, The	7.56
Barnabas Fund (J)	7.57
Barnardo's	7.57
Batchworth Trust (J)	7.60
BBC Media Action	7.61
Bell Educational Trust Ltd	7.64
BEN-Motor & Allied Trades Benevolent Fund (J)	7.64
Berkshire Maestros (J)	7.66
bet365 Foundation	7.67
BirdLife International (J)	7.70
Black Country Living Museum Trust	7.74
Blenheim Foundation, The (J)	7.75
Blind Veterans UK	7.76
Bloodwise	7.76
Bluecoat, The	7.77
BMS World Mission	7.77
Book Aid International (J)	7.79
Booth Charities (J)	7.79
Bowerman Charitable Trust	7.82
Bradford Diocesan Board of Finance, The (J)	7.83
Brathay Trust (J)	7.85
BRE Trust	7.85
Breast Cancer Campaign	7.86
Brendoncare Foundation	7.87
Bridgewood Trust (J)	7.88
Bright Red Dot Foundation	7.88
British & Foreign School Society, The	7.91
British Heart Foundation	7.93
British Home & Hospital for Incurables	7.94
British Library (J)	7.95
British Safety Council	7.98
British School of Osteopathy	7.98

British Small Animal Veterinary Assoc	7.99
Brooke Hospital for Animals	7.101
BSS	7.102
Burton Family Charitable Trust, The	7.105
Business in the Community	7.105
Butterwick	7.106
C Alma Baker Trust	7.106
Caldecott Foundation Limited (J)	7.108
Cambridge Foundation	7.109
Cancer Recovery Foundation UK	7.112
CARE International UK (J)	7.114
Care South (J)	7.114
Carers Trust	7.114
Carpenters' Company Charitable Trust	7.117
Catch22	7.118
Cats Protection	7.120
Caudwell Children	7.120
CAYSH	7.121
Central Foundation Schools of London (J)	7.122
Central Manchester Univ Hosp NHS Trust	7.123
Centre for Effective Dispute Resolution	7.124
Centre for Eng. & Manufacturing Excellence	7.124
Cerebra (J)	7.125
Certified Accountants Educational Trust	7.125
Chabad Lubavitch UK	7.125
Chance to Shine Foundation Ltd	7.126
Changing Lives	7.127
Chapter 1	7.127
Charity of Sir Richard Whittington	7.129
Charles Elsie Sykes Trust	7.131
Chartered Institute of Housing	7.133
CharteredInstitute of Logistics&Transport UK	7.133
Chartered Institute of Purchasing & Supply	7.134
Chartered Management Institute	7.135
Chatham Historic Dockyard Trust	7.135
Chelmsford Diocesan Board Finance (J)	7.136
Chelsea F C Foundation Limited	7.137
Chevras Tsedokoh Limited	7.138
Chichester Diocesan Fd Bd Finance	7.138
Chicken Shed Theatre Trust, The	7.139
Children's Society	7.142
Choice Support	7.143
Christ's Hospital Foundation	7.144
Christian Conference Trust	7.145
Christie Charitable Fund, The	7.146
Church Army (J)	7.147
Church Mission Society	7.148
Church of God of Prophecy Trust (J)	7.148
Church of Pentecost - UK, The (J)	7.149
CITB-ConstructionSkills	7.151
Citizens Advice	7.152
City of Glasgow College Foundation (J)	7.153
City of Sheffield Theatre Trust	7.154
Clacton Family Trust	7.154
CLIC Sargent Cancer Care for Children (J)	7.156
College Estate Endowment Charity, The	7.160
College Optometrists	7.160
Community Foundation for Manchester (J)	7.162
Comm Fdn (Tyne&Wear&Northumberland)	7.164
Compassion UK	7.169
Compton Hospice	7.169
Compton Verney	7.169
Concern Worldwide (UK) (J)	7.170
Congregation of La Sainte Union	7.171
Daughters of the Holy Ghost	7.173
CongregationDominicanSistersofMaltaTrst	7.173
Congregation of the Sisters of Nazareth Trust	7.174
Conservation Education & Research Trust (J)	7.177
Constance Green Foundation	7.177
Consumers' Association	7.178
Contemporary Dance Trust	7.178
Coquet Trust, The	7.179
Cornwall Hospice Care	7.180
Corporation of Trinity House	7.181
Council for Awards in Care,Health&Education	7.182
Country Houses Foundation	7.182
County Air Ambulance Trust (J)	7.183
Creative and Cultural Industries Limited	7.184
Crime Reduction Initiatives	7.186
Cruse Bereavement Care	7.187
Cyngor Alcohol Information Service Limit	7.190
D'Oyly Carte Charitable Trust	7.191
Dartington Hall Trust, The	7.192
David Tannen Charitable Trust	7.195
Deflog V Q Trust Limited, The	7.196
Denville Hall	7.197
Design Museum (J)	7.199
Diabetes Research & Wellness Foundation	7.200

Diabetes UK (J)	7.200	Hampstead Theatre Foundation	7.299	Liverpool PSS	7.393
Disabilities Trust	7.201	Hampstead Wells & Campden Trust	7.299	Llamau Limited	7.394
Disasters Emergency Committee (J)	7.202	Hampton Fuel Allotment Charity	7.300	London Academy of Music and Dramatic Art (J)	7.397
Ditchley Foundation, The	7.202	Handmaids of the Sacred Heart of Jesus (J)	7.300	London City Mission	7.397
Dogs Trust	7.203	Haynes International Motor Museum	7.304	London Cyrenians Housing	7.398
Dollond Charitable Trust	7.203	HCT Group	7.304	London Diocesan Board for Schools	7.398
Donkey Sanctuary	7.206	Healthcare Management Trust, The	7.306	London Diocesan Fund	7.398
Douglas Haig Memorial Homes (J)	7.209	Hearing Dogs for Deaf People	7.306	London Library	7.399
Downside Abbey General Trust	7.210	Heart of Kent Hospice, The	7.307	Lonia Ltd	7.402
Drive	7.212	Helen & Douglas House (J)	7.307	Lord Belstead Charitable Trust, The	7.402
Dulwich Estate	7.214	Help for Heroes (J)	7.308	Lord Crewe's Charity	7.402
Dulwich Picture Gallery	7.215	HelpAge International	7.308	Lord Leverhulme's Charitable Trust	7.402
E Hayes Dashwood Foundation (J)	7.218	Helping Foundation, The (J)	7.308	Lowry Centre Trust	7.403
Earl Fitzwilliam Charitable Trust	7.218	Henshaws Society for Blind People	7.309	Lyric Hammersmith	7.404
Earl of Northampton's Charity	7.219	Heritage Care	7.310	Marie Stopes International (J)	7.410
East Anglia's Children's Hospices (J)	7.220	Hestia Housing and Support	7.310	Marine Society & Sea Cadets (J)	7.411
East End Community Foundation	7.221	Higher Education Academy, The (J)	7.311	Martha Trust	7.413
East Malling Research	7.222	Hillsong Church London	7.313	Martin House	7.413
East Malling Trust, The	7.222	Historic Royal Palaces	7.314	Martlets Hospice Limited (J)	7.413
East of England Agricultural Society	7.223	Holstein UK	7.315	Mary Kinross Charitable Trust	7.414
Edinburgh Leisure (J)	7.225	Horder Healthcare	7.317	Mary Stevens Hospice (J)	7.415
Education & Services for People with Autism	7.226	Hospice in the Weald (J)	7.319	Maurice & Vivienne Wohl Philanthropic Fdn	7.417
Education and Training Foundation (J)	7.227	Hospital of God at Greatham	7.321	Maurice Wohl Charitable Foundation	7.417
Edward Penley Abraham Research Fund (J)	7.228	Howletts Wild Animal Trust, The	7.322	Melow Charitable Trust	7.420
Eighty Eight Foundation, The	7.228	Hull Trinity House Charities	7.323	Mental Health Matters	7.421
Ellenor Lions Hospices	7.231	Huntingdon Freemen's Trust (J)	7.325	Mercers' Charitable Foundation	7.422
Elton John Aids Foundation	7.231	Ian Askew Charitable Trust	7.326	MERLIN (J)	7.423
Ely Diocesan Board of Finance, The	7.231	ifs School of Finance	7.328	Methodist Homes (J)	7.424
Encompass (Dorset)	7.233	Injured Jockeys Fund	7.331	Middlesbrough Diocesan Trust	7.425
Engineering Construction Training Board	7.234	Institute of Daughters of Mary Help	7.334	Midlands Air Ambulance Charity	7.426
English Stage Company Ltd	7.236	Institute of Development Studies (J)	7.334	Mike Gooley Trailfinder Charity	7.427
Entindale	7.237	Institute of Food Research	7.335	Millennium Awards Trust, The (J)	7.427
Essex & Herts Air Ambulance Trust (J)	7.240	Inst of Marine Engineering, Science & Tech	7.335	Millennium Point Trust	7.428
Essex Wildlife Trust	7.240	Institution of Engineering and Technology	7.338	Milton Keynes Parks Trust Ltd (J)	7.428
Evelyn Trust	7.242	Institution of Eng Technology Ben Fund (J)	7.338	Morgan Foundation	7.434
Exilarch's Foundation (J)	7.244	Institution of Structural Engineers	7.339	Morley Agricultural Foundation, The	7.434
F Glenister Woodger Trust, The	7.245	International Centre for Life Trust	7.341	Motability (J)	7.435
Fairley House School	7.246	International HIV/AIDS Alliance	7.342	Motability Tenth Anniversary Trust, The	7.435
FARA Foundation	7.248	Intl Institute for Environment&Development	7.343	Movember Europe (J)	7.436
FARM-Africa (J)	7.248	International Medical Corps (UK)	7.343	Mrs D M France-Hayhurst Charitable Trust	7.437
Fauna & Flora International	7.249	Intl Planned Parenthood Federation	7.344	Mrs L D Rope Third Charitable Settlement	7.438
FIA Foundation for Automobile & Society	7.252	Ironbridge Gorge Museum Trust Limited	7.346	Multiple Sclerosis Society	7.438
Fidelity UK Foundation	7.252	Islamic Relief Worldwide (J)	7.347	National Autistic Society	7.442
Field Studies Council	7.253	Islamic Trust (J)	7.347	National Children's Bureau (J)	7.444
Finchley Charities	7.254	Jamie Oliver Food Foundation	7.351	National Council Voluntary Organisations	7.444
Fire Fighters Charity (J)	7.254	Jesus House (J)	7.353	National Motor Museum Trust Ltd	7.450
Fitzwilliam Wentworth Amenity Trust	7.255	Jewish Care (J)	7.354	National Rifle Association	7.451
Football Foundation	7.256	JNF Charitable Trust	7.355	National Skills Academy For Social Care	7.452
Football League (Community) Limited, The	7.257	John Black Charitable Foundation	7.357	NSPCC (J)	7.452
Fostering Network	7.258	John Innes Centre	7.358	National Space Science Centre (J)	7.453
Fdn&Friends of RoyalBotanicGardens, Kew (J)	7.259	John Innes Foundation	7.358	National Trust	7.454
Foundation for Credit Counselling	7.259	John Marshall's Charity (J)	7.359	National Waterfront Museum Swansea	7.454
Foundation for Social Entrepreneurs (J)	7.259	Joseph Rank Trust, The	7.363	Nazareth Care Charitable Trust	7.455
Foundation of Edward Storey	7.260	Joshua Trust Group, The (J)	7.364	NCFE (J)	7.455
Foundation of Light	7.260	JTL	7.364	New Kadampa Tradition (J)	7.458
Foundation Trust Network, The (J)	7.261	Juvenile Diabetes Research Foundation	7.365	New Testament Church of God (J)	7.458
Francis C Scott Charitable Trust (J)	7.262	Kathleen & Michael Connolly Foundation UK (J)	7.366	New Wine Trust	7.458
Frankgiving Limited	7.263	Kent Autistic Trust	7.368	Newbury & Thatcham Hospital Trust (J)	7.459
Freeways Trust	7.264	Kent Wildlife Trust	7.369	Newcastle Diocesan Board Finance	7.459
Future Leaders Charitable Trust Ltd	7.267	Keren Association	7.369	Newcastle Healthcare Charity	7.459
GarfieldWestonTrustforWestminsterAbbey	7.269	Keychange Charity	7.370	Newlife Foundation for Disabled Children	7.461
Genome Analysis Centre, The	7.271	Kidney Research UK	7.371	NHS Confederation	7.462
Geoffrey Watling Charity, The	7.272	KIDS	7.371	Nightingale Hammerson (J)	7.463
Gilmoor Benevolent Fund Limited	7.274	Kirklees Active Leisure	7.374	Norfolk Community Foundation	7.464
Girls Friendly Soc in England & Wales	7.275	Kisharon	7.375	Norfolk Wildlife Trust (J)	7.464
Girton Town Charity	7.275	L H A London Limited (J)	7.376	North Country Leisure	7.465
Global Charities	7.277	L M Kendon Settlement (J)	7.376	North East Autism Society (J)	7.466
Gloucester Diocesan Board Finance	7.278	Lady Hewleys Charity	7.376	North London Hospice	7.467
Gloucestershire Care Partnership	7.278	Land Restoration Trust	7.378	North Music Trust	7.467
Gloucestershire Everyman Theatre (J)	7.278	Lawes Agricultural Trust (J)	7.380	Northampton Theatres Trust	7.468
God's House in Ewelme	7.279	League Football Education	7.381	Northamptonshire Arts Management Trust	7.469
Goldman Sachs Gives (UK)	7.280	Legacy Trust UK	7.383	N Police Convalescent & Treatment Centre	7.471
Goldsmiths Centre, The (J)	7.280	Legal Education Foundation, The (J)	7.383	Norwich Consolidated Charities	7.471
Goldsmiths' Company Charity (J)	7.281	Leicester Diocesan Board Finance	7.383	Norwich Diocesan Board of Finance, The	7.471
Goodenough College	7.281	Lempriere Pringle Charitable Trust, The (J)	7.384	Norwich Town Close Estate Charity	7.472
Goshen Trust	7.282	Leonard Cheshire Disability	7.385	Norwood (J)	7.472
Gosling Sports Park	7.282	LEPRA	7.385	Nottingham Playhouse Trust Ltd	7.473
Grace Eyre Foundation	7.283	Leprosy Mission England (J)	7.385	Nuffield Foundation	7.474
Grand Charity, The (J)	7.284	Leprosy Mission International	7.385	Nuffield Health (J)	7.474
Grange Farm Centre Trust	7.284	Les Filles de la Croix	7.386	Nuffield Oxford Hospitals Fund (J)	7.474
Great Hospital, Norwich	7.285	Leverhulme Trade Charities Trust	7.386	Nuffield Trust for Forces of the Crown	7.475
Greenham Common Community Trust (J)	7.286	Leverhulme Trust	7.386	Oasis Charitable Trust	7.477
Guide Dogs for the Blind Association (J)	7.291	Lincs&Notts Air Ambulance Ch Tst	7.390	Oasis Community Learning	7.477
Guild Estate Endowment	7.291	Lincolnshire Wildlife Trust	7.390	Open Doors with Brother Andrew (J)	7.480
Hackney Empire	7.295	Lind Trust	7.390	Open Society Foundation	7.481
Haig Housing Trust (J)	7.296	Little Way Association (J)	7.391	Opportunity International United Kingdom	7.481
Hall for Cornwall Trust	7.296	Livability	7.391	ORBIS Charitable Trust	7.482
Hampstead Theatre	7.299	Liverpool Merchants Guild	7.393	Order of Hermit Friars of St Augustine	7.483

Order St Augustine Mercy Jesus (J)	7.483	RSAS AgeCare	7.576	Thames Reach (J)	7.675
Order St John Priory for Wales	7.483	Ruddock Foundation for the Arts	7.577	Theatre Royal Bath Ltd	7.675
Orders St John Care Trust	7.483	Rustington Convalescent Home Carpenters Co	7.578	Thera Trust (J)	7.676
Ormiston Families	7.484	Said Foundation	7.581	Thomas Parsons Charity	7.677
Ormiston Trust	7.484	Sainsbury Laboratory	7.582	Thompson Family Charitable Trust (J)	7.678
Oshwal Association of the UK	7.485	Salford Diocesan Trust (J)	7.582	Thornton-Smith and Plevins Trust (J)	7.679
Outward Bound Trust	7.485	Samaritan's Purse International	7.585	Three C's Support	7.679
Outward Housing	7.486	Save the Children International (J)	7.588	TLC Care Attendant Service (J)	7.681
Oxford Archaeological Unit Ltd	7.487	SEMTA	7.589	Together Trust	7.681
Oxford Group	7.488	Science Museum Foundation	7.589	Traffic International	7.684
Oxfordshire Care Partnership, The	7.488	Science Museum Group	7.590	Tudor Trust	7.690
P H Holt Foundation	7.489	Scottish Catholic International Aid Fund (J)	7.591	Turning Point	7.691
Pallant House Gallery	7.490	Scout Association	7.594	Ty Hafan (J)	7.692
Papworth Trust (J)	7.490	Seckford Foundation	7.595	UFI Charitable Trust	7.692
Parmiter's School Foundation	7.492	Send a Cow	7.596	UK Biobank Ltd (J)	7.692
Patrick & Helena Frost Foundation, The	7.492	Servants Fellowship International	7.598	UK Islamic Mission	7.693
Paul Bassham Charitable Trust	7.493	Severn Hospice (J)	7.598	UK Youth	7.693
Paul Strickland Scanner Centre	7.493	SheffCare	7.600	Ulverscroft Foundation	7.694
People 1st	7.496	Sheffield Theatres Crucible Trust	7.602	Unipol Student Homes (J)	7.695
People in Action	7.496	Sheffield Theatres Trust	7.602	United Jewish Israel Appeal	7.696
Percy Hedley Foundation	7.497	Shooting Star CHASE (J)	7.605	United Learning Trust	7.696
Peterborough Diocesan Board Finance	7.500	Shree Kutch Satsang Swaminarayan Temple (J)	7.606	Univ Old Members' Trust, The (J)	7.699
Philip King Charitable Trust	7.501	Shulem B. Association Ltd	7.607	UCKG HelpCentre	7.699
Pilgrims Hospices in East Kent (J)	7.503	Sir Halley Stewart Trust	7.610	UCAS	7.699
Plan International (J)	7.505	Sir Malcolm Stewart Bart Gen. Trust	7.612	University Hospital Birmingham Charities	7.700
PLUS (Providence Linc United Services)	7.505	Sir Robert Geffery's Almhouse Trust	7.612	UOHC Foundation	7.701
Police Rehabilitation Centre	7.507	Siri Guru Nanak Darbar (Sikh Temple) (J)	7.613	USPG	7.702
Pony Club	7.508	Sisters of Mercy, Gravesend	7.614	Valley Leisure (J)	7.702
Portsmouth Diocesan Board Of Finance	7.509	Sisters Notre Dame Namur	7.614	Vardy Foundation (J)	7.703
Positive Steps	7.510	Skills Active UK	7.617	Varrier Jones Foundation (J)	7.703
Practical Action	7.512	Skills for Care (J)	7.617	Veolia Environmental Trust, The (J)	7.704
Premier Christian Media Trust (J)	7.512	Sobell House Hospice Charity Limited	7.619	Vibrance	7.704
Premier League Charitable Fund	7.513	Social Care Institute for Excellence	7.620	Vivacity Culture & Leisure	7.708
Presbyterian Church of Wales	7.513	Social Investment Business Foundation (J)	7.620	Vodafone Foundation, The	7.708
Princess Alice Hospice	7.514	Society for Promoting Christian Knowledge	7.620	Voluntary Service Overseas (J)	7.709
Punchdrunk (J)	7.518	Society of Mary Reparatrice	7.622	W A Handley Charity Trust	7.710
Quarriers (J)	7.519	Society of Petroleum Engineers Europe	7.623	W O Street Charitable Foundation	7.710
Queen Alexandra Hospital Home	7.519	Society Salutation Mary Virgin Ltd	7.624	Wales Council for Voluntary Action	7.711
Racing Welfare	7.523	Soka Gakkai International UK (J)	7.625	Walton-on-Thames Charity	7.713
Raphael Freshwater Memorial Association Ltd	7.526	SSAFA (J)	7.626	Watch Tower Bible Tract Society Britain	7.714
Rayne Foundation	7.526	SOS Children's Villages UK (J)	7.628	WaterAid	7.715
Rayne Trust	7.527	S Lon Ch Fund&Sthwk Diocesan Bd Fin (J)	7.629	WCMC 2000	7.716
Redeemed Christian Church of God (J)	7.528	South Street Green Room Foundation	7.630	Weldmar Hospicecare Trust (J)	7.717
Regent's Park Theatre Limited (J)	7.530	Southside Partnership	7.631	Welsh Air Ambulance Charitable Trust	7.718
Regent's University London	7.530	Sparks Charity	7.632	Wessex Children's Hospice Trust (J)	7.719
Relief International UK (I)	7.531	Sports Council Trust Company	7.634	West Kirby Residential School	7.720
Rennie Grove Hospice Care	7.531	Springboard Sunderland Trust	7.634	West London YMCA	7.721
Response Organisation	7.532	Spurgeons	7.635	West Lothian Leisure (J)	7.721
Restless Development	7.533	St Albans Diocesan Board Finance	7.635	West Midlands Special Needs Transport (J)	7.721
Retail Trust (J)	7.533	St Catherine's Hospice Limited	7.639	Westway Trust	7.724
Reuben Foundation	7.534	St Clare West Essex Hospice Care Trust (J)	7.640	Whale Dolphin Conservation Society	7.724
ReVitalise Respite Holidays	7.535	St Francis Hospice	7.642	Wilberforce Trust	7.728
Rhondda Cynon Taff Welsh Church Fund	7.535	St George's Police Children Trust	7.643	Wildlife Trust BCNP, The	7.728
R. Ormonde Shuttleworth Remembrance Trust	7.536	St Giles Trust	7.644	Wilf Ward Family Trust	7.728
R.Watts&Rochester CityAlmshouseCharities	7.536	St James's Place Foundation (J)	7.644	William Brake Charitable Trust	7.730
Richmond Charities' Almshouses (J)	7.537	St John Ambulance	7.644	William Palmer College Educational Trust	7.731
Richmond Parish Lands Charity	7.538	St John of God Hospitaller Services Ltd	7.645	Wiltshire Wildlife Trust	7.731
River and Rowing Museum Foundation	7.539	St Joseph's Hospice, Hackney (J)	7.646	Winston Churchill Memorial Trust (J)	7.732
RMCC (Ronald McDonald House Charities)	7.540	St Joseph's Society for Foreign Missions	7.646	Wirral Autistic Society (J)	7.733
Robert Owen Communities (J)	7.541	St Luke's Hospice Plymouth	7.648	Wiseheights	7.733
Roch. Diocesan Society & Bd of Fin	7.542	St Margaret's Somerset Hospice	7.649	WJEC CBAC	7.734
Missionary Franciscan Sisters	7.544	St Michael's and All Saints Charity	7.650	Woking & Sam Beare Hospices (J)	7.735
Rontades Limited (J)	7.544	St Nicholas Hospice Care	7.652	Wolfson Family Charitable Trust	7.735
Rose Foundation	7.545	St Oswald's Hospice (J)	7.653	Wolfson Foundation	7.735
Roundhouse Trust (J)	7.547	St Peter & St James Charitable Trust	7.653	Wolverhampton Grand Theatre (1982)	7.735
Rowans Hospice	7.547	St Saviour's Medical Charity	7.654	Wordsworth Trust	7.738
Roy Castle Lung Cancer Foundation	7.548	St Wilfrid's Hospice (Eastbourne)	7.655	World Cancer Research Fund (WCRF UK) (J)	7.739
Royal Agricultural Benevolent Institution (J)	7.550	Stansted Park Foundation	7.656	World Energy Council	7.740
Royal Air Force Benevolent Fund (J)	7.550	Starling Family Charitable Trust, The	7.656	World Federation - Muslim Communities (J)	7.740
Royal Air Force Charitable Trust, The	7.550	Staying First	7.657	World Villages for Children	7.741
Royal Air Force Museum	7.551	Steel Charitable Trust (J)	7.657	Y Care International (J)	7.743
Royal Ballet School	7.552	Stoneleigh Abbey Limited	7.660	YMCA England	7.745
Royal Ballet School Endowment Fund (J)	7.553	Stonewall Equality Ltd	7.660	YMCA Norfolk	7.746
Royal British Legion Industries Ltd	7.554	Stowe House Preservation Trust	7.661	YMCA Training	7.746
Royal British Legion Poppy Factory Limited (J)	7.554	Stratford Upon Avon Town Trust	7.661	York Diocesan Board Finance Ltd	7.747
Royal College of General Practitioners	7.556	Street League (J)	7.661	Yorkshire Agricultural Society	7.748
RoyalCol.of Obstetricians & Gynaecologists	7.556	Stroke Association	7.662	Yorkshire Wildlife Trust	7.749
Royal College of Psychiatrists	7.558	Suffolk Agricultural Association	7.663	Zochonis Charitable Trust	7.752
Royal Hospital Chelsea Appeal Ltd (J)	7.561	Suffolk Foundation, The (J)	7.663	Zoological Society of London	7.752
Royal London Society for the Blind (J)	7.564	Suffolk Wildlife Trust	7.664	Zurbaran Trust, The	7.752
Royal Mencap Society	7.566	Sunfield Children's Homes Limited	7.664		
Royal National Children's Foundation (J)	7.566	Surrey Community Development Trust	7.665	BNP PARIBAS FORTIS, 5 Aldermanbury Square,	
Royal National College for the Blind	7.566	Sutton's Hospital in Charterhouse	7.666	London, EC2V 7HR. Tel: 0207 369 4800.	
Royal National Lifeboat Institution	7.567	Tagmarsh Charity Limited	7.667	Fax: 0207 369 4888.	
Royal Naval Benevolent Trust	7.568	Talbot Village Trust (J)	7.668	Internet: www.privatebanking.uk.fortis.com.	
Royal Shakespeare Company	7.571	Teach First	7.670		
Royal Trinity Hospice (J)	7.574	Teenage Cancer Trust (J)	7.671	Y Care International (J)	7.743
Royal Voluntary Service	7.575	TRAID	7.674		

BROWN SHIPLEY, Founders Court, Lothbury, London, EC2R 7HE. Tel: 020 7606 9833. Fax: 020 7282 3399. E-mail: info@brownshipley.co.uk. Internet: www.brownshipley.com.

Dowager Countess Eleanor Peel Trust (J)	7.210

C HOARE & CO, 37 Fleet Street, London, EC4P 4DQ. Tel: 020 7353 4522. Fax: 020 7353 4521. E-mail: enquiries@hoaresbank.co.uk. Internet: www.hoaresbank.co.uk.

A Team Foundation	7.4
African Medical & Research Foundation UK (J)	7.16
Architects Benevolent Society (J)	7.38
Backstage Trust	7.53
Band Trust	7.55
Beaverbrook Foundation (J)	7.63
Bulldog Trust	7.104
Charles Skey Charitable Trust	7.131
Childwick Trust	7.142
Corporation of the Sons of the Clergy (J)	7.181
Dr Mortimer & Theresa Sackler Fdtn (J)	7.211
Dunhill Medical Trust	7.216
Fairfield Charitable Trust	7.246
February Foundation, The	7.250
Golden Bottle Trust	7.280
Gray's Inn Scholarships Trust	7.284
Great Britain Sasakawa Foundation	7.284
Haberdashers' Benevolent Foundation, The (J)	7.295
Haberdashers' Educational Foundation (J)	7.295
Help for Heroes (J)	7.308
Hintze Family Charitable Foundation, The (J)	7.313
Hispanic Luso Brazilian Council	7.313
Institute of Psychoanalysis	7.337
John R Murray Charitable Trust	7.360
London Academy of Music and Dramatic Art (J)	7.397
Michael Uren Foundation, The	7.425
Mr Willats' Charity (J)	7.437
Nigel Vinson Charitable Trust	7.463
Normanby Charitable Trust	7.465
Phillips & Rubens Charitable Trust (J)	7.501
Radcliffe Trust, The	7.523
Rothermere Foundation	7.546
Royal College of Physicians of London (J)	7.557
Royal College of Surgeons (J)	7.558
Royal Society of Chemistry (J)	7.572
Royal Trinity Hospice (J)	7.574
Sackler Trust, The (J)	7.579
Samworth Foundation (J)	7.586
Suva Foundation Limited, The	7.666
Tate (J)	7.669
Tavistock Inst of Medical Psychology (J)	7.670
Tellus Mater Foundation Ltd (J)	7.672
Titsey Foundation	7.681
Will Charitable Trust	7.729
Will Woodlands	7.729

CAF BANK LTD, 25 Kings Hill Avenue, Kings Hill, West Malling, Kent, ME19 4JQ. Tel: 03000 123 444. Fax: 03000 123 007. E-mail: managingmoney@cafonline.org. Internet: www.cafonline.org/charities. Charity specialists: Charlotte Jago.

Actors' Benevolent Fund (J)	7.13
Afghanaid (J)	7.15
Africa Educational Trust (J)	7.15
Alcohol Research UK	7.23
All Saints Educational Trust	7.25
Ambika Paul Foundation	7.29
Ambitious about Autism (J)	7.29
Analytical Chemistry Trust Fund	7.31
Andrews Charitable Trust	7.32
Article 19 Research & Information Centre (J)	7.41
Asfari Foundation, The	7.43
Baily Thomas Charitable Fund, The	7.54
Barnes Workhouse Fund	7.57
Bath Wells Diocesan Board Finance (J)	7.60
Berkshire Maestros (J)	7.66
Bethphage Mission (Great Britain) (J)	7.68
Bill Brown's Charitable Settlement 1989	7.70
BirdLife International (J)	7.70
Blatchington Court Trust (J)	7.75
Book Aid International (J)	7.79
Bournemouth Young Men's Christian Assoc (J)	7.82
Bridgewood Trust (J)	7.88
Bristol Benevolent Institution	7.89

British Medical Association Scholarship	7.96
British Museum Friends (J)	7.96
Buckinghamshire Hospitals NHS Trust (J)	7.103
Butchers & Drovers Charitable Inst	7.105
Caring for Life (J)	7.115
Caritas Care (J)	7.115
Central England Quakers (CEQ) (J)	7.122
Cerebra (J)	7.125
Charles Hayward Foundation	7.131
Chelsea & Westminster Health Charity	7.136
Church Growth Trust	7.147
CLC International (UK) (J)	7.156
Colonel W H Whitbread Charitable Trust	7.161
Community of St Mary at the Cross (J)	7.166
Community of the Resurrection (J)	7.167
Conservation Education & Research Trust (J)	7.177
Cotswold Archaeological Trust	7.181
County Air Ambulance Trust (J)	7.183
Culture Coventry	7.188
D D McPhail Charitable Settlement (J)	7.191
Dr Edwards Bishop King's Fulham Charity	7.211
Drinkaware Trust, The	7.212
Durham Aged Mineworkers' Homes Assoc (J)	7.216
E F Bulmer Benevolent Fund (J)	7.217
E P A Cephalosporin Fund	7.218
Earley Charity (J)	7.219
Education Endowment Foundation, The	7.227
Edward Penley Abraham Research Fund (J)	7.228
Essex & Herts Air Ambulance Trust (J)	7.240
Estate Charity of William Hatcliffe (J)	7.241
Fairtrade Foundation (J)	7.247
Ffestiniog & Welsh Highland Railways Trust (J)	7.252
Fight For Sight (J)	7.254
Fdn&Friends of RoyalBotanicGardens, Kew (J)	7.259
Foundling Museum (J)	7.261
Foyle Foundation	7.261
Frances Augustus Newman Foundation	7.262
Friends Provident Charitable Foundation (J)	7.266
Groundwork South Trust Limited, The (J)	7.290
Guy Newton Research Fund (J)	7.293
Hamps & Isle of Wight Air Ambulance (J)	7.298
Health and Social Care Alliance, The (J)	7.305
Health Poverty Action (J)	7.305
Henry Barber Trust (J)	7.308
Holburne Museum	7.314
Institute of Grocery Distribution (J)	7.335
Institution of Chemical Engineers (J)	7.337
Institution of Mechanical Engineers (J)	7.338
Intl Society for Krishna Consciousness (J)	7.344
Jean Sainsbury Animal Welfare Trust	7.352
Jewish Joint Burial Society (J)	7.354
John Marshall's Charity (J)	7.359
John Martin's Charity (J)	7.360
Joseph Rowntree Charitable Trust (J)	7.363
Journalists' Charity (J)	7.364
Kabbalah Centre (J)	7.365
Kent Community Foundation	7.369
Leprosy Mission England (J)	7.385
Lifeline Community Projects (J)	7.388
London Catalyst	7.397
London Community Foundation (J)	7.397
Magen David Adom UK (J)	7.406
Manchester & District Home for Lost Dogs (J)	7.408
Merchant Navy Welfare Board	7.422
Moravian Church	7.433
Mount Saint Bernard Abbey (J)	7.436
Mrs E M Bates Trust	7.437
National Fed'n of Women's Institutes (J)	7.445
National Foundation for Youth Music (J)	7.446
Needham Research Institute (J)	7.456
Norman Family Charitable Trust	7.464
Open Doors with Brother Andrew (J)	7.480
Pargiter Trust	7.490
Peacock Charitable Trust	7.495
People Potential Possibilities (J)	7.496
People's Health Trust (J)	7.497
Peter Stebbings Memorial Charity	7.500
Pilgrims Hospices in East Kent (J)	7.503
Prison Advice & Care Trust (PACT)	7.515
Quaker International Educational Trust (J)	7.518
Queen Mary's Roehampton Trust	7.520
Queen's Nursing Institute (J)	7.520
R L Glasspool Charity Trust	7.522
Rainbow Trust Children's Charity (J)	7.524
Richard Cloudesley's Charity	7.536
Richard Reeve's Foundation	7.536
Rosminian Sisters Providence	7.545
Roundhouse Trust (J)	7.547

Saddlers' Company Charitable Fund (J)	7.580
Samworth Foundation (J)	7.586
Shakespeare Globe Trust (J)	7.599
Shipwrecked Mariners' Society (J)	7.605
SMB Charitable Trust	7.619
Society for Protection of Animals Abroad (J)	7.621
SOS Children's Villages UK (J)	7.628
South Yorkshire Community Foundation (J)	7.631
Southampton Row Trust Limited	7.631
St Mary Redcliffe Vestry	7.650
Summerfield Charitable Trust	7.664
Sussex Community Foundation (J)	7.665
Tavistock Inst of Medical Psychology (J)	7.670
Thames Hospicecare	7.675
Tree of Hope (J)	7.685
Triangle Trust 1949 Fund	7.686
UK Community Foundations	7.692
United Reformed Church (South Western) (J)	7.696
United Reformed Church Wessex Trust Ltd	7.697
University of Newcastle DevelopmentTrust	7.701
Voluntary Action Fund	7.709
W F Southall Trust	7.710
Waterloo Foundation, The (J)	7.715
Weldmar Hospicecare Trust (J)	7.717
Westbank Community Health and Care (J)	7.721
Westminster Almshouses Foundation	7.722
Wigmore Hall Trust (J)	7.727
Winston Churchill Memorial Trust (J)	7.732
Wyggeston's Hospital	7.743
York Conservation Trust	7.747
Zurich Community (UK) Trust (J)	7.753

CALEDONIAN BANK PLC, 8 St Andrew Square, Edinburgh, G2 2TU. Tel: 0131 556 8235. Fax: 0131 557 1259.

Rosslyn Chapel Trust (J)	7.545

CATER ALLEN PRIVATE BANK, 9 Nelson Street, Bradford, West Yorkshire, BD1 5AN. Tel: 0800 092 3300. Fax: 0870 240 6263. Internet: www.caterallen.co.uk.

Congregation of the Passion Jesus Christ (J)	7.174
Gloucestershire Everyman Theatre (J)	7.278
J A Clark Charitable Trust (J)	7.348
P F Charitable Trust (J)	7.489
Royal Society of Chemistry (J)	7.572
Toynbee Hall (J)	7.684

CCLA, Senator House, 85 Queen Victoria Street, London, EC4V 4ET. Tel: 0800 022 3505. Fax: 0844 561 5126. Internet: www.ccla.co.uk.

African Medical & Research Foundation UK (J)	7.16
Alice Ellen Cooper-Dean Charitable Fndtn (J)	7.24
Art Services Grants Ltd (J)	7.40
Central Young Men's Christian Association (J)	7.123
Charity Roman Union Order St Ursula (J)	7.130
Conciliation Resources (J)	7.170
Congregation of the Sisters of St Anne (J)	7.175
Dowager Countess Eleanor Peel Trust (J)	7.210
Eveson Charitable Trust (J)	7.243
Fdn&Friends of RoyalBotanicGardens, Kew (J)	7.259
Hamps & Isle of Wight Air Ambulance (J)	7.298
Ibbett Trust (J)	7.327
Leprosy Mission England (J)	7.385
London Community Foundation (J)	7.397
Louis Baylis Charitable Trust (J)	7.403
Nat Soc CoE for Promoting Religious Ed (J)	7.452
New Kadampa Tradition (J)	7.458
Newby Trust (J)	7.459
Norfolk Wildlife Trust (J)	7.464
Nuffield Oxford Hospitals Fund (J)	7.474
Nuffield Trst for Res.&Pol.Studies in Health (J)	7.475
Robert Owen Communities (J)	7.541
Royal Corps Signals Benevolent Fund (J)	7.559
Royal Navy Submarine Museum (J)	7.568
Sheffield Hospitals Trust & Related Charities (J)	7.602
Society for Assistance of Ladies (J)	7.621
St Joseph's Hospice, Hackney (J)	7.646

CENTRAL FINANCE BOARD OF THE CHURCH OF ENGLAND, Senator House, 85 Queen Victoria Street, London, EC1A 9BD.

Community of St John Baptist General (J)	7.165

CHARITY BANK, Fosse House, 182 High Street, Tonbridge, Kent, TN9 1BE. Tel: 01732 441 900. E-mail: enquiries@charitybank.org. Internet: www.charitybank.org.

Chester Diocesan Board Finance (J)	7.138
John Ellerman Foundation (J)	7.358
Westbank Community Health and Care (J)	7.721

CHILD & CO, 1 Fleet Street, London, EC4Y 1BD. Tel: 020 7353 9865. Fax: 020 7353 1122.

Alan Babette Sainsbury Charitable Fund	7.22
Ashden Charitable Trust	7.43
Catholic Apostolic Church (J)	7.118
Emmott Foundation Ltd	7.232
Gatsby Charitable Foundation	7.270
Glass House Trust	7.276
Headley Trust	7.305
Indigo Trust	7.331
J J Charitable Trust	7.349
Jerusalem Trust	7.352
Kay Kendall Leukaemia Fund	7.366
Linbury Trust	7.389
Mark Leonard Trust	7.412
Monument Trust	7.432
Royal Naval Ben. Society for Officers	7.567
Staples Trust	7.656
Tedworth Charitable Trust	7.671
Three Guineas Trust	7.679
True Colours Trust	7.687
Woodward Charitable Trust	7.737

CIMB BANK BERHAD, 27 Knightsbridge, London, SW1X 7YB. Tel: 020 7201 3150.

Islamic Trust (J)	7.347

CITIBANK, Citibank House, 335-336 The Strand, London, WC2R 1HB. Tel: 0800 00 55 00. Internet: www.citibank.co.uk.

Africa Centre Limited (J)	7.15
Church of Jesus Christ of Latter Day Saints (J)	7.149
North Bristol NHS Trust Charitable Funds (J)	7.465
Thomson Reuters Foundation	7.678
University of Notre Dame (USA) in England	7.701
Vincent Wildlife Trust (J)	7.706

CLOSE BROTHERS LIMITED, 10 Crown Place, London, EC2A 4FT. Tel: 020 7426 4000. Fax: 020 7426 4044. E-mail: enquiries@closebrothers.co.uk. Internet: www.closebrothers.co.uk.

Booth Charities (J)	7.79
Company of Biologists Limited (J)	7.168
Mountview Academy of Theatre Arts (J)	7.436
National Assoc for Colitis and Crohn's (J)	7.442
Norfolk Wildlife Trust (J)	7.464
People's Health Trust (J)	7.497
Royal Collection Trust (J)	7.555
Royal Society of Chemistry (J)	7.572

CLYDESDALE BANK PLC, 30 Vincent Place, Glasgow, G1 2HL. Tel: 0141 248 7070. Fax: 0141 223 2559. Internet: www.clydesdalebank.co.uk.

Aberdeen Endowments Trust (J)	7.5
Aberdeen Foyer	7.6
Ambitious about Autism (J)	7.29
Archdiocese of Glasgow, The	7.37
Beatson Oncology Centre Fund	7.63
Bernard Sunley Charitable Foundation	7.66
Brain Research Trust	7.84
Bransby Horses	7.85
Buttle Trust	7.106
Cattanach Charitable Trust	7.120
Cobalt Unit Appeal Fund (J)	7.159
Community Lifestyles Limited	7.164
Community Safety Glasgow	7.167
Cora Foundation	7.179
Cripplegate Foundation (J)	7.186
Culture NL Limited	7.189
Essex & Herts Air Ambulance Trust (J)	7.240
Free Church of Scotland (J)	7.264
Gloucester Charities Trust (J)	7.277
Good Shepherd Centre Bishopton, The (J)	7.281
Guild Care	7.291
High Life Highland	7.311

Horniman Public Museum and Public Park	7.318
Huntingdon Freemen's Trust (J)	7.325
Inspire (Partnership Through Life) Ltd	7.332
James Hutton Institute, The	7.350
Joseph Levy Charitable Foundation	7.362
Letchworth Garden City Heritage Foundation (J)	7.386
Lincolnshire Agricultural Society (J)	7.389
London Philharmonic Orchestra	7.400
Margaret Blackwood Housing Association (J)	7.409
Mark Benevolent Fund, The	7.411
Medical Aid for Palestinians (J)	7.418
Millennium Link Trust	7.427
Mount Stuart Trust, The	7.436
National Assoc for Colitis and Crohn's (J)	7.442
North Ayrshire Leisure	7.465
North Lanarkshire Leisure Ltd	7.467
Northern Housing Company (J)	7.470
Nuffield Trst for Res.&Pol.Studies in Health (J)	7.475
Rank Foundation Limited (J)	7.525
Raystede Centre for Animal Welfare	7.527
RCAHMS	7.527
Riverside Inverclyde	7.539
RMIG Endowment Trust	7.540
Robert Luff Foundation Limited	7.540
Rowett Research Institute	7.548
Rufford Foundation, The	7.577
Scottish Catholic International Aid Fund (J)	7.591
SSPCA (J)	7.592
Shetland Amenity Trust	7.604
Shetland Recreational Trust	7.605
Sport Aberdeen	7.633
St Mary's Kenmure	7.650
Strathcarron Hospice (J)	7.661
Underwood Trust	7.694
YMCA Watford & District Branch (J)	7.716
West Dunbartonshire Leisure Trust	7.720
YWCA Central Club	7.751

COIF, Senator House, 85 Queen Victoria Street, London, EC4V 4ET.

Francis C Scott Charitable Trust (J)	7.262
John Ellerman Foundation (J)	7.358
Joseph Rowntree Charitable Trust (J)	7.363

CONSOLIDATED CREDITS BANK LIMITED, Chelsea House, West Gate, London, W5 1DR.

David & Ruth Lewis Family Charitable Trust	7.194

COUTTS & CO, St Martins Office, 440 Strand, London, WC2R 0QS. Tel: 020 7753 1000. Fax: 020 7753 1066. Internet: www.coutts.com. Charity specialists: Katherine Parrot. S L Fielding (Client Group Head).

AIM Foundation	7.20
Albert Hunt Trust	7.23
Art Fund	7.40
Artists' General Benevolent Institution	7.41
Ashley Family Foundation, The	7.44
Bankers Benevolent Fund, The	7.55
Basil Samuel Charitable Trust	7.59
Biochemical Society (J)	7.70
Blagrave Trust, The	7.74
British Editorial Society Bone Joint Surgery	7.92
Burdett Trust for Nursing	7.104
Cadogan Charity	7.107
Catholic Foreign Missions	7.119
CBHA	7.121
Childhood First	7.140
Churches Conservation Trust	7.150
Colyer-Fergusson Charitable Trust	7.161
Corporation of the Church House	7.180
Cullum Family Trust	7.188
David Hockney Foundation (UK) Limited	7.194
Donmar Warehouse Projects	7.207
Duchy of Lancaster Benevolent Fund	7.213
Duchy of Lancaster Jubilee Trust	7.213
Edith Murphy Foundation	7.226
English National Ballet	7.235
English National Opera	7.235
English Speaking Union Commonwealth	7.236
Fair Share Trust (J)	7.246
Family Action	7.247
Farmington Trust	7.249
Florence Nightingale Aid Sickness Trust	7.256
Garfield Weston Foundation	7.269
Geological Society of London	7.272
Gilbert Trust for the Arts	7.274

Grand Charity, The (J)	7.284
Great Steward of Scotland's Dumfries Hse Tst	7.285
Gwyneth Forrester Trust	7.294
H D H Wills 1965 Charitable Trust	7.294
Hampshire & Isle of Wight Community Fdn	7.298
Harris (Belmont) Charity (J)	7.303
Help for Heroes (J)	7.308
Horse Trust	7.318
Hospice UK	7.320
Jean Shanks Foundation (J)	7.352
Jewish Care (J)	7.354
Jewish Museum London	7.354
John Armitage Charitable Trust	7.357
John Ellerman Foundation (J)	7.358
John Horseman Trust, The	7.358
John Lyon's Charity	7.359
Jordan Charitable Foundation (J)	7.362
Journalists' Charity (J)	7.364
Kings Place Music Foundation	7.373
Landmark Trust	7.378
Lawes Agricultural Trust (J)	7.380
Leeds Teaching Hospitals Charitable Fdn (J)	7.382
Lister Institute of Preventive Medicine	7.391
Liz and Terry Bramall Charitable Trust, The	7.394
LTA Trust, The	7.404
Marie Louise Von Motesiczky Charitable Trust	7.410
Maud Elkington Charitable Trust	7.416
Mental Health Foundation	7.421
Moorfields Eye Hospital Special Trustees	7.433
Muriel Jones Foundation, The	7.439
National Gallery (J)	7.447
National Gallery Trust	7.447
NGT Foundation	7.461
Nordoff Robbins Music Therapy Centre	7.464
Nuffield Trst for Res.&Pol.Studies in Health (J)	7.475
Ogden Trust (J)	7.479
Old Possum's Practical Trust	7.479
Opera North (J)	7.481
Padwa Charitable Foundation, The	7.489
Peabody Trust	7.494
Peter Harrison Foundation (J)	7.499
Prince of Wales's Charitable Fndtn	7.514
Prince's Trust (J)	7.514
Prism The Gift Fund	7.515
Queen Elizabeth Diamond Jubilee Trust (J)	7.519
Queen's Trust, The	7.521
Rainbow Trust Children's Charity (J)	7.524
Reed Foundation, The	7.529
Regent's Park Theatre Limited (J)	7.530
Resolution Trust, The (J)	7.532
Roddick Foundation, The	7.542
Rothschild Foundation (Hanadiv) Europe (J)	7.547
Royal Air Force Club	7.551
Royal Albert Hall	7.551
Royal Collection Trust (J)	7.555
Royal Life Saving Society UK	7.563
Royal Literary Fund	7.563
Royal National Theatre	7.567
Royal Opera House Covent Garden	7.569
Royal Opera House Endowment Fund 2000	7.569
Royal Opera House Foundation	7.569
Royal Society of Arts	7.571
RSPCA	7.572
Sadler's Wells Trust	7.580
Serpentine Trust	7.597
Sino-British Fellowship Trust	7.609
Sir John Cass's Foundation	7.611
Skills for Justice (J)	7.618
Society of Antiquaries of London	7.621
SSAFA (J)	7.626
Stone Family Foundation, The	7.660
Suffolk Foundation, The (J)	7.663
Swire Educational Trust	7.667
Tate (J)	7.669
Tate Foundation	7.669
Tate Members	7.669
Tennis Foundation (J)	7.672
Thompson Family Charitable Trust (J)	7.678
Thrombosis Research Institute	7.680
Tuixen Foundation, The	7.690
Union Jack Club, The	7.694
University College London Hospitals Charity	7.700

CREDIT SUISSE, 5 Cabot Square, London, E14 4QR. Tel: 020 7888 8000. Fax: 020 7888 8891.

Dr Mortimer & Theresa Sackler Fdtn (J)	7.211

ESCRS Limited (J) 7.242
Hintze Family Charitable Foundation, The (J) 7.313
Ingram Trust 7.331
Kabbalah Centre (J) 7.365
Sackler Trust, The (J) 7.579

CROWN AGENTS FINANCIAL SERVICES LIMITED, St Nicholas House, St Nicholas Road, Sutton, Surrey, SM1 1EL. Tel: 0208 643 3311. Fax: 0208 643 6250.

Homeless International (J) 7.316
Institute of Development Studies (J) 7.334

CUMBERLAND BUILDING SOCIETY, Castle Street, Carlisle, Cumbria, CA3 8RX. Internet: www.cumberland.co.uk.

Brathay Trust (J) 7.85
Cumbrian Community Foundation (J) 7.189

D Z BANK, 150 Cheapside, London, EC2V 6ET. Tel: 020 7776 6000. Fax: 020 7776 6100. E-mail: london@dzbank.de.

4 Charity Foundation (J) 7.3

DANSKE BANK, IFSC Advisory Centre, 3 Harbourmaster Pl, Dublin 1, Dublin. Tel: 1890 866 866. Internet: www.danskebank.ie.

Action Cancer 7.9
Action Mental Health 7.11
Disability Action (J) 7.201
ESCRS Limited (J) 7.242
Exceed Worldwide 7.243
Northern Ireland Assoc for Mental Health 7.470
Northern Ireland Hospice 7.470
Simon Community Northern Ireland 7.609
Ulster Independent Clinic 7.693

DEUTSCHE BANK AG, 1 Great Winchester Street, London, EC2N 2DB. Tel: 020 7545 8000. Fax: 020 7971 7455.

Federation European Biochemical Societies (J) 7.250
Marchig Animal Welfare Trust 7.409

ECOBANK, EBI SA Representative Office, 2nd Floor, 20 Old Broad Street, London, EC2N 1DP. Tel: 0203 582 8820. Fax: 020 7382 0671.

Save the Children International (J) 7.588

EFG PRIVATE BANK LIMITED, Leconfield House, Curzon Street, London, W1J 5JB. Tel: 020 7491 9111. Fax: 020 7872 3706. Internet: www.efgl.com.

Beaverbrook Foundation (J) 7.63

EUROPE ARAB BANK PLC, 13-15 Moorgate, London, EC2R 6AD. Tel: 020 7315 8500. Fax: 020 7600 7620. Internet: www.eabplc.co.uk.

A M Qattan Foundation (J) 7.3
Medical Aid for Palestinians (J) 7.418

FIRST TRUST BANK, 4 Queen's Square, Belfast, County Antrim, BT1 3DT. Tel: 028 9032 5599. Fax: 028 9043 8338.

Bryson Charitable Group 7.102
Community Foundation for N Ireland 7.163
Teresa Ball International Solidarity Fund (J) 7.673
United Christian Broadcasters (J) 7.695

FURNESS BUILDING SOCIETY, 51-55 Duke Street, Barrow-in-Furness, Cumbria, LA14 1RT. Tel: 01229 824 560. Fax: 01229 837 043. Internet: www.furnessbs.co.uk.

Cumbrian Community Foundation (J) 7.189

GOLDMAN SACHS INTERNATIONAL, Peterborough Court, 133 Fleet Street, London, EC4A 2BB. Tel: 0207 774 1000.

David Elaine Potter Charitable Foundation (J) 7.194

GOVERNMENT BANKING SERVICE, Southern House, 7th Floor, Wellesley Grove, Croydon, Surrey, CR9 1WW. Tel: 020 8929 2794. Internet: www.hmrc.gov.uk/gbs/about.htm.

British Library (J) 7.95

Buckinghamshire Hospitals NHS Trust (J) 7.103
Cardiff and Vale Health Charity (J) 7.113
National Gallery (J) 7.447
Royal United Hospital Bath NHS Trust Ch Fd 7.574

HABIB BANK AG ZURICH, Habib House, 42 Moorgate, London, EC2R 6JJ. Tel: 020 7452 0200. Fax: 020 7628 8583. E-mail: contactus@habibbank.com. Internet: www.habibbank.com.

Edhi International Foundation UK (J) 7.224
World Federation - Muslim Communities (J) 7.740

HANDELSBANKEN, 3 Thomas More Square, London, E1W 1WY. Tel: 020 7578 8000. Fax: 020 7578 8300. Internet: www.handelsbanken.co.uk.

AKO Foundation 7.21
Andrew Lloyd Webber Foundation, The 7.31
Bransford Trust, The 7.85
Coalfields Regeneration Trust (J) 7.158
Frank Jackson Foundation, The 7.263
Greenham Common Community Trust (J) 7.286
Higher Education Academy, The (J) 7.311
Milton Keynes Parks Trust Ltd (J) 7.428
Oaklea Trust, The 7.477
Pilling Trust Fund, The 7.504
Royal Bath and West of England Society 7.553
Sir John Fisher Foundation 7.611
Solent Mind (J) 7.626
SS Great Britain Trust (J) 7.635
St John's Hospital 7.645
St Luke's Hospice (J) 7.647
Tees Valley Community Foundation (J) 7.671
Unipol Student Homes (J) 7.695
Wallscourt Foundation (J) 7.712
Woking & Sam Beare Hospices (J) 7.735

HSBC BANK PLC, 8 Canada Square, London, E14 5HQ. Tel: 020 7991 8888. Internet: www.hsbc.com. Charity specialists: B Furneau-Harris.

1893 Derby RSD Company 7.2
29th May 1961 Charitable Trust 7.2
4Children 7.3
ABF The Soldiers Charity 7.6
Academies Enterprise Trust 7.7
Action for Children 7.10
Addiction Dependency Solutions (J) 7.14
Adolescent and Children's Trust, The 7.14
Al-Khair Foundation (J) 7.21
Al-Shirkatul Islamiyyah (J) 7.22
Alan Edward Higgs Charity 7.22
Alternative Futures Group Ltd 7.27
Alzheimer's Society 7.28
Amnesty International Limited 7.30
Andrew Anderson Trust 7.31
Anglo-European College of Chiropractic 7.32
Anheddau Cyf 7.33
APASENTH 7.34
Arundel and Brighton Diocesan Trust 7.42
ASDAN 7.42
Assoc of Anaesthetists of GB & Ireland 7.46
Baptist Union Corporation 7.56
Baptist Union of Great Britain 7.56
Barnwood House Trust 7.58
Barrow Cadbury Trust (J) 7.59
BBC Children in Need 7.61
Beacon Centre for the Blind (J) 7.62
Beatson Institute for Cancer Research 7.62
Beaverbrook Foundation (J) 7.63
Benjamin Foundation, The 7.66
Betel of Britain 7.67
Beverley Consolidated Charity 7.68
Bible & Gospel Trust (J) 7.69
Birmingham Museums Trust 7.72
Birmingham Royal Ballet 7.73
Bishop Radford Trust, The 7.73
Bishopsgate Foundation 7.73
Blatchington Court Trust (J) 7.75
Bletchley Park Trust 7.76
Bradford Trident Ltd 7.83
Brahma Kumaris World Spiritual UniversityUK 7.83
Breakthrough Breast Cancer (J) 7.86
Breast Cancer Care 7.86
Brentwood Roman Catholic Diocesan Trust 7.87
Bristol Charities 7.89

Bristol, Clifton, & West of England Zoo (J) 7.89
British Council 7.92
British Journal of Anaesthesia, The (J) 7.95
British Lung Foundation (J) 7.96
British Motor Industry Heritage Trust 7.96
British Museum Friends (J) 7.96
British Pregnancy Advisory Service 7.97
British Union of Seventh-Day Adventists 7.99
Britten-Pears Foundation (J) 7.100
Brookvale 7.101
Buckinghamshire Hospitals NHS Trust (J) 7.103
Burton Constable Foundation 7.105
Cabrini Children's Society 7.107
Cambridge Union Society, The (J) 7.109
Campden Charities Trustee 7.110
CARE International UK (J) 7.114
Caritas Care (J) 7.115
Carlisle Diocesan Board of Finance 7.116
Catherine Cookson Charitable Trust (J) 7.118
Catholic Trust for England and Wales 7.120
CDP Worldwide (J) 7.121
Chapter of Order of the Holy Paraclete 7.128
Charity for Roman Catholic Congregation (J) 7.128
Charity of Elizabeth Jane Jones, The (J) 7.129
Chartered Institute of Arbitrators 7.132
Chartered Institute Building 7.132
Chartered Institute of Environmental Health 7.133
Chartered Institute of Taxation 7.134
Chaseley Trust 7.135
Chatham Maritime Trust 7.136
Chief Fire Officers Association, The 7.139
Children s Family Trust 7.140
Children's Hospice South West 7.141
Children's Investment Fund Foundation 7.141
China Fleet Trust 7.143
Christian Aid (J) 7.145
Church of Jesus Christ of Latter Day Saints (J) 7.149
City of Birmingham Symphony Orchestra 7.153
CLC International (UK) (J) 7.156
Climate Group, The 7.157
College of Occupational Therapists 7.160
Comm. Foundation for Wiltshire & Swindon 7.163
Community of St Mary at the Cross (J) 7.166
Community of the Resurrection (J) 7.167
Congregation of Sisters of Jesus & Mary 7.172
Congregation of the Daughters of Wisdom 7.173
Congregation of Servants of Mary(London) 7.174
Congregation of the Sisters of St Anne (J) 7.175
Conservation Education & Research Trust (J) 7.177
Council for World Mission (J) 7.182
Coventry Freemen's Charity 7.184
Creative Skillset - Skillset Sector Skills Council 7.185
Croftlands Trust 7.187
Cumbrian Community Foundation (J) 7.189
Cutty Sark Trust (J) 7.189
David and Claudia Harding Foundation, The 7.193
Dawat-e-Hadiyah Trust (United Kingdom) (J) 7.195
Dawliffe Hall Educational Foundation (J) 7.195
Debra 7.196
Denys Eyre Bower Bequest, The (J) 7.197
Depaul International 7.197
Devon Air Ambulance Trust 7.200
Dibden Allotments Fund 7.201
Diocese of Hexham and Newcastle 7.201
Djanogly Learning Trust 7.202
Doncaster Deaf Trust 7.205
Douglas Turner Trust 7.210
Earley Charity (J) 7.219
East London Mosque Trust Ltd, The (J) 7.221
Edge Foundation 7.224
EDP - Drug and Alcohol Services 7.226
Ed & TrainingTst of Chartered Insurance Inst 7.227
Electrical Safety Council 7.229
Elizabeth Frankland Moore & Star Fdn 7.230
Engineering UK (J) 7.234
Euro Charity Trust 7.241
Ezer V'Hatzalah Ltd 7.245
Fairfield (Croydon) (J) 7.246
Fairtrade Foundation (J) 7.247
Federation European Biochemical Societies (J) 7.250
Federation of Synagogues 7.251
Felix Thornley Cobold Agricultural Trust 7.251
Fishmongers' Company's Charitable Trust 7.255
Forum for the Future, The 7.258
Foundation of Lady Katherine Leveson, The 7.260
FOUNDATION66 7.261
Francis Crick Insitute Limited, The 7.262
Friends of the Elderly 7.265

Future of Russia Foundation	7.267
General Conference of the New Church (J)	7.270
GOAL (International)	7.279
Goodman Foundation, The	7.281
Grace Trust, The	7.283
GreaterManchester AccessibleTransport (J)	7.286
Groundwork South Trust Limited, The (J)	7.290
Groundwork UK (J)	7.290
Guide Dogs for the Blind Association (J)	7.291
Guideposts Trust	7.291
Gurkha Welfare Trust (J)	7.292
GVEP International	7.293
Health Poverty Action (J)	7.305
Help for Heroes (J)	7.308
Henry Barber Trust (J)	7.308
Higher Education Statistics Agency	7.312
Hope House Children's Hospices	7.317
Hospice of Hope Romania Limited	7.319
Hospital of Gilbert, Earl of Shrewsbury	7.320
Hospital of St John and St Elizabeth	7.321
HSF Health Plan	7.323
Hull Truck Theatre Company	7.323
Human Relief Foundation (J)	7.324
Humberside Engineering Training Assoc	7.325
ICAEW Foundation & Educational Charities (J)	7.327
Imagine Independence	7.328
Institute of Advanced Motorists	7.333
Institute of Cancer Research	7.334
Institute of Grocery Distribution (J)	7.335
Institute of Physics	7.336
Institution of Civil Engineers	7.338
Intl Agency for the Prevention of Blindness (J)	7.340
Int. Baccalaureate Org (UK)	7.340
Intl Foundation for Aids to Navigation	7.342
International Fund for Animal Welfare	7.342
International Health Partners (UK) Ltd	7.342
International Inst for Strategic Studies	7.343
International Students House	7.345
International Water Association	7.345
Islamia Schools Trust	7.346
Islamic Help	7.347
Isle of Anglesey Charitable Trust, The	7.347
ITF Seafarers Trust	7.348
J Isaacs Charitable Trust	7.348
Jack Petchey Foundation	7.349
James Pantyfedwen Foundation	7.350
John Laing Charitable Trust	7.359
Joseph Rowntree Charitable Trust (J)	7.363
Joseph Rowntree Foundation	7.363
Journalists' Charity (J)	7.364
Julia's House	7.364
Keep Britain Tidy	7.367
Kelmarsh Trust	7.367
Keswick Foundation	7.370
King Fahad Academy Limited	7.372
King Henry VIII Endowed Trust Warwick	7.372
Kusuma Trust UK (J)	7.375
Lancaster Roman Catholic Diocesan Trust	7.378
Laureus Sport for Good Foundation	7.380
Leathersellers Company Charitable Fund	7.381
Leeds Diocesan Trust (J)	7.382
Lempriere Pringle Charitable Trust, The (J)	7.384
LHASA (J)	7.387
Life Opportunities Trust	7.388
Lifeline Community Projects (J)	7.388
Liverpool Charity and Voluntary Services (J)	7.392
Liverpool Roman Catholic Archdiocesan	7.393
London Academy of Music and Dramatic Art (J)	7.397
London Transport Museum	7.401
Lumos Foundation	7.404
MacIntyre Care	7.405
Maggie Keswick Jencks Cancer Trust (J)	7.406
Malaria Consortium	7.407
Marcela Trust, The	7.409
Maria Assumpta Trust	7.410
Marine Stewardship Council	7.411
Market Harborough & the Bowdens Charity	7.412
Medical Aid for Palestinians (J)	7.418
Medical Foundation for Victims of Torture (J)	7.419
Mercy Corps Scotland (J)	7.422
Methodist Central Hall Westminster	7.423
Methodist Church In Great Britain, The	7.423
Methodist Homes (J)	7.424
Michael Bishop Foundation	7.425
Midlands Arts Centre (J)	7.426
Mudiad Meithrin	7.438
Muscular Dystrophy Campaign (J)	7.439
Musicians Benevolent Fund	7.440

National Benevolent Charity, The	7.443
National Energy Action	7.445
National Maritime Museum (J)	7.449
National Memorial Arboretum Company Ltd (J)	7.450
National Star Foundation	7.453
Netherhall Educational Association (J)	7.457
New Victoria Hospital Limited, The	7.458
Newcastle Theatre Royal Trust (J)	7.460
Newcastle upon Tyne Hospitals NHS Charity (J)	7.460
Nicholas Chamberlaine School Foundation	7.462
North Humberside Hospice Project	7.466
Notre Dame de France Trust	7.472
Nuffield Health (J)	7.474
Nugent Care	7.475
Nursing & Midwifery Council	7.476
Oakhaven Trust	7.476
Office of the Ind. Adjudicator for Higher Ed.	7.478
Old Swinford Hospital	7.479
Old Vic Theatre Trust 2000	7.479
Opera North (J)	7.481
Oxford Trust, The	7.488
Passage 2000	7.492
Percy Bilton Charity	7.497
Perthyn (J)	7.498
Pharmacist Support (J)	7.500
Plymouth Marine Laboratory	7.506
Portland College	7.509
Prior's Court Foundation	7.515
Prospect Foundation	7.516
Prudential Staff Charitable Trust	7.517
Quality Assurance Agency for HE	7.518
R&A Foundation, The (J)	7.521
Rachel Charitable Trust	7.522
Ramakrishna Vedanta Centre	7.524
Ranyard Charitable Trust	7.526
Rathbone Training	7.526
Refuge	7.529
Regent's Park Theatre Limited (J)	7.530
Rehabilitation for Addicted Prisoners	7.530
Religious Sisters of Charity	7.531
Resolution Trust, The (J)	7.532
Retreat York, The	7.534
Richmond Charities' Almshouses (J)	7.537
Riders for Health	7.538
Robert Owen Communities (J)	7.541
Roffey Park Institute	7.542
Roman Catholic Diocese Hallam Trust	7.543
RC Diocese of Hexham & Newcastle	7.543
Rotherham Hospice Trust (J)	7.546
Royal Academy of Dance	7.549
Royal Aeronautical Society	7.550
Royal Astronomical Society (J)	7.552
Royal College of Pathologists	7.557
Royal College of Surgeons (J)	7.558
Royal Institution of Great Britain	7.562
Royal Liverpool Philharmonic Society	7.563
Royal School for Blind Liverpool	7.570
Royal School for the Deaf Derby	7.570
Royal Town Planning Institute	7.574
Royal Welsh Agricultural Society Limited	7.575
S F Foundation	7.578
SistersoftheSacred Hearts of Jesus & Mary	7.580
Salvation Army International Trust (J)	7.584
Samjo Limited	7.585
Samuel Sebba Charitable Trust	7.586
Scripture Union	7.594
Secular Clergy Common Fund	7.596
Services Sound Vision Corporation	7.598
Shakespeare Birthplace Trust	7.599
Shottermill Rec. Ground & Swimming Pool	7.606
Shree Kutch Satsang Swaminarayan Temple (J)	7.606
Sightsavers International (J)	7.608
Sigrid Rausing Trust	7.608
Sir James Knott Trust	7.610
Sir James Reckitt Charity, The	7.611
Sir John Priestman Charity Trust	7.611
Sisters of Charity of St Vincent de Paul	7.613
Sisters of the Holy Cross	7.615
Skills for Care (J)	7.617
Skills for Health Limited	7.617
Smile Train UK, The	7.619
Sobell Foundation	7.619
Society of Chemical Industry	7.622
Society of Jesus	7.622
Society of the Sacred Heart	7.624
Solace Women's Aid	7.625
South England Seventh-Day Adventists	7.628
South London YMCA	7.629

South Yorkshire Community Foundation (J)	7.631
Special Air Service Regimental Association	7.632
St Catherine's Hospice Trust	7.639
St Cecilia's Abbey Ryde Isle of Wight	7.639
St Christopher's Hospice	7.640
St Clare West Essex Hospice Care Trust (J)	7.640
St Gemma's Hospice Leeds	7.643
St John's Hospital Lichfield	7.645
St Luke's Parochial Trust	7.648
St Mungo Community Housing Association	7.652
Montessori St Nicholas Charity, The (J)	7.652
St Rocco's Hospice	7.654
Starlight Children's Foundation (J)	7.656
Stevenage Leisure	7.658
Stonyhurst Charitable Fund	7.660
Sutton Coldfield Municipal Charities	7.666
Tearfund	7.670
Tenovus	7.673
Tesco Charity Trust	7.674
Thames Valley Air Ambulance	7.675
TLC Care Attendant Service (J)	7.681
Tree of Hope (J)	7.685
St Benedict's Abbey Ealing (J)	7.688
Congregation of Christian Brothers	7.688
Franciscan Sisters Minoress	7.689
Trustees of the London Clinic Limited	7.689
TTE Technical Training Group, The	7.690
Twycross Zoo (J)	7.691
Ty Hafan (J)	7.692
UK Biobank Ltd (J)	7.692
UNICEF-UK	7.694
United Christian Broadcasters (J)	7.695
United Reformed Church	7.696
United St Saviour's Charities	7.698
Univ Old Members' Trust, The (J)	7.699
Universities & Colleges Christian F'ship	7.699
Urdd Gobaith Cymru	7.701
Valley Leisure (J)	7.702
Victoria Foundation, The	7.705
Waqf Al-Birr Educational Trust	7.714
Watershed Arts Trust Limited	7.715
YMCA Watford & District Branch (J)	7.716
Weizmann Institute Foundation (J)	7.717
Wellcome Trust	7.718
WFSC Foundation (J)	7.719
West Lancashire Freemasons' Charity	7.720
Westminster RC Diocesan Trust	7.723
Whizz-Kidz (J)	7.726
Wigan & Leigh Hospice	7.727
Windhorse Trust, The (J)	7.732
Wirral Autistic Society (J)	7.733
Wirral Hospice St John's	7.733
Wixamtree Trust	7.734
WomanCare Global	7.736
World Mission Agency	7.741
Worth Abbey (J)	7.742
Yesamach Levav (J)	7.744
Ymddiriedolaeth Clough Williams-Ellis Fdn (J)	7.746
York Citizens Theatre Trust	7.747
York Minster Fund	7.748
York Museums Trust	7.748
Young Enterprise	7.750
Young Foundation, The	7.750
Yusuf Islam Foundation	7.751
Zurich Community (UK) Trust (J)	7.753

I M WEALTH SERVICES, 2 Multrees Walk, Edinburgh, EH1 3DQ. Tel: 0131 247 5000. Internet: www.multrees.com.

P F Charitable Trust (J)	7.489

ICICI BANK UK PLC, 21 Knightsbridge, London, SW1X7LY. Internet: www.icicibank.co.uk.

Kusuma Trust UK (J)	7.375

INVESTEC BANK (UK) LIMITED, 2 Gresham Street, London, EC2V 7QP. Tel: 020 7597 1250. Internet: www.investec.co.uk/products-and-services/investing/charity-services.html.

Catherine Cookson Charitable Trust (J)	7.118
CHK Charities Limited	7.143
Pharmacist Support (J)	7.500
Soka Gakkai International UK (J)	7.625
Viscount Amory's Charitable Trust (J)	7.707

IRISH BANK RESOLUTION CORPORATION LIMITED, 10 Old Jewry, London, EC2R 8DN.

Architectural Association Incorporated (J) 7.38

ISLAMIC BANK OF BRITAIN, Edgbaston House, 3 Duchess Place, Birmingham, West Midlands, B16 8NH.

Al-Khair Foundation (J)	7.21
East London Mosque Trust Ltd, The (J)	7.221
Harrow Central Mosque and Islamic Centre (J)	7.303
Muslim Hands (J)	7.441

ISRAEL DISCOUNT BANK, Nightingale House, 65 Curzon Street, London, W1J 8PE.

Magen David Adom UK (J)	7.406

J P MORGAN CHASE BANK, London Branch, 25 Bank Street, Canary Wharf, London, E14 5JP.

Dr Mortimer & Theresa Sackler Fdtn (J)	7.211
Sackler Trust, The (J)	7.579

JPMORGAN, 125 London Wall, London, EC2Y 5AJ. Tel: 020 7777 2000. Fax: 020 7777 4165.

Aimwell Charitable Trust (J)	7.20
Claude and Sofia Marion Foundation, The	7.155
Movember Europe (J)	7.436
National Fund	7.446

JULIAN HODGE BANK LTD, 10 Windsor Place, Cardiff, CF1 3BX. Tel: 029 2022 0800. Fax: 029 2034 4061.

Booth Charities (J)	7.79
Jane Hodge Foundation	7.351

KINGDOM BANK, Ruddington Fields Business Park, Mere Way, Ruddington, Nottinghamshire, NG11 6JS. Tel: 0115 921 7250. Fax: 0115 921 7251. E-mail: info@kingdombank.co.uk. Internet: www.kingdombank.co.uk.

Christians Against Poverty (J)	7.146
Jesus House (J)	7.353

KLEINWORT BENSON PRIVATE BANK, 14 St. George Street, London, W1S 1FE. Tel: 020 3207 7000. Fax: 020 3207 7659. E-mail: charities@kbpb.co.uk. Internet: www.kbpb.co.uk. Charity specialists: G Rizk (Head of Charities).

Company of Biologists Limited (J)	7.168
Ernest Kleinwort Charitable Trust	7.239
Ibbett Trust (J)	7.327

LEEDS BUILDING SOCIETY, 41 Kingsway, London, WC2B 6TP. Internet: www.leedsbuildingsociety.co.uk.

Hinrichsen Foundation	7.313

LLOYDS BANK CORPORATE MARKETS, 4th Floor, 25 Gresham Street, London, EC2V 7HN. Tel: 020 7661 4986. Fax: 0207 356 2485. E-mail: richard.farr@lloydsbanking.com. Internet: lloydsbankcorporatemarkets.com. Charity specialists: Richard Farr (Relationship Director, London & South East).

Ability Housing Association (J)	7.7
Absolute Return for Kids (ARK)	7.7
Academy of Medical Sciences	7.8
Acorn Villages	7.8
Africa Educational Trust (J)	7.15
Aga Khan Foundation (United Kingdom)	7.16
Age UK Lancashire	7.17
Aimwell Charitable Trust (J)	7.20
Aldingbourne Trust	7.24
Alzheimer's Research UK (J)	7.28
Amateurs Trust, The	7.29
Amgueddfa Cymru	7.30
Anchor Trust	7.31
Aquarius Action Projects	7.36
Architects Benevolent Society (J)	7.38
Architectural Association Incorporated (J)	7.38
Army Cadet Force Association	7.39
Army Dependants' Trust, The	7.39
Arundel Castle Trustees	7.42
Ashdown Medway Accomodation Trust	7.43
Ashridge (Bonar Law Memorial) Trust (J)	7.44
Association of Accounting Technicians (J)	7.46
Autism East Midlands	7.49

Azure Charitable Enterprises	7.52
B E Perl Charitable Trust	7.53
Babraham Institute	7.53
Barbara Ward Children's Foundation	7.56
Barnsley Hospice Appeal (J)	7.58
Baron Davenport's Charity	7.58
Batchworth Trust (J)	7.60
Bath Wells Diocesan Board Finance (J)	7.60
BCS, The Chartered Institute for IT	7.61
BFI Trust	7.68
Bible & Gospel Trust (J)	7.69
Birmingham Dogs Home	7.72
Birmingham Hippodrome Theatre Trust Ltd	7.72
Bond's Hospital Estate Charity	7.79
Borrow Foundation, The	7.81
Bournemouth Young Men's Christian Assoc (J)	7.82
Bradford Diocesan Board of Finance, The (J)	7.83
Brain Tumour Charity	7.84
Brandon Trust	7.84
Break	7.86
Brian Mercer Charitable Trust	7.87
Bridge Estate	7.87
British Assoc Counselling & Psychotherapy	7.92
British Film Institute	7.93
British Kidney Patient Association	7.95
British Library (J)	7.95
Brook Young People	7.101
BRUNELCARE (J)	7.102
Burberry Foundation, The	7.104
C B and H H Taylor 1984 Trust	7.107
Cambridge Union Society, The (J)	7.109
CAMFED International	7.110
Canterbury Cathedral Trust Fund	7.112
Canterbury Diocesan Board of Finance	7.112
Carnegie Trust for Universities Scotland	7.116
Castel Froma	7.117
Catholic Blind Institute	7.119
Central England Quakers (CEQ) (J)	7.122
Centre 404	7.123
CFBT Education Trust	7.125
Chain of Hope	7.126
Chapter (Cardiff)	7.127
Charity of the Congregation of Our Lady	7.129
Chartered Inst of Personnel & Development	7.134
Chartered Quality Institute (J)	7.135
Cheltenham Festival	7.137
Cheshire Residential Homes (J)	7.137
Children's Trust	7.142
Chippenham Borough Lands Charity	7.143
Christian Blind Mission (United Kingdom)	7.145
Christians Against Poverty (J)	7.146
Church of Pentecost - UK, The (J)	7.149
CIPFA	7.151
City Bridge Trust, The	7.153
Civil Service Benevolent Fund, The	7.154
Claire House Appeal	7.155
CLIC Sargent Cancer Care for Children (J)	7.156
Clore Duffield Foundation	7.157
Coal Industry Social Welfare Organisation	7.158
Cobalt Unit Appeal Fund (J)	7.159
Collegiate Charitable Foundation, The	7.161
Colt Foundation	7.161
Community Integrated Care	7.164
Community Links (Northern)	7.164
Company of Biologists Limited (J)	7.168
Consolidated Charity of Burton upn Trent	7.177
Constance Travis Charitable Trust	7.178
Cornwall Care	7.180
Cottage and Rural Enterprises Limited	7.181
Countryside Restoration Trust (J)	7.182
County Air Ambulance Trust (J)	7.183
CVQO Limited	7.189
Daiwa Anglo Japanese Foundation	7.192
Dame Alice Owen's Foundation	7.192
Dame Hannah Rogers Trust (J)	7.192
David Elaine Potter Charitable Foundation (J)	7.194
Derwen College	7.198
Design Council	7.199
Dorneywood Trust, The	7.208
Douglas Macmillan Hospice	7.209
Drug Safety Research Trust, The	7.212
Duke of Edinburgh's Award Intl Foundation	7.214
Duke of Edinburgh's Award	7.214
Dynamic Earth Charitable Trust	7.217
Dyslexia Action	7.217
Edhi International Foundation UK (J)	7.224
Edward Cadbury Charitable Trust	7.228
Elim Foursquare Gospel Alliance (J)	7.230

Elizabeth Finn Care	7.230
Energy Institute	7.233
Englefield Charitable Trust	7.234
Epping Forest	7.237
Equinox Care	7.237
ESCRS Limited (J)	7.242
EveryChild (J)	7.243
ExtraCare Charitable Trust	7.245
Farleigh Hospice	7.248
Father Hudson's Society	7.249
Forum Trust Limited	7.258
Fdn&Friends of RoyalBotanicGardens, Kew (J)	7.259
General Optical Council (J)	7.271
George Cadbury Fund B Account	7.272
Global Alliance For Livestock Vet Med.	7.277
Glyndebourne Arts Trust	7.278
Glyndebourne Productions Limited	7.279
Godinton House Preservation Trust	7.279
Gofal Housing Trust	7.280
Gosling Foundation Limited	7.282
Greensleeves Homes Trust	7.287
Grenadier Guards Charity, The	7.288
GroceryAid	7.289
Groundwork London	7.289
Guildford Diocesan Board of Finance	7.292
Guiting Manor Amenity Trust	7.292
Guy Newton Research Fund (J)	7.293
Hamps & Isle of Wight Air Ambulance (J)	7.298
Hampstead Heath	7.299
Handmaids of the Sacred Heart of Jesus (J)	7.300
Harrogate District Hospice Care	7.303
Healthcare Quality Improvement Partnership	7.306
Help for Heroes (J)	7.308
Henry Moore Foundation (J)	7.309
Hereford Diocesan Board Finance	7.309
HF Trust Limited	7.311
Hill Foundation, The	7.312
HMS Victory Preservation Company, The	7.314
Hobson Charity Limited	7.314
Hollybank Trust	7.315
Hospice in the Weald (J)	7.319
Hospice St Francis Berkhamsted Limited	7.319
Housing for Women	7.322
Hughes Travel Trust	7.323
Hult International Business School	7.324
Ibbett Trust (J)	7.327
In Kind Direct	7.330
Institute of Materials, Minerals & Mining	7.336
Institution of Eng Technology Ben Fund (J)	7.338
Intl Society for Krishna Consciousness (J)	7.344
Jaffray Care Society	7.349
JCA Charitable Foundation	7.351
Jean Shanks Foundation (J)	7.352
Jesus House (J)	7.353
Jewish Secondary Schools Movement	7.355
Jisc	7.355
Joffe Charitable Trust	7.356
John Martin's Charity (J)	7.360
John Roan Foundation	7.360
John Townsend Trust, The	7.361
JW3 Trust Limited (J)	7.365
Katharine House Hospice	7.366
Kennedy Trust for Rheumatology Research	7.368
Khodorkovsky Foundation	7.370
King's College Hospital Charity	7.372
Kirkwood Hospice	7.374
L M Kendon Settlement (J)	7.376
Langdon Community	7.378
Langdon Foundation	7.379
LankellyChase Foundation, The (J)	7.379
Lichfield Diocesan Board Of Education, The	7.387
Lichfield Diocesan Board Of Finance	7.387
Lilian Faithfull Homes Limited	7.389
Linkage Community Trust	7.390
Liverpool & Merseyside Theatres Trust	7.392
Liverpool Diocesan Board of Finance, The	7.392
Lloyds Foundation for England and Wales	7.395
Lolev Charitable Trust, The	7.396
London Grid for Learning Trust	7.399
London Symphony Orchestra	7.401
Longfield	7.401
Making Space	7.407
Margaret Blackwood Housing Association (J)	7.409
Marine Biological Association United Kingdom	7.411
Martin Foundation, The	7.413
Martlets Hospice Limited (J)	7.413
Mary Rose Trust	7.414
Mathematics in Education and Industry	7.416

Mayfair Charities	7.417
Meath Epilepsy Trust	7.418
Medical Research Council Technology	7.419
Medical Research Foundation (J)	7.419
Medlock Charitable Trust	7.420
Memralife Group	7.420
Mental Health Concern	7.421
Metropolitan City Police Orphans Fund	7.424
Metropolitan Support Trust	7.424
Moondance Foundation	7.432
Moor House School	7.432
Motor Neurone Disease Association	7.435
Museum of London	7.440
Museum of London Archaeology	7.440
Muslim Aid	7.440
Myton Hospices, The	7.441
National Army Museum	7.442
National Assoc for Colitis and Crohn's (J)	7.442
Nat Centre for Young People with Epilepsy	7.443
National Childbirth Trust	7.444
National Film and Television School	7.445
National Foundation for Youth Music (J)	7.446
Nat Institute of Agricultural Botany Trust	7.448
National Marine Aquarium	7.449
National Memorial Arboretum Company Ltd (J)	7.450
National Museum of Royal Navy, The	7.450
National Osteoporosis Society (J)	7.451
NCFE (J)	7.455
Nene Park Trust	7.456
Nesta	7.456
NIAB	7.462
North East Autism Society (J)	7.466
Northern Ballet Theatre	7.469
Northern Rock Foundation (J)	7.471
Notts Roman Catholic Diocesan Trustees	7.473
Novalis Trust	7.474
Oakdale Trust	7.476
Ogden Trust (J)	7.479
Ombersley Conservation Trust	7.480
Papworth Trust (J)	7.490
Parkhaven Trust	7.491
Paul Mellon Centre for Studies British Art	7.493
PDSA	7.494
People Potential Possibilities (J)	7.496
Peter Lang Children's Trust Limited (J)	7.499
Phillips & Rubens Charitable Trust (J)	7.501
Phyllis Tuckwell Memorial Hospice (J)	7.501
Pilgrim Homes	7.502
Pilgrim Trust	7.503
Pilgrims' Friend Society	7.503
Pilgrims Hospices in East Kent (J)	7.503
Pirbright Institute	7.504
Place2Be	7.504
Polish Catholic Mission, The	7.507
Polonsky Foundation, The (J)	7.508
Portsmouth RC Diocesan Trustees	7.510
Postcode Global Trust (J)	7.511
Postcode Green Trust	7.511
Postcode Heroes Trust	7.511
PROSPECTS	7.516
Queen Elizabeth Diamond Jubilee Trust (J)	7.519
Railway Housing Association and Benefit Fund	7.524
Redeemed Christian Church of God (J)	7.528
Representative Body of the Church in Wales	7.532
Richmond Church Charity Estates	7.537
Robert McAlpine Foundation	7.540
Robert Owen Communities (J)	7.541
Rochester Bridge Trust	7.541
Rothamsted Research Ltd	7.546
Royal Air Force Benevolent Fund (J)	7.550
Royal Air Forces Association	7.551
Royal Artillery Charitable Fund, The	7.552
Royal Ballet School Endowment Fund (J)	7.553
Royal British Legion	7.554
Royal Collection Trust (J)	7.555
Royal College of Emergency Medicine, The	7.555
Royal College of Physicians of London (J)	7.557
Royal Corps Signals Benevolent Fund (J)	7.559
Royal Engineers Association	7.559
Royal Entomological Society of London	7.559
Royal Foundation of St Katharine, The	7.560
Royal Hospital Chelsea Appeal Ltd (J)	7.561
Royal Institute of British Architects	7.562
Royal Institute International Affairs	7.562
Royal Marsden Cancer Campaign (J)	7.564
Royal Natl Mission to Deep Sea Fishermen	7.567
Royal Navy Submarine Museum (J)	7.568
Royal Society for Prevention of Accidents	7.571

RSPB (J)	7.572
Royal Society of Medicine (J)	7.573
Royal Zoological Society of Scotland	7.576
Ruach Inspirational Church of God	7.576
Ruskin Mill Trust (J)	7.578
S O V A	7.579
Salisbury City Almshouse and Welfare	7.583
Salisbury Diocesan Board of Education	7.583
Samaritans (J)	7.585
Science, Tech, Eng & Mathematics Network	7.590
SeeAbility	7.596
Shared Lives South West	7.599
Shell Foundation	7.603
SHELTER	7.603
Sherburn House Charity	7.604
Shooting Star CHASE (J)	7.605
Sir Thomas White's Charity	7.612
Siri Guru Nanak Darbar (Sikh Temple) (J)	7.613
Sisters of Charity of St Paul	7.613
Skills for Care (J)	7.617
Smallpeice Trust	7.618
Society for Assistance of Ladies (J)	7.621
Society of St Pius X	7.623
Somerset Redstone Trust (J)	7.627
South Bank Centre (J)	7.628
South West Environmental Parks Limited	7.630
South West Grid for Learning Trust	7.630
South West Lakes Trust	7.630
Southwell Diocesan Board Finance	7.631
Spectrum	7.632
Sports Aid Trust	7.633
SS Great Britain Trust (J)	7.635
St Andrew Holborn Charity	7.636
St Andrew Holborn Church Foundation	7.636
St Andrew's Healthcare	7.636
St Basil's	7.638
St Clement Danes Holborn Estate Charity	7.641
St David's Diocesan Board of Finance	7.641
St Giles Hospice	7.643
St Luke Centre Management Company	7.647
St Luke's Hospice (J)	7.647
St Martin's Trust	7.649
St Mary Magdalene & Holy Jesus Trust (J)	7.649
St Michael's Hospice Hastings	7.651
St Michael's Hospice (North Hampshire)	7.651
Montessori St Nicholas Charity, The (J)	7.652
Steinberg Family Charitable Trust, The	7.657
Stewardship Services (UKET) Ltd	7.658
Sue Ryder	7.663
Sustrans (J)	7.666
Talbot Village Trust (J)	7.668
Thalidomide Trust	7.674
Theatre Royal (Norwich) Trust	7.676
Thomas Hickman's Charity (J)	7.677
Together: Working for Wellbeing (J)	7.682
Tompkins Foundation	7.683
Tony Blair Governance Initiative	7.683
Transforming Education in Norfolk	7.685
Treloar Trust	7.685
Trinity College London	7.686
Trust for London	7.688
United Reformed Church (South Western) (J)	7.696
United Response	7.697
Valentine Charitable Trust, The	7.702
Valley Leisure (J)	7.702
Vardy Foundation (J)	7.703
Victim Support	7.704
Virgin Unite	7.706
Viscount Amory's Charitable Trust (J)	7.707
Wales Millennium Centre	7.711
Wallace Collection	7.712
Wallich Clifford Community	7.712
Welsh National Opera (J)	7.718
Western Community Leisure	7.722
Weston Hospicecare	7.723
Whitechapel Gallery	7.725
Whiteley Homes Trust (J)	7.725
Whitley Wildlife Conservation Trust, The	7.726
Wigmore Hall Trust (J)	7.727
William Adlington Cadbury Charitable Trust	7.729
William Harding's Charity (J)	7.730
William Leech Charity	7.730
William Leech Charity Trust	7.730
William Leech Foundation Trust	7.731
Woking & Sam Beare Hospices (J)	7.735
Womankind (Worldwide) (J)	7.736
Woodbrooke Quaker Study Centre	7.737
Woodland Trust	7.737

Diocese of Worcester	7.738
World Cancer Research Fund (WCRF UK) (J)	7.739
World Horse Welfare	7.740
World Vision UK (J)	7.741
Yesamach Levav (J)	7.744
YHA (England and Wales) (J)	7.744
YMCA London South West	7.746
Ymddiriedolaeth Clough Williams-Ellis Fdn (J)	7.746
Yorkshire Air Ambulance (J)	7.749
Yorkshire Cancer Research	7.749
Yorkshire Sculpture Park	7.749
You Trust	7.750
Youth Sport Trust (J)	7.751
Zurich Community (UK) Trust (J)	7.753

LLOYDS TSB, Lloyds TSB Commercial, Sedgemoor House, Deane Gate Avenue, Taunton, Somerset, TA1 2UF. Tel: 01823 446801.
Internet: www.lloydstsb.com/community.

Associated Board Royal Schools Music (J)	7.45
Booth Charities (J)	7.79
Britten-Pears Foundation (J)	7.100
Jewish Blind & Disabled (J)	7.353
Joseph Strong Frazer Trust	7.363
NorthamptonshireMusic&PerformingArtsTst	7.469
Retired Greyhound Trust	7.534
Royal Navy & Royal Marines Children's Fund	7.568
Salisbury Diocesan Board Finance	7.583

METRO BANK, 1 Southampton Row, London, WC1B 5HA.
Internet: www.metrobankonline.co.uk.

SignHealth	7.608

N & P BUILDING SOCIETY, Peterborough Business Park, Lynch Wood, Peterborough, PE2 6WZ. Tel: 01733 372372. Fax: 01733 372373.

Community All Hallows Ditchingham Norfolk (J)	7.165

N.M. ROTHSCHILD & SONS (C.I.) LIMITED, P.O. Box 58, St. Julian's Court, St Peter Port, Guernsey, GY1 3BP.

Booth Charities (J)	7.79
Eranda Foundation	7.238
Neil Kreitman Foundation	7.456

NATIONAL SAVINGS BANK, Millburn Gate House, Durham, County Durham, DH99 1NS. Tel: 0191 386 4900. Fax: 0191 374 5495.

Charity of Thomas Dawson (J)	7.130

NATIONWIDE BUILDING SOCIETY, 101-107 Finsbury Court, Moorgate, London, EC2A. Tel: 020 7705 1600. Fax: 020 7705 1606.

Booth Charities (J)	7.79
Methodist Homes (J)	7.424
Newbury & Thatcham Hospital Trust (J)	7.459
People's Health Trust (J)	7.497
Skills for Care (J)	7.617

NATIONWIDE INTERNATIONAL, 5-11 St Georges Street, Douglas, Isle of Man, IM99 1RN.

Essex & Herts Air Ambulance Trust (J)	7.240
Norfolk Wildlife Trust (J)	7.464

NATWEST, 2nd Floor, Argyll House, 246 Regent Street, London, W1B 3PB. Tel: 020 7432 4107. Fax: 020 7432 4142.
Internet: www.rbs.co.uk/commercial.

1610 Limited	7.2
A M Qattan Foundation (J)	7.3
Abbeycroft Leisure	7.4
Abbeyfield Kent Society, The (J)	7.5
Action Medical Research	7.11
Action on Addiction	7.11
Active Life Ltd	7.12
Active Nation UK Ltd	7.12
Actors' Benevolent Fund (J)	7.13
Addington Fund, The	7.14
Affinity Trust (J)	7.15
Ahmadiyya Muslim Association UK	7.19
Ahmadiyya Muslim Jamaat International	7.19
Aid to the Church in Need (UK) (J)	7.20
Al-Shirkatul Islamiyyah (J)	7.22

Allchurches Trust	7.25	Cecil Alan Pilkington Trust Fund	7.121	Elim Foursquare Gospel Alliance (J)	7.230
Alliance House Foundation	7.26	Cecil Pilkington Charitable Trust	7.122	Elizabeth and Prince Zaiger Trust	7.230
Almeida Theatre Company	7.27	Central Foundation Schools of London (J)	7.122	Elrahma Charity Trust	7.231
Alpha International	7.27	Charities Aid Foundation	7.128	Embrace the Middle East	7.232
Ambitious about Autism (J)	7.29	Charity for the Sisters of Mercy Midhurst	7.129	EMIH	7.232
American Museum in Britain	7.29	Charity of Thomas Dawson (J)	7.130	Enable Care & Home Support	7.233
Animal Health Trust	7.33	Charity of Walter Stanley	7.130	England and Wales Cricket Trust	7.234
Arch (North Staffs)	7.36	Chartered Inst of Building Services Engineers	7.134	English Province of our Lady of Charity	7.235
Archbishops' Council	7.37	Chelmsford Diocesan Board Finance (J)	7.136	Enham	7.236
Art Services Grants Ltd (J)	7.40	Cheshire Residential Homes (J)	7.137	Enid Linder Foundation	7.236
Arthritis Care	7.40	Chester Diocesan Board Finance (J)	7.138	Ernest Cook Trust	7.239
Arthritis Research UK	7.40	Chetham's Hospital School and Library	7.138	Essex & Herts Air Ambulance Trust (J)	7.240
Asda Foundation Limited	7.42	Children with Cancer UK	7.142	Essex Community Foundation	7.240
Ashorne Hill Management College	7.44	Christ Embassy	7.144	Eveson Charitable Trust (J)	7.243
Association of Commonwealth Universities	7.47	Christ's Hospital of Abingdon	7.144	Ex-Services Mental Welfare Society (J)	7.243
Asthma UK	7.47	Christadelphian Care Homes	7.144	Exeter Diocesan Board of Finance, The	7.244
Aston-Mansfield Charitable Trust	7.47	Christian Vision (J)	7.146	Exeter Royal Academy for Deaf Education	7.244
Autistic Wessex	7.50	Christopher Laing Foundation	7.146	Exilarch's Foundation (J)	7.244
Bader International Study Centre	7.54	Church Commissioners for England	7.147	Fairfield (Croydon) (J)	7.246
Barnabas Fund (J)	7.57	Church Communities UK	7.147	Family Fund, The	7.247
Barristers' Benevolent Association	7.59	Church Lands Charity	7.148	Farmland Reserve UK Limited	7.249
Bath Wells Diocesan Board Finance (J)	7.60	Church of God of Prophecy Trust (J)	7.148	Federation of Jewish Services (J)	7.250
Battersea Dogs & Cats Home	7.60	Church Urban Fund	7.150	Federation London Youth Clubs	7.250
Beacon Centre for the Blind (J)	7.62	Cinema and Television Benevolent Fund (J)	7.150	Fellowship of School of Economic Science	7.251
Beamish Museum Limited	7.62	City Gateway	7.153	Ffestiniog & Welsh Highland Railways Trust (J)	7.252
Beatrice Laing Trust	7.62	COLET	7.154	Fight For Sight (J)	7.254
Belgrade Theatre Trust (Coventry)	7.64	Clare Milne Trust	7.155	Fire Fighters Charity (J)	7.254
Benenden Hospital Trust	7.65	Clifton Diocesan Trust	7.156	FitzRoy Support	7.255
Benevolent Fund Institution of Civil Engineers	7.65	Coalfields Regeneration Trust (J)	7.158	Forest Young Men's Christian Association	7.257
IMechE Benevolent Fund	7.65	Cobalt Unit Appeal Fund (J)	7.159	Foundation (J)	7.258
Bible & Gospel Trust (J)	7.69	Colchester Catalyst Charity	7.159	Foundation for Liver Research	7.259
BID Services	7.69	College of Estate Management	7.160	Foundling Museum (J)	7.261
Bideford Bridge Trust (J)	7.69	Comic Relief (J)	7.162	Framework Housing Association	7.262
Big Local Trust (J)	7.70	Common Purpose Charitable Trust	7.162	Franciscan Missionaries Charitable Trust	7.263
Biochemical Society (J)	7.70	Community All Hallows Ditchingham Norfolk (J)	7.165	Fusion Lifestyle	7.266
Birmingham MIND	7.71	Community of St John Baptist General (J)	7.165	Game & Wildlife Conservation Trust	7.268
Birmingham Children's Hospital Charities (J)	7.71	Community of St Mary the Virgin	7.166	Garsington Opera	7.269
Birmingham Diocesan Trust	7.71	Community of the Holy Cross	7.166	Geffrye Museum	7.270
Birmingham Repertory Theatre	7.72	Community Options	7.167	George Gibson Almshouses Foundation	7.272
Birtenshaw	7.73	Compassion in World Farming	7.168	George Muller Charitable Trust [The]	7.273
Blackburn Diocesan Board Finance Limited	7.74	Congregation of La Retraite Trustees	7.171	Gerald Palmer Eling Trust Company	7.273
Blanchminster Trust	7.75	Congregation of the Sisters of St Anne (J)	7.175	Gerald Ronson Foundation, The	7.273
Blenheim CDP	7.75	Congregation of the Sisters of St Martha (J)	7.175	Get Kids Going	7.273
Blue Cross	7.76	Sisters of the Finding of Jesus (J)	7.175	Girlguiding UK	7.274
Board of Trustees for the Royal Armouries	7.78	Congregational Federation	7.176	Global Partners (UK)	7.277
Boltini Trust, The	7.78	Conservation Volunteers, The	7.177	Gloucester Charities Trust (J)	7.277
Bolton Community Leisure Limited	7.78	Cope Children's Trust	7.179	Grace & Compassion Benedictines	7.283
Book Trust	7.79	Coram	7.179	Greenwich & Bexley Comm. Hospice Ltd	7.287
Bootstrap Company (Blackburn)	7.80	Corporation of the Sons of the Clergy (J)	7.181	Greggs Foundation	7.288
Borough Market (Southwark)	7.80	County Air Ambulance Trust (J)	7.183	Groundwork North East (J)	7.289
Borough of Havant Sport & Leisure Trust	7.81	County Durham Community Foundation	7.183	Groundwork Oldham and Rochdale	7.290
Bourne United Charities	7.81	Cranstoun Drug Services	7.184	Gurdjieff Society Limited, The	7.292
Bournemouth Symphony Orchestra	7.82	Creative Foundation Limited - Group, The	7.185	Guy Pilkington Memorial Home Limited	7.293
Bournemouth Young Men's Christian Assoc (J)	7.82	Cremation Society of Great Britain, The	7.185	Guy's & St Thomas' Charity	7.293
Brighton & Sussex Univ Hospitals NHS Trust	7.88	CSV	7.187	Gwent Assoc of Voluntary Organisation	7.294
Bristol, Clifton, & West of England Zoo (J)	7.89	Culham St Gabriel's Trust	7.188	H B Allen Charitable Trust	7.294
Bristol Diocesan Board Finance Ltd	7.89	Cutty Sark Trust (J)	7.189	Hafal	7.296
Bristol Music Trust	7.90	D D McPhail Charitable Settlement (J)	7.191	Halo Leisure Services Limited	7.297
Bristol Old Vic and Theatre Royal Trust Ltd	7.90	Dartmouth Trust	7.193	Hampshire Autistic Society	7.298
British Academy of Film & Television Arts	7.91	David Lewis Centre	7.194	Handmaids of the Sacred Heart of Jesus (J)	7.300
British & Foreign Bible Society	7.91	Dawat-e-Hadiyah Trust (United Kingdom) (J)	7.195	Hannah Susan Samuel Victor Greig Fund	7.300
British Association for Adoption & Fostering (J)	7.92	De Haan Charitable Trust	7.195	Harborne Parish Lands Charity	7.301
British Gas Energy Trust	7.93	Demelza House Children's Hospice	7.196	Harewood House Trust	7.302
British Horse Society	7.94	Denys Eyre Bower Bequest, The (J)	7.197	Harlow Health Centres Trust Ltd	7.302
BLESMA	7.95	Derby Diocesan Board Finance Ltd	7.198	Harris (Belmont) Charity (J)	7.303
British Museum Friends (J)	7.96	Design Museum (J)	7.199	Harrow Central Mosque and Islamic Centre (J)	7.303
British Museum	7.97	DHL UK Foundation (J)	7.200	Harrow Development Trust	7.303
British Museum Trust Limited, The	7.97	Diabetes UK (J)	7.200	Havens Christian Hospice	7.304
British Red Cross Society	7.98	Diverse Abilities Plus Limited	7.202	HCPT - The Pilgrimage Trust (J)	7.304
British Refugee Council	7.98	Doris Field Charitable Trust	7.207	Healthcare Financial Management Association	7.306
British Trust for Ornithology (J)	7.99	Dorothy House Foundation Ltd	7.208	Heathcoat Trust	7.307
Broadway Homelessness and Support	7.100	Dorothy Kerin Trust	7.208	Helen & Douglas House (J)	7.307
Bromley Trust	7.100	Dorset Wildlife Trust	7.209	Higher Education Careers Services Unit	7.311
BRUNELCARE (J)	7.102	Douai Abbey	7.209	Home Devenish	7.315
Brunts Charity	7.102	Dudley and W Midlands Zoological Society	7.213	Homeless International (J)	7.316
Burghley House Preservation Trust	7.104	Dulverton Trust	7.214	Honourable Artillery Company (J)	7.316
Butterfly Conservation	7.106	Dyers Company Charitable Trust	7.217	Hospice Care for Burnley and Pendle	7.318
Caldecott Foundation Limited (J)	7.108	E F Bulmer Benevolent Fund (J)	7.217	Hospice of Our Lady & St John	7.319
Cambridge Arts Theatre Trust Ltd, The	7.108	Ealing Community Transport	7.218	Hospice of the Good Shepherd Ltd	7.320
Cambridge Commonwealth Trust	7.108	Earl Mountbatten Hospice	7.219	Hospiscare	7.320
Camden Society	7.109	Earth Trust	7.220	Hospital of St Cross Foundation	7.321
Camelia Botnar Foundation	7.109	East Anglia's Children's Hospices (J)	7.220	Hospital of the Blessed Mary	7.321
Campaign to Protect Rural England	7.110	East Anglian Air Ambulance	7.220	Hospital of the Holy & Undivided Trinity (J)	7.322
Camphill Village Trust Limited	7.111	East Lancashire Hospice	7.221	Housing Pathways Trust	7.322
Canal & River Trust	7.111	Crossroads Care East Midlands	7.222	Human Appeal International	7.324
Canterbury Oast Trust	7.113	EBM Charitable Trust	7.223	Human Relief Foundation (J)	7.324
Cardiff and Vale Health Charity (J)	7.113	Echoes of Service	7.223	ICAEW Foundation & Educational Charities (J)	7.327
Cartrefi Cymru	7.117	Edward James Foundation Limited	7.228	Imperial College Healthcare Charity	7.329

Imperial Society of Teachers of Dancing	7.329	Missionaries of Africa (The White Fathers)	7.431	RBS PeopleCharity, The	7.527
Imperial War Museum	7.329	Money Advice Trust	7.431	RCN Foundation	7.528
Impetus Private Equity Foundation	7.330	Monmouth Diocesan Board of Finance	7.431	RedR UK	7.528
Inc Council of Law Reporting England Wales	7.330	Monmouth Diocesan Trust	7.432	Redwings Horse Sanctuary	7.528
Independent Age	7.331	Morden College	7.433	Refugee Action	7.529
Institute for Fiscal Studies	7.332	Mothers' Union	7.435	Relate	7.530
Institute for War Peace Reporting Limited	7.333	Mount Saint Bernard Abbey (J)	7.436	Retail Trust (J)	7.533
Institute of Biomedical Science	7.333	Mr & Mrs J A Pye's Charitable Settlement	7.437	Rhodes Trust	7.535
Institute of Fundraising	7.335	Mr Willats' Charity (J)	7.437	Rich Mix Cultural Foundation	7.535
Institution of Chemical Engineers (J)	7.337	Mulberry Bush Organisation Limited, The	7.438	Rikkyo School in England Trust	7.538
Institution of Mechanical Engineers (J)	7.338	Muslim Hands (J)	7.441	Ripon Diocesan Board of Finance	7.539
Inst. of Occupational Safety & Health	7.339	NACRO	7.442	Roger Raymond Charitable Trust	7.542
Insurance Charities (J)	7.339	National Botanic Garden Wales	7.443	Roman Catholic Diocese of East Anglia	7.543
International Alert	7.340	National Centre for Social Research	7.443	Roman Catholic Diocese of Southwark	7.544
International Fellowship Evangelical Students	7.341	National Children's Bureau (J)	7.444	TrusteesofCongregattionofMostHolyRedeemer	7.544
Intl Network for Availability Of Scientific Pub	7.344	National Deaf Children's Society	7.444	Rothschild Foundation	7.547
International Rescue Committee UK (J)	7.344	NEBOSH	7.445	Rowcroft House Foundation Limited	7.548
Islamic Relief Worldwide (J)	7.347	NFER	7.446	Royal Academy of Engineering	7.549
Islamic Trust (J)	7.347	National Library of Wales, The	7.449	Royal Agricultural Benevolent Institution (J)	7.550
J A Clark Charitable Trust (J)	7.348	National Maritime Museum Cornwall Trust	7.449	Royal Astronomical Society (J)	7.552
Jagclif Charitable Trust	7.350	Nat Museums & Galleries on Merseyside	7.450	Royal College of Ophthalmologists	7.556
Jah-Jireh Charity Homes	7.350	National Osteoporosis Society (J)	7.451	Royal College of Radiologists	7.558
James Tudor Foundation, The	7.351	National Portrait Gallery	7.451	Royal Exchange Theatre Company	7.560
Jesus Hospital Charity in Chipping Barnet	7.353	National Society for Epilepsy	7.452	Royal Horticultural Society	7.561
Jewish Blind & Disabled (J)	7.353	National Youth Advocacy Service	7.454	Royal Hospital for Neuro-disability	7.562
Jewish Community Secondary School Trust	7.354	National Youth Agency	7.454	Royal Masonic Hospital Charity	7.565
Jewish Joint Burial Society (J)	7.354	Natural History Museum	7.455	Royal Masonic Trust For Girls and Boys (J)	7.565
John Coates Charitable Trust	7.357	Needham Research Institute (J)	7.456	Royal Medical Benevolent Fund	7.565
John James Bristol Foundation	7.359	NETA Training Trust	7.457	Royal Philharmonic Orchestra (J)	7.569
Jones 1986 Charitable Trust	7.362	New College Development Fund	7.457	Royal Sailors' Rests	7.570
Keech Hospice Care	7.367	New Testament Church of God (J)	7.458	Royal Society of Chemistry (J)	7.572
Kent, Surrey & Sussex Air Ambulance Trust	7.369	Newground Together	7.460	Royal Society of Wildlife Trusts	7.573
King Edward VII's Hospital Sister Agnes	7.372	Newmarston Limited Group	7.461	Royal Star & Garter Home, The	7.574
King's Fund, The	7.373	Nightingale Hammerson (J)	7.463	Rumi Foundation, The	7.577
Kingsway International Christian Centre	7.373	Norfolk Wildlife Trust (J)	7.464	Saddlers' Company Charitable Fund (J)	7.580
Kingwood Trust	7.373	North Devon Hospice	7.466	Sailors Society (J)	7.581
L'Arche (J)	7.375	North England Seventh-Day Adventists	7.466	Salisbury District Hospital Charitable Fund	7.583
Lady Elizabeth Hastings' Charities	7.376	North York Moors Historical Railway (J)	7.468	Salvation Army International Trust (J)	7.584
Lantra	7.379	Northampton RC Diocesan Trust	7.468	Sandra Charitable Trust	7.586
Leeds Grand Theatre and Opera House	7.382	Norwood and Newton Settlement	7.472	Save the Children	7.588
Leeds Teaching Hospitals Charitable Fdn (J)	7.382	Nottingham University Hospitals General Fund	7.473	Scope	7.590
Leeds Theatre Trust	7.382	NYU in London	7.476	Seafarers UK	7.594
Legal Education Foundation, The (J)	7.383	Oblates of Mary Immaculate	7.478	Sears Group Trust	7.595
Leicester Theatre Trust	7.383	Ofenheim Charitable Trust	7.478	Sense National Deafblind & Rubella Assoc	7.597
Leics Independent Educational Trust	7.384	OMF International (UK)	7.480	Sequoia Trust, The	7.597
Letchworth Garden City Heritage Foundation (J)	7.386	Operation Mobilisation	7.481	Severn Hospice (J)	7.598
Life Path Trust Ltd	7.388	Order of Friars Minor	7.482	Sheffield Galleries and Museums Trust	7.601
Lifeline Project	7.388	Order of Friars Minor (Capuchin) Province	7.482	Sheiling Trust	7.603
Lincoln Diocesan Trust Board Finance Ltd	7.389	Orthopaedic Research UK	7.484	SHP	7.606
Lincolnshire Agricultural Society (J)	7.389	Outlook Care	7.485	Shri Vallabh Nidhi - UK (J)	7.607
Liversage Trust	7.393	Outreach 3 Way	7.485	Shri Venkateswara (Balaji) Temple of UK (J)	7.607
Llandaff Diocesan Board Finance	7.394	Overseas Bishoprics Fund	7.486	Simon Gibson Charitable Trust	7.609
Lloyd's Benevolent Fund	7.395	Overseas Development Institute	7.486	Sir Edward Lewis Foundation	7.610
Local Solutions	7.395	Oxford Diocesan Board Finance	7.487	Sir Harold Hood Charitable Trust	7.610
Local Trust (J)	7.396	Oxford Diocesan Council For Social Work	7.487	Sir Jules Thorn Charitable Trust	7.612
Loddon School Company	7.396	Panacea Society	7.490	Sisters Hospitallers of the Sacred Heart (J)	7.613
London Early Years Foundation, The	7.398	Paul Hamlyn Foundation	7.493	Sisters of Mercy St Anthony's Convent	7.614
London Mathematical Society	7.400	Peace Hospice Care	7.494	Sisters of the Holy Family	7.616
London Oratory Charity	7.400	Penderels Trust	7.495	Skills for Justice (J)	7.618
London School for the Performing Arts	7.401	Performances Birmingham Ltd	7.498	Social Investment Business Foundation (J)	7.620
Lord's Taverners	7.403	Perseverance Trust	7.498	Society for Protection of Animals Abroad (J)	7.621
Louis Baylis Charitable Trust (J)	7.403	Petans	7.499	Society of St James	7.623
Magdalen Lasher Charity	7.406	Pharmacist Support (J)	7.500	Society ofthe Holy Child Jesus Eur.Province	7.624
Magen David Adom UK (J)	7.406	Philharmonia	7.500	Soka Gakkai International UK (J)	7.625
Magna Trust	7.407	Phoenix House	7.501	Solicitors Benevolent Association	7.626
Make-A-Wish Foundation (UK)	7.407	Picker Institute Europe	7.502	Soll (Vale)	7.627
Malvern Theatres Trust Ltd	7.408	Pickering & Ferens Homes	7.502	Somerset House Trust	7.627
Mare and Foal Sanctuary	7.409	Pilgrims Hospices in East Kent (J)	7.503	S Lon Ch Fund&Sthwk Diocesan Bd Fin (J)	7.629
Marine Society & Sea Cadets (J)	7.411	Plymouth Diocesan Trust	7.505	Spiritualists National Union	7.632
Marston Vale Trust	7.412	Plymouth Secular Clergy Fund	7.506	Sports Coach UK	7.633
Marwell Wildlife (J)	7.414	Polonsky Foundation, The (J)	7.508	St Asaph Diocesan Board of Finance	7.638
Mary Hare School	7.414	Postal Heritage Trust	7.510	St Barnabas Hospice Lincolnshire Trust	7.638
Mary Stevens Hospice (J)	7.415	Potanin Foundation	7.511	St Barnabas Hospices (Sussex) Ltd	7.638
Masonic Samaritan Fund	7.415	Pre-school Learning Alliance	7.512	St Catherine's Hospice (Lancashire)	7.639
Mayflower Theatre Trust	7.417	Premier Christian Media Trust (J)	7.512	St Christopher's Fellowship	7.640
MCCH Society	7.418	Prince's Trust (J)	7.514	St Cuthberts Care	7.641
Med Col of St Bartholomew's Hospital	7.419	Printing Charity, The (J)	7.514	St David's Foundation Hospice Care	7.642
Medical Foundation for Victims of Torture (J)	7.419	Prostate Cancer UK	7.517	St George's Hospital Charity	7.643
Meningitis Now	7.421	PRS For Music Members Benevolent Fund	7.517	St Helena Hospice	7.644
Mercy Corps Scotland (J)	7.422	Queen Elizabeth's Fndtn For Disabled People	7.520	St James's Place Foundation (J)	7.644
MGS Trust	7.424	Queenscourt Hospice	7.521	St John's Winchester Charity	7.645
Microbiology Society	7.425	Quintin Hogg Trust	7.521	St Leonard's Hospice York	7.646
Midland Sports Centre for the Disabled	7.426	RAC Foundation for Motoring	7.522	St Loye's Foundation	7.646
Milestones Trust (J)	7.427	Radha Soami Satsang Beas British Isles	7.523	St Luke's (Cheshire) Hospice	7.647
Mirus-Wales	7.429	Raleigh International Trust	7.524	St Luke's Hospice (J)	7.647
Mission Aviation Fellowship International	7.430	Rambert Trust	7.525	St Margaret's Convent (Uckfield)	7.648
Mission Aviation Fellowship UK	7.430	Rank Foundation Limited (J)	7.525	St Mary Magdalene & Holy Jesus Trust (J)	7.649
Mission Care	7.430	Rank Prize Fund	7.525	St Mary's Hospice	7.650

St Monica Trust	7.651
St Olave, St Thomas and St John United	7.653
St Oswald's Hospice (J)	7.653
St Peter's Home and Sisterhood	7.653
St Peter's Hospice	7.654
St Richard's Hospice Foundation	7.654
St Wilfrid's Hospice (South Coast)	7.655
Steps to Work (Walsall) Limited	7.657
Stewards Company	7.658
Stoller Charitable Trust	7.659
Strode Pk Foundation for Disabled People	7.662
Style Acre	7.663
Supported Fostering Services Charitable Trust	7.665
Swanswell Charitable Trust	7.667
Talisman Charitable Trust	7.668
Tavistock Inst of Medical Psychology (J)	7.670
Teikyo Foundation UK	7.672
Tennis Foundation (J)	7.672
Terrence Higgins Trust	7.673
Thames Reach (J)	7.675
Theatre Royal (Plymouth)	7.676
Thera Trust (J)	7.676
Thinkaction	7.676
Three Counties Agricultural Society	7.679
Threshold Housing Project	7.680
Thurrock Community Leisure	7.680
Thursford Collection, The	7.680
Together: Working for Wellbeing (J)	7.682
Tommy's, the baby charity	7.682
Tomorrow's People Trust	7.682
Tone Leisure (Taunton Deane) Limited	7.683
Toynbee Hall (J)	7.684
Training 2000	7.685
Trident Reach the People Charity	7.686
Trinity Hospice & Palliative Care Services	7.686
Truro Diocesan Board Finance Ltd	7.687
Trust Thamesmead	7.689
Twycross Zoo (J)	7.691
Ty Hafan (J)	7.692
UK Sailing Academy	7.693
Unipol Student Homes (J)	7.695
United Bible Societies Association, The (J)	7.695
United Reformed Church (Yorkshire) Trust	7.697
Universities UK	7.700
V&A Foundation, The	7.702
Valley Leisure (J)	7.702
Variety the Children's Charity	7.703
Varrier Jones Foundation (J)	7.703
Victoria and Albert Museum	7.705
Victory Services Association Ltd	7.705
Viridor Credits Environmental Company	7.706
Virunga Foundation	7.707
Vista	7.707
Vocational Training Charitable Trust	7.708
Voiceability Advocacy	7.708
Walcot Educational Foundation	7.711
Walk the Walk Worldwide	7.712
Wallscourt Foundation (J)	7.712
Walsingham	7.713
Weldmar Hospicecare Trust (J)	7.717
Welsh National Opera (J)	7.718
WESC Foundation (J)	7.719
Westbank Community Health and Care (J)	7.721
Westminster Society	7.723
Weston Park Foundation	7.724
Wheler Foundation, The	7.725
Whitgift Foundation (J)	7.726
Whitley Animal Protection Trust	7.726
Wicksteed Charitable Trust	7.727
Wildfowl and Wetlands Trust	7.728
Will Trust of Gerald Segelman Deceased, The	7.729
Willowbrook Hospice	7.731
Winchester Diocesan Board of Finance	7.732
Wine & Spirit Education Trust Ltd	7.732
Womankind (Worldwide) (J)	7.736
Woodlands Hospice Charitable Trust Limited	7.737
World Assoc of Girl Guides & Girl Scouts	7.739
Wrexham (Parochial) Educational Fdn	7.742
Wycliffe UK Ltd	7.743
Yale University Press London (J)	7.744
Yesamach Levav (J)	7.744
York Archaeological Trust	7.747
Youth Sport Trust (J)	7.751
Youth United Foundation	7.751

NEDBANK, 1st Floor Millenium Bridge House, 2 Lambeth Hill, London, EC4V 4GG. Internet: www.nedbank.co.za.

Kathleen & Michael Connolly Foundation UK (J)	7.366

NORTHERN TRUST (GUERNSEY) LIMITED, P O Box 71, Trafalgar Court, Les Banques, ST Peter Port, Guernsey, Channel Islands, GY1 3DA. Tel: 01481 745000. Fax: 01481 745050. Internet: www.northerntrust.com.

Blenheim Foundation, The (J)	7.75

THE CO-OPERATIVE BANK PLC, Charity Co-operative & Social Enterprise Banking, 3rd Floor, 1 Balloon Street, Manchester, Greater Manchester, M60 4EP. Tel: 0161 201 1965. Fax: 020 7248 0863. E-mail: charities@co-operativebank.co.uk. Internet: co-operativebank.co.uk/corporate.

Acorns Children's Hospice Trust	7.9
Action for Blind People (J)	7.10
Action Housing & Support Limited (J)	7.10
ActionAid	7.12
Active Luton (J)	7.12
Addaction	7.13
Addiction Dependency Solutions (J)	7.14
Age UK Lincoln	7.18
Allen Lane Foundation	7.26
Amnesty International UK Section	7.30
Aquaterra Leisure	7.36
Arts Council England	7.41
Arts Council of Wales, The	7.41
Aspire Sports and Cultural Trust	7.45
Autism West Midlands	7.50
Barnsley Premier Leisure	7.58
BAC	7.60
BEN-Motor & Allied Trades Benevolent Fund (J)	7.64
Berks, Bucks & Oxon Wildlife Trust	7.66
Bernie Grant Centre Partnership	7.67
Bethphage Mission (Great Britain) (J)	7.68
Big Local Trust (J)	7.70
Blyth Valley Arts and Leisure Ltd	7.77
Booth Charities (J)	7.79
Breakthrough Breast Cancer (J)	7.86
Britten-Pears Foundation (J)	7.100
Building and Social Housing Foundation	7.103
Carers UK	7.115
Changeworks (J)	7.127
Children's Links	7.141
Christian Aid (J)	7.145
Co-operative Community Inv Foundation	7.158
Coalfields Regeneration Trust (J)	7.158
Community Foundation for Manchester (J)	7.162
Community Foundation for Leeds	7.163
Community Links Trust	7.165
Cripplegate Foundation (J)	7.186
Dacorum Sports Trust (J)	7.191
Dame Hannah Rogers Trust (J)	7.192
Developing Initiatives, Support in Community	7.199
Disasters Emergency Committee (J)	7.202
Dolphin Square Charitable Foundation, The	7.203
Doncaster Culture and Leisure Trust	7.204
Durham Aged Mineworkers' Homes Assoc (J)	7.216
Eleanor Rathbone Charitable Trust [The]	7.229
Estate Charity of William Hatcliffe (J)	7.241
Fairtrade Foundation (J)	7.247
Foundation (J)	7.258
Foundation Trust Network, The (J)	7.261
Francis House Family Trust	7.263
Friends of the Earth Trust	7.265
Furniture Resource Centre	7.266
GreaterManchester AccessibleTransport (J)	7.286
Greenpeace Environmental Trust	7.287
Groundwork North East (J)	7.289
Groundwork UK (J)	7.290
Harpur Trust, The	7.302
Health and Social Care Alliance, The (J)	7.305
Help for Heroes (J)	7.308
Hymns Ancient and Modern	7.326
ICAN	7.327
Institute for Government	7.333
Institute of Grocery Distribution (J)	7.335
Institute of Our Lady of Mercy, The	7.336
Institute of the Blessed Virgin Mary (J)	7.337
Isabel Hospice	7.346
King David Schools (Manchester)	7.371
Leadership Foundation for Higher Education	7.381
Leeds Diocesan Trust (J)	7.382
Leprosy Mission England (J)	7.385
LHASA (J)	7.387

Live Active Leisure Limited	7.392
Liverpool Charity and Voluntary Services (J)	7.392
Living Streets (The Pedestrians' Association)	7.394
Local Trust (J)	7.396
Luton Cultural Services Trust	7.404
Manchester & District Home for Lost Dogs (J)	7.408
Manchester Sport and Leisure Trust	7.408
Mary Ward Settlement	7.415
Medical Aid for Palestinians (J)	7.418
Medical Foundation for Victims of Torture (J)	7.419
MERLIN (J)	7.423
Milestones Trust (J)	7.427
National Children's Bureau (J)	7.444
National Fed'n of Women's Institutes (J)	7.445
National Gardens Scheme Charitable Trust	7.447
NSPCC (J)	7.452
NECA (J)	7.455
Newcastle Theatre Royal Trust (J)	7.460
Norfolk Wildlife Trust (J)	7.464
North of England Zoological Society (J)	7.467
North West Air Ambulance	7.468
Northern College for Residential Adult Ed	7.470
PayPal Giving Fund UK	7.494
People's Health Trust (J)	7.497
People's History Museum (J)	7.497
Perennial	7.498
Places for People Scotland Care & Support Ltd	7.505
PohWER	7.506
PACEY (J)	7.515
Pure Innovations Limited	7.518
Relief International UK (J)	7.531
Rethink Mental Illness	7.534
Richmond Fellowship	7.537
Rochdale Boroughwide Cultural Trust	7.541
Rotherham Hospice Trust (J)	7.546
Roundhouse Trust (J)	7.547
Royal College of Anaesthetists	7.555
RSPB (J)	7.572
Saferworld	7.581
Sandwell Leisure Trust (J)	7.587
Scottish Catholic International Aid Fund (J)	7.591
Severn Trent Water Charitable Trust Fund	7.598
Sheffield City Trust	7.601
Shlomo Memorial Fund	7.605
Sisters of St Joseph of Peace (J)	7.615
Skills for Care (J)	7.617
Solaraid	7.626
St Joseph's Hospice, Hackney (J)	7.646
St Vincent de Paul Society	7.655
Street League (J)	7.661
Support for Ordinary Living	7.664
Sustrans (J)	7.666
Tameside Sports Trust	7.668
Tees Valley Community Foundation (J)	7.671
Thomas Pocklington Trust	7.678
Trafford Community Leisure Trust	7.684
Tree of Hope (J)	7.685
Veolia Environmental Trust, The (J)	7.704
vInspired	7.706
Walthamstow&Chingford Almshouse Charity	7.713
War Child	7.714
Warwickshire Wildlife Trust	7.714
Wave Leisure Trust Limited	7.716
Wentworth Castle & Stainborough Park Trust	7.719
Wessex Archaeology Ltd	7.719
Westbank Community Health and Care (J)	7.721
Whitgift Foundation (J)	7.726
Wigan Leisure and Cultural Trust	7.727
Witton Lodge Community Association	7.734
WIEGO Ltd (J)	7.736
Workers' Educational Assoc South Wales Ltd	7.739
World Cancer Research Fund (WCRF UK) (J)	7.739
World Society for the Protection of Animals	7.741
WWF UK	7.743
Yale University Press London (J)	7.744
YHA (England and Wales) (J)	7.744

PERSHING SECURITIES LTD, Capstan House, One Clove Crescent, London, E14 2BH.

Parham Park Trust (1984) (J)	7.491

PICTET ET CIE, 29 bd Georges-Favon, 1204 Geneva.

Birmingham Children's Hospital Charities (J)	7.71

PUNJAB NATIONAL BANK (INTERNATIONAL) LTD, 87 Gresham Street, London, EC2V 7HQ.

Sarjudas Foundation	7.587
Shri Vallabh Nidhi - UK (J)	7.607
Shri Venkateswara (Balaji) Temple of UK (J)	7.607

RELIANCE BANK LIMITED, Faith House, 23 - 24 Lovat Lane, London, EC3R 8EB. Tel: 020 7398 5400. Fax: 020 7398 5401.
E-mail: info@reliancebankltd.com.
Internet: www.reliancebankltd.com.

Salvation Army International Trust (J)	7.584
Salvation Army Officers Pension Fund	7.584
Salvation Army Social Work Trust	7.584
Salvation Army Trust	7.584

ROTHSCHILD, New Court, St Swithin's Lane, London, EC4N 8AL. Tel: 0207 280 1732.
E-mail: nandu.patel@rothschild.com.

ROYAL BANK OF SCOTLAND GROUP PLC, THE, 2nd Floor, Argyll House, 246 Regent Street, London, W1B 3PB. Tel: 020 7432 4107.
Fax: 020 7432 4142.
Internet: www.natwest.com/business/services/market-expertise/charities-and-social-enterprise.aspx.

A S Charitable Trust	7.3
Aberdeen Endowments Trust (J)	7.5
Aberlour Child Care Trust	7.6
Abernethy Trust	7.6
ACT Foundation	7.9
Action Housing & Support Limited (J)	7.10
Active Stirling Limited	7.13
After Adoption	7.16
Akshar Educational Trust	7.21
Alabarė Christian Care Centres	7.22
Alexandra Palace and Park (J)	7.24
Alexian Brothers of Province of Sacred Heart	7.24
Alliance Family Foundation	7.26
Apostolic Church, The	7.35
AQA Education	7.35
Archange Lebrun Trust Limited	7.37
Ark Housing Association	7.39
Army Central Fund, The	7.39
Asser Bishvil Foundation	7.45
Association for Cultural Exchange Ltd	7.46
Atlantic Charitable Trust	7.48
Autlsm Anglia	7.49
Autism Initiatives UK	7.49
Autism Sussex Ltd	7.50
Baring Foundation	7.57
Barts and The London Charity	7.59
Belvedere Trust	7.64
Bield Housing Association	7.69
Blair Drummond Camphill Trust Limited	7.74
Bluebell Wood Children's Hospice	7.77
Bolton Hospice	7.78
Borders Sport & Leisure Trust	7.80
Borough Care Services	7.80
Box Moor Trust	7.82
Brighton Dome and Festival Limited	7.88
British Academy	7.91
British Psychological Society	7.97
British Trust for Ornithology (J)	7.99
Broadening Choices for Older People	7.100
Brothers of Charity Services (Scotland) (J)	7.101
Buccleuch Living Heritage Trust, The	7.103
C-Change Scotland	7.107
Cambridge Crystallographic Data Centre	7.108
Camphill Rudolf Steiner Estates	7.111
Camphill Rudolf Steiner Schools	7.111
Capability Scotland	7.113
Care South (J)	7.114
Carmelite Charitable Trust	7.116
Carr-Gomm Scotland	7.117
Catholic Agency for Overseas Development	7.118
Catholic Apostolic Church (J)	7.118
Catholic Institute for International Relations	7.119
Central Young Men's Christian Association (J)	7.123
Centre for Economic Policy Research	7.123
Centre for the Moving Image	7.124
Centrepoint	7.124
Charity for Roman Catholic Congregation (J)	7.128
Marist Sisters	7.130
Charity Roman Union Order St Ursula (J)	7.130
Chartered Accountants' Benevolent Assoc	7.132
Chatsworth House Trust	7.136
Chest Heart & Stroke Scotland (J)	7.137

Church of England Pensions Board	7.148
Church of Pentecost - UK, The (J)	7.149
Church of Scotland General Trustees	7.149
Church of Scot Uninc. Councils Cttees (J)	7.149
Citizens Advice Scotland (J)	7.152
City and Guilds of London Institute	7.152
Clara E Burgess Charity	7.155
CLIC Sargent Cancer Care for Children (J)	7.156
Clyde Gateway URC	7.157
Colefax Charitable Trust	7.159
Community Foundation Wales	7.163
Faithful Companions of Jesus	7.166
Community Security Trust	7.167
Compass	7.168
Concern Universal (J)	7.170
Concern Worldwide (UK) (J)	7.170
Conciliation Resources (J)	7.170
Congregation of the Jesus Charitable Trust	7.171
Good Shepherd Sisters	7.171
Sisters of Bon Secours of Paris	7.172
Congregation of the Brothers of Charity (J)	7.172
Cong of the Daughters of the Cross of Liege	7.173
Congregation of the Little Sisters of the Poor	7.174
Congregation of the Passion Jesus Christ (J)	7.174
Cong. of the Sisters of Nazareth Generalate	7.175
Congregation of the Sisters of St Martha (J)	7.175
Sisters of the Finding of Jesus (J)	7.175
Congregation of the Ursulines of Jesus	7.176
Congregational & General Charitable Trust	7.176
Council for World Mission (J)	7.182
Northampton County Council on Addiction	7.183
Crimestoppers Trust	7.186
Cripplegate Foundation (J)	7.186
Crisis	7.186
Culture and Sport Glasgow	7.188
CXK Limited	7.190
Cyclists' Touring Club	7.190
Cystic Fibrosis Trust	7.190
D&AD	7.191
Dacorum Sports Trust (J)	7.191
Daughters of Jesus, The	7.193
Daughters Mary Joseph English Province	7.193
Dawliffe Hall Educational Foundation (J)	7.195
Derian House Children's Hospice	7.198
Dominican Council	7.203
Dominican Sisters Congregation Newcastle	7.204
Doncaster & Bassetlaw Hospitals Trust	7.204
Douglas Haig Memorial Homes (J)	7.209
E Hayes Dashwood Foundation (J)	7.218
Earl Haig Fund Scotland	7.219
East Cheshire Hospice	7.220
East Lothian Housing Association (J)	7.222
Edina Trust	7.224
Edinburgh Festival Fringe Society Ltd	7.225
Edinburgh International Festival Society	7.225
Edinburgh Leisure (J)	7.225
Edinburgh Military Tattoo (Charities) Ltd	7.225
Education and Training Foundation (J)	7.227
Eduserv	7.227
ELCAP	7.229
English Dominican Congregation Ch Fund	7.235
Eric Wright Trust	7.238
Erskine	7.239
Esmée Fairbairn Foundation	7.240
Ex-Services Mental Welfare Society (J)	7.243
Family Fed for World Peace & Unification	7.247
Federation European Biochemical Societies (J)	7.250
Fife Cultural Trust	7.253
Fife Sports & Leisure Trust Ltd	7.253
Find A Future	7.254
Foundation Scotland	7.260
Friends Royal Academy	7.265
Fylde Coast YMCA	7.267
Garvald Edinburgh	7.269
General Conference of the New Church (J)	7.270
General Medical Council	7.271
General Optical Council (J)	7.271
Gideons International British Isles	7.274
Glasgow Science Centre Limited	7.275
Glasgow Science Centre Charitable Trust	7.276
Glasgow Simon Community	7.276
Goldsmiths Centre, The (J)	7.280
Goldsmiths' Company Charity (J)	7.281
Gowrie Care Limited	7.283
Great North Air Ambulance	7.285
Great Ormond St Hosp Children's Charity	7.285
Greater Manchester Arts Centre	7.286
Greenwich Royal Naval College Foundation (J)	7.288

Gurkha Welfare Trust (J)	7.292
Haig Housing Trust (J)	7.296
Hallé Concerts Society	7.297
HALO Trust	7.297
Hanover (Scotland) Housing Association	7.301
Hansel Foundation	7.301
Harbour Foundation	7.301
Harmeny Education Trust	7.302
Health Foundation, The	7.305
Hedley Foundation Limited	7.307
Hertsmere Leisure	7.310
Higher Education Academy, The (J)	7.311
Homeless International (J)	7.316
Honourable Society Middle Temple Trust	7.316
Hope and Homes for Children	7.317
Hulme Trust Estates (Educational) Fndn	7.324
Hyde Park Place Estate Charity	7.326
IES London	7.328
Imperial College Trust (J)	7.329
INCLUDEM	7.330
Institute of Brewing & Distilling	7.334
Institute of the Blessed Virgin Mary (J)	7.337
Institute of the Franciscan Missionaries	7.337
Integrate (Preston and Chorley)	7.339
International Aid Trust (J)	7.340
Inverness Leisure Limited	7.345
IVCC	7.348
J Paul Getty Jnr General Charitable Trust	7.349
Jerwood Charitable Foundation	7.353
Johnson & Johnson Corporate Citizenship Trust	7.361
Jordan Charitable Foundation (J)	7.362
Joshua Trust Group, The (J)	7.364
Kabbalah Centre (.I)	7.365
Kennedy Memorial Fund	7.368
Kibble Education and Care Centre	7.371
L'Arche (J)	7.375
Lancashire Wildlife Trust	7.377
LankellyChase Foundation, The (J)	7.379
Lawrence Atwell's Charity	7.380
Leeds Castle Foundation (J)	7.381
I OROS	7.384
LGS General Charitable Trust	7.387
Lloyd's Register Foundation	7.395
London Housing Foundation	7.399
Loretto Care	7.403
Macmillan Cancer Support	7.405
Maggie Keswick Jencks Cancer Trust (J)	7.406
Manchester & District Home for Lost Dogs (J)	7.408
Manchester Diocesan Board of Finance	7.408
Marie Curie Cancer Care	7.410
Marine Society & Sea Cadets (.I)	7.411
Maudsley Charity	7.416
Merchant Taylors' Consolidated Charities	7.422
Methodist Homes (J)	7.424
MIND	7.428
Mines Advisory Group	7.429
Missio	7.429
Momentum Scotland	7.431
Motability (J)	7.435
Mungo Foundation, The	7.439
Muscular Dystrophy Campaign (J)	7.439
NABS	7.441
National Galleries of Scotland (J)	7.446
National Heart & Lung Inst. Foundation, The	7.448
National Library of Scotland (J)	7.448
National Maritime Museum (J)	7.449
National Museums Scotland	7.451
Nat Soc CoE for Promoting Religious Ed (J)	7.452
National Theatre of Scotland	7.453
National Trust for Scotland	7.453
Newton Dee Camphill Community Ltd	7.461
NHS Gtr Glasgow & Clyde Endowments	7.462
North Bristol NHS Trust Charitable Funds (J)	7.465
Northern Housing Company (J)	7.470
Norwood (J)	7.472
Nuffield Health (J)	7.474
Officers Association	7.478
Onside Youth Zones	7.480
Ormerod Home Trust Limited	7.484
Oxfam GB	7.486
Papworth Trust (J)	7.490
Parham Park Trust (1984) (J)	7.491
Park Charitable Trust, The	7.491
Parkinson's UK	7.491
Partners for Inclusion	7.492
Physiological Society, The	7.502
Police Dependants' Trust Limited, The	7.507
Poole Arts Trust	7.508

Poor Servants of the Mother of God	7.508
Portsmouth Naval Base Property Trust	7.510
Postcode Global Trust (J)	7.511
Prince and Princess of Wales Hospice	7.513
Professional Footballers Assoc Educ Fund	7.516
Professional Footballers Benevolent Fund	7.516
Queen's Cross Workspace	7.520
Queen's Nursing Institute (J)	7.520
R&A Foundation, The (J)	7.521
Religious of the Assumption	7.531
Richmond Fellowship Scotland	7.537
Rifles Benevolent Trust, The	7.538
Rokpa Trust	7.543
Rosslyn Chapel Trust (J)	7.545
Royal Academy of Arts	7.548
Royal Academy Trust	7.549
Royal Blind	7.553
Royal Botanic Garden Edinburgh	7.553
Royal Botanic Gardens, Kew	7.554
Royal College of Paediatrics	7.556
Royal Col. Physicians & Surgeons Glasgow	7.557
Royal Commission for the 1851 Exhibition	7.558
Royal Electrical & Mech Eng Central Trust	7.559
Royal Highland Agricultural Soc Scotland	7.561
Royal Institution of Naval Architects	7.563
Royal Logistic Corps Association Trust	7.564
Royal National Children's Foundation (J)	7.566
Royal National Institute of Blind People	7.566
Royal Navy and Royal Marines Charity	7.568
Royal Scottish Corporation	7.570
Royal Society Musicians Great Britain	7.573
Royal Society, The	7.573
Royal Yacht Britannia Trust	7.575
Salesians of Don Bosco UK	7.582
Salford Diocesan Trust (J)	7.582
Sandwell Leisure Trust (J)	7.587
Savitri Waney Charitable Trust	7.588
Savoy Educational Trust	7.588
Scottish Autism	7.591
Scottish Ballet (J)	7.591
Scottish Catholic International Aid Fund (J)	7.591
SCVO	7.592
Scottish Opera	7.592
Scottish Veterans Garden City Association Inc	7.593
Scottish War Blinded	7.593
Scottish Wildlife Trust	7.593
Scottish Youth Hostels Association	7.594
Seamen's Hospital Society	7.595
Seashell Trust	7.595
Shakespeare Globe Trust (J)	7.599
Shaw Trust	7.599
Sheffield Church Burgesses Trust	7.600
Sheffield Futures	7.601
Sheffield Hospitals Trust & Related Charities (J)	7.602
Shipwrecked Mariners' Society (J)	7.605
Diocese of ShrewsburyTrust	7.607
Sir Andrew Judd Foundation	7.609
Sisters of St Joseph of Annecy	7.614
Sisters of St Joseph Province (J)	7.615
Sisters of the Cross and Passion (J)	7.615
Sisters Holy Family Bordeaux	7.616
Presentation Sisters	7.616
Skill Force Development	7.617
Skills for Care (J)	7.617
Society of African Missions	7.621
Society of the Helpers of the Holy Souls	7.624
Soho Theatre Company	7.625
SSAFA (J)	7.626
Sons of the Sacred Heart of Jesus, The	7.627
South Lanarkshire Leisure Ltd	7.629
St Andrew's Hospice (Lanarkshire)	7.637
St Andrews Links Trust (J)	7.637
St Ann's Hospice	7.637
St Columba's Hospice	7.641
St Edmundsbury & Ipswich Diocesan Bd of Fin	7.642
St Elizabeth Hospice (Suffolk)	7.642
St Michael's Hospice	7.651
Stanley Picker Trust, The	7.655
Stockport Cerebral Palsy Society	7.659
Strathcarron Hospice (J)	7.661
Talbot Association Limited	7.668
Tayside NHS Board Endowment Fund	7.670
Teenage Cancer Trust (J)	7.671
Teesside Hospice Care Foundation	7.671
Teresa Rosenbaum Golden Charitable Trust	7.673
Thistle Foundation	7.677
Thornton-Smith and Plevins Trust (J)	7.679
Tottenham Grammar School Foundation	7.683

Little Company of Mary	7.688
Trustees of the Bernadine Sisters Charity	7.689
Trusthouse Charitable Foundation	7.690
United Synagogue	7.698
United Utilities Trust Fund	7.698
VAMW Care	7.703
Victim Support Scotland	7.704
Viewpoint Housing Association	7.705
Vincent Wildlife Trust (J)	7.706
Vision Redbridge Culture & Leisure	7.707
Wakefield Hospice	7.711
WCS Care Group Limited (J)	7.717
Weavers Company Benevolent Fund	7.717
Wessex Children's Hospice Trust (J)	7.719
West Lothian Leisure (J)	7.721
Westminster Drug Project	7.722
Westminster Foundation	7.723
White Horse Care Trust, The	7.725
Whizz-Kidz	7.726
Wigmore Hall Trust (J)	7.727
Wise Group	7.733
WIEGO Ltd (J)	7.736
Workers' Educational Association (J)	7.739
World Cancer Research Fund (WCRF UK) (J)	7.739
Worldwide Cancer Research	7.742
YMCA Downslink Group	7.745

ROYAL LONDON CASH MANAGEMENT, 55 Gracechurch Street, London, EC3V 0RL.

Henry Moore Foundation (J)	7.309
Royal Masonic Trust For Girls and Boys (J)	7.565
Y Care International (J)	7.743

SANTANDER UK PLC, 2 Triton Square, Regent's Place, London, NW1 3AN. Tel: 0870 607 6000. Internet: www.santander.co.uk.

1989 Willan Charitable Trust	7.2
A W Charitable Trust	7.4
Ashridge (Bonar Law Memorial) Trust (J)	7.44
Associated Board Royal Schools Music (J)	7.45
Autism Plus Limited	7.50
B G Campbell Trust Fund	7.53
Booth Charities (J)	7.79
Bridgewood Trust (J)	7.88
British Association for Adoption & Fostering (J)	7.92
Caldecott Foundation Limited (J)	7.108
Cerebra (J)	7.125
City of Glasgow College Foundation (J)	7.153
Congregation of the Sisters of St Martha (J)	7.175
DHL UK Foundation (J)	7.200
EveryChild (J)	7.243
Foundation (J)	7.258
Greenhouse Schools Project Limited	7.286
Helping Foundation, The (J)	7.308
Imperial College Trust (J)	7.329
International Aid Trust (J)	7.340
International Aid Trust (J)	7.340
Letchworth Garden City Heritage Foundation (J)	7.386
London Marathon Charitable Trust Limited	7.399
London's Air Ambulance Ltd	7.400
Maggie Keswick Jencks Cancer Trust (J)	7.406
Muslim Hands (J)	7.441
National Osteoporosis Society (J)	7.451
Norfolk Wildlife Trust (J)	7.464
North of England Zoological Society (J)	7.467
North York Moors Historical Railway (J)	7.468
Nuffield Health (J)	7.474
Oakhaven Trust (J)	7.476
Open Doors with Brother Andrew (J)	7.480
Peter Harrison Foundation (J)	7.499
Phyllis Tuckwell Memorial Hospice (J)	7.501
Punchdrunk (J)	7.518
Redeemed Christian Church of God (J)	7.528
Santander UK Foundation Limited	7.587
Scottish Catholic International Aid Fund (J)	7.591
Shree Kutch Satsang Swaminarayan Temple (J)	7.606
Skills for Care (J)	7.617
Somerset Redstone Trust (J)	7.627
Street League (J)	7.661
Sussex Community Foundation (J)	7.665
Sustrans (J)	7.666
YHA (England and Wales) (J)	7.744
Youth Sport Trust (J)	7.751

SCHRODERS & CO LIMITED, 12 Moorgate, London, EC2R 6DA. Tel: 020 7658 3636. Fax: 020 7658 3087. Internet: www.cazenovecharities.com.

SCOTTISH WIDOWS BANK PLC, PO Box 12757, 67 Morrison Street, Edinburgh, EH3 8YJ. Tel: 0845 845 0829. Fax: 0845 846 0829. Internet: www.scottishwidows.co.uk.

Alice Ellen Cooper-Dean Charitable Fndtn (J)	7.24
Association of Accounting Technicians (J)	7.46
Bethphage Mission (Great Britain) (J)	7.68
Bideford Bridge Trust (J)	7.69
Bradford Diocesan Board of Finance, The (J)	7.83
Bridgewood Trust (J)	7.88
Britten-Pears Foundation (J)	7.100
Chartered Quality Institute (J)	7.135
Company of Biologists Limited (J)	7.168
Conservation Education & Research Trust (J)	7.177
Dowager Countess Eleanor Peel Trust (J)	7.210
Engineering UK (J)	7.234
Groundwork UK (J)	7.290
Inspiring Scotland (J)	7.332
JW3 Trust Limited (J)	7.365
London Community Foundation (J)	7.397
Medical Research Foundation (J)	7.419
Midlands Arts Centre (J)	7.426
Nuffield Trst for Res.&Pol.Studies in Health (J)	7.475
People's Health Trust (J)	7.497
Printing Charity, The (J)	7.514
Regent's Park Theatre Limited (J)	7.530
Royal London Society for the Blind (J)	7.564
Scottish Catholic International Aid Fund (J)	7.591
St Andrews Links Trust (J)	7.637
Valley Leisure (J)	7.702
Westbank Community Health and Care (J)	7.721

SG HAMBROS BANK LIMITED, Norfolk House, 31 St James's Square, London, SW1Y 4JR. Tel: 020 7597 3000. Fax: 020 7587 3056.

Kennedy Leigh Charitable Trust	7.368
Maurice Hilda Laing Charitable Trust (J)	7.416

SIEMENS BANK GMGH, Bavaria House, 13-14 Appold Street, London, EC2S 2NB.

Nuffield Health (J)	7.474

SKIPTON BUILDING SOCIETY, The Bailey, Skipton, North Yorkshire, BD23 1DN. Internet: www.skipton.co.uk.

Bradford Diocesan Board of Finance, The (J)	7.83
Sisters of St Joseph of Peace (J)	7.615

STANDARD BANK JERSEY LIMITED, Standard Bank House, PO Box 583, St Helier, Jersey, JE4 8XR. Tel: 01534 881188.

Joe and Rosa Frenkel Charitable Trust, The	7.356

STANDARD BANK PLC, 20 Gresham Street, London, EC2V 7JE. Tel: 020 3145 5000. Fax: 020 3189 5000. Internet: www.standardbank.com.

Christian Aid (J)	7.145
Save the Children International (J)	7.588

STANDARD CHARTERED BANK (CI) LIMITED, PO Box 830, Conway Street, St Helier, Jersey, JE4 0UF.

Africa Centre Limited (J)	7.15
Concern Universal (J)	7.170
Hadley Trust	7.296
Intl Agency for the Prevention of Blindness (J)	7.340
International Rescue Committee UK (J)	7.344
Marie Stopes International (J)	7.410
Save the Children International (J)	7.588
Sightsavers International (J)	7.608
Thailand Border Consortium	7.674
Voluntary Service Overseas (J)	7.709

STANDARD LIFE WEALTH, 1 George Street, Edinburgh, EH2 2LL. Tel: 0845 279 8880. Internet: www.standardlifeinvestments.co.uk.

Sangha Tri-National Trust Fund Ltd	7.587

STATE BANK OF INDIA, 15 King Street, London, EC2V 8EA. Tel: 020 7454 4367. Internet: www.sbiuk.com.

TRIODOS BANK, Brunel House, 11 The Promenade, Bristol, BS8 3NN. Tel: 0800 328 2181. Fax: 0117 973 9303. E-mail: mail@triodos.co.uk. Internet: www.triodos.co.uk.

Abbeyfield Kent Society, The (J)	7.5
Art Services Grants Ltd (J)	7.40
Barrow Cadbury Trust (J)	7.59
Bristol Drugs Project (J)	7.90
Caring for Life (J)	7.115
Changeworks (J)	7.127
Charity Roman Union Order St Ursula (J)	7.130
Conciliation Resources (J)	7.170
Countryside Restoration Trust (J)	7.182
Fairtrade Foundation (J)	7.247
Foundation for Social Entrepreneurs (J)	7.259
Friends Provident Charitable Foundation (J)	7.266
Health and Social Care Alliance, The (J)	7.305
Joseph Rowntree Charitable Trust (J)	7.363
Margaret Blackwood Housing Association (J)	7.409
Marwell Wildlife (J)	7.414
Millennium Awards Trust, The (J)	7.427
Polden Puckham Charitable Foundation	7.506
Robert Owen Communities (J)	7.541
Ruskin Mill Trust (J)	7.578
Sheepdrove Trust, The	7.600
Soil Association	7.625
St Christopher's School (Bristol)	7.640
St Joseph's Hospice, Hackney (J)	7.646
Sustrans (.I)	7.666
Tellus Mater Foundation Ltd (J)	7.672
Waterloo Foundation, The (J)	7.715
Windhorse Trust, The (J)	7.732

UBS AG, 1 Finsbury Avenue, London, EC2M 2AN. Tel: 020 7567 5757. Fax: 020 7567 5656. Internet: www.ubs.com/charities-uk.

BirdLife International (J)	7.70
FARM-Africa (J)	7.248
John Booth Charitable Foundation, The	7.357

ULSTER BANK LIMITED, University Road, Dublin, BT7 1NN. Tel: 00 35 31 8403411. Fax: 00 35 31 8404088. Internet: www.ulsterbank.com.

Disability Action (J)	7.201
Insurance Charities (J)	7.339
Open Doors with Brother Andrew (J)	7.480

UNITED NATIONAL BANK, 2 Brook Street, London, W15 1BQ. Tel: 0121 753 6009. Fax: 0121 773 9872. Internet: www.ubluk.com.

Edhi International Foundation UK (J)	7.224

UNITY TRUST BANK PLC, Nine Brindleyplace, Birmingham, West Midlands, B1 2HB. Tel: 0345 140 1000. Fax: 0345 113 0033. E-mail: us@unity.co.uk. Internet: www.unity.co.uk. Charity specialists: N Price.

Action Housing & Support Limited (J)	7.10
Age UK Northumberland	7.18
Becht Family Charitable Trust, The	7.63
Bristol Drugs Project (J)	7.90
CDP Worldwide (J)	7.121
CILIP (J)	7.133
Church Army (J)	7.147
Contact a Family	7.178
Developing Health and Independence	7.199
Eiris Foundation	7.229
Equity Charitable Trust	7.238
Five Lamps Organisation	7.255
Hampshire & Isle of Wight Wildlife Trust	7.298
Homeless Link	7.316
Imagine Act and Suceed	7.328
Keyring-Living Support Networks	7.370
LIONHEART	7.391
Locality (UK)	7.396
Midland Mencap	7.426
Mountview Academy of Theatre Arts (J)	7.436
Murray Hall Community Trust	7.439
NUMAST Welfare Funds	7.475
People's History Museum (J)	7.497
Porchlight	7.509
Ramblers Association	7.525
Robert Owen Communities (J)	7.541
Sheffield Media and Exhibition Centre	7.602
Sheppard Trust	7.604
Skills for Care (J)	7.617
Solent Mind (J)	7.626
St Anne's Community Services	7.637
StreetGames UK	7.662
Tiverton Almshouse Charity	7.681
West Midlands Special Needs Transport (J)	7.721
Westbank Community Health and Care (J)	7.721
Westhill Endowment	7.722
Worcester Consolidated Municipal Charity	7.738
Worcestershire YMCA Limited	7.738
YMCA Black Country Group	7.744
YWCA England & Wales	7.752

VIRGIN MONEY, Jubilee House, Gosforth, Tyne and Wear, NE3 4PL.

Bradford Diocesan Board of Finance, The (J)	7.83
Federation of Jewish Services (J)	7.250
Ibbett Trust (J)	7.327
Marwell Wildlife (J)	7.414
Medical Research Foundation (J)	7.419
National Osteoporosis Society (J)	7.451
Norfolk Wildlife Trust (J)	7.464
Northern Rock Foundation (J)	7.471
People's Health Trust (J)	7.497
Scottish Ballet (J)	7.591
Valley Leisure (J)	7.702

WEATHERBYS BANK LIMITED, Sanders Road, Wellingborough, Northamptonshire, NN8 4BX. Tel: 01933 304 777. Fax: 01933 304 888. Internet: www.weatherbysbank.com.

Racing Foundation, The	7.523

WELLS FARGO BANK, One Plantation Place, 30 Fenchurch Street, London, EC3M 3BD. Tel: 020 7149 8100. Fax: 020 7149 8393. Internet: www.wellsfargo.com.

United Bible Societies Association, The (J)	7.695

YORKSHIRE BANK PLC, 20 Merrion Way, Leeds, West Yorkshire, LS2 8NZ. Internet: www.ybonline.co.uk.

Arch Initiatives	7.36
Baltic Flour Mills Visual Arts Trust	7.55
Barnsley Hospice Appeal (.I)	7.58
Booth Charities (J)	7.79
Catholic Care (Diocese of Leeds)	7.119
Child Action Northwest	7.139
Children's Food Trust, The	7.140
Community Foundation for Calderdale	7.162
Hospital of the Holy & Undivided Trinity (J)	7.322
Lamport Hall Preservation Trust	7.377
Leeds Teaching Hospitals Charitable Fdn (J)	7.382
National Space Science Centre (J)	7.453
NECA (J)	7.455
Newcastle upon Tyne Hospitals NHS Charity (J)	7.460
Pharmacist Support (J)	7.500
Preston Rd Neigbourhood Development Co.	7.513
Sheffield Diocesan Board of Finance	7.601
Skills for Care (J)	7.617
South Yorkshire Community Foundation (J)	7.631
St Mary Magdalene & Holy Jesus Trust (J)	7.649
St Oswald's Hospice (J)	7.653
Wakefield Diocesan Board Finance	7.710
Yorkshire Air Ambulance (J)	7.749

Break the chain

Rawlinson & Hunter specialises in advising on the formation, management and administration of charitable trusts both in the UK and overseas.

Our practice is founded on the long term relationships we have forged with our clients and fellow professionals over many years. We constantly develop our services to meet the ever increasing compliance and regulatory burdens placed on charities. We aim to break the chains hampering trustees, allowing them to focus on the effective management and development of their charity.

Our Charity Specialist Team are Chris Bliss FCA, Simon Jennings FCA and Frances Jennings ACA.

RAWLINSON & HUNTER

www.rawlinson-hunter.com

UK, Australia, Bermuda, British Virgin Islands, Cayman Islands, Guernsey, Jersey, New Zealand, Singapore, Switzerland

FINANCIAL ADVISERS AND THEIR CHARITY

CLIENTS

ASPIRE, 2 Infirmary Street, Leeds, West Yorkshire, LS1 2JP. Tel: 0113 236 8368.

St Oswald's Hospice   7.653

BARCLAYS WEALTH, Tay House, 300 Bath Street, Glasgow, G2 4LH.

Milestones Trust   7.427

BARRATT & COOKE, 5/6 Opie Street, Norwich, Norfolk, NR1 3DW. Tel: 01603 624236. Fax: 01603 665757. Internet: www.barrattandcooke.co.uk. Charity specialists: A Mann.

Norfolk Wildlife Trust   7.464

BUZZACOTT FINANCIAL PLANNING, 130 Wood Street, London, EC2V 6DL. Tel: 020 7556 1200. Fax: 020 7556 1212. Internet: www.buzzacott.co.uk/specialist-teams/financial-planning.

Essex Wildlife Trust   7.240

CAMBRIDGE ASSOCIATES LIMITED, 4th Floor, 80 Victoria Street, Cardinal Place, London, SW1E 5JL. Tel: 020 7592 2200. Fax: 020 7592 2201. Internet: www.cambridgeassociates.com.

Medlock Charitable Trust   7.420

CLAY RATNAGE STREVENS & HILLS, Construction House, Runwell Road, Wickford, Essex, SS11 7HQ. Tel: 01268 735363.

L M Kendon Settlement   7.376

DEUTSCHE BANK PRIVATE WEALTH MANAGEMENT, Royal Liver Building, Pier Head, Liverpool, Merseyside, L3 1NY. Tel: 0151 255 3000. Fax: 0151 236 1252. Charity specialists: P Hartley.

Austin Hope Pilkington Trust   7.49
Pilkington Charities Fund   7.503

DODD & CO, Warwick House, Allenbrook Road, Carlisle, Cumbria, CA1 2UT.

Cumbrian Community Foundation   7.189

FIDELIUS LTD, 20 Little Britain, London, EC1A 7DH. Tel: 020 3651 5530. Internet: www.fidelius.co.uk.

R L Glasspool Charity Trust   7.522

FOSTER DENOVO LTD, Ruxley House, 2 Hamm Moor Lane, Addlestone, Surrey, KT15 2SA. Tel: 0845 838 6060. Fax: 0845 838 6060.

Papworth Trust   7.490

HUTCHINSON LILLEY INVESTMENTS LTD, 43 Portland Place, London, W1B 1QH. Tel: 0207 612 7391. Fax: 0207 612 7390. E-mail: robert.hutchinson@hlinv.com.

David Elaine Potter Charitable Foundation   7.194

L & P FINANCIAL TRUSTEES (UK) LIMITED, 2/3 Terminus Mills, Clonskeagh Road, Dublin. Tel: +353 1 283 8788. Fax: +353 1 283 8988. E-mail: info@lpgroup.ie. Internet: www.lpgroup.ie.

Teresa Ball International Solidarity Fund   7.673
Congregation of Christian Brothers   7.688

MY 1ST CONSULTANCY LTD, 320a Romford Road, Forest Gate, London, E7 8BD.

Palestinians Relief and Development Fund   7.489

RAWLINSON & HUNTER

RAWLINSON & HUNTER, Eighth Floor, 6 New Street Square, New Fetter Lane, London, EC4A 3AQ. Tel: 020 7842 2000. Fax: 020 7842 2080. E-mail: charity@rawlinson-hunter.com. Internet: www.rawlinson-hunter.com.

Rawlinson & Hunter's dedicated charity team offers tailor made services to charity clients. For over 80 years we have been providing high levels of service to our charity clients by applying our private client advisory approach for which we are renowned.

This specialist unit offers services which include, but are not limited to, accounting, outsourcing, audit and independent examination and other specialist services such as investment and performance monitoring, IT support and taxation advice.

We are constantly developing our services as a result of increasing regulatory burdens being placed on trustees. We aim to minimise these burdens to allow the trustees to concentrate on managing the charity effectively.

Charity specialists: C J A Bliss FCA. S P Jennings FCA. F J Jennings ACA.

SKERRITT CONSULTANTS LTD, Skerritt House, 23 Coleridge Street, Hove, Brighton & Hove, BN3 5AB. Tel: 01273 204999. Fax: 01273 204480. E-mail: enquiries@skerritts.co.uk. Internet: www.skerritts.co.uk.

Crime Reduction Initiatives   7.186

SMITH & WILLIAMSON, 25 Moorgate, London, EC2R 6AY. Tel: 020 7131 4000. Fax: 020 7131 4001. Internet: www.smith.williamson.co.uk. Charity specialists: J Biddell.

Eurocentres UK   7.241
London Cyrenians Housing   7.398

SMITH & WILLIAMSON, Imperial House, 18-21 Kings Park Road, Southampton, Hampshire, SO15 2AT. Tel: 023 8082 7600. Internet: www.smith.williamson.co.uk.

Vocational Training Charitable Trust   7.708

STEWART FINANCIAL MANAGEMENT, 2 Woodside Place, Glasgow, G3 7QF. Tel: 0141 332 6688. Internet: www.stewartfm.co.uk.

Mungo Foundation, The   7.439

TOWERGATE FINANCIAL, Baton House, Holly Bank Road, Lindley, Huddersfield, West Yorkshire, HD3 3JE.

Caring for Life   7.115

TRADERISKS LTD, 21 Great Winchester Street, London, EC2N 2JA. Tel: 020 7382 0900. Internet: www.traderisks.com.

Church of England Pensions Board   7.148

UBS WEALTH MANAGEMENT, 2 St James' Gate, Newcastle upon Tyne, Tyne and Wear, NE4 7JH. Tel: 0191 211 1000. Fax: 0191 211 1001. E-mail: adrew.elliot@ubs.com. Internet: www.ubs.com/uk. Charity specialists: Vinay Bedi. Andrew Elliot.

1989 Willan Charitable Trust   7.2
Ballinger Charitable Trust   7.55

WM COMPANY, World Markets House, Crewe Toll, Edinburgh, EH4 2PY. Tel: 0131 315 2000. Fax: 0131 315 2999.

Hampstead Wells & Campden Trust   7.299

INSURANCE BROKERS AND THEIR CHARITY CLIENTS

ACCESS INSURANCE, Selsdon House, 212-220 Addington Road, South Croydon, Surrey, CR2 8LD.
E-mail: insure@accessinsurance.co.uk.
Internet: www.accessunderwriting.co.uk.

Fellowship of School of Economic Science 7.251

ALLIANZ INSURANCE PLC, 1 Wellington Place, Tower Square, Wellington Street, Leeds, West Yorkshire, LS1 4AJ. Tel: 0113 284 8200.
Internet: www.allianz.co.uk.

Congregation of the Passion Jesus Christ 7.174

AON UK LIMITED, 5th Floor, The Fountain Precinct, Sheffield, South Yorkshire, S1 2JA. Tel: 0114 203 4600.
Internet: www.rewritinginsurance.aon.co.uk/charities.aspx.

ARTHUR J GALLAGHER, 89 High Road, South Woodford, London, E18 2RH.

Thomas Pocklington Trust 7.678

ARTHUR J GALLAGHER, Charity & Healthcare Division, Temple Point 7th Floor, 1 Temple Row, Birmingham, West Midlands, B2 5YB. Tel: 0121 200 4939. Fax: 0870 197 3289.
Internet: www.ajginternational.com.
Charity specialists: P Eden. E Flaherty. A Waite. G Hockey.

ARTHUR J GALLAGHER, 5 Western Boulevard, Leicester, Leicestershire, LE2 7EX. Tel: 0116 254 6221. Internet: www.ajginternational.com.

Woodland Trust 7.737

AVIVA, 8 Surrey Street, Norwich, Norfolk, NR1 3NG. Internet: www.aviva.co.uk.

Blanchminster Trust 7.75

BARTLETT & CO LIMITED, Broadway Hall, Horsforth, Leeds, West Yorkshire, LS18 4RS. Tel: 0845 605 4155. Fax: 0113 258 5081.
E-mail: mail@bartlettgroup.com.
Internet: www.bartlettgroup.com.
Charity specialists: I Roberts. S Mockett.

CIPFA (J)	7.151
Institute of Psychoanalysis	7.337
LGS General Charitable Trust	7.387

BERKELEY APPLEGATE WEBB, Lowcroft, Church Road, Wombourne, Wolverhampton, West Midlands, WV5 9EZ. Tel: 01902 324194. Fax: 01902 324993.
Internet: www.bawinsurance.co.uk/services/churches-and-charities.

BLUEFIN, Fountain House, 130 Fenchurch Street, London, EC3M 5DJ. Tel: 020 7335 1646. Fax: 020 7338 0112.
E-mail: charity@bluefingroup.co.uk.
Internet: www.bluefingroup.co.uk.
Charity specialists: S Holt (Schemes Manager). D Maskell (Accounts Executive).

Campden Charities Trustee 7.110

BLUEFIN, Castlemead, Lower Castle Street, Bristol, BS1 3AG. Tel: 0117 929 3344. Fax: 0845 521 5576.
Internet: www.bluefingroup.co.uk.

Dame Hannah Rogers Trust 7.192

Holburne Museum (J) 7.314

BLUEFIN, Suite D, Galleon House, 12 Lion and Lamb Yard, Farnham, Surrey, GU9 7LL.
Internet: www.bluefingroup.co.uk.

Wine & Spirit Education Trust Ltd 7.732

BLUEFIN, Stephenson House, 7-10 The Grove, Gravesend, Kent, DA12 1DU. Tel: 01474 537 777. E-mail: charity@bluefingroup.co.uk.
Internet: www.bluefingroup.co.uk.

Camphill Village Trust Limited	7.111
Marist Sisters	7.130
Treloar Trust	7.685

BLUEFIN, Applicon Centre, Exchange Street, Stockport, Greater Manchester, SK3 0EY. Tel: 0161 429 9032. Fax: 0161 480 2215.

Chetham's Hospital School and Library	7.138
Wilf Ward Family Trust	7.728

CASE INSURANCE, James House, Emlyn Lane, Leatherhead, Surrey, KT22 7EP. Tel: 0845 2252288. Internet: www.caseinsurance.co.uk.

Society for Promoting Christian Knowledge 7.620

CATHOLIC CHURCH INSURANCE ASSOCIATION, Oakley House, Mill Street, Aylesbury, Buckinghamshire, HP20 1BN. Tel: 01296 422030. Internet: www.ccia.org.uk.

Arundel and Brighton Diocesan Trust	7.42
Notts Roman Catholic Diocesan Trustees	7.473
Roman Catholic Diocese Hallam Trust	7.543
Diocese of ShrewsburyTrust	7.607

CHESHAM INSURANCE BROKERS, MW House, 1 Penman Way, Grove Park, Leicester, Leicestershire, LE19 1SY.

R.Watts&Rochester CityAlmshouseCharities 7.536

CODAL LIMITED, 90 Fenchurch Street, London, EC3M 4ST. Tel: 020 7283 4646. Fax: 020 7204 2565.
E-mail: codal.enquiries@thomasmiller.com.
Internet: www.codalltd.com.

College of Estate Management 7.160

D E FORD INSURANCE BROKERS LTD, Poppleton Grange, Low Poppleton Lane, York, North Yorkshire, YO26 6GZ. Tel: 01904 784141. Fax: 01904 790880.
E-mail: cwalton@deford.co.uk.
Internet: www.deford.co.uk.

E COLEMAN AND CO LIMITED, 8 Albany Park, Cabot Lane, Poole, Dorset, BH17 7AZ. Tel: 01202 647400. Fax: 01202 647422.
Internet: www.colemaninsurance.co.uk.
Charity specialists: P Moody.

Buckfast Abbey Trust 7.103

ECCLESIASTICAL INSURANCE, Ecclesiastical Insurance Office, Beaufort House, Brunswick Road, Gloucester, Gloucestershire, GL1 1JZ. Tel: 0845 777 3322.
E-mail: information@ecclesiastical.com.
Internet: www.ecclesiastical.com.

Blackburn Diocesan Board Finance Limited	7.74
Bradford Diocesan Board of Finance, The (J)	7.83
Bristol Diocesan Board Finance Ltd	7.89
Coventry Diocesan Board of Finance	7.184

Derby Diocesan Board Finance Ltd	7.198
Exeter Diocesan Board of Finance, The	7.244
Guildford Diocesan Board of Finance	7.292
Lichfield Diocesan Board Of Education, The	7.387
Lichfield Diocesan Board Of Finance	7.387
Lincoln Diocesan Trust Board Finance Ltd	7.389
London Diocesan Fund	7.398
Norwich Diocesan Board of Finance, The	7.471
Oxford Diocesan Board Finance	7.487
Ripon Diocesan Board of Finance	7.539
Salisbury Diocesan Board Finance	7.583
St Edmundsbury & Ipswich Diocesan Bd of Fin	7.642
Truro Diocesan Board Finance Ltd	7.687
Winchester Diocesan Board of Finance	7.732
Diocese of Worcester	7.738

GALLAGHER HEATH, 2nd Floor, Station Square, 1 Gloucester Street, Swindon, Wiltshire, SN1 1GW. Tel: 020 7560 3000.
Internet: www.gallagherheath.com.

Whitechapel Gallery 7.725

GRIFFITHS & ARMOUR INSURANCE BROKERS, Drury House, 19 Water Street, Liverpool, Merseyside, L2 ORL. Tel: 0151 236 5656. Fax: 0151 227 2216.
Internet: www.griffithsandarmour.com.

Retail Trust	7.533
RSPB	7.572

GRIFFITHS & ARMOUR INSURANCE BROKERS, 44 Peter Street, Manchester, Greater Manchester, M2 5GP. Tel: 0161 817 4450. Fax: 0161 817 4477.
E-mail: info@griffithsandarmour.com.
Internet: www.griffithsandarmour.com.

Keep Britain Tidy 7.367

H W WOOD , The Baltic Exchange, 38 St. Mary Axe, London, EC3A 8BH. Tel: 020 7398 9000. Fax: 020 7398 9001.
E-mail: london@hwint.com.
Internet: www.hwint.com/uk.

Guy's & St Thomas' Charity 7.293

HEATH GALLAGHER GROUP, 2nd Floor, Station Square, 1 Gloucester Street, Swindon, Wiltshire, SN1 1GW. Tel: 020 7560 3000.
Internet: www.gallagherheath.com.

Bath Wells Diocesan Board Finance 7.60

HENDERSON INSURANCE BROKERS LTD, No 1 Whitehall Riverside, Leeds, West Yorkshire, LS1 4BN. Tel: 0113 261 5088. Fax: 0113 261 5099. Internet: www.hibl.co.uk.

HENDERSON INSURANCE BROKERS LTD, 1st floor, The Forum, Minerva Business Park, Lynchwood, Peterborough, PE2 6FT. Tel: 01733 404488. Fax: 01733 404480.
Internet: www.hibl.co.uk.

Engineering UK 7.234

HETTLE ANDREWS & ASSOCIATES LIMITED, Eleven Brindleyplace, 9th Floor, 2 Brunswick Square, Brindleyplace, Birmingham, West Midlands, B1 2LP. Tel: 0121 423 6200.
Internet: www.hettleandrews.co.uk.

Portland College 7.509

HUBERT MITCHELL (INSURANCE BROKERS) LIMITED, Kinauld Court, 350a Lanark Road West, Currie, Edinburgh, EH14 5RR. Tel: 0131 449 9002. Fax: 0131 449 9001. Internet: www.hubertmitchell.co.uk. Charity specialists: R Shaw.

Walcot Educational Foundation	7.711

JARDINE LLOYD THOMPSON, City Plaza, Temple Row, Birmingham, West Midlands, B2 5AB. Tel: 0121 633 3377. Fax: 0121 633 4214. Internet: www.jltgroup.com.

City of Birmingham Symphony Orchestra	7.153

JARDINE LLOYD THOMPSON, St James House, 7 Charlotte Street, Manchester, Greater Manchester, M1 4DZ. Tel: 020 7528 4444. Internet: www.jltgroup.com.

Raleigh International Trust	7.524

JARDINE LLOYD THOMPSON, Threefield House, Threefield Lane, Southampton, Hampshire, SO14 3RP. Tel: 023 8037 4890. Internet: www.jltgroup.com.

Royal Hospital for Neuro-disability	7.562

JELF GROUP, Kabel House, 15 Quay Street, Manchester, Greater Manchester, M3 3HN. Tel: 0161 228 0444. Internet: www.jelfgroup.com.

Langdon Community	7.378
Langdon Foundation	7.379

KEEGAN & PENNYKID (INSURANCE BROKERS) LTD, 50 Queen Street, Edinburgh, EH2 3NS. Tel: 0131 225 6005. Fax: 0131 226 3811. E-mail: mail@keegan-pennykid.com. Internet: www.keegan-pennykid.com. Charity specialists: K H C Pennykid.

Carr-Gomm Scotland	7.117

LARK INSURANCE BROKING GROUP, 9th Floor, Colman House, King Street, Maidstone, Kent, ME14 1DN. Tel: 01622 687476. Fax: 01622 670991. E-mail: mailbox@larkinsurance.co.uk. Internet: www.larkinsurance.co.uk.

Royal Commission for the 1851 Exhibition	7.558

LOCKTON INTERNATIONAL, 138 Houndsditch, The St. Botolph Building, London, EC3A 7AG. Tel: 0207 933 2634. Fax: 0207 933 0912.

Alzheimer's Society	7.28

MARKEL (UK) LIMITED, Riverside West, Whitehall Road, Leeds, West Yorkshire, LS1 4AW. Tel: 0113 261 5824. Fax: 0845 351 2601. E-mail: socialwelfare@markeluk.com. Internet: www.markeluk.com/socialwelfare.

Arch Initiatives	7.36
Oxford Diocesan Council For Social Work	7.487

MARSH BROKERS, Tower Place, 1 Tower Place West, London, EC3R 5BU. Tel: 020 7357 1000. Fax: 020 7929 2705. Internet: www.marsh.co.uk.

Royal Highland Agricultural Soc Scotland	7.561

MARSH BROKERS, Capital House, 1-5 Perrymount Road, Haywards Heath, West Sussex, RH16 3SY. Tel: 01444 458144. Fax: 01444 415088. Internet: www.marsh.co.uk. Charity specialists: P J Newnham.

Harpur Trust, The	7.302
Lawrence Atwell's Charity	7.380
Moor House School	7.432
Sir Andrew Judd Foundation	7.609

MARSH LTD, International House, George Curl Way, Southampton, Hampshire, SO18 2RZ. Tel: 02380 218700. Fax: 02380 318394. Internet: uk.marsh.com.

Regent's University London	7.530

MARSH LTD, 39 King Hill Avenue, Kings Hill, West Malling, Kent, ME19 4ER. Tel: 01732 877500. Internet: www.marsh.co.uk. Charity specialists: J Ram. M Singfield. Libby Hammerton. J Kerwin. Amy Green. Kym Ongley.

United Response	7.697

MILLER & CO INSURANCE BROKERS, High Street, Hambledon, Waterlooville, Hampshire, PO7 4RS. Tel: 023 9263 2555. Internet: www.millerinsuranceltd.co.uk.

Mary Rose Trust	7.414

NFU MUTUAL, No. 1 North Pallant, Chichester, West Sussex, PO19 1TJ. Tel: 01243 784022. Fax: 01243 539276. E-mail: chichester@nfumutual.co.uk. Internet: www.nfumutual.co.uk.

Edward James Foundation Limited	7.228

OVAL FINANCIAL SERVICES LIMITED, 5 Western Boulevard, Leicester, Leicestershire, LE2 7EX. Tel: 0116 254 6221. Fax: 0116 247 0140.

South West Environmental Parks Limited	7.630

OVAL INSURANCE BROKING LIMITED, Temple Circus House, Temple Way, Bristol, BS1 6HG. Tel: 0117 3006161. Internet: www.theovalgroup.com.

Whitley Wildlife Conservation Trust, The	7.726

OVAL INSURANCE BROKING LIMITED, 8-10 South Parade, Wakefield, West Yorkshire, WF1 1LR. Tel: 01924 371991. Internet: www.theovalgroup.com.

Inst. of Occupational Safety & Health	7.339

PAVEY GROUP, Minerva House, Orchard Way, Edginswell Park, Torquay, Devon, TQ2 7FA.

Shared Lives South West	7.599

QBE INSURANCE (EUROPE) LIMITED, Plantation Place, 30 Fenchurch Street, London, EC3M 3BD.

Norfolk Wildlife Trust	7.464

RKH GROUP, Woodlands, Manton Lane, Bedford, Bedfordshire, MK41 7LW. Tel: 01234 305 555. Fax: 01234 408 676. Internet: www.rkhgroup.com.

Ombersley Conservation Trust	7.480

ROBERTSON TAYLOR W&P LONGREACH, America House, 2 America Square, London, EC3N 2LU. Tel: 020 7510 1234. Fax: 020 7510 1134. E-mail: enquiries@rtworldwide.com. Internet: www.rtworldwide.com. Charity specialists: Andrew Rudge. Bev Hewes.

Shakespeare Globe Trust	7.599

SCRUTTON BLAND, 820 The Crescent, Colchester Business Park, Colchester, Essex, CO4 9YQ. Tel: 01206 838400.

Independent Age	7.331

SPINK INSURANCE CONSULTANTS LTD, Kirtlington Business Centre, Building C, Slade Farm, Portway, Kirtlington, Oxford, Oxfordshire, OX5 3JA. Tel: 01869 221 327. Fax: 01869 352 712.

Charity of Thomas Dawson	7.130

STACKHOUSE POLAND INSURANCE BROKERS, New House, Bedford Road, Guildford, Surrey, GU1 4SJ. Tel: 01483 407440. Fax: 01483 407441. E-mail: keithhester@stackhouse.co.uk. Internet: www.stackhouse.co.uk/charity. Charity specialists: Susan Westaway.

Breast Cancer Campaign	7.86
Rainbow Trust Children's Charity	7.524

SUTTON WINSON LTD, Town Hall Chambers, Heath Road, Petersfield, Hampshire, GU31 4TF. Tel: 0845 688 9088. Internet: www.suttonwinson.com.

Roffey Park Institute	7.542

SYDNEY PACKETT & SONS LTD, Salts Wharf, Ashley Lane, Shipley, West Yorkshire, BD17 7DB. Tel: 01274 206500. Fax: 01274 206506. E-mail: mail@packetts.com. Internet: www.packetts.com.

Chartered Institute of Arbitrators	7.132
Chartered Inst of Personnel & Development	7.134
Guide Dogs for the Blind Association	7.291
Hollybank Trust	7.315
Royal College of Pathologists	7.557
Royal College of Physicians of London	7.557
St John Ambulance	7.644

TOWERGATE MIA, Kings Court, London Road, Stevenage, Hertfordshire, SG1 2GA. Tel: 01438 739787. Fax: 01438 747465. E-mail: m.a@towergate.co.uk. Internet: www.towergatemia.co.uk.

St Clare West Essex Hospice Care Trust	7.640
St Oswald's Hospice	7.653

TOWERGATE RISK SOLUTIONS, Towergate House, 1 Canal Place, Leeds, West Yorkshire, LS12 2DU. Tel: 0113 243 3533. Fax: 0113 384 4100. Internet: www.towergateinsurance.co.uk.

Bradford Diocesan Board of Finance, The (J)	7.83
Leicester Diocesan Board Finance	7.383

TOWERGATE RISK SOLUTIONS, Towergate House, The Embankment, Heaton Mersey, Stockport, Greater Manchester, SK4 3GN. Tel: 0161 443 0700. Internet: www.towergateinsurance.co.uk.

Nugent Care	7.475

TOWNSEND MCCORMACK LTD, 6 Lloyds Avenue, London, EC3N 3AX.

Loddon School Company	7.396

UMAL AND UM ASSOCIATION (SPECIAL RISKS) LTD, Woburn House, Tavistock Square, London, WC1H 9HW. Tel: 020 7388 9222. Fax: 020 7388 9229.

UTTINGS INSURANCE BROKERS, 16 The Fairland, Hingham, Norwich, Norfolk, NR9 4HN. Tel: 01953 850459. Fax: 01953 850629. E-mail: julie.edmunds@uttingsinsurance.co.uk. Internet: www.uttingsinsurance.co.uk.

British Trust for Ornithology	7.99
World Horse Welfare	7.740

WILLIS LTD, Ten Trinity Square, London, EC3P 3AX. Tel: 020 7488 8111. Fax: 020 7488 8223. Internet: www.willis.com. Charity specialists: Janice Ashby.

Barts and The London Charity	7.59

WILLIS LTD, 285 Queen Street, Broughty Ferry, Dundee, DD5 2HD. Tel: 08700 100 410. Fax: 01382 735135. Internet: www.willis.com.

Penumbra	7.496

WILLIS LTD, Stuart House, Caxton Road, Fulwood, Preston, Lancashire, PR2 9RW. Tel: 01772 664000. Fax: 01772 651221. Internet: www.willis.com.

Sense - National Deafblind & Rubella Assoc	7.597

WRIGHTSURE SERVICES LTD, Wrightsure House, 799 London Road, West Thurrock, Essex, RM20 3LH.

English Stage Company Ltd	7.236

ZURICH MUNICIPAL INSURANCE, Southwood Crescent, Farnborough, Hampshire, GU14 0NJ. Tel: 0870 2418050. E-mail: info@zurichmunicipal.com. Internet: www.zurichmunicipal.com.

Scripture Union (J)	7.594

ZURICH MUNICIPAL INSURANCE, Zurich House, Stanhope Road, Portsmouth, Hampshire, PO1 1DU. Tel: 02392 822200. E-mail: info@zurichmunicipal.com. Internet: www.zurichmunicipal.com.

Rethink Mental Illness   7.534

ZURICH MUNICIPAL INSURANCE, Mountbatten House, Grosvenor Square, Southampton, Hampshire, SO15 2RP. Tel: 0845 600 3184. Fax: 0845 762 6822. E-mail: zurichthirdsector@uk.zurich.com. Internet: www.zurich.co.uk.

CIPFA (J)   7.151

ZURICH MUNICIPAL INSURANCE, The Zurich Centre, 3000 Parkway, Whiteley, Hampshire, PO15 7JZ. E-mail: info@zurichmunicipal.com. Internet: www.zurichmunicipal.com.

Caring for Life   7.115

INVESTMENT CONSULTANTS AND THEIR CHARITY CLIENTS

ALAN STEEL ASSET MANAGEMENT, Nobel House, Regent Centre, Linlithgow, Lothian, EH49 7HU. Tel: 01506 842365. Fax: 01506 845074. E-mail: info@alansteel.com. Internet: www.alansteel.com.

Doris Field Charitable Trust	7.207

ALLENBRIDGE INVESTMENT CONSULTANTS, 26th Floor, 125 Old Broad Street, London, EC2N 1AR. Tel: +44 (0)20 7079 1000. Internet: www.allenbridgeis.com.

Maurice & Vivienne Wohl Philanthropic Fdn	7.417
Maurice Wohl Charitable Foundation	7.417
Phillips & Rubens Charitable Trust	7.501
Richmond Church Charity Estates	7.537
Samuel Sebba Charitable Trust	7.586

AON HEWITT LTD, 8 Devonshire Square, London, EC2M 4PL. Tel: 020 7086 8000. Internet: www.aon.com.

Institution of Engineering and Technology	7.338

ARGENTIS FINANCIAL MANAGEMENT, London Road Office Park, London Road, Salisbury, SP1 3HP. Tel: 01722 343130. Fax: 01722 349103. Internet: www.argentisfm.co.uk.

Royal Natl Mission to Deep Sea Fishermen	7.567

BARCLAYS WEALTH, 1 Churchill Place, London, E14 5HP. Tel: 0203 134 2842. Internet: www.barclays.com/wealth.

Charity of Walter Stanley	7.130
Chartered Institute of Purchasing & Supply	7.134
Father Hudson's Society	7.249
Geoffrey Watling Charity, The	7.272
Milestones Trust	7.427
Myton Hospices, The	7.441
Royal United Hospital Bath NHS Trust Ch Fd	7.574
RSAS AgeCare	7.576
Severn Trent Water Charitable Trust Fund	7.598

BARING ASSETS MANAGEMENT, 155 Bishopsgate, London, EC2M 3XY. Tel: 020 7214 1807. Internet: www.barings.com/charities.

National Fund	7.446
Wessex Children's Hospice Trust	7.719

BARNETT WADDINGHAM LLP, Cheapside House, 138 Cheapside, London, EC2V 6BW. Tel: 020 7776 2200. Fax: 020 7776 3800. E-mail: info@barnett-waddingham.co.uk. Internet: www.barnett-waddingham.co.uk.

RAC Foundation for Motoring	7.522
SEMTA	7.589

BARRATT & COOKE, 5 Opie Street, Norwich, Norfolk, NR1 3DW. Tel: 01603 624236. Fax: 01603 665757. E-mail: info@barrattandcooke.co.uk. Internet: www.barrattandcooke.co.uk.

Norwich Diocesan Board of Finance, The (J)	7.471
Starling Family Charitable Trust, The (J)	7.656

BLACKROCK, Accounts Payable, 12 Throgmorton Avenue, London, EC2N 2DL. Tel: 020 7743 2175. Fax: 020 7743 1000. Internet: www.blackrock.co.uk.

Analytical Chemistry Trust Fund	7.31
NSPCC (J)	7.452

BROOKS MACDONALD ASSET MANAGEMENT, 10 Melville Crescent, Edinburgh, EH3 9GL. Tel: 0131 240 3900. Internet: www.brooksmacdonald.com.

Scottish Wildlife Trust	7.593

CAMBRIDGE ASSOCIATES LIMITED, 4th Floor, 80 Victoria Street, Cardinal Place, London, SW1E 5JL. Tel: 020 7592 2200. Fax: 020 7592 2201. Internet: www.cambridgeassociates.com.

29th May 1961 Charitable Trust	7.2
Burdett Trust for Nursing	7.104
Drapers Charities Pooling Scheme	7.211
Health Foundation, The	7.305
Henry Smith Charity	7.309
King's Fund, The	7.373
National Gallery Trust	7.447
Nuffield Foundation	7.474
St Monica Trust	7.651
Trusthouse Charitable Foundation	7.690

CAPITAL GENERATION PARTNERS LLP, Berkeley Square House, Berkeley Square, London, W1J 6BX. Tel: 020 7543 1500. Fax: 020 7543 1520. E-mail: info@capgenpartners.com. Internet: www.capgenpartners.com.

Said Foundation	7.581

CAZENOVE CAPITAL MANAGEMENT, Regency Court, Glategny Esplanade, St Peter Port, Guernsey, GY1 3UF. Tel: 01481 703700. Internet: www.cazenovecapital.com.

CAZENOVE CAPITAL MANAGEMENT LIMITED, 12 Moorgate, London, EC2R 6DA. Tel: 020 3479 0102. Fax: 020 3479 0054.

CCLA INVESTMENT MANAGEMENT LIMITED, Senator House, 85 Queen Victoria Street, London, EC4V 4ET. Tel: 0800 022 3505. Fax: 0844 561 5126. Internet: www.ccla.co.uk.

Derby Diocesan Board Finance Ltd	7.198
Lichfield Diocesan Board Of Education, The	7.387
Lichfield Diocesan Board Of Finance (J)	7.387
Norwich Diocesan Board of Finance, The (J)	7.471
St Edmundsbury & Ipswich Diocesan Bd of Fin	7.642
Truro Diocesan Board Finance Ltd	7.687
Diocese of Worcester	7.738
York Diocesan Board Finance Ltd (J)	7.747

CHARLES STANLEY & CO. LIMITED, 55 Calthorpe Road, Birmingham, West Midlands, B15 1TH. Tel: 0121 452 2900. Internet: www.charles-stanley.co.uk.

Shakespeare Birthplace Trust	7.599

CHARLES STANLEY & CO. LIMITED, Mey House, Bridport Road, Poundbury, Dorchester, Dorset, DT1 3QY. Internet: www.charles-stanley.co.uk.

Encompass (Dorset)	7.233

CROWE CLARK WHITEHILL FINANCIAL PLANNING LTD, Carrick House, Lyppiatt Road, Cheltenham, Gloucestershire, GL50 2QJ.

Quality Assurance Agency for HE	7.518

DEAN WETTON ADVISORY LTD, 100 Pall Mall, London, SW1Y 5NQ. Tel: 020 3422 5000.

Hammersmith United Charities	7.297

EFG HARRIS ALLDAY, 33 Great Charles Street, Birmingham, West Midlands, B3 3JN. Tel: 0121 233 1222. Fax: 0121 236 2587. E-mail: simon.raggett@efgha.com/ronald.treverton-jones@efgha.com. Internet: www.efgha.com.

Lichfield Diocesan Board Of Finance (J)	7.387

ENHANCE INVESTMENTS LIMITED, 9 Hope Street, St Helier, Jersey, JE2 3NS.

British Kidney Patient Association	7.95

EPOCH WEALTH MANAGEMENT, The Tramshed, Beehive Yard, Bath, Bath & North East Somerset, BA1 5BB. Tel: 0845 3009 822. E-mail: enquiries@epochwm.co.uk. Internet: www.epochwm.co.uk.

Demelza House Children's Hospice	7.196
Family Action	7.247
Woodland Trust	7.737

ETHICAL SCREENING, Formal House, 60 St. George's Place, Cheltenham, Gloucestershire, GL50 3PN. Tel: 01242 539850. Internet: www.ethicalscreening.co.uk.

Compassion in World Farming	7.168

HENDERSON GLOBAL INVESTORS, 201 Bishopsgate, London, EC2M 3AF. Tel: 020 7818 1818. Fax: 020 7818 1819. Internet: www.henderson.com.

NSPCC (J)	7.452

HYMANS ROBERTSON, 20 Waterloo Street, Glasgow, G2 6DB. Tel: 0141 566 7777. Fax: 0141 566 7788. Internet: www.hymans.co.uk.

Shetland Charitable Trust	7.604

IIMIA FINANCIAL PLANNING, Heliting House, 35 Richmond Hill, Bournemouth, Dorset, BH2 6HT. Tel: 01202 446400.

Borough of Havant Sport & Leisure Trust	7.81

INVESTEC WEALTH & INVESTMENT, 2 Gresham Street, London, EC2V 7QN. Tel: 020 7597 1250.

Burton Constable Foundation	7.105
Marine Society & Sea Cadets	7.411
St Olave, St Thomas and St John United	7.653

JAGGER & ASSOCIATES, Ground Floor, 14 Exchange Quay, Salford Quays, Manchester, Greater Manchester, M5 3EQ. Tel: 0161 873 9350. Fax: 0161 877 4851. E-mail: enquiries@jaggerandassociates.co.uk. Internet: www.jaggerandassociates.co.uk.

Gannochy Trust	7.268

JLT BENEFIT SOLUTIONS, St Albans, Hertfordshire, AL1 3AB.

Royal Society of Chemistry	7.572

JM FINN & CO, 33 Park Place, Leeds, West Yorkshire, LS1 2RY. Tel: 0113 220 6240. Internet: www.jmfinn.com.

Linkage Community Trust	7.390

KANE GROUP, Westpoint House, 32/34 Albert Street, Fleet, Hampshire, GU51 3RW. Tel: 01252 816644. Fax: 01252 815568. E-mail: info@thekanegroup.co.uk. Internet: www.thekanegroup.co.uk.

Borrow Foundation, The 7.81

L J ATHENE INVESTMENT ADVISORS, 9 Clifford Street, London, W1S 2FT. Tel: 020 7195 1400.

Royal Corps Signals Benevolent Fund 7.559

LANE CLARK & PEACOCK LLP, 95 Wigmore Street, London, W1U 1DQ. Tel: 020 7439 2266. E-mail: enquiries@lcp.uk.com. Internet: www.lcp.uk.com.

Independent Age 7.331
Royal National Lifeboat Institution 7.567

M&G INVESTMENTS, Governors House, Laurence Pountney Hill, London, EC4R 0HH. Tel: 020 7548 3661 / 020 7548 3731. Internet: www.mandg.co.uk/charities.

NSPCC (J) 7.452

MAZARS FINANCIAL PLANNING LTD, Tower Bridge House, St Katharine's Way, London, E1W 1DD. Tel: 020 7063 4259. E-mail: wealthmanagement@mazars.co.uk. Internet: www.mazars.co.uk.

Hampton Fuel Allotment Charity 7.300
Institution of Civil Engineers 7.338

MERRILL LYNCH PORTFOLIO MANAGERS LTD, Bank of America Merrill Lynch Financial Centre, 2 King Edward Street, London, EC1A 1HQ.

Dollond Charitable Trust 7.203

NEWTON INVESTMENT MANAGEMENT LIMITED, 160 Queen Victoria Street, London, EC4V 4LA. Tel: 0800 917 6594. E-mail: charities@newton.co.uk. Internet: www.newton.co.uk/charities.

World Horse Welfare 7.740

PEEL HUNT LLP, 120 London Wall, London, EC2Y 5ET. Tel: 020 7418 8900. Internet: www.peelhunt.com.

Grocers' Charity 7.289

QUILTER CHEVIOT, One Kingsway, London, WC2B 6AN. Tel: 020 7150 4000. Internet: www.quiltercheviot.com.

Jewish Care 7.354

QUILTER CHEVIOT, 39 Bennetts Hill, Birmingham, West Midlands, B2 5SN. Tel: +44 (0)121 212 2120. Fax: +44 (0)121 212 3130. Internet: www.quiltercheviot.com.

Sir Thomas White's Charity 7.612

RATHBONE INVESTMENT MANAGEMENT LTD, 1 Curzon Street, London, W1J 3ER.

Pilgrim Homes 7.502

Pilgrims' Friend Society 7.503
Rayne Trust 7.527

RATHBONE INVESTMENT MANAGEMENT LTD, The Stables, Levens Hall, Kendal, Cumbria, LA8 0PB. Tel: 015395 61457. Internet: www.rathbones.com.

Brothers of Charity Services (Scotland) 7.101

RATHBONE INVESTMENT MANAGEMENT LTD, Earl Grey House, 75-85 Grey Street, Newcastle upon Tyne, Tyne and Wear, NE1 6EF. Tel: 0191 255 1440. E-mail: james.garbutt@rathbones.com. Internet: www.rathbones.com/charities.

NCFE 7.455

REDBOURNE WEALTH MANAGEMENT LTD, Belmont House, Shrewsbury Business Park, Shrewsbury, Shropshire, SY2 6LG. Tel: 01743 273273. Internet: www.redbournewm.com.

Hope House Children's Hospices 7.317

ROWAN DARTINGTON & CO, 23 North Street, Chichester, West Sussex, PO19 1LB. Tel: 01243 771886. Fax: 01243 771986. Internet: www.rowan-dartington.co.uk.

F Glenister Woodger Trust, The 7.245

ROYAL LONDON CASH MANAGEMENT, 55 Gracechurch Street, London, EC3V 0UF. Tel: 020 7506 6625. Fax: 020 7506 6796. Internet: www.rlcm.co.uk.

Brooke Hospital for Animals 7.101

RUFFER LLP, 80 Victoria Street, London, SW1E 5JL. Tel: 0207 963 8100. Fax: 0207 963 8175. Internet: www.ruffer.co.uk.

Hampstead Wells & Campden Trust 7.299

SARABAITE LIMITED, North House, 27 Great Peter Street, London, SW1P 3LN.

Backstage Trust 7.53
Gatsby Charitable Foundation 7.270

SARASIN & PARTNERS LLP, Juxon House, 100 St Paul's Churchyard, London, EC4M 8BU. Tel: 020 7038 7000. Fax: 020 7038 6864. E-mail: john.handford@sarasin.co.uk. Internet: www.sarasinandpartners.com.

SEI, Time & Life Building, 4th Floor, 1 Bruton Street, London, W1J 6TL.

Kennedy Trust for Rheumatology Research 7.368

SMITH & WILLIAMSON INVESTMENT MANAGEMENT LTD, 25 Moorgate, London, EC2R 6AY. Tel: 020 7131 4200. Fax: 020 7131 4001. Internet: www.sandwcharities.com.

Andrew Anderson Trust 7.31

SMITH & WILLIAMSON INVESTMENT MANAGEMENT LTD, 9 Colmore Row, Birmingham, West Midlands, B3 2BJ. Tel: 0121 710 5200. Fax: 0121 710 5201. Internet: www.smith.williamson.co.uk.

York Diocesan Board Finance Ltd (J) 7.747

STAMFORD ASSOCIATES LIMITED, 19 - 21 Old Bond Street, London, W1S 4PX. Tel: 020 7629 5225. Fax: 020 7629 7355. E-mail: info@stamfordassociates.com. Internet: www.stamfordassociates.com.

Blenheim Foundation, The 7.75

STANDARD LIFE WEALTH, No 1 Leeds, 26 Whitehall Road, Leeds, West Yorkshire, LS12 1BE. Internet: www.standardlifewealth.com.

Community Foundation for Leeds 7.163
JGW Patterson Foundation, The 7.355

TOWERS WATSON, 21 Tothill Street, Westminster, London, SW1H 9LL. Tel: 020 7222 8033. Fax: 020 7222 9182.

Intl Foundation for Aids to Navigation 7.342

UBS WEALTH MANAGEMENT, 1 Finsbury Avenue, London, EC2M 2AN. Tel: 020 7567 5757. Fax: 020 7567 5656. Internet: www.ubs.com/uk.

NSPCC (J) 7.452

WALKER CRIPS STOCKBROKERS LIMITED, Finsbury Tower, 103-105 Bunhill Row, London, EC1Y 8LZ. Tel: 020 3100 8000. Internet: www.wcgplc.co.uk.

Will Trust of Gerald Segelman Deceased, The 7.729

WHITING & PARTNERS WEALTH MANAGEMENT LTD, 12/13 The Crescent, Wisbech, Cambridgeshire, PE13 1EH. Tel: 01945 581937. Fax: 01945 660333. Internet: www.whitingandpartnersfs.co.uk.

Starling Family Charitable Trust, The (J) 7.656

WILTON ASSOCIATES, 10 Liberia Road, London, N5 1JR. Tel: 0207 7049 497. E-mail: angela.docherty@wiltonassociates.co.uk . Internet: www.wiltonassociates.co.uk.

Leverhulme Trust 7.386

WINDMILL HILL ASSET MANAGEMENT LIMITED, Windmill Hill, Silk Street, Waddesdon, Aylesbury, Buckinghamshire, HP18 0JZ.

Future of Russia Foundation 7.267

XAFINITY, 10 South Parade, Leeds, West Yorkshire, LS1 5AL. Tel: 0113 244 0200. Internet: www.xafinity.com.

Inst of Marine Engineering, Science & Tech 7.335

INVESTMENT MANAGERS AND THEIR CHARITY CLIENTS

ABERDEEN ASSET MANAGEMENT, Bow Bells House, 1 Bread Street, London, EC4M 9HH. Tel: 020 7463 6158. E-mail: roger.curtis@aberdeen-asset.com. Internet: www.aberdeen-asset.com/charities.

Bernard Sunley Charitable Foundation (J)	7.66
Sisters of Bon Secours of Paris (J)	7.172
Coram (J)	7.179
Edmund Rice Bicentennial Trust Ltd (J)	7.226
Nuffield Foundation (J)	7.474
Royal Air Force Benevolent Fund (J)	7.550
Royal Mencap Society (J)	7.566
SEMTA	7.589
University of Newcastle DevelopmentTrust (J)	7.701

ABERDEEN ASSET MANAGERS, 10 Queen's Terrace, Aberdeen, Grampian, AB10 1YG. Tel: 020 7463 6158. E-mail: roger.curtis@aberdeen-asset.com. Internet: www.aberdeen-asset.com/charities. Charity specialists: David Bailey. Victor Beamish. Bill Greenhalgh.

Health Foundation, The (J)	7.305
Henry Moore Foundation (J)	7.309
Northern Rock Foundation	7.471
Royal Blind	7.553
Scottish War Blinded	7.593

ACADIAN ASSET MANAGEMENT, 110 Cannon Street, 4th Floor, London, EC4N 6EU. Tel: 020 7398 7280. Fax: 020 7398 /281. E-mail: info@acadian-asset.com. Internet: www.acadian-asset.com.

Nuffield Foundation (J)	7.474

ACPI, Pegasus House, 37-43 Sackville Street, London, W1S 3EH.

Stoller Charitable Trust	7.659

ADAM & COMPANY INVESTMENT MANAGEMENT LIMITED, 25 St Andrew Square, Edinburgh, EH2 1AF. Tel: 0131 225 8484. Fax: 0131 220 2357. E-mail: AIM@adambank.com. Internet: www.adambank.com.

Children's Hospice Association Scotland (J)	7.141
Equity Charitable Trust (J)	7.238
Henshaws Society for Blind People (J)	7.309
Hopetoun House Preservation Trust	7.317
Royal Botanic Garden Edinburgh	7.553
Royal College of Physicians of Edinburgh	7.557

ADAM & COMPANY INVESTMENT MANAGEMENT LIMITED, 22 King Street, London, SW1Y 6QY. Tel: 020 7839 4615. Fax: 020 7839 5994. Internet: www.adambank.com.

Battersea Dogs & Cats Home	7.60

ALAN BOSWELL & COMPANY LIMITED, Harbour House, All Saints Green, Norwich, Norfolk, NR1 3GA.

Norfolk Community Foundation (J)	7.464

ALBERT E SHARP , Seven Elm Court, Arden Street, Stratford-upon-Avon, Warwickshire, CV37 6PA. Tel: 01789 404000. Fax: 01789 404001.

Westhill Endowment (J)	7.722

ALLIANCE TRUST, 107 George Street, Edinburgh, EH2 3ES.

Joseph Rowntree Charitable Trust (J)	7.363

ALLIANCE TRUST INVESTMENTS, 8 West Marketgair, Dundee, DD1 1QN. Tel: 01382 321000.

Tudor Trust	7.690

ALTA ADVISERS LTD, 8 Lancelot Place, London, SW7 1DR. Tel: 020 7590 5010.

Sigrid Rausing Trust	7.608

ANDREW GRANGER & CO LLP, 2 High Street, Loughborough, Leicestershire, LE11 2PY.

Leicester Diocesan Board Finance (J)	7.383

ANTIN INFRASTRUCTURE PARTNERS, 15 Sackville Street, London, W1S 3DJ. Tel: 020 7494 6950. Internet: www.antin-ip.com.

Church of England Pensions Board (J)	7.148

AON HEWITT LTD, Payments Processing, C/O Capital Capture, Post Room, 8 Devonshire Square, London, EC2M 4PL. Tel: 020 7086 8000. Internet: www.aon.com.

Royal National Institute of Blind People	7.566

AQR CAPITAL MANAGEMENT EUROPE LLP, Charles House, 5-11 Regent Street, London, SW1Y 4LR. Tel: 020 3130 7800. Fax: 020 3110 7810.

Foundation for Social Entrepreneurs (J)	7.259
Millennium Awards Trust, The (J)	7.427

ARROWSTREET CAPITAL LP, 1 Berkeley Street, London, W1J 8DJ. Tel: 020 7016 8834. Internet: www.arrowstreetcapital.com.

Church of England Pensions Board (J)	7.148

ARTEMIS ASSET MANAGEMENT LTD, 42 Melville Street, Edinburgh, EH3 7HA. Tel: 0131 225 7300. Internet: www.artemisonline.co.uk.

ARTEMIS FUND MANAGERS LIMITED, Cassini House, 57 St James's Street, London, SW1A 1LD. Internet: www.artemisonline.co.uk.

City Bridge Trust, The (J)	7.153
Dulverton Trust (J)	7.214
Henry Moore Foundation (J)	7.309
University of Newcastle DevelopmentTrust (J)	7.701

ASHBURN WEALTH MANAGEMENT LIMITED, Ashburn House,, 84 Grange Road, Darlington, County Durham, DL1 5NP.

Stewardship Services (UKET) Ltd (J)	7.658

ASHCOURT ROWAN ASSET MANAGEMENT LIMITED, 60 Queen Victoria Street, London, EC4N 4TR. Tel: 020 7871 7250. E-mail: michaeljohnstone@ashcourtrowan.com. Internet: www.ashcourtrowan.com. Charity specialists: M Johnstone. C Simkins.

Maurice Hilda Laing Charitable Trust	7.416
Rufford Foundation, The	7.577

ASSET RISK CONSULTANTS LTD, 46 Chancery Lane, London, WC2A 1JE. Tel: 0207 442 5955. E-mail: info@assetrisk.com. Internet: www.assetrisk.com.

Rank Foundation Limited	7.525

AURUM FUNDS LIMITED, Ixworth House, 37 Ixworth Place, London, SW3 3QH. Tel: 020 7589 1130. Fax: 020 7581 1780. Internet: www.aurum.com.

Maurice & Vivienne Wohl Philanthropic Fdn (J)	7.417
Samuel Sebba Charitable Trust (J)	7.586

AVIVA INVESTORS, No.1 Poultry, London, EC2R 8EJ. Tel: 020 7809 6000. Internet: www.avivainvestors.co.uk.

Trust for London (J)	7.688

AXA FRAMLINGTON, 7 Newgate Street, London, EC1A 7NX. Tel: 020 7003 1000. Internet: www.axaframlington.com. Charity specialists: C A Walton.

Society of Jesus (J)	7.622

BABSON CAPITAL, 61 Aldwych, London, WC2B 4AE. Tel: 020 3206 4500. Fax: 020 3206 4591.

Dulverton Trust (J)	7.214

BAILLIE GIFFORD & CO, Calton Square, 1 Greenside Row, Edinburgh, EH1 3AN. Tel: 0131 275 2000. Fax: 0131 275 3975. E-mail: anthony.dickson@bailliegifford.com. Internet: www.bailliegifford.com.

Baillie Gifford is a privately owned investment management company which manages £123 billion of investments for UK and international clients. This includes equities, bonds and diversifying assets managed on either a segregated or a pooled basis for charities with varied requirements.

Contact

Anthony Dickson
0131 275 2725
anthony.dickson@bailliegifford.com

or Piers Lowson
0131 275 2738
piers.lowson@bailliegifford.com

Charity specialists: A Dickson.

Arthritis Research UK (J)	7.40
Baring Foundation (J)	7.57
Eveson Charitable Trust (J)	7.243
Independent Age (J)	7.331
Jordan Charitable Foundation (J)	7.362
Walcot Educational Foundation (J)	7.711

BANK OF SCOTLAND, New Uberior House, 11 Earl Grey Street, Edinburgh, EH3 9BN.

BSS   7.102

BARCLAYS WEALTH AND INVESTMENT MANAGEMENT, 1 Churchill Place, London, E14 5HP. Tel: 020 3134 2842. E-mail: sasha.wiggins@barclays.com. Internet: www.barclays.com/wealth. Charity specialists: Sasha Wiggins.

Africa Educational Trust	7.15
Alexian Brothers of Province of Sacred Heart	7.24
Amgueddfa Cymru	7.30
Cardiff RC Archdiocesan Trust (J)	7.37
Arundel and Brighton Diocesan Trust	7.42
Birmingham Diocesan Trust	7.71
Bransby Horses (J)	7.85
Chartered Management Institute	7.135
Chippenham Borough Lands Charity	7.143
Community Foundation for Manchester	7.162
Community of St Mary the Virgin (J)	7.166
CongregationDominicanSistersofMaltaTrst	7.173
Congregation of the Passion Jesus Christ	7.174
Daughters Mary Joseph English Province	7.193
Deflog V Q Trust Limited, The	7.196
Doris Field Charitable Trust (J)	7.207
Eighty Eight Foundation, The	7.228
George Muller Charitable Trust [The] (J)	7.273
Hannah Susan Samuel Victor Greig Fund	7.300
Henshaws Society for Blind People (J)	7.309
Higher Education Careers Services Unit	7.311
Hospice St Francis Berkhamsted Limited	7.319
Imperial College Healthcare Charity	7.329
Institute of the Blessed Virgin Mary (J)	7.337
Jewish Care (J)	7.354
John Roan Foundation	7.360
JTL (J)	7.364
L H A London Limited	7.376
Legacy Trust UK	7.383
Make-A-Wish Foundation (UK)	7.407
Monmouth Diocesan Board of Finance	7.431
Monmouth Diocesan Trust	7.432
Newlife Foundation for Disabled Children	7.461
Norfolk Community Foundation (J)	7.464
Ormiston Trust	7.484
Prince and Princess of Wales Hospice (J)	7.513
Professional Footballers Assoc Educ Fund (J)	7.516
Professional Footballers Benevolent Fund (J)	7.516
Quality Assurance Agency for HE (J)	7.518
R S Macdonald Charitable Trust (J)	7.522
Roman Catholic Diocese of East Anglia	7.543
Roman Catholic Diocese of Southwark	7.544
Missionary Franciscan Sisters (J)	7.544
Royal College of Psychiatrists	7.558
Duke & Duchess of Cambridge & Prince Harry	7.560
Royal Shakespeare Company	7.571
Royal Welsh Agricultural Society Limited	7.575
Scottish Association for Mental Health	7.591
Shetland Amenity Trust	7.604
Sir Halley Stewart Trust	7.610
Sisters of St Joseph Province (J)	7.615
Sisters Holy Family Bordeaux (J)	7.616
Sisters of the Sacred Heart of Mary UK	7.616
St Giles Hospice (J)	7.643
Thomson Reuters Foundation	7.678
Little Company of Mary	7.688
Ty Hafan (J)	7.692
UK Youth	7.693
Whale Dolphin Conservation Society	7.724
Wheler Foundation, The	7.725
Wilberforce Trust (J)	7.728
Wiltshire Wildlife Trust	7.731

BARING ASSET MANAGEMENT LIMITED, 155 Bishopsgate, London, EC2M 3XY. Tel: 020 7214 1763. E-mail: paul.fleming@barings.com. Internet: www.barings.com/charities. Charity specialists: Malcolm Herring (Director, Charities). Alison Huang (Fund Manager, Charities). Paul Fleming (UK Institutional Relationship Manager).

Bristol Charities (J)	7.89
Civil Service Benevolent Fund, The	7.154
College of Estate Management	7.160
D D McPhail Charitable Settlement	7.191
Duke of Edinburgh's Award Intl Foundation (J)	7.214
Duke of Edinburgh's Award (J)	7.214
French Huguenot Church Ldn Charitable Trust	7.265

GroceryAid (J)	7.289
Groundwork UK (J)	7.290
John Ellerman Foundation (J)	7.358
John Swire 1989 Charitable Trust	7.361
Maurice & Vivienne Wohl Philanthropic Fdn (J)	7.417
Police Dependants' Trust Limited, The	7.507
Regent's University London	7.530
Samuel Sebba Charitable Trust (J)	7.586
Shipwrecked Mariners' Society	7.605
Sports Council Trust Company	7.634
Watts Gallery	7.716

BARRATT & COOKE, 5/6 Opie Street, Norwich, Norfolk, NR1 3DW. Tel: 01603 624236. Fax: 01603 665757. E-mail: info@barrattandcooke.co.uk. Internet: www.barrattandcooke.co.uk. Charity specialists: C W L Barratt.

Community All Hallows Ditchingham Norfolk	7.165
Jones 1986 Charitable Trust (J)	7.362
Morley Agricultural Foundation, The	7.434
Norfolk Community Foundation (J)	7.464
Paul Bassham Charitable Trust	7.493

BASEL ASSET MANAGEMENT, One Rockefeller Plaza, Suite 1505, New York, NY 10020.

Clore Duffield Foundation   7.157

BESTINVEST, 6 Chesterfield Gardens, Mayfair, London, W1J 5BQ. Tel: 020 7189 9999. Internet: www.bestinvest.co.uk.

St Mary Magdalene & Holy Jesus Trust (J)   7.649

BLACKROCK®

BLACKROCK, 12 Throgmorton Avenue, London, EC2N 2DL. Tel: 020 7743 3000. Internet: www.blackrock.co.uk/charities.

BlackRock has been investing on behalf of charities and endowments for over thirty years and today manages approximately £3 billion for over 3,000 UK charities*. Our dedicated team aims to give every charity the support they need to flourish.

We offer six Common Investment Funds – Charinco, Charishare, Charishare Restricted, ChariTrak, Charifaith and the Armed Forces Common Investment Fund – as well as a discretionary service for charities with sizeable accounts. We also offer a range of funds with ethical considerations. To discuss your needs further, please call 0207 743 2049 to speak to a relationship manager.

*As at 30/09/2015

Charity specialists: Candida de Silva. Mike Marsham. Luke Twyman.

BNP PARIBAS FORTIS, 5 Aldermanbury Square, London, EC2V 7HR. Internet: www.privatebanking.fortis.com.

Augustinians of the Assumption (J)   7.48

BNY MELLON, The Bank of New York, Mellon Centre, 160 Queen Victoria Street, London, EC4V 4LA. Tel: 020 7163 4300. Internet: www.bnymellon.com.

Buckfast Abbey Trust (J)	7.103
Downside Abbey General Trust	7.210
R S Macdonald Charitable Trust (J)	7.522

BNY MELLON, PO Box 12041, Brentwood, Essex, CM14 9LS.

Amateurs Trust, The (J)	7.29
Brighton & Sussex Univ Hospitals NHS Trust	7.88
Jean Sainsbury Animal Welfare Trust (J)	7.352

BNY MELLON, 1 Piccadilly Gardens, Manchester, Greater Manchester, M1 1RN. Tel: 0161 725 3000. Internet: www.bnymellon.com.

Foyle Foundation (J)   7.261

BORDIER & CIE (UK) PLC, 23 King Street, St James's, London, SW1Y 6QY. Tel: 020 7667 6600. Internet: www.bordieruk.com.

Glass House Trust	7.276
Merchant Navy Welfare Board	7.422

BREWIN DOLPHIN, 12 Smithfield Street, London, EC1A 9BD. Tel: 0203 201 3483/ 0203 201 3924. Fax: 0845 213 1001 (UK only) / 0203 201 3001. Internet: www.brewin.co.uk. Charity specialists: Ruth Murphy (Head of Charities Business Development).

1989 Willan Charitable Trust	7.2
Cardiff RC Archdiocesan Trust (J)	7.37
Bishop Radford Trust, The (J)	7.73
Bolton Hospice (J)	7.78
Bond's Hospital Estate Charity	7.79
British Academy of Film & Television Arts (J)	7.91
Campden Charities Trustee (J)	7.110
Chapter of Order of the Holy Paraclete	7.128
Charity Roman Union Order St Ursula (J)	7.130
Chartered Institute Building	7.132
Chelmsford Diocesan Board Finance (J)	7.136
Chest Heart & Stroke Scotland	7.137
Christian Vision	7.146
Community Foundation for Leeds (J)	7.163
Comm Fdn (Tyne&Wear&Northumberland) (J)	7.164
Community of St John Baptist General	7.165
Community of the Resurrection	7.167
Congregation of La Retraite Trustees (J)	7.171
Congregation of La Sainte Union	7.171
Congregation of the Daughters of Wisdom	7.173
Congregation of the Sisters of St Anne (J)	7.175
Cope Children's Trust	7.179
Earl Mountbatten Hospice	7.219
Erskine	7.239
Fauna & Flora International	7.249
Florence Nightingale Aid Sickness Trust	7.256
Foundation Scotland (J)	7.260
Free Church of Scotland	7.264
Gannochy Trust	7.268
GarfieldWestonTrustforWestminsterAbbey	7.269
General Optical Council	7.271
George Muller Charitable Trust [The] (J)	7.273
Gloucester Charities Trust (J)	7.277
Gofal Housing Trust	7.280
Greggs Foundation	7.288
H B Allen Charitable Trust	7.294
Hamps & Isle of Wight Air Ambulance (J)	7.298
Jane Hodge Foundation	7.351
Kirby Laing Foundation (J)	7.374
Leicester Diocesan Board Finance (J)	7.383
Les Filles de la Croix	7.386
Manchester & District Home for Lost Dogs	7.408
Marine Biological Association United Kingdom	7.411
Martin House	7.413
Mount Saint Bernard Abbey	7.436
Mrs E M Bates Trust	7.437
Musicians Benevolent Fund (J)	7.440
National Institute of Adult Education	7.448
National Library of Scotland (J)	7.448
National Youth Advocacy Service	7.454
Nuffield Oxford Hospitals Fund	7.474
Ofenheim Charitable Trust	7.478
Order St John Priory for Wales	7.483
Percy Bilton Charity	7.497
Plymouth Marine Laboratory	7.506
PRS For Music Members Benevolent Fund (J)	7.517
Rowcroft House Foundation Limited	7.548
Rowett Research Institute	7.548
RSABI	7.576
SSPCA	7.592
Scottish Veterans Garden City Association Inc	7.593
Sherburn House Charity	7.604
Shooting Star CHASE	7.605

Sir Edward Lewis Foundation	7.610
Sir John Priestman Charity Trust	7.611
Sisters of the Holy Family	7.616
Spiritualists National Union	7.632
St Ann's Hospice	7.637
St Clement Danes Holborn Estate Charity (J)	7.641
St John's Hospital Lichfield	7.645
St Joseph's Society for Foreign Missions (J)	7.646
St Luke's Hospice Plymouth	7.648
Steinberg Family Charitable Trust, The (J)	7.657
Stockport Cerebral Palsy Society	7.659
Sunfield Children's Homes Limited	7.664
Tenovus	7.673
Thistle Foundation	7.677
Thompson Family Charitable Trust (J)	7.678
Together Trust	7.681
Ulverscroft Foundation	7.694
United Reformed Church (Yorkshire) Trust	7.697
VSA (J)	7.709
Weavers Company Benevolent Fund	7.717
Wilberforce Trust (J)	7.728
Yorkshire Air Ambulance (J)	7.749

BRIDGES COMMUNITIES VENTURES LTD, 1 Craven Hill, London, W2 3EN. Tel: 020 7262 5566. Fax: 020 7262 6389. E-mail: info@bridgesventures.com. Internet: www.bridgesventures.com.

Comic Relief (J)	7.162

BRIDGEWATER ASSOCIATES LP LTD, Dashwood House, 69 Old Broad Street, London, EC2M 1QS. Internet: www.bwater.com.

Church of England Pensions Board (J)	7.148

BROADSTONE, 55 Baker Street, London, W1U 7EU. Tel: 020 7893 3456. Fax: 020 7487 3686. Internet: www.broadstoneltd.co.uk.

Worth Abbey	7.742

BROWN SHIPLEY, Founders Court, Lothbury, London, EC2R 7HE. Tel: 020 7606 9833. Internet: www.brownshipley.com.

Institute of Brewing & Distilling (J)	7.334

BROWN SHIPLEY, 2 Multrees Walk, Edinburgh, EH1 3DQ. Tel: 0131 524 1270. Fax: 0131 557 1128. E-mail: paul.embleton@brownshipley.co.uk. Internet: www.brownshipley.com. Charity specialists: P Embleton.

National Library of Scotland (J)	7.448

BROWN SHIPLEY, 3 Hardman Street, Manchester, Greater Manchester, M3 3HF. Tel: 0161 214 6500. Fax: 0161 214 6950. Internet: www.brownshipley.com.

Dowager Countess Eleanor Peel Trust	7.210
Training 2000	7.685

C HOARE & CO, 37 Fleet Street, London, EC4P 4DQ. Tel: 020 7353 4522. Fax: 020 7353 4521. E-mail: Charities.Team@hoaresbank.co.uk. Internet: www.hoaresbank.co.uk.

CAMBRIDGE ASSOCIATES LIMITED, 4th Floor, 80 Victoria Street, Cardinal Place, London, SW1E 5JL. Tel: 020 7592 2200. Fax: 020 7592 2201. Internet: www.cambridgeassociates.com. Charity specialists: Evelyn Curtin (Senior Business Development Associate).

CANACCORD GENUITY WEALTH MANAGEMENT, 8th Floor, 41 Lothbury, London, EC2R 7AE. Tel: 020 7665 4500. E-mail: charities@collinsstewart.com. Internet: www.canaccordgenuity.com.

C Alma Baker Trust	7.106
Constance Travis Charitable Trust	7.178
Dollond Charitable Trust (J)	7.203
JTL (J)	7.364
LTA Trust, The (J)	7.404
R.Watts&Rochester CityAlmshouseCharities	7.536
Royal College of Pathologists	7.557
Royal Corps Signals Benevolent Fund	7.559

St Giles Hospice (J)	7.643
Thompson Family Charitable Trust (J)	7.678
Whitley Animal Protection Trust	7.726

CANTAB ASSET MANAGEMENT, 35 Hills Road, Cambridge, Cambridgeshire, CB2 1NT. Tel: 01223 52 2000. Internet: www.cantabam.com.

Health Foundation, The (J)	7.305

CAPITA FINANCIAL MANAGERS LTD, 2 The Boulevard, City West One Office Park, Gelderd Road, Leeds, West Yorkshire, LS12 6NT.

Holburne Museum (J)	7.314
ICAN	7.327

CAPITAL INTERNATIONAL LIMITED, 40 Grosvenor Place, London, SW1X 7GG. Tel: 020 7864 5000. Fax: 020 7864 5001.

Leverhulme Trust (J)	7.386

CARDIFF COUPLAND ASSET MANAGEMENT LLP, 31-32 St. James's Street, London, SW1A 1HD. Tel: +44 207 321 3470 Fax: +44 207 321 3471. Fax: +44 207 321 3471. E-mail: enquiries@ccam-asia.com. Internet: www.couplandcardiff.com.

Dulverton Trust (J)	7.214

CASTLEFIELD, 9th Floor, 111 Piccadilly, Manchester, Greater Manchester, M1 2HY. Tel: 0161 233 4890. Fax: 0161 233 4899. E-mail: queries@castlefield.com. Internet: www.castlefield.com.

Cheshire Residential Homes (J)	7.137
Chetham's Hospital School and Library	7.138
Christie Charitable Fund, The	7.146
Hulme Trust Estates (Educational) Fndn	7.324
Seashell Trust	7.595
Society of African Missions (J)	7.621
St Luke's (Cheshire) Hospice	7.647

CAVE & SONS, Lockgates House, Rushmills, Northampton, Northamptonshire, NN4 7YB. Tel: 01604 621 421. Fax: 01604 234 335. E-mail: info@caves.co.uk. Internet: www.caves.co.uk.

Market Harborough & the Bowdens Charity (J)	7.412

CAVENDISH ASSET MANAGEMENT LIMITED, Chelsea House, West Gate, London, W5 1DR. Tel: 020 8810 8041. E-mail: info@cavendishmanagers.com. Internet: www.cavendishmanagers.co.uk/asset/ .

David & Ruth Lewis Family Charitable Trust	7.194

CAZENOVE CAPITAL MANAGEMENT LIMITED, Edinburgh Quay, 133 Fountainbridge, Edinburgh, EH3 9QG. Tel: 0131 270 3000. Fax: 0131 270 3001.

CBRE GLOBAL INVESTORS, Third Floor, One New Change, London, EC4M 9AF. Tel: 020 7809 9000. Fax: 020 7809 9002. Internet: www.cbreglobalinvestors.com.

Church of England Pensions Board (J)	7.148

CCLA INVESTMENT MANAGEMENT LIMITED, Senator House, 85 Queen Victoria Street, London, EC4V 4ET. Tel: 0800 022 3505. Fax: 0844 561 5126. E-mail: clientservices@ccla.co.uk. Internet: www.ccla.co.uk.

Action Mental Health	7.11
Age UK Hertfordshire	7.17
Aldeburgh Music	7.23
Archbishops' Council (J)	7.37
Army Dependants' Trust, The (J)	7.39
Bath Wells Diocesan Board Finance (J)	7.60
IMechE Benevolent Fund (J)	7.65
Big Local Trust	7.70
Birmingham Children's Hospital Charities (J)	7.71
Birmingham Dogs Home (J)	7.72
Blackburn Diocesan Board Finance Limited	7.74
Bradford Diocesan Board of Finance, The (J)	7.83
Bristol Diocesan Board Finance Ltd	7.89
British Home & Hospital for Incurables	7.94
Brunts Charity (J)	7.102
Burdett Trust for Nursing (J)	7.104
Butchers & Drovers Charitable Inst (J)	7.105
Carlisle Diocesan Board of Finance	7.116
Carmelite Charitable Trust (J)	7.116
Catch22 (J)	7.118
Catholic Apostolic Church	7.118
Chartered Inst of Building Services Engineers	7.134
Chelmsford Diocesan Board Finance (J)	7.136
Chester Diocesan Board Finance	7.138
Chichester Diocesan Fd Bd Finance (J)	7.138
Christian Aid (J)	7.145
Church of England Pensions Board (J)	7.148
Church Urban Fund	7.150
City and Guilds of London Institute	7.152
Community Foundation for Calderdale (J)	7.162
Community Foundation for Leeds (J)	7.163
Comm. Foundation for Wiltshire & Swindon (J)	7.163

Community Foundation Wales (J)	7.163
Comm Fdn (Tyne&Wear&Northumberland) (J)	7.164
Congregation of the Jesus Charitable Trust (J)	7.171
County Durham Community Foundation	7.183
Coventry Diocesan Board of Finance (J)	7.184
Cripplegate Foundation (J)	7.186
Culham St Gabriel's Trust	7.188
Cumbrian Community Foundation (J)	7.189
Dulverton Trust (J)	7.214
Durham Diocesan Board of Finance, The	7.216
Dyslexia Action	7.217
East End Community Foundation (J)	7.221
Edward James Foundation Limited (J)	7.228
Ely Diocesan Board of Finance, The (J)	7.231
Essex Community Foundation (J)	7.240
EveryChild	7.243
Felix Thornley Cobold Agricultural Trust	7.251
Foundation of Lady Katherine Leveson, The (J)	7.260
Friends of the Elderly	7.265
Gerald Palmer Eling Trust Company	7.273
Gloucester Diocesan Board Finance	7.278
GroceryAid (J)	7.289
Guildford Diocesan Board of Finance	7.292
Hampshire & Isle of Wight Community Fdn (J)	7.298
Hinrichsen Foundation	7.313
Hospital of St Cross Foundation	7.321
Huntingdon Freemen's Trust (J)	7.325
Hyde Park Place Estate Charity (J)	7.326
Independent Age (J)	7.331
Institution of Mechanical Engineers	7.338
Inst. of Occupational Safety & Health	7.339
Jesus Hospital Charity in Chipping Barnet (J)	7.353
John Marshall's Charity	7.359
John Martin's Charity	7.360
Joseph Rowntree Charitable Trust (J)	7.363
King Henry VIII Endowed Trust Warwick (J)	7.372
Land Restoration Trust	7.378
LankellyChase Foundation, The (J)	7.379
Leicester Diocesan Board of Finance (J)	7.383
LGS General Charitable Trust	7.387
LIONHEART	7.391
Liverpool Diocesan Board of Finance, The	7.392
Living Streets (The Pedestrians' Association)	7.394
Local Trust	7.396
London Community Foundation	7.397
London Diocesan Board for Schools	7.398
London Diocesan Fund	7.398
Magdalen Lasher Charity	7.406
Manchester Diocesan Board of Finance	7.408
Market Harborough & the Bowdens Charity (J)	7.412
Mental Health Foundation	7.421
Metropolitan City Police Orphans Fund	7.424
Mothers' Union	7.435
National Children's Bureau	7.444
National Fed'n of Women's Institutes	7.445
National Star Foundation	7.453
Newcastle Diocesan Board Finance	7.459
Newcastle upon Tyne Hospitals NHS Charity	7.460
Norfolk Community Foundation (J)	7.464
Norman Family Charitable Trust (J)	7.464
Overseas Bishoprics Fund	7.486
Peterborough Diocesan Board Finance	7.500
Portsmouth Diocesan Board Of Finance	7.509
Prospect Foundation	7.516
Quartet Community Foundation (J)	7.519
Queenscourt Hospice (J)	7.521
Ramblers Association	7.525
Ripon Diocesan Board of Finance	7.539
Royal Horticultural Society (J)	7.561
Royal Naval Benevolent Trust (J)	7.568
S L G Charitable Trust (J)	7.578
Salisbury City Almshouse and Welfare (J)	7.583
Salisbury Diocesan Board of Education	7.583
Salisbury Diocesan Board of Finance (J)	7.583
Samaritans (J)	7.585
Skills for Care	7.617
Society of Jesus (J)	7.622
S Lon Ch Fund&Sthwk Diocesan Bd Fin (J)	7.629
St Albans Diocesan Board Finance	7.635
St Giles Hospice (J)	7.643
St Giles Trust	7.644
St Joseph's Hospice, Hackney	7.646
St Luke's Parochial Trust (J)	7.648
St Mary Magdalene & Holy Jesus Trust (J)	7.649
St Michael's Hospice (North Hampshire)	7.651

Strode Pk Foundation for Disabled People	7.662
Suffolk Foundation, The (J)	7.663
Sussex Community Foundation	7.665
Thames Valley Air Ambulance	7.675
Tree of Hope	7.685
University College London Hospitals Charity	7.700
USPG (J)	7.702
Wakefield Diocesan Board Finance	7.710
YMCA Watford & District Branch	7.716
Weston Hospicecare (J)	7.723
Whitgift Foundation	7.726
William Palmer College Educational Trust	7.731
Winchester Diocesan Board of Finance	7.732
Wirral Autistic Society (J)	7.733
Woodbrooke Quaker Study Centre	7.737
World Energy Council (J)	7.740
World Federation - Muslim Communities	7.740
Young Foundation, The	7.750

CEDAR ROCK CAPITAL FUND PLC, 110 Wigmore Street, London, W1U 3RW. Tel: 020 7563 1100. Fax: 020 7563 1111.

Dunhill Medical Trust (J)	7.216

**CENTRAL FINANCE BOARD OF THE METHODIST CHURCH, 2nd Floor, 9 Bonhill Street, London, EC2A 4PE. Tel: 020 7496 3600. Fax: 020 7496 3631.
E-mail: admin@cfbmethodistchurch.org.uk.
Internet: www.cfbmethodistchurch.org.uk.**

Action for Children	7.10
Methodist Church In Great Britain, The	7.423
Methodist Homes	7.424
Southwell Diocesan Board Finance (J)	7.631

**CERNO CAPITAL PARTNERS, 34 Sackville Street, London, W1S 3ED. Tel: 020 7036 4117. Fax: 020 7036 4122.
E-mail: info@cernocapital.com.
Internet: www.cernocapital.com.**

John Booth Charitable Foundation, The	7.357

CG ASSET MANAGEMENT, 25 Moorgate, London, EC2R 5AY.

Burdett Trust for Nursing (J)	7.104
Dulverton Trust (J)	7.214

**CHARITIES AID FOUNDATION, 25 Kings Hill Avenue, Kings Hill, West Malling, Kent, ME19 4TA. Tel: 03000 123 444. Fax: 03000 123 007. Internet: www.cafonline.org/charities.
Charity specialists:** Mark Hodkinson. N Poynton. Linda Sheridan.

**CHARITIES PROPERTY FUND, c/o Cordea Savills, 33 Margaret Street, London, W1G 0JD. Tel: 020 3107 5439. Fax: 0845 409 1281.
E-mail: cpf@cordeasavills.com.
Internet: www.cpfund.org.uk.**

College Estate Endowment Charity, The	7.160
Corporation of the Sons of the Clergy (J)	7.181
Dunhill Medical Trust (J)	7.216
Foundation for Social Entrepreneurs (J)	7.259
Foundation of Lady Katherine Leveson, The (J)	7.260
Guild Estate Endowment	7.291
Hampton Fuel Allotment Charity (J)	7.300
Henry Moore Foundation (J)	7.309
John Ellerman Foundation (J)	7.358
Millennium Awards Trust, The (J)	7.427
S Lon Ch Fund&Sthwk Diocesan Bd Fin (J)	7.629
St Luke's Parochial Trust (J)	7.648
Trusthouse Charitable Foundation (J)	7.690
Westhill Endowment (J)	7.722

**CHARLES STANLEY & CO. LIMITED, 2 Westover Road, Bournemouth, Dorset, BH1 2BY. Tel: 01202 317788. Fax: 01202 317754.
E-mail: charities@charles-stanley.co.uk.
Internet: www.charles-stanley.co.uk.**

Alice Ellen Cooper-Dean Charitable Fndtn	7.24
Journalists' Charity	7.364
Stewards Company (J)	7.658
Valentine Charitable Trust, The (J)	7.702

CHARLES STANLEY & CO. LIMITED, 24a Wilbury Grove, Hove, Brighton & Hove, BN3 3JQ. Tel: 01273 229880. Fax: 01273 229881. Internet: www.charles-stanley.co.uk.

Blatchington Court Trust	7.75

**CHARLES STANLEY & CO. LIMITED, Charities Department, 25 Luke Street, London, EC2A 4AR. Tel: 020 7739 8200. Fax: 020 7739 7798. E-mail: charities@charles-stanley.co.uk. Internet: www.charles-stanley.co.uk.
Charity specialists:** Emma Foden-Pattinson MCSI. Nic Muston Chartered FCSI (Director of Private Clients & Charities).

Bath Wells Diocesan Board Finance (J)	7.60
Bransby Horses (J)	7.85
British Medical Association Scholarship	7.96
Charity for the Sisters of Mercy Midhurst	7.129
Charity Roman Union Order St Ursula (J)	7.130
Chartered Institute of Housing	7.133
Chichester Diocesan Fd Bd Finance (J)	7.138
Daughters of the Holy Ghost	7.173
Corporation of the Sons of the Clergy (J)	7.181
Equity Charitable Trust (J)	7.238
G C Gibson Charitable Trust	7.267
Grace & Compassion Benedictines	7.283
Handmaids of the Sacred Heart of Jesus (J)	7.300
Holstein UK	7.315
Ian Karten Charitable Trust	7.326
Imperial Society of Teachers of Dancing	7.329
Institute of Our Lady of Mercy, The	7.336
John Laing Charitable Trust	7.359
Kathleen & Michael Connolly Foundation UK (J)	7.366
Lamport Hall Preservation Trust (J)	7.377
Leicester Diocesan Board Finance (J)	7.383
Missionaries of Africa (The White Fathers)	7.431
Nene Park Trust	7.456
Padwa Charitable Foundation, The	7.489
Portsmouth RC Diocesan Trustees	7.510
Raystede Centre for Animal Welfare	7.527
Sisters of the Cross and Passion	7.615
St Cecilia's Abbey Ryde Isle of Wight	7.639
Suffolk Foundation, The (J)	7.663

**CHARLES STANLEY & CO. LIMITED, 2 Multrees Walk, St Andrew Square, Edinburgh, EH1 3DQ. Tel: 0131 550 1200. Fax: 0131 550 1250.
E-mail: charities@charles-stanley.co.uk.
Internet: www.charles-stanley.co.uk.**

Foundation Scotland (J)	7.260
Moredun Foundation, The	7.433

CHARLES STANLEY & CO. LIMITED, Broadwalk House, Southernhay West, Exeter, Devon, EX1 1TS. Tel: 01392 453600. Fax: 01392 410422. Internet: www.charles-stanley.co.uk.

Norman Family Charitable Trust (J)	7.464

CHARLES STANLEY & CO. LIMITED, 70-72 Chertsey Street, Guildford, Surrey, GU1 4HL. Tel: 01483 230810. Fax: 01483 230818. Internet: www.charles-stanley.co.uk.

Community of St Mary at the Cross	7.166

CHARLES STANLEY & CO. LIMITED, Abbey House, 121 St Aldates, Oxford, Oxfordshire, OX1 1EA. Tel: 01865 320000. Fax: 01865 209048. Internet: www.charles-stanley.co.uk.

Kirkhouse Trust	7.374
Society Salutation Mary Virgin Ltd	7.624

**CHARLES STANLEY PAN ASSET, 25 Luke Street, London, EC2A 4AR. Tel: 020 7799 5454. Fax: 020 7340 9299.
E-mail: enquiries@pan-asset.co.uk.
Internet: www.pan-asset.co.uk.**

Congregation of Our Lady of Sion (J)	7.172
Royal Commission for the 1851 Exhibition (J)	7.558

CHARLES STANLEY PAN ASSET CAPITAL MANAGEMENT LTD, 5th Floor, 131 Finsbury Pavement, London, EC2A 1NT.

Bernard Sunley Charitable Foundation (J)	7.66

CITIBANK, Citigroup Centre, 25 Canada Square, Canary Wharf, London, E14 5LB.
Internet: www.citibank.co.uk.

Charity for Roman Catholic Congregation (J)	7.128
Maurice Wohl Charitable Foundation (J)	7.417
Suva Foundation Limited, The	7.666
Tellus Mater Foundation Ltd	7.672

CLOSE BROTHERS ASSET MANAGEMENT, 10 Exchange Square, Primrose Street, London, EC2A 2BY. Tel: 020 7426 4337. Fax: 020 7426 4707.
E-mail: jonathan.moon@closebrothers.com.
Internet: www.closebrothersam.com.
Charity specialists: Penny Lovell (Head of Client Services). Jonathan Moon (Business Development Director).

COLCHESTER GLOBAL INVESTORS, 20 Savile Row, London, W1S 3PR. Tel: 020 7292 6920. Fax: 020 7292 6932.
Internet: www.colchesterglobal.com.

Church of England Pensions Board (J)	7.148
Dunhill Medical Trust (J)	7.216
Trusthouse Charitable Foundation (J)	7.690

CORDEA SAVILLS INVESTMENT MANAGEMENT LTD, Lansdowne House, 33 Margaret Street, London, W1G 0JD. Tel: +44 (0)20 7877 4700. Fax: +44 (0)20 7877 4777.
E-mail: cpf@cordeasavills.com.
Internet: www.cordeasavills.com.

IMechE Benevolent Fund (J)	7.65
Burdett Trust for Nursing (J)	7.104
Church of England Pensions Board (J)	7.148
Council for World Mission (J)	7.182
Health Foundation, The (J)	7.305
Leicester Diocesan Board Finance (J)	7.383
Maurice Wohl Charitable Foundation (J)	7.417
Samuel Sebba Charitable Trust (J)	7.586
Sisters of Charity of St Vincent de Paul (J)	7.613
Society of Jesus (J)	7.622
St John's Hospital (J)	7.645
Stewards Company (J)	7.658
UFI Charitable Trust (J)	7.692
USPG (J)	7.702

CORNELIAN ASSET MANAGERS LIMITED, 30 Charlotte Square, Edinburgh, EH2 4DF. Tel: 0131 243 4130. Fax: 0131 243 4131.
Internet: www.cornelianam.com.

Chartered Institute of Taxation	7.134
National Galleries of Scotland	7.446
Robertson Trust	7.541
Worldwide Cancer Research	7.742

COUTTS & CO, 440 Strand, London, WC2R 0QS. Tel: 020 7753 1000. Fax: 020 7753 1061. Internet: www.coutts.com.
Charity specialists: Ian Flemng (Head of Charity Investing). Suzanne Collins (Head of UK & Ireland Marketing at Coutts). Sarah Wyse (Head of UK Business Development). Carol Attwater (Administration Officer).

Basil Samuel Charitable Trust	7.59
Breast Cancer Campaign	7.86
BFHU (J)	7.93
Catholic Foreign Missions	7.119
Cinnamon Trust (J)	7.150
Clara E Burgess Charity	7.155
Cullum Family Trust	7.188
Edith Murphy Foundation	7.226
Field Lane Foundation	7.253
Gwyneth Forrester Trust	7.294
Marie Louise Von Motesiczky Charitable Trust	7.410
Maurice Wohl Charitable Foundation (J)	7.417
Muriel Jones Foundation, The	7.439
Pilgrims Hospices in East Kent	7.503
Roddick Foundation, The	7.542
Royal Life Saving Society UK	7.563
Sisters Hospitallers of the Sacred Heart	7.613
Society of African Missions (J)	7.621
Stone Family Foundation, The (J)	7.660
Tuixen Foundation, The	7.690

CQS INVESTMENT MANAGEMENT LTD, 5th Floor, 33 Grosvenor Place, London, WIG 0JD.

Stewards Company (J)	7.658

CREDIT SUISSE ASSET MANAGEMENT LIMITED, 1 Cabot Square, London, E14 4QJ. Tel: 0207 888 1000. Fax: 0207 883 9487.
Internet: www.credit-suisse.com/uk.

Dollond Charitable Trust (J)	7.203
FIA Foundation for Automobile & Society (J)	7.252
Liz and Terry Bramall Charitable Trust, The (J)	7.394
Ogden Trust	7.479

CUNNINGHAM COATES LIMITED, The Linenhall, 32-38 Linenhall Street, Belfast, County Antrim, BT2 8BG. Tel: 028 9072 3000. Fax: 028 9072 3001.
E-mail: gordon.mcdougall@ccstockbrokers.com . Internet: www.ccstockbrokers.com.
Charity specialists: G McDougall.

Action Cancer (J)	7.9

DALTON CAPITAL LTD, First Floor, Tudor House, St Peter Port, Guernsey, Channel Islands, GY1 1DB. Tel: 01481 716 850. Fax: 01481 726 590. Internet: www.daltonsp.com.

Dunhill Medical Trust (J)	7.216

DAVIDSON KEMPNER CAPITAL MANAGEMENT, The Bank of New York Mellon, 101 Barclay Street, 20th Floor West, New York, NY 10286.

Said Foundation (J)	7.581

DAVY STOCKBROKERS, 49 Dawson Street, Dublin. Tel: 00 353 1 614 8780.
E-mail: ian.brady@davy.ie.
Internet: www.davy.ie.

Congregation of La Retraite Trustees (J)	7.171

DEUTSCHE BANK PRIVATE WEALTH MANAGEMENT, 1 Great Winchester Street, London, EC2N 2DB. Tel: 020 7545 8000. Fax: 020 7545 6155.
Internet: www.pwm.db.com.

Community of the Holy Cross (J)	7.166
Federation European Biochemical Societies	7.250
Islamic Trust (J)	7.347

DEUTSCHE BANK PRIVATE WEALTH MANAGEMENT, Baskerville House, Centenary Square, Birmingham, West Midlands, B1 2ND. Tel: 0121 232 5700. Fax: 0121 627 6288.

Birmingham Dogs Home (J)	7.72
East of England Agricultural Society (J)	7.223

DEUTSCHE BANK PRIVATE WEALTH MANAGEMENT, 25 Melville Street, Edinburgh, EH3 7PE. Tel: 0131 243 1000. Fax: 0131 220 4199.
Charity specialists: A Hartley (Director). G G Milne (Director). D Henderson (Director).

Aberdeen Endowments Trust (J)	7.5
Michael Bishop Foundation (J)	7.425
Royal Zoological Society of Scotland	7.576
Volant Charitable Trust	7.709

DEUTSCHE BANK PRIVATE WEALTH MANAGEMENT, 130 St Vincent Street, Glasgow, G2 5SE. Tel: 0141 227 2400. Fax: 0141 221 5962.
Charity specialists: C Pedley.

British Journal of Anaesthesia, The	7.95

DEXIA ASSET MANAGEMENT, 200 Aldersgate Street, London, EX1A 4HD. Internet: www.dexia-am.com.

Edmund Rice Bicentennial Trust Ltd (J)	7.226

DIMENSIONAL FUND ADVISORS LTD, 5th Floor, 20 Triton Street, London, NW1 3BF.

Foundation for Social Entrepreneurs (J)	7.259
Millennium Awards Trust, The (J)	7.427

Charity specialists: Mike Goddings (Head of Charity Market Development).

Ely Diocesan Board of Finance, The (J)	7.231
Sisters of Charity of St Vincent de Paul (J)	7.613
St Asaph Diocesan Board of Finance (J)	7.638

EDENTREE INVESTMENT MANAGEMENT LTD (FORMERLY ECCLESIASTICAL INVESTMENT MANAGEMENT LTD.), Beaufort House, Brunswick Road, Gloucester, Gloucestershire, GH1 1JZ. Tel: 0345 777 3322.
Internet: www.edentreeim.com.

Coventry Diocesan Board of Finance (J)	7.184
St Mary Magdalene & Holy Jesus Trust (J)	7.649

EDINBURGH PARTNERS LTD, 27-31 Melville Street, Edinburgh, EH3 7JF. Tel: 0131 270 3800. Fax: 0131 270 3801.
Internet: www.edinburghpartners.com.

Church of England Pensions Board (J)	7.148

EFG HARRIS ALLDAY, 33 Great Charles Street, Birmingham, West Midlands, B3 3JN. Tel: 0121 233 1222. Fax: 0121 236 2587.
E-mail: simon.raggett@efgha.com/ronald.treverton-jones@efgha.com.
Internet: www.efgha.com.
Charity specialists: Ronald Treverton-Jones. Simon Raggett (Senior Director). James Holroyd (Director, Charities). Christopher Morley.

Addington Fund, The	7.14
St Martin's Trust	7.649
Stoneleigh Abbey Limited	7.660

EFG HARRIS ALLDAY, 25a St Leonard's Close, Bridgnorth, Shropshire, WV16 4EL. Tel: 01746 761 444. Fax: 01746 765 209.
E-mail: bridgnorthw@efgha.com.
Internet: www.efgha.com.

G J W Turner Trust	7.268

EGERTON CAPITAL (UK) LLP, Stratton House, 5 Stratton Street, W1J 8LA. Tel: 020 7410 9090.
E-mail: info@egercap.co.uk.
Internet: www.egertoncapital.com.

Royal Marsden Cancer Campaign (J)   7.564

EPWORTH INVESTMENT MANAGEMENT LIMITED, 9 Bonhill Street, London, EC2A 4PE. Tel: 020 7496 3636. Fax: 020 7496 3637. E-mail: admin@epworthinvestment.co.uk. Internet: www.epworthinvestment.co.uk. Charity specialists: Peter Forward.

Carmelite Charitable Trust (J)	7.116
Christian Aid (J)	7.145
Congregation of the Jesus Charitable Trust (J)	7.171
Congregation of the Sisters of St Anne (J)	7.175
English Province of our Lady of Charity	7.235
Handmaids of the Sacred Heart of Jesus (J)	7.300
Joseph Rowntree Charitable Trust (J)	7.363
Maria Assumpta Trust (J)	7.410
Religious of the Assumption (J)	7.531
S L G Charitable Trust (J)	7.578
Sisters of Charity of St Vincent de Paul (J)	7.613
Spurgeons	7.635
St Luke's Parochial Trust (J)	7.648

EVOLVE FINANCIAL PLANNING LTD, No. 1 Ropemaker Street, London, EC2Y 9HT. Tel: 0845 602 7875. Internet: www.evolvefp.com.

ITF Seafarers Trust   7.348

F & C MANAGEMENT LIMITED, Exchange House, Primrose Street, London, EC2A 2NY. Tel: 020 7628 8000. Fax: 020 7011 5487. Internet: www.fandc.com.

Edmund Rice Bicentennial Trust Ltd (J)   7.226

FF & P ASSET MANAGEMENT LIMITED, 15 Suffolk Street, London, SW1Y 4HG. Tel: 020 7036 5000. Fax: 020 7036 5601. Internet: www.ffandp.com.

Bernard Sunley Charitable Foundation (J)	7.66
Englefield Charitable Trust	7.234
King's Fund, The	7.373
Royal Opera House Covent Garden (J)	7.569
Royal Opera House Endowment Fund 2000 (J)	7.569

FIDELITY INVESTMENTS LIMITED, Oakhill House, 130 Tonbridge Road, Hildenborough, Kent, TN11 9DZ. Tel: 01732 361144. Fax: 01732 838886. Internet: www.fidelity.co.uk.

Robert Luff Foundation Limited   7.540

FINDLAY PARK PARTNERS LLP, Almack House, 4th Floor, 28 King Street, London, SW1Y 6QW. Tel: 020 7968 4900. Fax: 020 7000 1321. Internet: www.findlaypark.co.uk.

Dulverton Trust (J)	7.214
Dunhill Medical Trust (J)	7.216

FIRST STATE INVESTMENT MANAGEMENT (UK) LIMITED, 23 St Andrews Square, Edinburgh, EH2 1BB. Tel: 0800 587 4141. Fax: 0131 473 2516. E-mail: enquiries@firststate.co.uk. Internet: www.firststate.co.uk.

Church of England Pensions Board (J)	7.148
Joseph Rowntree Charitable Trust (J)	7.363

FISKE PLC, Salisbury House, London Wall, London, EC2M 5QS. Tel: 020 7638 4681. Fax: 020 7256 5365. Internet: www.fiskeplc.com.

SMB Charitable Trust   7.619

FOSTER DENOVO, 15 Brenkley Way, Blezard Business Park, Wideopen, Newcastle upon Tyne, Tyne and Wear, NE13 6DS. Tel: 0191 217 3903. Fax: 0191 217 3909. E-mail: newcastle@fosterdenovo.com. Internet: www.fosterdenovogroup.com.

Age UK North Tyneside	7.18
Book Trust	7.79

FRANKLIN TEMPLETON, The Adelphi, 1 - 11 John Adam Street, London, WC2N 6HT. Tel: 0800 305 306. Internet: www.franklintempleton.co.uk.

Council for World Mission (J)   7.182

FULCRUM ASSET MANAGEMENT, Marble Arch House, 66 Seymour Street, London, W1H 5BT. Tel: 0207 016 6450. Fax: 0207 016 6460. Internet: www.fulcrumasset.com.

Birmingham Children's Hospital Charities (J)	7.71
Grand Charity, The (J)	7.284
Masonic Samaritan Fund (J)	7.415
Royal Masonic Benevolent Institution	7.565
Royal Masonic Trust For Girls and Boys (J)	7.565

GAM LONDON LIMITED, 20 King Street, London, SW1Y 6QY. Tel: 020 7393 8776. E-mail: charitieslondon@gam.com. Internet: www.gam.com/en/Charities/Overview. htm.

Kent, Surrey & Sussex Air Ambulance Trust	7.369
Univ Old Members' Trust, The (J)	7.699

GENERATION INVESTMENT MANAGEMENT LLP, 20 Air Street, London, W1B 5AN. Tel: 0207 534 4700. Fax: 0207 534 4701. Internet: www.generationim.com.

Joseph Rowntree Charitable Trust (J)	7.363
Society of Jesus (J)	7.622

GMO (UK) LTD, No. 1 London Bridge, London, SE1 9BG. Tel: 020 7814 7600. Fax: 020 7814 7605. E-mail: peter.froude@gmo.com. Internet: www.GMO.com.

Burdett Trust for Nursing (J)	7.104
City Bridge Trust, The (J)	7.153
Intl Planned Parenthood Federation	7.344

GOLDMAN SACHS INTERNATIONAL LIMITED, Christchurch Court, 10-15 Newgate Street, London, EC1A 7HD. Tel: 020 7774 1000. Internet: www.gs.com.

AQA Education (J)	7.35
Education Endowment Foundation, The (J)	7.227
Fdn&Friends of RoyalBotanicGardens, Kew (J)	7.259
Foundation for Social Entrepreneurs (J)	7.259
Ingram Trust (J)	7.331
Islamic Trust (J)	7.347
Kusuma Trust UK (J)	7.375
Millennium Awards Trust, The (J)	7.427
Nightingale Hammerson (J)	7.463
Souter Charitable Trust (J)	7.628

GOLDMAN SACHS INTERNATIONAL LIMITED, Peterborough Court, 133 Fleet Street, London, EC4A 2BB. Tel: 020 7774 1000. Internet: www2.goldmansachs.com.

bet365 Foundation	7.67
Hadley Trust	7.296
Health Foundation, The (J)	7.305
Khodorkovsky Foundation (J)	7.370
Potanin Foundation (J)	7.511

HARGREAVE HALE LTD, Accurist House, 44 Baker Street, London, W1U 7AL. Tel: 020 7009 4900. Fax: 020 7009 4999. E-mail: london@hargreave-hale.co.uk. Internet: www.hargreave-hale.co.uk.

Masonic Samaritan Fund (J)	7.415
Royal Masonic Hospital Charity	7.565

HARGREAVE HALE LTD, 30 Dean Street, Bangor, Gwynedd, LL57 1UR. Tel: 01248 353 242. Fax: 01248 361 745. E-mail: bangor@hargreave-hale.co.uk. Internet: www.hargreave-hale.co.uk.

Urdd Gobaith Cymru	7.701
West Lancashire Freemasons' Charity	7.720

HARGREAVES LANSDOWN, One College Square South, Anchor Road, Bristol, BS1 5HL. Tel: 0117 900 9000. Internet: www.h-l.co.uk.

Echoes of Service	7.223
St Rocco's Hospice	7.654

HEARTWOOD INVESTMENT MANAGEMENT, 1 Kingsway, London, WC2B 6AN. Tel: 020 7045 1375. Fax: 020 7045 1321. E-mail: guy.davies@heartwoodgroup.co.uk. Internet: www.heartwoodgroup.co.uk. Charity specialists: Guy Davies (Head of Charities).

Hugh Tottenham (Client Director - Charities). Natalie Wilkinson (Client Associate). Noland Carter (Chief Investment Officer). Jaisal Pastakia (Investment Manager). Jade Fu (Investment Manager). David Absolon (Investment Director). Scott Ingham (Investment Director). Martin Perry (Investment Director). Alan Sippetts (Investment Director). Saajan Mahbubani (Investment Associate). Benjamin Matthews (Investment Associate). Michael Stanes (Investment Director).

Fdn&Friends of RoyalBotanicGardens, Kew (J)	7.259
Great Britain Sasakawa Foundation	7.284
Hospice in the Weald	7.319
Lawrence Atwell's Charity	7.380
London Oratory Charity	7.400
Maurice Wohl Charitable Foundation (J)	7.417
Royal London Society for the Blind	7.564
Sir Andrew Judd Foundation	7.609

HEARTWOOD INVESTMENT MANAGEMENT, 77 Mount Ephraim, Tunbridge Wells, Kent, TN4 8BS. Tel: 01892 701801. Internet: www.heartwoodgroup.co.uk.

Fellowship of School of Economic Science (J)   7.251

HEDLEY & CO, 13b Winckley Square, Preston, Lancashire, PR1 3JJ. Tel: 01772 887 880. E-mail: mail@hedleyandco.co.uk. Internet: www.hedleyandco.co.uk.

Institute of the Blessed Virgin Mary (J)   7.337

HENDERSON GLOBAL INVESTORS, 201 Bishopsgate, London, EC2M 3AE. Tel: 020 7818 1818. Fax: 020 7818 1819. Internet: www.henderson.com.

Health Foundation, The (J)	7.305
St Joseph's Society for Foreign Missions (J)	7.646

HERMES INVESTMENT MANAGEMENT, Lloyds Chambers, 1 Portsoken Street, London, E1 8HZ. Tel: 020 7702 0888. E-mail: marketing@hermes-investment.com. Internet: www.hermes-investment.com.

Clothworkers' Foundation (J)	7.157
Sisters of Charity of St Vincent de Paul (J)	7.613
S Lon Ch Fund&Sthwk Diocesan Bd Fin (J)	7.629

HERONBRIDGE INVESTMENT MANAGEMENT, 24 Gay Street, Bath, Bath & North East Somerset, BA1 2PD. Tel: 01225 328 300. Fax: 01225 442 839. E-mail: tom@heronbridge.com. Internet: www.heronbridge.com.

29th May 1961 Charitable Trust (J)	7.2
Dunhill Medical Trust (J)	7.216
Foyle Foundation (J)	7.261
Westminster Foundation (J)	7.723

HILL OSBORNE & CO, Permanent House, Horsefair Street, Leicester, Leicestershire, LE1 5BU.

Franciscan Sisters Minoress   7.689

HOLDEN & PARTNERS, The Piano Works, 117 Farringdon Road, London, EC1R 3BX. Tel: 020 7812 1460. Internet: www.holden-partners.co.uk.

International Fund for Animal Welfare (J)   7.342

HSBC GLOBAL ASSET MANAGEMENT (UK) LTD, Wealth Charity Service, 78 St James's Street, London, SW1A 1EJ. Tel: +44(0) 8456 066 286. Fax: +44 (0) 20 7024 1913. E-mail: dwm.enquiries@hsbc.com. Internet: www.assetmanagement.hsbc.com/uk. Charity specialists: Sridhar Chandrasekharan (Global Chief Executive Officer). George Efthimiou (Global Chief Operating Officer). Guy Blackden. Alistair Peel.

Albert Hunt Trust	7.23
Sisters of Charity of Jesus and Mary (J)	7.94
Camphill Village Trust Limited	7.111
CFBT Education Trust (J)	7.125
Congregation of Servants of Mary(London)	7.174
Electrical Safety Council	7.229
European Renal Association	7.242
G M Morrison Charitable Trust	7.268

Great Ormond St Hosp Children's Charity (J)	7.285
Isle of Anglesey Charitable Trust, The	7.347
Maudsley Charity	7.416
Medical Research Council Technology	7.419
Mrs L D Rope Third Charitable Settlement	7.438
NFER (J)	7.446
National Osteoporosis Society	7.451
Royal Institution of Great Britain	7.562
Salisbury District Hospital Charitable Fund	7.583
Secular Clergy Common Fund	7.596
Sino-British Fellowship Trust	7.609
St John of God Hospitaller Services Ltd	7.645
United Bible Societies Association, The	7.695
Victoria Foundation, The (J)	7.705
World Energy Council (J)	7.740

HYMANS ROBERTSON, 20 Waterloo Street, Glasgow, G2 6DB. Tel: 0141 566 7777. Fax: 0141 566 7788. Internet: www.hymans.co.uk. Charity specialists: B Lindsay.

Scottish Sports Council Trust Company	7.593

IGNIS ASSET MANAGEMENT, Britannic Court, 50 Bothwell Street, Glasgow, G2 6HR. Tel: 0141 222 8000. Fax: 0141 222 8300. Internet: www.britannicasset.com.

Comic Relief (J)	7.162

IMPAX ASSET MANAGEMENT, Norfolk House, 31 St James Square, London, SW1Y 4JR.

Joseph Rowntree Charitable Trust (J)	7.363

INGENIOUS ASSET MANAGEMENT, 15 Golden Square, London, W1F 9JG. Tel: 020 7319 4215. Fax: 020 7319 4001. E-mail: www.ingeniousmedia.co.uk/asset-management. Internet: craig.wright@ingeniousam.co.uk.

British Academy of Film & Television Arts (J)	7.91
Comic Relief (J)	7.162

INSIGHT INVESTMENT, 160 Queen Victoria Street, London, EC4V 4LA. Tel: 020 7163 4000. Internet: www.insightinvestment.com.

Church of England Pensions Board (J)	7.148
Shetland Charitable Trust	7.604

INTERNATIONAL ASSET MANAGEMENT, 7 Clifford Street, London, W1S 2FT. Tel: 020 7734 8488. Fax: 020 7287 7129. Internet: www.iam.uk.com.

Maurice Wohl Charitable Foundation (J)	7.417

INVESCO GLOBAL INVESTMENTS LIMITED, 30 Finsbury Square, London, EC2A 1AG.

Said Foundation (J)	7.581

INVESTEC WEALTH & INVESTMENT, 2 Gresham Street, London, EC2V 7QN. Tel: 020 7597 1250. E-mail: Caroline.Jarvis@investecwin.co.uk. Internet: www.investecwin.co.uk/charities. Charity specialists: Caroline Jarvis (Client Development Director). Louise Hall (Head of Charities). James Minett (Investment Manager). John Ross (Investment Manager). Bryan Burrough (Investment Manager). David Richardson (Investment Manager). John Hildebrand (Investment Manager). Michael Turner (Investment Manager). Elliot Bancroft (Investment Manager). Tom Quicke (Investment Manager).

Action Cancer (J)	7.9
Alcohol Research UK	7.23
Architects Benevolent Society	7.38
Army Cadet Force Association	7.39
Assoc of Anaesthetists of GB & Ireland	7.46
Augustinians of the Assumption (J)	7.48
Band Trust (J)	7.55
Barristers' Benevolent Association	7.59
Beverley Consolidated Charity	7.68
Bill Brown's Charitable Settlement 1989	7.70
Blagrave Trust, The (J)	7.74
BMS World Mission	7.77
Bradford Diocesan Board of Finance, The (J)	7.83
British & Foreign School Society, The	7.91

BFHU (J)	7.93
British Safety Council	7.98
Bulldog Trust	7.104
Cabrini Children's Society	7.107
Catholic Trust for England and Wales	7.120
Charles Skey Charitable Trust	7.131
CharteredInstitute of Logistics&Transport UK	7.133
Christ's Hospital of Abingdon	7.144
Christadelphian Care Homes	7.144
CITB-ConstructionSkills	7.151
Claire House Appeal	7.155
Colyer-Fergusson Charitable Trust	7.161
Comm Fdn (Tyne&Wear&Northumberland) (J)	7.164
Community of St Mary the Virgin (J)	7.166
Compton Hospice	7.169
Congregational & General Charitable Trust	7.176
County Air Ambulance Trust	7.183
D'Oyly Carte Charitable Trust	7.191
Doncaster & Bassetlaw Hospitals Trust	7.204
Donkey Sanctuary	7.206
Douglas Turner Trust	7.210
E F Bulmer Benevolent Fund	7.217
E P A Cephalosporin Fund	7.218
Earley Charity	7.219
East End Community Foundation (J)	7.221
East of England Agricultural Society (J)	7.223
Embrace the Middle East	7.232
Essex Community Foundation (J)	7.240
February Foundation, The	7.250
FIA Foundation for Automobile & Society (J)	7.252
Finchley Charities	7.254
Garfield Weston Foundation	7.269
Gloucester Charities Trust (J)	7.277
Grange Farm Centre Trust	7.284
Great Hospital, Norwich	7.285
Great Ormond St Hosp Children's Charity (J)	7.285
Havens Christian Hospice	7.304
Health Foundation, The (J)	7.305
HF Trust Limited	7.311
Home Devenish	7.315
Hospital of the Holy & Undivided Trinity	7.322
Insurance Charities	7.339
Jewish Joint Burial Society	7.354
John Ellerman Foundation (J)	7.358
Joseph Strong Frazer Trust	7.363
Kirkwood Hospice	7.374
Leeds Diocesan Trust	7.382
London City Mission	7.397
Louis Baylis Charitable Trust (J)	7.403
Mark Benevolent Fund, The (J)	7.411
Med Col of St Bartholomew's Hospital (J)	7.419
Morden College	7.433
Mrs D M France-Hayhurst Charitable Trust	7.437
Muscular Dystrophy Campaign	7.439
NFER (J)	7.446
National Library of Wales, The	7.449
National Rifle Association	7.451
Nordoff Robbins Music Therapy Centre	7.464
North West Air Ambulance	7.468
Outward Bound Trust	7.485
Oxford Trust, The	7.488
Pharmacist Support	7.500
Phyllis Tuckwell Memorial Hospice	7.501
Presbyterian Church of Wales	7.513
Professional Footballers Assoc Educ Fund (J)	7.516
Professional Footballers Benevolent Fund (J)	7.516
Quintin Hogg Trust	7.521
Ramakrishna Vedanta Centre	7.524
Rank Prize Fund	7.525
Rethink Mental Illness	7.534
RMIG Endowment Trust	7.540
Roger Raymond Charitable Trust (J)	7.542
Roman Catholic Diocese Hallam Trust	7.543
Royal Liverpool Philharmonic Society	7.563
Royal Mencap Society (J)	7.566
Sailors Society	7.581
Salisbury City Almshouse and Welfare (J)	7.583
Services Sound Vision Corporation (J)	7.598
Sheffield Hospitals Trust & Related Charities	7.602
Sheppard Trust	7.604
Sir Jules Thorn Charitable Trust (J)	7.612
Sisters of Mercy-St Anthony's Convent	7.614
Society for Assistance of Ladies (J)	7.621
Solicitors Benevolent Association	7.626
South Yorkshire Community Foundation	7.631
Southside Partnership	7.631
St Catherine's Hospice Trust	7.639
St Gemma's Hospice Leeds	7.643

St George's Hospital Charity	7.643
St Luke's Hospice	7.647
St Margaret's Convent (Uckfield)	7.648
St Vincent de Paul Society	7.655
Sylvanus Lysons Charity	7.667
Tank Museum, The	7.669
Tate	7.669
Tate Foundation	7.669
Tees Valley Community Foundation	7.671
Thames Hospicecare	7.675
Tiverton Almhouse Charity	7.681
Tolkien Trust	7.682
Trusthouse Charitable Foundation (J)	7.690
UK Sailing Academy	7.693
United St Saviour's Charities	7.698
UCAS	7.699
Vincent Wildlife Trust (J)	7.706
Walthamstow&Chingford Almshouse Charity	7.713
Walton-on-Thames Charity	7.713
WESC Foundation	7.719
Westhill Endowment (J)	7.722
Whitley Wildlife Conservation Trust, The	7.726
Wilf Ward Family Trust (J)	7.728
William Leech Charity	7.730
Wirral Hospice St John's	7.733
Woodlands Hospice Charitable Trust Limited	7.737
Wyggeston's Hospital	7.743
YWCA England & Wales (J)	7.752

J.P. MORGAN, 1 Knightsbridge, London, SW1X 7LX. Tel: 020 7742 2819. Fax: 020 7742 2990. E-mail: tom.rutherford@jpmorgan.com. Internet: www.jpmorganassetmanagement.co.uk /institutional. Charity specialists: Tom Rutherford (Head of Charities Team).

Aimwell Charitable Trust	7.20
Alzheimer's Society	7.28
Balcombe Charitable Trust	7.54
Education Endowment Foundation, The (J)	7.227
Eranda Foundation	7.238
Handmaids of the Sacred Heart of Jesus (J)	7.300
Hospital of God at Greatham	7.321
Institute of Biomedical Science	7.333
Kusuma Trust UK (J)	7.375
Liz and Terry Bramall Charitable Trust, The (J)	7.394
Macmillan Cancer Support	7.405
Maurice & Vivienne Wohl Philanthropic Fdn (J)	7.417
Moorfields Eye Hospital Special Trustees	7.433
National Trust (J)	7.454
Natural History Museum	7.455
Potanin Foundation (J)	7.511
Reta Lila Howard Foundation (J)	7.533
Reta Lila Weston Tst for Medical Research (J)	7.533
Royal Commission for the 1851 Exhibition (J)	7.558
Samuel Sebba Charitable Trust (J)	7.586
Seamen's Hospital Society	7.595
Services Sound Vision Corporation (J)	7.598
United Synagogue	7.698
Weston Provident Fund	7.724
Whitechapel Gallery	7.725
Woodward Charitable Trust	7.737

J STERN & CO LLP, 21 Knightsbridge, London, SW1X 7LY. Tel: 020 3478 1800. Fax: 020 3478 1799. E-mail: info@jsternco.com. Internet: www.jsternco.com.

Vincent Wildlife Trust (J)	7.706

JAMES BREARLEY & SONS, 5 Grimshaw Street, Burnley, Lancashire, BB11 2AS. Tel: 01282 422042. Fax: 01282 831724. Internet: www.jbrearley.co.uk.

Hospice Care for Burnley and Pendle	7.318

JAMES BREARLEY & SONS, 7 South Preston Office Village, Cuerden Way, Bamber Bridge, Preston, Lancashire, PR5 6BL. Tel: 01772 318760. Fax: 01772 318799. Internet: www.jbrearley.co.uk.

Trinity Hospice & Palliative Care Services (J)	7.686

JAMES HAMBRO & PARTNERS, 3rd Floor, Ryder Court, 14 Ryder Street, London, SW1Y 6QB. Tel: 0203 817 3402. E-mail: fmatson@.jameshambro.com.

Internet: www.jameshambro.com/charities.
Charity specialists: Nicola Barber (Head of Charities). J Langrish (Head of Investments). Fiona Matson (Business Development Manager - Charities).

Brooke Hospital for Animals (J)	7.101
PRS For Music Members Benevolent Fund (J)	7.517
Racing Foundation, The (J)	7.523
Samaritans (J)	7.585
Society of the Holy Child Jesus Eur.Province (J)	7.624

JAMES SHARP & CO, Exchange House, 5 Bank Street, Bury, Lancashire, BL9 0DN. Tel: 0161 764 4043. Fax: 0161 764 1628.
Charity specialists: R D Calrow.

Zochonis Charitable Trust	7.752

JLT WEALTH MANAGEMENT, 23 Cathedral Yard, Exeter, Devon, EX1 1HB. Tel: 01752 660 282.
E-mail: exeter@jltwm.com.
Internet: www.iimia.co.uk.

Elizabeth Finn Care (J)	7.230

JMFinn&Co

JM FINN & CO, 4 Coleman Street, London, EC2R 5TA. Tel: 020 7600 1660. Fax: 020 7600 1661. E-mail: charities@jmfinn.com.
Internet: www.jmfinn.com.

> For further information please see our full page profile at the front of the book.

Charity specialists: Mark Powell. Sam Barty-King. Alison Finney.

Beacon Centre for the Blind	7.62
Catherine Cookson Charitable Trust	7.118
Central Foundation Schools of London (J)	7.122
Charity of the Congregation of Our Lady	7.129
Chichester Diocesan Fd Bd Finance (J)	7.138
Christopher Laing Foundation (J)	7.146
Sisters of the Finding of Jesus	7.175
Council for World Mission (J)	7.182
East Anglia's Children's Hospices	7.220
Elizabeth and Prince Zaiger Trust	7.230
Geoffrey Watling Charity, The	7.272
Gosling Foundation Limited	7.282
Institute of Advanced Motorists (J)	7.333
Mark Benevolent Fund, The (J)	7.411
Meath Epilepsy Trust	7.418
Nat Soc CoE for Promoting Religious Ed	7.452
Norwich Diocesan Board of Finance, The	7.471
Order of Friars Minor	7.482
Oxford Centre Hebrew & Jewish Studies	7.487
Pargiter Trust	7.490
Royal Aeronautical Society	7.550
Sisters Notre Dame Namur	7.614
Trustees of the Bernadine Sisters Charity	7.689
Wilf Ward Family Trust (J)	7.728

JUBILEE ABSOLUTE RETURN FUND PCC LTD, Arnold House, St Julian's Avenue, St Peter Port, Guernsey, GY1 3NF.

Council for World Mission (J)	7.182

JULIUS BAER INTERNATIONAL LIMITED, 1 St Martin's Le Grand, London, EC1A 4AS.
Tel: 0203 481 8100. Fax: 0203 481 8181.
Internet: www.juliusbaer.com.

Sisters of Charity of Jesus and Mary (J)	7.94
Grand Charity, The (J)	7.284
Islamic Trust (J)	7.347
Phillips & Rubens Charitable Trust (J)	7.501
Royal British Legion Industries Ltd	7.554
Waterloo Foundation, The	7.715

JUPITER ASSET MANAGEMENT LIMITED, Jupiter Private Clients & Charities, 1 Grosvenor Place, London, SW1X 7JJ. Tel: 020 7314 5574.
Internet: www.jupiteronline.com.
Charity specialists: Melanie Wotherspoon (Private Clients & Charities Director).

Blind Veterans UK	7.76
Huntingdon Freemen's Trust (J)	7.325
Institution of Chemical Engineers (J)	7.337
Joseph Rowntree Foundation (J)	7.363
Multiple Sclerosis Society	7.438

KAMES CAPITAL, 4th Floor, 77 Gracechurch Street, London, EC3V 0AS.
Internet: www.kamescapital.com.

Royal Society of Chemistry	7.572
Sisters of Charity of St Vincent de Paul (J)	7.613

KENNOX ASSET MANAGEMENT LTD, 28 Drumshengh Gardens, Edinburgh, EH37RN. Tel: 0131 563 5440.
E-mail: enquiries@kennox.co.uk.
Internet: www.kennox.co.uk.
Charity specialists: P Boyle (Managing Director). C Heenan (Investment Director). G Legg (Investment Manager).

P H Holt Foundation (J)	7.489

KLEINWORT BENSON, 14 St George Street, Mayfair, London, W1S 1FE. Tel: +44 (0)20 3207 7400. Fax: +44 (0)20 3207 7001.
Internet: www.kleinwortbenson.com.

British Assoc Counselling & Psychotherapy	7.92
Cambridge Union Society, The	7.109
Colefax Charitable Trust	7.159
Company of Biologists Limited	7.168
Dyers Company Charitable Trust	7.217
Ely Diocesan Board of Finance, The (J)	7.231
Ernest Kleinwort Charitable Trust	7.239
Hull Trinity House Charities	7.323
Viscount Amory's Charitable Trust	7.707

L & P FINANCIAL TRUSTEES (UK) LIMITED, Manchester, Greater Manchester, M22 5PP.

Institute of the Franciscan Missionaries	7.337

L & P FINANCIAL TRUSTEES (UK) LIMITED, 3rd Floor, New Oxford House, 75 Dale Street, Liverpool, Merseyside, L2 2HT. Tel: 0151 255 1553. Fax: 0151 255 1533.
E-mail: info@lpsystems.com.
Internet: www.lpgroup.ie.

Sisters of Bon Secours of Paris (J)	7.172

LANE CLARK & PEACOCK, 95 Wigmore Street, London, W1U 1DQ. Tel: 020 7439 2266.
Internet: www.lcp.uk.com.

UFI Charitable Trust (J)	7.692

LANSDOWNE PARTNERS LTD, 15 Davies Street, London, W1K 3AG. Tel: 020 7290 5500. Fax: 020 7409 1122.
E-mail: info@lansdownepartners.com.
Internet: www.lansdownepartners.com.

Royal Marsden Cancer Campaign (J)	7.564

LAZARD ASSET MANAGEMENT LIMITED, 50 Stratton Street, London, W1J 8LL. Tel: 020 7448 2339. Fax: 020 7659 5797.
Internet: www.uk.lazardnet.com.

Savoy Educational Trust	7.588

LEGAL & GENERAL INVESTMENT MANAGEMENT (LGIM), One Coleman Street, London, EC2R 5AA. Tel: +44 (0)20 3124 3000.
Internet: www.lgim.com.

Action for Blind People	7.10
British Library	7.95
Church of England Pensions Board (J)	7.148
Clothworkers' Foundation (J)	7.157
Hampton Fuel Allotment Charity (J)	7.300
ICAEW Foundation & Educational Charities	7.327
King's College Hospital Charity	7.372
National Trust (J)	7.454
Stewards Company (J)	7.658

LIONTRUST ASSET MANAGEMENT PLC, 2 Savoy Court, London, WC2R 0EZ. Tel: 020 7412 1766. Fax: 020 7412 1779.
Internet: www.liontrust.co.uk.

Grocers' Charity	7.289

LLOYDS TSB PRIVATE BANKING LIMITED, 25 Gresham Street, London, EC2V 7HN. Tel: 020 7493 7722. Fax: 020 7495 0398.
Internet: www.lloydstsb.com.
Charity specialists: G Hughes. Linda Pollard.

Edmund Rice Bicentennial Trust Ltd (J)	7.226
Steinberg Family Charitable Trust, The (J)	7.657

LLOYDS TSB PRIVATE BANKING LIMITED, Butt Dyke House, 33 Park Row, Nottingham, Nottinghamshire, NG1 6GY. Tel: 0115 947 1267. Fax: 0115 947 1276.
Internet: www.lloydstsb.com.

Portland College	7.509

LONGVIEW PARTNERS LLP, Thames Court, 1 Queenhithe, London, EC4V 3RL. Tel: 020 7809 4100. Fax: 020 7809 4199.
E-mail: info@longview-partners.com.
Internet: www.longview-partners.com.

Church of England Pensions Board (J)	7.148
Henry Moore Foundation (J)	7.309
National Trust (J)	7.454
Nuffield Foundation (J)	7.474

LORD NORTH STREET LIMITED, 105 Wigmore Street, London, W1U 1QY. Tel: 020 7290 4915.
Internet: www.lordnorthstreet.com.

Edward Penley Abraham Research Fund (J)	7.228
Guy Newton Research Fund (J)	7.293
William Brake Charitable Trust	7.730

LOTHBURY INVESTMENT MANAGEMENT LIMITED, 155 Bishopsgate, London, EC2M 3TQ. Tel: 020 3551 4900. Fax: 020 3551 4920.
E-mail: LothburyIMinvestorrelations@lothburyim.com. **Internet:** www.lothburyim.com.

Council for World Mission (J)	7.182

M&G SECURITIES LTD, Laurence Pountney Hill, London, EC4R 0HH. Tel: 020 7548 3731. Fax: 020 7548 3058.
E-mail: charities@mandg.co.uk.
Internet: www.mandg.co.uk/charities.

> For more information see our profile in the front colour section

Charity specialists: Peter Knapton (Director of Charities). Richard Macey (Director of Charities). James Potter (Charity Relationship Executive).

MCCARTHY TAYLOR LIMITED, 100 High Street Evesham, Worcester, Worcestershire, WR11 4EU. Tel: 01386 422611. Fax: 01386 422612. E-mail: advice@mccarthytaylor.co.uk.
Internet: www.mccarthytaylor.co.uk.

Bransford Trust, The	7.85

MCINROY & WOOD LTD, Easter Alderston, Haddington, East Lothian, EH41 3SF. Tel: 01620 825 867. Fax: 01620 826 295.
E-mail: enquiry@mcinroy-wood.co.uk.
Internet: www.mcinroy-wood.co.uk.

Philip King Charitable Trust (J)	7.501
Royal Academy of Dramatic Art	7.549

MAJEDIE ASSET MANAGEMENT LTD, 10 Old Bailey, London, EC4M 7NG. Tel: 020 7618 3900. Fax: 020 7618 3933. E-mail: info@majedie.com. Internet: www.majedie.com.

University of Newcastle DevelopmentTrust (J)   7.701

MARATHON ASSET MANAGEMENT LIMITED, Orion House, 5 Upper St Martin's Lane, London, WC2H 9EA. Tel: 020 7497 2211. Fax: 020 7497 2399.

Westminster Foundation (J)   7.723

MARTIN CURRIE INVESTMENT MANAGEMENT LIMITED, Saltire Court, 20 Castle Terrace, Edinburgh, EH1 2ES. Tel: 0131 229 5252. Fax: 0131 228 5959. E-mail: kburdon@martincurrie.com. Internet: www.martincurrie.com. Charity specialists: Keith Burdon (Director, client services). D Townsend.

Carnegie Trust for Universities Scotland	7.116
Liverpool Roman Catholic Archdiocesan	7.393
Medical Research Scotland	7.420
National Trust for Scotland (J)	7.453
Nugent Care	7.475
Trust for London (J)	7.688

MARYLEBONE PARTNERS LLP, 1st Floor, Clearwater House, 4-7 Manchester Street, London, W1U 3AE. Tel: 020 3468 9910. Fax: 020 3468 9912. E-mail: contacts@marylebonepartners.com. Internet: www.marylebonepartners.com.

Motability Tenth Anniversary Trust, The (J)   7.435

MAUNBY INVESTMENT MANAGEMENT LIMITED, 3rd Floor, The Exchange, Station Parade, Harrogate, North Yorkshire, HG1 1TJ. Tel: 01423 523553. Fax: 01423 530356. E-mail: hello@maunby.com. Internet: www.maunby.com. Charity specialists: P A Hill-Walker.

Yorkshire Agricultural Society (J)   7.748

MAYFAIR CAPITAL INVESTMENT MANAGEMENT LTD, 2 Cavendish Square, London, W1G 0PU. Tel: 020 7495 1929.

Mayfair Capital is a privately owned property fund management business. We manage a series of pooled property funds and segregated portfolios on behalf of professional clients, charities, pensions and institutions. We have a strong performance record attributable to our focus on strategy, deal sourcing capabilities and asset management.

The Property Income Trust for Charities is a Pooled Fund specifically designed to enable charities to enjoy an attractive income yield through investing in UK commercial property on a tax efficient basis. Importantly, all property purchases are exempt from SDLT (currently 4% on all commercial property transactions over £500,000).

For further information visit www.pitch-fund.co.uk or contact James Thornton/James Lloyd on Tel: +44 (0)20 7495 1929

Army Dependants' Trust, The (J)	7.39
Bernard Sunley Charitable Foundation (J)	7.66
Burdett Trust for Nursing (J)	7.104
Church of England Pensions Board (J)	7.148
Edward James Foundation Limited (J)	7.228
Foundation of Lady Katherine Leveson, The (J)	7.260
Hampshire & Isle of Wight Community Fdn (J)	7.298
National Trust for Scotland (J)	7.453
S Lon Ch Fund&Sthwk Diocesan Bd Fin (J)	7.629
Southwell Diocesan Board Finance (J)	7.631
UFI Charitable Trust (J)	7.692
YWCA England & Wales (J)	7.752

MAYFLOWER MANAGEMENT CO. LTD, 2 Gresham Street, London, EC2V 7QN. Tel: 020 7303 1487.

Clothworkers' Foundation (J)   7.157

MERCER UK, 1 Tower Place West, Tower Place, London, EC3R 5BU. Tel: 020 7626 6000. Fax: 020 7929 7445. Internet: www.mercer.com.

Stewards Company (J)   7.658

MFS INVESTMENT MANAGEMENT, Paternoster House, 65 St Paul's Churchyard, London, EC4M 8AM.

Health Foundation, The (J)   7.305

MIDAS CAPITAL PARTNERS LTD, Martins Building, Water Street, Liverpool, Merseyside, L2 3SP. Tel: 0151 906 2450.

Steinberg Family Charitable Trust, The (J)   7.657

MILLBANK INVESTMENT MANAGERS LIMITED, Pollen House, 10/12 Cork Street, London, W1S 3LW.

Parham Park Trust (1984)   7.491

MMIP INVESTMENT MANAMENT LTD, Trafalgar Court, Les Banques, St Peter Port, Guernsey, GY1 2JA. Tel: 01481 745153.

Blenheim Foundation, The   7.75

MONDRIAN INVESTMENT PARTNERS LIMITED, Fifth Floor, 10 Gresham Street, London, EC2V 7JD. Tel: 020 7477 7001. Fax: 020 7776 8512. Internet: ww.mondrian.com.

Health Foundation, The (J)   7.305

MORGAN STANLEY INVESTMENT MANAGEMENT, 25 Cabot Square, Canary Wharf, London, E14 4QA. Tel: 020 7425 8000. Fax: 020 7425 8990. Internet: www.morganstanley.com.

FIA Foundation for Automobile & Society (J)	7.252
Khodorkovsky Foundation (J)	7.370
Royal Ballet School Endowment Fund (J)	7.553
Royal College of Physicians of London (J)	7.557
Sloane Robinson Foundation	7.618
Teresa Ball International Solidarity Fund (J)	7.673

MORNINGSTAR ASSOCIATES EUROPE LTD, 1 Olivers Yard, 55/71 City Road, London, EC1Y 1HQ.

Reta Lila Howard Foundation (J)	7.533
Reta Lila Weston Tst for Medical Research (J)	7.533

NATIXIS GLOBAL ASSOCIATES UK, Cannon Bridge Street, 25 Dowgate Hill, London, EC4R 2YA. Tel: 020 3216 9757. Fax: 020 3216 9776. Internet: www.ngam.natixis.co.uk.

Council for World Mission (J)   7.182

NEUBERGER BERMAN MANAGEMENT LLC, Lansdowne House, 57 Berkeley Square, 4th Floor, London, W1J 6ER. Tel: 020 3214 9000. Internet: www.nb.com.

Council for World Mission (J)   7.182

NEWTON INVESTMENT MANAGEMENT LIMITED, The Bank of New York Mellon Centre, 160 Queen Victoria Street, London, EC4V 4LA. Tel: 0800 917 6594. E-mail: charities@newton.co.uk. Internet: www.newton.co.uk/charities.

Charity specialists: Hilary Meades (Portfolio Manager). Jeremy Wells (Investment Relationship Manager). Stephanie Gore (Charity Business Development Manager). Alan Goodwin (Head of Institutional&CharityInv Relationship Mgmt). Oliver Larminie (Portfolio Manager). Christopher Metcalfe (Portfolio Manager). Paul Mitchell (Investment Relationship Manager). Richard Sankey (Investment Relationship Manager). Bhavin Shah (Portfolio Manager). Robert Stewart (Portfolio Manager). Claire Blackwell (Head of Marketing). Kelly Tran.

Association of Commonwealth Universities	7.47
Biochemical Society	7.70
British Academy of Film & Television Arts (J)	7.91
British Museum	7.97
British Museum Trust Limited, The	7.97
Brooke Hospital for Animals (J)	7.101
Catch22 (J)	7.118
Central Foundation Schools of London (J)	7.122
CFBT Education Trust (J)	7.125
Charles Hayward Foundation (J)	7.131
Chartered Institute of Arbitrators	7.132
Chartered Quality Institute	7.135
Children's Society (J)	7.142
Cripplegate Foundation (J)	7.186
Croydon Almshouse Charities	7.187
Duchy of Lancaster Benevolent Fund	7.213
Duchy of Lancaster Jubilee Trust	7.213
Dulverton Trust (J)	7.214
Edward James Foundation Limited (J)	7.228
Fire Fighters Charity	7.254
Fishmongers' Company's Charitable Trust	7.255
Foundation of Lady Katherine Leveson, The (J)	7.260
General Conference of the New Church (J)	7.270
Goldsmiths' Company Charity	7.281
Great Ormond St Hosp Children's Charity (J)	7.285
GroceryAid (J)	7.289
Guide Dogs for the Blind Association (J)	7.291
Institute of Physics (J)	7.336
John Ellerman Foundation (J)	7.358
Lamport Hall Preservation Trust (J)	7.377
Leverhulme Trade Charities Trust (J)	7.386
Leverhulme Trust (J)	7.386
Marie Curie Cancer Care	7.410
Mary Kinross Charitable Trust	7.414
Medical Research Foundation	7.419
National Trust (J)	7.454
Newcastle Healthcare Charity	7.459
North Devon Hospice	7.466
North London Hospice	7.467
Order of Friars Minor (Capuchin) Province (J)	7.482
Oxford Diocesan Board Finance	7.487
PDSA (J)	7.494
Phillips & Rubens Charitable Trust (J)	7.501
Plymouth Diocesan Trust (J)	7.505
Plymouth Secular Clergy Fund (J)	7.506
RBS PeopleCharity, The	7.527
Representative Body of the Church in Wales	7.532
Royal Air Force Benevolent Fund (J)	7.550
Royal Astronomical Society	7.552
Royal British Legion Poppy Factory Limited	7.554
Royal College of Anaesthetists	7.555
Royal Geographical Society (J)	7.561
Royal Institute International Affairs	7.562
Royal Medical Benevolent Fund (J)	7.565
Royal Naval Benevolent Trust (J)	7.568
Royal Navy and Royal Marines Charity	7.568
Royal Opera House Covent Garden (J)	7.569
Royal Opera House Endowment Fund 2000 (J)	7.569
Rustington Convalescent Home Carpenters Co	7.578
Save the Children	7.588
Sir James Knott Trust	7.610
Sisters Holy Family Bordeaux (J)	7.616
Society for Promoting Christian Knowledge	7.620
Society for Assistance of Ladies (J)	7.621
Society of Jesus (J)	7.622
Montessori St Nicholas Charity, The (J)	7.652
Sutton's Hospital in Charterhouse (J)	7.666
University of Newcastle DevelopmentTrust (J)	7.701
Victim Support	7.704
Westminster Society (J)	7.723
William Adlington Cadbury Charitable Trust	7.729
WWF UK	7.743
Zoological Society of London	7.752

NORTHERN TRUST GLOBAL INVESTMENTS LTD,
50 Bank Street, Canary Wharf, London,
E14 5NT.

Church of England Pensions Board (J)　　　7.148

NORTHERN TRUST INVESTOR SERVICES
(IRELAND) LTD, Ulster Bank Group Centre,
George's Quay, Dublin.

Foyle Foundation (J)　　　　　　　　　7.261

NW BROWN INVESTMENT MANAGEMENT,
Richmond House, 16-20 Regent Street,
Cambridge, Cambridgeshire, CB2 1DB.
Tel: 01223 720 207.
E-mail: investment.management@nwbrown.co.u
k. Internet: www.nwbrown.co.uk.

BirdLife International　　　　　　　　7.70
Cambridge Crystallographic Data Centre　　7.108
Ely Diocesan Board of Finance, The (J)　　7.231
Leicester Diocesan Board Finance (J)　　　7.383

OBJECTIVE COMPLETION, M3 House, 71
London Road, Sevenoaks, Kent, TN13 1AX.
Tel: 01732 468 020.
Internet: www.objectivecompletion.co.uk.

Nuffield Foundation (J)　　　　　　　　7.474

OCM WEALTH MANAGEMENT, 3 Bouverie Court,
The Lakes, Northampton, Northamptonshire,
NN4 7YD. Tel: 0845 338 1971. Fax: 01604
628 396.
Internet: www.ocmwealthmanagement.co.uk.

Rosminian Sisters Providence　　　　　　7.545

ODEY ASSET MANAGEMENT, 12 Upper
Grosvenor Street, London, W1K 2ND. Tel: 020
72081400.

Joseph Rank Trust, The　　　　　　　　7.363
Royal Commission for the 1851 Exhibition (J)　7.558

ODIN INVESTMENT MANAGEMENT LIMITED,
Centenary House, La Grande Route de St
Pierre, Jersey, JE3 7AY.

Constance Green Foundation　　　　　　7.177

OLD MUTUAL FUND MANAGERS LTD, 2
Lambeth Place, London, EC4V 4AD. Tel: 020
7332 7500. Fax: 020 7489 5253.
Internet: www.omam.co.uk.

Trusthouse Charitable Foundation (J)　　7.690

OLDFIELD PARTNERS LLP, 130 Buckingham
Palalce Road, London, SW1W 9SA. Tel: 020
7259 1000. Fax: 020 7259 1010.
E-mail: info@oldfieldpartners.com.
Internet: www.oldfieldpartners.com.
Charity specialists: Jamie Carter. David Jones.

OLIM LIMITED, 15 Berkeley Street, London,
W1J 8DY. Tel: 020 7408 7290. Fax: 020 7408
7296. E-mail: julia_willis@olim.co.uk.
Internet: www.olim.co.uk.
Charity specialists: Angela M Lascelles (Portfolio).

Alan Edward Higgs Charity (J)　　　　　7.22
Burdett Trust for Nursing (J)　　　　　7.104
Royal Academy of Engineering　　　　　7.549
Smallpeice Trust　　　　　　　　　　7.618
Special Air Service Regimental Association　7.632
Stock Exchange Benevolent Fund　　　　7.659

ORIGIN FINANCIAL LTD, 28/29 Hagley Mews,
Hall Drive, Hagley, Stourbridge, West Midlands,
DY9 9LQ. Tel: 0800 0858 858.
E-mail: simon.williams@origin.eu.com.
Internet: www.origin.eu.com.

Groundwork UK (J)　　　　　　　　　7.290

OXFORD INVESTMENT PARTNERS, Christ
Church, Oxford, Oxfordshire, OX1 1DP.

Montessori St Nicholas Charity, The (J)　　7.652

PARTNERS CAPITAL

PARTNERS CAPITAL LLP, 5 Young Street,
London, W8 5EH. Tel: 020 7938 5200.
Fax: 020 7938 5201. Internet: www.partners-
cap.com.

> For more information see our profile in
> the front colour section

Charity specialists: Kelly Shek. N Rider.

PAYDEN & RYGEL GLOBAL LTD, 1 Bartholomew
Lane, London, EC2N 2AX. Tel: 020 7621 3000.
Fax: 020 7626 0897.
Internet: www.payden.com.

Council for World Mission (J)　　　　　7.182
Jordan Charitable Foundation (J)　　　　7.362

PICTET ASSET MANAGEMENT UK LTD, Moor
House, Level 11, 120 London Wall, London,
EC2Y 5ET. Tel: 020 7847 5000. Fax: 020 7847
5300.

Foundation for Social Entrepreneurs (J)　7.259
Marchig Animal Welfare Trust　　　　　7.409
Millennium Awards Trust, The (J)　　　　7.427

PIMCO EUROPE LTD., 11 Baker Street, London,
W1U 3AH. Tel: +44 (0) 20 3640 1000.
Fax: +44-(0) 20 3640 1007.
Internet: www.pimco.co.uk.

Dulverton Trust (J)　　　　　　　　　7.214
Leverhulme Trade Charities Trust (J)　　7.386
Leverhulme Trust (J)　　　　　　　　7.386
Westminster Foundation (J)　　　　　　7.723

PIRHO INVESTMENT CONSULTING LIMITED, 13
Austin Friars, London, WC2N 2HE. Tel: 44 (0)20
7489 6190.

Consumers' Association　　　　　　　7.178

POCOCK RUTHERFORD & COMPANY LTD,
Langwood House, 63-81 High Street,
Rickmansworth, Hertfordshire, WD3 1EQ.
Tel: 01727 833466.
E-mail: enquiries@pocockrutherford.com.
Internet: www.pocockrutherford.com.

NABS　　　　　　　　　　　　　　7.441

PREMIER ASSET MANAGEMENT LTD, Eastgate
Court, High Street, Guildford, Surrey, GU1 3DE.
Tel: 01483 306090.
Internet: www.premierassetmanagement.co.uk.

Society of St Columban for Foreign Missions　7.623

PRODIGY FINANCE LTD, Palladium House, 1-4
Argyll Street, London, W1F 7LD. Tel: 020 7193
2832. E-mail: info@prodigyfinance.com.
Internet: www.prodigyfinance.com.

Said Foundation (J)　　　　　　　　　7.581

PRYFORD INTERNATIONAL PLC, 95 Wigmore
Street, London, W1U 1HH. Tel: 020 7495 4641.
Fax: 020 7399 2204.
Internet: www.bmo.com/pyrford.

City Bridge Trust, The (J)　　　　　　7.153

PSIGMA INVESTMENT MANAGEMENT, 11
Strand Street, London, WC2N 5HR. Tel: 020
3327 5400. Fax: 020 7681 3963.
E-mail: info@psigmainvestments.com.
Internet: www.psigmaim.com.

Allen Lane Foundation　　　　　　　7.26
EBM Charitable Trust (J)　　　　　　7.223

PSIGMA INVESTMENT MANAGEMENT, 7 Castle
Street, Edinburgh, EH2 3AH. Tel: 0131
2300294. Fax: 01318778173.
Internet: www.psigma.com.

Mr & Mrs J A Pye's Charitable Settlement　7.437

QUILTER CHEVIOT
INVESTMENT MANAGEMENT

QUILTER CHEVIOT, One Kingsway, London,
WC2B 6AN. Tel: +44 (0)20 7150 4005.
Fax: +44 (0)20 7845 6155.
Internet: www.quiltercheviot.com.

Charity specialists: William Reid (Head of Charity Investment Management).

Alzheimer's Research UK	7.28
Beatrice Laing Trust	7.62
Bransby Horses (J)	7.85
British Small Animal Veterinary Assoc	7.99
Caritas Care	7.115
Marist Sisters	7.130
Christopher Laing Foundation (J)	7.146
Cinnamon Trust (J)	7.150
Colt Foundation	7.161
Cumbrian Community Foundation (J)	7.189
Daughters of Jesus, The (J)	7.193
East Cheshire Hospice	7.220
Elizabeth Frankland Moore & Star Fdn	7.230
Fairfield Charitable Trust	7.246
Inc Council of Law Reporting England Wales	7.330
International Students House	7.345
John Innes Foundation	7.358
Kathleen & Michael Connolly Foundation UK (J)	7.366
Kingsway International Christian Centre	7.373
Kirby Laing Foundation (J)	7.374
Lancaster Roman Catholic Diocesan Trust	7.378
Louis Baylis Charitable Trust (J)	7.403
Maria Assumpta Trust (J)	7.410
Needham Research Institute	7.456
Notts Roman Catholic Diocesan Trustees	7.473
Patrick & Helena Frost Foundation, The (J)	7.492
Poor Servants of the Mother of God	7.508
Redwings Horse Sanctuary	7.528
Religious of the Assumption (J)	7.531
TrusteesofCongregattionofMostHolyRedeemer	7.544
Royal College of Emergency Medicine, The	7.555
Royal Society Musicians Great Britain	7.573
Shaw Trust	7.599
Sir James Reckitt Charity, The	7.611
Sobell House Hospice Charity Limited	7.619
Society of Mary Reparatrice	7.622
St Barnabas Hospice Lincolnshire Trust	7.638
Talisman Charitable Trust	7.668
World Assoc of Girl Guides & Girl Scouts	7.739

QUILTER CHEVIOT, 8th Floor, 2 Snowhill, Birmingham, West Midlands, B4 6GA. Tel: +44 (0)121 212 2120. Fax: +44 (0)121 212 3130. Internet: www.quiltercheviot.com.

Edward Cadbury Charitable Trust	7.228
Ironbridge Gorge Museum Trust Limited	7.346
Johnson Association, The	7.361
St Mary's Hospice	7.650

QUILTER CHEVIOT, Queen's Quay, 33-35 Queen Square, Bristol, BS1 4LU. Tel: 0117 927 3377. Fax: 0117 927 3263. Internet: www.quiltercheviot.com.

Get Kids Going	7.273

QUILTER CHEVIOT, Delta House, 50 West Nile Street, Glasgow, G1 2NP. Tel: 0141 222 4000. Fax: 0141 222 4050. Internet: www.quiltercheviot.com.

Aberlour Child Care Trust	7.6
Prince and Princess of Wales Hospice (J)	7.513

QUILTER CHEVIOT, Provincial House, 37 New Walk, Leicester, Leicestershire, LE1 6TU. Tel: +44 (0)116 249 3000. Fax: +44 (0)116 247 1555. Internet: www.quiltercheviot.com.

Coventry Freemen's Charity	7.184
General Charity (Coventry)	7.270
King Henry VIII Endowed Trust Warwick (J)	7.372
Nicholas Chamberlaine School Foundation	7.462

QUILTER CHEVIOT, 4th Floor, The Pinnacle, 73 King Street, Manchester, Greater Manchester, M2 4NG. Tel: 0161 832 9979. Fax: 0161 832 9030. Internet: www.quiltercheviot.com.

Trinity Hospice & Palliative Care Services (J)	7.686
Yorkshire Cancer Research	7.749

QUILTER CHEVIOT, PO Box 276, 4th Floor, 28 - 30 The Parade, St Helier, Jersey, JE4 8TE. Tel: +44 (0)1534 506070. Fax: +44 (0)1534 768108. Internet: www.quiltercheviot.com.

Amateurs Trust, The (J)	7.29

RAHN & BODMER, Talstrasse 15, Postfach, Zurich.

Roger Raymond Charitable Trust (J)	7.542

Rathbone Greenbank Investments

RATHBONE GREENBANK INVESTMENTS, 10 Queen Square, Bristol, BS1 4NT. Tel: 020 7399 0000. E-mail: greenbank@rathbone.com. Internet: www.rathbonegreenbank.com.

Increasing numbers of charities are considering how to ensure that their investments are consistent with their mission, or indeed how the nature of their investments might further that mission.

Rathbone Greenbank Investments is a specialist ethical investment team, providing personalised and professional investment services for charities who wish to ensure that their investments take account of their environmental, social and ethical concerns whilst still achieving their financial aims.

Rathbone Greenbank Investments is part of Rathbone Investment Management Limited (A subsidiary of Rathbone Brothers Plc) through which it has the backing of one of the UK's largest and longest-established providers of high-quality discretionary investment management services.

The value of investments and income arising from them may fall as well as rise and you might get back less than you originally invested. Rathbone Investment Management Ltd is authorised and regulated by the Financial Services Authority. Please note, the FSA will be replaced as our regulator by the Financial Conduct Authority (FCA) and the Prudential Regulatory Authority (PRA) within the first half of 2013.

Charity specialists: John David (Head of Rathbone Greenbank Investments). Nicola Day (Investment Director, Bristol). Kate Elliot. Victoria Hoskins (Investment Director London). Jane Wilcock.

Brit.YearlyMtngofTheReligiousSocietyofFriends	7.90
Polden Puckham Charitable Foundation	7.506

RATHBONE GREENBANK INVESTMENTS, Port of Liverpool Building, Pier Head, Liverpool, Merseyside, L3 1NW. Tel: 0151 236 6666.

Blagrave Trust, The (J)	7.74
Joseph & Annie Cattle Trust	7.362

Rathbones
Look forward

RATHBONE INVESTMENT MANAGEMENT LTD, 1 Curzon Street, London, W1J 5FB. Tel: 020 7399 0359. E-mail: james.brennan@rathbones.com. Internet: www.rathbones.com/charities.

Rathbones welcomes charities of all shapes and sizes

We like to work in partnership with our charity clients which means you will have direct access to the person managing your charity's investments, resulting in a portfolio that accurately meets your needs and is as individual as your charity.

Key facts

- £3.53 billion of charitable funds under management
- Over 1,000 charities
- Segregated or pooled investment
- Dedicated team of charity investment specialists
- A history grounded in philanthropy

All figures as at 31st December 2015

Charity specialists: Ivo Clifton (Head of Charities and Specialist Business). James Brennan (Head of Business Development - Charities). Alex Dow. James Codrington. James Pettit. Alex Turnbull. Andrew Pitt (Head of Charities - London). Libby Barrett. Olivia Merrick. Gareth Pearl.

Aberdeen Endowments Trust (J)	7.5
Alan Edward Higgs Charity (J)	7.22
Alder Hey Children's Charity, The	7.23
Ambitious about Autism	7.29
Asthma UK	7.47
B G Campbell Trust Fund	7.53
Band Trust (J)	7.55
Benevolent Fund Institution of Civil Engineers	7.65
Blue Cross	7.76
Booth Charities (J)	7.79
British School of Osteopathy	7.98
Brunts Charity (J)	7.102
Butchers & Drovers Charitable Inst (J)	7.105
Catholic Blind Institute	7.119
Cats Protection	7.120
Cecil Alan Pilkington Trust Fund (J)	7.121
Charity for Roman Catholic Congregation (J)	7.128
Charity of Sir Richard Whittington (J)	7.129
Charity of Thomas Dawson	7.130
Chatham Maritime Trust	7.136
COLET (J)	7.154
Clare Milne Trust (J)	7.155
Coal Industry Social Welfare Organisation	7.158
Community Foundation for Calderdale (J)	7.162
Community Foundation Wales (J)	7.163
Community of the Holy Cross (J)	7.166
Compassion in World Farming	7.168
Congregation of La Retraite Trustees (J)	7.171
Good Shepherd Sisters	7.171
Congregation of Our Lady of Sion (J)	7.172
Congregation of the Brothers of Charity	7.172
Congregation of the Sisters of St Anne (J)	7.175
Coram (J)	7.179
Countryside Restoration Trust	7.182
Daughters of Jesus, The (J)	7.193
Dibden Allotments Fund	7.201
Disabilities Trust	7.201
Dominican Sisters Congregation Newcastle	7.204
Doris Field Charitable Trust (J)	7.207
Dorothy House Foundation Ltd	7.208
Dulwich Picture Gallery	7.215
Dunhill Medical Trust (J)	7.216
Earl of Northampton's Charity (J)	7.219

East End Community Foundation (J)	7.221
East Kilbride District Eng Grp Training Assoc	7.221
Eleanor Rathbone Charitable Trust [The]	7.229
Emmanuel Community Charitable Trust Ltd	7.232
Evan Cornish Foundation	7.242
General Conference of the New Church (J)	7.270
Goodenough College	7.281
Hamps & Isle of Wight Air Ambulance (J)	7.298
Hampshire & Isle of Wight Community Fdn (J)	7.298
Healthcare Management Trust, The	7.306
Heathcoat Trust	7.307
Hereford Diocesan Board Finance	7.309
Hospice of Our Lady & St John	7.319
Hyde Park Place Estate Charity (J)	7.326
ifs School of Finance	7.328
Institution of Chemical Engineers (J)	7.337
Institution of Eng Technology Ben Fund	7.338
International Fund for Animal Welfare (J)	7.342
Jesus Hospital Charity in Chipping Barnet (J)	7.353
John Innes Foundation (J)	7.358
Jones 1986 Charitable Trust (J)	7.362
Lamport Hall Preservation Trust (J)	7.377
Leathersellers Company Charitable Fund	7.381
Leeds Teaching Hospitals Charitable Fdn	7.382
Leeds Theatre Trust	7.382
Leprosy Mission International	7.385
Liverpool Merchants Guild	7.393
Liverpool PSS	7.393
Llandaff Diocesan Board Finance	7.394
Lord Crewe's Charity	7.402
Martlets Hospice Limited	7.413
Merchant Taylors' Consolidated Charities	7.422
Mercy Ships - UK	7.423
Midlands Air Ambulance Charity	7.426
Musicians Benevolent Fund (J)	7.440
National Benevolent Charity, The	7.443
National Childbirth Trust	7.444
New England Company	7.457
Newby Trust	7.459
Norfolk Community Foundation (J)	7.464
Northampton RC Diocesan Trust (J)	7.468
Orthopaedic Research UK	7.484
Panacea Society	7.490
Perennial (J)	7.498
Perseverance Trust	7.498
Peter Lang Children's Trust Limited	7.499
Pilling Trust Fund, The	7.504
Quality Assurance Agency for HE (J)	7.518
Queen's Nursing Institute (J)	7.520
Radcliffe Trust, The	7.523
Rayne Foundation	7.526
Rochester Bridge Trust	7.541
Roy Castle Lung Cancer Foundation	7.548
Royal Agricultural Benevolent Institution	7.550
Royal Air Forces Association	7.551
Royal Alfred Seafarers' Society	7.552
Royal Society for Prevention Accidents	7.571
Royal Society, The	7.573
Salesians of Don Bosco UK	7.582
Sandra Charitable Trust (J)	7.586
Scripture Union	7.594
Sir Harold Hood Charitable Trust	7.610
Sir Malcolm Stewart Bart Gen. Trust	7.612
Sisters of St Joseph Province (J)	7.615
Presentation Sisters	7.616
SS Great Britain Trust	7.635
St Asaph Diocesan Board of Finance (J)	7.638
St Barnabas Hospices (Sussex) Ltd	7.638
St Clement Danes Holborn Estate Charity (J)	7.641
St David's Diocesan Board of Finance	7.641
St Margaret's Somerset Hospice	7.649
St Michael's Hospice Hastings	7.651
St Nicholas Hospice Care (J)	7.652
St Olave's & St Saviour's Schools Foundation	7.652
St Peter & St James Charitable Trust	7.653
St Peter's Home and Sisterhood	7.653
Stewardship Services (UKET) Ltd (J)	7.658
Suffolk Foundation, The (J)	7.663
Sutton Coldfield Municipal Charities	7.666
Talbot Village Trust	7.668
Teesside Hospice Care Foundation	7.671
Ty Hafan (J)	7.692
Union Sisters Mercy Great Britain	7.695
USPG (J)	7.702
Victoria Foundation, The (J)	7.705
W F Southall Trust	7.710
Walcot Educational Foundation (J)	7.711
Walk the Walk Worldwide	7.712
Weldmar Hospicecare Trust	7.717
Weston Hospicecare (J)	7.723
Wrexham (Parochial) Educational Fdn	7.742
Wycliffe UK Ltd	7.743

RBC WEALTH MANAGEMENT, Riverbank House, 2 Swan Lane, London, EC4R 3BF. Tel: 020 7653 4594.
Charity specialists: Pat Moody.

Babraham Institute	7.53
John Moores Foundation	7.360

RCM, 155 Bishopsgate, London, EC2M 3AD. Tel: 020 7859 9000. Fax: 020 7638 3507. E-mail: philip.dawes@uk.rcm.com; helen.palmer@uk.rcm.com.
Charity specialists: P Dawes.

Islamic Trust (J)	7.347

REDMAYNE BENTLEY, 9 Bond Court, Leeds, West Yorkshire, S1 2JZ. Tel: 0113 243 6941. E-mail: info@redmayne.co.uk. Internet: www.redmayne.co.uk.

Yorkshire Air Ambulance (J)	7.749

RIVER & MERCANTILE ASSET MANAGEMENT LLP, 30 Coleman Street, London, EC2R 5 AL. Tel: 020 7601 6262. Fax: 020 7600 2426. E-mail: www.riverandmercantile.com. Internet: 20 7600 2426.

Health Foundation, The (J)	7.305

ROTHSCHILD (CI) LIMITED, St Julian's Court, St Peter Port, Guernsey, Channel Islands, GY1 3BP. Tel: 01481 713713. Fax: 01481 727715.

Sheepdrove Trust, The	7.600

ROTHSCHILD WEALTH MANAGEMENT (UK) LIMITED, New Court, St. Swithin's Lane, London, EC4N 8AL. Tel: 020 7280 1732. Fax: 020 7280 1514. E-mail: nandu.patel@rothschild.com. Internet: www.rothschild.com.

A charity's assets are precious, and usually irreplaceable.

Any investment strategy must focus on preserving and growing these assets.

At Rothschild, we have developed a distinctive investment approach that meets a charity's long-term spending needs as well as growing its portfolio ahead of inflation, without jeopardising capital.

We build portfolios with two distinct parts - one side focused on 'return assets' or opportunities for growth and the other on mitigating risk through 'diversifying assets' that offer protection.

By combining assets in the way we do, the portfolio can deliver inflation-beating returns while cushioning against inevitable challenges on the investment road.

In our seventh generation of family controlled ownership, Rothschild is a safe and secure home for a charity's assets.

Our approach is being welcomed by an increasing number of charities, endowments and foundations, which rely on our dedicated and experienced Charities Team to advise on and manage their investments.

Charity specialists: Nandu Patel (Head of Charities). Tracy Collins (Director). Dario Siciliano (Associate). Abel Seow (Analyst).

Central Young Men's Christian Association	7.123
Charity of Sir Richard Whittington (J)	7.129
Cinema and Television Benevolent Fund	7.150
Earl of Northampton's Charity (J)	7.219
Glyndebourne Arts Trust	7.278
Glyndebourne Productions Limited	7.279
Kennedy Leigh Charitable Trust	7.368
Kusuma Trust UK (J)	7.375
Mercers' Charitable Foundation	7.422
Rothschild Archive Ltd	7.546
Sterling Charity, The	7.658
Weizmann Institute Foundation	7.717

ROYAL LONDON

ROYAL LONDON ASSET MANAGEMENT, 55 Gracechurch Street, London, EC3V ORL. Tel: +44(0)20 7506 6754. Fax: +44(0)20 7506 6796. E-mail: philip.clifford@rlam.co.uk. Internet: www.rlam.co.uk.

Royal London Asset Management (RLAM) is one of the UK's leading investment companies for the charity sector. RLAM has built a strong reputation as an innovative manager, investing across all major asset classes and delivering consistent long-term outperformance. RLAM manages over £83 billion of assets*, split between equities, fixed interest, property and cash, with a market leading capability in sustainable investing.

RLAM has around 150 charity clients from a wide variety of areas, including medical, religious and educational foundations. We are proud to manage £2.4 billion* on their behalf. We pride ourselves on the breadth and quality of the investment options we offer, and we recognise that your main focus is your charitable activity; ours is to construct the best possible investment portfolio to meet your risk and return objectives. Whatever your requirements, we are well positioned to offer a solution.

Over 150 clients across

- Education
- Religious bodies
- Health
- Financial and professional bodies
- Royal societies

*As at 30th September 2015

Charity specialists: Philip Clifford.

Please mention

Top 3000 Charities

when responding to advertisements

RUFFER LLP, 80 Victoria Street, London, SW1E 5JL. Tel: 0207 963 8100. Fax: 0207 963 8175. E-mail: cqueree@ruffer.co.uk. Internet: www.ruffer.co.uk.

At Ruffer, we have a distinctive approach to investing focused on delivering consistent positive returns, regardless of how the financial markets perform. Instead of following benchmarks, Ruffer simply aims not to lose money on a 12 month rolling basis and to deliver a return greater than the return on cash. We believe that the majority of the investment industry continues to suffer from benchmarking against market-weighted indices, which has the unintended consequence of moving the management of market risk from investment managers (where it belongs) to the trustees. At Ruffer, we believe this is wrong and work to protect and grow the value of charities' assets throughout the market cycle. Ruffer Group manages £18 billion to include over £2 billion for a diverse range of charity clients.

Ruffer LLP is authorised and regulated by the Financial Conduct Authority

29th May 1961 Charitable Trust (J)	7.2
Action Medical Research	7.11
Addenbrooke's Charitable Trust	7.13
Anna Freud Centre	7.33
Archbishops' Council (J)	7.37
Arthritis Research UK (J)	7.40
Arundel Castle Trustees	7.42
Association of Accounting Technicians	7.46
Baily Thomas Charitable Fund, The (J)	7.54
Bankers Benevolent Fund, The	7.55
Baring Foundation (J)	7.57
Barnardo's	7.57
Booth Charities (J)	7.79
Buckfast Abbey Trust (J)	7.103
Burdett Trust for Nursing (J)	7.104
Buttle Trust	7.106
Campaign to Protect Rural England	7.110
Campden Charities Trustee (J)	7.110
Charles Hayward Foundation (J)	7.131
Children's Society (J)	7.142
Childwick Trust	7.142
Church Army	7.147
City Bridge Trust, The (J)	7.153
COLET (J)	7.154
Comm. Foundation for Wiltshire & Swindon (J)	7.163
Compton Verney Fund (J)	7.170
Coram (J)	7.179
Country Houses Foundation	7.182
Cripplegate Foundation (J)	7.186
Cumbrian Community Foundation (J)	7.189
DHL UK Foundation	7.200
Duke of Edinburgh's Award Intl Foundation (J)	7.214
Duke of Edinburgh's Award (J)	7.214
Edge Foundation	7.224
Essex Community Foundation (J)	7.240
Fellowship of School of Economic Science (J)	7.251
Foyle Foundation (J)	7.261
Game & Wildlife Conservation Trust	7.268
Grand Charity, The (J)	7.284
Great Ormond St Hosp Children's Charity (J)	7.285

Grimsthorpe and Drummond Castle Trust	7.288
Help for Heroes (J)	7.308
Henry Moore Foundation (J)	7.309
Holburne Museum (J)	7.314
Institute of Advanced Motorists (J)	7.333
Institute of Physics (J)	7.336
Institution of Chemical Engineers (J)	7.337
Jean Sainsbury Animal Welfare Trust (J)	7.352
John Ellerman Foundation (J)	7.358
Joseph Rowntree Foundation (J)	7.363
LankellyChase Foundation, The (J)	7.379
Leeds Castle Foundation	7.381
Lempriere Pringle Charitable Trust, The	7.384
Liz and Terry Bramall Charitable Trust, The (J)	7.394
Med Col of St Bartholomew's Hospital (J)	7.419
Northampton RC Diocesan Trust (J)	7.468
Nuffield Trst for Res.&Pol.Studies in Health	7.475
Oakhaven Trust	7.476
Oxford Radcliffe Hospitals Charitable Fund	7.488
P H Holt Foundation (J)	7.489
Patrick & Helena Frost Foundation, The (J)	7.492
Plymouth Diocesan Trust (J)	7.505
Plymouth Secular Clergy Fund (J)	7.506
Racing Foundation, The (J)	7.523
Rainbow Trust Children's Charity	7.524
Royal College of General Practitioners	7.556
Royal College of Physicians of London (J)	7.557
Royal Geographical Society (J)	7.561
Royal Masonic Trust For Girls and Boys (J)	7.565
Royal Medical Benevolent Fund (J)	7.565
Seafarers UK (J)	7.594
Sir Jules Thorn Charitable Trust (J)	7.612
Southwell Diocesan Board Finance (J)	7.631
St Leonard's Hospice York	7.646
St Saviour's Medical Charity	7.654
St Wilfrid's Hospice (South Coast)	7.655
Stewards Company (J)	7.658
Treloar Trust	7.685
UFI Charitable Trust (J)	7.692
Univ Old Members' Trust, The (J)	7.699
Valentine Charitable Trust, The (J)	7.702
Westminster Foundation (J)	7.723
Westminster Society (J)	7.723
Weston Park Foundation	7.724

RUSSELL INVESTMENTS LIMITED, Rex House, 10 Regent Street, London, SW1Y 4PE. Tel: 020 7024 6000. Internet: www.russell.com.

Papworth Trust	7.490

RUSSELL ULYATT FINANCIAL SERVICES LTD, 1 The Triangle, ng2 Business Park, Nottingham, Nottinghamshire, NG2 1AE. Tel: 0115 907 5100. Fax: 0115 986 6306. E-mail: info@russellulyatt.co.uk. Internet: www.russellulyatt.co.uk.

British Trust for Ornithology	7.99

RWC PARTNERS LTD, 60 Petty France, London, SW1H 9EU. Tel: +44 20 7227 6000. Fax: +44 20 7227 6003. E-mail: invest@rwcpartners.com. Internet: www.rwcpartners.com.

Dulverton Trust (J)	7.214

SAND AIRE LIMITED, 105 Wigmore Street, London, W1U 1QY. Tel: 020 7290 5200. Fax: 020 7495 0240. E-mail: info@sandaire.co.uk. Internet: www.sandaire.com.

Francis C Scott Charitable Trust (J)	7.262
Ingram Trust (J)	7.331
Peacock Charitable Trust	7.495
Stone Family Foundation, The (J)	7.660

SANLAM PRIVATE WEALTH, Bank House, 55 Main Street, Kirkby Lonsdale, Cumbria, LA6 2AH. Fax: 015242 72941. Internet: www.spi.sanlam.co.uk.

Bolton Hospice (J)	7.78
Brathay Trust	7.85

SANTANDER ASSET MANAGEMENT UK LIMITED, 2 Triton Square, Regent's Place, London, NW1 3AN. Internet: www.santanderam.co.uk.

Wirral Autistic Society (J)	7.733

SANTANDER ASSET MANAGEMENT UK LIMITED, 287 St. Vicent Street, Glasgow, G2 5NB.

Santander UK Foundation Limited	7.587

SARASIN
& PARTNERS

SARASIN & PARTNERS LLP, Juxon House, 100 St Paul's Churchyard, London, EC4M 8BU. Tel: 020 7038 7000. Fax: 020 7038 6864. E-mail: john.handford@sarasin.co.uk. Internet: www.sarasinandpartners.com.

Sarasin & Partners manage investments of £5.3 billion* for a variety of 370 charities, representing over 39% of our total Assets under Management.

Underpinning our personalised service is the philosophy that we provide investment strategies to suit any charity's specific needs. Our particular expertise is determining and reviewing the appropriate mix of asset classes suitable to meet the circumstances of each charity.

We are well known for our commitment to education having trained over 3,800 trustees. The reference for this training is our Compendium of Investment – written to support charities plan their investment policy in conjunction with their chosen manager –its 20th edition will be published March 2016.

*As at 31 December 2015. Sarasin & Partners LLP is a limited liability partnership registered in England and Wales with registered number OC329859 and is authorised and regulated by the Financial Conduct Authority.

Charity specialists: R J Maitland - specialist area: Head of Charities. O R H Bates. M J G Black. R G R Boddington. H F Boucher. R Dunluce. L J M Harris. S Jeffries. J G E Monson. S M Rivett-Carnac. R Duncan. J Fishbourne. J Hutton. C Pease. M Roberts. E Salvesen. A True. R White. H Clarfelt. J Handford (Head of Charity Marketing) - specialist area: Head of Charity Marketing.

SETANTA ASSET MANAGEMENT, College Park House, 20 Nassau Street, Dublin 2, Dublin. E-mail: info@setanta-asset.com. Internet: www.setanta-asset.com.

Teresa Ball International Solidarity Fund (J)	7.673

SEVEN INVESTMENT MANAGEMENT LTD, 125 Old Broad Street, London, EC2N 1AR. Tel: 0207 760 8777. Fax: 0207 760 8799. E-mail: information@7im.co.uk. Internet: www.7im.co.uk.

Norwood	7.472
Sisters of Charity of St Vincent de Paul (J)	7.613

SG HAMBROS BANK LIMITED, Norfolk House, 31 St James's Square, London, SW1Y 4JR. Tel: +44 20 7597 3000. Internet: www.privatebanking.societegenerale.co.uk.

Douai Abbey	7.209

Jones 1986 Charitable Trust (J)   7.362
Maurice & Vivienne Wohl Philanthropic Fdn (J)   7.417

SILCHESTER INTERNATIONAL INVESTORS LTD,
1 Bruton Street, London, W1J 6TL. Tel: 020
7468 5900.

Dunhill Medical Trust (J)   7.216

SLATER INVESTMENT LIMITED, Nicholas House,
3 Laurence Pountney Hill, London, EC4R 0EU.
Tel: 020 7220 9460. Fax: 020 7220 9469.
E-mail: ralphb@slaterinvestments.com.
Internet: www.slaterinvestments.com.

Aspinall Foundation, The   7.44

SMITH & WILLIAMSON INVESTMENT
MANAGEMENT LTD, 25 Moorgate, London,
EC2R 6AY. Tel: 020 7131 4200. Fax: 020 7131
4001.
E-mail: willie.hartleyrussell@smith.williamson.co
.uk. Internet: www.sandwcharities.com.

Action on Hearing Loss   7.11
Aston-Mansfield Charitable Trust   7.47
Brampton Trust   7.84
Bristol Charities (J)   7.89
British Heart Foundation (J)   7.93
British Kidney Patient Association   7.95
Burdett Trust for Nursing (J)   7.104
Chatsworth House Trust   7.136
Cheshire Residential Homes (J)   7.137
Cong of the Daughters of the Cross of Liege   7.173
Duke of Devonshire's Charitable Trust   7.213
Elizabeth Finn Care (J)   7.230
Francis C Scott Charitable Trust (J)   7.262
James Tudor Foundation, The   7.351
John Ellerman Foundation (J)   7.358
NFER (J)   7.446
Nigel Vinson Charitable Trust   7.463
Nottingham University Hospitals General Fund   7.473
Old Swinford Hospital   7.479
Philip King Charitable Trust (J)   7.501
Retail Trust   7.533
Samuel Sebba Charitable Trust (J)   7.586
Society ofthe Holy Child Jesus Eur.Province (J)   7.624
St Andrew's Healthcare   7.636
St Catherine's Hospice Limited   7.639
Summerfield Charitable Trust   7.664
Thomson Media Foundation, The   7.678
Vocational Training Charitable Trust   7.708

SMITH & WILLIAMSON INVESTMENT
MANAGEMENT LTD, 9 Colmore Row,
Birmingham, West Midlands, B3 2BJ. Tel: 0121
710 5200. Fax: 0121 710 5201.
E-mail: adrian.taylor@smith.williamson.co.uk.
Internet: www.smith.williamson.co.uk.

Acorns Children's Hospice Trust   7.9
Birmingham Diocesan Board Finance   7.71
Birmingham Royal Ballet   7.73
Booth Charities (J)   7.79
George Cadbury Fund B Account   7.272
Harborne Parish Lands Charity   7.301
Lady Elizabeth Hastings' Charities   7.376
LOROS   7.384
Salford Diocesan Trust   7.582
Severn Hospice   7.598
Sisters of Charity of St Paul   7.613

SMITH & WILLIAMSON INVESTMENT
MANAGEMENT LTD, Portwall Place, Portwall
Lane, Bristol, BS1 6NA. Tel: 0117 376 2223.
Fax: 0117 376 2001.
E-mail: ian.richley@smith.williamson.co.uk.
Internet: www.smith.williamson.co.uk.

Bristol Benevolent Institution   7.89
Bristol, Clifton, & West of England Zoo   7.89
Clifton Diocesan Trust   7.156
Clifton Suspension Bridge Trust   7.156
Comm. Foundation for Wiltshire & Swindon (J)   7.163
North Bristol NHS Trust Charitable Funds   7.465
Quartet Community Foundation (J)   7.519
St John's Hospital (J)   7.645
St Mary Redcliffe Vestry   7.650
St Peter's Hospice   7.654

SOMERSET CAPITAL MANAGEMENT LLP, Third
Floor, 146 Buckingham Palace Road, London,
SW1W 9TR. Tel: 020 7499 1815. Fax: 020
7259 0514. Internet: www.somersetcm.com.

Dunhill Medical Trust (J)   7.216
Henry Moore Foundation (J)   7.309

SPEIRS & JEFFREY LTD, George House, 50
George Square, Glasgow, G2 1EH. Tel: 0141
248 4311. Fax: 0141 552 7175.
E-mail: russell.crichton@speirsjeffrey.co.uk.
Internet: www.speirsjeffrey.co.uk.
Charity specialists: R Crichton (Chief Executive). M
Wilson.

Baird Trust   7.54
Foundation Scotland (J)   7.260
Foyle Foundation (J)   7.261
National Galleries of Scotland Foundation   7.447
Nineveh Charitable Trust   7.463
Oxford Group   7.488
Quarriers   7.519
Royal Col. Physicians & Surgeons Glasgow   7.557
Royal Society of Edinburgh   7.572
Souter Charitable Trust (J)   7.628
YHA (England and Wales)   7.744

ST JAMES'S PLACE, St. James's Place House,
1 Tetbury Road, Cirencester, Gloucestershire,
GL7 1FP. Tel: 0800 0138 137.
Internet: www.sjp.co.uk.

Edmund Rice Bicentennial Trust Ltd (J)   7.226
Salisbury Diocesan Board Finance (J)   7.583

STANDARD LIFE INVESTMENTS, 1 George
Street, Edinburgh, EH2 2LL. Tel: 0131 245
0055. Fax: 0131 245 6105.
Internet: www.standardlifeinvestments.co.uk.

Children's Hospice Association Scotland (J)   7.141
City Bridge Trust, The (J)   7.153
Duke of Edinburgh's Award Intl Foundation (J)   7.214
Duke of Edinburgh's Award (J)   7.214
Guide Dogs for the Blind Association (J)   7.291
Inst of Marine Engineering, Science & Tech   7.335
PDSA (J)   7.494
Queenscourt Hospice (J)   7.521
R S Macdonald Charitable Trust (J)   7.522
Said Foundation (J)   7.581
Scottish Catholic International Aid Fund   7.591
Stewards Company (J)   7.658
Trusthouse Charitable Foundation (J)   7.690
VSA (J)   7.709
Yorkshire Agricultural Society (J)   7.748

STANDARD LIFE WEALTH, 30 St Mary Axe, 14th
Floor, London, EC3A 8EP. Tel: 020 7868 5700.
Internet: www.standardlifewealth.com.

Catholic Care (Diocese of Leeds)   7.119
Community Foundation for Leeds (J)   7.163
Consolidated Charity of Burton upn Trent   7.177
Cornwall Hospice Care   7.180
Foundation Scotland (J)   7.260
Liz and Terry Bramall Charitable Trust, The (J)   7.394
LTA Trust, The (J)   7.404
Queen's Nursing Institute (J)   7.520
St Mary Magdalene & Holy Jesus Trust (J)   7.649
St Nicholas Hospice Care (J)   7.652

STANHOPE CONSULTING, 35 Portman Square,
London, W1H 6LR. Tel: 020 7725 1800.
Fax: 020 7725 1801.
E-mail: enquiries@stanhopecapital.com.
Internet: www.stanhopecapital.com.

Alternative Futures Group Ltd   7.27
Baily Thomas Charitable Fund, The (J)   7.54
Barnwood House Trust   7.58
British Heart Foundation (J)   7.93
Dunhill Medical Trust (J)   7.216
Earl Fitzwilliam Charitable Trust (J)   7.218
Eveson Charitable Trust (J)   7.243
Fitzwilliam Wentworth Amenity Trust   7.255
Henry Moore Foundation (J)   7.309
Lennox Wyfold Foundation   7.384
Motability Tenth Anniversary Trust, The (J)   7.435

STATE STREET GLOBAL ADVISORS, 20 Churchill
Place, Canary Wharf, London, E14 5HJ.
Tel: 020 3395 6000. Fax: 020 3395 6350.

Education Endowment Foundation, The (J)   7.227

STONE HARBOR INVESTMENT PARTNERS, 48
Dover Street, 5th Floor, London, W1S 4FF.
Tel: 020 3205 4100.

Health Foundation, The (J)   7.305

T ROWE PRICE INTERNATIONAL LTD, 60 Queen
Victoria Street, London, EC4N 4TZ. Tel: 020
7651 8200.
Internet: www.corporate.troweprice.com.

Church of England Pensions Board (J)   7.148

TAUBE HODSON STONEX PARTNERS, Cassini
House, 57-59 St James's Street, London,
SW1A 1LD. Tel: 020 7659 4220. Fax: 020
7659 4222. Internet: www.thspartners.com.

Foundation for Social Entrepreneurs (J)   7.259
Millennium Awards Trust, The (J)   7.427

THE CO-OPERATIVE ASSET MANAGEMENT,
22nd Floor, Miller Street, Manchester, Greater
Manchester, M60 0AL. Tel: 0161 903 9986.
Fax: 0161 903 5896. Internet: http://co-
operativeassetmanagement.co.uk.

Vibrance (J)   7.704

THESIS ASSET MANAGEMENT PLC, St John's
Street, Chichester, West Sussex, PO19 1UP.
Tel: 01243 531234. Fax: 01243 539094.
E-mail: michael.lally@thesis-plc.com.
Internet: www.thesis-plc.com.

A Team Foundation   7.4
Aldingbourne Trust   7.24
Institute of Brewing & Distilling (J)   7.334
St Michael's Hospice   7.651

THOMAS MILLER INVESTMENT LTD, 90
Fenchurch Street, London, EC3M 4ST. Tel: 020
7204 2200. Fax: 020 7204 2737.
E-mail: invest@thomasmiller.com.
Internet: www.tminvestment.com.

Society of Chemical Industry   7.622

THREADNEEDLE INVESTMENTS, 60 St. Mary's
Axe, London, EC3A 8JQ. Tel: 020 7464 5540.
Fax: 020 7464 5793.
Internet: www.threadneedle.com.
Charity specialists: Jennifer Athill.

Zurich Community (UK) Trust   7.753

THURLEIGH INVESTMENT MANAGERS LLP, 3rd
Floor, Foxglove House, 166 Piccadilly, London,
W1J 9EF. Tel: 020 7016 3040.
Internet: www.thurleigh.com.

Edward Penley Abraham Research Fund (J)   7.228
Guy Newton Research Fund (J)   7.293
Hintze Family Charitable Foundation, The   7.313

TILNEY BESTINVEST, Royal Liver Building, Pier
Head, Liverpool, Merseyside, L3 1NY. Tel: 0151
515 4526. Internet: www.tilneybestinvest.co.uk.

Cecil Alan Pilkington Trust Fund (J)   7.121
Cecil Pilkington Charitable Trust   7.122
Derian House Children's Hospice   7.198
James Pantyfedwen Foundation   7.350
Lady Hewleys Charity   7.376
MGS Trust   7.424
NUMAST Welfare Funds   7.475
P H Holt Foundation (J)   7.489

TOWER WATSON INVESTMENT MANAGEMENT,
21 Tothill Street, Westminster, London,
SW1H 9LL. Tel: 020 7222 8033. Fax: 020
7222 9182. Internet: www.towerswatson.com.

Gray's Inn Scholarships Trust   7.284

TRADITION (UK) LIMITED, Beaufort House, 15
St Botolph Street, London, EC3A 7QX.

London Housing Foundation   7.399

TRILOGY GLOBAL ADVISORS LP, 23 Austin Friars, London, EC2N 2QP. Tel: 0203 170 8057. Fax: 0203 427 3029. Internet: www.trilogyadvisors.com.

Church of England Pensions Board (J)	7.148

TROY ASSET MANAGEMENT LIMITED, 33 Davies Street, London, W1K 4BP. Tel: 0207 290 7850. Fax: 0207 491 2445. E-mail: fvw@taml.co.uk. Internet: www.taml.co.uk.

Baring Foundation (J)	7.57
Burdett Trust for Nursing (J)	7.104
Gatsby Charitable Foundation	7.270
Henry Moore Foundation (J)	7.309
Kay Kendall Leukaemia Fund	7.366
Linbury Trust (J)	7.389
Med Col of St Bartholomew's Hospital (J)	7.419
New College Development Fund	7.457
P H Holt Foundation (J)	7.489
Racing Welfare	7.523
Royal Ballet School Endowment Fund (J)	7.553
Royal Horticultural Society (J)	7.561
Royal Opera House Covent Garden (J)	7.569
Royal Opera House Endowment Fund 2000 (J)	7.569
Sobell Foundation	7.619
Stansted Park Foundation	7.656
Sutton's Hospital in Charterhouse (J)	7.666
Tennis Foundation	7.672
Westminster Foundation (J)	7.723
Winston Churchill Memorial Trust	7.732

UBS GLOBAL ASSET MANAGEMENT (UK) LTD., 21 Lombard Street, London, EC3V 9AH.

S Lon Ch Fund&Sthwk Diocesan Bd Fin (J)	7.629

UBS WEALTH MANAGEMENT, 1 Finsbury Avenue, London, EC2M 2PP. Tel: 020 7568 5805. Fax: 020 7567 5656. Internet: www.ubs.com/charities-uk.

VANGUARD INVESTMENTS UK, 50 Cannon Street, London, EC4N 6JJ. Tel: 0800 408 2065. Internet: www.vanguard.co.uk.

Clothworkers' Foundation (J)	7.157
Foyle Foundation (J)	7.261
World Society for the Protection of Animals	7.741

VERITAS ASSET MANAGEMENT(UK) LTD, Elizabeth House, 6th Floor, 39 York Road, London, SE1 7NQ. Tel: 020 7961 1600. Fax: 020 7961 1602. E-mail: privateclientservices@veritas-asset.com. Internet: www.veritas-asset.com.

AQA Education (J)	7.35
Bishop Radford Trust, The (J)	7.73
Children's Society (J)	7.142
City Bridge Trust, The (J)	7.153
Coram (J)	7.179
Foyle Foundation (J)	7.261
Help for Heroes (J)	7.308
Jewish Care (J)	7.354
John Coates Charitable Trust	7.357
Maurice Wohl Charitable Foundation (J)	7.417
Michael Bishop Foundation (J)	7.425
Motability Tenth Anniversary Trust, The (J)	7.435
Nightingale Hammerson (J)	7.463
Nuffield Foundation (J)	7.474
Overseas Development Institute	7.486

Phillips & Rubens Charitable Trust (J)	7.501
Royal Horticultural Society (J)	7.561
Royal Navy & Royal Marines Children's Fund	7.568
Samuel Sebba Charitable Trust (J)	7.586
Seafarers UK (J)	7.594
Trust for London (J)	7.688
Westminster Foundation (J)	7.723

VESTRA WEALTH LLP, 14 Cornhill, London, EC3V 3NR. Tel: 0203 207 8000. Fax: 0203 207 8001. E-mail: info@vestrawealth.com. Internet: www.vestrawealth.com.

WALKER CRIPS STOCKBROKERS LIMITED, Finsbury Tower, 103-105 Bunhill Row, London, EC1Y 8LZ. Tel: 020 3100 8000. Internet: www.wcgplc.co.uk.

Pennington Mellor Munthe Charity Trust	7.495
St Benedict's Abbey Ealing	7.688

WATSON MOORE INDEPENDENT FINANCIAL ADVISERS LIMITED, 63 Butts Green Road, Hornchurch, Essex, RM11 2JS. Tel: 01708 437006. Fax: 01708 437005. E-mail: e-mail@watsonmooreifa.com. Internet: www.watsonmooreifa.com. Charity specialists: S Pickering. Mella Quinlan. C Moore. Alison Rose. J Watson (Director). J Watson. Fleur Webb.

Missionary Franciscan Sisters (J)	7.544

WAVERTON

CHARITIES

WAVERTON INVESTMENT MANAGEMENT, 16 Babmaes Street, London, SW1Y 6AH. Tel: 020 7484 2065. Fax: 020 7484 7400. E-mail: erobertson@waverton.co.uk. Internet: www.waverton.co.uk.

Waverton Investment Management, formerly J O Hambro Investment Management, has been providing discretionary investment management to charities since its inception. We understand how to manage charitable investment assets in a prudent, pragmatic and flexible way and offer:

- a dedicated charity team
- Direct relationship with your portfolio manager
- Tailored mandates
- Long term performance
- Trustee Training

Our investment approach is also ideally suited to managing charities with an ethical policy.

Charity specialists: Katrina Norris. Emma Robertson. James Pike (Head of Charities). Ian Enslin.

29th May 1961 Charitable Trust (J)	7.2
Burdett Trust for Nursing (J)	7.104
Carpenters' Company Charitable Trust	7.117
Compton Verney Fund (J)	7.170
EBM Charitable Trust (J)	7.223
Foundation for Liver Research	7.259
Godinton House Preservation Trust	7.279
Grand Charity, The (J)	7.284
Hedley Foundation Limited	7.307
Jerwood Charitable Foundation	7.353
Microbiology Society	7.425
Old Possum's Practical Trust	7.479
Order of Friars Minor (Capuchin) Province (J)	7.482
Richard Reeve's Foundation	7.536
Roundhouse Trust	7.547
Royal Masonic Trust For Girls and Boys (J)	7.565
Sandra Charitable Trust (J)	7.586
Soka Gakkai International UK	7.625
Stroke Association	7.662
Sutton's Hospital in Charterhouse (J)	7.666
Thornton-Smith and Plevins Trust	7.679
Whiteley Homes Trust	7.725

WELLINGTON MANAGEMENT INTERNATIONAL LTD., 80 Victoria Street, London, SW1E 5JL.

City Bridge Trust, The (J)	7.153

WH IRELAND, 24 Martin Lane, London, EC4R 0DR. Tel: 020 7220 1666. Fax: 020 7220 1667. Internet: www.wh-ireland.co.uk/.

College of Occupational Therapists	7.160
George Gibson Almshouses Foundation	7.272
Perennial (J)	7.498
Police Rehabilitation Centre	7.507
Simon Gibson Charitable Trust	7.609
St Michael's and All Saints Charity	7.650

WHEB ASSET MANAGEMENT, 2 Fitzhardinge Street, London, W1H 6EE. Tel: 020 3219 3441. Fax: 020 3219 3451. Internet: www.whebam.com.

Ashridge (Bonar Law Memorial) Trust	7.44
Sisters of St Joseph of Peace	7.615

WILLIAMS INVESTMENT MANAGEMENT LLP, 34 Victoria Avenue, Harrogate, North Yorkshire, HG1 5PR. Tel: 01423 705123. Fax: 01423 528905. E-mail: info@williams-im.com. Internet: www.williams-im.com.

Harrogate District Hospice Care	7.303

WINDMILL HILL ASSET MANAGEMENT LIMITED, Windmill Hill Silk Street, Waddesdon, Aylesbury, Buckinghamshire, HP18 0JZ.

Linbury Trust (J)	7.389
Rothschild Foundation	7.547

WINTON CAPITAL MANAGEMENT LTD, 1-5 St. Mary Abbot's Place, London, W8 6LS. Tel: 020 7610 5350. Internet: www.wintoncapital.com.

Church of England Pensions Board (J)	7.148
Said Foundation (J)	7.581

LEGAL ADVISERS AND THEIR CHARITY CLIENTS

A & L GOODBODY, 42-46 Fountain Street, Belfast, County Antrim, BT1 5EB. Tel: 028 9031 4466. Internet: www.algoodbody.com.

Action Mental Health (J)	7.11

A J LUTLEY, Springfield, Rookery Hill, Ashtead Park, Ashstead, Surrey, KT21 1HY. Tel: 01372 279066. E-mail: andrew@ajlutley.co.uk. Internet: www.charitysolicitors.com. Charity specialists: A Lutley (Principal).

Gurkha Welfare Trust (J)	7.292
Marie Stopes International (J)	7.410
Muscular Dystrophy Campaign (J)	7.439
National Autistic Society (J)	7.442

A4ID, The Broadgate Tower, 20 Primrose Street, London, EC2A 2RS. Tel: 020 3116 2798.

Fairtrade Foundation (J)	7.247

AARON & PARTNERS, Grosvenor Court, Foregate Street, Chester, Cheshire, CH1 1HG. Tel: 01244 405555. Fax: 01244 405566. E-mail: simon.ellis@aaronandpartners.com. Internet: www.aaronandpartners.com. Charity specialists: S Ellis.

North of England Zoological Society (J)	7.467

ACTONS, 20 Regent Street, Nottingham, Nottinghamshire, NG1 5BQ. Tel: 0115 910 0200. Fax: 0115 910 0290. E-mail: enquiries@actons.co.uk. Internet: www.actons.co.uk.

Framework Housing Association (J)	7.262

ACUITY LEGAL LIMITED, 3 Assembly Square Britannia Quay, Cardiff Bay, Cardiff, CF10 4PL. Tel: 029 2048 2288. Fax: 029 2049 5588. E-mail: info@acuitylegal.co.uk. Internet: www.acuitylegal.co.uk. Charity specialists: Craig Giffiths. Jon Lawley. Steve Morris.

Aspire Sussex Limited	7.45
National Botanic Garden Wales	7.443
Welsh National Opera (J)	7.718

ADAMS & REMERS, Trinity House, School Hill, Lewes, East Sussex, BN7 2NN. Tel: 01273 480616. Fax: 01273 480618. E-mail: chris.walker@adams-remers.co.uk. Internet: www.adams-remers.co.uk. Charity specialists: C J R Walker.

Glyndebourne Arts Trust	7.278
Glyndebourne Productions Limited	7.279
Raystede Centre for Animal Welfare	7.527
St Peter & St James Charitable Trust	7.653

ADAMS HARRISON, 52a High Street, Haverhill, Suffolk, CB9 8AR. Tel: 01223 832939. E-mail: enquiries@adams-harrison.co.uk. Internet: www.adams-harrison.co.uk.

Spiritualists National Union (J)	7.632

ADDLESHAW GODDARD LLP, 150 Aldersgate Street, London, EC1A 4EJ. Tel: 020 7606 8855. Fax: 020 7606 4390. Internet: www.addleshawgoddard.com. Charity specialists: R Preston.

In Kind Direct (J)	7.330

ADDLESHAW GODDARD LLP, Sovereign House, PO Box 8, Leeds, West Yorkshire, LS1 1HQ. Tel: 0113 209 2000. Fax: 0113 209 2060. E-mail: pervinder.atcha@addleshawgoddard.com. Internet: www.addleshawgoddard.com. Charity specialists: Pervinder Atcha. P Howell. Sylvie Nunn. N Shaw. A Sturrock.

Northern Ballet Theatre (J)	7.469
Yorkshire Sculpture Park	7.749

ADDLESHAW GODDARD LLP, 100 Barbirolli Square, Manchester, Greater Manchester, M2 3AB. Tel: 0161 934 6000. Fax: 0161 934 6060. Internet: www.addleshawgoddard.com. Charity specialists: Alan Sturrock. Nick Shaw.

Christie Charitable Fund, The (J)	7.146
Royal Exchange Theatre Company (J)	7.560
Salesians of Don Bosco UK	7.582

AGNEW ANDRESS HIGGINS & CO, 92 High Street, Belfast, County Antrim, BT1 5ED. Tel: 028 9032 0035. Fax: 028 9032 8063. E-mail: srobb@aah.uk.com. Charity specialists: R Higgins.

Simon Community Northern Ireland	7.609

ALCOCK, GRIMDITCH & RIGLEY, Byron House, Commercial Street, Mansfield, Nottinghamshire, NG181EE. Tel: 01623 460444. Fax: 01623 460445. E-mail: enquiries@alcockgrimditchrigley.co.uk. Internet: www.alcockgrimditchrigley.co.uk.

Brunts Charity	7.102

ALLEN & OVERY LLP, One Bishops Square, London, E1 6AD. Tel: 020 3088 0000. Fax: 020 3088 0088.

Homeless International (J)	7.316
Institute of Materials, Minerals & Mining (J)	7.336
Thornton-Smith and Plevins Trust	7.679

ALLINGTON HUGHES, 2 Vicars Lane, Chester, Cheshire, CH1 1QX. Tel: 01244 312166. Fax: 01244 348876. E-mail: EnquiriesC@allingtonhughes.co.uk. Internet: www.allingtonhughes.co.uk.

Hospice of the Good Shepherd Ltd	7.320
Wrexham (Parochial) Educational Fdn	7.742

ALLINGTON HUGHES, 10 Grosvenor Road, Wrexham, LL11 1SD. Tel: 01978 291 000. Fax: 01978 290 493. E-mail: enquiriesw@allingtonhughes.co.uk. Internet: www.allingtonhughes.co.uk.

Wrexham Diocesan Trust	7.742

AN LAW, Warnford Court, 29 Throgmorton Street, London, EC2N 2AT. Tel: 020 7947 4121. Internet: www.anlaw.org.

Ealing Community Transport (J)	7.218

ANDERSON BEATON LAMOND, Bordeaux House, 31 Kinnoull Street, Perth, Perth and Kinross, PH1 5EN. Tel: 01738 639999. Fax: 01738 630063. Internet: www.abl-law.co.uk.

Live Active Leisure Limited	7.392

ANDERSON STRATHERN LLP, 1 Rutland Court, Edinburgh, EH3 8EY. Tel: 0131 270 7700. Fax: 0131 270 7788.

E-mail: info@andersonstrathern.co.uk. Internet: www.andersonstrathern.co.uk. **Charity specialists:** R M Stimpson.

Abbotsford Trust	7.5
British Horse Society (J)	7.94
Buccleuch Living Heritage Trust, The	7.103
Carnegie UK Trust (J)	7.116
Culture NL Limited	7.189
Dynamic Earth Charitable Trust	7.217
East Lothian Housing Association	7.222
ELCAP	7.229
HALO Trust (J)	7.297
National Trust for Scotland (J)	7.453
Royal Zoological Society of Scotland	7.576
RSABI	7.576
Sailors Society (J)	7.581

ANDREW & CO, St Swithins Court, 1 Flavian Road, Nettleham Road, Lincoln, Lincolnshire, LN2 4GR. Tel: 01522 512123. Fax: 01522 546713. E-mail: catriona.wheeler@andrew-solicitors.co.uk. Internet: www.andrew-solicitors.co.uk. Charity specialists: Catriona Wheeler.

Lincolnshire Agricultural Society	7.389
Lincolnshire Wildlife Trust	7.390
Royal Society of Wildlife Trusts (J)	7.573
St Barnabas Hospice Lincolnshire Trust	7.638

ANDREW JACKSON, Marina Court, Castle Street, Hull, East Riding of Yorkshire, HU1 1TJ. Tel: 01482 325242. Fax: 01482 212974. E-mail: enquiries@andrewjackson.co.uk. Internet: www.andrewjackson.co.uk.

Pickering & Ferens Homes	7.502

ANN C BENNETT, Shelley House, 1 Chelsea Embankment, London, SW3 4LG.

Dawliffe Hall Educational Foundation	7.195

ANSONS, St Mary's Chambers, 5-7 Breadmarket Street, Lichfield, Staffordshire, WS13 6LQ. Tel: 01543 263 456. Fax: 01543 250 942. E-mail: info@ansonsllp.com. Internet: www.ansonsllp.com.

St John's Hospital Lichfield	7.645

ANTHONY COLLINS SOLICITORS LLP, 134 Edmund Street, Birmingham, West Midlands, B3 2ES. Tel: 0121 214 3693. Fax: 0121 212 7438. E-mail: shivaji.shiva@anthonycollins.com. Internet: www.anthonycollins.com. Charity specialists: Phil Watts (Senior Associates) - specialist area: Charity Law. Jenny Smith (Associate) - specialist area: Charity Law. Edwina Turner (Associate) - specialist area: Charity Law. Shivaji Shiva (Senior Associate) - specialist area: Charity Law. Sarah Tomlinson (Associate).

Anchor Trust (J)	7.31
Autism West Midlands (J)	7.50
Baptist Union Corporation	7.56
Baptist Union of Great Britain (J)	7.56
Barnwood House Trust	7.58
Birmingham Diocesan Trust (J)	7.71
Birmingham Hippodrome Theatre Trust Ltd (J)	7.72
Black Country Living Museum Trust (J)	7.74
BMS World Mission (J)	7.77
Bradford Trident Ltd (J)	7.83
Brahma Kumaris World Spiritual UniversityUK (J)	7.83
Brandon Trust (J)	7.84
British & Foreign Bible Society	7.91

British Library (J)	7.95
British Union of Seventh-Day Adventists	7.99
Broadening Choices for Older People	7.100
Building and Social Housing Foundation (J)	7.103
Camphill Village Trust Limited (J)	7.111
Carers Trust	7.114
Chapter 1 (J)	7.127
Children s Family Trust (J)	7.140
Children's Society (J)	7.142
Christian Vision (J)	7.146
Christians Against Poverty	7.146
Church Army (J)	7.147
Church Growth Trust (J)	7.147
Church Mission Society (J)	7.148
Church of God of Prophecy Trust (J)	7.148
Church of Pentecost - UK, The	7.149
Church Urban Fund (J)	7.150
Community Integrated Care (J)	7.164
Community of St Mary the Virgin (J)	7.166
Compassion UK (J)	7.169
Congregational Federation (J)	7.176
Cornwall Care (J)	7.180
Cottage and Rural Enterprises Limited (J)	7.181
County Air Ambulance Trust	7.183
Cyclists' Touring Club	7.190
Disabilities Trust (J)	7.201
Crossroads Care East Midlands (J)	7.222
Echoes of Service (J)	7.223
EDP - Drug and Alcohol Services (J)	7.226
Edward Cadbury Charitable Trust	7.228
Elim Foursquare Gospel Alliance (J)	7.230
Embrace the Middle East (J)	7.232
ExtraCare Charitable Trust (J)	7.245
Field Studies Council (J)	7.253
FitzRoy Support (J)	7.255
Fostering Network (J)	7.258
Friends of the Earth Trust (J)	7.265
Friends of the Elderly (J)	7.265
Gideons International British Isles (J)	7.274
Goodwin Development Trust Limited	7.282
Greenpeace Environmental Trust (J)	7.287
Groundwork London (J)	7.289
Groundwork South Trust Limited, The (J)	7.290
Groundwork UK (J)	7.290
HF Trust Limited (J)	7.311
Institution of Engineering and Technology (J)	7.338
Institution of Eng Technology Ben Fund	7.338
International Fellowship Evangelical Students	7.341
John Martin's Charity (J)	7.360
Keychange Charity (J)	7.370
Keyring-Living Support Networks (J)	7.370
Kingsway International Christian Centre (J)	7.373
Leonard Cheshire Disability (J)	7.385
Lincoln Diocesan Trust Board Finance Ltd (J)	7.389
Livability (J)	7.391
Locality (UK) (J)	7.396
London City Mission (J)	7.397
MacIntyre Care (J)	7.405
Martha Trust	7.413
MCCH Society (J)	7.418
Memralife Group	7.420
Methodist Homes (J)	7.424
MIND (J)	7.428
Mission Aviation Fellowship UK	7.430
National Autistic Society (J)	7.442
Nat Centre for Young People with Epilepsy (J)	7.443
National Society for Epilepsy (J)	7.452
North England Seventh-Day Adventists	7.466
Norwich Consolidated Charities (J)	7.471
Norwood (J)	7.472
Open Doors with Brother Andrew	7.480
Outreach 3 Way (J)	7.485
Outward Housing (J)	7.486
Papworth Trust (J)	7.490
Peabody Trust (J)	7.494
People Potential Possibilities (J)	7.496
Presbyterian Church of Wales (J)	7.513
PROSPECTS (J)	7.516
Response Organisation (J)	7.532
Rothamsted Research Ltd	7.546
Royal Academy of Arts (J)	7.548
RoyalCol.of Obstetricians & Gynaecologists (J)	7.556
Royal Life Saving Society UK (J)	7.563
Royal Mencap Society (J)	7.566
Royal National Institute of Blind People (J)	7.566

S4E Limited	7.579
Scope (J)	7.590
Sense - National Deafblind & Rubella Assoc (J)	7.597
SignHealth (J)	7.608
Social Care Institute for Excellence	7.620
Solace Women's Aid (J)	7.625
South England Seventh-Day Adventists	7.628
Spectrum (J)	7.632
Spurgeons (J)	7.635
St Mary's Hospice	7.650
Stewards Company (J)	7.658
Stewardship Services (UKET) Ltd (J)	7.658
Stratford Upon Avon Town Trust (J)	7.661
Sustrans (J)	7.666
Tearfund (J)	7.670
Thera Trust (J)	7.676
Trident Reach the People Charity (J)	7.686
Tudor Trust (J)	7.690
Turning Point (J)	7.691
UK Islamic Mission	7.693
United Christian Broadcasters (J)	7.695
United Response (J)	7.697
Universities & Colleges Christian F'ship	7.699
Vibrance (J)	7.704
Westbank Community Health and Care	7.721
Wirral Autistic Society (J)	7.733
Witton Lodge Community Association (J)	7.734
Woodbrooke Quaker Study Centre	7.737
World Vision UK (J)	7.741
YMCA Black Country Group (J)	7.744
Young Foundation, The (J)	7.750

AQUABRIDGE LAW, Aquabridge House, 3 Freebournes Court, Newland Street, Witham, Essex, CM8 2BL. Tel: 0333 405 0327. Internet: www.aquabridgelaw.co.uk.

Outlook Care	7.485

ARCHERS LAW, Lakeside House, Kingfisher Way, Stockton-on-Tees, TS18 3NB. Tel: 01642 636 500. Fax: 01642 636 502. E-mail: enquiries@archerslaw.co.uk. Internet: www.archerslaw.co.uk. Charity specialists: D A Collier. Christopher Todd.

Butterwick	7.106
Goshen Trust	7.282
Hospital of God at Greatham	7.321

ARCHON SOLICITORS LLP, Martin House, 5 Martin Lane, London, EC4R 0DP. Tel: 020 7397 9650. Internet: www.archonlaw.co.uk.

World Energy Council (J)	7.740

ARMITAGE SYKES LLP, 72 New North Road, Huddersfield, West Yorkshire, HD1 5NW. Tel: 01484 538 121. Fax: 01484 518 968. E-mail: info@armitagesykes.co.uk. Internet: www.armitagesykes.co.uk.

Kirkwood Hospice	7.374

ARNOLD & PORTER, Tower 42, 25 Old Broad Street, London, EC2N 1HQ. Tel: 020 7786 6100. Fax: 020 7786 6299.

African Agricultural Technology Foundation	7.16

ARNOLD DAVIES VINCENT EVANS, 33 High Street, Lampeter, Dyfed, SA48 7BB. Tel: 01570 422517. Fax: 01570 423244. E-mail: post@adve.co.uk.

Presbyterian Church of Wales (J)	7.513

ARNOLD FOOKS CHADWICK & CO, 15 Bolton Street, Picadilly, London, W1J 8AR. Tel: 020 7499 3007. Fax: 020 7491 4695. E-mail: info@afclaw.co.uk. Internet: www.afclaw.co.uk. Charity specialists: J E Bates.

Little Way Association (J)	7.391

ASB LAW, Origin Two, 106 High Street, Crawley, West Sussex, RH10 1BF. Tel: 01293 603603. Fax: 01293 603666. E-mail: enquiries@asb-law.com. Internet: www.asb-law.com.

Disabilities Trust (J)	7.201
Rochester Bridge Trust	7.541

ASHFORDS, Ashford House, Grenadier Road, Exeter, Devon, EX1 3LH. Tel: 01392 337000. Fax: 01392 337001. E-mail: info@ashfords.co.uk. Internet: www.ashfords.co.uk.

South West Grid for Learning Trust (J)	7.630
Spectrum (J)	7.632

ASHFORDS, Gotham House, Phoenix Lane, Tiverton, Devon, EX16 6LT. Tel: 01884 203000. Fax: 01884 203001. E-mail: info@ashfords.co.uk. Internet: www.ashfords.co.uk.

Heathcoat Trust	7.307
Tiverton Almhouse Charity	7.681
Viscount Amory's Charitable Trust	7.707

ASHTON KCJ, 81 Guildhall Street, Bury St Edmunds, Suffolk, IP33 1PZ. Tel: 01284 762 331. Fax: 01284 762 331. E-mail: enquiries.bury@ashtonkcj.co.uk. Internet: www.ashtonkcj.co.uk.

Ormiston Families	7.484

ASHTON KCJ, Chequers House, 77-81 Newmarket Road, Cambridge, Cambridgeshire, CB5 8EU. Tel: 01223 363111. Fax: 01223 323370. E-mail: enquiries.cambridge@ashtonkcj.co.uk. Internet: www.ashtonkcj.co.uk.

Nat Institute of Agricultural Botany Trust (J)	7.448

ASHTON KCJ, Waterfront House, Wherry Quay, Ipswich, Suffolk, IP4 1AS. Tel: 01473 232425. Fax: 01473 230505. E-mail: enquiry@ashtonkcj.co.uk. Internet: www.ashtonkcj.co.uk.

Age UK Suffolk	7.19
BMS World Mission (J)	7.77
Ormiston Trust (J)	7.484

ASHURST, Broadwalk House, 5 Appold Street, London, EC2A 2HA. Tel: 020 7638 1111. Fax: 020 7638 1112. Internet: www.ashurst.com. Charity specialists: A Cook. M C Johns.

CARE International UK	7.114
Roddick Foundation, The	7.542
Teach First (J)	7.670
Union Jack Club, The	7.694

B P COLLINS LLP, Collins House, 32-38 Station Road, Gerrards Cross, Buckinghamshire, SL9 8EL. Tel: 01753 889995. Fax: 01753 889851. E-mail: charitylaw@bpcollins.co.uk. Internet: www.bpcollins.co.uk.

Keech Hospice Care (J)	7.367
National Society for Epilepsy (J)	7.452

BACHES, Lombard House, Cronehills Linkway, West Bromwich, West Midlands, B70 7PL. Tel: 0121 553 3286. Fax: 0121 500 5204. E-mail: reception@baches.co.uk.

Charity of Walter Stanley	7.130

BAKER & MCKENZIE, 100 New Bridge Street, London, EC4V 6JA. Tel: 020 7242 6531. Fax: 020 7831 8611. Internet: www.bakernet.com. Charity specialists: R D A Pick. Vicki Reynolds.

London Symphony Orchestra	7.401
NSPCC (J)	7.452
UCAS	7.699

BALFOUR+MANSON LLP, 54-66 Frederick Street, Edinburgh, EH2 1LS. Tel: 0131 200 1200. Fax: 0131 200 1300. E-mail: john.hodge@balfour-manson.co.uk. Internet: www.balfour-manson.co.uk. Charity specialists: John M Hodge WS. Alan Gilfillan.

Bethany Christian Trust	7.67
Free Church of Scotland (J)	7.264
Penumbra	7.496
R S Macdonald Charitable Trust	7.522

Workers' Educational Association (J) 7.739

BAND HATTON, 1 Copthall House, Station Square, Coventry, West Midlands, CV1 2FY. Tel: 024 7663 2121. Fax: 024 7622 9038. E-mail: law@bandhatton.co.uk. Internet: www.bandhatton.co.uk.

Sir Thomas White's Charity 7.612

BARBER TITLEYS, 6 North Park Road, Harrogate, North Yorkshire, HG1 5PA. Tel: 0142 350 2211. Fax: 0412 381 7238. E-mail: judith.long@barbertitleys.co.uk. Internet: www.barbertitleys.co.uk.

Charles Elsie Sykes Trust 7.131

BARLOW ROBBINS LLP, The Oriel, Sydenham Road, Guildford, Surrey, GU1 3SR. Tel: 01483 562901. Fax: 01483 464260. E-mail: enquiries@barlowrobbins.com. Internet: www.barlowrobbins.com.

Journalists' Charity 7.364
National Rifle Association (J) 7.451
PohWER (J) 7.506
Shooting Star CHASE (J) 7.605
St Peter's Home and Sisterhood 7.653

BASSETS, 75 High Street, Chatham, ME4 4EE.

Ashdown Medway Accomodation Trust 7.43

BATCHELORS, Charles House, 35 Widmore Road, Bromley, Kent, BR1 1RW. Tel: 020 8768 7000. Fax: 020 8768 7045. E-mail: batchelors@batchelors.co.uk. Internet: www.batchelors.co.uk. Charity specialists: D Field.

Douglas Haig Memorial Homes (J) 7.209

BATES WELLS BRAITHWAITE (LONDON), 2-6 Cannon Street, London, EC4M 6YH. Tel: 020 7551 7777. Fax: 020 7551 7800. E-mail: mail@bwbllp.com. Internet: www.bwbllp.com. Charity specialists: Julian Blake (Joint Head of Charity). Philip Kirkpatrick (Joint Head of Charity). Luke Fletcher (Partner). Thea Longley (Partner). Rosamund McCarthy (Partner). Lord Phillips of Sudbury OBE (Founder) - specialist area: Charity business. Abbie Rumbold (Partner). Lawrence Simanowitz (Partner). Mary Groom (Partner). Stephanie Biden (Partner). Laura Soley (Partner). Simon Steeden (Partner).

Abbeyfield Society 7.5
Action on Addiction (J) 7.11
Action on Hearing Loss (J) 7.11
ActionAid (J) 7.12
Africa Centre Limited 7.15
Alan Edward Higgs Charity (J) 7.22
Alcohol Research UK 7.23
Alexandra Palace and Park 7.24
Alzheimer's Society (J) 7.28
Amanat Charitable Trust (J) 7.28
Ambitious about Autism (J) 7.29
Amnesty International UK Section (J) 7.30
Anna Freud Centre (J) 7.33
Anthony Nolan (J) 7.34
Architects Benevolent Society (J) 7.38
Architectural Association Incorporated (J) 7.38
Architectural Heritage Fund (J) 7.38
Army Cadet Force Association 7.39
Arthritis Research UK (J) 7.40
Article 19 Research & Information Centre 7.41
Asthma UK (J) 7.47
Autism West Midlands (J) 7.50
Bankers Benevolent Fund, The 7.55
Baring Foundation 7.57
Barnardo's (J) 7.57
Barrow Cadbury Trust (J) 7.59
Battersea Dogs & Cats Home (J) 7.60
Blenheim CDP (J) 7.75
Blue Cross (J) 7.76
Book Aid International (J) 7.79
Brain Research Trust 7.84
Brain Tumour Charity (J) 7.84
Breast Cancer Campaign (J) 7.86
Breast Cancer Care (J) 7.86
Bright Red Dot Foundation 7.88
British Council 7.92
BFHU 7.93
British Lung Foundation 7.96
British Red Cross Society (J) 7.98
Brooke Hospital for Animals (J) 7.101
Business in the Community (J) 7.105
Carers UK 7.115
Catholic Agency for Overseas Development (J) 7.118
Central Foundation Schools of London 7.122
Centre for Economic Policy Research 7.123
Centre for Effective Dispute Resolution 7.124
CFBT Education Trust (J) 7.125
Charities Aid Foundation (J) 7.128
Charity of Sir Richard Whittington 7.129
Chartered Accountants' Benevolent Assoc (J) 7.132
CILIP 7.133
Children's Society (J) 7.142
Children with Cancer UK (J) 7.142
Christian Aid (J) 7.145
Church Communities UK 7.147
Church of Jesus Christ of Latter Day Saints (J) 7.149
Citizens Advice (J) 7.152
CLIC Sargent Cancer Care for Children (J) 7.156
Community Security Trust (J) 7.167
Compton Verney 7.169
Compton Verney Collection Settlement 7.169
Compton Verney Fund 7.170
Council for Awards in Care,Health&Education 7.182
Council for World Mission 7.182
Crime Reduction Initiatives (J) 7.186
Crimestoppers Trust 7.186
Design Council (J) 7.199
Diabetes UK (J) 7.200
Disasters Emergency Committee (J) 7.202
Dogs Trust (J) 7.203
Donmar Warehouse Projects 7.207
Douglas Haig Memorial Homes (J) 7.209
Duke of Edinburgh's Award Intl Foundation 7.214
Duke of Edinburgh's Award (J) 7.214
Ealing Community Transport (J) 7.218
Earl of Northampton's Charity 7.219
East Malling Trust, The (J) 7.222
Eden Trust (J) 7.224
Education and Training Foundation (J) 7.227
Eiris Foundation (J) 7.229
Elim Foursquare Gospel Alliance (J) 7.230
Elizabeth Finn Care (J) 7.230
Engineering UK 7.234
England and Wales Cricket Trust (J) 7.234
English National Opera 7.235
Equinox Care (J) 7.237
EveryChild (J) 7.243
Fairtrade Foundation (J) 7.247
Family Fed for World Peace & Unification 7.247
Farleigh Hospice 7.248
Federation London Youth Clubs 7.250
Fidelity UK Foundation 7.252
Find A Future 7.254
Football Foundation 7.256
Forum for the Future, The 7.258
Fostering Network (J) 7.258
Fdn&Friends of RoyalBotanicGardens, Kew (J) 7.259
Foundation for Credit Counselling (J) 7.259
Foundation for Social Entrepreneurs 7.259
FOUNDATION66 (J) 7.261
Framework Housing Association (J) 7.262
French Huguenot Church Ldn Charitable Trust 7.265
Friends of the Earth Trust (J) 7.265
Fusion Lifestyle (J) 7.266
Get Kids Going 7.273
Girlguiding UK 7.274
Girls Friendly Soc in England & Wales 7.275
Golden Bottle Trust 7.280
Goldman Sachs Gives (UK) 7.280
Gosling Sports Park (J) 7.282
Grand Charity, The (J) 7.284
Greenpeace Environmental Trust (J) 7.287
Groundwork London (J) 7.289
Groundwork South Trust Limited, The (J) 7.290
Groundwork UK (J) 7.290
GVEP International 7.293
Hackney Empire 7.295
Hampstead Wells & Campden Trust (J) 7.299
Harrow Central Mosque and Islamic Centre (J) 7.303
HCT Group 7.304
Health Foundation, The (J) 7.305
Heritage Care (J) 7.310
Hillsong Church London 7.313
Hospice St Francis Berkhamsted Limited (J) 7.319
Hospice UK 7.320
Hymns Ancient and Modern 7.326
Imperial Society of Teachers of Dancing (J) 7.329
Independent Age (J) 7.331
Institute for War Peace Reporting Limited 7.333
Institute of Fundraising 7.335
Intl Agency for the Prevention of Blindness 7.340
International Alert (J) 7.340
International Fund for Animal Welfare (J) 7.342
International HIV/AIDS Alliance (J) 7.342
Intl Institute for Environment&Development 7.343
International Medical Corps (UK) 7.343
Intl Society for Krishna Consciousness 7.344
Islamic Relief Worldwide (J) 7.347
Jamie Oliver Food Foundation 7.351
John Ellerman Foundation 7.358
Joseph Rank Trust, The 7.363
Joseph Rowntree Charitable Trust (J) 7.363
Kent Community Foundation (J) 7.369
L H A London Limited (J) 7.376
LankellyChase Foundation, The (J) 7.379
Lempriere Pringle Charitable Trust, The 7.384
Leonard Cheshire Disability (J) 7.385
Leprosy Mission England (J) 7.385
Lifeline Project (J) 7.388
Livability (J) 7.391
Liverpool Charity and Voluntary Services 7.392
Locality (UK) (J) 7.396
London Community Foundation 7.397
London Early Years Foundation, The 7.398
London Library 7.399
London Mathematical Society 7.400
Macmillan Cancer Support (J) 7.405
Magen David Adom UK 7.406
Medecins sans Frontieres (UK) (J) 7.418
Medical Aid for Palestinians 7.418
Medical Foundation for Victims of Torture (J) 7.419
Mental Health Foundation (J) 7.421
Mercers' Charitable Foundation 7.422
Millennium Awards Trust, The 7.427
MIND (J) 7.428
Mines Advisory Group 7.429
Motor Neurone Disease Association (J) 7.435
Mountview Academy of Theatre Arts 7.436
National Assoc for Colitis and Crohn's (J) 7.442
National Centre for Social Research 7.443
National Council Voluntary Organisations (J) 7.444
National Deaf Children's Society 7.444
National Fed'n of Women's Institutes 7.445
NFER 7.446
National Gardens Scheme Charitable Trust 7.447
National Rifle Association (J) 7.451
National Skills Academy For Social Care 7.452
NSPCC (J) 7.452
National Youth Agency 7.454
New Victoria Hospital Limited, The 7.458
Nigel Vinson Charitable Trust 7.463
Nordoff Robbins Music Therapy Centre (J) 7.464
Northampton Theatres Trust (J) 7.468
Northamptonshire Arts Management Trust (J) 7.469
NorthamptonshireMusic&PerformingArtsTst 7.469
Nuffield Foundation 7.474
NYU in London 7.476
Old Vic Theatre Trust 2000 (J) 7.479
Open Society Foundation 7.481
ORBIS Charitable Trust (J) 7.482
Ormiston Trust (J) 7.484
Oxfam GB (J) 7.486
Pargiter Trust 7.490
PayPal Giving Fund UK 7.494
People's Health Trust 7.497
Peter Lang Children's Trust Limited 7.499
Peter Moores Charitable Trust 7.499
PohWER (J) 7.506
Practical Action 7.512
Premier League Charitable Fund (J) 7.513
Prince of Wales's Charitable Fndtn (J) 7.514
Prudential Staff Charitable Trust 7.517
RAC Foundation for Motoring 7.522
Ramblers Association (J) 7.525
Rank Foundation Limited (J) 7.525
Rank Prize Fund 7.525
RCN Foundation 7.528
RedR UK 7.528
Reed Foundation, The (J) 7.529
Refugee Action (J) 7.529

Rehabilitation for Addicted Prisoners	7.530
Resolution Trust, The	7.532
Rethink Mental Illness	7.534
Richard Cloudesley's Charity (J)	7.536
Richmond Fellowship (J)	7.537
Royal British Legion (J)	7.554
RoyalCol.of Obstetricians & Gynaecologists (J)	7.556
Duke & Duchess of Cambridge & Prince Harry	7.560
Royal Institute of British Architects (J)	7.562
Royal Masonic Benevolent Institution (J)	7.565
Royal Medical Benevolent Fund (J)	7.565
Royal Shakespeare Company (J)	7.571
Royal Society of Arts (J)	7.571
RSPCA (J)	7.572
Royal Town Planning Institute	7.574
Saferworld	7.581
Said Foundation	7.581
Samaritan's Purse International	7.585
Samaritans	7.585
Save the Children (J)	7.588
SEMTA (J)	7.589
Scout Association (J)	7.594
Services Sound Vision Corporation (J)	7.598
Shakespeare Globe Trust (J)	7.599
Sheffield Futures (J)	7.601
SHELTER (J)	7.603
Sightsavers International (J)	7.608
Sigrid Rausing Trust	7.608
Smile Train UK, The	7.619
Spoore, Merry & Rixman Foundation, The (J)	7.633
St Wilfrid's Hospice (Eastbourne)	7.655
Tennis Foundation	7.672
Thames Hospicecare (J)	7.675
Thames Reach (J)	7.675
Thomson Media Foundation, The (J)	7.678
Trinity College London	7.686
Trust Thamesmead (J)	7.689
Tudor Trust (J)	7.690
UFI Charitable Trust	7.692
UK Sailing Academy (J)	7.693
United Christian Broadcasters (J)	7.695
Victoria Foundation, The	7.705
vInspired (J)	7.706
Vodafone Foundation, The	7.708
War Child	7.714
WaterAid (I)	7.715
YMCA Watford & District Branch	7.716
Watts Gallery	7.716
Westway Trust (J)	7.724
Whitechapel Gallery (J)	7.725
Windhorse Trust, The (J)	7.732
WIEGO Ltd	7.736
Wordsworth Trust	7.738
Workers' Educational Association (J)	7.739
World Cancer Research Fund (WCRF UK) (J)	7.739
World Society for the Protection of Animals (J)	7.741
World Vision UK (J)	7.741
Wycliffe UK Ltd	7.743
Y Care International	7.743
YMCA England (J)	7.745
YMCA London South West	7.746
Young Foundation, The (J)	7.750

BATT BROADBENT SOLICITORS, Minster Chambers, 42/44 Castle Street, Salisbury, SP1 3TX. Tel: 01722 411 141. Fax: 01722 411 566. E-mail: service@battbroadbent.co.uk. Internet: www.battbroadbent.co.uk.

L H A London Limited (J)	7.376

BATTENS, Mansion House, Princes Street, Yeovil, Somerset, BA20 1EP. Tel: 01935 846000. Fax: 01935 846001. E-mail: enquiries@battens.co.uk. Internet: www.battens.co.uk.

Dorset Wildlife Trust	7.209

BAWTRESS LLP, 65 Newland Street, Witham, Essex, CM8 1AB. Tel: 01376 513491. Fax: 01376 510713. E-mail: mail@bawtrees.co.uk. Internet: www.bawtrees.co.uk.

Royal Masonic Trust For Girls and Boys (J)	7.565

BAZELEY BARNES & BAZELEY, 24 Bridgeland Street, Bideford, Devon, EX39 2QB. Tel: 01237 473122.

Bideford Bridge Trust	7.69

BEALE AND COMPANY SOLICITORS LLP, Garrick House, 27-32 King Street, London, WC2E 8JB. Tel: 020 7240 3474. Fax: 020 7240 9111. E-mail: reception@beale-law.com. Internet: www.beale-law.com. Charity specialists: M Archer.

Chartered Inst of Building Services Engineers	7.134
Institution of Structural Engineers (J)	7.339

BENTLEYS, 182 Hoe Street, London, E17 4QH. Tel: 020 8521 8751.

R L Glasspool Charity Trust (J)	7.522

BERRY SMITH, Haywood House, Dumfries Place, Cardiff, CF10 3GA. Tel: 029 2034 5511. Fax: 029 2034 5945. E-mail: cardiff@berrysmith.com. Internet: www.berrysmith.com.

Llandaff Diocesan Board Finance	7.394

BERWIN LEIGHTON PAISNER LLP, Adelaide House, London Bridge, London, EC4R 9HA. Tel: 020 7760 1000. Fax: 020 7760 1111. E-mail: Charities@blplaw.com. Internet: www.blplaw.com. Charity specialists: Janet Turner QC (Head of Charities). Martin Paisner CBE (Partner). Jonathan Kropman (Partner). Neasa Coen (Associate Director). Tora Smith (Associate). Clarissa Lyons (Associate).

BEVAN BRITTAIN, Fleet Place House, 2 Fleet Place, Holborn Viaduct, London, EC4M 7RF. Tel: 0870 194 1000. Fax: 0870 194 7800. Internet: www.bevanbrittan.com.

Future Leaders Charitable Trust Ltd	7.267

BEVAN BRITTAIN, Kings Orchard, 1 Queen Street, Bristol, BS2 0HQ. Tel: 0870 194 1000. Fax: 0870 194 1001. Internet: www.bevanbrittan.com.

Action for Children (J)	7.10
BRUNELCARE (J)	7.102
Healthcare Financial Management Association	7.306
Newbury & Thatcham Hospital Trust	7.459
Royal United Hospital Bath NHS Trust Ch Fd	7.574

BEVAN KIDWELL, 113-117 Farringdon Road, London, EC1R 3BX. Tel: 020 7843 1820. Fax: 020 7278 4685.

SEMTA (J)	7.589

BEVERIDGE, PHILIP & ROSS, 22 Bernard Street, Leith, Edinburgh, EH6 6PP. Tel: 0131 554 6244.

Elim Foursquare Gospel Alliance (J)	7.230

BHP LAW, Kepier House, Belmont Business Park, Durham, County Durham, DH1 1TW. Tel: 0191 384 0840. Fax: 0191 384 1523. E-mail: info@bhplaw.co.uk. Internet: www.bhplaw.co.uk.

County Durham Community Foundation (J)	7.183
RC Diocese of Hexham & Newcastle (J)	7.543

BIRCHAM DYSON BELL LLP, 50 Broadway, London, SW1H 0BL. Tel: 020 7713 3537. Fax: 020 7222 3480. E-mail: pennychapman@bdb-law.co.uk. Internet: www.bdb-law.co.uk. Charity specialists: Penny J Chapman (Partner, Head of Charities Group). Alice Unwin (Solicitor) - specialist area: Charity Law. Daisy Scaife (Solicitor) - specialist area: Real Estate. Kevin Poulter (Senior Associate) - specialist area: Employment Law. Nick Le Riche (Senior Associate) - specialist area: Employment Law. Caroline Yarrow (Partner) - specialist area: Employment Law. Katie Smith (Solicitor) - specialist area: Litigation. Jonathan Brinsden (Partner) - specialist area: Charity Law. Felix Appelbe. Jonathan Bracken (Special Counsel) - specialist area: Public Law. Nicholas W Brown (Partner) - specialist area: Government & Infrastructure and Charity Law. Jesper Christensen (Partner) - specialist area: Employment. Alastair J C

Collett (Partner) - specialist area: Charity Law. John Darnton (Partner) - specialist area: Litigation. David Darvill (Partner) - specialist area: Real Estate. Jonathan Fewster (Partner) - specialist area: Real Estate. Neil M Emerson (Partner) - specialist area: Litigation. Richard Langley (Partner) - specialist area: Litigation. Ian McCulloch (Partner) - specialist area: Government & Infrastructure and Charity Law. David Mundy (Partner) - specialist area: Public Law. Paul Voller (Partner) - specialist area: Commercial & Charity Law. Simon P Weil (Partner) - specialist area: Charity Law. Nicola J Evans (Senior Associate & Charities Prof Support Lawyer) - specialist area: Charity Law. Ben Brice (Associate) - specialist area: Charity Law. Andrew Mackie (Solicitor) - specialist area: Charity Law. Henrietta Newman (Associate) - specialist area: Charity Law. Sarah Williams (Associate) - specialist area: Charity Law.

ABF The Soldiers Charity (J)	7.6
Alzheimer's Society (J)	7.28
Apollo Foundation, The	7.35
Asfari Foundation, The (J)	7.43
Balcombe Charitable Trust	7.54
Barts and The London Charity (J)	7.59
BBC Children in Need	7.61
IMechE Benevolent Fund	7.65
Biochemical Society (J)	7.70
Blind Veterans UK (J)	7.76
Blue Cross (J)	7.76
British Film Institute (J)	7.93
British Pregnancy Advisory Service (J)	7.97
Burdett Trust for Nursing	7.104
Cancer Recovery Foundation UK	7.112
Catholic Care (Diocese of Leeds) (J)	7.119
Central Young Men's Christian Association	7.123
Centrepoint	7.124
Charity of Elizabeth Jane Jones, The	7.129
Chartered Institute for Securities &Investment	7.132
Chartered Institute of Arbitrators	7.132
Children's Hospice South West (J)	7.141
Children's Investment Fund Foundation	7.141
Children with Cancer UK (J)	7.142
Church of Scotland General Trustees	7.149
Climate Group, The (J)	7.157
Coalfields Regeneration Trust	7.158
Colonel W H Whitbread Charitable Trust	7.161
Consumers' Association	7.178
Corporation of the Church House	7.180
Dawat-e-Hadiyah Trust (United Kingdom)	7.195
Denville Hall	7.197
Diabetes Research & Wellness Foundation	7.200
Donkey Sanctuary (J)	7.206
Ealing Community Transport (J)	7.218
Eurocentres UK	7.241
Fairfield (Croydon) (J)	7.246
Father Hudson's Society (J)	7.249
Federation of Synagogues (J)	7.251
Fight For Sight	7.254
FOUNDATION66 (J)	7.261
Foundling Museum	7.261
Goldsmiths Centre, The (J)	7.280
Great Ormond St Hosp Children's Charity (J)	7.285
HALO Trust (J)	7.297
Health Foundation, The (J)	7.305
Healthcare Management Trust, The	7.306
Henshaws Society for Blind People (J)	7.309
Hospital of St John and St Elizabeth (J)	7.321
Imperial College Healthcare Charity (J)	7.329
In Kind Direct (J)	7.330
Intl Planned Parenthood Federation (J)	7.344
International Students House (J)	7.345
International Water Association	7.345
Jewish Care (J)	7.354
John James Bristol Foundation	7.359
JTL	7.364
Kathleen Hannay Memorial Charity	7.366
King Edward VII's Hospital Sister Agnes (J)	7.372
Marine Biological Association United Kingdom	7.411
Mothers' Union	7.435
Neil Kreitman Foundation	7.456
Nordoff Robbins Music Therapy Centre (J)	7.464
Nuffield Health (J)	7.474
Oxford Group	7.488
Police Dependants' Trust Limited, The	7.507
Prison Advice & Care Trust (PACT)	7.515
Richmond Fellowship (J)	7.537
Royal Air Force Benevolent Fund (J)	7.550

Royal Brompton Hospital Charity	7.555
Royal College of Emergency Medicine, The (J)	7.555
Royal College of Surgeons (J)	7.558
Royal Highland Agricultural Soc Scotland (J)	7.561
Royal Horticultural Society (J)	7.561
Royal Institution of Naval Architects	7.563
Royal Life Saving Society UK (J)	7.563
RSAS AgeCare	7.576
Scope (J)	7.590
Seafarers UK (J)	7.594
SeeAbility (J)	7.596
Shakespeare Birthplace Trust (J)	7.599
Shaw Trust (J)	7.599
Sheppard Trust (J)	7.604
Solace Women's Aid (J)	7.625
St John Ambulance (J)	7.644
St Margaret's Convent (Uckfield) (J)	7.648
St Vincent de Paul Society (J)	7.655
Starlight Children's Foundation	7.656
Stonewall Equality Ltd (J)	7.660
Stroke Association (J)	7.662
Sutton's Hospital in Charterhouse (J)	7.666
Swanswell Charitable Trust	7.667
Swire Educational Trust	7.667
Thomas Pocklington Trust (J)	7.678
Tony Blair Governance Initiative	7.683
Union Sisters Mercy Great Britain (J)	7.695
University of Notre Dame (USA) in England	7.701
Variety the Children's Charity	7.703
Westminster Almshouses Foundation	7.722
Westway Trust (J)	7.724
Whitgift Foundation (J)	7.726
Wigmore Hall Trust (J)	7.727
WomanCare Global	7.736
Wood Green Animal Shelters (J)	7.736
World Assoc of Girl Guides & Girl Scouts	7.739
YMCA Training	7.746
Zoological Society of London (J)	7.752

BIRD & BIRD, 15 Fetter Lane, London, EC4A 1JP. Tel: 020 7415 6000. Fax: 020 7415 6111. Internet: www.twobirds.com. Charity specialists: Jane Gunter.

Inc Council of Law Reporting England Wales	7.330

BIRKETT LONG, Essex House, 42 Crouch Street, Colchester, Essex, CO3 3HH. Tel: 01206 217300. Fax: 01206 572393. E-mail: enquiry@birkettlong.co.uk. Internet: www.birkettlong.co.uk. Charity specialists: B R Ballard. D J Cammack. A Livesley.

Colchester Catalyst Charity	7.159
Essex Community Foundation	7.240
St Helena Hospice (J)	7.644

BIRKETTS LLP, 22 Station Road, Cambridge, Cambridgeshire, CB1 2JD. Tel: 01223 326763. Fax: 01223 326629. E-mail: sara-sayer@birketts.co.uk. Internet: www.birketts.co.uk. Charity specialists: Erika Clarke. James Hall. S Jones. Sara Sayer.

Nat Institute of Agricultural Botany Trust (J)	7.448
NIAB (J)	7.462
Suffolk Wildlife Trust	7.664

BIRKETTS LLP, 24-26 Museum Street, Ipswich, Suffolk, IP1 1HZ. Tel: 01223 326763. Fax: 01223 326629. E-mail: sara-sayer@birketts.co.uk. Internet: www.birketts.co.uk.

Redwings Horse Sanctuary (J)	7.528
Suffolk Agricultural Association	7.663
Suffolk Foundation, The	7.663

BIRKETTS LLP, Kingfisher House, 1 Gilders Way, Norwich, Norfolk, NR3 1UB. Tel: 01603 232300. Fax: 01603 230533. E-mail: erika-clarke@birketts.co.uk. Internet: www.birketts.co.uk.

British Trust for Ornithology	7.99
Genome Analysis Centre, The (J)	7.271
Institute of Food Research (J)	7.335
John Innes Centre (J)	7.358
Morley Agricultural Foundation, The	7.434
Norwich Diocesan Board of Finance, The (J)	7.471

Sir Malcolm Stewart Bart Gen. Trust	7.612

BISCOES, 62-66 Kingston Place, Kingston Crescent, North End, Portsmouth, Hampshire, PO2 8AQ. Tel: 023 9266 0261. Fax: 023 9266 2970. E-mail: rsalvetti@biscoes-law.co.uk. Internet: www.biscoes-law.co.uk.

Rowans Hospice (J)	7.547

BISHOP & SEWELL, 59-60 Russell Square, London, WC1B 3HP. Tel: 020 7631 4141. Fax: 020 7636 5369. Internet: www.bishopandsewell.co.uk. Charity specialists: Jill P Sewell.

Ahmadiyya Muslim Jamaat International	7.19

BKS SOLICITORS, 107 High Street, London, SE20 7DT. Tel: 020 8776 9388. Internet: www.balkir.co.uk.

Addaction (J)	7.13

BLACKADDERS, 30/34 Reform Street, Dundee, DD1 1RJ. Tel: 01382 229222. Fax: 01382 342220. E-mail: solicitors@blackadders.co.uk. Internet: www.blackadders.co.uk.

Dundee Repertory Theatre	7.215

BLACKADDERS, 5 Rutland Square, Edinburgh, EH1 2AX. Tel: 0131 222 8000. Fax: 0131 222 8008. Internet: www.blackadders.co.uk.

Salvation Army Social Work Trust (J)	7.584
Salvation Army Trust (J)	7.584

BLACKETT, HART & PRATT INCORP DEAS MALLEN SOUTER, Eldon Chambers, 23 The Quayside, Newcastle upon Tyne, Tyne and Wear, NE1 3DE. Tel: 0191 221 0898. Fax: 0191 232 0930. Internet: www.bhplaw.co.uk. Charity specialists: A Mallen.

Diocese of Hexham and Newcastle (J)	7.201
National Energy Action	7.445

BLACKHURST BUDD LLP, 22 Edward Street, Blackpool, Lancashire, FY1 1BA. Tel: 01253 629300. Fax: 01253 629333. Internet: www.blackhurstbudd.co.uk.

Trinity Hospice & Palliative Care Services	7.686

BLACKHURST SWAINSON GOODIER LLP, 3 & 4 Aalborg Sqaure, Lancaster, Lancashire, LA1 1GG. Tel: 01524 386500. Fax: 01534 386515. E-mail: info@bsglaw.co.uk. Internet: www.bsglaw.co.uk. Charity specialists: M Belderbos.

Lancaster Roman Catholic Diocesan Trust	7.378

BLACKS, Hanover House, 22 Clarendon Road, Leeds, West Yorkshire, LS2 9NZ. Tel: 0113 243 3311. Fax: 0113 242 1703.

Sports Coach UK	7.633

BLAIR CADELL, The Bond House, 5 Breadalbane Street, Edinburgh, EH6 5JH. Tel: 0131 555 5800. Fax: 0131 555 1022. E-mail: office@blaircadell.com. Internet: www.blaircadell.com.

Chest Heart & Stroke Scotland	7.137

Please mention

Top 3000 Charities

when responding
to advertisements

BLAKE MORGAN, New Kings Court, Tollgate, Chandler's Ford, Eastleigh, Hampshire, SO53 3LG. Tel: 023 808 57011. E-mail: elizabethdavies@blakemorgan.co.uk. Internet: www.blakemorgan.co.uk.

Blake Morgan is a Top 50 law firm with offices in London, Oxford, Reading, Southampton, Portsmouth and Cardiff. We provide a full range of charity and commercial law services across all of our offices.

Our nationally recognised Charities team works for over 500 charities. Whether large or small, national or international, regionally-centred or community-centred, clients value our ability to provide the full range of legal advice which is practical, commercially focused and relevant to their charity's circumstances.

Contacts: Elizabeth Davis, Chris Williams.

Charity specialists: Liz Brownsell (Associate). Louise Brooks. Kirsteen Hook (Solicitor). Claire Lamkin. Jane Robinson. Philip Collins (Senior Associate). Rachel Sales. Anna Larbi (Senior Associate). Christopher Williams (Partner). Mererid McDaid (Associate). Delme Griffiths (Associate). Virginia Henley. Elizabeth Davis (Head of Charities Team).

Borough of Havant Sport & Leisure Trust	7.81
Brendoncare Foundation	7.87
British Kidney Patient Association	7.95
Bromley Trust	7.100
Catch22 (J)	7.118
Children's Trust (J)	7.142
Concern Universal (J)	7.170
Cranstoun Drug Services (J)	7.184
D D McPhail Charitable Settlement	7.191
Dartington Hall Trust, The (J)	7.192
Doris Field Charitable Trust	7.207
Earth Trust	7.220
Edward James Foundation Limited (J)	7.228
Enham	7.236
Ex-Services Mental Welfare Society (J)	7.243
FitzRoy Support (J)	7.255
Grace Trust, The (J)	7.283
Hampshire & Isle of Wight Community Fdn	7.298
Hope and Homes for Children (J)	7.317
Keyring-Living Support Networks (J)	7.370
MacIntyre Care (J)	7.405
Malaria Consortium	7.407
Mary Rose Trust	7.414
Mary's Meals	7.415
Merchant Navy Welfare Board	7.422
Mission to Seafarers (J)	7.430
Nominet Charitable Trust	7.463
Overseas Development Institute	7.486
Oxford Centre Hebrew & Jewish Studies (J)	7.487
Pilgrim Homes	7.502
Pilgrims' Friend Society	7.503
Portsmouth Naval Base Property Trust (J)	7.510
Portsmouth RC Diocesan Trustees	7.510
Quaker International Educational Trust	7.518
Rifles Benevolent Trust, The	7.538
Rowans Hospice (J)	7.547
Royal Agricultural Benevolent Institution (J)	7.550
Royal National Lifeboat Institution (J)	7.567
Royal National Lifeboat Institution (J)	7.567
Royal Naval Benevolent Trust (J)	7.568
Sailors Society (J)	7.581

Seafarers UK (J)	7.594
Shipwrecked Mariners' Society (J)	7.605
Sobell House Hospice Charity Limited (J)	7.619
Society of St James	7.623
Solent Mind	7.626
St Barnabas Hospices (Sussex) Ltd	7.638
St John's Winchester Charity	7.645
Tenovus (J)	7.673
Terrence Higgins Trust (J)	7.673
Thames Hospicecare (J)	7.675
Vocational Training Charitable Trust (J)	7.708
Wessex Children's Hospice Trust (J)	7.719
Winchester Diocesan Board of Finance	7.732
World Vision UK (J)	7.741
YMCA Fairthorne Group	7.745

BLANCHARDS BAILEY LLP, Bunbury House, Stour Park, Blandford Forum, Dorset, DT11 9LQ. Tel: 01258 459361. Fax: 01258 483610.
E-mail: bunbury@blanchardsbailey.co.uk.
Internet: www.blanchardsbailey.co.uk.

Weldmar Hospicecare Trust (J)	7.717

BLANDY & BLANDY LLP, One Friar Street, Reading, Berkshire, RG1 1DA. Tel: 0118 951 6851. Fax: 08701 975381.
E-mail: nick.burrows@blandy.co.uk.
Internet: www.blandy.co.uk.
Charity specialists: Nick Burrows. Rosie Brass. Katja Wigham. Tim Clark.

Adviza	7.14
CXK Limited	7.190
Gerald Palmer Eling Trust Company	7.273
Institution of Structural Engineers (J)	7.339
Oxford Diocesan Council For Social Work (J)	7.487
Rhodes Trust (J)	7.535
Thames Valley Air Ambulance (J)	7.675

BOLT BURDON, 16 Theberton Street, London, N1 0QX. Tel: 020 7288 4700. Fax: 020 7288 4701. E-mail: boltburdon@boltburdon.co.uk.
Internet: www.boltburdon.co.uk.

Richard Cloudesley's Charity (J)	7.536

BOND DICKINSON LLP, 4 More London Riverside, London, SE1 2AU. Tel: 0345 415 6000. Fax: 0345 415 6200.
Internet: www.bonddickinson.com.
Charity specialists: Emma Moody (Charities). Alexandra Casley (Charities). Samantha Pritchard (Charities). M Honeywell (Charities). Kimberley levins (Charities). Barbara Painter (Real Estate). Claire-Jane Nicol (Employment). C Moore (Real Estate). Jackie Gray (Data Protection). Jenny Atkin (Real Estate). M Woodward (Private Wealth). Sue Pattie (Debt Recovery). Tracy Walsh (Pensions). W Sander (Commercial).

Addaction (J)	7.13
Age UK North Tyneside (J)	7.18
Age UK Northumberland	7.18
Ballinger Charitable Trust (J)	7.55
Bauer Radio's Cash for Kids Charities	7.61
Bristol Charities (J)	7.89
British & Foreign School Society, The (J)	7.91
China Fleet Trust	7.143
Dame Hannah Rogers Trust (J)	7.192
Developing Initiatives, Support in Community	7.199
Diocese of Hexham and Newcastle (J)	7.201
English Province of our Lady of Charity (J)	7.235
Halo Leisure Services Limited (J)	7.297
Higher Education Academy, The (J)	7.311
Institution of Chemical Engineers (J)	7.337
J A Clark Charitable Trust	7.348
Lord Crewe's Charity	7.402
Masonic Samaritan Fund (J)	7.415
Mental Health Matters (J)	7.421
NSPCC (J)	7.452
NCFE	7.455
Oaklea Trust, The	7.477
Opera North (J)	7.481
Percy Hedley Foundation (J)	7.497
Preston Rd Neigbourhood Development Co.	7.513
ReVitalise Respite Holidays (J)	7.535
RC Diocese of Hexham & Newcastle (J)	7.543
Royal Academy of Dramatic Art	7.549
Royal Masonic Hospital Charity (J)	7.565

Royal National Lifeboat Institution (J)	7.567
Scope (J)	7.590
Shaw Trust (J)	7.599
Shears Foundation	7.600
Sisters of Mercy-St Anthony's Convent	7.614
Springboard Sunderland Trust	7.634
St Gemma's Hospice Leeds (J)	7.643
St Mary Magdalene & Holy Jesus Trust (J)	7.649
St Oswald's Hospice (J)	7.653
Theatre Royal (Plymouth) (J)	7.676
Thomas Pocklington Trust (J)	7.678
TTE Technical Training Group, The (J)	7.690
Vincent Wildlife Trust (J)	7.706
William Leech Charity	7.730
William Leech Charity Trust	7.730
William Leech Foundation Trust	7.731

BOODLE HATFIELD, 89 New Bond Street, London, W1S 1DA. Tel: 020 7629 7411.
Fax: 020 7629 2621.
E-mail: law@boodlehatfield.co.uk.
Internet: www.boodlehatfield.com.
Charity specialists: Natasha Hassall. Eleanor Sepanski. G Todd. D J Way.

A Team Foundation	7.4
Absolute Return for Kids (ARK) (J)	7.7
Honourable Artillery Company (J)	7.316
Lennox Wyfold Foundation	7.384
Suva Foundation Limited, The	7.666
Tellus Mater Foundation Ltd	7.672
Westminster Foundation	7.723

BOYCE HATTON, 12 Tor Hill Road, Castle Circus, Torquay, Devon, TQ2 5RB. Tel: 01803 403 403. Fax: 01803 214 876.
Internet: www.boycehatton.co.uk.

Boltini Trust, The	7.78

BOYD & HUTCHINSON, 154 Tooley Street, London, SE1 2TZ. Tel: 0207 4070 770.

Ruach Inspirational Church of God (J)	7.576

BOYES SUTTON & PERRY, 20 Wood Street, Barnet, Hertfordshire, EN5 4BJ. Tel: 020 8449 9155. Fax: 020 8441 3584.
E-mail: solicitors@boyessuttonperry.co.uk.
Internet: www.boyessuttonperry.co.uk.

Congregation of the Sisters of St Martha (J)	7.175
Jesus Hospital Charity in Chipping Barnet	7.353

BOYS & MAUGHAN, India House, Hawley Street, Margate, Kent, CT9 1PZ. Tel: 01843 234000. Fax: 01843 234002.
E-mail: ctj@boysandmaughan.co.uk.
Internet: www.boysandmaughan.co.uk.
Charity specialists: C T James.

John Townsend Trust, The (J)	7.361

BPE SOLICITORS LLP, St James's House, St James' Square, Cheltenham, Gloucestershire, GL50 3PR. Tel: 01242 224 433. Fax: 01242 574 285. E-mail: bpe@bpe.co.uk.
Internet: www.bpe.co.uk.

Children s Family Trust (J)	7.140
Gloucestershire Everyman Theatre	7.278
Meningitis Now	7.421
Physiological Society, The	7.502
Smallpeice Trust	7.618

BRABNERS, Horton House, Exchange Flags, Liverpool, Merseyside, L2 3YL. Tel: 0151 600 3000. Fax: 0151 227 3185.
E-mail: daj@brabnerscs.com.
Internet: www.brabners.com.

Arch Initiatives	7.36
Austin Hope Pilkington Trust	7.49
Autism Initiatives UK	7.49
Cecil Pilkington Charitable Trust	7.122
Co-operative Community Inv Foundation	7.158
Coal Industry Social Welfare Organisation (J)	7.158
Furniture Resource Centre	7.266
IVCC	7.348
Liverpool & Merseyside Theatres Trust (J)	7.392
Liverpool PSS	7.393
Local Solutions (J)	7.395
P H Holt Foundation	7.489

Pilkington Charities Fund	7.503
Queenscourt Hospice (J)	7.521
Royal Liverpool Philharmonic Society	7.563
Sisters Notre Dame Namur (J)	7.614
Wirral Hospice St John's (J)	7.733

BRABNERS, 55 King Street, Manchester, Greater Manchester, M2 4LQ. Tel: 0161 836 8800. Fax: 0161 836 8801.
E-mail: daj@brabners.com.
Internet: www.brabners.com.

Professional Footballers Assoc Educ Fund	7.516
Professional Footballers Benevolent Fund	7.516
Shaw Trust (J)	7.599
Sisters of St Joseph Province	7.615

BRACHERS, 31 Southampton Row, London, WC1B 5HJ. Tel: 020 7242 1250. Fax: 020 7405 4352. E-mail: @brachers.co.uk.
Internet: www.brachers.co.uk.

Tate (J)	7.669

BRACHERS, Somerfield House, 59 London Road, Maidstone, Kent, ME16 8JH. Tel: 01622 690691. Fax: 01622 681430.
E-mail: simonpalmer@brachers.co.uk.
Internet: www.brachers.co.uk.
Charity specialists: Simon Palmer. Ruth Pannell.

Benenden Hospital Trust (J)	7.65
East Malling Research	7.222
East Malling Trust, The (J)	7.222
Royal British Legion Industries Ltd (J)	7.554
Royal Engineers Association	7.559

BRADFORD & CO, 144 High Street, Nailsea, North Somerset, BS48 1AP. Tel: 01275 856 302. Fax: 01275 810 123.
Internet: www.bradfordlaw.co.uk.

Congregation of La Retraite Trustees (J)	7.171

BREADY & CO, 225 Dumbarton Road, Glasgow, G11 6AB.

Marie Curie Cancer Care (J)	7.410

BRECHER, 4th Floor, 64 North Row, London, W1K 7DA. Tel: 020 7563 1000. Fax: 020 7518 8420. Internet: www.brecher.co.uk.

Elrahma Charity Trust	7.231

BRETHERTONS, Montague House, 2 Clifton Road, Rugby, Warwickshire, CV21 3PX. Tel: 01788 579579. Fax: 01788 570949.
Internet: www.brethertons.co.uk.
Charity specialists: C B Cooper.

British Assoc Counselling & Psychotherapy (J)	7.92

BRIDGE MCFARLAND, 9 Cornmarket, Louth, Lincolnshire, LN11 9PY. Tel: 01507 605883. Fax: 01507 605708.
Internet: www.bridgemcfarland.co.uk.
Charity specialists: P R E McFarland.

Linkage Community Trust	7.390

BRIGNALLS BALDERSTON WARREN, Broadway Chambers, Letchworth, Hertfordshire, SG6 3AD. Tel: 01462 482 248. Fax: 01462 480 052. Internet: www.bbwlaw.biz.

Letchworth Garden City Heritage Foundation (J)	7.386

BRINDLEY, TWIST, TAFFT & JAMES, Lowick Gate, Siskin Drive, Coventry, Warwickshire, CV3 4FJ. Tel: 024 7653 1532. Fax: 024 7630 1300. Internet: www.bttj.com.

Alan Edward Higgs Charity (J)	7.22

BRISTOWS LLP, 100 Victoria Embankment, London, EC4Y 0DH. Tel: 020 7400 8000. Fax: 020 7400 8050.
Internet: www.bristows.com.
Charity specialists: Mark Hawes - specialist area: Charity, Corporate, Royal Charter. Miranda Cass - specialist area: Taxation, Charity. Teresa Edmund - specialist area: Real Estate. Linda R Farrell - specialist area: Human Resources, Professional Disciplinary Issues. Laura Anderson - specialist area: Intellectual Property. Dr Mark Watts - specialist

area: Information Technology, Data Protection.
Matthew Warren - specialist area: Intellectual
Property. Kevin E Appleton - specialist
area: Litigation.

Analytical Chemistry Trust Fund	7.31
Atlantic Charitable Trust	7.48
BRE Trust (J)	7.85
Electrical Safety Council	7.229
Geological Society of London	7.272
Institution of Civil Engineers (J)	7.338
Institution of Engineering and Technology (J)	7.338
Institution of Mechanical Engineers	7.338
Retired Greyhound Trust	7.534
Royal Academy of Engineering	7.549
Royal Astronomical Society	7.552

**BRM SOLICITORS, Gray Court, 99 Saltergate,
Chesterfield, Derbyshire, S40 1LD. Tel: 01246
555 111. Fax: 01246 554 411.
E-mail: info@brmlaw.co.uk.
Internet: www.brmlaw.co.uk.**

Arthritis Research UK (J)	7.40

**BRODIES LLP, Brodies House, 31-33 Union
Grove, Aberdeen, Aberdeenshire, AB10 6SD.
Tel: 01224 392 242. Fax: 01224 392 244.
Internet: www.brodies.com.**

Newton Dee Camphill Community Ltd	7.461

**BRODIES LLP, 15 Atholl Crescent, Edinburgh,
EH3 8HA. Tel: 0131 228 3777. Fax: 0131 228
3878. E-mail: andrew.dalgleish@brodies.co.uk.
Internet: www.brodies.co.uk.
Charity specialists:** A M C Dalgleish - specialist
area: Trusts, Tax, Charities & Estate Planning.
Brenda C Scott. H J Stevens.

Camphill Rudolf Steiner Estates	7.111
Camphill Rudolf Steiner Schools	7.111
National Galleries of Scotland (J)	7.446
Royal Botanic Garden Edinburgh (J)	7.553
Turning Point Scotland	7.691

**BRODIES LLP, 110 Queen Street, Glasgow,
G1 3BX. Tel: 0141 248 4672. Fax: 0141 221
9270. E-mail: mailbox@brodies.co.uk.
Internet: www.brodies.co.uk.**

Breast Cancer Care (J)	7.86
Capability Scotland (J)	7.113
Community Safety Glasgow (J)	7.167
Ex-Services Mental Welfare Society (J)	7.243
Quarriers (J)	7.519
Rokpa Trust (J)	7.543

**BROWN RUDNICK, 8 Clifford Street, London,
W1S 2LQ. Tel: 020 7851 6000. Fax: 020 7851
6100. Internet: www.brownrudnick.com.**

Worth Abbey (J)	7.742

**BROWNE JACOBSON, Victoria Square House,
Victoria Square, Birmingham, West Midlands,
B2 4BU. Tel: 0121 337 3900. Fax: 0121 236
1291. E-mail: info@brownejacobson.com.
Internet: www.brownejacobson.com.**

Oasis Charitable Trust (J)	7.477

**BROWNE JACOBSON, Ground Floor, 3 Piccadilly
Place, Manchester, Greater Manchester,
M1 3BN. Tel: 0161 300 8100.
Internet: www.brownejacobson.com.**

YHA (England and Wales) (J)	7.744

**BROWNE JACOBSON, Mowbray House, Castle
Meadow Road, Nottingham, Nottinghamshire,
NG2 1 BJ. Tel: 0115 976 6000. Fax: 0115 947
5246. E-mail: info@brownejacobson.com.
Internet: www.brownejacobson.com.
Charity specialists:** R Oakes. P J Ellis (Head of
Commercial Litigation) - specialist area: Intellectual
Property Litigation.

Baron Davenport's Charity	7.58
Children's Links (J)	7.141
Notts Roman Catholic Diocesan Trustees (J)	7.473
Diocese of ShrewsburyTrust (J)	7.607
Wyggeston's Hospital	7.743

**BRUTTON & CO, West End House, 288 West
Street, Fareham, Hampshire, PO16 0AJ.
Tel: 01329 236 171. Fax: 01329 289 915.**

Portsmouth Diocesan Board Of Finance	7.509
Royal Natl Mission to Deep Sea Fishermen (J)	7.567

**BTO, One Edinburgh Quay, 133 Fountainbridge,
Edinburgh, EH3 9QG. Tel: 0131 222 2939.
Fax: 0131 222 2949.
E-mail: lawyers@bto.co.uk.
Internet: www.bto.co.uk.**

Richmond Fellowship Scotland	7.537

**BTO, 48 St. Vincent Street, Glasgow, G2 5HS.
Tel: 0141 221 8012. Fax: 0141 221 7803.
E-mail: lawyers@bto.co.uk.
Internet: www.bto.co.uk.
Charity specialists:** A C Borthwick - specialist
area: Corporate Property and Charities.

Architectural Heritage Fund (J)	7.38
Baird Trust	7.54
Children's Hospice Association Scotland (J)	7.141
Community Lifestyles Limited	7.164
Great Steward of Scotland's Dumfries Hse Tst	7.285
Greenock Arts Guild Limited	7.287
Quarriers (J)	7.519
Queen's Cross Workspace	7.520
Royal National Lifeboat Institution (J)	7.567

**BUCKLES SOLICITORS LLP, Grant House, 101
Bourges Boulevard, Peterborough, PE1 1NG.
Tel: 01733 888 888. Fax: 01733 888 990.
E-mail: enquiries@buckles-law.co.uk.
Internet: www.buckles-law.co.uk.**

Chartered Institute of Purchasing & Supply	7.134

**BURGES SALMON LLP, One Glass Wharf,
Bristol, BS2 0ZX. Tel: 0117 902 2739.
Fax: 0117 902 4400. E-mail: email@burges-
salmon.com. Internet: www.burges-salmon.com.
Charity specialists:** T Gauterin. Rosie Parr (Head of
Charities Unit). C Wyld.

At-Bristol Ltd	7.48
Board of Trustees for the Royal Armouries	7.78
Children's Hospice South West (J)	7.141
Farmington Trust	7.249
Fdn&Friends of RoyalBotanicGardens, Kew (J)	7.259
Freeways Trust	7.264
Holstein UK (J)	7.315
Old Swinford Hospital	7.479
Royal Botanic Gardens, Kew	7.554
Sheepdrove Trust, The	7.600
Soil Association (J)	7.625

**BURNESS PAULL LLP, 120 Bothwell Street,
Glasgow, G2 7JL. Tel: 0141 248 4933.
Fax: 0141 204 1601.
E-mail: stephen.phillips@burnesspaull.com.
Internet: www.burnesspaull.com.**

Aberdeen Foyer	7.6
Action for Children (J)	7.10
Beatson Institute for Cancer Research	7.62
Capital City Partnership Limited	7.113
Changeworks	7.127
Clyde Gateway URC	7.157
Community Safety Glasgow (J)	7.167
Culture and Sport Glasgow	7.188
Fife Cultural Trust	7.253
Fife Sports & Leisure Trust Ltd	7.253
Glasgow Association for Mental Health	7.275
Glasgow Science Centre Limited	7.275
Glasgow Science Centre Charitable Trust	7.276
Health and Social Care Alliance, The (J)	7.305
INCLUDEM	7.330
Inspire (Partnership Through Life) Ltd	7.332
Irvine Bay Urban Regeneration Company (J)	7.346
Jobs & Business Glasgow	7.356
Riverside Inverclyde	7.539
Royal Col. Physicians & Surgeons Glasgow	7.557
Royal Natl Mission to Deep Sea Fishermen (J)	7.567
SCVO (J)	7.592
Thistle Foundation	7.677
VSA	7.709
Wise Group	7.733

**BURNETTS, 6 Victoria Place, Carlisle, Cumbria,
CA1 1ES. Tel: 01228 552222. Fax: 01228
522399. E-mail: info@burnetts.co.uk.
Internet: www.burnetts.co.uk.
Charity specialists:** T S Leach.

Croftlands Trust	7.187

**BURY & WALKERS, Britannic House, Regent
Street, Barnsley, South Yorkshire, S70 2EQ.
Tel: 01226 733533. Fax: 01226 207610.
Internet: www.burywalkers.com.**

Barnsley Premier Leisure	7.58

**BUSS MURTON LAW LLP, 31 High Street,
Cranbrook, Kent, TN17 3EE. Tel: 01892
510222. Fax: 01892 510333.
E-mail: gedwards@bussmurton.co.uk.
Internet: www.bussmurton.co.uk.**

SMB Charitable Trust (J)	7.619

**BUTCHER & BARLOW, 34 Railway Road, Leigh,
Lancashire, WN7 4AU. Tel: 01942 674144.
Fax: 01942 262217.
E-mail: enquiries@butcher-barlow.co.uk.
Internet: www.butcher-barlow.co.uk.**

Chetham's Hospital School and Library (J)	7.138

**BUTCHER & BARLOW, 31 Middlewich Road,
Sandbach, Cheshire, CW11 1HW. Tel: 01270
762521. Fax: 01270 764795.
E-mail: enquiries@butcher-barlow.co.uk.
Internet: www.butcher-barlow.co.uk.**

Booth Charities	7.79

**BUTCHER ANDREWS, 1 Old Post Office Street,
Fakenham, Norfolk, NR21 9BL. Tel: 01328
863131. Fax: 01328 864705.
E-mail: anne@butcherandrews.co.uk.
Internet: www.butcherandrews.co.uk.**

Break	7.86

**CALVERT SMITH & SUTCLIFFE, Onslow House, 9
The Green, Richmond, Surrey, TW9 1PU.
Tel: 020 8940 0017. Fax: 020 8948 8498.**

Barnes Workhouse Fund	7.57
Richmond Charities' Almshouses	7.537
Richmond Church Charity Estates	7.537
Royal British Legion Poppy Factory Limited (J)	7.554

**CAMERONS SOLICITORS LLP, 70 Wimpole
Street, London, W1G 8AX. Tel: 020 7467 5424.
Fax: 020 7486 8171.
E-mail: michaelstewart@camerons.co.uk.**

Healthcare Quality Improvement Partnership	7.306
Royal College of Ophthalmologists (J)	7.556
Royal College of Radiologists (J)	7.558

**CANNINGS CONNOLLY, 16 St. Martin's-le-
Grand, London, EC1A 4EE. Tel: 020 7329
9000. Internet: www.cclaw.co.uk.**

Ed & TrainingTst of Chartered Insurance Inst	7.227

**CAPITAL LAW, One Caspian Point, Caspian Way,
Cardiff, CF10 4DQ. Tel: 0870 224 1819.
Fax: 0870 224 9091.
Internet: www.capitallaw.co.uk.**

Mudiad Meithrin	7.438

**CAPSTICKS, 1 St George's Road, Wimbledon,
London, SW19 4DR. Tel: 020 8780 2211.
Fax: 020 8780 1141.
Internet: www.capsticks.com.**

Buckinghamshire Hospitals NHS Trust (J)	7.103
Hospital of St John and St Elizabeth (J)	7.321
Housing for Women	7.322
NHS Confederation	7.462
Royal Institute of British Architects (J)	7.562
SeeAbility (J)	7.596
Terrence Higgins Trust (J)	7.673
United Response (J)	7.697

CARPENTERS ROSE, 26 The Broadway, London, NW7 3NL. Tel: 020 8906 0088. Fax: 020 8959 1281. E-mail: general@carpentersrose.co.uk. Internet: www.carpentersrose.co.uk.

Melow Charitable Trust   7.420

CARREG LAW, 74 Rhosmaen Street, Llandeilo, Dyfed, SA19 6EN. Tel: 01558 678009. Internet: www.carreglaw.co.uk.

St David's Diocesan Board of Finance (J)   7.641

CARSON MCDOWELL, Murray House, Murray Street, Belfast, County Antrim, BT1 6HS. Tel: 028 9024 4951. Fax: 028 9024 5768. Internet: www.carson-mcdowell.com. Charity specialists: R D J Nixon.

Ulster Independent Clinic   7.693

CARTER LEMON CAMERONS, 10 Aldersgate Street, London, EC1A 4HJ. Tel: 020 7406 1000. Fax: 020 7406 1010. E-mail: duncantuft@cartercamerons.co.uk. Internet: www.cartercamerons.com. Charity specialists: D Tuft.

West London YMCA   7.721

CARTER-RUCK SOLICITORS, 6 St Andrew Street, London, EC4A 3AE.

Palestinians Relief and Development Fund   7.489

CARTMELL & CO SOLICITORS LTD, 12 High Street, Chalfont St Giles, Buckinghamshire, HP8 4QA. Tel: 01494 870075. E-mail: office@cartmell-solicitors.co.uk. Internet: www.cartmell-solicitors.co.uk.

Spoore, Merry & Rixman Foundation, The (J)   7.633

CASSELL MOORE, Edward Pavilion, Albert Dock, Liverpool, Merseyside, L3 4AF. Tel: 0151 375 9940. Fax: 0845 578 5722. E-mail: info@cassellmoore.com. Internet: www.cassellmoore.com.

Alternative Futures Group Ltd (J)   7.27

CHADWICKS SOLICITORS, 9-11 Towngate, Tudor House, Leyland, Lancashire, PR25 2EN. Tel: 01772 424 080. Fax: 01772 424 070. E-mail: law@chadwickssolicitors.co.uk. Internet: chadwicks-solicitors.co.uk.

International Aid Trust   7.340

CHAFES, 32 London Road, Alderley Edge, Cheshire, SK9 7DZ. Tel: 01625 585404.

David Lewis Centre (J)   7.194

CHALLENOR & SON, Stratton House, Bath Street, Abingdon, Oxfordshire, OX14 3LA. Tel: 01235 520013. Fax: 01235 534311.

Christ's Hospital of Abingdon   7.144

CHARLES RUSSELL SPEECHLYS LLP, 5 Fleet Place, London, EC4M 7RD. Tel: 020 7203 5000. Fax: 020 7203 0200. E-mail: mike.scott@crsblaw.com. Internet: www.charlesrussellspeechlys.com.

CHARLES RUSSELL SPEECHLYS LLP, Compass House, Lypiatt Road, Cheltenham, Gloucestershire, GL50 2QJ. Tel: 01242 221122. Fax: 01242 584700. E-mail: julia.cox@crsblaw.com. Internet: www.charlesrussellspeechlys.com.

CHARLES RUSSELL SPEECHLYS LLP, One London Square, Cross Lanes, Guildford, Surrey, GU1 1UN. Tel: 01483 252525. Fax: 01483 252550. E-mail: kate.parkinson@crsblaw.com. Internet: www.charlesrussellspeechlys.com.

At Charles Russell Speechlys we have one of the largest charity and not-for-profit practices in the country. The group spans the entire firm, sharing expertise, knowledge and resources to provide our clients with the support and advice they need to help them respond to the challenges they face. With strength in depth, we bring expertise from the firm's very broad general practice, both in the UK and internationally.

We act for a diverse range of charities and not-for-profit organisations. Our clients include household names, national and international charities, family charitable trusts, foundations, schools and professional and governing bodies.

We have particular knowledge of and involvement in the arts, environment, healthcare, museums and heritage, higher education, military, philanthropy, religious organisations, schools and sport.

Charity specialists: Michael Scott (Partner) - specialist area: Charity law, governance, mergers, trading. Sally Ashford (Partner) - specialist area: Legacy, Tax, trusts and estate planning. Jessica Arrol (Associate) - specialist area: Charity funds & investment structures. Vanessa Barnett (Partner) - specialist area: IT, digital & social media for charities. Nancy Battell (Associate) - specialist area: Charity property. Jonathan Bayliss (Partner) - specialist area: Charity funds & investment structures. Trevor Bettany (Partner) - specialist area: Charity employment. Robert Bond (Partner) - specialist area: Intellectual Property, charities and CSR. Ian Brothwood (Partner) - specialist area: Charity property. Simon Butterworth (Partner) - specialist area: Charity property. Andrew Cameron (Partner) - specialist area: Education charities and trustee issues. Louise Clark (Partner) - specialist area: Property litigation. Andrew Collins (Partner) - specialist area: Mergers, finance, joint ventures. Julia Cox (Partner) - specialist area: Philanthropy, tax, trusts & estate planning. George Duncan (Partner) - specialist area: Religious charities, tax & trusts. Duncan Elson (Partner) - specialist area: Legacy & disputes. David Green (Partner) - specialist area: Charity employment. Martin Griffiths (Senior Associate) - specialist area: Charity tax. Roberta Harvey (Partner) - specialist area: Legacy & disputes. Helen Hutton (Senior Associate) - specialist area: Planning & environmental. Michael M Jones (Partner) - specialist area: Charity pensions. Richard Kirby (Consultant) - specialist area: Charity, tax planning & international. Graeme Kleiner (Partner) - specialist area: Legacy & disputes. Ashley Kopitko (Partner) - specialist area: Charity property. Dominic Lawrance (Partner) - specialist area: Charity, tax planning & international. Nigel Morton (Partner) - specialist area: Charity property. Christopher Page (Partner) - specialist area: Philanthropy, tax, trusts & estate planning. Bart Peerless (Partner) - specialist area: Philanthropy, tax, trusts & estate planning. Jennifer Pierce (Partner) - specialist area: IP & IT. Lynn Povey (Partner) - specialist area: Charity Property & charity law. Prav Reddy (Partner) - specialist area: Corporate insolvency. Sarah Rowley (Associate) - specialist area: Charity law, governance, mergers, trading. Archie Sherbrooke (Senior Associate) - specialist area: Charity property. Ben Smith (Senior Associate) - specialist area: Charity employment. Sarah Jane Brostoff (Partner) -

specialist area: Charity employment. John Ward (Partner) - specialist area: Charity, tax planning & international trust. Andy Williams (Legal Director) - specialist area: Charity employment. Ruth Williams (Associate) - specialist area: Charity property. James Bradford (Associate) - specialist area: Philanthropy and tax planning. Henry Fea (Partner) - specialist area: Charity, tax planning & international. Christina Flemming (Associate) - specialist area: IP. Mark Harvey (Consultant) - specialist area: Charity law and governance. Debra Kent (Partner) - specialist area: Charity property. James Lister (Senior Associate) - specialist area: Legacy & disputes. Kate Parkinson (Associate) - specialist area: Charity commercial and corporate. Tamasin Perkins (Senior Associate) - specialist area: Legacy & disputes. Jason Saiban (Partner) - specialist area: Commercial. Tanya Wilkie (Associate) - specialist area: Charity law. Sara Wilson (Legal Director) - specialist area: Charity employment and employment disputes.

Baily Thomas Charitable Fund, The	7.54
BCS, The Chartered Institute for IT	7.61
Brampton Trust (J)	7.84
Church Commissioners for England (J)	7.147
City and Guilds of London Institute (J)	7.152
Colt Foundation	7.161
Company of Biologists Limited (J)	7.168
Design Museum (J)	7.199
Dorneywood Trust, The	7.208
Dulwich Estate (J)	7.214
EBM Charitable Trust	7.223
Ernest Cook Trust (J)	7.239
GarfieldWestonTrustforWestminsterAbbey	7.269
Godinton House Preservation Trust	7.279
Grocers' Charity	7.289
Guildford Diocesan Board of Finance	7.292
Hackney Joint Estate Charity (J)	7.295
Honourable Artillery Company (J)	7.316
Ian Askew Charitable Trust	7.326
Imperial Society of Teachers of Dancing (J)	7.329
London Philharmonic Orchestra	7.400
Louis Baylis Charitable Trust	7.403
Marie Curie Cancer Care (J)	7.410
Marie Louise Von Motesiczky Charitable Trust	7.410
Merchant Taylors' Consolidated Charities	7.422
National Army Museum	7.442
National Museum of Royal Navy, The	7.450
NSPCC (J)	7.452
Ombersley Conservation Trust	7.480
Pennington Mellor Munthe Charity Trust	7.495
Pirbright Institute (J)	7.504
Racing Welfare	7.523
Rainbow Trust Children's Charity	7.524
R. Ormonde Shuttleworth Remembrance Trust	7.536
RMIG Endowment Trust (J)	7.540
Roch. Diocesan Society & Bd of Fin (J)	7.542
Royal Air Force Benevolent Fund (J)	7.550
Royal Air Force Charitable Trust, The (J)	7.550
Royal Albert Hall (J)	7.551
Royal Electrical & Mech Eng Central Trust	7.559
Royal National Lifeboat Institution (J)	7.567
Royal Navy and Royal Marines Charity	7.568
RSPB (J)	7.572
RSPB (J)	7.572
Sandra Charitable Trust	7.586
SEMTA (J)	7.589
Society of Antiquaries of London (J)	7.621
St Andrew Holborn Charity	7.636
St Andrew Holborn Church Foundation	7.636
St Luke's Parochial Trust	7.648
St Olave's & St Saviour's Schools Foundation	7.652
Summerfield Charitable Trust	7.664
Victory Services Association Ltd	7.705

CHATTERTONS MCKINNELLS, 23 West Parade, Lincoln, Lincolnshire, LN1 1NW. Tel: 01522 541 181. Fax: 01522 513 764. E-mail: info@mckinnells.co.uk. Internet: www.chattertons.com.

Bransby Horses (J)   7.85

CHRISTOPHER B MITCHELL , New Zealand House, 9th Floor, 80th Haymarket, London, SW1Y 4TQ. Charity specialists: C Mitchell.

Dr Mortimer & Theresa Sackler Fdtn (J)   7.211
Sackler Trust, The (J)   7.579

CHUBB BULLEID, Langler House, Market Place, Somerton, Somerset, TA11 7LZ. Tel: 01458 271930. Fax: 01458 274019.
Internet: www.chubb-bulleid.co.uk.

Elizabeth and Prince Zaiger Trust	7.230

CLARION SOLICITORS, Britannia Chambers, 4 Oxford Place, Leeds, West Yorkshire, LS1 3AX. Tel: 0113 246 0622. Fax: 0113 246 7488.
E-mail: enquiries@clarionsolicitors.com.
Internet: clarionsolicitors.com.
Charity specialists: Marie Pugh. Alison Batty. Susannah Bottomley. Victoria Clark. R Hutton. Claire King. Sara Rogers. John Mackle.

Community Foundation for Leeds (J)	7.163
Outward Bound Trust (J)	7.485
RSPCA (J)	7.572

CLARKE MAIRS LLP, Royal House, 5-7 Market Street, Newcastle upon Tyne, Tyne and Wear, NE1 6JN.

Lonia Ltd	7.402

CLARKE WILLMOTT, 138 Edmund Street, Birmingham, West Midlands, B3 2ES. Tel: 0845 209 1001. Fax: 0845 209 2001.
Internet: www.clarkewillmott.com.

BEN-Motor & Allied Trades Benevolent Fund	7.64
West Midlands Special Needs Transport (J)	7.721

CLARKE WILLMOTT, Blackbrook Gate, Blackbrook Park Avenue, Taunton, Somerset, TA1 2PG. Tel: 01823 442 266. Fax: 01823 259643. Internet: www.clarkewillmott.com.

St Margaret's Somerset Hospice	7.649

CLARKSLEGAL LLP, Caspian Point, Caspian Way, Cardiff, CF10 4DQ. Tel: 029 2055 7500.
Internet: www.clarkslegal.com.

Wallich Clifford Community	7.712

CLARKSLEGAL LLP, 1 Forbury Square, The Forbury, Reading, Berkshire, RG1 3EB. Tel: 0118 958 5321. Fax: 0118 960 4611.
E-mail: msippitt@clarkslegal.com.
Internet: www.clarkslegal.com.

CFBT Education Trust (J)	7.125
Earley Charity (J)	7.219
International Alert (J)	7.340
Kaleidoscope Project Limited	7.365
Mr & Mrs J A Pye's Charitable Settlement (J)	7.437

CLARKSON WRIGHT & JAKES LTD, Valiant House, 12 Knoll Rise, Orpington, Kent, BR6 0PG. Tel: 01689 887808. Fax: 01689 887888. E-mail: amanda.mehlin@cwj.co.uk.
Internet: www.cwj.co.uk.

Mytime Active (J)	7.441
St Christopher's Hospice (J)	7.640

CLEAVER FULTON RANKIN, 50 Bedford Street, Belfast, County Antrim, BT2 7FW. Tel: 028 9024 3141. Fax: 028 9024 9096.
E-mail: info@cfrlaw.co.uk.
Internet: www.cfrlaw.co.uk.
Charity specialists: A J Rankin (Probate, Wills, Inheritance Tax, Charity). Jennifer E Ebbage.

Action for Children (J)	7.10
Action Mental Health (J)	7.11
Bryson Charitable Group	7.102
Disability Action (J)	7.201

CLIFFORD CHANCE LLP, 10 Upper Bank Street, London, E14 5JJ. Tel: 020 7006 1000.
Fax: 020 7006 5555.
Internet: www.cliffordchance.com.
Charity specialists: M Smyth. Cathy Jones.

Daiwa Anglo Japanese Foundation	7.192
Hertford British Hospital, Paris (J)	7.310
Impetus Private Equity Foundation (J)	7.330
National Autistic Society (J)	7.442
NSPCC (J)	7.452
Norwood (J)	7.472
RSPB (J)	7.572
Sadler's Wells Trust	7.580

Teach First (J)	7.670
Tottenham Grammar School Foundation	7.683
Victim Support	7.704

CLIFTON INGRAM LLP, 22-24 Broad Street, Wokingham, Berkshire, RG40 1BA. Tel: 0118 978 0099. Fax: 0118 977 1122.
E-mail: jimpaterson@cliftoningram.co.uk.
Internet: www.cliftoningram.co.uk.

Cinema and Television Benevolent Fund (J)	7.150
Donnington Hospital Trust	7.207

CLIVE TANT, PALMERS SOLICITORS, 19 Town Square, Basildon, Essex, SS14 1BD. Tel: 01268 240000. Fax: 01268 240001.

William Palmer College Educational Trust	7.731

CLYDE & CO, St Botolph Building, 138 Houndsditch, London, EC3A 7AR. Tel: 020 7876 5000. Fax: 020 7876 5111.
E-mail: infolondon@clydeco.com.
Internet: www.clydeco.com.

Art Services Grants Ltd	7.40
Mercy Ships - UK	7.423
Royal Aeronautical Society	7.550

CMS CAMERON MCKENNA, Mitre House, 160 Aldersgate Street, London, EC1A 4DD. Tel: 020 7367 3000. Fax: 020 7367 2000.
E-mail: info@cmck.com. Internet: www.cms-cmck.com.
Charity specialists: A J Crawford. Pamela Castle (Head of Environmental Law).

Chartered Accountants' Benevolent Assoc (J)	7.132
Contemporary Dance Trust (J)	7.178
Francis Crick Insitute Limited, The (J)	7.262
Henry Moore Foundation (J)	7.309
Inst of Marine Engineering, Science & Tech (J)	7.335
National Maritime Museum (J)	7.449
Nuffield Health (J)	7.474
Royal Geographical Society (J)	7.561
Science Museum Group (J)	7.590
Wellcome Trust (J)	7.718
Whitechapel Gallery (J)	7.725

CMS CAMERON MCKENNA, Saltire Court, 20 Castle Terrace, Edinburgh, EH1 2EN. Tel: 0131 228 8000. Fax: 0131 228 8888.
Internet: www.cms-cmck.com.

Inspiring Scotland (J)	7.332
James Hutton Institute, The (J)	7.350
Moredun Foundation, The (J)	7.433
Moredun Research Institute (J)	7.434
National Galleries of Scotland (J)	7.446
National Museums Scotland	7.451
Sacro	7.580

CMS CAMERON MCKENNA, 191 West George Street, Glasgow, G2 2LD. Tel: 0141 222 2200. Fax: 0141 222 2201. Internet: www.cms-cmck.com.

Robertson Trust (J)	7.541

COASTER LEGAL, Well House, Hunstrete, Pensford, Bristol, BS39 4NT. Tel: 01761 490 358. E-mail: anita.coaster@coasterlegal.co.uk.
Internet: www.coasterlegal.co.uk.

Gideons International British Isles (J)	7.274

COFFIN MEW SOLICITORS, 1000 Lakeside, North Harbour, Western Road, Portsmouth, Hampshire, PO6 3EN. Tel: 023 9238 8021. Fax: 023 9238 0952.
E-mail: info@coffinmew.co.uk.
Internet: www.coffinmew.co.uk.

Marwell Wildlife	7.414
Stewardship Services (UKET) Ltd (J)	7.658

COFFIN MEW SOLICITORS, Kings Park House, 22 Kings Park Road, Southampton, Hampshire, SO15 2UF. Tel: 023 8033 4661. Fax: 023 8033 0956. Internet: www.coffinmew.co.uk.

Hampshire & Isle of Wight Wildlife Trust	7.298

COLLYER BRISTOW, 4 Bedford Row, London, WC1R 4TF. Tel: 020 7242 7363. Fax: 020 7405 0555. E-mail: cblaw@collyerbristow.com.
Internet: www.collyerbristow.com.

Fellowship of School of Economic Science (J)	7.251
Hispanic Luso Brazilian Council	7.313
Royal Philharmonic Orchestra	7.569

CONWAY, FLOOD & TODD, 22 Market Square, Antrim, County Antrim, BT41 4DT.

Sisters of the Cross and Passion (J)	7.615

COODES, Elizabeth House, Castle Street, Truro, Cornwall, TR1 3AP. Tel: 01872 246200. Fax: 01872 241122.
Internet: www.coodes.co.uk.

Hall for Cornwall Trust	7.296

COOPERBURNETT, Napier House, 14-16 Mount Ephraim Road, Tunbridge Wells, Kent, TN1 1EE. Tel: 01892 515022. Fax: 01892 515088.
E-mail: tal@cooperburnet.com.
Internet: www.cooperburnett.com.

Church Army (J)	7.147

CORNFIELD LAW LLP, 47 Cornfield Road, Eastbourne, Sussex, BN21 4QN. Tel: 01323 412512. Fax: 01323 411611.
E-mail: elake@cornfieldlaw.co.uk.
Internet: www.cornfieldlaw.co.uk.
Charity specialists: A Board.

Chaseley Trust (J)	7.135

COVINGTON & BURLING LLP, 265 Strand, London, WC2R 1BH. Tel: 020 7067 2000.
Fax: 020 7067 2222. Internet: www.cov.com.

Solaraid	7.626

COZENS-HARDY LLP, Castle Chambers, Opie Street, Norwich, Norfolk, NR1 3DP. Tel: 01603 625231. Fax: 01603 627160.
E-mail: macollins@cozens-hardy.com.
Internet: www.cozens-hardy.com.

Anguish's Educational Foundation	7.33
Norfolk Wildlife Trust	7.464
Norwich Consolidated Charities (J)	7.471
Norwich Town Close Estate Charity	7.472

CRANE & WALTON, 113 - 117 London Road, Leicester, Leicestershire, LE2 0RG. Tel: 0116 2551901. Fax: 0116 2555864.
Internet: www.craneandwalton.co.uk.

Edith Murphy Foundation	7.226

CRESCENT LAW, 81 London Road, Morden, Surrey, SM4 5HP. Tel: 020 8640 2300.
Fax: 020 8640 6778.
Internet: www.crescentlaw.com.
Charity specialists: Imran Uddin.

Ahmadiyya Muslim Association UK	7.19

CRIPPS HARRIES HALL LLP, Wallside House, 12 Mount Ephraim Road, Tunbridge Wells, Kent, TN1 1EG. Tel: 01892 515121. Fax: 01892 544878. E-mail: peter.scott@crippslaw.com.
Internet: www.crippslaw.com.
Charity specialists: S D Leney - specialist area: Charity formation, reorganisations. Peter Scott (Principal in Charities Group) - specialist area: Charities & Taxplanning.

Abbeyfield Kent Society, The	7.5
Chatham Historic Dockyard Trust	7.135
Dorothy Kerin Trust	7.208
General Conference of the New Church (J)	7.270
Goodenough College	7.281
Heart of Kent Hospice, The	7.307
Horder Healthcare	7.317
John Marshall's Charity	7.359
Kelmarsh Trust	7.367
Moravian Church	7.433
Mrs E M Bates Trust (J)	7.437
Porchlight	7.509
Royal Geographical Society (J)	7.561
South West Environmental Parks Limited (J)	7.630
Whitley Wildlife Conservation Trust, The (J)	7.726

CRIPPS HARRIES HALL LLP, 53 Chandos Place, Covent Garden, London, WC2N 4HS. Tel: 020 7930 7879. Internet: www.crippslaw.com.

General Conference of the New Church (J)   7.270

CROMBIE WILKINSON, Forsyth House, Market Place, Malton, North Yorkshire, YO17 7LR. Tel: 01653 600070. Fax: 01653 600049. E-mail: malton@crombiewilkinson.co.uk. Internet: www.crombiewilkinson.co.uk.

Wilf Ward Family Trust (J)   7.728

CROMBIE WILKINSON, Clifford House, 19 Clifford Street, York, North Yorkshire, YO1 1RJ. Tel: 01904 624185. Fax: 01904 623078. E-mail: york@crombiewilkinson.co.uk. Internet: www.crombiewilkinson.co.uk.

York Citizens Theatre Trust   7.747

CROWLEY & CO, 10 - 16 Vere Street, Cardiff, CF24 3DS. Tel: 02920 458895. Fax: 02920 458894. E-mail: admin@crowleysolicitors.co.uk. Charity specialists: H Bhamjee OBE. Anna M Stewart.

Wales Council for Voluntary Action (J)   7.711

CULLEN KILSHAW, 27 Market Street, Galashiels, Borders, TD1 3AF.

Brothers of Charity Services (Scotland)   7.101

CULLIMORE DUTTON, Friars, White Friars, Chester, Cheshire, CH1 1XS. Tel: 01244 321 066. Fax: 01244 312 582. E-mail: info@bclaw.co.uk. Internet: www.bclaw.co.uk.

Cheshire Residential Homes   7.137
Chester Diocesan Board Finance   7.138

CUMBERLAND ELLIS LLP, Atrium Court, 15 Jockey's Fields, London, WC1R 4QR. Tel: 020 7242 0422. Fax: 020 7831 9081. Internet: www.cumberlandellis.com/home. Charity specialists: S Howell.

Rikkyo School in England Trust   7.538

CUNNINGHAM & DICKEY, 68 Upper Church Lane, Belfast, County Antrim, BT1 4LG. Tel: 028 9024 5896. Fax: 028 9032 7657. Internet: www.cdlegal.com.

Elim Foursquare Gospel Alliance (J)   7.230

CURREY & CO, 21 Buckingham Gate, London, SW1E 6LS. Tel: 020 7828 4091/8. Fax: 020 7828 5049. Charity specialists: E R H Perks.

Arundel Castle Trustees   7.42
Chatsworth House Trust (J)   7.136
CHK Charities Limited   7.143
Duke of Devonshire's Charitable Trust   7.213
Earl Fitzwilliam Charitable Trust (J)   7.218
Fitzwilliam Wentworth Amenity Trust (J)   7.255
Francis C Scott Charitable Trust   7.262
G M Morrison Charitable Trust   7.268
Horniman Public Museum and Public Park   7.318
John R Murray Charitable Trust   7.360
P F Charitable Trust   7.489
Parham Park Trust (1984)   7.491

CURRY POPECK, 380 Kenton Road, Kenton, Middlesex, HA3 8DP. Tel: 020 8907 2000. Fax: 020 8927 0499. E-mail: cpinfo@currypopeck.com. Internet: www.currypopeck.com.

St Luke's Hospice (Harrow & Brent)   7.648

D J DUMBLETON ESQ, 8 & 9 The Quadrant, Coventry, West Midlands, CV1 2EG.

Myton Hospices, The   7.441

DAC BEACHCROFT LLP, 100 Fetter Lane, London, EC4A 1BN. Tel: 020 7242 1011. Fax: 020 7894 6640. E-mail: info@dacbeachcroft.com.

Internet: www.dacbeachcroft.com. Charity specialists: Rt Hon Lord D J F Hunt of Wirral MBE - specialist area: Financial Services.

Chartered Institute Building   7.132
CIPFA (J)   7.151
College of Occupational Therapists   7.160
Congregation of the Passion Jesus Christ (J)   7.174
Higher Education Academy, The (J)   7.311
ifs School of Finance   7.328
Jisc (J)   7.355
Making Space (J)   7.407
Marine Stewardship Council   7.411
Norwood (J)   7.472
Royal College of Paediatrics (J)   7.556
SistersoftheSacred Hearts of Jesus & Mary (J)   7.580
Tompkins Foundation   7.683

DAC BEACHCROFT LLP, Portwall Place, Portwall Lane, Bristol, BS99 7UD. Tel: 0117 918 2000. Fax: 0117 918 2100. Internet: www.dacbeachcroft.com.

Foundation Trust Network, The (J)   7.261
National Osteoporosis Society (J)   7.451
North Bristol NHS Trust Charitable Funds (J)   7.465

DAC BEACHCROFT LLP, 7 Park Square, Leeds, West Yorkshire, LS1 2LW. Tel: 0113 251 4700. Fax: 0113 251 4900.

Internet: www.dacbeachcroft.com.

Doncaster & Bassetlaw Hospitals Trust   7.204
Higher Education Statistics Agency (J)   7.312

DAC BEACHCROFT LLP, Winton House, St Peter Street, Winchester, Hampshire, SO23 8BW. Tel: 01962 705 500. Fax: 01962 705 510. Internet: www.dacbeachcroft.com.

Salisbury District Hospital Charitable Fund   7.583

DALE & CO, 11 Beaumont Fee, Lincoln, Lincolnshire, LN1 1HU. Tel: 01522 513399.

Age UK Lincoln   7.18

DARBYS, Richmond House, Heath Road, Hale, Altrincham, Cheshire, WA14 2XP. Tel: 08000 843 780, Fax: 0161 2411446.

Pharmacist Support (J)   7.500

DARBYS, Midland House, West Way, Botley, Oxford, Oxfordshire, OX2 0PH. Tel: 01865 811700. Fax: 01865 811777. E-mail: info@darbys.co.uk. Internet: www.darbys.co.uk.

Berks, Bucks & Oxon Wildlife Trust (J)   7.66
British Horse Society (J)   7.94
E P A Cephalosporin Fund   7.218
Edward Penley Abraham Research Fund   7.228
Guy Newton Research Fund   7.293
Intl Network for Availability Of Scientific Pub   7.344
Mr & Mrs J A Pye's Charitable Settlement (J)   7.437
People 1st   7.496
Society Salutation Mary Virgin Ltd   7.624
St Michael's and All Saints Charity   7.650

DAVEY LAW LTD, 10/12 Dollar Street, Cirencester, Gloucestershire, GL7 2AL. Tel: 01285 654875. Fax: 01285 650963. E-mail: enquiries@daveylaw.co.uk. Internet: www.daveylaw.co.uk.

Longfield (J)   7.401

DAVID CONWAY & CO, 1 Great Cumberland Place, Marble Arch, London, W1H 7AL. Tel: 020 7258 3000. Fax: 020 7258 3390.

Rose Foundation   7.545

DAVID JEACOCK, 41 Church Street, Wootton Bassett, Swindon, Wiltshire, SN4 7BQ. Tel: 01793 854 111 Internet: www.lawandlegal.co.uk.

Alliance House Foundation (J)   7.26

DAVID PROSSER & CO SOLICITORS, 3 Court Road, Bridgend, CF31 1BL. Tel: 01656 645921. E-mail: enquiries@davidprosser.co.uk. Internet: www.davidprosser.co.uk.

Gofal Housing Trust (J)   7.280

DE CRUZ SOLICITORS, 1 Green Street, Mayfair, London, W1K 6RG. Tel: 020 7493 4265. Fax: 020 7318 7247. E-mail: info@decruz.net. Internet: www.decruz.net.

ESCRS Limited   7.242

DEAN WILSON LLP, Ridgeley House, 165 Dyke Road, Brighton, Sussex, BN3 1TL. Tel: 01273 249 200. Fax: 01273 770 913. E-mail: e-mail.thelawyers@deanwilson.co.uk. Internet: www.deanwilson.co.uk.

Blatchington Court Trust   7.75
Camelia Botnar Foundation   7.109

DEBENHAMS OTTAWAY, Ivy House, 107 St Peter's Street, St Albans, Hertfordshire, AL1 3EW. Tel: 01727 837161. Fax: 01727 830506. E-mail: lawyers@debenhamsottaway.co.uk. Internet: www.debenhamsottaway.co.uk. Charity specialists: Ruth Boulton. Kate Carroll. D Cheetham. J Foy. M Henry. A Stovin. N Turner. A Yates.

Childwick Trust (J)   7.142
Church Lands Charity   7.148
Life Opportunities Trust   7.388
National Assoc for Colitis and Crohn's (J)   7.442
St Albans Diocesan Board Finance (J)   7.635

DEBEVOISE & PLIMPTON, Tower 42, International Financial Centre, London, EC2N 1HT. Tel: 020 7786 9000. Fax: 0207 7588 4180. Internet: www.debevoise.com.

Disasters Emergency Committee (J)   7.202

DECHERT, 160 Queen Victoria Street, London, EC4V 4QQ. Tel: 020 7184 7000. Fax: 020 7184 7001. E-mail: advice@titmuss-dechert.com. Internet: www.dechert.com. Charity specialists: C Carman. M Stapleton.

Netherhall Educational Association   7.457
Sears Group Trust   7.595

DENTONS UKMEA LLP, One Fleet Place, London, EC4M 7WS. Tel: 020 7242 1212. Fax: 020 7246 7777. Internet: www.dentons.com/en. Charity specialists: Kathy Vanderhook.

CAMFED International   7.110
Gatsby Charitable Foundation   7.270
Henry Smith Charity   7.309
Kay Kendall Leukaemia Fund   7.366
Lloyds Foundation for England and Wales (J)   7.395
Order St Augustine Mercy Jesus (J)   7.483
Royal Albert Hall (J)   7.551
Whitgift Foundation (J)   7.726

DEVONSHIRES, Salisbury House, London Wall, London, EC2M 5QY. Tel: 020 7628 7576. Fax: 020 7256 7318. E-mail: info@devonshires.co.uk. Internet: www.devonshires.com.

Ability Housing Association   7.7
Church of Jesus Christ of Latter Day Saints (J)   7.149
Cripplegate Foundation   7.186
Dolphin Square Charitable Foundation, The (J)   7.203
Farmland Reserve UK Limited   7.249
Heritage Care (J)   7.310
Homeless International (J)   7.316
London Housing Foundation   7.399
Outward Housing (J)   7.486
Royal Air Force Museum   7.551
SHP   7.606
South London YMCA (J)   7.629
Surrey Community Development Trust   7.665
TLC Care Attendant Service   7.681
United St Saviour's Charities   7.698

DF LEGAL LLP, 1 North Place, Cheltenham, Gloucestershire, GL50 4DW. Tel: 01242 583434. Fax: 01242 583435. Internet: www.dflegal.com.

Elim Foursquare Gospel Alliance (J)   7.230

DICKINSON MANSER LLP, 5 Parkstone Road, Poole, Dorset, BH15 2NL. Tel: 01202 673071. Fax: 01202 680470.
E-mail: mjd@dmsolicitors.co.uk.
Internet: www.dickinsonmanser.co.uk.
Charity specialists: G Cox.

Talbot Village Trust	7.668

DILWYNS, Oxford Chambers, Temple Street, Llandrindod Wells, Powys, LD1 5DL. Tel: 01597 822 707. Internet: www.dilwyns-solicitors.co.uk.

Royal Welsh Agricultural Society Limited	7.575

DIXON WARD, 16 The Green, Richmond, Surrey, TW9 1QD. Tel: 020 8940 4051. Fax: 020 8940 3901.

Hilden Charitable Fund	7.312
Richmond Parish Lands Charity	7.538

DLA PIPER UK LLP, 3 Noble Street, London, EC2V 7EE. Tel: 08700 111111. Fax: 020 7796 6666. Internet: www.dlapiper.com.
Charity specialists: Karen E Friebe - specialist area: Charity Law & Property. Catherine Usher. T Leek. M Collins (National Banking Group Head).

Ambitious about Autism (J)	7.29
Catholic Trust for England and Wales (J)	7.120
Esmée Fairbairn Foundation (J)	7.240
Howletts Wild Animal Trust, The (J)	7.322
Marie Curie Cancer Care (J)	7.410
NSPCC (J)	7.452

DLA PIPER UK LLP, Victoria Square House, Victoria Square, Birmingham, West Midlands, B2 4DL. Tel: 0845 7262 728. Fax: 0121 212 5794. Internet: www.dlapiper.com.

SEMTA (J)	7.589

DLA PIPER UK LLP, Princes Exchange Princes Square, Leeds, West Yorkshire, LS1 4BY. Tel: 08700 111 111. Fax: 0113 369 2949. Internet: www.dlapiper.com.

Leeds Diocesan Trust	7.382
London Grid for Learning Trust	7.399
South West Grid for Learning Trust (J)	7.630

DLA PIPER UK LLP, India Buildings, Water Street, Liverpool, Merseyside, L2 0NH. Tel: 0151 227 3060. Fax: 0151 236 1079. Internet: www.dlapiper.com.
Charity specialists: D Mason. M Pinfold.

Parkhaven Trust	7.491

DLA PIPER UK LLP, 101 Barbirolli Square, Manchester, Greater Manchester, M2 3DL. Tel: 08700 111 111. Fax: 0161 235 4111. Internet: www.dlapiper.com.

Higher Education Careers Services Unit	7.311

DLA PIPER UK LLP, 1 St Paul's Place, Sheffield, South Yorkshire, S1 2JX. Tel: 08700 111 111. Fax: 0114 270 0568.
Internet: www.dlapiper.com.

Magna Trust	7.407
St Luke's Hospice (J)	7.647

DMH STALLARD, 98 Queens Road, Brighton, Brighton & Hove, BN1 3YB. Tel: 01273 329833. Fax: 01273 747500.
Internet: www.dmhstallard.com.

International HIV/AIDS Alliance (J)	7.342
Order St Augustine Mercy Jesus (J)	7.483

DMH STALLARD, Gainsborough House, Pegler Way, Crawley, Sussex, RH11 7FZ. Tel: 01293 663 481. Fax: 01293 663 480.
Internet: www.dmhstallard.com.

Arundel and Brighton Diocesan Trust (J)	7.42
Congregation of the Sisters of St Martha (J)	7.175
Crime Reduction Initiatives (J)	7.186
Institute of Development Studies (J)	7.334
Worth Abbey (J)	7.742

DONNELLY & ELLIOTT LTD, 38 Stoke Road, Gosport, Hampshire, PO12 1JG. Tel: 023 9250 5500. Fax: 023 9250 3980.
E-mail: EWQ@donnelly-elliott.co.uk.
Internet: www.donnelly-elliott.co.uk.

Stansted Park Foundation	7.656

DORSEY & WHITNEY, 21 Wilson Street, London, EC2M 2TD. Tel: 020 7588 0800.
Internet: www.dorsey.com.

Punchdrunk	7.518

DOUGLAS-JONES MERCER, 16 Axis Court, Mallard Way, Swansea Vale, Swansea, SA7 0AJ. Tel: 01792 650000. Fax: 01792 656500. Internet: www.djm.law.co.uk.
Charity specialists: P Graham. K Morgan. M Snowdon.

Action for Children (J)	7.10

DOWLE SMITH & RUTHERFORD, St.Olaf's Hall, Church Road, Lerwick, Shetland, ZE1 0FD. Tel: 01595 695583. Fax: 01595 695310.
E-mail: solicitors@d-s-r.co.uk. Internet: www.d-s-r.co.uk.
Charity specialists: C J W Dowle. P J W Rutherford.

Shetland Amenity Trust	7.604
Shetland Recreational Trust	7.605

DOWNS, 156 High Street, Dorking, Surrey, RH4 1BQ. Tel: 01306 880110. Fax: 01306 876577. Internet: www.downslaw.co.uk.
Charity specialists: T Hughes.

Chief Fire Officers Association, The	7.139

DOYLE CLAYTON, One Crown Court, Cheapside, London, EC2V 6LR. Tel: 020 7329 9090.
E-mail: info@doyleclayton.co.uk.
Internet: www.doyleclayton.co.uk.

Marie Curie Cancer Care (J)	7.410

DRIVERS, 56a, Bootham, York, North Yorkshire, YO30 7BZ. Tel: 01904 625661. Fax: 01904 646259. Internet: www.drivers-solicitors.co.uk.

John Horseman Trust, The	7.358
York Conservation Trust	7.747

DRUCES LLP, Salisbury House, London Wall, London, EC2M 5PS. Tel: 020 7638 9271.
Fax: 020 7628 7525. E-mail: info@druces.com.
Internet: www.druces.com.

Alexian Brothers of Province of Sacred Heart	7.24
Dogs Trust (J)	7.203
Institute of Daughters of Mary Help (J)	7.334
Sisters of the Holy Family	7.616
Sisters Holy Family Bordeaux (J)	7.616

DRUMMOND MILLER WS, 32 Moray Place, Edinburgh, EH3 6BZ. Tel: 0131 226 5151.
Fax: 0131 225 2608.
E-mail: mail@drumil.demon.co.uk.
Internet: www.drummondmiller.co.uk.

Edina Trust	7.224
Kirkhouse Trust	7.374

DTM LEGAL LLP, Archway House, Station Road, Chester, Cheshire, CH1 3DR. Tel: 01244 354 800. Fax: 01244 403 485.
E-mail: alisonbrennan@dtmlegal.com.
Internet: www.dtmlegal.com.

North of England Zoological Society (J)	7.467

DUNCAN MCLEAN & CO, 81 John Finnie Street, Kilmarnock, Ayrshire, KA1 1BG.

Partners for Inclusion	7.492

DUTTON GREGORY, 48/50 Parkstone Road, Poole, Dorset, BH15 2PG. Tel: 01202 466669. Fax: 01202 668614.
Internet: www.duttongregory.co.uk.

Bournemouth Young Men's Christian Assoc	7.82

DUTTON GREGORY LLP, Trussell House, 23 St Peter Street, Winchester, Hampshire, SO23 8BT. Tel: 01962 844333. Fax: 01962 863582. Internet: www.duttongregory.co.uk.
Charity specialists: Gill Longman. Mr Keighley.

E Hayes Dashwood Foundation (J)	7.218

DWF LLP, Bridgewater Place, Water Lane, Leeds, West Yorkshire, LS11 5DY. Tel: 0113 261 6187.
E-mail: catherine.rustomji@dwf.co.uk.
Internet: www.dwf.co.uk.
Charity specialists: Catherine Rustomji (Director, Charities). Sarah Morgan (Director, Empolyment). Derek Ellery (Partner, Corporate). Richard S Williams (Partner, Affordable Housing). David Walton (Partner, Property). Kathy Halliday (Partner, Emploment). Emma Roe (Partner, Corporate). Tim Scott (Partner, Employment). Adam Heather (Partner, Real Estate). Mitch Brown (Partner, Social Housing).

Action Against Hunger (UK) (J)	7.9
Alternative Futures Group Ltd (J)	7.27
Amateurs Trust, The	7.29
Architectural Heritage Fund (J)	7.38
Arthritis Research UK (J)	7.40
Avocet Trust (J)	7.52
Birmingham Royal Ballet (J)	7.73
Canal & River Trust (J)	7.111
Central England Quakers (CEQ) (J)	7.122
Chetham's Hospital School and Library (J)	7.138
Cottage and Rural Enterprises Limited (J)	7.181
East Cheshire Hospice	7.220
ICAN	7.327
Joseph Rowntree Charitable Trust (J)	7.363
Joseph Rowntree Foundation (J)	7.363
Kings Place Music Foundation	7.373
Kirklees Active Leisure	7.374
Liverpool & Merseyside Theatres Trust (J)	7.392
Living Streets (The Pedestrians' Association)	7.394
Manchester & District Home for Lost Dogs (J)	7.408
Marie Curie Cancer Care (J)	7.410
Mental Health Matters (J)	7.421
Multiple Sclerosis Society (J)	7.438
Nat Museums & Galleries on Merseyside (J)	7.450
Nordoff Robbins Music Therapy Centre (J)	7.464
North Country Leisure (J)	7.465
North Lanarkshire Leisure Ltd	7.467
PDSA (J)	7.494
Percy Hedley Foundation (J)	7.497
Performances Birmingham Ltd	7.498
Pilling Trust Fund, The	7.504
Pony Club	7.508
Ramblers Association (J)	7.525
Rathbone Training	7.526
Richmond Fellowship (J)	7.537
Royal British Legion (J)	7.554
Skills Active UK (J)	7.617
Skills for Care	7.617
Society of African Missions (J)	7.621
St Ann's Hospice (J)	7.637
St Anne's Community Services	7.637
St Cuthberts Care (J)	7.641
St Gemma's Hospice Leeds (J)	7.643
St George's Police Children Trust (J)	7.643
St Mungo Community Housing Association (J)	7.652
St Oswald's Hospice (J)	7.653
Sue Ryder (J)	7.663
Tees Valley Community Foundation (J)	7.671
Trafford Community Leisure Trust	7.684
Training 2000 (J)	7.685
TTE Technical Training Group, The (J)	7.690
Turning Point (J)	7.691
Voiceability Advocacy (J)	7.708
Wirral Autistic Society (J)	7.733
YMCA Glasgow (J)	7.745
Yorkshire Air Ambulance	7.749
Yorkshire Cancer Research (J)	7.749
Young Enterprise	7.750

E J MOYLE, 2a Broadmark Parade, Rustington, West Sussex, BN16 2NE. Tel: 01903 784447. Fax: 01903 787822.
E-mail: rustmail@moyle.co.uk.
Internet: www.moyle.co.uk.

Bowerman Charitable Trust (J)	7.82

EDC LORD & CO, Link House, 1200 Uxbridge Road, Hayes, Middlesex, UB4 8JD. Tel: 0208 848 9988. Fax: 0208 561 0101.
E-mail: ealing@edclord.com.
Internet: www.edclord.com.

YMCA England (J)   7.745

EDDOWES WALDRON, 12 St Peter's Churchyard, Derby, Derbyshire, DE1 1TZ. Tel: 01332 348484. Fax: 01332 291312.
Internet: www.ewlaw.co.uk.

Derby Diocesan Board Finance Ltd   7.198

EDELL JONES & LESSERS, 1 Ron Leighton Way, East Ham, London, E6 1JA. Tel: 020 8548 5700. Fax: 020 8548 5720.

Cranstoun Drug Services (J)   7.184

EDMONDSON HALL, 25 Exeter Road, Newmarket, Suffolk, CB8 8AR. Tel: 01638 560556. Fax: 01638 561656.
E-mail: solicitors@edmonsonhall.com.
Internet: www.edmonsonhall.com.
Charity specialists: Anna Hall.

Injured Jockeys Fund (J)   7.331

EDWARD HANDS & LEWIS, The Old School Rooms, 346 Loughborough Road, Loughborough, Leicestershire, LE4 5PJ. Tel: 0110 266 5394. Fax: 0110 266 6446.
E-mail: info@ehlsolicitors.co.uk.
Internet: www.ehlsolicitors.co.uk.

Rosminian Sisters Providence   7.545

EDWARD HARTE LLP, 6 Pavilion Parade, Brighton, Brighton & Hove, BN2 1RA. Tel: 01273 662750. Fax: 01273 662755.
Internet: www.edward-harte.co.uk.

Windhorse Trust, The (J)   7.732

EDWARDS & CO, 28 Hill Street, Belfast, County Antrim, BT1 2LA. Tel: 028 9032 1863.
Fax: 028 9033 2723.
E-mail: jenny.ebbage@edwardsandcompany.co.uk. Internet: www.edwardsandcompany.co.uk.
Charity specialists: R Murphy.

Northern Ireland Assoc for Mental Health   7.470

EDWARDS DUTHIE, 9/15 York Road, Ilford, Essex, IG1 3AD. Tel: 020 8514 9000. Fax: 020 8514 9009. Internet: www.edwardsduthie.com.

Montessori St Nicholas Charity, The   7.652

EDWIN COE LLP, 2 Stone Buildings, Lincoln's Inn, London, WC2A 3TH. Tel: 020 7691 4000.
Fax: 020 7691 4111.
E-mail: marketing@edwincoe.com.
Internet: www.edwincoe.com.
Charity specialists: David Goepel (Head of Charities Group).

Association of Accounting Technicians	7.46
BPR Trust	7.83
Gosling Foundation Limited	7.282
PohWER (J)	7.506

EEF, Broadway House, Tothill St, London, SW1H 9NQ.

Design Council (J)   7.199

ELDRIDGES, 36 St James Street, Newport, Isle of Wight, PO30 1LF. Tel: 01983 524741.
Fax: 01983 521421.
E-mail: info@eldridges.co.uk.
Internet: www.eldridges.co.uk.

St Cecilia's Abbey Ryde Isle of Wight (J)   7.639

ELLIOTT DUFFY GARRETT, 2nd Floor, Royston House, 34 Upper Queen Street, Belfast, BT1 6FD. Tel: 028 9024 5034. Fax: 028 9024 1337. E-mail: michael.wilson@edglegal.com.
Internet: www.edglegal.com.
Charity specialists: M Wilson.

Disability Action (J)	7.201
Northern Ireland Hospice	7.470

ELLIS FERMOR AND NEGUS, 2 Devonshire Avenue, Beeston, Nottingham, Nottinghamshire, NG9 1BS. Tel: 0115 922 1591. Fax: 0115 925 9341. E-mail: beeston@ellis-fermor.co.uk.
Internet: www.ellis-fermor.co.uk.

Church Growth Trust (J)   7.147

ELLIS FERMOR AND NEGUS, 5 Market Place, Ripley, Derbyshire, DE5 3BS. Tel: 01773 744 744. Fax: 01773 570 047. E-mail: ripley@ellis-fermor.co.uk. Internet: www.ellis-fermor.co.uk.

Nottingham YMCA   7.473

ELLISONS, Headgate Court, Head Street, Colchester, Essex, CO1 1NP. Tel: 01206 764477. Fax: 01206 764455.
Internet: www.ellisonslegal.com.

Acorn Villages (J)	7.8
Clacton Family Trust	7.154

ELMHIRST PARKER LLP, 17/19 Regent Street, Barnsley, South Yorkshire, S70 2HP. Tel: 01226 282238. Fax: 01226 244153.
E-mail: barnsley@elmhirstparker.com.
Internet: www.elmhirstparker.com.

Barnsley Hospice Appeal   7.58

EMMS GILMORE LIBERSON, Lancaster House, 67 Newhall Street, Birmingham, West Midlands, B3 1NQ. Tel: 0121 236 6639.

West Midlands Special Needs Transport (J)   7.721

EMW LAW, Seebeck House, 1 Seebeck Place, Milton Keynes, Buckinghamshire, MK5 8FR. Tel: 0845 070 6000.
E-mail: enquiries@emwllp.com.
Internet: www.emwllp.com.

Milton Keynes Community Foundation   7.428

ENDEAVOUR PARTNERSHIP LLP, Westminster, St Mark's Court, Teesdale Business Park, Teesside, Stockton-on-Tees, TS17 6QP. Tel: 01642 610300. Fax: 01642 610330.
E-mail: enquiries@endeavourpartnership.com
Internet: www.endeavourpartnership.com.

NETA Training Trust   7.457

ENN ADVOKATBYRA, Strandvägen 47, 114 56, Stockholm. Tel: 00 46(0)8 545 688 30. Fax: 00 46(0)8 545 688 39.
E-mail: info@enadvokatbyra.se.
Internet: www.enadvokatbyra.se.

Philharmonia (J)   7.500

EVERSHEDS, 1 Wood Street, London, EC2V 7WS. Tel: 0845 497 9797.
Internet: www.eversheds.com/education.
Charity specialists: R McCreath. N Morris. C Sly. Sue Taylor. R K Lewis - specialist area: Pension Law.

Anchor Trust (J)	7.31
Bolton Community Leisure Limited	7.78
Elton John Aids Foundation	7.231
FIA Foundation for Automobile & Society (J)	7.252
Institute of Physics	7.336
Jane Hodge Foundation	7.351
Joseph Rowntree Foundation (J)	7.363
Newcastle Healthcare Charity (J)	7.459
Newlife Foundation for Disabled Children	7.461
Northern College for Residential Adult Ed	7.470
Onside Youth Zones (J)	7.480
South Bank Centre (J)	7.628
Sports Aid Trust (J)	7.633
Sue Ryder (J)	7.663
Trustees of the London Clinic Limited (J)	7.689
Turning Point (J)	7.691
Universities UK	7.700
Welsh National Opera (J)	7.718

EVERYS, Magnolia House, Church Street, Exmouth, Devon, EX8 1HQ. Tel: 01395 264384.
Fax: 01395 267643.
E-mail: john.hawkins@everys.co.uk.
Internet: www.everys.co.uk.

Norman Family Charitable Trust   7.464

F J CLEVELAND LLP, Hillbrow House, Hillbrow Road, Esher, Surrey, KT10 9NW.
Internet: www.cleveland-ip.com.

British Small Animal Veterinary Assoc (J)   7.99

FARRER & CO LLP, 66 Lincoln's Inn Fields, London, WC2A 3LH. Tel: 020 3375 7000.
Fax: 020 3375 7001.
E-mail: enquiries@farrer.co.uk.
Internet: www.farrer.co.uk.
Charity specialists: T Bruce. J Carleton. Elizabeth Jones (Senior Associate). S Macdonald. J Maloney (Senior Associate). Anne-Marie Piper. Laetitia Ransley (Solicitor). P Reed. J Smith. Maria Strauss. Hannah Whyatt.

Age UK (J)	7.17
AIM Foundation	7.20
Albert Hunt Trust	7.23
Allchurches Trust	7.25
Ambitious about Autism (J)	7.29
Art Fund	7.40
Associated Board Royal Schools Music	7.45
Bader International Study Centre	7.54
Bell Educational Trust Ltd (J)	7.64
Bible & Gospel Trust	7.69
Bishopsgate Foundation	7.73
Breast Cancer Care (J)	7.86
British Academy of Film & Television Arts	7.91
British Film Institute (J)	7.93
British Gas Energy Trust	7.93
Burghley House Preservation Trust	7.104
Church Commissioners for England (J)	7.147
Churches Conservation Trust	7.150
Clothworkers' Foundation	7.157
Colyer-Fergusson Charitable Trust	7.161
Cong of the Daughters of the Cross of Liege	7.173
Country Houses Foundation	7.182
Cremation Society of Great Britain, The	7.185
Cullum Family Trust	7.188
DHL UK Foundation	7.200
Dominican Council	7.203
Dominican Sisters Congregation Newcastle (J)	7.204
Duchy of Lancaster Benevolent Fund	7.213
Duchy of Lancaster Jubilee Trust	7.213
Duke of Edinburgh's Award (J)	7.214
Dulverton Trust (J)	7.214
Dulwich Picture Gallery (J)	7.215
Elizabeth Finn Care (J)	7.230
Elizabeth Frankland Moore & Star Fdn	7.230
Exilarch's Foundation (J)	7.244
FamilyLives	7.248
February Foundation, The	7.250
Fishmongers' Company's Charitable Trust	7.255
Florence Nightingale Aid Sickness Trust	7.256
Football League (Community) Limited, The	7.257
Fdn&Friends of RoyalBotanicGardens, Kew (J)	7.259
Future of Russia Foundation	7.267
Grace Trust, The (J)	7.283
Great Britain Sasakawa Foundation	7.284
Greenwich Royal Naval College Foundation	7.288
H D H Wills 1965 Charitable Trust	7.294
Haberdashers' Benevolent Foundation, The	7.295
Haberdashers' Educational Foundation	7.295
Hand in Hand International	7.300
Historic Royal Palaces	7.314
Hospital of St John and St Elizabeth (J)	7.321
Hughes Travel Trust (J)	7.323
Injured Jockeys Fund (J)	7.331
Institute of Cancer Research (J)	7.334
Institution of Structural Engineers (J)	7.339
Intl Foundation for Aids to Navigation	7.342
International Inst for Strategic Studies (J)	7.343
Islamic Help	7.347
Islamic Trust	7.347
King's Fund, The	7.373
Laureus Sport for Good Foundation	7.380
Lawrence Atwell's Charity	7.380
Leathersellers Company Charitable Fund	7.381
Linbury Trust	7.389
LTA Trust, The	7.404
Lumos Foundation	7.404
Lyric Hammersmith (J)	7.404
Marine Society & Sea Cadets (J)	7.411
Med Col of St Bartholomew's Hospital	7.419
Museum of London	7.440
National Gallery	7.447
National Gallery Trust	7.447

National Maritime Museum (J)	7.449
National Portrait Gallery (J)	7.451
Natural History Museum	7.455
Paul Hamlyn Foundation (J)	7.493
Paul Mellon Centre for Studies British Art	7.493
People Potential Possibilities (J)	7.496
Pilgrim Trust	7.503
Police Rehabilitation Centre (J)	7.507
Prince of Wales's Charitable Fndtn (J)	7.514
Prism The Gift Fund	7.515
Queen's Trust, The	7.521
Rank Foundation Limited (J)	7.525
Rayne Foundation	7.526
Rhodes Trust (J)	7.535
Riders for Health (J)	7.538
Rothschild Foundation (Hanadiv) Europe	7.547
Rothschild Foundation	7.547
Royal Air Force Club	7.551
Royal British Legion (J)	7.554
Royal Collection Trust	7.555
Royal College of Surgeons (J)	7.558
Royal Commission for the 1851 Exhibition	7.558
Royal Hospital for Neuro-disability (J)	7.562
Royal Institute International Affairs (J)	7.562
Royal Institution of Great Britain (J)	7.562
Royal Literary Fund	7.563
Royal Marsden Cancer Campaign	7.564
Royal National Institute of Blind People (J)	7.566
Royal Opera House Endowment Fund 2000	7.569
Save the Children (J)	7.588
Science Museum Foundation	7.589
Science Museum Group (J)	7.590
Seckford Foundation (J)	7.595
Sino-British Fellowship Trust	7.609
Sir Andrew Judd Foundation	7.609
Sir Edward Lewis Foundation	7.610
Solicitors Benevolent Association (J)	7.626
Somerset House Trust (J)	7.627
St Christopher's Hospice (J)	7.640
St John Ambulance (J)	7.644
Stanley Picker Trust, The	7.655
Tommy's, the baby charity	7.682
Trust for London	7.688
United Jewish Israel Appeal (J)	7.696
V&A Foundation, The	7.702
Victoria and Albert Museum	7.705
Wellcome Trust (J)	7.718
Weston Park Foundation	7.724
Whiteley Homes Trust (J)	7.725
Will Charitable Trust (J)	7.729
Will Woodlands (J)	7.729
Wood Green Animal Shelters (J)	7.736
Worth Abbey (J)	7.742
WWF UK (J)	7.743
Ymddiriedolaeth Clough Williams-Ellis Fdn	7.746

FASKEN MARTINEAU LLP, 17 Hanover Square, Mayfair DX 82984, London, W1S 1HU. Tel: 0207 917 8500. Fax: 0207 917 8555. E-mail: london@fasken.co.uk. Internet: www.fasken.com.

Raleigh International Trust (J)	7.524

FBC MANBY BOWDLER LLP, Routh House, Hall Court, Hall Park Way, Telford, Shropshire, TF3 4NJ. Tel: 01952 292129. Fax: 01952 291716. E-mail: info@fbcmb.co.uk.. Internet: www.fbcmb.co.uk.

Lichfield Diocesan Board Of Finance	7.387

FIELD SEYMOUR PARKES, 1 London Street, Reading, Berkshire, RG1 4PN. Tel: 0118 951 6200. Fax: 0118 950 2704. E-mail: enquiry@fsp-law.com. Internet: www.fsp-law.com. Charity specialists: Sue Vandersteen.

Berkshire Maestros	7.66
Office of the Ind. Adjudicator for Higher Ed.	7.478
Style Acre	7.663
United Bible Societies Association, The	7.695

FIELDFISHER, Riverbank House, 2 Swan Lane, London, EC4R 3TT. Tel: 020 7861 4000. Fax: 020 7488 0084. E-mail: info@fieldfisher.com. Internet: www.fieldfisher.com.

Architectural Association Incorporated (J)	7.38

Beaverbrook Foundation	7.63
Bloodwise (J)	7.76
East of England Agricultural Society	7.223
Fellowship of School of Economic Science (J)	7.251
Marie Curie Cancer Care (J)	7.410
National Heart & Lung Inst. Foundation, The	7.448
Nursing & Midwifery Council	7.476
Royal Academy of Dance	7.549
Royal College of Physicians of London	7.557
Royal Institution of Great Britain (J)	7.562
Royal London Society for the Blind (J)	7.564
Walcot Educational Foundation (J)	7.711

FIELDINGS PORTER, Silverwell House, Silverwell Street, Bolton, Greater Manchester, BL1 1PT. Tel: 01204 540900. Fax: 01204 362129. Internet: www.fieldingsporter.co.uk.

Human Relief Foundation	7.324
Onside Youth Zones (J)	7.480
Salford Diocesan Trust (J)	7.582

FINN GLEDHILL, 1-4 Harrison Road, Halifax, West Yorkshire, HX1 2AG. Tel: 01422 330000. Fax: 01422 342604. Internet: www.finngledhill.co.uk.

Community Foundation for Calderdale	7.162

FISHER JONES GREENWOOD LLP, Newcomen Way, Severalls Business Park, Colchester, Essex, CO4 9YA. Tel: 01206 835230. Fax: 01206 835239. E-mail: info@fjg.co.uk. Internet: www.fjg.co.uk.

St Helena Hospice (J)	7.644

FLADGATE LLP, 16 Queen Street, London, WC2B 5DG. Tel: 02030367000. Fax: 02030367600. E-mail: fladgate@fladgate.com. Internet: www.fladgate.com. Charity specialists: P Sewell.

A W Charitable Trust	7.4
Bowerman Charitable Trust (J)	7.82
Federation of Synagogues (J)	7.251
Institute of Biomedical Science	7.333
S F Foundation	7.578

FOOT ANSTEY LLP, Senate Court, Southernhay Gardens, Exeter, Devon, EX1 1NT. Tel: 01392 411221. Fax: 01392 685220. E-mail: contact@footanstey.com. Internet: www.footanstey.com.

FOOT ANSTEY LLP, Salt Quay House, Sutton Harbour, Plymouth, Devon, PL4 0BN. Tel: 01752 675 000. Fax: 01752 675 500. E-mail: contact@footanstey.com. Internet: www.footanstey.com.

FOOT ANSTEY LLP, High Water House, Malpas Road, Truro, Cornwall, TR1 1QH. Tel: 01872 243 300. Fax: 01872 242 458. E-mail: contact@footanstey.com. Internet: www.footanstey.com. Charity specialists: James Evans. Anna Roderick. Lucy Gill. Alex Rogers. Emma Facey. Emilie Gingell. Anna Phillips.

Age UK (J)	7.17
Barnabas Fund (J)	7.57
British Horse Society (J)	7.94
Cornwall Care (J)	7.180
Dame Hannah Rogers Trust (J)	7.192
Dartington Hall Trust, The (J)	7.192
Dogs Trust (J)	7.203
Eden Trust (J)	7.224
EDP - Drug and Alcohol Services (J)	7.226
Exeter Royal Academy for Deaf Education	7.244
Family Action (J)	7.247
Hamps & Isle of Wight Air Ambulance	7.298
National Marine Aquarium	7.449
North Devon Hospice	7.466
Royal Shakespeare Company (J)	7.571
Scope (J)	7.590
South West Environmental Parks Limited (J)	7.630
Theatre Royal (Plymouth) (J)	7.676

FORBES HALL LLP, New City House, 71 Rivington Street, London, EC2A 3AY. Tel: 020 7729 9111. Fax: 020 77299050. E-mail: info@forbeshall.co.uk. Internet: www.forbeshall.co.uk. Charity specialists: B Hall.

Royal Masonic Benevolent Institution (J)	7.565

FORBES SOLICITORS, Rutherford House, 4 Wellington Street (St Johns), Blackburn, Lancashire, BB1 8DD. Tel: 01254 54374. Fax: 01254 52347. E-mail: enquiries@forbessolicitors.co.uk. Internet: www.forbessolicitors.co.uk. Charity specialists: Daniel Milnes (Partner). Pauline Rigby (Associate). Charlotte Wood (Solicitor). Alexandra Sagar (Solicitor). Sarah Wilkinson (Solicitor).

Child Action Northwest	7.139

FORBES SOLICITORS, Ribchester House, Langcaster Road, Preston, Lancashire, PR1 2QL. Tel: 01772 220022. Fax: 01772 220166. Internet: www.forbessolicitors.co.uk.

Lancaster Foundation	7.377

FORD & WARREN, Westgate Point, Westgate, Leeds, West Yorkshire, LS1 2AX. Tel: 0113 243 6601. Fax: 0113 242 0905. Internet: www.forwarn.com. Charity specialists: K Hearn.

Retreat York, The	7.534

FORRESTER SYLVESTER MACKETT, Castle Street, Trowbridge, Wiltshire, BA14 8AX. Tel: 01225 755621. Fax: 01225 769055. E-mail: enquiries@fsmsolicitors.co.uk. Internet: www.fsmsolicitors.co.uk. Charity specialists: M G Jones.

Wiltshire Wildlife Trust (J)	7.731

FORSHAWS DAVIES RIDGWAY, 21 Bold Street, Warrington, Cheshire, WA1 1DG. Tel: 01925 231000. Fax: 01925 230616. Internet: www.fdrlaw.co.uk.

St Rocco's Hospice	7.654

FORSTERS LLP, 31 Hill Street, London, W1J 5LS. Tel: 020 7863 8333. Fax: 020 7863 8444. E-mail: mail@forsters.co.uk. Internet: www.forsters.co.uk. Charity specialists: A H Penny. D C Willis.

BLESMA	7.95
Corporation of Trinity House (J)	7.181
Ernest Kleinwort Charitable Trust	7.239
Gerald Ronson Foundation, The	7.273
Goldsmiths Centre, The (J)	7.280
Goldsmiths' Company Charity	7.281
Royal Ballet School	7.552
Royal National Children's Foundation	7.566
Sheppard Trust (J)	7.604

FOSKETT MARR GADSBY & HEAD LLP, 181 High Street, Epping, Essex, CM16 4BQ. Internet: www.foskettmarr.co.uk.

Grange Farm Centre Trust	7.284

FOSKETT MARR GADSBY & HEAD LLP, 106/108 High Road, Loughton, Essex, IG10 4HN. Tel: 020 8502 3991. Fax: 020 8502 2261. E-mail: email@foskettmarr.co.uk. Internet: www.foskettmarr.co.uk.

Harlow Health Centres Trust Ltd	7.302

FREETHS LLP (TRADING AS HENMANS FREETH), 5000 Oxford Business Park South, Oxford, Oxfordshire, OX4 2BH. Tel: 01865 781000. Fax: 01865 778504. E-mail: welcome@henmansfreeth.co.uk. Internet: http://HenmansFreeth.co.uk. Charity specialists: Nigel Roots (Partner, National Head of Charities Practice Group). Angela Bowman (Partner). Iain Davis (Partner). Lesley Pollock (Partner). Malcolm Sadler (Partner). Veronica Cowdrey (Senior Associate). Robert Nieri (Senior Associate, Freeth LLP).

Acorns Children's Hospice Trust (J)	7.9
Action for Blind People (J)	7.10
Action Medical Research (J)	7.11
Action on Hearing Loss (J)	7.11
ActionAid (J)	7.12
Age UK (J)	7.17
Air Ambulance Service	7.20
Alzheimer's Research UK (J)	7.28
Alzheimer's Society (J)	7.28
Amnesty International UK Section (J)	7.30
Arthritis Research UK (J)	7.40
Ashgate Hospice	7.43
Ashridge (Bonar Law Memorial) Trust (J)	7.44
Asthma UK (J)	7.47
Baptist Union of Great Britain (J)	7.56
Barnardo's (J)	7.57
Battersea Dogs & Cats Home (J)	7.60
Berks, Bucks & Oxon Wildlife Trust (J)	7.66
Bloodwise (J)	7.76
Blue Cross (J)	7.76
Bransby Horses (J)	7.85
British Heart Foundation (J)	7.93
British Psychological Society	7.97
British Red Cross Society (J)	7.98
BRUNELCARE (J)	7.102
Buckinghamshire Hospitals NHS Trust (J)	7.103
Building and Social Housing Foundation (J)	7.103
Butterfly Conservation (J)	7.106
Campaign to Protect Rural England (J)	7.110
Cancer Research UK (J)	7.112
Catholic Agency for Overseas Development (J)	7.118
Cats Protection (J)	7.120
Chatsworth House Trust (J)	7.136
Children with Cancer UK (J)	7.142
Christian Aid (J)	7.145
Church Commissioners for England (J)	7.147
CLIC Sargent Cancer Care for Children (J)	7.156
Comic Relief (J)	7.162
Community of St Mary the Virgin (J)	7.166
Community of the Holy Cross	7.166
Compassion in World Farming (J)	7.168
Diabetes UK (J)	7.200
Dogs Trust (J)	7.203
Donkey Sanctuary (J)	7.206
Dulverton Trust (J)	7.214
Crossroads Care East Midlands (J)	7.222
Elizabeth Finn Care (J)	7.230
Fire Fighters Charity	7.254
Friends of the Earth Trust (J)	7.265
Game & Wildlife Conservation Trust (J)	7.268
Grace & Compassion Benedictines (J)	7.283
Great Ormond St Hosp Children's Charity (J)	7.285
Greenpeace Environmental Trust (J)	7.287
Guide Dogs for the Blind Association (J)	7.291
Hearing Dogs for Deaf People (J)	7.306
Help for Heroes (J)	7.308
Imperial College Healthcare Charity (J)	7.329
Institution of Civil Engineers (J)	7.338
International Fund for Animal Welfare (J)	7.342
Jerry Green Dog Rescue (J)	7.352
Jewish Care (J)	7.354
Kent, Surrey & Sussex Air Ambulance Trust	7.369
Kidney Research UK (J)	7.371
LOROS (J)	7.384
Leonard Cheshire Disability (J)	7.385
Lincs&Notts Air Ambulance Ch Tst (J)	7.390
Little Way Association (J)	7.391
Luton Cultural Services Trust (J)	7.404
Macmillan Cancer Support (J)	7.405
Manchester & District Home for Lost Dogs (J)	7.408
Marie Stopes International (J)	7.410
Martin House (J)	7.413
Mary Stevens Hospice (J)	7.415
Milton Keynes Parks Trust Ltd (J)	7.428
MIND (J)	7.428
Multiple Sclerosis Society (J)	7.438
Muslim Hands	7.441
NSPCC (J)	7.452
National Trust (J)	7.454
North Bristol NHS Trust Charitable Funds (J)	7.465
North London Hospice	7.467
Nottingham Playhouse Trust Ltd	7.473
Oakhaven Trust (J)	7.476
Oxfam GB (J)	7.486
Oxford Radcliffe Hospitals Charitable Fund (J)	7.488

Oxford Trust, The	7.488
Parkinson's UK (J)	7.491
PDSA (J)	7.494
People Potential Possibilities (J)	7.496
Pilgrims Hospices in East Kent (J)	7.503
Portland College	7.509
Prospect Foundation (J)	7.516
Redwings Horse Sanctuary (J)	7.528
Reed Foundation, The (J)	7.529
Response Organisation (J)	7.532
Roy Castle Lung Cancer Foundation (J)	7.548
Royal Academy of Arts (J)	7.548
Royal Agricultural Benevolent Institution (J)	7.550
Royal Air Forces Association (J)	7.551
Royal British Legion (J)	7.554
Royal Mencap Society (J)	7.566
Royal National Institute of Blind People (J)	7.566
Royal National Lifeboat Institution (J)	7.567
Royal Natl Mission to Deep Sea Fishermen (J)	7.567
RSPCA (J)	7.572
RSPB (J)	7.572
RUSI (J)	7.575
Salvation Army Trust (J)	7.584
Save the Children (J)	7.588
Scope (J)	7.590
Seafarers UK (J)	7.594
SHELTER (J)	7.603
Diocese of ShrewsburyTrust (J)	7.607
Sobell House Hospice Charity Limited (J)	7.619
Society for Protection of Animals Abroad (J)	7.621
St Francis Hospice	7.642
St Helena Hospice (J)	7.644
St John Ambulance (J)	7.644
St Leonard's Hospice York (J)	7.646
St Mungo Community Housing Association (J)	7.652
St Peter's Hospice (J)	7.654
Stonewall Equality Ltd (J)	7.660
Stroke Association (J)	7.662
Sue Ryder (J)	7.663
Tearfund (J)	7.670
Tenovus (J)	7.673
Terrence Higgins Trust (J)	7.673
Thames Valley Air Ambulance (J)	7.675
UNICEF UK (J)	7.694
United Jewish Israel Appeal (J)	7.696
Vista	7.707
WaterAid (J)	7.715
Weldmar Hospicecare Trust (J)	7.717
Wigan & Leigh Hospice (J)	7.727
Wildfowl and Wetlands Trust (J)	7.728
Wood Green Animal Shelters (J)	7.736
World Horse Welfare (J)	7.740
World Society for the Protection of Animals (J)	7.741
Worldwide Cancer Research (J)	7.742
WWF UK (J)	7.743
Yorkshire Cancer Research (J)	7.749

**FRESHFIELDS BRUCKHAUS DERINGER, 65 Fleet
Street, London, EC4Y 1HS. Tel: 020 7936
4000. Fax: 020 7832 7001.
E-mail: email@freshfields.com.
Internet: www.freshfields.com.
Charity specialists:** Sarah Burton (Business
Development & Communications Dr).

City and Guilds of London Institute (J)	7.152
Depaul International	7.197
Education Endowment Foundation, The (J)	7.227
Oxfam GB (J)	7.486
Refuge (J)	7.529
Relief International UK	7.531

**FRETTENS SOLICITORS, The Saxon Centre, 11
Bargates, Christchurch, Dorset, BH23 1PZ.
Tel: 01202 499255.
Internet: www.frettens.co.uk.**

Anglo-European College of Chiropractic (J)	7.32

**FRIDAY LEGAL, 5 Oak House, Medlicott Close,
Northampton, Northamptonshire, NN18 9NF.
Tel: 01536 218 888.**

Wicksteed Charitable Trust	7.727

**FRONT ROW LEGAL, Foundry St, Leeds, West
Yorkshire, LS11 5QP. Tel: 0113 394 4395.**

Horse Trust (J)	7.318

**FURLEY PAGE LLP, 39 St Margaret's Street,
Canterbury, Kent, CT1 2TX. Tel: 01227
763939. Fax: 01227 762829.
E-mail: info@furleypage.co.uk.
Internet: www.furleypage.co.uk.**

Christ Embassy	7.144
John Townsend Trust, The (J)	7.361
Pilgrims Hospices in East Kent (J)	7.503
Strode Pk Foundation for Disabled People	7.662

**GABBS LLP, 14 Broad Street, Hereford,
Herefordshire, HR4 9AP. Tel: 01432 353481.
Fax: 01432 353537.
E-mail: hereford@gabbs.biz.
Internet: www.gabbs.biz.**

E F Bulmer Benevolent Fund	7.217

**GABY HARDWICKE, 34 Wellington Square,
Hastings, East Sussex, TN34 1PN. Tel: 01424
438 011. Fax: 01424 722 409.**

Magdalen Lasher Charity	7.406
St Michael's Hospice Hastings	7.651

**GARDENER LEADER, White Hart House, Market
Place, Newbury, Berkshire, RG14 5BA.
Tel: 01635 508080. Internet: www.gardner-
leader.co.uk.**

Wessex Children's Hospice Trust (J)	7.719

**GARNER CANNING & CO, 11 Aldergate,
Tamworth, Staffordshire, B79 7DL. Tel: 01827
314004. Fax: 01827 60327.
Internet: www.garnercanning.co.uk.**

Thera Trust (J)	7.676

**GARNER CANNING & CO, 301-303 Chester
Road, Birmingham, West Midlands, B36 0JG.
Tel: 0121 749 5577. Fax: 0121 749 2765.
Internet: www.garnercanning.co.uk.
Charity specialists:** K Garner.

Camden Society (J)	7.109

**GATELEY LLP, One Eleven, Edmund Street,
Birmingham, West Midlands, B3 2HJ. Tel: 0121
234 0000. Fax: 0121 234 0001.
E-mail: info@gateleyuk.com.
Internet: www.gateleyuk.com.
Charity specialists:** S Spencer.

Acorns Children's Hospice Trust (J)	7.9
Birmingham Diocesan Trust (J)	7.71
Father Hudson's Society (J)	7.249
NACRO	7.442

**GELDARDS LLP, Dumfries House, Dumfries
Place, Cardiff, CF10 3ZF. Tel: 029 2023 8239.
Fax: 029 2023 7268.
E-mail: info@geldards.co.uk.
Internet: www.geldards.com.
Charity specialists:** H R C Williams - specialist
area: Public Law & Charities. Giselle A Davies
(Charity Law) - specialist area: Charities & Trusts.

Amgueddfa Cymru	7.30
Arts Council of Wales, The	7.41
Cartrefi Cymru (J)	7.117
Community Foundation Wales	7.163
Gofal Housing Trust (J)	7.280
Lloyd's Register Foundation (J)	7.395
Mirus-Wales (J)	7.429
National Library of Wales, The	7.449
Perthyn	7.498
Royal Voluntary Service	7.575
St David's Diocesan Board of Finance (J)	7.641
Ty Hafan (J)	7.692
Wales Council for Voluntary Action (J)	7.711
Wales Millennium Centre	7.711
WJEC CBAC	7.734

**GELDARDS LLP, Pride Park, Derby, Derbyshire,
DE24 8QR. Tel: 01332 331631. Fax: 01332
294295. Internet: www.geldards.com.**

English Speaking Union Commonwealth	7.236
Lichfield Diocesan Board Of Education, The (J)	7.387
Liversage Trust	7.393

GELDARDS LLP, The Arc, Enterprise Way, Nottingham, Nottinghamshire, NG2 1EN. Tel: 0115 983 3650. Fax: 0115 983 3761. Internet: www.geldards.com.

Djanogly Learning Trust	7.202

GEOFFREY LEAVER SOLICITORS LLP, 251 Upper Third Street, Central Milton Keynes, Buckinghamshire, MK9 1DR. Tel: 01908 692769. Fax: 01908 692772. E-mail: legal@geoffreyleaver.com. Internet: www.geoffreyleaver.com. Charity specialists: T Warner. R Willis.

Hospice of Our Lady & St John	7.319
Milton Keynes Parks Trust Ltd (J)	7.428
New Testament Church of God	7.458

GEORGE GREEN LLP, 195 High Street, Cradley Heath, West Midlands, B64 5HW. Tel: 01384 410 410. Fax: 01384 634 237. E-mail: jcoles@georgegreen.co.uk. Internet: www.georgegreen.co.uk.

Birmingham Dogs Home	7.72

GEORGE IDE PHILLIPS, 52 North Street, Chichester, West Sussex, PO19 1NQ. Tel: 01243 786 668. Fax: 01243 831 000. Internet: www.georgeidephillips.co.uk.

Shipwrecked Mariners' Society (J)	7.605

GEPP & SONS LLP, 58 New London Road, Chelmsford, Essex, CM2 0PA. Tel: 01245 493939. Fax: 01245 493940. Internet: www.geppandsons.co.uk. Charity specialists: J Douglas-Hughes.

New England Company	7.457

GIBSON DUNN & CRUTCHER, 2-4 Temple Avenue, London, EC4Y 0HB. Tel: 020 7071 4000. Fax: 020 7071 4244. Internet: www.gibsondunn.com.

UK Youth (J)	7.693

GILBERT STEPHENS, 7 Broad Street, Ottery St. Mary, Devon, EX11 1BS. Tel: 01404 812 228. Fax: 01404 815 270. E-mail: osmlaw@gilbertstephens.co.uk. Internet: www.gilbertstephens.co.uk.

Donkey Sanctuary (J)	7.206

GILL TURNER & TUCKER, Colman House, King Street, Maidstone, Kent, ME14 1JE. Tel: 01622 759051. Fax: 01622 762192. Internet: www.gillturnertucker.com.

William Brake Charitable Trust	7.730

GILLESPIE GIFFORD & BROWN LLP, 135 Irish Street, Dumfries, Dumfries and Galloway, DG1 2NT. Tel: 01387 255351. Fax: 01387 257306. E-mail: mail@ggblaw.co.uk. Internet: www.ggblaw.co.uk. Charity specialists: G S Scott.

Holywood Trust	7.315

GILLESPIE MACANDREW LLP, 5 Atholl Crescent, Edinburgh, EH3 8EJ. Tel: 0131 225 1677. Fax: 0131 225 4519. E-mail: mail@gillespiemacandrew.co.uk. Internet: www.gillespiemacandrew.co.uk. Charity specialists: T K Murray.

Earl Haig Fund Scotland	7.219
Johnson & Johnson Corporate Citizenship Trust	7.361
Mount Stuart Trust, The	7.436
Royal College of Physicians of Edinburgh	7.557
Scottish Veterans Garden City Association Inc	7.593

GIRLINGS SOLICITORS, Stourside Place, Station Road, Ashford, Kent, TN23 1PP. Tel: 01233 664711. Fax: 01233 664722. Internet: www.girlings.com.

Active Life Ltd	7.12
Pilgrims Hospices in East Kent (J)	7.503

GIRLINGS SOLICITORS, 16 Rose Lane, Canterbury, Kent, CT1 2UR. Tel: 01227 768 374. Internet: www.girlings.com.

Thinkaction (J)	7.676

GLAISYERS, 10 Rowchester Court, Printing House Street, Birmingham, West Midlands, B4 6DZ. Tel: 0121 233 2971. Fax: 0121 236 1534. Internet: www.glaisyers.co.uk.

Sisters of Charity of St Paul	7.613

GLANVILLES, The Courtyard, St Cross Business Park, Monks Brook, Newport, Isle of Wight, PO30 5BF. Tel: 01983 527878. Internet: www.glanvilles.co.uk.

Earl Mountbatten Hospice (J)	7.219

GLOVERS, 6 York Street, London, W1U 6QD. Tel: 020 7935 8882. Fax: 020 7486 7666. E-mail: central@glovers.co.uk. Internet: www.glovers.co.uk. Charity specialists: Frances Dewhurst.

Royal Society of Arts (J)	7.571

GLP SOLICITORS, 85 Chapel Street, Manchester, Greater Manchester, M3 5DF. Tel: 0161 834 6721. Fax: 0161 834 2015. E-mail: manchester@glplaw.com. Internet: www.glplaw.com.

Cogent SSC Limited	7.159

GODWINS SOLICITORS LLP, 12 St Thomas Street, Winchester, Hampshire, SO23 9HF. Tel: 01962 841484. Fax: 01962 841554. Internet: www.godwins-law.co.uk. Charity specialists: A Cowgill. Anna Spencer. N Spicer.

Hospital of St Cross Foundation	7.321

GOLDKORN MATHIAS, 6 Coptic Street, Bloomsbury, London, WC1A 1NW. Tel: 020 7631 1811.

Kennedy Leigh Charitable Trust	7.368

GOODMAN DERRICK LLP, 10 St Bride Street, London, EC4A 4AD. Tel: 020 7404 0606. Fax: 020 7831 6407. Internet: www.gdlaw.co.uk. Charity specialists: Diana Rawstron - specialist area: Charity Law, Wills, Estates & Tax, Trust drafts. I Bradshaw - specialist area: Charity Law, Wills, Estates & Tax, Trust drafts.

Anna Freud Centre (J)	7.33
Borrow Foundation, The	7.81
Dollond Charitable Trust	7.203
Sir Jules Thorn Charitable Trust	7.612
Soho Theatre Company (J)	7.625
Thrombosis Research Institute	7.680
Yale University Press London	7.744

GOODYBURRETT LLP, St. Martin's House, 63 West Stockwell Street, Colchester, Essex, CO1 1HE. Tel: 01206 577676. Fax: 01206 548704. E-mail: law@goodyburrett.co.uk. Internet: www.goodyburrett.co.uk.

Autism Anglia	7.49

GORDON DADDS, 6 Agar Street, London, WC2N 4HN. Tel: 020 7493 6151. Fax: 020 7491 1065. E-mail: rogerpeters@gordondads.com. Internet: www.gordendadds.com. Charity specialists: R M Peters.

Actors' Benevolent Fund	7.13
Exilarch's Foundation (J)	7.244
Forest Young Men's Christian Association (J)	7.257
Skill Force Development	7.617

GORDONS LLP, Forward House, 8 Duke Street, Bradford, West Yorkshire, BD1 3QX. Tel: 01274 202 202. Fax: 01274 202 100. E-mail: mail@gordonslegal.com.

Bradford Diocesan Board of Finance, The	7.83
Bradford Trident Ltd (J)	7.83

GORVINS SOLICITORS, Dale House, Tiviot Dale, Stockport, Cheshire, SK1 1TA. Tel: 0161 930 5278. Fax: 0161 930 5252. E-mail: paul.longmire@gorvins.com. Internet: www.gorvins.com. Charity specialists: Val Bown. Tasoula Crosby. Michael Smoult. Christine Thornley.

Age UK (J)	7.17
Alzheimer's Society (J)	7.28
Seashell Trust (J)	7.595
Together Trust (J)	7.681

GOSSCHALKS, Queens Gardens, Dock Street, Hull, HU1 3DZ.

North Humberside Hospice Project (J)	7.466

GOTELEES, 31-41 Elm Street, Ipswich, Suffolk, IP1 2AY. Tel: 01473 211121. Fax: 01473 230387. E-mail: info@gotelee.co.uk. Internet: www.gotelee.co.uk.

Seckford Foundation (J)	7.595

GRAHAM & ROSEN, 8 Parliament Street, Hull, HU1 2BB. Tel: 01482 323123. Fax: 01482 223542. Internet: www.graham-rosen.co.uk. Charity specialists: R Palmer.

North Humberside Hospice Project (J)	7.466

GRANT SAW SOLICITORS LLP, Norman House, 110-114 Norman Road, London, SE10 9EH. Tel: 020 8858 6971. Fax: 020 8858 5796. Internet: www.grantsaw.com.

Estate Charity of William Hatcliffe	7.241
Ruach Inspirational Church of God (J)	7.576

GRAYS, Duncombe Place, York, North Yorkshire, YO1 7DY. Tel: 01904 634771. Fax: 01904 610711. E-mail: enquires@grayssolicitors.co.uk. Internet: www.grayssolicitors.co.uk. Charity specialists: Mrs H A I Mellors. F A Lawton.

Catholic Care (Diocese of Leeds) (J)	7.119
Lady Elizabeth Hastings' Charities	7.376
Middlesbrough Diocesan Trust	7.425

GREENE & GREENE, 80 Guildhall Street, Bury St Edmunds, Suffolk, IP33 1QB. Tel: 01284 762211. Fax: 01284 717499. Internet: www.greene-greene.com.

Special Air Service Regimental Association	7.632

GREENWOOD & CO, Premier House, 12 & 13 Hatton Garden, London, EC1N 8AN. Tel: 020 7831 8386. Fax: 020 7404 0523.

Chalfords Limited	7.126

GREENWOODS SOLICITORS LLP, Monkstone House, City Road, Peterborough, PE1 1JE. Tel: 01733 887700. Fax: 01733 887701. E-mail: mail@greenwoods.co.uk. Internet: www.greenwoods.co.uk.

Nene Park Trust	7.456

GREGG LATCHAMS LLP, 6 Queen Street, Bristol, BS1 4JE. Tel: 0117 906 9400. Fax: 0117 906 9401. Internet: www.latchams.co.uk.

Bristol Drugs Project	7.90

GREGORY ROWCLIFFE MILNERS, 1 Bedford Row, London, WC1R 4BZ. Tel: 020 7242 0631. Fax: 020 7242 6652. E-mail: law@grm.co.uk. Internet: www.grm.co.uk. Charity specialists: C Bannister. Christopher Barber. Christopher J Harder. Jane Laidler. J Sharpe.

Christian Aid (J)	7.145
Mrs E M Bates Trust (J)	7.437
Newby Trust	7.459
Officers Association	7.478
Royal Naval Ben. Society for Officers	7.567

GRIFFITH SMITH FARRINGTON WEBB LLP, 47 Old Steyne, Brighton, Brighton, Sussex, BN1 1NW. Tel: 01273 324041. Fax: 01273 384000. E-mail: t.smitth@gsfsolicitors.co.uk. Internet: www.gsfwsolicitors.co.uk.

Grace Eyre Foundation	7.283
Guild Care	7.291

GRIFFITHS ROBERTSON, 7-11 Queen Victoria Street, Reading, Berkshire, RG1 1SY. Tel: 01189 585049. Fax: 01189 585659. E-mail: admin@griffithsrobertson.co.uk.

Oxford Diocesan Council For Social Work (J)	7.487

GRINDEYS, Glebe Court, Stoke-on-Trent, ST4 1ET. Tel: 01782 846441. Fax: 01782 416220. E-mail: grindeys@aol.com. Internet: www.grindeys.co.uk. Charity specialists: A Rushton.

Camphill Village Trust Limited (J)	7.111
Douglas Macmillan Hospice	7.209
St John of God Hospitaller Services Ltd	7.645

GROSS & CO, 84 Guildhall Street, Bury St Edmunds, Suffolk, IP33 1PR. Tel: 01284 763333. Fax: 01284 762207.

St Nicholas Hospice Care	7.652

GROVE TOMPKINS BOSWORTH, 54 Newhall Street, Birmingham, West Midlands, B3 3QG. Tel: 0121 236 9341. Fax: 0121 236 5169. E-mail: jrd@gtb-solicitors.com.

Henry Barber Trust (J)	7.308

GS SOLICITORS, 23 Station Road, Hinckley, Leicestershire, LE10 1AW. Tel: 01455 618763. Fax: 01455 623660. E-mail: mgoodman@gssolicitors.co.uk.

Medlock Charitable Trust (J)	7.420

GULLANDS, 16 Mill Street, Maidstone, Kent, ME15 6XT. Tel: 01622 678 341. Fax: 01622 757 735. E-mail: mailbox@gullands.com. Internet: www.gullands.com. Charity specialists: A B Gulland.

Kent Community Foundation (J)	7.369
Kent Wildlife Trust	7.369

HAGUE & DIXON, Bank House, 1 The Square, Stamford Bridge, York, YO4 1AG. Tel: 01759 371634. Fax: 01759 372910. Internet: www.hague-dixon.co.uk. Charity specialists: R Dixon.

St Leonard's Hospice York (J)	7.646

HAGUE LAMBERT, Knutsford, Cheshire, WA16 6EJ.

Oblates of Mary Immaculate	7.478

HALLMARKHULME, 3, 4-5 Sansome Place, Worcester, Worcestershire, WR1 1UQ. Tel: 01905 726 600. Fax: 01905 74 33 66. E-mail: enquiries@hallmarkhulme.co.uk. Internet: www.hallmarkhulme.co.uk.

St Richard's Hospice Foundation	7.654

HAMERS SOLICITORS, Company & Commercial Dept, 5 Earls Court, Priory Park East, Hull, HU4 7DY. Tel: 01482 639674. Fax: 01482 639801. E-mail: lhowes@hamers.com. Internet: www.hamers.com.

Deflog V Q Trust Limited, The	7.196

HAMLINS, Roxburghe House, 273-287 Regent's Street, London, W1B 2AD. Tel: 020 7355 6000. Fax: 020 7518 9100. E-mail: admin@hamlins.co.uk. Internet: www.hamlins.co.uk.

NGT Foundation	7.461
Order of Friars Minor (Capuchin) Province (J)	7.482
Youth Sport Trust	7.751

HAND MORGAN & OWEN, 17 Martin Street, Stafford, Staffordshire, ST16 2LF. Tel: 01785 211 411. Fax: 01785 248 537. E-mail: info@hmo.co.uk. Internet: www.hmo.co.uk.

Katharine House Hospice	7.366

HANSELLS, 13 The Close, Norwich, Norfolk, NR1 4DS. Tel: 01603 615 731. Fax: 01603 633 585. E-mail: philipnorton@hansells.co.uk. Internet: www.hansells.co.uk.

East Anglian Air Ambulance	7.220

HARBOTTLE & LEWIS LLP, Hanover House, 14 Hanover Square, London, W1S 1HP. Tel: 020 7667 5000. Fax: 020 7667 5100. E-mail: david.scott@harbottle.com. Internet: www.harbottle.com. Charity specialists: D W Scott (Head of Charities Group) - specialist area: Charity Law, Tax. G L Harbottle. R K Reilly - specialist area: Property/Charity/Planning/Environment. C M Howes - specialist area: Corporate, Charities & Theatre.

Cinema and Television Benevolent Fund (J)	7.150
Comic Relief (J)	7.162
Equity Charitable Trust	7.238
London Academy of Music and Dramatic Art (J)	7.397
Lyric Hammersmith (J)	7.404
Queen Elizabeth Diamond Jubilee Trust	7.519
Regent's Park Theatre Limited	7.530
Royal Exchange Theatre Company (J)	7.560
Royal Shakespeare Company (J)	7.571
Services Sound Vision Corporation (J)	7.598
Virgin Unite	7.706
Wigmore Hall Trust	7.727

HARBOTTLE ASSOCIATES, 2 Kentish Buildings, 125 Borough High Street, London, SE1 1NP. Tel: 020 7234 0001. Fax: 020 7234 0002.

Lantra	7.379

HARLAND & CO, 18 St Saviourgate, York, North Yorkshire, YO1 8NS. Tel: 01904 655555. Fax: 01904 611162. Charity specialists: K Sutcliffe.

Wilberforce Trust	7.728
Yorkshire Wildlife Trust (J)	7.749

HARPER MACLEOD LLP, Citypoint, 65 Haymarket Terrace, Edinburgh, EH12 5HD. Tel: 0131 247 2500. E-mail: info@harpermacleod.co.uk. Internet: www.harpermacleod.co.uk.

Edinburgh Leisure (J)	7.225

HARPER MACLEOD LLP, The Ca'd'oro, 45 Gordon Street, Glasgow, G1 3PE. Tel: 0141 221 8888. E-mail: info@harpermacleod.co.uk. Internet: www.harpermacleod.co.uk.

Cattanach Charitable Trust	7.120
Children's Hospice Association Scotland (J)	7.141
Health and Social Care Alliance, The (J)	7.305
Retail Trust	7.533

HARRIS & HARRIS, 14 Market Place, Wells, Somerset, BA5 2RE. Tel: 01749 674 747. Fax: 01749 834060. E-mail: jacqui.jackson@harris-harris.co.uk. Internet: www.harris-harris.co.uk. Charity specialists: Tim Berry (Diocesan Registrar). John Clare (Partner). Roland Callaby (Partner). Alison Macaulay (Partner). Neil Howlett (Partner). Annemarie Swainson (Partner). Kathryn Lander (Partner). Christopher Jones (Associate). Joshua Eva (Associate). Andy Hambleton. Jacqui Jackson.

Andrews Charitable Trust	7.32
Bristol Diocesan Board Finance Ltd	7.89
Church of God of Prophecy Trust (J)	7.148
General Conference of the New Church (J)	7.270

HARRISON CLARK RICKERBYS, Ellenborough House, Wellington Street, Cheltenham, Gloucestershire, GL50 1YD. Tel: 01242 224422. Fax: 01242 518428. Internet: www.hcrlaw.com.

British Small Animal Veterinary Assoc (J)	7.99
Longfield (J)	7.401
National Star Foundation	7.453
Royal Air Force Charitable Trust, The (J)	7.550

HARRISON CLARK RICKERBYS, 5 Deansway, Worcester, Worcestershire, WR1 2JG. Tel: 01905 612001. Fax: 01905 204333. Internet: www.hcrlaw.com.

Bransford Trust, The	7.85
Malvern Theatres Trust Ltd	7.408

HARVEY INGRAM LLP, 20 New Walk, Leicester, Leicestershire, LE1 6TX. Tel: 0116 254 5454. Fax: 0116 255 4559. E-mail: mark.dunkley@harveyingram.com. Internet: www.harveyingram.com. Charity specialists: M Dunkley. Paula Fowle. D Perry.

Franciscan Sisters Minoress (J)	7.689

HATCH LEGAL, 1 Sella Bank, Seascale, Cumbria, CA20 1QU. Tel: 0194 672 1715. E-mail: info@hatchlegal.co.uk.

Horse Trust	7.318
Unipol Student Homes (J)	7.695

HAY & KILNER, Merchant House, 30 Cloth Market, Newcastle upon Tyne, Tyne and Wear, NE1 1EE. Tel: 0191 232 8345. Fax: 0191 261 7704. E-mail: jonathan.waters@hay-kilner.co.uk. Internet: www.hay-kilner.co.uk. Charity specialists: J Luke.

Mental Health Matters (J)	7.421

HAYES AND STORR, 18/19 Market Place, Fakenham, Norfolk, NR21 9BH. Tel: 01328 863231. Fax: 01328 855455. E-mail: law@hayes-storr.com. Internet: www.hayesandstorr.co.uk.

Thursford Collection, The (J)	7.680

HAYGARTH JONES, 8 Hardshaw Street, St Helens, Merseyside, WA10 1RE. Tel: 01744 26153. Fax: 01744 24036.

Willowbrook Hospice	7.731

HC SOLICITORS LLP, 35 Thorpe Road, Peterborough, PE3 6AG. Tel: 01733 882 800. Fax: 01733 552 748. E-mail: helen.wilson@hcsolicitors.co.uk. Internet: www.hcsolicitors.co.uk.

Peterborough Diocesan Board Finance (J)	7.500

HCB SOLICITORS, 20 Lichfield Street, Walsall, West Midlands, WS1 1TJ. Tel: 01922 720 000. E-mail: reception@hcbsolicitors.com. Internet: www.hcbsolicitors.com.

Steps to Work (Walsall) Limited	7.657

HEALD HEFFRON, Ashton House, 471 Silbury Boulevard, Milton Keynes, Buckinghamshire, MK9 2AH. Tel: 01908 662277. Fax: 01908 675667. E-mail: info@healdlaw.com. Internet: www.healdlaw.com. Charity specialists: P Crawley.

British Sports Trust	7.99

HEMPSONS

HEMPSONS, Hempsons House, 40 Villiers Street, London, WC2N 6NJ. Tel: 020 7839 0278. Fax: 020 7839 8212.
E-mail: charities@hempsons.co.uk.
Internet: www.hempsons.co.uk.

HEMPSONS, The Exchange, Station Parade, Harrogate, North Yorkshire, HG1 1DY.
Tel: 01423 522331. Fax: 01423 724047.
E-mail: charities@hempsons.co.uk.
Internet: www.hempsons.co.uk.

HEMPSONS, City Tower, Piccadilly Plaza, Manchester, Greater Manchester, M1 4BT.
Tel: 0161 228 0011. Fax: 0161 236 6734.
E-mail: charities@hempsons.co.uk.
Internet: www.hempsons.co.uk.

HEMPSONS, West One, Forth Banks, Newcastle upon Tyne, Tyne and Wear, NE1 3PA. Tel: 0191 230 0669. Fax: 0191 231 2669.
E-mail: charities@hempsons.co.uk.
Internet: www.hempsons.co.uk.

Hempsons prides itself on its provision of pragmatic and appropriate solutions, and this expertise has been appreciated by many of the best known national charities. Our charities and social enterprise team also works for a wide variety of other charities and not-for-profit organisations, both large and small – in all over 350 of them. In addition to its specialist charity legal skills, other lawyers are experienced in advising such organisations in all their operational needs.

Charity specialists: Ian D Hempseed (Head of Charities & Social Enterprise) - specialist area: Charities/Commercial Law/Social Enterprises. Fiona Wilson (Legacies) - specialist area: Charities/Legacies. Martin Cheyne (Employment). Faisal Dhalla (Social Enterprise). Jamie Foster (Social Enterprise). Crispin Pettifer (Projects/Construction). Graham Lea (Real Estate). Richard Nolan (Commercial Dispute/Mediation). Adrian Parker (Commercial/Procurement). Simon Lee (Charities/Social Enterprise).

Age UK North Tyneside (J)	7.18
Anchor Trust (J)	7.31
Anthony Nolan (J)	7.34
APS (J)	7.35
Assoc of Anaesthetists of GB & Ireland (J)	7.46
Autism Plus Limited (J)	7.50
Avenues Trust Group, The	7.52
Avocet Trust (J)	7.52
Battersea Dogs & Cats Home (J)	7.60
Birtenshaw (J)	7.73
British Heart Foundation (J)	7.93
British Home & Hospital for Incurables	7.94
Camden Society (J)	7.109
Central Manchester Univ Hosp NHS Trust	7.123
Children's Trust (J)	7.142
Christie Charitable Fund, The (J)	7.146
Church of England Pensions Board (J)	7.148
Conservation Volunteers, The	7.177
Dame Alice Owen's Foundation	7.192
Demelza House Children's Hospice	7.196
Energy Institute	7.233
European Assoc for Cardio Thoracic Surgery	7.241
Federation of Jewish Services	7.250
Foundation Trust Network, The (J)	7.261
Hallé Concerts Society (J)	7.297
Kennedy Trust for Rheumatology Research (J)	7.368
Letchworth Garden City Heritage Foundation (J)	7.386

Lowry Centre Trust (J)	7.403
Macmillan Cancer Support (J)	7.405
Muscular Dystrophy Campaign (J)	7.439
National Childbirth Trust (J)	7.444
National Maritime Museum (J)	7.449
North Country Leisure (J)	7.465
Pilgrims Hospices in East Kent (J)	7.503
Pure Innovations Limited	7.518
Ramblers Association (J)	7.525
ReVitalise Respite Holidays (J)	7.535
Richmond Fellowship (J)	7.537
Royal College of Emergency Medicine, The (J)	7.555
RoyalCol.of Obstetricians & Gynaecologists (J)	7.556
Royal College of Paediatrics (J)	7.556
Royal College of Radiologists (J)	7.558
Royal Mencap Society (J)	7.566
Salvation Army Social Work Trust (J)	7.584
Sheffield Hospitals Trust & Related Charities (J)	7.602
Skills Active UK (J)	7.617
St Ann's Hospice (J)	7.637
St Gemma's Hospice Leeds (J)	7.643
St George's Police Children Trust (J)	7.643
St Luke's (Cheshire) Hospice	7.647
Sue Ryder (J)	7.663
Tees Valley Community Foundation (J)	7.671
TTE Technical Training Group, The (J)	7.690
Turning Point (J)	7.691
Vibrance (J)	7.704
Voiceability Advocacy (J)	7.708
Wilf Ward Family Trust (J)	7.728
Wirral Autistic Society (J)	7.733
Yorkshire Cancer Research (J)	7.749
Young Foundation, The (J)	7.750
Zoological Society of London (J)	7.752

HERBERT SMITH, Exchange House, Primrose Street, London, EC2A 2HS. Tel: 020 7374 8000. Fax: 020 7374 0888.
E-mail: john.wood@herbertsmith.com.
Internet: www.herbertsmith.com.
Charity specialists: M Wood - specialist area: Trusts & Charities.

FIA Foundation for Automobile & Society (J)	7.252
Francis Crick Insitute Limited, The (J)	7.262
Refuge (J)	7.529
Somerset House Trust (J)	7.627
South Bank Centre (J)	7.628
Weston Provident Fund	7.724

HEWETTS, 55-57 London Street, Reading, Berkshire, RG1 4PS. Tel: 0118 957 5337. Fax: 0118 939 3073.
Internet: www.hewetts.co.uk.

PROSPECTS (J)	7.516

HEWITSONS, Shakespeare House, 42 Newmarket Road, Cambridge, Cambridgeshire, CB5 8EP. Tel: 01223 461155. Fax: 01223 316511. E-mail: chrisknight@hewitsons.com.
Internet: www.hewitsons.co.uk.
Charity specialists: Chris Knight. M Robinson.

Bourne United Charities	7.81
Cambridge Crystallographic Data Centre	7.108
Canal & River Trust (J)	7.111
Constance Travis Charitable Trust	7.178
Evelyn Trust	7.242
Girton Town Charity	7.275
Harris (Belmont) Charity	7.303
Henry Moore Foundation (J)	7.309
Lamport Hall Preservation Trust	7.377
Market Harborough & the Bowdens Charity	7.412
Riders for Health (J)	7.538
RSPB (J)	7.572
Royal Society of Chemistry (J)	7.572
Services Sound Vision Corporation (J)	7.598
Southside Partnership	7.631
St Andrew's Healthcare	7.636
United Learning Trust	7.696
Wildlife Trust BCNP, The	7.728
Wood Green Animal Shelters (J)	7.736

HEWITT & GILPIN, Thomas House, 14-16 James Street South, Belfast, County Antrim, BT2 7GA. Tel: 028 9057 3573. Fax: 028 9057 3590.
E-mail: law@hewittandgilpin.co.uk.
Internet: www.hewittandgilpin.co.uk.
Charity specialists: D Hewitt.

Marie Curie Cancer Care (J)	7.410

HIGGS & SONS, 3 Waterfront Business Park, Brierley Hill, West Midlands, DY5 1LX. Tel: 0845 111 5050. Fax: 01384 327290.
E-mail: law@higgsandsons.co.uk.
Internet: www.higgsandsons.co.uk.

Douglas Turner Trust (J)	7.210
Mary Stevens Hospice (J)	7.415
SignHealth (J)	7.608

HILL & ROBB SOLICITORS LIMITED, 3 Pitt Terrace, Stirling, FK8 2EY. Tel: 01786 450 985.
E-mail: info@hillandrobb.co.uk.
Internet: www.hillandrobb.co.uk.

Society of African Missions (J)	7.621

HILL DICKINSON LLP, No 1, St Paul's Square, Liverpool, Merseyside, L3 9SJ. Tel: 0151 236 5400. Fax: 0151 236 2175.
Internet: www.hilldickinson.com.
Charity specialists: D R Swaffield.

David Lewis Centre (J)	7.194
Islamia Schools Trust	7.346
Liverpool Diocesan Board of Finance, The	7.392
Nugent Care	7.475
NUMAST Welfare Funds	7.475
Congregation of Christian Brothers (J)	7.688
Waqf Al-Birr Educational Trust	7.714
Woodlands Hospice Charitable Trust Limited	7.737
Yusuf Islam Foundation	7.751

HILL DICKINSON LLP, 50 Fountain Street, Manchester, Greater Manchester, M2 2AS. Tel: 0161 276 8800. Fax: 0161 276 8801.
Internet: www.hilldickinson.com.

Dowager Countess Eleanor Peel Trust	7.210
Lifeline Project (J)	7.388

HILL DICKINSON LLP, The Balance, Pinfold Street, Sheffield, South Yorkshire, S1 2GU. Tel: 0114 229 7907. Fax: 0114 229 8001.

Action Housing & Support Limited (J)	7.10

HILL HOFSTETTER LIMITED, Trigen House, Central Boulevard, Blythe Valley Park, Solihull, West Midlands, B90 8AB. Tel: 0121 210 6000. Fax: 0121 210 6499.
Internet: www.hillhofstetter.com.

Institution of Chemical Engineers (J)	7.337

HILLYER MCKEOWN, Murlain House, Union Street, Chester, Cheshire, CH1 1QP. Tel: 01244 318131. E-mail: mail@law.uk.com.
Internet: www.hillyermckeown.co.uk.

Wirral Hospice St John's (J)	7.733

HLW KEEBLE HAWSON LLP, Old Cathedral Vicarage, St James' Row, Sheffield, South Yorkshire, S1 1XA. Tel: 0114 272 2061. Fax: 0114 270 0813.
E-mail: info@hlwkeeblehawson.co.uk.
Internet: www.hlwkeeblehawson.co.uk.

Sheffield Hospitals Trust & Related Charities (J)	7.602
St Luke's Hospice (J)	7.647

HMG LAW LLP, 126 High Street, Oxford, Oxfordshire, OX1 4DG. Tel: 01865 244661. Fax: 01865 721263. E-mail: info@hmg-law.co.uk. Internet: www.hmg-law.co.uk.

Charity of Thomas Dawson	7.130
Ditchley Foundation, The	7.202
God's House in Ewelme	7.279
Mulberry Bush Organisation Limited, The	7.438
Nuffield Oxford Hospitals Fund	7.474
Nuffield Trust for Forces of the Crown	7.475
Sobell House Hospice Charity Limited (J)	7.619

HODGE HALSALL LLP, 565 Liverpool Avenue, Ainsdale, Southport, Merseyside, PR8 3LU. Tel: 01704 577 171. Fax: 01704 576 517.
E-mail: info@hhlegal.co.uk.
Internet: www.hodgehalsall.co.uk.

Queenscourt Hospice (J)	7.521

HOGAN LOVELLS LLP, Atlantic House, Holborn, London, EC1A 2FG. Tel: +44 (0)20 7296 2000. Fax: +44 (0)20 7296 2001. E-mail: enquiry@lovells.com. Internet: www.hoganlovells.com.

Assoc of Anaesthetists of GB & Ireland (J)	7.46
Dyslexia Action	7.217
FARM-Africa	7.248
Greenhouse Schools Project Limited	7.286

HOLMES & HILLS, Bocking End, Braintree, Essex, CM7 9AJ. Tel: 01376 320 456. Fax: 01376 342 156. E-mail: legaladvice@holmes-hills.co.uk. Internet: www.holmes-hills.co.uk.

Charity of the Congregation of Our Lady	7.129

HOLMES MACKILLOP, 109 Douglas Street, Blythswood Square, Glasgow, G2 4HB. Tel: 0141 226 4942. Fax: 0141 204 0736. Internet: www.holmesmackillop.co.uk.

Abernethy Trust	7.6
Sisters of Charity of St Vincent de Paul (J)	7.613

HOLROYD & CO, Market Street, Milnsbridge, Huddersfield, West Yorkshire, HD3 4ND. Tel: 01484 645464.

Bridgewood Trust (J)	7.88

HORSEY LIGHTLY, 48 Warwick Street, London, W1B 5NL. Tel: 020 7222 8844. Fax: 020 7222 4123. E-mail: www.horseylightly.com. Internet: lon@horseylightly.com.

Soka Gakkai International UK (J)	7.625

HOWARD KENNEDY FSI, 19 Cavendish Square, London, W1A 2AW. Tel: 020 7636 1616. Fax: 020 7491 2899. E-mail: marketing@hkfsi.com. Internet: www.howardkennedyfsi.com.

Congregation of Our Lady of Sion	7.172
Sir John Cass's Foundation	7.611

HOWARD KENNEDY FSI, 179 Great Portland Street, London, W1W 5LS. Tel: 020 3350 3350. Fax: 020 3350 3351. E-mail: marketing@howardkennedyfsi.com. Internet: www.howardkennedyfsi.com. Charity specialists: P A Carter.

Britten-Pears Foundation	7.100
Jewish Museum London	7.354
Old Vic Theatre Trust 2000 (J)	7.479

HOWELL JONES & COMPANY, 36 Station Road, Llanrwst, Conwy, LL26 0DA. Tel: 01492 640 277. Fax: 01492 640583. E-mail: enquiries@howelljoneslaw.co.uk. Internet: www.howelljoneslaw.co.uk.

Hope House Children's Hospices	7.317

HOWES PERCIVAL, 3 The Osiers Business Centre, Leicester, Leicestershire, LE19 1DX. Tel: 0116 247 3500. Fax: 0116 247 3539. Internet: www.howespercival.com.

Institute of Materials, Minerals & Mining (J)	7.336
Leicester Theatre Trust	7.383

HOWES PERCIVAL, The Guildyard, 51 Colegate, Norwich, Norfolk, NR3 1DD. Tel: 01603 762103. Fax: 01603 762104. E-mail: jeremy.heal@howespercival.com. Internet: www.howespercival.com. Charity specialists: J P W Heal - specialist area: Tax and Trusts.

Mrs L D Rope Third Charitable Settlement	7.438
Paul Bassham Charitable Trust	7.493

HUGH CARTWRIGHT & AMIN, 12 John Street, London, WC1N 2EB. Tel: 020 7632 4200. Fax: 020 7831 8171.

Akshar Educational Trust	7.21
Sarjudas Foundation	7.587

HUGH JAMES, 114 - 116 St. Mary Street, Cardiff, CF10 1DY. Tel: 029 2022 4871. Fax: 029 2038 8222. Internet: www.hughjames.com.

Drive (J)	7.212
Wales Council for Voluntary Action (J)	7.711

HUMPHRIES KIRK, 40 High West Street, Dorchester, Dorset, DT1 1UR. Tel: 01305 251007. Fax: 01305 251045. E-mail: dorchester@hklaw.eu. Internet: www.humphrieskirk.co.uk.

Encompass (Dorset)	7.233

HUNT & HUNT, Lambourne House, 7 Western Road, Romford, Essex, RM1 3LT. Tel: 01708 764433. Fax: 01708 733613. Internet: www.hunt-hunt.co.uk. Charity specialists: J E F Hunt.

Walthamstow&Chingford Almshouse Charity (J)	7.713

HUNTERS

INCORPORATING

MAY, MAY & MERRIMANS

HUNTERS INCORPORATING MAY, MAY & MERRIMANS, 9 New Square, Lincoln's Inn, London, WC2A 3QN. Tel: 020 7412 0050. Fax: 020 7412 0049. E-mail: paa@hunters-solicitors.co.uk. Internet: www.hunters-solicitors.co.uk.

Hunters are experts in social enterprises & charity law. The firm has practised from Lincoln's Inn for nearly 300 years and have a dedicated charities and not-for-profit team that provides practical and intelligent advice with a commercial steer. The firm delivers a broad range of expertise to ensure that all clients receive clear specialist advice on every aspect of their affairs to a high standard.

Contact: Paul Almy, the partner who heads the Charity Group. For more information see our profile in the front colour section.

Charity specialists: Paul Almy. Dominik Opalinski. James Vernor-Miles. Wilfrid Vernor-Miles. Louise Walker. Andrew Parry.

Architects Benevolent Society (J)	7.38
Charities Aid Foundation (J)	7.128
Congregation of the Little Sisters of the Poor	7.174
Gray's Inn Scholarships Trust	7.284
Gwyneth Forrester Trust	7.294
Insurance Charities	7.339
Missionaries of Africa (The White Fathers) (J)	7.431
Society of St Pius X	7.623

HUTCHINSON MAINPRICE, 45 Lower Belgrave Street, London, SW1W 0LS. Tel: 020 7259 0121. Fax: 020 7259 0051. E-mail: ah@htmp.co.uk.

Alliance House Foundation (J)	7.26

IBB SOLICITORS, Capital Court, 30 Windsor Street, Uxbridge, Middlesex, UB8 1AB. Tel: 01895 230941. Fax: 08456 381351. Internet: www.ibblaw.co.uk. Charity specialists: Eva Abeles. Jo Coleman (Partner) - specialist area: Charities.

Academy of Medical Sciences	7.8
Archbishops' Council (J)	7.37
Barnardo's (J)	7.57
Brentwood Roman Catholic Diocesan Trust	7.87
CLIC Sargent Cancer Care for Children (J)	7.156

Croydon Almshouse Charities (J)	7.187
Daughters of Jesus, The	7.193
Embrace the Middle East (J)	7.232
Groundwork South Trust Limited, The (J)	7.290
HSF Health Plan	7.323
Institute of Our Lady of Mercy, The	7.336
Musicians Benevolent Fund	7.440
PRS For Music Members Benevolent Fund	7.517
Richard Reeve's Foundation	7.536
Royal College of Pathologists (J)	7.557
S L G Charitable Trust	7.578
Sisters of Charity of St Vincent de Paul (J)	7.613
Teenage Cancer Trust (J)	7.671
Union Sisters Mercy Great Britain (J)	7.695
United Synagogue	7.698

INGRAM WINTER GREEN, Bedford House, 21a John Street, London, WC1N 2BL. Tel: 020 7845 7400. Fax: 020 7845 7401. E-mail: back-chat@iwg.co.uk. Internet: www.iwg.co.uk.

Norwood (J)	7.472

INTERNATIONAL VOLUNTARY SERVICE - NORTHERN IRELAND, 34 Shaftesbury Square, Belfast, Northern Ireland, BT2 7DB.

Royal Bath and West of England Society	7.553

IRWIN MITCHELL, 31 Temple Street, Birmingham, West Midlands, B2 5DB. Tel: 0870 1500 100. Fax: 0121 643 6021. Internet: www.irwinmitchell.com.

YMCA Black Country Group (J)	7.744

IRWIN MITCHELL, 2 Wellington Place, Leeds, West Yorkshire, LS1 4BZ. Tel: 0870 1500 100. Fax: 0113 234 3322. Internet: www.irwinmitchell.com.

LHASA	7.387

IRWIN MITCHELL, Riverside East, 2 Millsands, Sheffield, South Yorkshire, S3 8DT. Tel: 0870 1500 100. Fax: 0114 275 3306. Internet: www.irwinmitchell.com. Charity specialists: T M Napier QC CBE - specialist area: Litigation.

Autism Plus Limited (J)	7.50
Breast Cancer Care (J)	7.86
Coal Industry Social Welfare Organisation (J)	7.158
Newham Training and Education Centre	7.460
SheffCare	7.600
Sheffield City Trust	7.601
Sheffield Futures (J)	7.601
St Luke's Hospice (J)	7.647

ISON HARRISON, Duke House, 54 Wellington Street, Leeds, West Yorkshire, LS1 2EE. Internet: isonharrison.co.uk.

Broadway Homelessness and Support	7.100

J & H MITCHELL WS, 51 Atholl Road, Pitlochry, Perth and Kinross, PH16 5BU. Tel: 01796 472606. Fax: 01796 473198. E-mail: j@hmitchell.co.uk. Internet: www.hmitchell.co.uk. Charity specialists: A C M Liddell WS (Senior Partner) - specialist area: Charities.

Dunard Fund	7.215
Pitlochry Festival Theatre	7.504

J G POOLE & CO LLP, E-Space South, 26 St. Thomas Place, Ely, Cambridge, Cambridgeshire, CB7 4EX. Tel: 01353 644028. Internet: www.jgpoole.co.uk.

Aston Student Villages	7.47

JACK GRANT & CO, 14 Hamilton Road, Motherwell, North Lanarkshire, ML1 1BB. Tel: 01698 254 636. Fax: 01698 275 121. E-mail: enquiries@jackgrantsolicitors.co.uk. Internet: www.jackgrantsolicitors.co.uk.

VAMW Care	7.703

JACKLYN DAWSON, Equity Chambers, John Frost Square, Newport, NP20 1PW. Tel: 01633 262 952. Internet: www.jacklyndawson.co.uk.

Monmouth Diocesan Board of Finance	7.431

Monmouth Diocesan Trust   7.432

JACKSONS LAW FIRM, Central Square, Forth Street, Newcastle upon Tyne, Tyne and Wear, EC2V 7QN. Tel: 0191 580 0183. Fax: 0191 231 3921. E-mail: info@jacksons-law.com. Internet: www.jacksons-law.com.

Joseph Strong Frazer Trust   7.363

JACKSONS LAW FIRM, Innovation House, Yarm Road, Stockton-on-Tees, TS18 3TN. Tel: 01642 356 500. Fax: 01642 356 501. E-mail: info@jacksons-law.com. Internet: www.jacksons-law.com.

Tees Valley Community Foundation (J)   7.671
Teesside Hospice Care Foundation   7.671

JCP SOLICITORS, Venture Court, Waterside Business Park, Valley Way, Enterprise Park, Swansea, SA6 8QP. Tel: 01792 773 773. Fax: 01792 774 775. E-mail: law@jcpsolicitors.co.uk. Internet: www.jcpsolicitors.co.uk.

Mirus-Wales (J)   7.429
Welsh Air Ambulance Charitable Trust   7.718

JEFFERIES BACHE, Vintners Place, 68 Upper Thames Street, London, EC4V 3BJ. Tel: 020 7029 8000. Internet: www.jefferies.com.

Asfari Foundation, The (J)   7.43

JEFFREY AITKEN SOLICITORS, Fortune House, 74 Waterloo Street, Glasgow, G2 7DA. Tel: 0141 221 5983.

C-Change Scotland   7.107

JEFFREY GREEN RUSSELL, Waverley House, 7-12 Noel Street, London, W1F 8GQ. Tel: 020 7339 7000. Fax: 020 7339 7001. Internet: www.jgrweb.com. Charity specialists: Penny Spencer.

World Energy Council (J)   7.740

JMW SOLICITORS LLP, 1 Byrom Place, Manchester, Greater Manchester, M3 3HG. Tel: 0345 872 6666. Internet: www.jmw.co.uk.

Pharmacist Support (J)   7.500

JOHN MARSHALL, 23 Aldersbrook Road, Wanstead, London, E12 5HH.

Secular Clergy Common Fund   7.596

JOHN OWENS SOLICITOR, Hanover House, The Roe, St Asaph, Denbighshire, LL17 0LT. E-mail: John.owens@johnowenssolicitor.co.uk. Internet: www.johnowenssolicitor.co.uk/.

Cyngor Alcohol Information Service Limit   7.190

JOHNS & SAGGAR LLP, 34-36 Grays Inn Road, London, WC1X 8HR. Tel: 0203 490 1475. Fax: 0207 831 3935. E-mail: info@johnsandsaggar.co.uk. Internet: www.johnsandsaggar.co.uk.

Al-Khair Foundation   7.21
Harrow Central Mosque and Islamic Centre (J)   7.303
Human Appeal International   7.324

JONES & CO, Cannon Square, Retford, Nottinghamshire, DN22 6PB. Tel: 01777 703827. Fax: 01777 707 713. Internet: www.jonessolicitors.co.uk.

Hospital of the Holy & Undivided Trinity   7.322

JONES DAY, 21 Tudor Street, London, EC4Y 0DJ. Tel: 020 7039 5959. Fax: 020 7039 5999. Internet: www.jonesday.com. Charity specialists: Jennett Davies. D P H Burgess.

Friends Royal Academy   7.265
Royal Academy of Arts (J)   7.548
Royal Academy Trust   7.549

JONES MYERS SOLICITORS, The Pearl Building, 22 East Parade, Leeds, West Yorkshire, LS1 5BZ. Tel: 0113 246 0055. Internet: www.jonesmyers.co.uk.

Catholic Trust for England and Wales (J)   7.120

KATTEN MUCHIN ROSENMAN LLP, 125 Old Broad Street, London, EC2N 1AR. Tel: 020 7776 7620. Fax: 020 7776 7621. Internet: www.kattenlaw.com.

Design Museum (J)   7.199
Roundhouse Trust   7.547

KEELYS LLP, 28 Dam Street, Lichfield, Staffordshire, WS13 6AA.

St Giles Hospice (J)   7.643

KEENE & MARSLAND, 6 Clanricarde Gardens, Tunbridge Wells, Kent, TN1 1PH. Tel: 01892 526 442. Fax: 01892 510 486. E-mail: enquiries@keenemarsland.co.uk. Internet: www.keenemarsland.co.uk.

Kent Autistic Trust   7.368

KENDALL & DAVIES, Station Road, Bourton-on-the-Water, Cheltenham, Gloucestershire, GL54 2AA. Tel: 01451 820277. Fax: 01451 822157. E-mail: bourton@kendallanddavies.co.uk. Internet: www.kendallanddavies.co.uk.

Guiting Manor Amenity Trust   7.292

KENNEDYS, Longbow House, 14-20 Chiswell Street, London, EC1Y 4TY. Tel: 020 7638 3688. Fax: 020 7638 2212. Internet: www.kennedys-law.com.

Scout Association (J)   7.594

KERMAN & CO LLP, 200 Strand, London, WC2R 1DJ. Tel: 020 7539 7272. Fax: 020 7240 5780. Internet: www.kermanco.com. Charity specialists: A Kerman.

Chabad Lubavitch UK   7.125

KEYSTONE LAW LTD, 53 Davies Street, London, W1K 5JH. Tel: 020 7152 6550. Fax: 0845 458 9398. E-mail: enquiries@keystonelaw.co.uk. Internet: www.keystonelaw.co.uk.

Marcela Trust, The   7.409
Virunga Foundation   7.707

KIDD RAPINET, 17 South Street, Farnham, Surrey, GU9 7QU. Tel: 01252 713242. Fax: 01252 737506. E-mail: gstones@kiddrapinet.co.uk. Internet: www.kiddrapinet.co.uk.

Truemark Trust   7.687

KING & CO, 238 High Street, Cottenham, Cambridge, Cambridgeshire, CB4 8RZ. Tel: 01954 206036. Fax: 01954 251672. Charity specialists: R S Covell.

Needham Research Institute   7.456

KING & WOOD MALLESONS, 10 Queen Street Place, London, EC4R 1BE. Tel: 020 7111 2222. Fax: 020 7111 2000. Internet: www.kwm.com.

Aspinall Foundation, The   7.44
Howletts Wild Animal Trust, The (J)   7.322

KINGSFORDS, 2 Elwick Road, Ashford, Kent, TN23 1PD. Tel: 01233 624545. Fax: 01233 610011. E-mail: timfagg@kingsfords.net. Internet: www.kingsfords-solicitors.com.

Caldecott Foundation Limited   7.108

KITSONS, Minerva House, Orchard Way, Edginswell Park, Torquay, Devon, TQ2 7FA. Tel: 01803 202020. Internet: www.kitsons-solicitors.co.uk.

Rowcroft House Foundation Limited   7.548

KLC EMPLOYMENT LAW CONSULTANTS LLP, Mill Pool House, Mill Lane, Godalming, Surrey, GU7 1EY.

Services Sound Vision Corporation (J)   7.598

KNIGHTS, 34 Cuppin Street, Chester, Cheshire, CH1 2BN.

Addiction Dependency Solutions (J)   7.14

KNIGHTS SOLICITORS LLP, The Brampton, Newcastle-under-Lyme, Staffordshire, ST5 0QW. Tel: 01782 619225. Fax: 01782 620410. E-mail: jenny.hampson@knightsllp.co.uk. Internet: www.knightsllp.co.uk.

Caudwell Children   7.120
United Christian Broadcasters (J)   7.695

KUIT STEINART LEVY, 3 St Mary's Parsonage, Manchester, Greater Manchester, M3 2RD. Tel: 0161 832 3434. Fax: 0161 832 6650. E-mail: grahamwood@kuits.com. Internet: www.kuits.com. Charity specialists: Lauren Clyne. Jan Fidler. C Rose. G Wood.

Henshaws Society for Blind People (J)   7.309
Park Charitable Trust, The   7.491
Stoller Charitable Trust   7.659
Tagmarsh Charity Limited   7.667

L G WILLIAMS & PRICHARD, 22 St Andrews Crescent, Cardiff, CF10 3DD. Tel: 029 2022 9716. Fax: 029 2037 7761. E-mail: slyons@cardiff-law.co.uk. Internet: www.cardiff-law.co.uk. Charity specialists: S Lyons.

Cardiff RC Archdiocesan Trust   7.37

LAMB BROOKS, Victoria House, 39 Winchester Street, Basingstoke, Hampshire, RG21 7EQ. Tel: 01256 844888. Fax: 01256 840427. Internet: www.lambbrooks.com.

Greenham Common Community Trust   7.286
Notre Dame de France Trust   7.472

LANGLEYS, Olympic House, Doddington Road, Lincoln, Lincolnshire, LN6 3SE. Tel: 01522 888555. Fax: 01522 888556. E-mail: info@langleys.co.uk. Internet: www.langleys.co.uk.

Lincs&Notts Air Ambulance Ch Tst (J)   7.390

LANGLEYS, Queens House, Micklegate, York, North Yorkshire, YO1 6WG. Tel: 01904 610886. Fax: 01904 611086. E-mail: info@langleys.co.uk. Internet: www.langleys.co.uk.

Burton Constable Foundation   7.105

LANYON BOWDLER, 39-41 Church Street, Oswestry, Shropshire, SY11 2SZ. Tel: 01691 652241. Internet: www.lblaw.co.uk.

Derwen College (J)   7.198

LANYON BOWDLER, Chapter House North, Abbey Lawn, Abbey Foregate, Shrewsbury, Shropshire, SY2 5DE. Tel: 01743 280280. Fax: 01743 282342. E-mail: info@lblaw.co.uk. Internet: www.lblaw.co.uk. Charity specialists: A Evans.

Severn Hospice   7.598

LARGE & GIBSON, Kent House, 49 Kent Road, Southsea, Hampshire, PO5 3EJ. Tel: 023 9229 6296. Fax: 023 9282 6134. Internet: www.largeandgibson.co.uk. Charity specialists: Vivien Bradley-Shaw. Peter Dymock. Erin Hunt. Tricia Longmore. Michael Rowland. Richard Wootton.

Royal Sailors' Rests   7.570

LATHAM & CO, Charnwood House, 2 & 4 Forest Road, Loughborough, Leicestershire, LE11 3NP. Tel: 01509 238822. Internet: www.lathamlawyers.co.uk.

Leicester Diocesan Board Finance   7.383

LATHAM & WATKINS LLP, 99 Bishopsgate, London, EC2M 3XF. Tel: 020 7710 1000.

BAC   7.60
Hospice of Hope Romania Limited   7.319
Norwood (J)   7.472
Rich Mix Cultural Foundation   7.535

LAURA DEVINE SOLICITORS, 100 Cannon Street, London, EC4N 6EU. Tel: 020 7469 6460. Fax: 020 7469 6461.
E-mail: enquiries@lauradevine.com.
Internet: www.lauradevine.com.

World Energy Council (J)	7.740

LAW BY DESIGN LTD, Kingsley Hall, 20 Bailey Lane, Manchester Airport, Manchester, Greater Manchester, M90 4AB.

Addiction Dependency Solutions (J)	7.14

LAYTONS, 50 Victoria Embankment, Blackfriars, London, EC4Y 0LS. Tel: 020 1483 407000. Fax: 020 1483 407070.
Internet: www.laytons.com.
Charity specialists: I A Burman.

Affinity Trust	7.15
Royal Mencap Society (J)	7.566
Sir Harold Hood Charitable Trust	7.610

LEATHES PRIOR SOLICITORS, 74 The Close, Norwich, Norfolk, NR1 4DR. Tel: 01603 610911. Fax: 01603 610088.
E-mail: info@leathesprior.co.uk.
Internet: www.leathesprior.co.uk.

Benjamin Foundation, The	7.66
Great Hospital, Norwich	7.285
RSPCA (J)	7.572
World Horse Welfare (J)	7.740

LEDINGHAM CHALMERS LLP, Johnstone House, 52-54 Rose Street, Aberdeen, Grampian, AB10 1HA. Tel: 01224 408 408. Fax: 01224 408 400.
E-mail: mail@ledinghamchalmers.com.
Internet: www.ledinghamchalmers.com.

Aberdeen Endowments Trust	7.5
Cornerstone Community Care	7.180

LEE BOLTON MONIER-WILLIAMS, 1 The Sanctuary, Westminster, London, SW1P 3JT. Tel: 020 7222 5381. Fax: 020 7222 7502.
E-mail: enquiries@lbmw.com.
Internet: www.lbmw.com.
Charity specialists: Nigel Urwin. Howard Dellar. Peter F B Beesley.

Adolescent and Children's Trust, The (J)	7.14
All Saints Educational Trust	7.25
Campden Charities Trustee	7.110
Canterbury Diocesan Board of Finance (J)	7.112
Clare Milne Trust	7.155
Ely Diocesan Board of Finance, The	7.231
Hereford Diocesan Board Finance	7.309
Nat Soc CoE for Promoting Religious Ed	7.452
Norwich Diocesan Board of Finance, The (J)	7.471
Printing Charity, The	7.514
Society of Petroleum Engineers Europe	7.623
St Albans Diocesan Board Finance (J)	7.635
Weavers Company Benevolent Fund	7.717
Whitgift Foundation (J)	7.726
Wine & Spirit Education Trust Ltd	7.732

LEES SOLICITORS LLP, 44/45 Hamilton Square, Birkenhead, Merseyside, CH41 5AR. Tel: 0151 647 9381. Fax: 0151 666 1445.
E-mail: info@lees.co.uk.
Internet: www.lees.co.uk.
Charity specialists: I MacGregor.

Claire House Appeal	7.155

LEGAL OFFICE, THE, THE ARCHBISHOPS' COUNCIL, Church House, Great Smith Street, London, SW1P 3NZ.

Archbishops' Council (J)	7.37
Church Urban Fund (J)	7.150

LEO ABSE & COHEN, 40 Churchill Way, Cardiff, CF10 2SS. Tel: 029 2038 3252.
Internet: www.leoabse.co.uk.

Workers' Educational Assoc South Wales Ltd	7.739

LESTER ALDRIDGE, WSP House, 70 Chancery Lane, London, WC2A 1AF. Tel: 0844 967 0785. Fax: 0207 400 9890.
Internet: www.lesteraldridge.com.

Honourable Society Middle Temple Trust	7.316

LESTER ALDRIDGE, Russell House, Oxford Road, Bournemouth, Dorset, BH8 8EX. Tel: 01202 786 161. Fax: 01202 786 110.
E-mail: geoff.trobridge@la-law.com.
Internet: www.lesteraldridge.com.
Charity specialists: Geoff Trobridge.

Autistic Wessex	7.50
Becht Family Charitable Trust, The	7.63
Bournemouth Symphony Orchestra	7.82
British Heart Foundation (J)	7.93
Camphill Village Trust Limited (J)	7.111
Care South	7.114
RBS PeopleCharity, The (J)	7.527

LEWIS FRANCIS BLACKBURN BRAY, 14-16 Paradise Square, Sheffield, South Yorkshire, S1 2DE. Tel: 0114 272 9721. Fax: 0114 275 4347. E-mail: info@lfbbsolicitors.co.uk.
Internet: www.lfbbsolicitors.co.uk.

Sheffield Media and Exhibition Centre	7.602

LEWIS SILKIN, 5 Chancery Lane, Clifford's Inn, London, EC4A 1BL. Tel: 020 7074 8000. Fax: 020 7864 1200.
E-mail: info@lewissilkin.com.
Internet: www.lewissilkin.com.
Charity specialists: M King (Head of BD and Marketing).

Book Aid International (J)	7.79
D&AD (J)	7.191
Oasis Charitable Trust (J)	7.477
Oasis Community Learning (J)	7.477
SeeAbility (J)	7.596

LEWIS SILKIN, King Charles House, Park End Street, Oxford, Oxfordshire, OX1 1JD. Tel: 020 7074 8000. Fax: 01865 724224.
E-mail: info@lewissilkin.com.
Internet: www.lewissilkin.com.

Rhodes Trust (J)	7.535

LEX SOLICITORS, 271 Derby Street, Bolton, Greater Manchester, BL3 6LA. Tel: 01204 387310.

Amanat Charitable Trust (J)	7.28

LINDSAY & KIRK, 39 Huntly Street, Aberdeen, Grampian, AB10 1TJ. Tel: 01224 641402. Fax: 01224 639974.
E-mail: law@lindsayandkirk.com.

LINDSAYS, Caledonian Exchange, 19A Canning Street, Edinburgh, EH3 8HE. Tel: 0131 229 1212. Fax: 0131 229 5611.
E-mail: alastairkeatinge@lindsays.co.uk.
Internet: www.lindsays.co.uk.
Charity specialists: Alastair J Keatinge. David Reith. Fiona Linklater.

Carnegie Trust for Universities Scotland	7.116
Carr-Gomm Scotland (J)	7.117
Citizens Advice Scotland	7.152
Garvald Edinburgh	7.269
Horsecross Arts Ltd	7.318
Inspiring Scotland (J)	7.332
Rosslyn Chapel Trust	7.545
Scottish Association for Mental Health	7.591
Scottish Autism	7.591
Scottish Youth Hostels Association	7.594

LINDSAYS, 1 Royal Bank Place, Glasgow, G1 3AA. Tel: 0141 221 6551. Fax: 0141 204 0507. E-mail: mail@lindsays.co.uk.
Internet: www.lindsays.co.uk.

Carnegie UK Trust (J)	7.116
Prince and Princess of Wales Hospice (J)	7.513

LINKLATERS, One Silk Street, London, EC2Y 8HQ. Tel: 020 7456 2000. Fax: 020 7456 2222. E-mail: enquiries@linklaters.com.
Internet: www.linklaters.com.
Charity specialists: A L Angel (Managing Partner) - specialist area: Head of Taxation.

Contemporary Dance Trust (J)	7.178
European Renal Association	7.242

Hadley Trust	7.296
ICAEW Foundation & Educational Charities	7.327
John Laing Charitable Trust	7.359
Kirby Laing Foundation	7.374
Maurice Hilda Laing Charitable Trust	7.416
Ogden Trust	7.479
Prince's Trust (J)	7.514
Royal Opera House Foundation	7.569
Rufford Foundation, The	7.577
Tate (J)	7.669
Toynbee Hall (J)	7.684

LODDERS SOLICITORS LLP, 10 Elm Court, Arden Street, Stratford-upon-Avon, Warwickshire, CV37 6PA. Tel: 01789 293259. Fax: 01789 268093.
E-mail: steven.baker@lodders.co.uk.
Internet: www.lodders.co.uk.
Charity specialists: S Baker. D Lodder. Ruth Shipman. M Wakeling.

Children s Family Trust (J)	7.140
College Estate Endowment Charity, The (J)	7.160
Guild Estate Endowment (J)	7.291
King Henry VIII Endowed Trust Warwick (J)	7.372
UK Youth (J)	7.693

LOOSEMORES, Alliance House, 18/19 High Street, Cardiff, CF10 1PT. Tel: 029 2022 4433. Fax: 029 2080 3100.
E-mail: post@loosemores.co.uk.
Internet: www.loosemores.co.uk.

Echoes of Service (J)	7.223
Llamau Limited	7.394
Stewards Company (J)	7.658
Ty Hafan (J)	7.692

LUPTON FAWCETT DENISON TILL, Yorkshire House, East Parade, Leeds, West Yorkshire, LS1 5BD. Tel: 0113 280 2097. Fax: 0113 280 2103. E-mail: duncan.milwain@lf-dt.com.
Charity specialists: Louise Connacher. Peter Foskett. Lionel Lennox. Duncan Milwain. Jonathan Warner-Reed. D Whitaker.

Higher Education Academy, The (J)	7.311
Hollybank Trust	7.315
LGS General Charitable Trust	7.387
United Reformed Church (Yorkshire) Trust	7.697
Yorkshire Cancer Research (J)	7.749

LUPTON FAWCETT DENISON TILL, Stamford House, Piccadilly, York, North Yorkshire, YO1 9PP. Tel: 01904 611 411. Fax: 01904 646 972. E-mail: info@lf-dt.com.
Internet: www.denisontill.com.
Charity specialists: L Lennox.

APS (J)	7.35
Chapter of Order of the Holy Paraclete	7.128
Unipol Student Homes (J)	7.695
York Diocesan Board Finance Ltd	7.747

LYNDALES, Lynton House, 7-12 Travistock Square, London, WC1H 9LT. Tel: 020 7391 1000. Fax: 020 7383 3494.
Internet: www.lyndales.co.uk.

Community Links Trust	7.165

LYONS DAVIDSON, Victoria House, 51 Victoria Street, Bristol, BS1 6AD. Tel: 0117 904 6000. Fax: 0117 904 6001.
E-mail: info@lyonsdavidson.co.uk.
Internet: www.lyonsdavidson.co.uk.
Charity specialists: R Acock. Amanda Hibbard.

Above and Beyond (J)	7.7
Milestones Trust	7.427
Soil Association (J)	7.625

MA LAW (SOLICITORS) LLP, 72-74 Edgware Road, London, W2 2EG.

Africa Educational Trust	7.15

MCCANN FITZGERALD, Riverside One, Sir John Rogerson's Quay, Dublin 2. Tel: +353 1 829 0000. Fax: +353 1 829 0010.

Sightsavers International (J)	7.608

MCCARTHY DENNING, 25 Southampton Buildings, London, WC2A 1AL. Tel: 020 7769 6741. E-mail: info@mccarthydenning.com. Internet: www.mccarthydenning.com. Charity specialists: B James (Head of Charities Group). Jayne Adams.

Breast Cancer Campaign (J)	7.86
St Vincent de Paul Society (J)	7.655
Walk the Walk Worldwide	7.712

MCCARTNEY STEWART, 1B Paisley Road, Paisley, Renfrewshire, PA4 8JH. Tel: 0141 885 1858. Fax: 0141 886 5425. E-mail: law@mccartneystewart.co.uk. Internet: www.mccartneystewart.co.uk.

Sustrans (J)	7.666

MCCLURE NAISMITH, 292 St Vincent Street, Glasgow, G2 5TQ. Tel: 0141 204 2700. Fax: 0141 248 3998. E-mail: glasgow@mcclurenaismith.com. Internet: www.mcclurenaismith.com.

Momentum Scotland	7.431

MCCORMICKS SOLICITORS, Wharfedale House, 37 East Parade, Harrogate, North Yorkshire, HG1 5LQ. Tel: 01423 530 630. Fax: 01423 530 709. E-mail: enquiries@mccormicks-solicitors.com. Internet: www.mccormicks-solicitors.com.

Outward Bound Trust (J)	7.485
Premier League Charitable Fund (J)	7.513

MCDERMOTT, WILL & EMERY, Heron Tower, 110 Bishopsgate, London, EC2N 4AY. Tel: 020 7577 6900. Internet: www.mwe.com.

Philharmonia (J)	7.500

MACDONALD HENDERSON, 94 Hope Street, Glasgow, G2 6PH. Tel: 0141 248 4957. Fax: 0141 248 4986. Internet: www.macdonaldhenderson.co.uk. Charity specialists: Christine S Henderson.

Active Stirling Limited	7.13

MACFARLANES LLP, 20 Cursitor Street, London, EC4A 1LT. Tel: 020 7831 9222. Fax: 020 7831 9607. E-mail: owen.clutton@macfarlanes.com; helen.darling@macfarlanes.com. Internet: www.macfarlanes.com.

29th May 1961 Charitable Trust	7.2
Ambitious about Autism (J)	7.29
Andrew Lloyd Webber Foundation, The	7.31
British Academy	7.91
D'Oyly Carte Charitable Trust	7.191
Education Endowment Foundation, The (J)	7.227
Guy's & St Thomas' Charity (J)	7.293
Hedley Foundation Limited	7.307
Impetus Private Equity Foundation (J)	7.330
John Armitage Charitable Trust	7.357
Lister Institute of Preventive Medicine	7.391
National Fund	7.446
Portsmouth Naval Base Property Trust (J)	7.510
Samworth Foundation	7.586
Savoy Educational Trust	7.588
Trusthouse Charitable Foundation	7.690
Whiteley Homes Trust (J)	7.725

MACHINS SOLICITORS LLP, Victoria Street, Luton, Bedfordshire, LU1 2BS. Tel: 01582 514000. Fax: 01582 535000. E-mail: enquiries@machins.co.uk. Internet: www.machins.co.uk. Charity specialists: Nic Pestell. Kevin Walsh.

MCINTYRE & COMPANY, 38 High Street, Fort William, Highland, PH33 6AT. Tel: 01397 703231. Internet: www.solicitors-scotland.com.

West Highland College UHI	7.720

MCKENZIE BELL, 19 John Street, Sunderland, Tyne and Wear, SR1 1JG. Tel: 0191 5674857. Internet: www.mckenzie-bell.co.uk.

Sir John Priestman Charity Trust	7.611

MACLAY MURRAY & SPENS LLP, One London Wall, London, EC2Y 5AB. Tel: 020 7002 8500. Fax: 020 7002 8501. Internet: www.mms.co.uk.

Avenues East	7.51
Avenues London	7.51
Avenues South East	7.51
Camden Society (J)	7.109
Thomas Pocklington Trust (J)	7.678

MACLAY MURRAY & SPENS LLP, Quartermile One, 15 Lauriston Place, Edinburgh, EH3 9EP. Tel: 0131 228 7000. Fax: 0131 228 7001. Internet: www.mms.co.uk. Charity specialists: E Easton.

Edinburgh International Festival Society	7.225
Global Alliance For Livestock Vet Med.	7.277
Shetland Charitable Trust (J)	7.604

MACLAY MURRAY & SPENS LLP, 1 George Square, Glasgow, G2 1AL. Tel: 0141 248 5011. Fax: 0141 248 5819. Internet: www.mms.co.uk. Charity specialists: A Murray.

Action Group Ltd (J)	7.10
Beatson Oncology Centre Fund	7.63
Blair Drummond Camphill Trust Limited	7.74
National Theatre of Scotland	7.453
Scottish Ballet (J)	7.591
Scottish Opera (J)	7.592

MACLEOD & MACCALLUM, 28 Queensgate, Inverness, Highland, IV1 1YN. Tel: 01463 239393. Fax: 01463 222879. E-mail: mail@macandmac.co.uk. Internet: www.macandmac.co.uk. Charity specialists: D Graham.

Highland Hospice	7.312
Inverness Leisure Limited	7.345

MACRAE & CO, 100 Cannon Street, London, EC4N 6EU. Tel: 020 7378 7716. Fax: 020 7407 4318. Internet: www.macraeco.com.

Hult International Business School	7.324

MACROBERTS LLP, Excel House, 30 Semple Street, Edinburgh, EH3 8BL. Tel: 0131 229 5046. Fax: 0131 229 0849. E-mail: maildesk@macroberts.com. Internet: www.macroberts.com.

Sense Scotland	7.597

MACROBERTS LLP, Capella, 60 York Street, Glasgow, G2 8JX. Tel: 0141 303 1100. Fax: 0141 332 8886. E-mail: maildesk@macroberts.com. Internet: www.macroberts.com. Charity specialists: D J C MacRobert. Carole McAlpine-Scott.

Scottish Opera (J)	7.592
Talbot Association Limited	7.668

MCSPARRAN & MCCORMICK, 19 Waterloo Street, Glasgow, G2 6AH. Tel: 0141 248 7962. Fax: 0141 204 2232. Internet: www.mcsparranmccormick.co.uk.

Archdiocese of Glasgow, The	7.37
Cora Foundation	7.179
Good Shepherd Centre Bishopton, The	7.281
Mungo Foundation, The	7.439
Scottish Catholic International Aid Fund	7.591
Sisters Notre Dame Namur (J)	7.614
St Mary's Kenmure	7.650

MAIER BLACKBURN, Prama House, 267 Banbury Road, Oxford, Oxfordshire, OX2 7HT. Tel: 01865 339330. Fax: 01865 339331. E-mail: info@maierblackburn.com. Internet: www.maierblackburn.com.

Tolkien Trust	7.682

MALE & WAGLAND, 4 Barnet Road, Potters Bar, Hertfordshire, EN6 2QT. Tel: 01707 657 171. Fax: 01707 646 336. E-mail: enquiry@mwlaw.co.uk. Internet: www.mwlaw.co.uk.

Finchley Charities	7.254

Foyle Foundation (J)	7.261

MANDER HADLEY & CO, 1 The Quadrant, Coventry, West Midlands, CV1 2DW. Tel: 024 7663 1212. Fax: 024 7663 3131. Internet: www.mander_hadley.co.uk.

Coventry Freemen's Charity	7.184
General Charity (Coventry)	7.270

MANUEL SWADEN, 340 West End Lane, London, NW6 ILN. Tel: 020 7431 4999. Fax: 020 7794 9900.

Hampstead Wells & Campden Trust (J)	7.299
Hannah Susan Samuel Victor Greig Fund	7.300

MAPLES TEESDALE LLP, 30 King Street, London, EC2V 8EE. Tel: 0207 600 3800. Fax: 0203 465 4400. E-mail: enq@maplesteesdale.co.uk. Internet: www.maplesteesdale.co.uk.

Cancer Research UK (J)	7.112
Percy Bilton Charity	7.497

MARRIOTT HARRISON, 12 Great James Street, London, WC1N 3DR. Tel: 020 7209 2000. Fax: 020 7209 2001. Internet: www.marriottharrison.com. Charity specialists: P Stuart-Buttle.

Thomson Media Foundation, The (J)	7.678

MARSONS, Amadeus House, 33-39 Elmfield Road, Bromley, Kent, BR1 1LT. Tel: 020 8313 1300. Internet: www.marsons.co.uk.

CAYSH	7.121

MARTIN & CO, 2 Wellington Square, Ayr, Strathclyde, KA7 1EN. Tel: 01292 265024. Fax: 01292 610192.

Ayrshire Hospice	7.52

MARTIN TOLHURST PARTNERSHIP, 7 Wrotham Road, Gravesend, Kent, DA11 0PD. Tel: 01474 325531. Fax: 01474 560771. E-mail: mtp.gravesend.kent@cableinet.co.uk. Internet: www.martintolhurst.co.uk.

Ellenor Lions Hospices (J)	7.231
Sisters of Mercy, Gravesend	7.614

MASSERS, Russell House, 9 Tudor Square, West Bridgford, Nottingham, Nottinghamshire, NG2 6BT. Tel: 0115 851 1666. Fax: 0115 851 1655. E-mail: martinw@massers.co.uk. Internet: www.massers.co.uk.

Notts Roman Catholic Diocesan Trustees (J)	7.473
Presentation Sisters	7.616

MATHIE MACLUCKIE, Wellington House, Dumbarton Road, Stirling, FK8 2RW. Tel: 01786 475112. Fax: 01786 450451.

Strathcarron Hospice	7.661

MATTHEW ARNOLD & BALDWIN, P O Box No 101, 21 Station Road, Watford, Hertfordshire, WD17 1HT. Tel: 01923 202020. Fax: 01923 215050. E-mail: info@mablaw.co.uk. Internet: www.mablaw.co.uk. Charity specialists: I Donaldson.

Institute of Grocery Distribution	7.335
Sports Aid Trust (J)	7.633

MATTHEW BOYER SOLICITORS, Appletree Barn, Chagford, Devon, TQ13 8JQ.

South West Lakes Trust (J)	7.630

MATTHEW WAITE & CO, Ariel House, Frogmore Street, Tring, Hertfordshire, HP23 5AU.

Rennie Grove Hospice Care (J)	7.531

MAURICE TURNOR GARDNER LLP, 201 Bishopsgate, London, EC2M 2AB. Tel: 020 7456 8610. Fax: 020 7012 8620. E-mail: info@mtgllp.com. Internet: www.mauriceturnorgardner.com.

Chartered Institute of Taxation	7.134
Childwick Trust (J)	7.142

Ingram Trust	7.331
Institute of Materials, Minerals & Mining (J)	7.336
Jean Shanks Foundation	7.352
Leverhulme Trade Charities Trust	7.386
Leverhulme Trust	7.386
Michael Bishop Foundation	7.425
Royal College of Anaesthetists	7.555

MAX BITEL GREENE, 1 Canonbury Place, London, N1 2NG. Tel: 020 7354 2767. Fax: 0207 226 1210. Internet: www.mbg.co.uk.

London Marathon Charitable Trust Limited (J)	7.399

MAX ENGEL & CO LLP, 8 Hazelwood Road, Northampton, Northamptonshire, NN1 1LP. Tel: 01604 887450. Fax: 01604 231465. E-mail: info@maxengel.co.uk. Internet: www.maxengel.co.uk.

Northampton County Council on Addiction	7.183

MAXWELL HODGE, 34 Grange Road, West Kirby, Wirral, CH48 4EF. Tel: 0151 625 9154. Fax: 0151 625 1162. Internet: www.maxweb.co.uk. Charity specialists: Mark Fergusson. Jonathon Gorman.

West Kirby Residential School	7.720

MAYER BROWN ROWE & MAW, 11 Pilgrim Street, London, EC4V 6RW. Tel: 020 7248 4282. Fax: 020 7248 2009. Internet: www.mayerbrownrowe.com. Charity specialists: Anne Radford.

Biochemical Society (J)	7.70

MAYO WYNNE BAXTER LLP, 20 Gilderedge Road, Eastbourne, East Sussex, BN21 4RP. Tel: 01323 730 543. Fax: 01323 737 214. E-mail: eastbourne@mayowynnebaxter.co.uk. Internet: www.mayowynnebaxter.co.uk.

Wave Leisure Trust Limited	7.716

MBM COMMERCIAL LLP, 5th Floor, 7 Castle Street, Edinburgh, EH2 3AH. Tel: 0131 226 8200. Fax: 0131 226 8240. E-mail: info@mbmcommercial.co.uk. Internet: www.mbmcommercial.co.uk.

Alliance of Sector Skills Councils	7.26

MDY LEGAL, St Nicholas House, St Nicholas Road, Sutton, Surrey, SM1 1EL. Tel: 020 8643 9794. Fax: 020 8770 9184. E-mail: liam.davies@mdy.co.uk. Internet: www.mdy.co.uk. Charity specialists: Kirsten Bryans. L Davies. Diane Harris. A Kirk. R Marriott. Karen Maurice-Jones. J Thorne. N Williamson. T Yapp.

Children's Food Trust, The	7.140

MEADE KING LLP, 11-12 Queen Square, Bristol, BS1 4NT. Tel: 0117 926 4121. Fax: 0117 929 7578. E-mail: sre@meadeking.co.uk. Internet: www.meadeking.co.uk. Charity specialists: Cathrine Anley. Simon East. James Hawking. Edward Langford.

Adolescent and Children's Trust, The (J)	7.14
BRUNELCARE (J)	7.102
George Muller Charitable Trust [The]	7.273
St Christopher's School (Bristol)	7.640

MERCERS, 50 New Street, Henley-on-Thames, Oxfordshire, RG9 2BX. Tel: 01491 572138. Fax: 01491 572223. Internet: www.mercerslaw.co.uk.

Church of England Pensions Board (J)	7.148

ME33R3 ROBERT LUNN & LOWTH, 2 Sheep Street, Stratford-upon-Avon, Warwickshire, CV37 6EJ.

Guild Estate Endowment (J)	7.291

METCALFE, COPEMAN AND PETTEFAR, Cage Lane, Thetford, Norfolk, IP24 2DT. Tel: 01842 756100. Fax: 01842 752818. E-mail: info@mcp-law.co.uk. Internet: www.mcp-law.co.uk.

Starling Family Charitable Trust, The	7.656

MFG, Adam House, Birmingham Road, Kidderminster, Worcestershire, DY10 2SH. Tel: 01562 820 181. Fax: 01562 820 066. E-mail: kidderminster@mfgsolicitors.com. Internet: www.mfgsolicitors.com.

Worcestershire YMCA Limited	7.738

MFG, Padmore House, Hall Court, Hall Park Way, Town Centre, Telford, Shropshire, TF3 4LX. Tel: 01952 641651. Fax: 01952 247441. E-mail: telford@mfgsolicitors.com. Internet: www.mfgsolicitors.com.

Whitley Animal Protection Trust	7.726

MICHAEL SIMKINS LLP, Lynton House, 7-12 Tavistock Square, London, WC1H 9LT. Tel: 020 7874 5600. Fax: 020 7874 5601. E-mail: info@simkins.com. Internet: www.simkins.com.

D&AD (J)	7.191

MICHELMORES, 48 Chancery Lane, London, WC2A 1JF. Tel: 020 7659 7660. Fax: 020 7659 7661. E-mail: enquiries@michelmores.com. Internet: www.michelmores.com.

Lord's Taverners	7.403

MICHELMORES, Woodwater House, Pynes Hill, Exeter, Devon, EX2 5WR. Tel: 01392 688 688. Fax: 01392 360 563. E-mail: tjc@michelmores.com. Internet: www.michelmores.com.

Cornwall Hospice Care	7.180
Devon Air Ambulance Trust	7.200
Dulwich Picture Gallery (J)	7.215
Exeter Diocesan Board of Finance, The	7.244
National Portrait Gallery (J)	7.451
Tempus Leisure Limited (J)	7.672
Truro Diocesan Board Finance Ltd (J)	7.687
WESC Foundation	7.719

MILLS & REEVE LLP, 8th and 9th Floor, 1 New York Street, Manchester, Greater Manchester, M1 4AD. Tel: 0161 235 5420. Fax: 0161 235 5421.

Hallé Concerts Society (J)	7.297
League Football Education (J)	7.381

MILLS & REEVE LLP, Francis House, 112 Hills Road, Cambridge, Cambridgeshire, CB2 1PH. Tel: 01223 222297. Fax: 01223 222220. E-mail: ted.powell@mills-reeve.com. Internet: www.mills-reeve.com. Charity specialists: Ted Powell.

Academies Enterprise Trust	7.7
Anglo-European College of Chiropractic (J)	7.32
Ashridge (Bonar Law Memorial) Trust (J)	7.44
BirdLife International (J)	7.70
Birmingham Children's Hospital Charities (J)	7.71
British & Foreign School Society, The (J)	7.91
Centre for Eng. & Manufacturing Excellence	7.124
Countryside Restoration Trust	7.182
Education and Training Foundation (J)	7.227
Fauna & Flora International	7.249
Forum Trust Limited	7.258
Huntingdon Freemen's Trust (J)	7.325
Imperial College Trust	7.329
Institute of Food Research (J)	7.335
Institution of Chemical Engineers (J)	7.337
John Innes Centre (J)	7.358
John Innes Foundation	7.358
Letchworth Garden City Heritage Foundation (J)	7.386
National Film and Television School	7.445
Norfolk Community Foundation	7.464
Regent's University London	7.530
Roman Catholic Diocese of East Anglia (J)	7.543
Royal Foundation of St Katharine, The	7.560
Royal Society of Chemistry (J)	7.572
Severn Trent Water Charitable Trust Fund	7.598
Transforming Education in Norfolk	7.685
WCMC 2000	7.716

MINAHAN HIRST & CO, 33 Station Rd, Cheadle, Cheshire, SK8 5AF. Tel: 0161 485 8131.

After Adoption (J)	7.16

MISHCON DE REYA, Summit House, 12 Red Lion Square, London, WC1R 4QD. Tel: 020 7440 7000. Fax: 020 7404 5982. E-mail: feedback@mishcon.co.uk. Internet: www.mishcon.com.

Coram	7.179
In Kind Direct (J)	7.330
JNF Charitable Trust (J)	7.355
Maggie Keswick Jencks Cancer Trust (J)	7.406
United Jewish Israel Appeal (J)	7.696

MJ BROWN, SON & CO, Dean Bank Lodge, 10 Dean Bank Lane, Edinburgh, EH3 5BS.

Carr-Gomm Scotland (J)	7.117

MKB SOLICITORS LLP, 1-11 Huddersfield Road, Barnsley, South Yorkshire, S70 2LP. Tel: 01226 210000. Fax: 01226 211110. E-mail: dw@mkbsolicitors.co.uk. Internet: www.mkbsolicitors.co.uk.

North York Moors Historical Railway (J)	7.468

MONRO FISHER WASBROUGH LLP, 8 Great James Street, London, WC1N 3DF. Tel: 020 7404 7001. Fax: 020 7404 7002. E-mail: law@monro-fisher.com. Internet: www.monro-fisher-wasbrough.com. Charity specialists: Olivia G Meekin. D D C Monro.

Saddlers' Company Charitable Fund	7.580

MOON BEEVER, Bedford House, 21a John Street, London, WC1N 2BF. Tel: 020 7400 7770. Fax: 020 7400 7799. E-mail: info@moonbeever.com. Internet: www.moonbeever.com. Charity specialists: Aishling J Davies. P A Sheils. R J Weetch. Baron P Temple-Morris - specialist area: Intl Affairs & UK Public Affairs.

Greensleeves Homes Trust (J)	7.287
Marine Society & Sea Cadets (J)	7.411

MOORCROFTS, 7 Church Road, Woolton, Liverpool, Merseyside, L25 5JE. Tel: 0151 428 1911. Internet: www.morecrofts.co.uk.

West Lancashire Freemasons' Charity	7.720

MOORCROFTS, James House, Mere Park, Dedmere Road, Marlow, Buckinghamshire, SL7 1FJ. Tel: 01628 470000. Fax: 01628 470001.

Lloyds Foundation for England and Wales (J)	7.395

MOORE BLATCH, 48 High Street, Lymington, Hampshire, SO41 9ZQ. Tel: 01590 625800. Fax: 01590 671224. E-mail: carla.brown@mooreblatch.com. Internet: www.mooreblatch.com.

Oakhaven Trust (J)	7.476

MOORHEAD JAMES LLP, Kildare House, 3 Dorset Rise, London, EC4Y 8EN. Tel: 020 7831 8888. Fax: 020 7936 3635. E-mail: mail@moorheadjames.com. Internet: www.moorheadjames.com.

Sports Council Trust Company	7.634

MORECROFTS, Cotton Exchange, Old Hall Street, Liverpool, Merseyside, L3 9LQ. Tel: 0151 236 8871. Fax: 0151 236 8109. E-mail: mail@morecroft.co.uk. Internet: www.morecroft.co.uk.

Caritas Care (J)	7.115

MORGAN, DENTON, JONES LTD, Ground Floor, Park House, Greyfriars Road, Cardiff, CF10 3AF. Tel: 029 20 537740. Fax: 029 20 537749. E-mail: pa@mdjlaw.co.uk. Internet: www.mdjlaw.co.uk.

Gwent Assoc of Voluntary Organisation	7.294

MORGAN LEWIS, Condor House, 5-10 St Paul's Churchyard, London, EC4M 8AL. Tel: 020 3210 5000. Fax: 020 3201 5001.
Internet: www.morganlewis.com.

New Wine Trust (J)   7.458

MORISONS LLP, Erskine House, 68 Queen Street, Edinburgh, EH2 4NN. Tel: 0313 226 6541. Fax: 0131 226 3156.
Internet: www.morisonsllp.com.

Children 1st   7.140

MORRISONS, Clarendon House, Clarendon Road, Redhill, Surrey, RH1 1FB. Tel: 01737 854 500. Fax: 01737 854 596.
E-mail: info@morrlaw.com.
Internet: www.morrlaw.com.

Chapter 1 (J)   7.127

MORTON FRASER LLP, Quartermile Two, 2 Lister Square, Edinburgh, EH3 9GL. Tel: 0131 247 1000. Fax: 0131 247 1007.
E-mail: infodesk@morton-fraser.com.
Internet: www.morton-fraser.com.
Charity specialists: A Bell. Scott A Rae WS.

Capability Scotland (J)	7.113
Harmeny Education Trust	7.302
Institute of Occupational Medicine	7.336
Mercy Corps Scotland (J)	7.422
Scottish Wildlife Trust	7.593
Social Investment Scotland	7.620

MORTON FRASER LLP, 145 St Vincent Street, Glasgow, G2 5JF. Tel: 0141 274 1100.
Internet: www.morton-fraser.com.

East Kilbride District Eng Grp Training Assoc   7.221

MOSS SOLICITORS LLP, 80-81 Wood Gate, Loughborough, Leicestershire, LE11 2XE. Tel: 01509 217770. Fax: 01509 233698.
E-mail: enquiries@moss-solicitors.co.uk.
Internet: www.moss-solicitors.co.uk.
Charity specialists: D J Pagett-Wright. Ms J L Tarr.

Mount Saint Bernard Abbey   7.436

MOWLL & MOWLL, Trafalgar House, Gordon Road, Whitfield, Dover, Kent, CT16 3PN. Tel: 01304 873344. Fax: 01304 873355.
E-mail: enquiries@mowll.co.uk.
Internet: www.mowll.co.uk.

Canterbury Diocesan Board of Finance (J)   7.112

MUCKLE LLP, Time Central, 32 Gallowgate, Newcastle upon Tyne, Tyne and Wear, NE1 4BF. Tel: 0191 211 7777. Fax: 0191 211 7788.
E-mail: advice@muckle-llp.com.
Internet: www.muckle-llp.com.

1989 Willan Charitable Trust (J)	7.2
Age UK North Tyneside (J)	7.18
Alnwick Garden Trust (J)	7.27
Azure Charitable Enterprises	7.52
Chelsea F C Foundation Limited	7.137
Comm Fdn (Tyne&Wear&Northumberland) (J)	7.164
Great North Air Ambulance Service	7.285
Mental Health Concern (J)	7.421
North East Autism Society	7.466
North Music Trust	7.467

MURPHY O'RAWE, Scottish Provident Buildings, 4th Floor, 7 Donegall Square West, Belfast, County Antrim, BT1 6LF. Tel: 028 9032 6636. Fax: 028 9082 8386. E-mail: info@murphy-orawe.com. Internet: www.murphy-orawe.com.

Praxis Care Group   7.512

MURRAY BEITH MURRAY, 3 Glenfinlas Street, Edinburgh, EH3 6AQ. Tel: 0131 225 1200. Fax: 0131 225 4412.
E-mail: mbm@murraybeith.co.uk.
Internet: www.murraybeith.co.uk.
Charity specialists: Carole Hope. J K Scott Moncrieff WS.

Action Group Ltd (J)   7.10

Dovecot Foundation   7.210

MURRAY DONALD LLP, Kinburn Castle, St Andrews, Fife, KY16 9DR. Tel: 01334 477107. Fax: 01334 476862.
E-mail: mail@murraydonald.co.uk.
Internet: www.murraydonald.co.uk.

St Andrews Links Trust   7.637

MURRAY SNELL, 40 North Castle Street, Edinburgh, EH2 3BN. Tel: 0131 625 6625. Fax: 0131 625 6626.
E-mail: mail@murraysnell.com.

National Library of Scotland (J)   7.448

MURRELL ASHWORTH LLP, 14 High Cross, Truro, Cornwall, TR1 2AJ. Tel: 01872 226990. Fax: 01872 278669.
Internet: www.murrellassociates.co.uk.

Cinnamon Trust (J)   7.150

NABARRO, Lacon House, Theobald's Road, London, WC1X 8RW. Tel: 020 7524 6000. Fax: 020 7524 6524.
Internet: www.nabarro.com.

4 Charity Foundation	7.3
Bloodwise (J)	7.76
Dolphin Square Charitable Foundation, The (J)	7.203
Raleigh International Trust (J)	7.524
Stowe House Preservation Trust	7.661

NABARRO, 1 South Quay, Victoria Quays, Sheffield, South Yorkshire, S2 5SY. Tel: 0114 279 4000. Fax: 0114 278 6123.
E-mail: info@nabarro.com.
Internet: www.nabarro.com.

Compass	7.168
Lowry Centre Trust (J)	7.403

NALDERS, Farley House, Falmouth Road, Truro, Cornwall, TR1 2HX. Tel: 01872 241414. Fax: 01872 242424.
Internet: www.nalders.co.uk.

Cinnamon Trust (J)   7.150

NAPTHENS, Greenbank Business Park, Greenbank Court, Challenge Way, Blackburn, Lancashire, BB1 5QB. Tel: 01254 667733. Fax: 01254 681166.
Internet: www.napthens.co.uk.
Charity specialists: J Kay.

Blackburn Diocesan Board Finance Limited	7.74
Positive Steps	7.510

NAPTHENS, 7 Winckley Square, Preston, Lancashire, PR1 3JD. Tel: 01772 883883. Fax: 01772 257805.
E-mail: reception@nepthens.co.uk.
Internet: www.napthens.co.uk.

Caritas Care (J)	7.115
Derian House Children's Hospice	7.198

NELSONS SOLICITORS, Provincial House, 37 New Walk, Leicester, Leicestershire, LE1 6TU. Tel: 0116 222 6666.
E-mail: newbusinessteam@nelsonslaw.co.uk.
Internet: www.nelsonslaw.co.uk.

National Space Science Centre   7.453

NELSONS SOLICITORS, Pennine House, 8 Stanford Street, Nottingham, Nottinghamshire, NG1 7BQ. Tel: 0115 958 6262.
E-mail: newbusinessteam@nelsonslaw.co.uk.
Internet: www.nelsonslaw.co.uk.
Charity specialists: S J Moore (Trust Executive).

Congregational Federation (J)   7.176

NEWMAN & BOND, 35 Church Street, Barnsley, South Yorkshire, S70 2AP. Tel: 01226 213434. Fax: 01226 213435.
E-mail: jill.leece@newmanandbond.co.uk.
Internet: www.newmanandbond.co.uk.

Earl Fitzwilliam Charitable Trust (J)	7.218
Fitzwilliam Wentworth Amenity Trust (J)	7.255

NEWMAN LAW, 10 Hendon Lane, Finchley Central, London, N3 1TR. Tel: 0208 349 2655. Fax: 0208 346 0270.
E-mail: info@newmanlaw.co.uk.
Internet: www.newmanlaw.co.uk.

Solicitors Benevolent Association (J)   7.626

NEWTONS, 22 Fitzjohn's Avenue, London, NW3 4PY.

Servants Fellowship International   7.598

NICHOLAS & CO., 18-22 Wigmore Street, London, W1U 2RG. Tel: 020 7323 4450. Internet: www.nicholassolicitors.com/nicholas.swf.

Archie Sherman Charitable Trust   7.38

NICHOLLS LINDSELL & HARRIS, 34/36 Park Lane, Poynton, Cheshire, SK12 1RE. Tel: 01625 876411. Fax: 01625 879947.
E-mail: enquiries@nichollslindsellharris.co.uk.
Internet: www.nichollslindsellandharris.co.uk.

Imagine Act and Suceed   7.328

NOCKOLDS SOLICITORS, Market Square, Bishop's Stortford, Hertfordshire, CM23 3UZ. Tel: 01279 755 777. Fax: 01279 260 047.
E-mail: enquiries@nockolds.co.uk.
Internet: www.nockolds.co.uk.

Essex & Herts Air Ambulance Trust   7.240

NORTON ROSE, 3 More London Riverside, London, SE1 2AQ. Tel: 020 7283 6000. Fax: 020 7283 6500.
Internet: www.nortonrose.com.
Charity specialists: D Lewis.

Debra (J)   7.196

NOWELL MELLER, 24 Market Place, Burslem, Stoke-on-Trent, ST6 4AX. Tel: 01782 813315. Fax: 01782 835782.

Addiction Dependency Solutions (J)   7.14

O'NEILL, ROBSON PALMER, 1 & 2 Lansdowne Terrace East, Gosforth, Newcastle upon Tyne, Tyne and Wear, NE3 1HL. Tel: 0191 246 4000. Fax: 0191 213 0134. E-mail: info@oneill-law.com. Internet: www.oneill-law.com.
Charity specialists: F A Jones.

Durham Aged Mineworkers' Homes Assoc   7.216

OLSWANG, 90 High Holborn, London, WC1V 6XX. Tel: 020 7067 3000. Fax: 020 7067 3999. Internet: www.olswang.com.
Charity specialists: A Bott. J S Goldstein (Chief Executive).

Design Council (J)	7.199
Joshua Trust Group, The	7.364
Rachel Charitable Trust	7.522
Royal Institution of Great Britain (J)	7.562

ORMERODS, 45 Friends Road, Croydon, Surrey, CR0 1ED. Tel: 020 8686 5000. Fax: 020 8680 0972. E-mail: peter.woods@ormerods.co.uk. Internet: www.solicitorscroydon.com.

Action Medical Research (J)   7.11

OSBORNE CLARKE, 2 Temple Back East, Temple Quay, Bristol, BS1 6EG. Tel: 0117 917 3000. Fax: 0117 917 3005.
E-mail: mark.woodward@osborneclarke.com; alexandra.casley@osborneclarke.com.
Internet: www.osborneclarke.com.
Charity specialists: Mark Woodward. Robert Drewett. Alexandra Casley.

Battersea Dogs & Cats Home (J)	7.60
Book Trust	7.79
Bristol, Clifton, & West of England Zoo (J)	7.89
Cancer Research UK (J)	7.112
Quartet Community Foundation (J)	7.519
Stone Family Foundation, The	7.660
Sustrans (J)	7.666

OUTSET (UK) LIMITED, Vinters Business Park, New Cut Road, Maidstone, Kent, ME14 5NZ. Tel: 01622 759900.
Internet: www.outsetuk.com.

South of England Foundation   7.629

PAGAN OSBORNE, Clarendon House, 116 George Street, Edinburgh, EH2 4LH. Tel: 0131 624 6820. Fax: 0131 220 1612.
E-mail: ed_web@pagan.co.uk.
Internet: www.paganosborne.com.

Miss Agnes H Hunter's Trust	7.429
Royal Blind	7.553
Scottish War Blinded	7.593

PANNONE LLP, 123 Deansgate, Manchester, Greater Manchester, M3 2BU. Tel: 0161 909 3000. Fax: 0161 909 4444.
E-mail: law@pannone.co.uk.
Internet: www.pannone.com.

Addiction Dependency Solutions (J)	7.14
Alternative Futures Group Ltd (J)	7.27
Manchester Sport and Leisure Trust	7.408
Tameside Sports Trust	7.668
UK Biobank Ltd	7.692

PARIS SMITH LLP, 1 London Road, Southampton, Hampshire, SO15 2AE. Tel: 023 8048 2482. Fax: 023 8048 2229.
E-mail: nicholas.vaughan@parissmith.co.uk.
Internet: www.parissmith.co.uk.
Charity specialists: N Vaughan - specialist area: Property, charities and public sector.

Drug Safety Research Trust, The	7.212
Mayflower Theatre Trust	7.417
Rank Foundation Limited (J)	7.525
Royal Navy Submarine Museum	7.568
UK Sailing Academy (J)	7.693

PARK WOODFINE HEALD MELLOWS LLP, 1 Lurke Street, Bedford, Bedfordshire, MK40 3TN. Tel: 01234 400000. Fax: 01234 401111. **Internet: www.pwhmllp.com.**
Charity specialists: R Levene.

Marston Vale Trust   7.412

PARKER BULLEN LLP, 45 Castle Street, Salisbury, SP1 3SS. Tel: 01722 412000. Fax: 01722 411822.
E-mail: mark.lello@parkerbullen.com.
Internet: www.parkerbullen.co.uk.

Salisbury Diocesan Board of Education   7.583

PASSMORES, 21 Tynewydd Road, Barry, Vale of Glamorgan, CF62 8HB. Tel: 01446 721000. Fax: 01446 746949.
Internet: www.passmores.com.

Cartrefi Cymru (J)	7.117
Drive (J)	7.212
Mirus-Wales (J)	7.429

PATTEN & PRENTICE, 2 Ardgowan Square, Greenock, Strathclyde, PA16 8PP. Tel: 01475 720 306. Fax: 01475 888 127.
Internet: www.patten.co.uk.

Inverclyde Leisure   7.345

PATTERSON GLENTON & STRACEY, Law Court Chambers, Waterloo Square, South Shields, Tyne and Wear, NE33 1AW. Tel: 0191 456 0281. Fax: 0191 455 7380.

W A Handley Charity Trust   7.710

PAUL WEISS RIFKIND WHARTON & GARRISON, Alder Castle, 10 Noble Street, London, EC2V 7JU. Tel: 020 7367 1600.
Charity specialists: Matthew Nimetz.

Anna Freud Centre (J)   7.33

PAYNE HICKS BEACH, 10 New Square, Lincoln's Inn, London, WC2A 3QG. Tel: 020 7465 4300. Fax: 020 7465 4400. **E-mail: mail@phb.co.uk.**
Internet: www.phb.co.uk.
Charity specialists: G S Brown. P J Black.

Bill Brown's Charitable Settlement 1989	7.70
Englefield Charitable Trust	7.234

Ernest Cook Trust (J)	7.239
Geffrye Museum	7.270
Royal College of Psychiatrists	7.558
Royal Society of Medicine (J)	7.573

PAYNE MARSH STILLWELL, 6 Carlton Crescent, Southampton, Hampshire, SO15 2EY. Tel: 023 8022 3957. Fax: 023 8022 5261.
E-mail: enquiries@pms.gs. Internet: www.pms-law.co.uk.

Jerry Green Dog Rescue (J)   7.352

PEARSON ROWE, 56 St Pauls Square, Birmingham, West Midlands, B3 1QS. Tel: 0121 236 7388. Fax: 0121 237 4307.
E-mail: info@pearson-rowe.co.uk.
Internet: www.pearson-rowe.co.uk.

Murray Hall Community Trust   7.439

PEMBERTON GREENISH, 45 Cadogan Gardens, London, SW3 2AQ. Tel: 020 7591 3333. Fax: 020 7591 3300. **E-mail: law@pglaw.co.uk. Internet: www.pglaw.co.uk.**
Charity specialists: A J F Stebbings - specialist area: Charities and Trusts.

Harrow Development Trust	7.303
John Lyon's Charity	7.359
Peter Stebbings Memorial Charity	7.500

PENMAN JOHNSON, 5 George Street, Watford, Hertfordshire, WD18 0SQ. Tel: 01923 225 212. Fax: 01923 223 522.
E-mail: pjlaw@penmanjohnson.com.
Internet: www.penmanjohnson.com.
Charity specialists: Julie Windsor.

Peace Hospice Care   7.494

PENNINGTONS MANCHES, Abacus House, 33 Gutter Lane, London, EC2V 8AR. Tel: 020 7457 3000. Fax: 020 7457 3240.
E-mail: info@penningtons.co.uk.
Internet: www.penningtons.co.uk.
Charity specialists: Joan Radley.

Almeida Theatre Company (J)	7.27
Institute for Fiscal Studies (J)	7.332
Science, Tech, Eng & Mathematics Network	7.590

PENNINGTONS MANCHES, Da Vinci House, Basing View, Basingstoke, Hampshire, RG21 4EQ. Tel: 01256 407 100. Fax: 01256 479 425. **Internet: www.penningtons.co.uk.**

Loddon School Company   7.396

PENNINGTONS MANCHES, Clarendon House, Clarendon Road, Cambridge, Cambridgeshire, CB2 8FH. Tel: 01223 465465. Fax: 01223 465400. **Internet: www.penningtons.co.uk.**

Company of Biologists Limited (J)   7.168

PENNINGTONS MANCHES, Highfield, Brighton Road, Godalming, Surrey, GU7 1NS. Tel: 01483 791800. Fax: 01483 424177.
Internet: www.penningtons.co.uk.

Make-A-Wish Foundation (UK)   7.407

PENNINGTONS MANCHES, 9400 Garsington Road, Oxford, Oxfordshire, OX4 2HN. Tel: 01865 722106. Fax: 01865 201012.
Internet: www.penningtons.co.uk.
Charity specialists: R Jonckheer. T Gilman.

Hearing Dogs for Deaf People (J)	7.306
Pirbright Institute (J)	7.504

PERRY HAY & CO, 25 The Green, Richmond, Surrey, TW9 1JY. Tel: 020 8940 8115. Fax: 020 8948 8013.
E-mail: peterhay@perryhay.co.uk.
Internet: www.perryhay.co.uk.

Royal Scottish Corporation   7.570

PETER LYNN & PARTNERS, 2nd Floor, Langdon House, Langdon Road, Swansea, Dyfed, SA1 8QY. Tel: 01792 450010. Fax: 01792 462881.
Internet: www.peterlynnandpartners.co.uk.

Hafal   7.296

PETER MCFARLANE & CO, Argyll House, Quarrywood Court, Livingston, Lothian, EH54 6AX. Tel: 01506 497160.

West Lothian Leisure   7.721

PETER, PETER & WRIGHT, 1 Queen Street, Bude, Cornwall, EX23 8AZ. Tel: 01288 352101. Fax: 01288 355860.
Internet: www.peterslaw.co.uk.
Charity specialists: A Bennett.

Blanchminster Trust   7.75

PHILIP J. WILLANS, 20 London Road, St Albans, Hertfordshire, AL1 1NP. Tel: 01727 840549. Fax: 01727 843179.
Internet: www.philipwillans.co.uk.

Royal Entomological Society of London   7.559

PICKERINGS, Etchell House, Etchell Court, Bonehill Road, Tamworth, Staffordshire, B78 3HQ. Tel: 01827 317070. Fax: 01827 317080. **E-mail: mail@pickerings-solicitors.com. Internet: www.pickerings-solicitors.com.**

St Giles Hospice (J)   7.643

PICTONS LLP, 28 Dunstable Road, Luton, Bedfordshire, LU1 1DY. Tel: 01582 870870. Fax: 01582 870872.
E-mail: info@pictons.co.uk.
Internet: www.pictons.com.
Charity specialists: R T Hodder.

Active Luton (J)   7.12

PINNEY TALFOURD LLP, 39-41 High Street, Brentwood, Essex, CM 14 4RH. Tel: 01277 211755. Fax: 01277 261154.
E-mail: brentwood@pinneytalfourd.co.uk.
Internet: www.pinneytalfourd.co.uk.

Keech Hospice Care (J)   7.367

PINNEY TALFOURD LLP, Crown House, 40 North Street, Hornchurch, Essex, RM11 1EW. Tel: 01708 511000. Fax: 01708 511040.
E-mail: mail@pinneytalfourd.co.uk.
Internet: www.pinneytalfourd.co.uk.

TRAID   7.674

PINSENT MASONS LLP, 30 Crown Place, London, EC2A 4ES. Tel: 020 7418 7000. Fax: 020 7418 7050.
Internet: www.pinsentmasons.com.

Delapage Ltd	7.196
Luton Cultural Services Trust (J)	7.404
Mary Hare School	7.414
SOS Children's Villages UK	7.628
South Bank Centre (J)	7.628
Trustees of the London Clinic Limited (J)	7.689

PINSENT MASONS LLP, 13 Queen's Road, Aberdeen, Aberdeenshire, AB15 4YL. Tel: 01224 377 900. Fax: 01224 377 901.
Internet: www.pinsentmasons.com.

Rowett Research Institute   7.548

PINSENT MASONS LLP, 3 Colmore Circus, Birmingham, West Midlands, B4 6BH. Tel: 0121 200 1050. Fax: 0121 626 1040.
E-mail: hugo.stephens@pinsentmasons.com.
Internet: www.pinsentmasons.com.

Birmingham Royal Ballet (J)	7.73
British Motor Industry Heritage Trust	7.96
Methodist Homes (J)	7.424
Royal Shakespeare Company (J)	7.571
Veolia Environmental Trust, The (J)	7.704

PINSENT MASONS LLP, 141 Bothwell Street, Glasgow, G2 7EQ. Tel: 0141 248 4858. Fax: 0141 248 6655.
Internet: www.pinsentmasons.com.

Sisters of Bon Secours of Paris	7.172
Millennium Link Trust	7.427
National Library of Scotland (J)	7.448
Prince and Princess of Wales Hospice (J)	7.513
Royal Yacht Britannia Trust	7.575

PINSENT MASONS LLP, 1 Park Row, Leeds, West Yorkshire, LS1 5AB. Tel: 0113 244 5000. Fax: 0113 244 8000.
E-mail: janet.hoskin@pinsentmasons.com.
Internet: www.pinsentmasons.com.

Asda Foundation Limited (J)   7.42

Unipol Student Homes (J)   7.695

PITMANS LLP, 46 The Avenue, Southampton, Hampshire, SO17 1AX. Tel: 023 8083 1919. E-mail: poppy@pitmans.com. Internet: www.pitmans.com.

Sheiling Trust (J)   7.603

PITMANS LLP, 1 Crown Court, 66 Cheapside, London, EC2V 6LR. Tel: 020 7634 4620. Fax: 020 7634 4621. Internet: www.pitmans.com.

England and Wales Cricket Trust (J)   7.234
River and Rowing Museum Foundation   7.539

PLATT & FISHWICK, The Old Bank, King Street, Wigan, Greater Manchester, WN1 1DB. Tel: 01942 243281. Fax: 01942 495522.

Wigan & Leigh Hospice (J)   7.727

PORTER DODSON, Central House, Church Street, Yeovil, Somerset, BA20 1HH. Tel: 01935 424 581. Fax: 01935 706 063. Internet: www.porterdodson.co.uk.

Haynes International Motor Museum (J)   7.304

PORTRAIT SOLICITORS, 21 Whitefriars Street, London, EC4Y 8JJ. Tel: 020 7092 6990. Fax: 020 7430 1242. Internet: www.portraitsolicitors.com. Charity specialists: Alison Burton. D Flynn. Judith S Portrait - specialist area: Charity Law, Private Client/Trust.

Pothecary Witham Weld | PWW solicitors

POTHECARY WITHAM WELD, 70 St George's Square, London, SW1V 3RD. Tel: 020 7821 8211. Fax: 020 7630 6484. E-mail: info@pwwsolicitors.co.uk. Internet: www.pwwsolicitors.co.uk.

Pothecary Witham Weld offers specialist advice in the following areas:

- Establishment and administration of charities and not for profit organisations operating both nationally and internationally
- Statutory obligations and governance
- Acting for Religious and Educational Institutions
- Trustee powers and liabilities
- Acquisition/disposal of property and assets
- Taxation, donations, legacies and investments
- Commercial activities and agreements, trading and fund raising
- Administration of grant-making charities
- Employment
- Dispute Resolution

Contact: Gerald Kidd on 020 7821 8211

Pothecary Witham Weld is authorised and regulated by the Solicitors Regulation Authority – No. 00446834

Charity specialists: Gerald Kidd - specialist area: Charity & Church. Alexa Beale. Patrick Herschan. Peter Holland. Nadeem Azhar. Catherine Durant. Jayne Day. Peter Spencer.

Brampton Trust (J)   7.84
British Editorial Society Bone Joint Surgery   7.92
Sisters of Charity of Jesus and Mary   7.94
Carmelite Charitable Trust (J)   7.116
Catholic Foreign Missions   7.119
Charity for Roman Catholic Congregation   7.128
Charity for the Sisters of Mercy Midhurst   7.129
Charity Roman Union Order St Ursula (J)   7.130
Congregation of the Jesus Charitable Trust (J)   7.171
Good Shepherd Sisters (J)   7.171
Daughters of the Holy Ghost   7.173
Congregation of the Ursulines of Jesus   7.176
English Province of our Lady of Charity (J)   7.235
Handmaids of the Sacred Heart of Jesus (J)   7.300
Institute of the Franciscan Missionaries   7.337
Methodist Central Hall Westminster   7.423
Methodist Church In Great Britain, The   7.423
Missio   7.429
Passage 2000   7.492
TrusteesofCongregattionofMostHolyRedeemer   7.544
SistersoftheSacred Hearts of Jesus & Mary (J)   7.580
Scripture Union (J)   7.594
Sisters of the Holy Cross   7.615
SMB Charitable Trust (J)   7.619
Society of Jesus (J)   7.622
Society of the Sacred Heart   7.624
Sons of the Sacred Heart of Jesus, The   7.627
St Joseph's Society for Foreign Missions   7.646

POTTER OWTRAM & PECK, 42 West Street, Haslemere, Surrey, GU27 2AN. Tel: 01428 642321. Fax: 01428 653643. Charity specialists: B E Farley.

FitzRoy Support (J)   7.255

POWELLS WITH CHAWNER GREY SOLICITORS, 7-13 Oxford Street, Weston-super-Mare, Somerset, BS23 1TE. Tel: 01934 623 501. Fax: 01394 635 036. E-mail: hannah@powellslaw.com. Internet: www.powellslaw.com. Charity specialists: T C Hannah.

Weston Hospicecare   7.723

PRESTON GOLDBURN SOLICITORS, Gwella House, 6B Falmouth Business Park, Falmouth, Cornwall, TR11 4SZ. Tel: 01326 318900. Fax: 01326 311275. E-mail: legal@prestongoldburn.com. Internet: www.prestongoldburn.com.

Tempus Leisure Limited (J)   7.672

PRESTON REDMAN, Hinton House, Hinton Road, Bournemouth, Dorset, BH1 2EN. Tel: 01202 292424. Fax: 01202 552758. E-mail: office@prestonredman.co.uk. Internet: www.prestonredman.co.uk. Charity specialists: D J E Neville-Jones - specialist area: Charity and Trust Law.

Alice Ellen Cooper-Dean Charitable Fndtn   7.24
Valentine Charitable Trust, The   7.702

PRETTYS, Elm House, 25 Elm Street, Ipswich, Suffolk, IP1 2AD. Tel: 01473 232121. Fax: 01473 230002. Internet: www.prettys.co.uk.

Aldeburgh Music   7.23
St Elizabeth Hospice (Suffolk)   7.642
Varrier Jones Foundation   7.703

PRINCE EVANS, 40-44 Uxbridge Road, Ealing, London, W5 2BS. Tel: 020 8567 3477. Fax: 020 8840 7757. E-mail: rjennings@prince-evans.co.uk. Charity specialists: T Lemon. L Robert - specialist area: Housing Associations.

Housing Pathways Trust   7.322

PROJECTS PARTNERSHIP LTD, Linton House, 164-180 Union Street, London, SE1 0LH.

Gloucestershire Care Partnership   7.278
Oxfordshire Care Partnership, The   7.488

PULHAM & CO, Egmere House, Market Place, Saxmundham, Suffolk, IP17 1AG. Tel: 01728 602084. Fax: 01728 603739. E-mail: jsp@pulham.co.uk. Internet: www.pulham.co.uk.

Congregation of Sisters of Jesus & Mary   7.172

PUNCH ROBSON, 35 Albert Road, Middlesbrough, Cleveland, TS1 1NU. Tel: 01642 230700. Fax: 01642 218923.

St Oswald's Hospice (J)   7.653

QUALITYSOLICITORS BURROUGHS DAY, Queen Square House, 18-21 Queen Square, Bristol, BS1 4NH. Tel: 0117 929 0333. Fax: 0117 929 0335. E-mail: contact@qsbdlaw.com. Internet: www.qsbdlaw.com/charities.

QUALITYSOLICITORS FJG, Norfolk House, Southway, Colchester, Essex, CO2 7BA. Tel: 01206 578282. Fax: 01206 760282. E-mail: info@qsfjg.co.uk. Internet: www.fjg.co.uk. Charity specialists: D Jones.

Missionary Franciscan Sisters   7.544

QUALITYSOLICITORS PGS LAW, Law Court Chambers, Waterloo Square, South Shields, Tyne and Wear, NE33 1AW. Tel: 0191 456 0281. Fax: 0191 455 7380. E-mail: pgslaw@qualitysolicitors.com. Internet: www.qualitysolicitors.com/pgslaw/south shields.

Mental Health Concern (J)   7.421

QUALITYSOLICITORS ROWBIS, Morroway House, Station Road, Gloucester, Gloucestershire, GL1 1DW. Tel: 01452 301903. Fax: 01452 411115. E-mail: enquiries@rowbis.co.uk. Internet: www.qualitysolicitors.com/rowbis.

Sylvanus Lysons Charity   7.667

QUALITYSOLICITORS RUBIN LEWIS O'BRIEN, Gwent House, Gwent Square, Cwmbran, Torfaen, NP44 1PL. Tel: 01633 867 000. Fax: 01633 626 389. E-mail: law@rlob.co.uk. Internet: www.QualitySolicitors.com/rlob.

Sisters of St Joseph of Annecy   7.614

QUALITYSOLICITORS WILSON BROWNE, Kettering Parkway South, Kettering Venture Park, Kettering, Northamptonshire, NN15 6WN. Tel: 01536 410 014. Fax: 01536 516 805. E-mail: enquiries@wilsonbrowne.co.uk. Internet: www.qualitysolicitors.com/wilson-browne.

Spurgeons (J)   7.635

QUINN LEGAL, The Beacon, 176 St Vincent Street, Glasgow, G2 5SG.

Apostolic Church, The (J)   7.35

R J L STONES, 91 Linden Way, London, N14 4NG.

Ffestiniog & Welsh Highland Railways Trust   7.252

Please mention

Top 3000 Charities

when responding
to advertisements

RadcliffesLeBrasseur

RADCLIFFESLEBRASSEUR, 85 Fleet Street, London, EC4Y 1AE. Tel: 020 7222 7040. Fax: 020 7222 6208. E-mail: philip.maddock@rlb-law.com. Internet: www.rlb-law.com.

RadcliffesLeBrasseur represents a substantial number of charities, many of which are well known and we are recognised for specialist knowledge and expertise.

Our Charities Group appreciates the issues affecting charities and provides focused, workable and commercial solutions. Our core team specialises in charity law and guides charities through the increasingly intricate demands of charity legislation and practice. The wider Group draws on the expertise of practitioners in all areas of law with a particular understanding of the needs of charity clients and covers:

- Charity Formation and Governance;
- Mergers and Reorganisations;
- Fundraising;
- Employment Law and Pensions;
- Immigration;
- Commercial Law and Trading Companies;
- Property issues; and
- Litigation and Dispute Resolution

Charity specialists: Philip Maddock - specialist area: Charities, Commercial and Corporate. Sejal Raja - specialist area: Employment. Antony Brougham - specialist area: Commercial Property. Lara Keenan - specialist area: Immigration. Victoria Fairley - specialist area: Charities and Tax & Private Clients.

Children's Society (J)	7.142
Church Commissioners for England (J)	7.147
Institution of Civil Engineers (J)	7.338
Microbiology Society	7.425
Orthopaedic Research UK	7.484
Parkinson's UK (J)	7.491
Royal College of General Practitioners	7.556

RAMSDENS SOLICITORS LLP, Ramsden Street, Huddersfield, West Yorkshire, HD1 2TH. Tel: 01484 821 500.

Community of the Resurrection (J)	7.167

RAWLINS DAVY, Rowland House, Hinton Road, Bournemouth, Dorset, BH1 2EG. Tel: 01202 558844. Fax: 01202 557175.

Diverse Abilities Plus Limited (J)	7.202

RAWLISON BUTLER LLP, Griffin House, 135 High Street, Crawley, Sussex, RH10 1DQ. Tel: 01293 527 744. Fax: 01293 520 202. E-mail: info@rawlisonbutler.com. Internet: www.rawlisonbutler.com.

London School for the Performing Arts	7.401

RAWLISON BUTLER LLP, 15 Carfax, Horsham, Sussex, RH12 1DY. Tel: 01403 252492. Fax: 01403 241545. Internet: www.rawlisonbutler.com.

St Catherine's Hospice Limited (J)	7.639

RAWORTHS, Eton House, 89 Station Parade, Harrogate, North Yorkshire, HG1 1HF. Tel: 01423 566666. Fax: 01423 504572. Internet: www.raworths.co.uk.

Harrogate District Hospice Care	7.303
Liz and Terry Bramall Charitable Trust, The	7.394
Yorkshire Agricultural Society	7.748

READ COOPER, Dorchester House, 15 Dorchester Place, Thame, Oxfordshire, OX9 2DL. Tel: 01844 260038. Fax: 01844 218923. Internet: www.read-cooper.co.uk.

Exceed Worldwide	7.243

RECULVER SOLICITORS, 12-16 Clerkenwell Road, London, EC1M 5PQ. Tel: 0207 324 6271. Fax: 0207 477 2276. E-mail: info@reculversolicitors.co.uk. Internet: www.reculversolicitors.co.uk.

Centre 404	7.123

REDKITE, 14-15, Spilman Street, Carmarthen, Carmarthenshire, SA31 1SR. Tel: 01267239000.

Cerebra (J)	7.125

REED SMITH, Broadgate Tower, 20 Primrose Street, London, EC2A 2RS. Tel: 020 3116 3000. Fax: 020 3116 3999. E-mail: kwallace@reedsmith.com. Internet: www.reedsmith.com.

Action Against Hunger (UK) (J)	7.9
Dulwich Estate (J)	7.214
Foyle Foundation (J)	7.261
Harbour Foundation	7.301
Medical Foundation for Victims of Torture (J)	7.419
Norwood (J)	7.472
Prince's Trust (J)	7.514
Rank Foundation Limited (J)	7.525
Reuben Foundation	7.534
Royal London Society for the Blind (J)	7.564
United Jewish Israel Appeal (J)	7.696
World Cancer Research Fund (WCRF UK) (J)	7.739

REYNOLDS PORTER CHAMBERLAIN LLP, Tower Bridge House, St Katharine's Way, London, E1W 1AA. Tel: 020 3060 6000. Fax: 020 3060 7000. E-mail: enquiries@rpc.co.uk. Internet: www.rpc.co.uk. Charity specialists: C J Russell. P D Nicholas.

British Pregnancy Advisory Service (J)	7.97
St Clement Danes Holborn Estate Charity	7.641
UCKG HelpCentre	7.699
World Villages for Children	7.741

RICH & CARR, Assurance House, 24 Rutland Street, Leicester, Leicestershire, LE1 9GX. Tel: 0116 253 8021. Fax: 0116 253 7427. Internet: www.richandcarr.co.uk.

Age UK Leicestershire & Rutland	7.18

RICHARD C HALL & PARTNERS, Redhill House, Hope Street, Chester, Cheshire, CH4 8BU.

Anheddau Cyf	7.33

RIX & KAY SOLICITORS LLP, The Courtyard, River Way, Uckfield, East Sussex, TN22 1SL. Tel: 01825 761555. Fax: 01825 764172. E-mail: uckfield@rixandkay.co.uk. Internet: www.rixandkay.co.uk.

Grace & Compassion Benedictines (J)	7.283

ROBERT DAVIES PARTNERSHIP LLP, Wentwood House, Langstone Business Village, Priory Drive, Newport, Gwent, NP18 2HJ. Tel: 01633 413 500. Fax: 01633 413 499. E-mail: info@rdplaw.co.uk. Internet: www.rdplaw.co.uk.

St David's Foundation Hospice Care (J)	7.642

ROBERT LUNN & LOWTH, 2 Sheep Street, Stratford-upon-Avon, Warwickshire, CV37 6EJ. Tel: 01789 292238. Fax: 01789 298443. E-mail: admin@robertlunnlowth.co.uk. Charity specialists: P I Hardy.

College Estate Endowment Charity, The (J)	7.160
Shakespeare Birthplace Trust (J)	7.599
Stratford Upon Avon Town Trust (J)	7.661

ROBINSONS SOLICITORS, St James Court, Friar Gate, Derby, Derbyshire, DE1 1BT. Tel: 01332 291 431. Fax: 01332 254 142. E-mail: info@robinsons-solicitors.co.uk. Internet: www.robinsons-solicitors.co.uk. Charity specialists: S Marshall (Charity Lead Partner).

Angel Foundation	7.32

ROLAND ROBINSON AND FENTONS, 87 Adelaide Street, Blackpool, Lancashire, FY1 4LX. Tel: 01253 621 432. Internet: www.rrfsolicitors.co.uk.

Jah-Jireh Charity Homes	7.350

ROLLITS, Wilberforce Court, High Street, Hull, HU1 1YJ. Tel: 01482 323239. Fax: 01482 326239. E-mail: gerry.morrison@rollits.com. Internet: www.rollits.co.uk.

EMIH	7.232
Hull Truck Theatre Company	7.323
North York Moors Historical Railway (J)	7.468

ROLLITS, Rowntree Wharf, Navigation Road, York, North Yorkshire, YO1 9WE. Tel: 01904 625 790. Fax: 01904 625 807. E-mail: gerry.morrison@rollits.com. Internet: www.rollits.co.uk.

Ampleforth Abbey Trust (J)	7.30
Family Fund, The	7.247
Sir James Reckitt Charity, The	7.611
York Archaeological Trust	7.747
Yorkshire Wildlife Trust (J)	7.749

ROPES & GRAY LLP, 5 New Street Square, London, EC4A 4BF.

Caribbean Biodiversity Fund	7.115

ROTHERA DAWSON, 2 Kayes Walk, Stoney Street, The Lace Market, Nottingham, Nottinghamshire, NG1 1PZ. Tel: 0115 9100 600. Fax: 0115 9100 800. E-mail: enquiries@rotheradowson.co.uk. Internet: www.rotheradowson.co.uk.

Southwell Diocesan Board Finance	7.631

ROTHERHAM & CO, 8 & 9 The Quadrant, Coventry, West Midlands, CV1 2EG. Tel: 024 7622 7331. Fax: 024 7622 1293. Internet: www.rotherham-solicitors.co.uk.

Bond's Hospital Estate Charity	7.79
Nicholas Chamberlaine School Foundation	7.462

ROYDS, 65 Carter Lane, London, EC4V 5HF. Tel: 020 7583 2222. Fax: 020 7583 2034. E-mail: jnr@royds.com. Internet: www.royds.com. Charity specialists: Julian Rampton (Partner). Tony Millson (Partner). Deanna Hart (Partner).

Chartered Management Institute	7.135
Royal Society Musicians Great Britain	7.573
Sacred Heart Fathers Trust	7.579
USPG (J)	7.702

ROYTHORNES LLP, Enterprise Way, Pinchbeck, Spalding, Lincolnshire, PE11 3YR. Tel: 01775 842500. Fax: 01775 725736. E-mail: vembermortlock@roythornes.co.uk. Internet: www.roythorne.co.uk.

Grimsthorpe and Drummond Castle Trust	7.288
Lincoln Diocesan Trust Board Finance Ltd (J)	7.389

RUSSEL & AITKEN, 22-24 Stirling Street, Denny, Falkirk, FK6 6AZ. Tel: 01324 822194. Fax: 01324 824560. E-mail: dem@radenny.co.uk. Internet: www.radenny.co.uk.

Alzheimer Scotland - Action on Dementia   7.28

RUSSELL-COOKE, 2 Putney Hill, London, SW15 6AB. Tel: 020 8789 9111. Fax: 020 8780 1194. E-mail: andrew.studd@russell-cooke.co.uk. Internet: www.russell-cooke.co.uk. Charity specialists: James Sinclair Taylor (Head of Charity Team) - specialist area: Charity Law, Governance and Consultancy. Jane Klauber - specialist area: Employment Law. James McCallum - specialist area: Property. Andrew Studd - specialist area: Charity Law & Governance. Mary Cheves - specialist area: Property.

4Children	7.3
ACT Foundation (J)	7.9
Action for Blind People (J)	7.10
Action for Children (J)	7.10
Afghanaid	7.15
Age UK (J)	7.17
Anthony Nolan (J)	7.34
Arthritis Care (J)	7.40
Aston-Mansfield Charitable Trust (J)	7.47
Ballinger Charitable Trust (J)	7.55
Barrow Cadbury Trust (J)	7.59
Blenheim CDP (J)	7.75
Borough Market (Southwark)	7.80
Brain Tumour Charity (J)	7.84
British Assoc Counselling & Psychotherapy (J)	7.92
British Heart Foundation (J)	7.93
British School of Osteopathy (J)	7.98
Brook Young People	7.101
Brooke Hospital for Animals (J)	7.101
Business in the Community (J)	7.105
Campaign to Protect Rural England (J)	7.110
Catch22 (J)	7.118
CBHA (J)	7.121
Chain of Hope	7.126
Charles Skey Charitable Trust	7.131
Chartered Quality Institute (J)	7.135
Choice Support	7.143
Civil Service Benevolent Fund, The (J)	7.154
Community Options	7.167
Community Security Trust (J)	7.167
Concern Worldwide (UK) (J)	7.170
Contact a Family	7.178
Cruse Bereavement Care	7.187
Depaul UK (J)	7.197
Dr Edwards Bishop King's Fulham Charity	7.211
Ealing Community Transport (J)	7.218
Earley Charity (J)	7.219
Edge Foundation	7.224
Eduserv	7.227
Elizabeth Finn Care (J)	7.230
Equinox Care (J)	7.237
Esmée Fairbairn Foundation (J)	7.240
Family Action (J)	7.247
GroceryAid	7.289
Groundwork London (J)	7.289
Hammersmith United Charities	7.297
Hestia Housing and Support	7.310
Homeless Link	7.316
Institute of Psychoanalysis	7.337
Int. Baccalaureate Org (UK) (J)	7.340
International House Trust	7.343
Intl Planned Parenthood Federation (J)	7.344
International Students House (J)	7.345
Kusuma Trust UK	7.375
LankellyChase Foundation, The (J)	7.379
Leonard Cheshire Disability (J)	7.385
London Academy of Music and Dramatic Art (J)	7.397
London City Mission (J)	7.397
Maria Assumpta Trust	7.410
Marine Society & Sea Cadets (J)	7.411
MCCH Society (J)	7.418
Medical Research Council Technology (J)	7.419
Money Advice Trust	7.431
Movember Europe	7.436
Muscular Dystrophy Campaign (J)	7.439
Nat Centre for Young People with Epilepsy (J)	7.443
National Childbirth Trust (J)	7.444
Nuffield Health (J)	7.474
Perennial	7.498
Plan International UK	7.505
Postal Heritage Trust	7.510
Pre-school Learning Alliance	7.512
Prostate Cancer UK	7.517
Queen's Nursing Institute	7.520

R L Glasspool Charity Trust (J)	7.522
Religious of the Assumption	7.531
Robert Owen Communities	7.541
Rokpa Trust (J)	7.543
Royal British Legion Poppy Factory Limited (J)	7.554
Royal London Society for the Blind (J)	7.564
Royal Trinity Hospice	7.574
S O V A	7.579
Shaw Trust (J)	7.599
Social Investment Business Foundation	7.620
Society of Chemical Industry (J)	7.622
Solace Women's Aid (J)	7.625
St Christopher's Fellowship (J)	7.640
St Giles Trust	7.644
St Mungo Community Housing Association (J)	7.652
Stonewall Equality Ltd (J)	7.660
Tearfund (J)	7.670
Thames Reach (J)	7.675
Thinkaction (J)	7.676
Thomas Pocklington Trust (J)	7.678
Three C's Support (J)	7.679
Tudor Trust (J)	7.690
UK Community Foundations	7.692
UK Youth (J)	7.693
UNICEF-UK (J)	7.694
Voiceability Advocacy (J)	7.708
Walcot Educational Foundation (J)	7.711
Woodland Trust (J)	7.737
World Vision UK (J)	7.741
YHA (England and Wales) (J)	7.744

RUTTERS, 2 Bimport, Shaftesbury, Dorset, SP7 8AY. Tel: 01747 852 377. Fax: 01747 851 989. E-mail: enquiries@rutterslaw.co.uk. Internet: www.rutterslaw.co.uk.

W F Southall Trust   7.710

SA CARR & CO, 416 Mare Street, Hackney, London, E8 1HP.

Adolescent and Children's Trust, The (J)   7.14

SA LAW, 60 London Road, St Albans, Hertfordshire, AL1 1NG. Tel: 01727 798000. Fax: 01727 798002. E-mail: info@salaw.com. Internet: www.salaw.com.

Box Moor Trust	7.82
Engineering Construction Training Board (J)	7.234
Gosling Sports Park (J)	7.282
Hospice St Francis Berkhamsted Limited (J)	7.319

SACKER & PARTNERS, 20 Gresham Street, London, EC2V 7JE. Tel: 020 7329 6699. Fax: 020 7248 0552. Internet: www.sackers.com.

Blind Veterans UK (J)	7.76
Royal National Lifeboat Institution (J)	7.567

SAINSBURY'S, 26-28 Ashton Road, Denton, Manchester, Greater Manchester, M34 3EX. Tel: 0161 336 7027. Fax: 0161 336 0535.

Salford Diocesan Trust (J)   7.582

SAMUEL PHILLIPS LAW FIRM, Gibb Chambers, 52 Westgate Road, Newcastle upon Tyne, Tyne and Wear, NE1 5XU. Tel: 0191 232 8451. Fax: 0191 232 7664. Internet: www.samuelphillips.co.uk.

NECA (J)	7.455
St Mary Magdalene & Holy Jesus Trust (J)	7.649

SAS DANIELS LLP, 30 Greek Street, Stockport, Greater Manchester, SK3 8AD. Tel: 0161 475 7676. Internet: www.sasdaniels.co.uk. Charity specialists: Kaye Whitby.

Training 2000 (J)   7.685

SAUNDERS ROBERTS, Solicitors, 1 Crown Court Yard, Bridge Street, Evesham, Worcestershire, WR11 4RY. Tel: 01386 442558. Fax: 01386 49448. E-mail: patrick.boyd@saundersroberts.co.uk. Internet: www.saundersroberts.co.uk. Charity specialists: Patrick Boyd.

East London Mosque Trust Ltd, The	7.221
John Martin's Charity (J)	7.360

SCHOFIELD SWEENEY, Church Bank House, Church Bank, Bradford, West Yorkshire, BD1 4DY. Tel: 01274 306000. Fax: 01274 306111. E-mail: law@schofieldsweeney.co.uk. Internet: www.schofieldsweeney.co.uk. Charity specialists: Andrew Hurst. Helen Hirst. Simon Petchey. Howard Allen. Jessica Blackwell.

Doncaster Culture and Leisure Trust (J)	7.204
Oasis Community Learning (J)	7.477
YMCA England (J)	7.745

SCHOFIELD SWEENEY, Springfield House, 76 Wellington Street, Leeds, West Yorkshire, LS1 2AY. Tel: 0113 220 6270. Fax: 0113 243 9326. E-mail: law@schofieldsweeney.co.uk. Internet: www.schofieldsweeney.co.uk. Charity specialists: Luisa D'Alessandro. Simon Shepherd. Catherine Rhodes.

Community Links (Northern)	7.164
PDSA (J)	7.494

SCULLY TWISS LLP, 71-75 Shelton Street, London, WC2H 9JQ. Tel: 020 3126 4940. Internet: www.scullytwiss.com.

Thomson Media Foundation, The (J)   7.678

SEAN EGAN CONSULTANTS LIMITED, 50 Sheen Park, Richmond, Surrey, TW9 1UW.

Soho Theatre Company (J)   7.625

SEDGWICK, PHELAN & PARTNERS, Royal London House, 56-58 Long Street, Middleton, Manchester, Lancashire, M24 6UQ. Tel: 0161 653 5299. Fax: 0161 653 3161. Internet: www.sedgwick-phelan.co.uk.

Institute of the Blessed Virgin Mary (J)   7.337

SEGENS BLOUNT PETRE, Glade House, 52-54 Carter Lane, London, EC4V 5EF. Tel: 020 7332 2222. Fax: 020 7236 2112. Internet: www.segens.com. Charity specialists: J C C Russell CBE - specialist area: Charity Law.

Marist Sisters (J)	7.130
Sisters of the Finding of Jesus	7.175
Order of Friars Minor	7.482
Order of Hermit Friars of St Augustine	7.483

SGH MARTINEAU, 1 Colmore Square, Birmingham, West Midlands, B4 6AA. Tel: 0800 7631000. Fax: 0800 7631001. E-mail: lawyers@sghmartineau.com. Internet: www.sghmartineau.com. Charity specialists: Keith Dudley. David Allison. Kate Wilcox.

Birmingham Royal Ballet (J)	7.73
British School of Osteopathy (J)	7.98
Castel Froma (J)	7.117
Christadelphian Care Homes	7.144
Christian Vision (J)	7.146
City of Birmingham Symphony Orchestra	7.153
Douglas Turner Trust (J)	7.210
G J W Turner Trust	7.268
Henry Barber Trust (J)	7.308
Inst. of Occupational Safety & Health	7.339
King Henry VIII Endowed Trust Warwick (J)	7.372
LIONHEART (J)	7.391
Quality Assurance Agency for HE	7.518
St Martin's Trust	7.649
University Hospital Birmingham Charities	7.700

SHAKESPEARES, Somerset House, Temple Street, Birmingham, West Midlands, B2 5DJ. Tel: 0121 632 4199. Fax: 0121 643 2257. E-mail: info@shakespeares.co.uk. Internet: www.shakespeares.co.uk. Charity specialists: A Jones. Gayle Ditchburn. I Sadiq.

Aquarius Action Projects	7.36
Jaffray Care Society	7.349
Royal National College for the Blind (J)	7.566

SHAKESPEARES, Greyfriars House, Greyfriars Lane, Coventry, Warwickshire, CV1 2GW. Internet: www.shma.co.uk.

Life Path Trust Ltd   7.388

SHAKESPEARES, Two Colton Square, Leicester, Leicestershire, LE1 1QH. Tel: 0116 254 5454. Fax: 0116 255 4559.
E-mail: info@shakespeares.co.uk.
Internet: www.shakespeares.co.uk.

Maud Elkington Charitable Trust	7.416
NEBOSH	7.445
National Institute of Adult Education	7.448
Sisters of St Joseph of Peace (J)	7.615

SHAKESPEARES, Chancery House, 199 Silbury Boulevard, Milton Keynes, Buckinghamshire, MK9 1JL. Tel: 01908 696 002. Fax: 01908 304 443. E-mail: info@shakespeares.co.uk.
Internet: www.shakespeares.co.uk.

Ibbett Trust (J)	7.327

SHAKESPEARES, Park House, Friar Lane, Nottingham, Nottinghamshire, NG1 6DN. Tel: 0115 945 3700. Fax: 0115 948 0234. E-mail: info@shakespeares.co.uk.
Internet: www.shakespeares.co.uk.

Jones 1986 Charitable Trust	7.362

SHAKESPEARES, Bridgeway House, Bridgeway, Stratford-upon-Avon, Warwickshire, CV37 6YX. Tel: 0845 630 8833. Fax: 0845 630 8844. E-mail: info@shakespeares.co.uk.
Internet: www.shakespeares.co.uk.

ExtraCare Charitable Trust (J)	7.245
Field Lane Foundation (J)	7.253
Fremantle Trust	7.264
SeeAbility (J)	7.596

SHEPHERD & WEDDERBURN, 1 Exchange Crescent, Conference Square, Edinburgh, EH3 8UL. Tel: 0131 228 9900. Fax: 0131 228 1222. E-mail: info@shepwedd.co.uk.
Internet: www.shepwedd.co.uk.

Ark Housing Association (J)	7.39
Children's Hospice Association Scotland (J)	7.141
Edinburgh Leisure (J)	7.225
Edinburgh Military Tattoo (Charities) Ltd	7.225
Festival City Theatres Trust	7.251
Maggie Keswick Jencks Cancer Trust (J)	7.406
Moredun Foundation, The (J)	7.433
Moredun Research Institute (J)	7.434
R&A Foundation, The	7.521
Royal Air Force Benevolent Fund (J)	7.550
Royal Botanic Garden Edinburgh (J)	7.553
Royal Society of Edinburgh	7.572
SCVO (J)	7.592
SSPCA	7.592
St Columba's Hospice	7.641
St Margaret's Hospice (Clydebank)	7.649
Victim Support Scotland (J)	7.704

SHEPHERD & WEDDERBURN, 191 West George Street, Glasgow, G2 2LB. Tel: 0141 566 9900. Fax: 0141 565 1222.
E-mail: info@shepwedd.co.uk.
Internet: www.shepwedd.co.uk.

Enjoy East Lothian	7.237
Foundation Scotland	7.260
North Ayrshire Leisure	7.465
South Lanarkshire Leisure Ltd	7.629

SHERIDANS, 14 Red Lion Square, London, WC1R 4QL. Tel: 020 7404 0444. Fax: 020 7831 1982. E-mail: info@sheridans.co.uk.
Internet: www.sheridans.co.uk.

Almeida Theatre Company (J)	7.27

SHERRARDS, 45 Grosvenor Road, St Albans, Hertfordshire, AL1 3AW. Tel: 01727 832 830. Fax: 01727 832833.
Internet: www.sherrards.com.

BRE Trust (J)	7.85
Rennie Grove Hospice Care (J)	7.531

SHOOSMITHS LLP, The Lakes, Northampton, Northamptonshire, NN4 7SH. Tel: 03700 863000. Fax: 03700 863001.
E-mail: northampton@shoosmiths.co.uk.
Internet: www.shoosmiths.co.uk.

Bletchley Park Trust	7.76
Engineering Construction Training Board (J)	7.234
Kidney Research UK (J)	7.371
Northampton Theatres Trust (J)	7.468
Northamptonshire Arts Management Trust (J)	7.469
Pharmacist Support (J)	7.500
Refugee Action (J)	7.529
Viewpoint Housing Association (J)	7.705

SHORT RICHARDSON & FORTH LLP, 4 Mosley Street, Newcastle upon Tyne, Tyne and Wear, NE1 1DE. Tel: 0191 2320283. Fax: 0191 2616956. E-mail: david.gibson@srflegal.co.uk.
Internet: www.srflegal.co.uk.
Charity specialists: Paul Bell. P Earnshaw. D Gibson. M D Winthrop.

St Cuthberts Care (J)	7.641

SHRANKS, Ruskin House, 40/41 Museum Street, London, WC1A 1LT. Tel: 020 7831 6677.

Gilmoor Benevolent Fund Limited	7.274

SILVERMAN SHERLIKER LLP, 7 Bath Place, London, EC2A 3DR. Tel: 020 7749 2700. Fax: 020 7739 4309.
E-mail: jtrs@silvermansherlikar.co.uk.
Internet: www.silvermansherliker.co.uk.

EveryChild (J)	7.243

SIMMONS & SIMMONS, City Point, One Ropemaker Street, London, EC2Y 9SS. Tel: 020 7628 2020. Fax: 020 7628 2070.
Internet: www.simmons-simmons.com.

Common Purpose Charitable Trust	7.162
English National Ballet	7.235
NSPCC (J)	7.452
vInspired (J)	7.706

SIMONS, MUIRHEAD & BURTON, 8-9 Frith Street, Soho, London, W1D 3JB. Tel: 020 3206 2700. Fax: 020 3206 2800.
Internet: www.smab.co.uk.
Charity specialists: S Goldberg.

English Stage Company Ltd	7.236

SIMPSON & MARWICK, 144 West George Street, Glasgow, G2 2HG. Tel: 0141 248 2666. Fax: 0141 248 9590.
Internet: www.simpmar.com.

Scottish Ballet (J)	7.591

SIMPSON & MARWICK, Albany House, 58 Albany Street, Edinburgh, EH1 3QR. Tel: 0131 557 1545. Fax: 0131 525 8651.
E-mail: john.miller@simpmar.co.uk.
Internet: www.simpmar.com.
Charity specialists: J K Miller.

Free Church of Scotland (J)	7.264

SIMS COOK & TEAGUE, 40 High Street, Thornbury, South Gloucestershire, BS35 2AJ.

United Reformed Church (South Western) (J)	7.696

SINGH KARRAN & CO, 480 Great West Road, Hounslow, Middlesex, TW5 0TA. Tel: 020 8570 5776. Fax: 020 8572 2286.
E-mail: law@singhkarran.com.

Radha Soami Satsang Beas British Isles	7.523

SINTONS LLP, The Cube, Barrack Road, Newcastle upon Tyne, Tyne and Wear, NE4 6DB. Tel: 0191 226 7878. Fax: 0191 226 7850. E-mail: law@sintons.co.uk.
Internet: www.sintons.co.uk.
Charity specialists: Pippa Aitken. Julie Garbutt. Sue Hennersey. Amanda Maskery.

Carlisle Diocesan Board of Finance	7.116
Congregation of the Passion Jesus Christ (J)	7.174
JGW Patterson Foundation, The	7.355
NECA (J)	7.455
Newcastle Diocesan Board Finance	7.459

SLATER AND GORDON LAWYERS, 50-52 Chancery Lane, London, WC2A 1HL. Tel: 020 7657 1555. Internet: www.slatergordon.co.uk.

Police Rehabilitation Centre (J)	7.507

SLATER HEELIS, Lloyds Bank Building, 16 School Road, Sale, Cheshire, M33 7XP. Tel: 0161 969 3131. Fax: 0161 973 1018. E-mail: intouch@slaterheelis.co.uk.
Internet: www.slaterheelis.co.uk.
Charity specialists: P J L Leyland.

Stockport Cerebral Palsy Society	7.659

SLAUGHTER AND MAY, One Bunhill Row, London, EC1Y 8YY. Tel: 020 7600 1200. Fax: 020 7090 5000.
Internet: www.slaughterandmay.com.

SLEIGH SON AND BOOTH, 1 Market Street, Denton, Manchester, Greater Manchester, M34 2BN. Tel: 0161 370 9524.

Birtenshaw (J)	7.73

SLOAN PLUMB WOOD LLP, Apollo House, Isis Way, Minerva Business Park, Lynch Wood, Peterborough, PE2 6QR. Tel: 01733 302410. Fax: 01733 390552. Internet: www.spw-law.co.uk.

Panacea Society	7.490

SMITH PARTNERSHIP, 158 High Street, Burton-on-Trent, Staffordshire, DE14 1JE. Tel: 01283 548282. Internet: www.smithpartnership.co.uk.

Consolidated Charity of Burton upn Trent	7.177

SMITH PARTNERSHIP, THE, 10 Pocklingtons Walk, Leicester, Leicestershire, LE1 6BN. Tel: 0116 255 6292. Fax: 0116 255 6294. E-mail: leicestercrime@smithpartnership.co.uk.
Internet: www.smithpartnership.co.uk.

Cope Children's Trust (J)	7.179

SMITH RODDAM, 56 North Bondgate, Bishop Auckland, County Durham, DL14 7PG. Tel: 01388 603073.
E-mail: hmm@smith.roddam.co.uk.

Durham Diocesan Board of Finance, The	7.216

SOLOMON TAYLOR & SHAW, 3 Coach House Yard, Hampstead High Street, London, NW3 1QD. Tel: 020 7794 3391. Fax: 020 7794 7485. Internet: www.aolts.co.uk.
Charity specialists: P Regan.

Jewish Blind & Disabled	7.353
Jewish Community Secondary School Trust (J)	7.354
Norwood (J)	7.472
Shakespeare Globe Trust (J)	7.599
Thompson Family Charitable Trust	7.678

SPARLINGS SOLICITORS, 13 High Street, Manningtree, Essex, CO11 1AQ. Tel: 01206 392201. Fax: 01206 396394.
E-mail: enquiries@sparlings.co.uk.
Internet: www.sparlings.co.uk.

Acorn Villages (J)	7.8

SPEARING WAITE LLP, 34 Pocklingtons Walk, Leicester, Leicestershire, LE1 6BU. Tel: 0116 262 4225. Fax: 0116 251 2009. E-mail: info@spearingwaite.com.
Internet: www.spearingwaite.com.

Cope Children's Trust (J)	7.179
LOROS (J)	7.384

SQUARE ONE LAW LLP, Anson House, Fleming Business Centre, Burdon Terrace, Newcastle upon Tyne, Tyne and Wear, NE2 3AE. Tel: 0843 224 7900. Internet: www.squareonelaw.com.

Betel of Britain	7.67

SQUIRE SANDERS, 7 Devonshire Square, London, EC2M 4YH. Tel: 020 7655 1000. Fax: 020 7655 1001.
Internet: www.squiresanders.com.

Islamic Relief Worldwide (J)	7.347

SQUIRE SANDERS, Rutland House, 148 Edmund Street, Birmingham, West Midlands, B3 2JR. Tel: 0121 222 3000. Fax: 0121 222 3001. Internet: www.squiresanders.com.

Land Restoration Trust (J)	7.378
Millennium Point Trust	7.428

STAFFORD YOUNG JONES, The Old Rectory, 29 Martin Lane, London, EC4R 0AU. Tel: 020 7623 9490. Fax: 020 7929 5704. E-mail: mail@syjlaw.co.uk.. Internet: www.syjlaw.co.uk. Charity specialists: Helen Wenham.

CLC International (UK)	7.156
Morden College (J)	7.433

STALLARD MARCH & EDWARDS, 8 Sansome Walk, Worcester, Worcestershire, WR1 1LW. Tel: 01905 723 561. Fax: 01905 723 812. E-mail: info@smesolicitors.co.uk. Internet: www.smesolicitors.co.uk.

Diocese of Worcester	7.738

STAMP JACKSON & PROCTER LLP, 5 Parliament Street, Hull, HU1 2AZ. Tel: 01482 324591. Fax: 01482 224048. E-mail: car@sjplaw.co.uk. Internet: www.sjplaw.co.uk. Charity specialists: Andrew Procter.

Humberside Engineering Training Assoc	7.325

STANDLEY & CO, 1612 High Street, Knowles, Solihull, West Midlands, B93 0JU. Tel: 01564 776287. Fax: 01564 774979. E-mail: enquiries@standley.co.uk. Internet: www.standley.co.uk.

Society of St Columban for Foreign Missions	7.623

STEELES (LAW) LLP, Bedford House, 21a John Street, London, WC1N 2BF. Tel: 020 7421 1720. Fax: 020 7421 1749. Internet: www.steeleslaw.co.uk.

CIPFA (J)	7.151

STEPHENS SCOWN LLP, Curzon House, Southernhay West, Exeter, Devon, EX1 1RS. Tel: 01392 210700. Fax: 01392 274010. E-mail: CharityLaw@stephens-scown.co.uk. Internet: www.stephens-scown.co.uk. Charity specialists: Helen Furneaux (Head of Charity).

Jean Sainsbury Animal Welfare Trust	7.352
Wiltshire Wildlife Trust (J)	7.731

STEPHENS SCOWN LLP, Osprey House, Malpas Road, Truro, Cornwall, TR1 1UT. Tel: 01872 265100. Fax: 01872 279137. E-mail: CharityLaw@stephens-scown.co.uk. Internet: www.stephens-scown.co.uk.

National Maritime Museum Cornwall Trust	7.449
Truro Diocesan Board Finance Ltd (J)	7.687

STEPHENSON HARWOOD, One Finsbury Circus, London, EC2M 7SH. Tel: 020 7329 4422. Fax: 020 7606 0822. E-mail: info@shlegal.com. Internet: www.shlegal.com. Charity specialists: W Corbett. R Blower. R M J Haldane - specialist area: Corporate Finance. M F Jennings. A Sutch.

JCA Charitable Foundation (J)	7.351
Jewish Care (J)	7.354
Rambert Trust	7.525

STEPHENSONS LLP, Northgate Close, Horwich, Bolton, Greater Manchester, BL6 6PQ. Tel: 01204 214245. Internet: www.stephensons.co.uk.

Wigan Leisure and Cultural Trust	7.727

STEVENS & BOLTON, Wey House, Farnham Road, Guildford, Surrey, GU1 4XS. Tel: 01483 302264. Fax: 01483 302254. E-mail: alison.maclennan@stevens-bolton.com. Internet: www.stevens-bolton.com/Default.aspx?sID=1003.

Compassion in World Farming (J)	7.168

SK STONE KING

STONE KING LLP, Boundary House, 91 Charterhouse Street, London, EC1M 6HR. Tel: 020 7796 1007 / 0800 111 4336. E-mail: charity@stoneking.co.uk. Internet: www.stoneking.co.uk.

> **For more information and contact details see our profile in the front colour section**

Charity specialists: Jonathan Burchfield (Head of Charity & Social Enterprise Sector Group). Ann Phillips (Chairman of Stone King LLP) - specialist area: Charity Law. Robert Meakin (Partner) - specialist area: Charity Law. Tim Rutherford (Partner) - specialist area: Charity Law. Hannah Kubie (Partner) - specialist area: Charity Law. Tom Murdoch (Partner) - specialist area: Charity Law. Michael King (Consultant) - specialist area: Charity Law. Vicki Bowles (Barrister) - specialist area: Charity Law. David Quentin - specialist area: Charity Law. Alexandra Whittaker - specialist area: Charity Law. Reema Mathur - specialist area: Charity Law. Sarah Clune - specialist area: Charity Law. Darren Hooker - specialist area: Charity Law. Sophie Pughe - specialist area: Charity Law. Clive Vergnaud - specialist area: Charity Law. Hugh Pearce (Partner) - specialist area: Head of Faith Charity Team. Roger Inman (Partner) - specialist area: Head of Education Team. Stephen Ravenscroft (Partner) - specialist area: Charity and Education Law. Michael Brotherton (Partner) - specialist area: Education Law. Lee Coley (Partner) - specialist area: Education Law. Richard Gold - specialist area: Education Law. Dan Harris - specialist area: Trusts & Estates. Paul Sutton (Partner) - specialist area: Charity Law Disputes. Sarah Eden (Charity Law Disputes). Brian Miller (Partner) - specialist area: IT, IP, Information Law.

Action on Addiction (J)	7.11
Action on Hearing Loss (J)	7.11
Addenbrooke's Charitable Trust (J)	7.13
Age UK (J)	7.17
Alzheimer's Society (J)	7.28
Arts Council England	7.41
Arundel and Brighton Diocesan Trust (J)	7.42
Benenden Hospital Trust (J)	7.65
Benevolent Fund Institution of Civil Engineers	7.65
BirdLife International (J)	7.70
Birmingham Diocesan Trust (J)	7.71
Bloodwise (J)	7.76
Blue Cross (J)	7.76
Book Aid International (J)	7.79
British Heart Foundation (J)	7.93
British Red Cross Society (J)	7.98
British Refugee Council	7.98
Butterfly Conservation (J)	7.106
Buttle Trust	7.106
Cabrini Children's Society (J)	7.107
Cancer Research UK (J)	7.112
Caritas Care (J)	7.115
Carmelite Charitable Trust (J)	7.116
Catholic Agency for Overseas Development (J)	7.118
Catholic Institute for International Relations	7.119
Catholic Trust for England and Wales (J)	7.120
Charities Aid Foundation (J)	7.128
Charles Hayward Foundation	7.131
Chartered Accountants' Benevolent Assoc (J)	7.132
CharteredInstitute of Logistics&Transport UK	7.133
Children with Cancer UK (J)	7.142
Christian Aid (J)	7.145
Civil Service Benevolent Fund, The (J)	7.154
CLIC Sargent Cancer Care for Children (J)	7.156
Concern Universal (J)	7.170
Concern Worldwide (UK) (J)	7.170
Congregation of the Jesus Charitable Trust (J)	7.171
Good Shepherd Sisters (J)	7.171
Congregation of the Sisters of Nazareth Trust	7.174

Conservation Education & Research Trust	7.177
Corporation of Trinity House (J)	7.181
Creative and Cultural Industries Limited	7.184
Cutty Sark Trust	7.189
Cystic Fibrosis Trust (J)	7.190
Debra (J)	7.196
Denys Eyre Bower Bequest, The	7.197
Diabetes UK (J)	7.200
Disabilities Trust (J)	7.201
Dogs Trust (J)	7.203
Dolphin Square Charitable Foundation, The (J)	7.203
Dominican Sisters Congregation Newcastle (J)	7.204
Donkey Sanctuary (J)	7.206
English Dominican Congregation Ch Fund	7.235
Fair Share Trust	7.246
Fairfield (Croydon) (J)	7.246
Foundation for Liver Research	7.259
Grace & Compassion Benedictines (J)	7.283
Grand Charity, The (J)	7.284
Guide Dogs for the Blind Association (J)	7.291
Hackney Joint Estate Charity (J)	7.295
Handmaids of the Sacred Heart of Jesus (J)	7.300
Haynes International Motor Museum (J)	7.304
Holburne Museum (J)	7.314
Holstein UK (J)	7.315
Hughes Travel Trust (J)	7.323
Institute for Fiscal Studies (J)	7.332
Institute of Advanced Motorists	7.333
Institute of the Blessed Virgin Mary (J)	7.337
JCA Charitable Foundation (J)	7.351
Kennedy Memorial Fund	7.368
Kennedy Trust for Rheumatology Research (J)	7.368
Kingsway International Christian Centre (J)	7.373
Kisharon	7.375
Landmark Trust	7.378
Langley House Trust (J)	7.379
Legacy Trust UK	7.383
Livability (J)	7.391
Lloyd's Register Foundation (J)	7.395
Lloyds Foundation for England and Wales (J)	7.395
London Marathon Charitable Trust Limited (J)	7.399
Lowry Centre Trust (J)	7.403
Macmillan Cancer Support (J)	7.405
Making Space (J)	7.407
Masonic Samaritan Fund (J)	7.415
Meath Epilepsy Trust	7.418
Medlock Charitable Trust (J)	7.420
Mission Aviation Fellowship International	7.430
Mission Care	7.430
Missionaries of Africa (The White Fathers) (J)	7.431
Moorfields Eye Hospital Special Trustees (J)	7.433
Multiple Sclerosis Society (J)	7.438
National Children's Bureau	7.444
National Council Voluntary Organisations (J)	7.444
National Maritime Museum (J)	7.449
National Osteoporosis Society (J)	7.451
NSPCC (J)	7.452
National Trust (J)	7.454
New College Development Fund	7.457
New Wine Trust (J)	7.458
Northampton RC Diocesan Trust	7.468
Nuffield Trst for Res.&Pol.Studies in Health	7.475
Oasis Charitable Trust (J)	7.477
Oasis Community Learning (J)	7.477
ORBIS Charitable Trust (J)	7.482
Order of Friars Minor (Capuchin) Province (J)	7.482
Ormiston Trust (J)	7.484
Oxfam GB (J)	7.486
Oxford Centre Hebrew & Jewish Studies (J)	7.487
Oxford Diocesan Board Finance (J)	7.487
PDSA (J)	7.494
Pears Family Charitable Foundation, The	7.495
Peterborough Diocesan Board Finance (J)	7.500
Philharmonia (J)	7.500
Polish Catholic Mission, The	7.507
Queen Mary's Roehampton Trust	7.520
RBS PeopleCharity, The (J)	7.527
Refugee Action (J)	7.529
RMIG Endowment Trust (J)	7.540
Royal Air Force Benevolent Fund (J)	7.550
RoyalCol.of Obstetricians & Gynaecologists (J)	7.556
Royal Geographical Society (J)	7.561
Royal Horticultural Society (J)	7.561
Royal Institute International Affairs (J)	7.562
Royal London Society for the Blind (J)	7.564
Royal Masonic Benevolent Institution (J)	7.565
Royal Masonic Trust For Girls and Boys (J)	7.565
Royal National Institute of Blind People (J)	7.566

Royal National Lifeboat Institution (J)	7.567
Royal Society of Arts (J)	7.571
RSPCA (J)	7.572
RSPB (J)	7.572
Royal Society of Medicine (J)	7.573
Royal Society of Wildlife Trusts (J)	7.573
Royal Society, The	7.573
Salvation Army Trust (J)	7.584
Samuel Sebba Charitable Trust	7.586
Save the Children (J)	7.588
Save the Children International	7.588
Send a Cow	7.596
Sightsavers International (J)	7.608
SignHealth (J)	7.608
Sisters of Charity of St Vincent de Paul (J)	7.613
Sisters Holy Family Bordeaux (J)	7.616
Sisters of the Sacred Heart of Mary UK	7.616
Society for Protection of Animals Abroad (J)	7.621
Society of Antiquaries of London (J)	7.621
Society of Chemical Industry (J)	7.622
Soka Gakkai International UK (J)	7.625
St Catherine's Hospice Limited (J)	7.639
St David's Foundation Hospice Care (J)	7.642
St John Ambulance (J)	7.644
St Joseph's Hospice, Hackney	7.646
St Margaret's Convent (Uckfield) (J)	7.648
St Vincent de Paul Society (J)	7.655
Sutton's Hospital in Charterhouse (J)	7.666
Theatre Royal Bath Ltd	7.675
Treloar Trust	7.685
Congregation of Christian Brothers (J)	7.688
Little Company of Mary	7.688
Ty Hafan (J)	7.692
Walthamstow&Chingford Almshouse Charity (J)	7.713
Westminster RC Diocesan Trust (J)	7.723
Will Woodlands (J)	7.729
World Energy Council (J)	7.740
World Horse Welfare (J)	7.740
WWF UK (J)	7.743
Youth United Foundation	7.751

STONE KING LLP, 13 Queen Square, Bath, Bath & North East Somerset, BA1 2HJ. Tel: 0800 111 4336 / 01225 337 599.
E-mail: charity@stoneking.co.uk.
Internet: www.stoneking.co.uk.

Above and Beyond (J)	7.7
Active Nation UK Ltd	7.12
Aid to the Church in Need (UK)	7.20
American Museum in Britain	7.29
BRUNELCARE (J)	7.102
Cerebra (J)	7.125
Marist Sisters (J)	7.130
Clifton Diocesan Trust	7.156
Faithful Companions of Jesus	7.166
Congregation of La Retraite Trustees (J)	7.171
Congregation of La Sainte Union	7.171
Congregation of the Daughters of Wisdom	7.173
Congregation of Servants of Mary(London)	7.174
Cong. of the Sisters of Nazareth Generalate	7.175
Congregation of the Sisters of St Martha (J)	7.175
Daughters Mary Joseph English Province	7.193
Downside Abbey General Trust	7.210
Edward James Foundation Limited (J)	7.228
Forest Young Men's Christian Association (J)	7.257
Franciscan Missionaries Charitable Trust	7.263
HCPT - The Pilgrimage Trust (J)	7.304
HF Trust Limited (J)	7.311
International Inst for Strategic Studies (J)	7.343
Jewish Community Secondary School Trust (J)	7.354
National Benevolent Charity, The	7.443
Nazareth Care Charitable Trust	7.455
Poor Servants of the Mother of God	7.508
Religious Sisters of Charity	7.531
Shooting Star CHASE (J)	7.605
Sisters Hospitallers of the Sacred Heart	7.613
Sisters of St Joseph of Peace (J)	7.615
Society of Jesus (J)	7.622
Somerset Redstone Trust (J)	7.627
St John's Hospital (J)	7.645
Teresa Ball International Solidarity Fund	7.673
Titsey Foundation	7.681
St Benedict's Abbey Ealing	7.688
Franciscan Sisters Minoress (J)	7.689
Union Sisters Mercy Great Britain (J)	7.695
Veolia Environmental Trust, The (J)	7.704
Wales Council for Voluntary Action (J)	7.711

YWCA Central Club	7.751

STONE KING LLP, Thirty Station Road, Cambridge, Cambridgeshire, CB1 2RE. Tel: 01223 351000 / 0800 111 4336.
E-mail: charity@stoneking.co.uk.
Internet: www.stoneking.co.uk.

Battersea Dogs & Cats Home (J)	7.60
Bell Educational Trust Ltd (J)	7.64
East Anglia's Children's Hospices (J)	7.220
Refuge (J)	7.529
Roman Catholic Diocese of East Anglia (J)	7.543
Scope (J)	7.590
Society of the Helpers of the Holy Souls	7.624
Spiritualists National Union (J)	7.632
Will Charitable Trust (J)	7.729

STONE MILWARD RAPERS, 50 West Gate, Chichester, West Sussex, PO19 3HE. Tel: 01243 780211. Fax: 01243 782619.
Internet: www.smrsolicitors.co.uk.

F Glenister Woodger Trust, The	7.245

STREATHERS SOLICITORS LLP, Accurist House, 44 Baker Street, London, W1U 7AL. Tel: 020 7034 4200. Internet: www.streathers.com.
Charity specialists: C Daynes. B G Streather.

Band Trust	7.55

STREETER MARSHALL, 74 High Street, Croydon, Surrey, CR9 2UU. Tel: 020 8680 2638. Fax: 020 8688 4105.
Internet: www.streetermarshall.com.

Croydon Almshouse Charities (J)	7.187
Whitgift Foundation (J)	7.726

STRONACHS, 34 Albyn Place, Aberdeen, Grampian, AB9 1FW. Tel: 01224 845 845. Fax: 01224 845 800.
Internet: www.stronachs.co.uk.

Sport Aberdeen	7.633

SWAYNE JOHNSON, Church House, High Street, St Asaph, Denbighshire, LL17 0RD. Tel: 01745 582 535. Fax: 01745 584 504.
Internet: www.swaynejohnson.com.

St Asaph Diocesan Board of Finance	7.638

T A MATTHEWS , 6 King Street, Hereford, Herefordshire, HR4 9BS. Tel: 01432 352121. Fax: 01432 352700.
Charity specialists: A Hing.

Eveson Charitable Trust	7.243
Halo Leisure Services Limited (J)	7.297
Three Counties Agricultural Society	7.679

T C YOUNG , 7 West George Street, Glasgow, G2 1BA. Tel: 0141 221 5562. Fax: 0141 221 5024. E-mail: mail@tcyoung.co.uk.
Internet: www.tcyoung.co.uk.
Charity specialists: A Cowan. M Ewing. Karen Harvie. S MacGregor. Christine Stuart.

Ark Housing Association (J)	7.39
Rield Housing Association	7.69
Erskine	7.239
Glasgow Simon Community	7.276
Hanover (Scotland) Housing Association	7.301
Loretto Care	7.403
Margaret Blackwood Housing Association	7.409
Places for People Scotland Care & Support Ltd	7.505
Thera Trust (J)	7.676
Viewpoint Housing Association (J)	7.705
YMCA Glasgow (J)	7.745

T G BAYNES & SONS, 5 Market Street, Dartford, Kent, DA1 1DB. Tel: 01322 295 555. Fax: 01322 295 501.

Trust Thamesmead (J)	7.689

TALKING LEGAL LAWYERS, The Granary, 2 The Barns, Longham Farm Close, Longham, Ferndown, Dorset, BH22 9DE. Tel: 01202 804 560. Internet: www.talkinglegallawyers.com.

Diverse Abilities Plus Limited (J)	7.202

TAYLOR & HENDERSON SOLICITORS, 65 High Street, Irvine, Ayrshire, KA12 0AL. Tel: 01294 278306. Fax: 01294 272886.
Internet: www.taylorandhenderson.co.uk.

Irvine Bay Urban Regeneration Company (J)	7.346
Sisters of the Cross and Passion (J)	7.615

TAYLOR & EMMET, 20 Arundel Gate, Sheffield, South Yorkshire, S1 2PP. Tel: 0114 218 4000. Fax: 0114 218 4223.
E-mail: info@tayloremmet.co.uk.
Internet: www.tayloremmet.co.uk.
Charity specialists: R Cooke. V Green.

Enable Care & Home Support	7.233
Roman Catholic Diocese Hallam Trust	7.543
Rotherham Hospice Trust	7.546
Skills for Justice	7.618
St Luke's Hospice (J)	7.647
YHA (England and Wales) (J)	7.744

TAYLOR VINTERS, Merlin Place, Milton Road, Cambridge, Cambridgeshire, CB4 0DP. Tel: 01223 423444. Fax: 01223 423486.
Internet: www.taylorvinters.com.
Charity specialists: Christine Berry. Caroline Eade. Julia Harkness. Jatinder Bahra. Patrick Farrant. Elizabeth Deyong. Oliver Pryke. Matt Meyer. Steven Beach. Jennifer Warren. Will Sanderson. Deborah Marshall.

Alzheimer's Research UK (J)	7.28
Animal Health Trust	7.33
Cambridge Union Society, The	7.109
Foundation of Edward Storey	7.260
Genome Analysis Centre, The (J)	7.271
Papworth Trust (J)	7.490
Royal Society of Chemistry (J)	7.572
Teenage Cancer Trust (J)	7.671
Workers' Educational Association (J)	7.739
World Horse Welfare (J)	7.740

TAYLOR WALTON, 28-44 Alma Street, Luton, Bedfordshire, LU1 2PL. Tel: 01582 731 161.
Internet: www.taylorwalton.co.uk.

Chartered Institute of Environmental Health	7.133

TAYLOR WESSING, 5 New Street Square, London, EC4A 3TW. Tel: 020 7300 7000. Fax: 020 7300 7100.
E-mail: london@taylorwessing.com.
Internet: www.taylorwessing.com.

Barts and The London Charity (J)	7.59
Forster Foundation CIO, The	7.257
Gilbert Trust for the Arts	7.274
Jerwood Charitable Foundation	7.353
Royal Hospital Chelsea Appeal Ltd	7.561
St John Ambulance (J)	7.644
Whitechapel Gallery (J)	7.725
Whizz-Kidz	7.726

TAYLORS, Ninth Floor, 80 Mosley Street, Manchester, Greater Manchester, M2 3FX. Tel: 0844 8000 263.
Internet: www.taylors.co.uk.

Lifeline Project (J)	7.388

TAYNTONS LLP, 8-10 Clarence Street, Gloucester, Gloucestershire, GL1 1DZ. Tel: 01452 522 047. Fax: 01452 424 659.
Internet: www.tayntons.co.uk.

Gloucester Charities Trust	7.277

TEACHER STERN LLP, 37/41 Bedford Roaw, London, WC1R 4JH. Tel: 020 7242 3191. Fax: 020 7242 1156.
E-mail: e.jones@teacherstern.com.
Internet: www.teacherstern.com.

Newmarston Limited Group	7.461

TEES LAW, Tees House, 95 London Road, Bishop's Stortford, Hertfordshire, CM23 3GW. Tel: 01279 755200. Fax: 01279 758400.
E-mail: lpg@teeslaw.co.uk.
Internet: www.teeslaw.co.uk.

Allan Nesta Ferguson Charitable Trust	7.25

THACKRAY WILLIAMS LLP, Kings House, 32-40 Widmore Road, Bromley, Kent, BR1 1RY. Tel: 020 8290 0440. Fax: 020 8464 5282. E-mail: info@thackraywilliams.com. Internet: www.thackraywilliams.com.

Dulwich Estate (J)	7.214

THE THOMAS HIGGINS PARTNERSHIP, Capitol Buildings, 10 Seaview Road, CH45 4TH.

Children's Links (J)	7.141

THOMAS CARROLL GROUP PLC, Pendragon House, Crescent Road, Caerphilly, CF83 1XX. Tel: 02920 887733. Fax: 02920 855230. E-mail: info@thomas-carroll.co.uk. Internet: www.thomascarroll.co.uk.

Innovate Trust	7.332

THOMAS COOPER & STIBBARD, Ibex House, 42-47 Minories, London, EC3N 1HA. Tel: 020 7481 8851. Fax: 020 7480 6097. Internet: www.thomascooperandstibbard.com. Charity specialists: T Goode.

Artists' General Benevolent Institution	7.41

THOMAS EGGAR LLP, 76 Shoe Lane, London, EC4A 3JB. Tel: 020 7842 0000. Fax: 020 7842 3900. E-mail: charities@thomaseggar.com. Internet: www.thomaseggar.com. Charity specialists: Julian Chadwick.

A M Qattan Foundation	7.3
College of Estate Management	7.160

THOMAS EGGAR LLP, The Corn Exchange, Baffin's Lane, Chichester, West Sussex, PO19 1GE. Tel: 01243 786 111. Fax: 01243 775 640. E-mail: charities@thomaseggar.com. Internet: www.thomaseggar.com. Charity specialists: Julian Chadwick. Gillian Dussek. Jane Futrille. Darran Fawcett. Iain MacLeod. Olga Powell.

Aldingbourne Trust	7.24
Hospital of the Blessed Mary	7.321
St Wilfrid's Hospice (South Coast)	7.655

THOMAS EGGAR LLP, Belmont House, Station Way, Crawley, West Sussex, RH10 1JA. Tel: 01293 742 700. Fax: 01293 742 999. E-mail: hello@thomaseggar.com. Internet: www.thomaseggar.com.

Christ's Hospital Foundation (J)	7.144
Roffey Park Institute	7.542
Sussex Community Foundation	7.665

THOMAS EGGAR LLP, Newbury House, 20 Kings Road West, Newbury, Berkshire, RG14 5XR. Tel: 01635 571 000. Fax: 01635 523 444. E-mail: hello@thomaseggar.com. Internet: www.thomaseggar.com.

Congregation of the Sisters of St Anne	7.175

THOMAS MAGNAY & CO LLP, 8 St Mary's Green, Whickham, Newcastle upon Tyne, Tyne and Wear, NE16 4DN. Tel: 0191 488 7459. Fax: 0191 488 8682.

Catherine Cookson Charitable Trust	7.118

THOMAS MCFARLANE, 2 Roman Road, Glasgow, G61 2SW. Tel: 0141 942 4455.

Keep Scotland Beautiful	7.367

THOMSON HAYTON WINKLEY, 114–116 Stricklandgate, Kendal, Cumbria, LA9 4QA. Tel: 01539 721945. Internet: www.thwlegal.co.uk.

Brathay Trust (J)	7.85

THOMSON SNELL & PASSMORE, 3 Lonsdale Gardens, Tunbridge Wells, Kent, TN1 1NX. Tel: 01892 510000. Fax: 01892 549884. E-mail: charlotte.eberlein@ts-p.co.uk. Internet: www.ts-p.co.uk. Charity specialists: Nick Hobden. James Partridge.

Avante Partnership	7.51
Chatham Maritime Trust	7.136

East Malling Trust, The (J)	7.222
Moor House School	7.432
Queen Elizabeth's Fndtn For Disabled People	7.520
Royal British Legion Industries Ltd (J)	7.554
Tomorrow's People Trust (J)	7.682
Worth Abbey (J)	7.742

THOMSON WILSON PATTINSON, Stonecliffe, Lake Road, Windermere, Cumbria, LA23 3AR. Tel: 015394 42233. Fax: 015394 88810. Internet: www.twpsolicitors.com. Charity specialists: D Scott.

Cumbrian Community Foundation	7.189

THORNTONS LAW LLP, Whitehall House, 33 Yeaman Shore, Dundee, DD1 4BJ. Tel: 01382 229111. Fax: 01382 202288. E-mail: dundee@thorntons-law.co.uk. Internet: www.thorntons-law.co.uk. Charity specialists: Prof S J Brymer WS - specialist area: Edu Law & Practice/Intellectual Property. A F McDonald.

Gowrie Care Limited	7.283
James Hutton Institute, The (J)	7.350
Northern Housing Company	7.470

THORNTONS LAW LLP, Kinburn Castle, St Andrews, Fife, KY16 9DR. Tel: 01334 477107. Fax: 01334 476862. Internet: www.thorntons-law.co.uk.

Worldwide Cancer Research (J)	7.742

THORPE & CO, 3 Bagdale, Whitby, North Yorkshire, YO21 1QL. Tel: 01947 603465. Fax: 01947 600068. Internet: www.thorpeandco.com.

St Catherine's Hospice Trust	7.639

THRINGS LLP, Kinnaird House, 1 Pall Mall East, London, SW1Y 5AU. Tel: 020 7766 5600. Fax: 020 7766 5675. E-mail: solicitors@thrings.com. Internet: www.thrings.com. Charity specialists: J Roney. J Whately.

Corporation of the Sons of the Clergy	7.181
Developing Health and Independence	7.199
Holburne Museum (J)	7.314
Mr Willats' Charity	7.437
St John's Hospital (J)	7.645

THRINGS LLP, 6 Drakes Meadow, Penny Lane, Swindon, Wiltshire, SN3 3LL. Tel: 01793 410800. Fax: 01793 539040. E-mail: solicitors@thrings.com. Internet: www.thrings.com.

Chippenham Borough Lands Charity	7.143
Dorothy House Foundation Ltd	7.208
Prospect Foundation (J)	7.516

TICKLE HALL CROSS, Charlton Chambers, 25 Hardshaw Street, St Helens, Merseyside, WA10 1RP. Tel: 01744 733 333. Fax: 01744 746 001. Internet: www.ticklehallcross.co.uk.

Guy Pilkington Memorial Home Limited	7.293

TLT LLP, One Redcliff Street, Bristol, BS1 6TP. Tel: 0117 917 7777. Fax: 0117 917 7778. E-mail: generalenquires@TCTsolicitors.com. Internet: www.TLTsolicitors.com. Charity specialists: T Pyper.

Brandon Trust (J)	7.84
Cottage and Rural Enterprises Limited (J)	7.181
HF Trust Limited (J)	7.311
Somerset Redstone Trust (J)	7.627
Watershed Arts Trust Limited	7.715

TMF CORPORATE SECRETARIAL SERVICES LTD, 400 Capability Green, Luton, Bedfordshire, LU1 3AE. Tel: 01582 439200. Internet: www.tmf-group.com.

Hertford British Hospital, Paris (J)	7.310

TODMANS SRE, Barringtons, Hockley Road, Rayleigh, Essex, SS6 8EH. Tel: 01268 774073. Fax: 01268 747110. E-mail: mail@todmans.co.uk. Internet: www.todmanssre.co.uk.

Havens Christian Hospice	7.304

TODS MURRAY LLP, Edinburgh Quay, 133 Fountainbridge, Edinburgh, EH3 9AG. Tel: 0131 656 2000. Fax: 0131 656 2020. E-mail: maildesk@todsmurray.com. Internet: www.todsmurray.com. Charity specialists: David Dunsire. J M H Biggar. A S Burrow.

Royal Highland Agricultural Soc Scotland (J)	7.561

TOLHURST FISHER, Marlborough House, Victoria Road South, Chelmsford, Essex, CM1 1LN. Tel: 01245 495111. Fax: 01245 494771. E-mail: pjt@tolhurstfisher.com. Internet: www.tolhurstfisher.com. Charity specialists: P J Tolhurst.

Raleigh International Trust (J)	7.524

TOWNS NEEDHAM & CO, Brook House, 64-72 Spring Gardens, Manchester, Greater Manchester, M2 2BQ. Tel: 0161 832 3721. Fax: 0161 835 3792. Internet: www.townsneedham.com.

United Reformed Church (J)	7.696

TOZERS LLP, Broadwalk House, Southernhay West, Exeter, Devon, EX1 1UA. Tel: 0139 220 7020. Fax: 0139 220 7019. E-mail: r.king@tozers.co.uk. Internet: www.tozers.co.uk.

Buckfast Abbey Trust	7.103
HCPT - The Pilgrimage Trust (J)	7.304
Les Filles de la Croix	7.386
Plymouth Diocesan Trust	7.505
Plymouth Secular Clergy Fund	7.506
Shared Lives South West	7.599
South West Lakes Trust (J)	7.630
St Cecilia's Abbey Ryde Isle of Wight (J)	7.639
Viridor Credits Environmental Company	7.706

TRAVERS SMITH, 10 Snow Hill, London, EC1A 2AL. Internet: www.traverssmith.com. Charity specialists: Catheryn Bowl.

Royal Institution of Great Britain (J)	7.562
Stock Exchange Benevolent Fund	7.659

TREASURY SOLICITOR, THE, 1 Kemble Street, London, WC2B 4TS. Tel: 020 7210 3000. Fax: 020 7210 3158. E-mail: thetreasurysolicitor@tsol.gsi.gov.uk. Internet: www.tsol.gov.uk.

British Library (J)	7.95

TRETHOWANS LLP, London Road Office Park, Salisbury, Wiltshire, SP1 3HP. Tel: 01722 412512. Fax: 01722 411300. E-mail: david.jones@trethowans.com. Internet: www.trethowans.com.

Salisbury City Almshouse and Welfare	7.583

TRETHOWANS LLP, 15 Rockstone Place, Southampton, Hampshire, SO15 2EP. Tel: 023 8032 1000. Fax: 023 8032 1001. E-mail: info@trethowans.com. Internet: www.trethowans.com.

Forest Trust, The	7.257
Hampshire Autistic Society	7.298

TROWERS & HAMLINS LLP, 3 Bunhill Row, London, EC1Y 8YZ. Tel: 020 7423 8000. Fax: 020 7423 8001. E-mail: enquiries@trowers.com. Internet: www.trowers.com.

Anglo-Omani Society, The	7.32
Aquaterra Leisure	7.36
Asthma UK (J)	7.47
Borough Care Services	7.80
Brandon Trust (J)	7.84
British School of Osteopathy (J)	7.98

CBHA (J)	7.121
Chartered Institute of Housing	7.133
Douglas Haig Memorial Homes (J)	7.209
E Hayes Dashwood Foundation (J)	7.218
Forest Young Men's Christian Association (J)	7.257
Haig Housing Trust	7.296
Keep Britain Tidy	7.367
Langley House Trust (J)	7.379
Leadership Foundation for Higher Education	7.381
Letchworth Garden City Heritage Foundation (J)	7.386
London Cyrenians Housing	7.398
Maudsley Charity	7.416
Metropolitan Support Trust	7.424
National Autistic Society (J)	7.442
Outreach 3 Way (J)	7.485
Patrick & Helena Frost Foundation, The	7.492
Peabody Trust (J)	7.494
PohWER (J)	7.506
Royal Star & Garter Home, The (J)	7.574
Science Museum Group (J)	7.590
St Christopher's Fellowship (J)	7.640
Together: Working for Wellbeing	7.682
Walsingham	7.713
YMCA England (J)	7.745

TROWERS & HAMLINS LLP, Heron House, Albert Square, Manchester, Greater Manchester, M2 5HD. Tel: 0161 211 0000. Fax: 0161 211 0001. Internet: www.trowers.com.

Diocese of ShrewsburyTrust (J)	7.607
YMCA Downslink Group	7.745

TUGHANS, Marlborough House, 30 Victoria Street, Belfast, County Antrim, BT1 3GS. Tel: 028 9055 3300. Fax: 028 9055 0096. Internet: www.tughans.com.

Action Mental Health (J)	7.11

TURCAN CONNELL

TURCAN CONNELL, Princes Exchange, 1 Earl Grey Street, Edinburgh, EH3 9EE. Tel: 0131 228 8111. Fax: 0131 228 8118. E-mail: charities@turcanconnell.com. Internet: www.turcanconnell.com.

Turcan Connell has Scotland's largest dedicated charity team acting for Scottish and UK charities, national institutions and grant-making trusts, with particular strength in heritage, conservation, the arts, philanthropy and charity mergers.

Fifteen Partners form Turcan Connell's Charity Unit together with other professionals across the firm including accountants and tax experts. Services include charity formation, reorganisation, SCIOs, regulatory advice, employment, philanthropy and legacies, tax and property.

Turcan Connell Charity Office enables grant-makers to outsource administration efficiently and cost-effectively. Turcan Connell is a partnership of Scottish Solicitors regulated by the Law Society of Scotland.

Charity specialists. Simon A Mackintosh. Gavin G R McEwan. Chris Sheldon.

Age Scotland	7.17
Centre for the Moving Image	7.124

Hopetoun House Preservation Trust	7.317
MacRobert Trust	7.405
Maggie Keswick Jencks Cancer Trust (J)	7.406
Mercy Corps Scotland (J)	7.422
National Galleries of Scotland (J)	7.446
National Trust for Scotland (J)	7.453
Robertson Trust (J)	7.541
RSPB (J)	7.572
Shetland Charitable Trust (J)	7.604
Souter Charitable Trust	7.628
Victim Support Scotland (J)	7.704
Volant Charitable Trust	7.709
Voluntary Action Fund	7.709

TURCAN CONNELL, Sutherland House, 149 St Vincent Street, Glasgow, G2 5NW. Tel: 0141 441 2111. Fax: 0141 221 9218. E-mail: charities@turcanconnell.com. Internet: www.turcanconnell.com. Charity specialists: Simon A Mackintosh. Gavin G R McEwan. Peter S Littlefield.

City of Glasgow College Foundation	7.153
Yorkhill Children's Charity	7.748

TWM SOLICITORS LLP, Broadoak House, Horsham Road, Cranleigh, Surrey, GU6 8DJ. Tel: 01483 273 515. Fax: 01483 278 075. Internet: www.twmsolicitors.com.

Community of St Mary at the Cross	7.166

TYNDALLWOODS, 29 Woodbourne Road, Edgbaston, Birmingham, West Midlands, B17 8BY. Tel: 0121 693 2222. Fax: 0121 693 0844. Internet: www.tyndallwoods.co.uk.

Witton Lodge Community Association (J)	7.734

UNDERHILLS, 7 Waterloo Road, Wolverhampton, West Midlands, WV1 4DW. Tel: 01902 423431. Fax: 01902 711696. Charity specialists: J V Taylor.

Compton Hospice	7.169
Lichfield Diocesan Board Of Education, The (J)	7.387

UNDERWOOD AND CO, 40 Welbeck Street, London, W1G 8LN. Tel: 020 7487 4461. Fax: 020 7486 8974. Charity specialists: Hilary Guest.

Derek Butler Trust, The	7.198
Horse Trust (J)	7.318
Royal Medical Benevolent Fund (J)	7.565

UNGOED THOMAS & KING, Gwynne House, 6 Quay Street, Carmarthen, Carmarthenshire, SA31 3JX. Tel: 01267 237 441. Fax: 01267 238 317. E-mail: enquiries@utk.co.uk. Internet: www.utk.co.uk.

St David's Diocesan Board of Finance (J)	7.641

VEALE WASBROUGH VIZARDS, Second Floor, 3 Brindley Place, Birmingham, West Midlands, B1 2JB. Tel: 0121 227 3700. Internet: www.vwv.co.uk.

Central England Quakers (CEQ) (J)	7.122
HelpAge International	7.308
Royal Society for Prevention Accidents	7.571
United Reformed Church (J)	7.696
United Reformed Church Wessex Trust Ltd	7.697

VEALE WASBROUGH VIZARDS, Orchard Court, Orchard Lane, Bristol, BS1 5WS. Tel: 0117 925 2020. Fax: 0117 925 2025. E-mail: calexander@vwv.co.uk. Internet: www.vwv.co.uk.

Alternative Futures Group Ltd (J)	7.27
Anthony Nolan (J)	7.34
ASDAN	7.42
Bristol Charities (J)	7.89
Bristol, Clifton, & West of England Zoo (J)	7.89
Bristol Old Vic and Theatre Royal Trust Ltd	7.90
CFBT Education Trust (J)	7.125
Christ's Hospital Foundation (J)	7.144
Citizens Advice (J)	7.152
Derwen College (J)	7.198
Doncaster Deaf Trust	7.205
Dunhill Medical Trust	7.216
Dutch Oak Tree Foundation	7.216

Equinox Care (J)	7.237
Fairley House School	7.246
Field Studies Council (J)	7.253
Game & Wildlife Conservation Trust (J)	7.268
Handmaids of the Sacred Heart of Jesus (J)	7.300
Harpur Trust, The	7.302
Jisc (J)	7.355
King Fahad Academy Limited	7.372
Kingsway International Christian Centre (J)	7.373
Lady Hewleys Charity	7.376
Leonard Cheshire Disability (J)	7.385
Mrs D M France-Hayhurst Charitable Trust	7.437
Novalis Trust	7.474
Perseverance Trust	7.498
Quartet Community Foundation (J)	7.519
Radcliffe Trust, The	7.523
Royal British Legion (J)	7.554
Royal National College for the Blind (J)	7.566
Ruskin Mill Trust	7.578
Seashell Trust (J)	7.595
Skills for Health Limited	7.617
St Mary Redcliffe Vestry	7.650
St Peter's Hospice (J)	7.654
Waterloo Foundation, The	7.715
Whitgift Foundation (J)	7.726
Wixamtree Trust	7.734
Worth Abbey (J)	7.742
Young Foundation, The (J)	7.750

VINCENTS, 10 Camden Place, Preston, Lancashire, PR1 3JL. Tel: 01772 555 176. Fax: 01772 881 233. Internet: www.vslaw.co.uk.

St Vincent de Paul Society (J)	7.655

VINGOE LLOYD, 33 St John's Street, Hayle, Cornwall, TR27 4LL. Tel: 01736 754075. Fax: 01736 756439.

Cinnamon Trust (J)	7.150

VIRTUAL LAW, Flints House, Eldernell Lane, Whittlesey, Peterborough, PE7 2DD. Tel: 0330 100 0320. Internet: www.virtuallaw.eu.

Livability (J)	7.391

VT LAW, 1 Olympic Way, Wembley, Middlesex, HA9 0NP. Tel: 020 8865 0363. E-mail: info@vt-law.co.uk. Internet: vt-law.co.uk.

Brahma Kumaris World Spiritual UniversityUK (I)	7.83

W DAVIES , Acorn House, 5 Chertsey Road, Woking, Surrey, GU21 5AB. Tel: 01483 744900. Fax: 01483 744901. E-mail: sjo@wdavies.com. Internet: www.wdavies.com.

Woking Homes	7.734
Woking & Sam Beare Hospices	7.735

WAKE SMITH LLP, 68 Clarkehouse Road, Sheffield, South Yorkshire, S10 2LJ. Tel: 0114 266 6660. Fax: 0114 267 1253. E-mail: legal@wake-smith.co.uk. Internet: www.wake-smith.co.uk. Charity specialists: M Tunbridge.

Hospital of Gilbert, Earl of Shrewsbury	7.320
Sheffield Diocesan Board of Finance	7.601

WALDRONS, Wychbury Court, Two Woods Lane, Merry Hill, Hertfordshire, DY5 1TA. Tel: 01384 811 833. Fax: 01384 811 822. Internet: www.waldrons.co.uk. Charity specialists: P Waldron.

Apostolic Church, The (J)	7.35

WALKER MORRIS LLP, Kings Court, 12 King Street, Leeds, West Yorkshire, LS1 2HL. Tel: 0113 283 2500. Fax: 0113 245 9412. Internet: www.walkermorris.co.uk.

NSPCC (J)	7.452
Yorkshire Wildlife Trust (J)	7.749

WARD HADAWAY, 1A Tower Square, Wellington Street, Leeds, West Yorkshire, LS1 4DL. Tel: 0113 205 6600. Fax: 0113 205 6700. Internet: www.wardhadaway.com.

Action Housing & Support Limited (J)	7.10

Doncaster Culture and Leisure Trust (J) 7.204
Land Restoration Trust (J) 7.378

WARD HADAWAY, Sandgate House, 102 Quayside, Newcastle upon Tyne, Tyne and Wear, NE1 3DX. Tel: 0191 204 4000. Fax: 0191 204 4001. E-mail: enquiries@wardhadaway.com. Internet: www.wardhadaway.com. Charity specialists: P R Allan OBE DL - specialist area: Corporate. C Hewitt.

1989 Willan Charitable Trust (J) 7.2
Alnwick Garden Trust (J) 7.27
Changing Lives 7.127
County Durham Community Foundation (J) 7.183
Foundation of Light 7.260
Northern Rock Foundation 7.471
Sherburn House Charity 7.604
Sir James Knott Trust 7.610
St Oswald's Hospice (J) 7.653
TTE Technical Training Group, The (J) 7.690

WARNERS, 16 South Park, Sevenoaks, Kent, TN13 1AN. Tel: 01732 747900. Fax: 01732 747919. Internet: www.warners-solicitors.co.uk.

Royal London Society for the Blind (J) 7.564

WARRENS BOYES & ARCHER, 20 Hartford Road, Huntingdon, Cambridgeshire, PE29 3QH. Tel: 01480 411331. Fax: 01480 459012. Internet: www.warrenslaw.co.uk. Charity specialists: C R Boyes.

C Alma Baker Trust 7.106
Huntingdon Freemen's Trust (J) 7.325

WATSON RAMSBOTTOM, 25-29 Victoria Street, Blackburn, Lancashire, BB1 6DN. Tel: 01254 672222. Fax: 01254 681723. Internet: www.watsonramsbottom.com.

Bootstrap Company (Blackburn) 7.80

WBW SOLICITORS, 9 Southernhay West, Exeter, Devon, EX1 1JG. Tel: 01392 202404. Fax: 01392 666555. E-mail: lawyer@wbw.co.uk. Internet: www.wbw.co.uk.

United Reformed Church (South Western) (J) 7.696

WEDLAKE BELL, 52 Bedford Row, London, WC1R 4LR. Tel: 020 7395 3000. Fax: 020 7395 3100. E-mail: legal@wedlakebell.com. Internet: www.wedlakebell.com. Charity specialists: C A Hicks. Eleanor C Metcalf.

Cabrini Children's Society (J) 7.107
Carpenters' Company Charitable Trust 7.117
Charity Roman Union Order St Ursula (J) 7.130
CongregationDominicanSistersofMaltaTrst 7.173
Morden College (J) 7.433
Roman Catholic Diocese of Southwark 7.544
Royal Alfred Seafarers' Society 7.552
Royal Masonic Trust For Girls and Boys (J) 7.565
Rustington Convalescent Home Carpenters Co 7.578
Society for Promoting Christian Knowledge (J) 7.620
Trustees of the Bernadine Sisters Charity 7.689

WEIGHTMANS LLP, 100 Old Hall Street, Liverpool, Merseyside, L3 9QJ. Tel: 0845 073 9900. Fax: 0845 073 9950. Internet: www.weightmans.com.

Local Solutions (J) 7.395
Nat Museums & Galleries on Merseyside (J) 7.450

WEIGHTMANS LLP, St Philips Point, Temple Row, Birmingham, West Midlands, B2 5AF. Tel: 0121 632 6100. Fax: 0121 632 5410. Internet: www.weightmans.com.

Ex-Services Mental Welfare Society (J) 7.243

WEIL, GOTSHAL & MANGES, 110 Fetter Lane, London, EC4A 1AY. Tel: 020 7903 1000. Fax: 020 7903 0990. Internet: www.weil.com/london.

Homeless International (J) 7.316
NSPCC (J) 7.452

Refuge (J) 7.529
Serpentine Trust 7.597
Tomorrow's People Trust (J) 7.682

WELLERS, 7-8 Grays Inn Square, London, WC1R 5JQ. Tel: 020 7242 7265. Internet: www.wellers.net.

Redeemed Christian Church of God 7.528

WELLERS, Tenison House, 45 Tweedy Road, Bromley, Kent, BR1 3NF. Tel: 020 8464 4242. Fax: 020 8464 6033. Internet: www.wellers.net. Charity specialists: P Martin.

Global Partners (UK) 7.277
OMF International (UK) 7.480
World Mission Agency 7.741

WHISKERS, 6 Mitre Buildings, Kitson Way, Harlow, Essex, CM20 1DR. Tel: 01279 439439. Fax: 01279 439100. E-mail: enquiries@whiskers.co.uk. Internet: www.whiskers.co.uk.

St Clare West Essex Hospice Care Trust 7.640

WHITAKER FIRTH, 1 Manor Row, Bradford, West Yorkshire, BD1 4PB. Tel: 01274 381900. Fax: 01274 392848. E-mail: reception@whitakerfirth.co.uk. Internet: www.whitakerfirth.co.uk.

Foundation 7.258

WHITE & CO, 190 Clarence Gate Gardens, Glentworth Street, London, NW1 6AD. Tel: 020 7258 0206. Fax: 020 7258 1096. E-mail: info@whiteandcosolicitors.com. Internet: www.whiteandcosolicitors.com.

Will Trust of Gerald Segelman Deceased, The 7.729

WHITE & CASE, 5 Old Broad Street, London, EC2N 1DW. Tel: 020 7532 1000. Fax: 020 7532 1001. Internet: www.whitecase.com.

International Rescue Committee UK 7.344

WHITMAN BREED, 960 Capability Green, Luton, Bedfordshire, LU1 3PE. Tel: 01582 635077. Fax: 01582 842787. Internet: www.whitmanbreedlaw.com.

Sterling Charity, The (J) 7.658

Wiggin Osborne Fullerlove
solicitors

WIGGIN OSBORNE FULLERLOVE, 95 The Promenade, Cheltenham, Gloucestershire, GL50 1HH. Tel: 01242 710200. E-mail: stephen.pallister@woflaw.com. Internet: www.woflaw.com. Charity specialists: Stephen Pallister.

College Estate Endowment Charity, The (J) 7.160
Dr Mortimer & Theresa Sackler Fdtn (J) 7.211
Guild Estate Endowment (J) 7.291
Ruddock Foundation for the Arts 7.577
Sackler Trust, The (J) 7.579
Sterling Charity, The (J) 7.658
Stratford Upon Avon Town Trust (J) 7.661

WILKES PARTNERSHIP, THE, 41 Church Street, Birmingham, West Midlands, B3 2RT. Tel: 0121 233 4333. Fax: 0121 233 4546. Internet: www.wilkes.co.uk. Charity specialists: R H Jaffa.

Euro Charity Trust 7.241

WILKIN CHAPMAN, The Hall, Lairgate, Beverley, East Riding of Yorkshire, HU17 8HL. Tel: 01482 398398. Fax: 01482 870913. Internet: www.wilkinchapman.co.uk. Charity specialists: M Adams.

Beverley Consolidated Charity 7.68
Hull Trinity House Charities 7.323

WILKIN CHAPMAN, New Oxford House, Town Hall Square, Grimsby, North East Lincolnshire, DN31 1EY. Tel: 01472 262626. Fax: 01472 360198. Internet: www.wilkinchapman.co.uk. Charity specialists: Julia Whittaker.

St Andrew's Hospice 7.636

WILLANS LLP, 28 Imperial Square, Cheltenham, Gloucestershire, GL50 1RH. Tel: 01242 514000. Fax: 01242 519079. E-mail: law@willans.co.uk. Internet: www.willans.co.uk. Charity specialists: Margaret Austen. Matthew Clayton. Alasdair Garbutt. Kate Hickey. Laurence Lucas. Nigel Whittaker.

Cheltenham Festival 7.137
Cobalt Unit Appeal Fund 7.159
Higher Education Statistics Agency (J) 7.312
Lilian Faithfull Homes Limited 7.389
Macmillan Cancer Support (J) 7.405
Marie Curie Cancer Care (J) 7.410
Scope (J) 7.590
SHELTER (J) 7.603
Sue Ryder (J) 7.663

WILLCOX LEWIS LLP, The Old Coach House, Bergh Apton, Norwich, Norfolk, NR15 1DD. Tel: 01508 480100. Fax: 01508 480001. E-mail: info@willcoxlewis.co.uk.

South Street Green Room Foundation 7.630

WILLIAM HEATH & CO, 16 Sale Place, Sussex Gardens, London, W2 1PX. Tel: 020 7402 3151. Fax: 020 7706 9139. E-mail: edwin.lee@williamheath.co.uk.

Mike Gooley Trailfinder Charity 7.427

WILLIAM STURGES & CO, Alliance House, 12 Caxton Street, London, SW1H 0QY. Tel: 020 7873 1000. Fax: 020 7873 1010. E-mail: michael.franks@williamsturges.co.uk. Internet: www.williamsturges.co.uk. Charity specialists: M H Lawson - specialist area: Commercial Trust, Charities,Insolvency. M M Franks. I G Brown.

Benesco Charity 7.65
Charles Wolfson Charitable Trust 7.131
Institute of Brewing & Distilling 7.334

WILLS CHANDLER, 76 Bounty Road, Basingstoke, Hampshire, RG21 3BZ. Tel: 01256 322911. Fax: 01256 327811. E-mail: legal@wills-chandler.co.uk. Internet: www.wills-chandler.co.uk.

St Michael's Hospice (North Hampshire) (J) 7.651

WILSON GUNN, 5th Floor, Blackfriars House, The Parsonage, Manchester, Greater Manchester, M3 2JA. Tel: 0161 827 9400. Fax: 0161 832 4905. E-mail: manchester@wilsongunn.com. Internet: www.wilsongunn.com.

Nat Museums & Galleries on Merseyside (J) 7.450

Wilsons
Solicitors

WILSONS SOLICITORS LLP, Alexandra House, St Johns Street, Salisbury, Wiltshire, SP1 2SB. Tel: 01722 412412. Fax: 01722 411500. E-mail: enquiries@wilsonslaw.com. Internet: www.wilsonslaw.com.

WILSONS SOLICITORS LLP, 4 Lincoln's Inn Fields, London, WC2A 3AA. Tel: 020 7998 0420. Fax: 020 7242 7661.

Our core team of twelve specialist lawyers, including a former Charity Commission lawyer, advise on a complete range of constitutional and governance issues, legacy management and contentious probate. They work with experts across the firm to deliver advice on property transactions, probate and trust administration, corporate law, employment and property litigation. Together they provide a one-stop shop for over 550 charity clients.

- Establishment and dissolution of charities
- Incorporation
- Property and employment
- Investment, trading and fund-raising
- Constitutional and Charity Commission issues
- Legacy administration
- Probate and estate administration
- Charity and probate litigation
- Inheritance Act claims
- Undue influence, proprietary estoppel
- Executor, trustee and solicitor claims

For more information please see our firm profile in the front colour section.

Charity specialists: Gillian Fletcher (Director of Charity Law and Governance). Peter Jeffreys. James Aspden. Fiona Campbell-White. Charlotte Watts. James Johnson. Amy Croxford. Caroline Walford. Emma Nigogosian. Alice Vale.

ABF The Soldiers Charity (J)	7.6
Absolute Return for Kids (ARK) (J)	7.7
ACT Foundation (J)	7.9
Action for Children (J)	7.10
Action Medical Research (J)	7.11
Action on Hearing Loss (J)	7.11
Age UK (J)	7.17
Alabaré Christian Care Centres	7.22
Alpha International	7.27
Alzheimer's Society (J)	7.28
Amnesty International Limited	7.30
Army Central Fund, The	7.39
Army Dependants' Trust, The	7.39
Arthritis Care (J)	7.40
Arthritis Research UK (J)	7.40
Asthma UK (J)	7.47
Barnardo's (J)	7.57
Battersea Dogs & Cats Home (J)	7.60
Blind Veterans UK (J)	7.76
Blue Cross (J)	7.76
BMS World Mission (J)	7.77
Brathay Trust (J)	7.85
Breast Cancer Care (J)	7.86

Bristol Charities (J)	7.89
British Heart Foundation (J)	7.93
British Red Cross Society (J)	7.98
Brooke Hospital for Animals (J)	7.101
BSS	7.102
Bulldog Trust (J)	7.104
Campaign to Protect Rural England (J)	7.110
Cancer Research UK (J)	7.112
Catholic Agency for Overseas Development (J)	7.118
Cats Protection (J)	7.120
Charities Aid Foundation (J)	7.128
Children's Hospice South West (J)	7.141
Children's Society (J)	7.142
Christ's Hospital Foundation (J)	7.144
Church Army (J)	7.147
Church Mission Society (J)	7.148
CLIC Sargent Cancer Care for Children (J)	7.156
Comm Fdn (Tyne&Wear&Northumberland) (J)	7.164
Concern Worldwide (UK) (J)	7.170
Cystic Fibrosis Trust (J)	7.190
Diabetes UK (J)	7.200
Dogs Trust (J)	7.203
Donkey Sanctuary (J)	7.206
Dulwich Estate (J)	7.214
Earl Mountbatten Hospice (J)	7.219
East Anglia's Children's Hospices (J)	7.220
Edward James Foundation Limited (J)	7.228
Elizabeth Finn Care (J)	7.230
Ellenor Lions Hospices (J)	7.231
Essex Wildlife Trust	7.240
Ex-Services Mental Welfare Society (J)	7.243
Field Lane Foundation (J)	7.253
Fdn&Friends of RoyalBotanicGardens, Kew (J)	7.259
Friends of the Elderly (J)	7.265
Game & Wildlife Conservation Trust (J)	7.268
Great Ormond St Hosp Children's Charity (J)	7.285
Greenpeace Environmental Trust (J)	7.287
Greensleeves Homes Trust (J)	7.287
Grenadier Guards Charity, The (J)	7.288
Guide Dogs for the Blind Association (J)	7.291
Gurkha Welfare Trust (J)	7.292
Help for Heroes (J)	7.308
IIF Trust Limited (J)	7.311
Hope and Homes for Children (J)	7.317
Imperial College Healthcare Charity (J)	7.329
Independent Age (J)	7.331
Institute of Cancer Research (J)	7.334
Institute of Development Studies (J)	7.334
International Fund for Animal Welfare (J)	7.342
Jewish Care (J)	7.354
JNF Charitable Trust (J)	7.355
King Edward VII's Hospital Sister Agnes (J)	7.372
Leonard Cheshire Disability (J)	7.385
Leprosy Mission England (J)	7.385
LIONHEART (J)	7.391
Macmillan Cancer Support (J)	7.405
Marie Curie Cancer Care (J)	7.410
Martin House (J)	7.413
Medecins sans Frontieres (UK) (J)	7.418
Mental Health Foundation (J)	7.421
Midlands Air Ambulance Charity	7.426
MIND (J)	7.428
Mission to Seafarers (J)	7.430
Motor Neurone Disease Association (J)	7.435
Multiple Sclerosis Society (J)	7.438
Muscular Dystrophy Campaign (J)	7.439
National Autistic Society (J)	7.442
National Motor Museum Trust Ltd	7.450
National Osteoporosis Society (J)	7.451
NSPCC (J)	7.452
National Trust (J)	7.454
Operation Mobilisation (J)	7.481
Oxfam GB (J)	7.486
Parkinson's UK (J)	7.491
Paul Strickland Scanner Centre	7.493
PDSA (J)	7.494
Picker Institute Europe	7.502
Pilgrims Hospices in East Kent (J)	7.503
Poole Arts Trust	7.508
Princess Alice Hospice	7.514
Redwings Horse Sanctuary (J)	7.528
Roy Castle Lung Cancer Foundation (J)	7.548
Royal Air Force Benevolent Fund (J)	7.550
Royal Artillery Charitable Fund, The	7.552
Royal British Legion (J)	7.554

Royal College of Ophthalmologists (J)	7.556
Royal College of Pathologists (J)	7.557
Royal Corps Signals Benevolent Fund	7.559
Royal Hospital for Neuro-disability (J)	7.562
Royal Institution of Great Britain (J)	7.562
Royal London Society for the Blind (J)	7.564
Royal Masonic Hospital Charity (J)	7.565
Royal Mencap Society (J)	7.566
Royal National College for the Blind (J)	7.566
Royal National Institute of Blind People (J)	7.566
Royal National Lifeboat Institution (J)	7.567
Royal Natl Mission to Deep Sea Fishermen (J)	7.567
Royal Naval Benevolent Trust (J)	7.568
RSPCA (J)	7.572
RSPB (J)	7.572
Royal Society of Wildlife Trusts (J)	7.573
Royal Star & Garter Home, The (J)	7.574
Salisbury Diocesan Board Finance	7.583
Save the Children (J)	7.588
Scripture Union (J)	7.594
Seafarers UK (J)	7.594
SeeAbility (J)	7.596
Sense - National Deafblind & Rubella Assoc (J)	7.597
Sheiling Trust (J)	7.603
SHELTER (J)	7.603
Sightsavers International (J)	7.608
Society for Protection of Animals Abroad (J)	7.621
Society ofthe Holy Child Jesus Eur.Province	7.624
St Catherine's Hospice (Lancashire)	7.639
St Christopher's Hospice (J)	7.640
St John's Hospital (J)	7.645
St Michael's Hospice (North Hampshire) (J)	7.651
Stroke Association (J)	7.662
Sue Ryder (J)	7.663
Thursford Collection, The (J)	7.680
UNICEF-UK (J)	7.694
USPG (J)	7.702
Valley Leisure	7.702
Vocational Training Charitable Trust (J)	7.708
Walton-on-Thames Charity	7.713
Wessex Archaeology Ltd	7.719
Wessex Children's Hospice Trust (J)	7.719
Wheler Foundation, The	7.725
Wildfowl and Wetlands Trust (J)	7.728
Wiltshire Wildlife Trust (J)	7.731
Wood Green Animal Shelters (J)	7.736
Woodland Trust (J)	7.737
World Cancer Research Fund (WCRF UK) (J)	7.739
World Horse Welfare (J)	7.740
World Society for the Protection of Animals (J)	7.741
World Vision UK (J)	7.741
WWF UK (J)	7.743
Yorkshire Cancer Research (J)	7.749

WINCH & WINCH, 5 New Road Avenue, Chatham, Kent, ME4 6AR. Tel: 01634 830111. Fax: 01634 408891. E-mail: solicitors@winch-winch.co.uk. Internet: www.winch-winch.co.uk.

R.Watts&Rochester CityAlmshouseCharities	7.536

WINCKWORTH SHERWOOD LLP, Minerva House, 5 Montague Close, London, SE1 9BB. Tel: 020 7593 5000. Fax: 020 7593 5099. E-mail: ocj@wslaw.co.uk. Internet: www.wslaw.co.uk.

Charity specialists: O G Carew-Jones. A R Hargreaves-Smith. P C E Morris. J Rees. Mr D R Fitton. R H A Macdonald. A J Murray.

Active Luton (J)	7.12
Canterbury Diocesan Board of Finance (J)	7.112
Chelmsford Diocesan Board Finance	7.136
Chichester Diocesan Fd Bd Finance	7.138
Diocese of Hexham and Newcastle (J)	7.201
Fusion Lifestyle (J)	7.266
London Diocesan Board for Schools	7.398
London Diocesan Fund	7.398
Mytime Active (J)	7.441
Roch. Diocesan Society & Bd of Fin (J)	7.542
S Lon Ch Fund&Sthwk Diocesan Bd Fin	7.629
South London YMCA (J)	7.629
Thurrock Community Leisure	7.680
Westminster RC Diocesan Trust (J)	7.723

WINCKWORTH SHERWOOD LLP, 16 Beaumont Street, Oxford, Oxfordshire, OX1 2LZ. Tel: 01865 297200. Fax: 01865 726274. E-mail: jrees@ws-oxford.co.uk. Internet: www.winckworths.co.uk.

Community of St Mary the Virgin (J)	7.166
Culham St Gabriel's Trust	7.188
Oxford Diocesan Board Finance (J)	7.487
Society for Promoting Christian Knowledge (J)	7.620

WINSTON & STRAWN, CityPoint, 1 Ropemaker Street, London, EC2Y 9HU. Tel: 020 7011 8700. Internet: www.winston.com.

Climate Group, The (J)	7.157

WITHERS LLP, 16 Old Bailey, London, EC4M 7EG. Tel: 020 7597 6000. Fax: 020 7597 6543. E-mail: enquiries.uk@withersworldwide.com. Internet: www.withersworldwide.com. Charity specialists: Alison Paines (Partner & Head of Charities & Philanthropy Team) - specialist area: Charity Law. Chris Priestley (Partner) - specialist area: Charity Law & Commercial Law. Clive Cutbill (Consultant) - specialist area: Charity Law & Philanthropy. Chris Groves (Partner) - specialist area: Estate Planning & Philanthropy. Richard Cassell (Partner) - specialist area: US Charity Law. Paul Hewitt (Partner) - specialist area: Legacies. Stephen Richards (Partner) - specialist area: Legacies. Paul Brecknell (Partner) - specialist area: Property. Jeremy Wakeham (Partner) - specialist area: Property. Meriel Schindler (Partner) - specialist area: Employment. Daniel Isaac (Partner) - specialist area: Employment. Graham Elliott (Consultant) - specialist area: VAT Tax. Anne Davies (Special Counsel) - specialist area: Health and Safety. Alana Lowe-Petraska (Special Counsel) - specialist area: Philanthropy. Michelle Chow (Consultant) - specialist area: Asia Charity Law and Philanthropy. Kenny Mullen (Partner) - specialist area: IP.

Addenbrooke's Charitable Trust (J)	7.13
Alzheimer's Research UK (J)	7.28
Assoc of Anaesthetists of GB & Ireland (J)	7.46
Barnabas Fund (J)	7.57
Barristers' Benevolent Association	7.59
Big Local Trust	7.70
Birmingham Children's Hospital Charities (J)	7.71
Blenheim Foundation, The	7.75
British Red Cross Society (J)	7.98
Bulldog Trust (J)	7.104
Butchers & Drovers Charitable Inst	7.105
Chartered Inst of Personnel & Development	7.134
Chartered Quality Institute (J)	7.135
Chaseley Trust (J)	7.135
Chelsea & Westminster Health Charity	7.136
Christ's Hospital Foundation (J)	7.144
College Optometrists	7.160
Concern Worldwide (UK) (J)	7.170
Creative Foundation Limited - Group, The	7.185
David and Claudia Harding Foundation, The	7.193
De Haan Charitable Trust	7.195
Edward James Foundation Limited (J)	7.228
Eighty Eight Foundation, The	7.228
Fdn&Friends of RoyalBotanicGardens, Kew (J)	7.259
Foyle Foundation (J)	7.261
Frances Augustus Newman Foundation	7.262
Frank Jackson Foundation, The	7.263
Game & Wildlife Conservation Trust (J)	7.268
Great Ormond St Hosp Children's Charity (J)	7.285
Guy's & St Thomas' Charity (J)	7.293
Inst of Marine Engineering, Science & Tech (J)	7.335
Int. Baccalaureate Org (UK) (J)	7.340
Joseph Levy Charitable Foundation	7.362
King's College Hospital Charity	7.372
Lawes Agricultural Trust	7.380
Local Trust	7.396
London Catalyst	7.397
London Oratory Charity	7.400
Macmillan Cancer Support (J)	7.405
Medical Research Foundation	7.419
Moondance Foundation	7.432
Moorfields Eye Hospital Special Trustees (J)	7.433
NSPCC (J)	7.452

Newcastle Healthcare Charity (J)	7.459
Nottingham University Hospitals General Fund	7.473
Old Possum's Practical Trust	7.479
Orders St John Care Trust	7.483
Oxford Radcliffe Hospitals Charitable Fund (J)	7.488
Paul Hamlyn Foundation (J)	7.493
PDSA (J)	7.494
Peter Harrison Foundation	7.499
Royal Air Forces Association (J)	7.551
RSPB (J)	7.572
Schroder Charity Trust	7.589
Schroder Foundation, The	7.589
Sheffield Hospitals Trust & Related Charities (J)	7.602
Shelterbox	7.603
Society for Protection of Animals Abroad (J)	7.621
SSAFA	7.626
St George's Hospital Charity	7.643
Stewardship Services (UKET) Ltd (J)	7.658
Talisman Charitable Trust	7.668
Tate (J)	7.669
Tate Foundation	7.669
Tate Members	7.669
Teach First (J)	7.670
Thalidomide Trust	7.674
Toynbee Hall (J)	7.684
Trustees of the London Clinic Limited (J)	7.689
University College London Hospitals Charity	7.700
W O Street Charitable Foundation	7.710
Whitechapel Gallery (J)	7.725
Winston Churchill Memorial Trust	7.732

WITHY KING SOLICITORS, Midland Bridge House, Midland Bridge Road, Bath, Bath & North East Somerset, BA2 3FP. Tel: 01225 730 100. Fax: 01225 730 101. E-mail: edward.cooke@withyking.com. Internet: www.withyking.co.uk.

Holburne Museum (J)	7.314
St John's Hospital (J)	7.645
Whale Dolphin Conservation Society	7.724
Wildfowl and Wetlands Trust (J)	7.728

WITHY KING SOLICITORS, 5 & 6 Northumberland Buildings, Queen Square, Bath, Bath & North East Somerset, BA1 2JE. Tel: 01225 352910. Fax: 01225 315562. E-mail: edward.cooke@withyking.co.uk. Internet: www.withyking.co.uk. Charity specialists: Richard Baxter. Jessica Bent. Andrew Chalk. Edward Cooke. Mike Cooper. Mark Emery. Malcom Gregory. Jaqueline Lagare. Samantha O'Sullivan.

Comm. Foundation for Wiltshire & Swindon	7.163
Wiltshire Wildlife Trust (J)	7.731

WITHY KING SOLICITORS, North Bailey House, New Inn Hall Street, Oxford, Oxfordshire, OX1 2EA. Tel: 01865 792 300. Internet: www.withyking.co.uk.

Helen & Douglas House	7.307

WOLFERSTANS, Deptford Chambers, 60-64 North Hill, Plymouth, Devon, PL4 8EP. Tel: 01752 663295. Fax: 01752 672021. Internet: www.wolferstans.com. Charity specialists: Jill M Buckler.

St Luke's Hospice Plymouth	7.648

WOLLEN MICHELMORE, 15-21 Market Street, Newton Abbot, Devon, TQ12 2RN. Tel: 01626 332266. Fax: 01626 331700. Internet: www.wollenmichelmore.co.uk. Charity specialists: M F Freeland.

South West Environmental Parks Limited (J)	7.630
Whitley Wildlife Conservation Trust, The (J)	7.726

WOODFINES LLP, 16 St Cuthberts Street, Bedford, Bedfordshire, MK40 3JG. Tel: 01234 270600. Fax: 01234 210128. E-mail: mail@woodfines.co.uk. Internet: www.woodfines.co.uk.

Ibbett Trust (J)	7.327

WOOLF SIMMONDS SOLICITORS, One Great Cumberland Place, London, W1H 7AL. Tel: 020 7262 1266. Fax: 020 7723 7159. E-mail: email@woolfsimmonds.co.uk. Internet: www.woolfsimmonds.co.uk.

Architectural Association Incorporated (J)	7.38

WOOLLEY, BEVIS & DIPLOCK, Lanes End House, 15 Prince Albert Street, Brighton, Sussex, BN1 1HY. Tel: 01273 323 231. Fax: 01273 820 350. E-mail: www.wooleybevis.com. Charity specialists: Amanda Epstein. C Bidwell.

Blind Veterans UK (J)	7.76

WORNHAM & CO, Ground Floor, 52 Albion Street, Jewellery Quarter, Birmingham, West Midlands, B1 3EA. Tel: 0121 236 7999.

Homeless International (J)	7.316

WORTHINGTONS, 21 Oxford Street, Belfast, County Antrim, BT1 3LA. Tel: 028 9043 4015. Fax: 028 9043 4016. Internet: www.worthingtonslaw.co.uk.

Action Cancer	7.9
Extern Organisation	7.244

WORTLEY BYERS LLP, Cathedral Place, Brentwood, Essex, CM14 4ES. Tel: 01277 268368. Fax: 01277 268369. E-mail: info@wortleybyers.co.uk. Internet: www.wortleybyers.co.uk.

Aston-Mansfield Charitable Trust (J)	7.47

WRAGGE LAWRENCE GRAHAM & CO, 4 More London Riverside, London, SE1 2AU. Tel: 0870 903 1000. Fax: 0870 903 1099. E-mail: mail@wragge-law.com. Internet: www.wragge-law.com. Charity specialists: Robert Smith.

Medical Research Council Technology (J)	7.419
Motability	7.435
Motability Tenth Anniversary Trust, The	7.435
NIAB (J)	7.462

WRAGGE LAWRENCE GRAHAM & CO, Two Snowhill, Birmingham, West Midlands, B4 6WR. Tel: 0870 903 1000. Fax: 0870 904 1099. E-mail: mail@wragge-law.com. Internet: www.wragge-law.com. Charity specialists: Julie A Fox - specialist area: Charities. J R A Crabtree OBE.

Birmingham Hippodrome Theatre Trust Ltd (J)	7.72
Birmingham Museums Trust	7.72
Black Country Living Museum Trust (J)	7.74
Dolphin Square Charitable Foundation, The (J)	7.203
Oxfam GB (J)	7.486
PDSA (J)	7.494
Sutton Coldfield Municipal Charities	7.666

WRIGHT HASSALL LLP, Olympus Avenue, Leamington Spa, Warwickshire, CV34 6BF. Tel: 01926 886688. Fax: 01926 885588. E-mail: mark.lewis@wrighthassall.co.uk. Internet: www.wrighthassall.co.uk. Charity specialists: Mark Lewis. Carol Matthews.

Addington Fund, The	7.14
Ashorne Hill Management College	7.44
Castel Froma (J)	7.117
Keychange Charity (J)	7.370
Trident Reach the People Charity (J)	7.686
Warwickshire Wildlife Trust	7.714
WCS Care Group Limited	7.717

WRIGHT JOHNSTON & MACKENZIE, 302 St Vincent Street, Glasgow, G2 5RZ. Tel: 0141 248 3434. Fax: 0141 221 1226. E-mail: enquiries@wjm.co.uk. Internet: www.wjm.co.uk.

Scottish Sports Council Trust Company	7.593

WRIGLEYS
— SOLICITORS —

WRIGLEYS SOLICITORS LLP, 19 Cookridge Street, Leeds, West Yorkshire, LS2 3AG. Tel: 0113 244 6100. Fax: 0113 244 6101. E-mail: malcolm.lynch@wrigleys.co.uk. Internet: www.wrigleys.co.uk.

Wrigleys advises charities nationally from its offices in Leeds and Sheffield. It has a long established team of lawyers specialising in the charity and social economy sector. For more information see our profile page in the front cover section.

Charity specialists: Chris Billington (Partner) - specialist area: Charities and Education Law, Employment Law. Malcolm Lynch (Partner) - specialist area: Charity Law, Charities and Trading. Matthew Wrigley (Partner) - specialist area: Charity Law and Heritage Charities. Sylvie Nunn (Partner) - specialist area: Charity Law. Elizabeth Wilson (Partner) - specialist area: Charity Property Law. Claris D'Cruz (Consultant) - specialist area: Charities and the Charity Commission. Tim Wrigley (Solicitor) - specialist area: Charity and Commercial Property. Clare Lawrence (Solicitor) - specialist area: Charity Law. Peter Parker (Solicitor) - specialist area: Charity Law, Trading & Social Finance. Natalie Johnson (Solicitor) - specialist area: Charity Law.

After Adoption (J)	7.16
Ampleforth Abbey Trust (J)	7.30
Asda Foundation Limited (J)	7.42
Bridgewood Trust (J)	7.88
Catholic Care (Diocese of Leeds) (J)	7.119
Circadian Trust	7.151
Community Foundation for Leeds (J)	7.163
Community Integrated Care (J)	7.164
Community of the Resurrection (J)	7.167
David Hockney Foundation (UK) Limited	7.194
Depaul UK (J)	7.197
Donisthorpe Hall	7.205
Donkey Sanctuary (J)	7.206
Dulverton Trust (J)	7.214
Eiris Foundation (J)	7.229
Esmée Fairbairn Foundation (J)	7.240
Foundation for Credit Counselling (J)	7.259
Friends Provident Charitable Foundation	7.266
Grenadier Guards Charity, The (J)	7.288
Harewood House Trust	7.302
Institute of Daughters of Mary Help (J)	7.334
L'Arche	7.375

League Football Education (J)	7.381
Newground Together	7.460
Northern Ballet Theatre (J)	7.469
Opera North (J)	7.481
Operation Mobilisation (J)	7.481
PACEY	7.515
Ripon Diocesan Board of Finance	7.539
Royal Horticultural Society (J)	7.561
RSPCA (J)	7.572
Sisters of the Cross and Passion (J)	7.615
Together Trust (J)	7.681
Wakefield Diocesan Board Finance	7.710
York Minster Fund	7.748

WRIGLEYS SOLICITORS LLP, 3rd Floor, Fountain Precinct, Balm Green, Sheffield, South Yorkshire, S1 2JA. Tel: 0114 267 5588. Fax: 0114 276 3176. E-mail: Godfrey.Smallman@wrigleys.co.uk. Internet: www.wrigleys.co.uk.
Charity specialists: Godfrey J Smallman (Partner) - specialist area: Grant-making Charities. Sue Greaves (Partner) - specialist area: Charities and Trading. Natalie Johnson (Solicitor) - specialist area: Charity Law.

Sheffield Church Burgesses Trust	7.600
Sheffield Hospitals Trust & Related Charities (J)	7.602

PROPERTY ADVISERS AND THEIR CHARITY CLIENTS

A R ARGYLE FRICS, 180 Horninglow Street, Burton-on-Trent, Staffordshire, DE14 1NG. Tel: 01283 538 222. Fax: 01283 564 333. E-mail: enquiries@argylefrics.co.uk. Internet: www.argylefrics.co.uk.

Consolidated Charity of Burton upn Trent	7.177

ALDER KING, 15 Pembroke Road, Bristol, BS8 3BA. Tel: 0117 317 1000. Fax: 0117 317 1001. Internet: www.alderking.com. Charity specialists: R Kneale.

Above and Beyond	7.7
Bristol Charities	7.89
St Monica Trust	7.651

ASSINDER TURNHAM AND CO, 6-7 Southernhay West, Exeter, Devon, EX1 1JG. Tel: 01392 499 091. Fax: 01392 499 097. E-mail: info@assinderturnham.co.uk.. Internet: www.assinderturnham.co.uk.

Tiverton Almhouse Charity	7.681

BALFOURS LLP CHARTERED SURVEYORS, Windsor House, Windsor Place, Shrewsbury, Shropshire, SY1 2BZ.

Weston Park Foundation	7.724

BAUHAUS PROPERTY COMPANY LIMITED, Island Studios, 22 St Peter's Square, London, W6 9NW. Tel: 020 8741 2203. Fax: 079 3206 0476.

Hammersmith United Charities	7.297

BIDWELLS, Trumpington Road, Cambridge, Cambridgeshire, CB2 9LD. Tel: 01223 559331. Fax: 01223 840294. E-mail: jbushell@bidwells.co.uk. Internet: www.bidwells.co.uk.

Kennedy Leigh Charitable Trust	7.368
Letchworth Garden City Heritage Foundation	7.386
Nat Institute of Agricultural Botany Trust	7.448
Nuffield Oxford Hospitals Fund	7.474
St Albans Diocesan Board Finance (J)	7.635
Varrier Jones Foundation	7.703

BISCOE CRAIG HALL, 5-6 Staple Inn, Holborn, London, WC1V 7QU. Tel: 020 7242 4321. Fax: 020 7242 4327. Charity specialists: J F Thompson.

Baptist Union Corporation	7.56
Baptist Union of Great Britain	7.56

BNP PARIBAS REAL ESTATE, 5 Aldermanbury Square, London, EC2V 7BP. Tel: 020 7338 4000. Internet: www.realestate.bnpparibas.com. Charity specialists: G A Cooke.

Corporation of the Sons of the Clergy	7.181

BRACKETTS, 27 High Street, Tunbridge Wells, Kent, TN1 1UU. Tel: 01892 533 733. Fax: 01892 512 201. E-mail: info@bracketts.co.uk. Internet: www.bracketts.co.uk.

SMB Charitable Trust (J)	7.619

BRAMLEYS, 14 St Georges Square, Huddersfield, West Yorkshire, HD1 1JF. Tel: 01484 530361. Fax: 01484 432318. E-mail: info@bramleys1.co.uk. Internet: www.bramleys.com.

Kirkwood Hospice	7.374

BROWN & CO, Market Chambers, 25-26 Tuesday Market Place, King's Lynn, Norfolk, PE30 1JJ. Tel: 01553 770771. Fax: 01553 770331. E-mail: kingslynn@brown-co.com. Internet: www.brown-co.com.

Geoffrey Watling Charity, The	7.272

BROWN & CO, The Atrium, St George's Street, Norwich, Norfolk, NR3 1AB. Tel: 01603 629871. Fax: 01603 616199. E-mail: norwich@brown-co.com. Internet: www.brown-co.com.

Norwich Consolidated Charities	7.471
Norwich Town Close Estate Charity	7.472

BRUTON KNOWLES, Greybrook House, 28 Brook Street, London, W1K 5DH. Tel: 0845 200 6489. E-mail: enquiries@brutonknowles.co.uk. Internet: www.brutonknowles.co.uk. Charity specialists: Paul Williams (Head of Third Sector).

Livability	7.391

BRUTON KNOWLES, Embassy House, 60 Church Street, Birmingham, West Midlands, B3 2DJ. Tel: 0845 200 6489. E-mail: enquiries@brutonknowles.co.uk. Internet: www.brutonknowles.co.uk. Charity specialists: Paul Williams (Head of Third Sector).

Harborne Parish Lands Charity	7.301
John Martin's Charity	7.360

BRUTON KNOWLES, Bisley House, Green Farm Business Park, Gloucester, Gloucestershire, GL2 4LY. Tel: 0845 200 6489. E-mail: enquiries@brutonknowles.co.uk. Internet: www.brutonknowles.co.uk. Charity specialists: Paul Williams (Head of Third Sector). Matthew Kitson.

Royal Mencap Society	7.566
Sylvanus Lysons Charity	7.667

BURNET WARE & GRAVES LTD, 13 Half Moon Lane, London, SE24 9JJ. Tel: 0207 733 1293. Fax: 0207 733 1255. E-mail: Michael.graves@burnetware.com. Internet: www.burnetware.com.

Notre Dame de France Trust	7.472
Poor Servants of the Mother of God	7.508

CAPITA SYMONDS LTD, 65 Greesham Street, London, EC2V 7NQ. Tel: 020 7709 4500. Fax: 020 7709 4501. Internet: www.capitaproperty.co.uk.

Corporation of Trinity House (J)	7.181

CARTER JONAS LLP, 5 & 6 Wood Street, Bath, Bath & North East Somerset, BA1 2JQ. Tel: 01225 747250. Internet: www.carterjonas.co.uk.

St John's Hospital (J)	7.645

CARTER JONAS LLP, 6-8 Hills Road, Cambridge, Cambridgeshire, CB2 1NH. Tel: 01223 368771. Fax: 01223 369950. E-mail: cambridge@carterjonas.co.uk. Internet: www.carterjonas.co.uk.

Ely Diocesan Board of Finance, The	7.231
Foundation of Edward Storey	7.260

CARTER JONAS LLP, Regent House, 13-15 Albert Street, Harrogate, North Yorkshire, HG1 1JX. Tel: 01423 523 423. Fax: 01423 521 373. Internet: www.carterjonas.co.uk.

Wheler Foundation, The	7.725

CARTER JONAS LLP, Anchor House, 269 Banbury Road, Oxford, Oxfordshire, OX2 7LL. Tel: 01865 511444. Fax: 01865 310653. Internet: www.carterjonas.co.uk. Charity specialists: G P Candy.

Doris Field Charitable Trust	7.207
Oxford Diocesan Board Finance (J)	7.487
Radcliffe Trust, The	7.523

CARTER JONAS LLP, South Pavilion, Sansaw Business Park, Hadnall, Shrewsbury, Shropshire, SY4 4AS. Tel: 01939 210171. E-mail: shrewsbury@carterjonas.co.uk. Internet: www.carterjones.co.uk.

Haberdashers' Benevolent Foundation, The	7.295
Haberdashers' Educational Foundation	7.295

CARTER JONAS LLP, 9-10 Jewry Street, Winchester, Hampshire, SO23 8RZ. Tel: 01962 833360. Internet: www.carterjones.co.uk.

Hospital of St Cross Foundation	7.321
St John's Winchester Charity	7.645
Winchester Diocesan Board of Finance	7.732

CASTLEFORD MANAGEMENT, 314-316 Bournemouth Road, Poole, Dorset, H14 9AP. Tel: 01202 757 050. Fax: 01202 768 997. E-mail: enquiries@castlefordmanage.co.uk. Internet: www.castlefordmanage.co.uk.

Institute of the Franciscan Missionaries	7.337

CAXTONS, 49-50 Windmill Street, Gravesend, Kent, DA12 1BG. Tel: 01474 537733. Internet: www.caxtons.com.

Colyer-Fergusson Charitable Trust	7.161

CB RICHARD ELLIS, Kingsley House, 1a Wimpole Street, London, W1G 0RE. Tel: 0207 182 2000. Fax: 0207 182 2001. Internet: www.cbre.co.uk.

Christ's Hospital Foundation (J)	7.144
English Province of our Lady of Charity	7.235

CBRE, The Quay, 30 Channel Way, Southampton, Hampshire, SO14 3TG. Tel: 023 8033 8811. Fax: 023 8033 6588. Internet: www.cbre.co.uk.

ACT Foundation	7.9
Royal College of Pathologists	7.557
Royal Free Hampstead Charitable Trust	7.560

CHAPMAN EMMETT CHARTERED SURVEYORS, 11 St James House, Bell Lane Office Village, Bell Lane, Little Chalfont, Buckinghamshire, HP6 6GL.

Housing Pathways Trust	7.322

CHAPMAN PETRIE, 12-14 Denman Street, London, W1D 7HJ. Tel: 020 7518 9400. E-mail: email@chapman-petrie.co.uk. Internet: www.chapman-petrie.co.uk.

Hampstead Wells & Campden Trust	7.299

CHEFFINS, Clifton House, 1-2 Clifton Road, Cambridge, Cambridgeshire, CB1 7EA. Tel: 01223 214214. Fax: 01223 271950. Internet: www.cheffins.co.uk.

Starling Family Charitable Trust, The	7.656

CLARKE & SIMPSON, Well Close Square, Framlingham, Suffolk, IP13 9DU. Tel: 01728 724200. Fax: 01728 724667. E-mail: email@clarkeandsimpson.co.uk. Internet: www.clarkeandsimpson.co.uk.

Harris (Belmont) Charity	7.303
St Edmundsbury & Ipswich Diocesan Bd of Fin	7.642

CLUTTONS, Portman House, 2 Portman Street, London, W1H 6DU. Tel: 020 7408 1010. Fax: 020 7629 3263. E-mail: info@cluttons.com. Internet: www.cluttons.com.

Breast Cancer Care	7.86
Campden Charities Trustee (J)	7.110
Congregation of the Passion Jesus Christ (J)	7.174
Corporation of Trinity House (J)	7.181
E Hayes Dashwood Foundation	7.218
John Lyon's Charity	7.359
Peter Stebbings Memorial Charity	7.500
Representative Body of the Church in Wales	7.532
Royal Commission for the 1851 Exhibition	7.558
St Olave's & St Saviour's Schools Foundation	7.652
Trust for London	7.688
Walcot Educational Foundation	7.711

CLUTTONS, Seacourt Tower, West Way, Oxford, Oxfordshire, OX2 0JJ. Tel: 01865 728 000. E-mail: oxford@cluttons.com. Internet: www.cluttons.com.

St Michael's and All Saints Charity	7.650

COLLIERS INTERNATIONAL, 12th Floor, Eleven Brindleyplace, 2 Brunswick Square, Brindleyplace, Birmingham, West Midlands, B1 2LP. Tel: 0121 265 7529. Fax: 0121 212 3010. E-mail: tarquin.Murray-Holgate@colliers.com. Internet: www.colliers.com.

College Estate Endowment Charity, The	7.160
Guild Estate Endowment	7.291
Stratford Upon Avon Town Trust	7.661

COLLINSON HALL, 9-11 Victoria Street, St Albans, Hertfordshire, AL1 3JJ. Tel: 01727 843222. Fax: 01727 835722. E-mail: stalbansmail@collinsonhall.co.uk. Internet: www.collinsonhall.co.uk.

Church Lands Charity	7.148

COLSTON & COLSTON, 1 Queen Square, Bath, Bath & North East Somerset, BA1 2HA. Tel: 01225 904704. Fax: 01225 904705. E-mail: info@colstonandcolston.com. Internet: www.colstonandcolston.com.

St John's Hospital (J)	7.645

CRANES CHARTERED SURVEYORS, 18, City Business Centre, Chichester, West Sussex. Tel: (01243) 783592. Fax: (01243) 530911.

F Glenister Woodger Trust, The	7.245

CURRELL RESIDENTIAL, 122/124 St John Street, London, EC1V 4JS. Tel: 020 7253 2533.

St Andrew Holborn Church Foundation (J)	7.636

CUSHMAN & WAKEFIELD LLP, 43-45 Portman Square, London, W1A 3BG. Tel: 020 7935 5000. Fax: 020 7152 5360. E-mail: @eur.cushwake.com. Internet: www.cushmanwakefield.com. Charity specialists: M Airey (Associate Director). Helen Basil (Media Relations Director).

Christ's Hospital Foundation (J)	7.144

DANIEL WATNEY, 165 Fleet Street, London, EC4A 2DW. Tel: 020 3077 3400. Fax: 020 3077 3477. E-mail: info@danielwatney.co.uk. Internet: www.danielwatney.co.uk. Charity specialists: Robert Thorling.

Carpenters' Company Charitable Trust	7.117
Dame Alice Owen's Foundation	7.192
Dulwich Estate	7.214
Estate Charity of William Hatcliffe	7.241
Richard Cloudesley's Charity	7.536
St John Ambulance (J)	7.644
Sutton's Hospital in Charterhouse (J)	7.666
YMCA London South West	7.746

DELOITTE REAL ESTATE, Athene Place, 66 Shoe Lane, London, EC4A 3BQ. Tel: 020 7007 9000. E-mail: chridavies@djdeloitte.co.uk. Internet: www.deloitterealestate.co.uk.

Christ's Hospital Foundation	7.144
Lawrence Atwell's Charity	7.380
Maudsley Charity (J)	7.416
Sir Andrew Judd Foundation	7.609

DRON & WRIGHT, 80 Cannon Street, London, EC4N 6HL. Tel: 020 7891 2345. Fax: 020 7891 2300. E-mail: droncity@donwright.co.uk. Internet: www.dronwright.co.uk.

University College London Hospitals Charity	7.700

DTZ DEBENHAM TIE LEUNG, 125 Old Broad Street, London, EC2N 2BQ. Tel: 020 3296 3000. Fax: 020 3296 3100. E-mail: chris.cobbold@dtz.com. Internet: www.dtz.com.

DTZ DEBENHAM TIE LEUNG, 10 Colmore Square, Birmingham, West Midlands, B4 6AJ. Tel: 0121 200 2050. Fax: 0121 200 3022. Internet: www.dtz.com.

St Martin's Trust	7.649
Sutton Coldfield Municipal Charities	7.666

DUNPHY & HAYES LIMITED, 164 Goldhawk Road, London, W12 8HJ.

Charity of Elizabeth Jane Jones, The	7.129

E C HARRIS, LONDON WC1, 34 York Way, London, N1 9AB.

Greenwich Royal Naval College Foundation (J)	7.288

EDWIN THOMPSON, 28 St John Street, Keswick, Cumbria, CA12 5AF. Tel: 01768 772988. Fax: 01768 774690. E-mail: ra.moss@edwin-thompson.co.uk. Internet: www.edwin-thompson.co.uk.

Cumbrian Community Foundation	7.189

FAREBROTHER, 27 Bream's Buildings, London, EC4A 1DZ. Tel: 020 7405 4545. Fax: 020 7404 4362. E-mail: enquiries@farebrother.net. Internet: www.farebrother.net.

Harpur Trust, The	7.302
Honourable Artillery Company	7.316
St Andrew Holborn Church Foundation (J)	7.636
Thomas Pocklington Trust	7.678

FINDERS KEEPERS, 226 Banbury Road, Oxford, Oxfordshire, OX2 7BY. Tel: 01865 556993.

Charity of Thomas Dawson (J)	7.130

FLETCHER KING, 61 Conduit Street, London, W1S 2GB. Tel: 020 7493 8400. Fax: 020 7491 2100. Internet: www.fletcherking.co.uk.

SEMTA	7.589
Sir John Cass's Foundation	7.611

FOWLER SANDFORD, 8 St James Street, Sheffield, South Yorkshire, S1 1XN. Tel: 0114 275 1441. Fax: 0114 275 4580. Charity specialists: N Robinson.

Sheffield Church Burgesses Trust	7.600

G V A GRIMLEY, 10 Stratton Street, London, W1J 8JR. Tel: 08449 02 03 04. Fax: 020 7911 2560. Internet: www.gva.co.uk.

Westway Trust	7.724

GEORGE ECKERT, 1-5 Summerland Gardens, London, N10 3QN. Tel: 020 8883 3232.

Foyle Foundation (J)	7.261

GERALD EVE, 72 Welbeck Street, London, W1G 0AY. Tel: 020 7493 3338. Fax: 020 7491 1825. E-mail: rmoir@geraldeve.com. Internet: www.geraldeve.com. Charity specialists: R A M Moir. S Chalwin. K Gibbs. J Orr. A Altman.

4 Charity Foundation	7.3
Barts and The London Charity (J)	7.59
Sisters of the Finding of Jesus	7.175
Greenwich Royal Naval College Foundation (J)	7.288
Morden College	7.433
Sisters of the Holy Cross	7.615
St Clement Danes Holborn Estate Charity	7.641

GOULD & CO, Hamilton House, Mabledon Place, London, WC1H 9BB. Tel: 020 7121 3310. Fax: 020 7388 1404. E-mail: lon@gouldco.co.uk. Internet: www.gouldco.co.uk.

Sightsavers International	7.608

GRAHAM & SIBBALD, 18 Newton Place, Glasgow, G3 7PY. Tel: 0141 332 1194. Fax: 0141 332 5914. E-mail: glasgowres@g-s.co.uk. Internet: www.g-s.co.uk.

Scottish Veterans Garden City Association Inc	7.593

GREENSLADE TAYLOR HUNT, 1 High Street, Chard, Somerset, TA20 1QF. Tel: 01460 238382. Fax: 01460 68266. Internet: www.gth.net.

Bath Wells Diocesan Board Finance	7.60

GRYPHON PROPERTY PARTNERS, 60 Gresham Street, London, EC2V 7BB. Tel: +44 (0)20 3440 9800.

Barts and The London Charity (J)	7.59

GVA, 10 Stratton Street, Mayfair, London, W1J 8JR. Tel: 08449 02 03 04. Fax: 020 7911 2560. Internet: www.gva.co.uk.

Diocese of Hexham and Newcastle (J)	7.201
RC Diocese of Hexham & Newcastle (J)	7.543

GVA, 3 Brindleyplace, Birmingham, West Midlands, B1 2JB. Tel: 08449 02 03 04. Fax: 0121 609 8314. Internet: www.gva.co.uk.

Nuffield Health	7.474

HALLS, 1 Kings Court, Charles Hastings Way, Worcester, Worcestershire, WR5 1JR. Tel: 01905 611066. E-mail: info@hallsworcester.com. Internet: www.hallsestateagents.co.uk.

Diocese of Worcester	7.738

HINDWOODS HUNTER PAYNE, 1 Charlton Road, Blackheath, West Midlands, SE3 7EY. Tel: 020 8858 3377. Internet: www.hhp-property.co.uk.

Spurgeons	7.635

HML SHAW & CO, First Floor, 9-11 The Quadrant, Richmond, North Yorkshire, TW9 1BP. Tel: 020 8948 3211. Fax: 020 8948 8734. E-mail: info@hmlshaw.com. Internet: www.hmlshaw.com. Charity specialists: M R Lee.

Richmond Charities' Almshouses	7.537
Richmond Church Charity Estates	7.537
Richmond Parish Lands Charity	7.538

HOOK MASON, 41 Widemarsh Street, Hereford, Herefordshire, HR4 9EA. Tel: 01432 352299. Fax: 01432 352272. E-mail: info@hookmason.co.uk. Internet: www.hookmason.co.uk.

Hereford Diocesan Board Finance	7.309

INGLEBY TRICE, 10 Foster Lane, London, EC2V 6HR. Tel: 020 7029 3610. Fax: 020 7900 6776. E-mail: enquiries@inglebytrice.co.uk. Internet: www.inglebytrice.co.uk.

Sutton's Hospital in Charterhouse (J)	7.666
USPG	7.702

INNES ENGLAND, 2 The Triangle, Enterprise Way, NG2 Business Park, Nottingham, Nottinghamshire, NG2 1AE. Tel: 0115 924 3243. Fax: 0115 924 2310.
E-mail: nottingham@innes-england.com.
Internet: www.innes-england.com.

Congregation of the Passion Jesus Christ (J)	7.174

J T S PARTNERSHIP LLP, Number One, The Drive, Great Warley, Brentwood, Essex, CM13 3DJ. Tel: 0127 722 4664. Fax: 0127 721 5487. Internet: www.jtspartnership.co.uk.

Institute of Our Lady of Mercy, The	7.336

JAS MARTIN & CO, 8 Bank Street, Lincoln, Lincolnshire, LN2 1DS. Tel: 01522 510234. Fax: 01522 511274.
E-mail: mailbox@jasmartin.co.uk.
Internet: www.jasmartin.co.uk.

Lincoln Diocesan Trust Board Finance Ltd	7.389

JHWALTER, 1 Mint Lane, Lincoln, Lincolnshire, LN1 1UD. Tel: 01522 526 526. Fax: 01522 512 720. E-mail: info@jhwalter.co.uk.
Internet: www.jhwalter.co.uk.

Bransby Horses	7.85

JOHN ARKWRIGHT & CO., 115 Mount Street, London, W1K 3NQ. Tel: 020 7495 7090.

Blagrave Trust, The	7.74

JONES LANG LASALLE, 30 Warwick Street, London, W1B 5NH. Tel: 020 7493 4933. Fax: 020 7248 0088.
Internet: www.joneslanglasalle.co.uk.

Drapers Charities Pooling Scheme	7.211

JONES LANG LASALLE, 40 Berkeley Square, Bristol, BS8 1HU. Tel: 0117 927 6691. Fax: 0117 929 9669.
Internet: www.joneslanglasalle.co.uk.
Charity specialists: E W Cussen - specialist area: Development and Planning.

St John's Hospital (J)	7.645
St Mary Redcliffe Vestry	7.650
Summerfield Charitable Trust	7.664

KEMSLEY WHITELEY & FERRIS, 8 Station Road, Romford, Essex, RM2 6AG. Tel: 01708 766 733. Fax: 01708 741 633.
E-mail: property@kwf.co.uk.
Internet: www.kwf.co.uk.

Ormiston Trust	7.484

KING STURGE LLP, 30, Warwick Street, London, W1B 5NH. Tel: 020 7493 4933. Fax: 020 7087 5555. Internet: www.kingsturge.co.uk.

Oxford Diocesan Board Finance (J)	7.487

KING WILKINSON & COMPANY, 15 Barnfield Road, Exeter, Devon, EX1 1RR. Tel: 01392 255884. Fax: 01392 422697.
E-mail: rwm@kingwilkinson.co.uk.
Internet: www.kingwilkinson.co.uk.

Hospiscare	7.320
Norman Family Charitable Trust	7.464

KINNEY GREEN, 27-32 Old Jewry, London, EC2R 8DQ. Tel: 020 7643 1500. Fax: 020 7643 1511. Internet: www.kinneygreen.com.

Asthma UK	7.47

KNIGHT FRANK LLP, 55 Baker Street, London, W1U 8AN. Tel: 020 7861 1003. Fax: 020 7861 1363. E-mail: emma.cleugh@knightfrank.com.
Internet: www.knightfrank.co.uk/residential/institutional.

Duke of Edinburgh's Award	7.214
Royal National Institute of Blind People	7.566

KNIGHT FRANK LLP, 1 Colmore Row, Birmingham, West Midlands, B3 2BJ. Tel: 0121 200 2220. Internet: www.knightfrank.co.uk.

Birmingham Diocesan Board Finance	7.71

LACY SCOTT AND KNIGHT, 10 Risbygate Street, Bury St Edmunds, Suffolk, IP33 3AA. Tel: 01284 748600.
E-mail: www.lskauctioncentre.co.uk.

Felix Thornley Cobold Agricultural Trust	7.251

LAMBERT SMITH HAMPTON, Midland House, West Way, Botley, Oxford, Oxfordshire, OX2 0PH. Tel: 01865 200 244. Fax: 01865 204 822. Internet: www.lsh.co.uk.

Charity of Thomas Dawson (J)	7.130

LAMBERTS, 387 City Road, London, EC1V 1NA. Tel: 020 7278 8191. Fax: 020 7837 5790.
E-mail: post@lambertsurv.co.uk.
Internet: www.lambertsurv.co.uk.

Bishopsgate Foundation	7.73

LASALLE INVESTMENT MANAGEMENT, One Curzon Street, London, W1J 5HD. Tel: 020 7852 4000.

Henry Smith Charity (J)	7.309

LESTER HARRISON ASSOCIATES, 15 Bolton Street, London, W1J 8BJ. Tel: 020 7629 4383. Internet: www.lesterharrison.co.uk.

Campden Charities Trustee (J)	7.110

LEVY REAL ESTATE LLP, Nuffield House, 41- 46 Piccadilly, London, W1J 0DS. Tel: 020 7747 0160. E-mail: paul.krendel@levyllp.co.uk.
Internet: www.levyllp.co.uk.

Foyle Foundation (J)	7.261

LONDON CLANCY, The Courtyard, 15 Winchester Road, Basingstoke, Hampshire, RG21 8UE.

Elrahma Charity Trust	7.231

LOVEITTS, Warwick Row, Coventry, West Midlands, CV1 1DY. Tel: 024 7622 8111. Fax: 024 7622 7187.
Internet: www.loveitts.co.uk.
Charity specialists: D Robinson.

Coventry Freemen's Charity	7.184
General Charity (Coventry)	7.270

LUBBOCK PROPERTY MANAGEMENT, The Old Vicarage, 107 Upper Tulse Hill, London, SW2 2RD.

SMB Charitable Trust (J)	7.619

MARTIN BLAKE ASSOCIATES LTD, 4 Miles's Buildings, Bath, Bath & North East Somerset, BA1 2QS. Tel: 01225 428977.

St John's Hospital (J)	7.645

MAUNDER TAYLOR, 1320 High Street, Whetstone, London, N20 9HP.

Sutton's Hospital in Charterhouse (J)	7.666

METRUS LIMITED, 8 - 10 Hallam Street, London, W1W 6NS. Tel: 020 7631 0550. Fax: 020 7636 3076.
E-mail: info@metrus.co.uk.
Internet: www.metrus.co.uk.

Benesco Charity	7.65
Charles Wolfson Charitable Trust	7.131

MILNER ASSOCIATES LTD, 4 St Georges House, Vernon Gate, Derby, Derbyshire, DE1 1UQ.

Liversage Trust	7.393

MONTAGU EVANS, 5 Bolton Street, London, W1J 8BA. Tel: 020 7493 4002. Fax: 020 7312 7548. Internet: www.montagu-evans.co.uk.

Age UK	7.17
British Heart Foundation	7.93
Central Young Men's Christian Association	7.123
Children's Society	7.142
FIA Foundation for Automobile & Society	7.252
NGT Foundation	7.461
Royal British Legion	7.554
Royal Horticultural Society	7.561
St John Ambulance (J)	7.644

MOTCOMB ESTATES, 4th Floor, Millbank Tower, 21-24 Millbank, London, SW1P 4QP.

Reuben Foundation	7.534

NORTHERN HOMES AND ESTATES LIMITED, Saville Chambers, 5 North Street, Newcastle upon Tyne, Tyne and Wear, NE1 8DF. Tel: 0191 232 7940.
Charity specialists: Ms S Penman.

William Leech Charity	7.730

PENNYCUICK COLLINS, 9 The Square, 111 Broad Street, Birmingham, West Midlands, B15 1AS. Tel: 0121 665 4150. Fax: 0121 665 4190. E-mail: info@pennycuick.co.uk.
Internet: www.pennycuick.co.uk.

Henry Barber Trust	7.308

PENRITH FARMERS' & KIDD'S PLC, Agricultural Hall, Skirsgill, Penrith, Cumbria, CA11 0DN.

Carlisle Diocesan Board of Finance (J)	7.116

PHILIP JENNINGS, 12 Chapel Row, Queen Square, Bath, Bath & North East Somerset, BA1 1HN. Tel: 01225 444070. Fax: 01225 444025. Internet: www.philip-jennings.co.uk.

St John's Hospital (J)	7.645

REEVES & PARTNERS, 2 Euston Place, Leamington Spa, Warwickshire, CV32 4LE. Tel: 01926 427 100. Fax: 01926 430 011. E-mail: leam@reevesandpartners.com.
Internet: www.reevesandpartners.com.

Birmingham Diocesan Trust	7.71
Father Hudson's Society	7.249

ROBERT POWELL & CO, Birmingham, West Midlands, B15 1PL.

University Hospital Birmingham Charities	7.700

RUMBALL SEDGWICK, 58 St Peters Street, St Albans, Hertfordshire, AL1 3HQ. Tel: 01727 852384. Fax: 01727 843177.
Internet: www.rumballsedgwick.co.uk.
Charity specialists: N Clarke.

St Albans Diocesan Board Finance (J)	7.635

SANDERSON WEATHERALL, 25 Wellington Street, Leeds, West Yorkshire, LS1 4WG. Tel: 0800 122 3050.
E-mail: enquiries@sw.co.uk. Internet: sw.co.uk.

Ripon Diocesan Board of Finance	7.539

SANDERSON WEATHERALL, 22-24 Grey Street, Newcastle upon Tyne, Tyne and Wear, NE1 6AD. Tel: 0191 261 2681. Fax: 0191 261 4761. E-mail: david.downing@sw.co.uk.
Internet: www.sw.co.uk.

Diocese of Hexham and Newcastle (J)	7.201
Leeds Diocesan Trust	7.382
RC Diocese of Hexham & Newcastle (J)	7.543

SANDERSON WEATHERALL, Robert House, Westpoint Road, Stockton-on-Tees, TS17 6BA. Tel: 0800 122 3050. Internet: www.sw.co.uk.

British & Foreign School Society, The	7.91

SAVILLS LTD, Olympic House, Doddington Road Doddington Road, Lincoln, Lincolnshire, LN6 3SE.

Corporation of Trinity House (J)	7.181

SAVILLS (UK) LTD, 20 Grosvenor Hill, London, W1K 3HQ. Tel: 020 7499 8644. Fax: 020 7495 3773. E-mail: westend@savills.com.
Internet: www.savills.co.uk.

Maudsley Charity (J)	7.416

SAVILLS (UK) LTD, Edgar House, 17 George Street, Bath, Bath & North East Somerset, BA1 2EN. Tel: 01225 474 500.
Internet: www.savills.co.uk.

St John's Hospital (J)	7.645

SIDLEYS, 6 King Edward Street, Oxford, Oxfordshire, OX1 4JL. Tel: 01865 726 016. Fax: 01865 791 493. Internet: sidleys-charteredsurveyor.co.uk.

Oxford Diocesan Board Finance (J)   7.487

SMART PROPERTY SOLUTIONS, 41 Havelock Road, Hastings, East Sussex, TN34 1BE. Tel: 01424 712555. Fax: 01424 717003. E-mail: info@smartpropertyonline.co.uk. Internet: www.smartpropertyonline.co.uk.

Magdalen Lasher Charity   7.406

SMITHS GORE, 17-18 Old Bond Street, London, W1S 4PT. Tel: 020 7409 9490. Fax: 020 7290 1617. Internet: www.smithsgore.co.uk.

Guy's & St Thomas' Charity   7.293

SMITHS GORE, 64 Warwick Road, Carlisle, Cumbria, CA1 1DR. Tel: 01228 527586.

Carlisle Diocesan Board of Finance (J)   7.116

SMITHS GORE, 26 Coniscliffe Road, Darlington, County Durham, DL3 7JX. Tel: 01325 462966. Fax: 01325 381139. E-mail: darlington@smithsgore.co.uk. Internet: www.smithsgore.co.uk.

Durham Diocesan Board of Finance, The   7.216

SMITHS GORE, 2-3 Sherbrook House, Swan Mews, Lichfield, Staffordshire, WS13 6TU. Tel: 01543 251221. Fax: 01543 251223. E-mail: lichfield@smithsgore.co.uk. Internet: www.smithsgore.co.uk.

Derby Diocesan Board Finance Ltd   7.198

SMITHS GORE, 42 High Street, Marlborough, Wiltshire, SN8 1HQ. Tel: 01672 529050. Fax: 01672 529051. E-mail: marlborough@smithsgore.co.uk. Internet: www.smithsgore.co.uk.

Salisbury Diocesan Board Finance   7.583

SMITHS GORE, Stuart House, City Road, Peterborough, PE1 1QF. Tel: 01733 567231. Fax: 01733 894649. E-mail: Peterborough@smithsgore.co.uk. Internet: www.smithsgore.co.uk.

Henry Smith Charity (J)   7.309
Nene Park Trust   7.456

SMITHS GORE, 23 Kings Hill Avenue, West Malling, Kent, ME19 4UA. Tel: 01732 879050. Fax: 01732 879051. E-mail: maidstone@smithsgore.co.uk. Internet: www.smithsgore.co.uk.

Roch. Diocesan Society & Bd of Fin   7.542

SPENCER BIRCH, 8 Claredon Street, Nottingham, Nottinghamshire, NG1 5HQ. Tel: 0115 941 3678. Fax: 0115 950 6235. Internet: www.spencerbirch.co.uk.

Notts Roman Catholic Diocesan Trustees   7.473

SPENCERS DRUCE LIMITED, 19 De Montfort Street, Leicester, Leicestershire, LE1 7GE.

Age UK Leicestershire & Rutland   7.18

STANLEY HICKS, 52 Bow Lane, London, EC4M 9ET. Tel: +44 (020) 7248 0241. Fax: +44 (020) 7489 1380. E-mail: mike.greensmith@stanleyhicks.co.uk. Internet: www.stanleyhicks.co.uk.

Roman Catholic Diocese of Southwark   7.544
St Andrew Holborn Church Foundation (J)   7.636

STILES HAROLD WILLIAMS, One Jubilee Street, Brighton, Sussex, BN1 1GE. Internet: www.shw.co.uk.

Whitgift Foundation   7.726

STRETTONS CHARTERED SURVEYORS, 1-3 Sun Street, London, EC2A 2EP. Tel: 020 7375 1801. E-mail: btobin@strettons.co.uk. Internet: www.strettons.co.uk.

STRUTT & PARKER, Coval Hall, Chelmsford, Essex, CM1 2QF. Tel: 01245 258201. Fax: 01245 254685. E-mail: chelmsford@struttandparker.com. Internet: www.struttandparker.com.

Chelmsford Diocesan Board Finance   7.136
Elizabeth Finn Care   7.230
New England Company   7.457

STRUTT & PARKER, 201 High Street, Lewes, Sussex, BN7 2NR. Tel: 01273 475411. Fax: 01273 478995. E-mail: lewes@struttandparker.co.uk. Internet: www.struttandparker.com. Charity specialists: Kate Moisson.

Ian Askew Charitable Trust   7.326
Titsey Foundation   7.681

STRUTT & PARKER, 41 Milford Street, Salisbury, Wiltshire, SP1 2BP. Tel: 01722 328741. Fax: 01722 411259. E-mail: salisbury@struttandparker.co.uk. Internet: www.struttandparker.com.

National Rifle Association   7.451
St John's Hospital (J)   7.645

SUNDERLANDS & THOMPSONS LLP, Offa House, St Peters Square, Hereford, Herefordshire, HR1 2PQ. Tel: 01432 356161. Fax: 01432 352954. E-mail: enquiries@st-hereford.co.uk. Internet: www.st-hereford.co.uk.

Eveson Charitable Trust   7.243

THOMAS CHARLES PROPERTY MANAGEMENT, 160 Castle Road, Bedford, Bedfordshire, MK40 3SW. Tel: 01234 290990. Fax: 01234 301301. Internet: www.tcea.co.uk.

Panacea Society   7.490

THOMPSON WILSON, 1 Amersham Hill, High Wycombe, Buckinghamshire, HP13 6NQ. Tel: 01494 474 234.

Roger Raymond Charitable Trust   7.542

VAIL WILLIAMS LLP, 540 Thames Valley Park, Reading, Berkshire, RG6 1RA. Tel: 0118 909 7400. Fax: 0118 909 7433. Internet: www.vailwilliams.com.

Rufford Foundation, The   7.577

WALKER SINGLETON, Property House, Lister Lane, Halifax, West Yorkshire, HX1 5AS. Tel: 01422 430000. Fax: 01422 430010.

United Reformed Church (Yorkshire) Trust   7.697

WALTER & RANDALL, Beaufort Court, Sir Thomas Longely Road, Rochester, Kent, ME2 2FA. Tel: 01634 841233. Fax: 01634 830580. Charity specialists: P Thomas.

R.Watts&Rochester CityAlmshouseCharities   7.536

WALTON GOODLAND LTD, 10 Lowther Street, Carlisle, Cumbria, CA3 8DA.

Carlisle Diocesan Board of Finance (J)   7.116

WORKMAN, Alliance House, 12 Caxton Street, London, SW1H 0QS. Tel: 020 7227 6200. Fax: 020 7227 6204. E-mail: info.london@workman.co.uk. Internet: www.workman.co.uk.

Barts and The London Charity (J)   7.59

STOCKBROKERS AND THEIR CHARITY CLIENTS

CHARLES STANLEY & CO. LIMITED, 25 Luke Street, London, EC2A 4AR. **Tel: 020 7739 8200. Fax: 020 7739 7798.**
Internet: www.charles-stanley.co.uk.

Actors' Benevolent Fund	7.13
Society of the Helpers of the Holy Souls	7.624
Spiritualists National Union	7.632

CUNNINGHAM COATES, The Linenhall, 32-38 Linenhall Street, Belfast, County Antrim, BT2 8BG. **Tel: 028 9072 3000. Fax: 028 9072 3001.**
E-mail: gordon.mcdougall@ccstockbrokers.com . Internet: www.ccstockbrokers.com.
Charity specialists: Christopher O'Neill.

Action Mental Health	7.11

DEUTSCHE BANK PRIVATE WEALTH MANAGEMENT, 130 St Vincent Street, Glasgow, G5 5SE. **Tel: 0141 227 2400. Fax: 0141 221 5962.**

Strathcarron Hospice	7.661

NEWTON INVESTMENT MANAGEMENT LIMITED, 160 Queen Victoria Street, London, EC4V 4LA. **Tel: 0800 917 6594.**
E-mail: charities@newton.co.uk.
Internet: www.newton.co.uk/charities.

Diocese of Hexham and Newcastle	7.201

CHARITY

FINANCIALS

The Top 3000 Charities 2016, now in its 24th edition
is the essential resource for those who work
for or with UK charities.

Our detailed Charity Financials section provides insight
into the success of top charities, and enables
easy comparison between charities.

Each profile includes:
A 5-year financial perspective
Charity aims, together with grant giving status
Named key personnel
Adviser details

The following pages are ONLY SAMPLES
of what can be found in the full edition.

For more information on the full edition of
Top 3000 Charities 2016,
or if you would like to place an order, please visit
www.wlrstore.com/charity-financials/top-3000-charities.aspx

Alternatively please email customerservices@wilmingtonplc.com
or call us on 020 7549 2571.

DOGS TRUST

INC 81 / £84.7m **EXP** 80 / £83.7m **FUNDS** 148 / £130m

ALTERNATIVE NAMES: National Canine Defence League. **AIMS:** Dogs Trust is working towards the day when all dogs can enjoy a happy life, free from the threat of unnecessary destruction. **GRANT MAKER:** No. **EXP ANALYSIS:** (31 Dec 14) Animal life - 100%.

EXECUTIVES: J Monteith (df); N Daniel (mkd); C Ferris. **EMPLOYEES:** 743 (663). **PAY:** £21.9m (£18.4m). **ADDRESS:** 17 Wakley Street, London, EC1V 7RQ. Tel: 020 7837 0006. Fax: 020 7713 8151. **INTERNET:** www.dogstrust.org.uk. **CC NO:** 227523. **OSCR NO:** SC037843.

AUDITORS: BDO LLP, London; audit fee £47k, non-audit fee £13k.

year ended 31 December		2010	2011	2012	2013	2014
legacies	£m	18.5	18.5	20.0	20.1	24.2
other voluntary income	£m	37.7	41.5	45.1	49.7	53.8
activities gen funds	£m	3.02	3.25	3.57	3.95	4.22
investment income	£m	1.38	1.69	2.16	1.65	1.36
charitable activities	£m	1.10	1.06	1.13	1.13	1.14
other incoming	£m	0.02	0.01	0.02	0.02	0.03
TOTAL INCOME	£m	61.7	66.0	72.0	76.6	84.7
voluntary costs	£m	18.1	20.4	21.4	21.2	23.4
cost generating funds	£m	1.38	1.64	1.80	2.23	2.51
investment costs	£m	0.12	0.11	0.10	0.18	0.19
charitable exp	£m	34.5	37.1	41.6	47.3	54.4
grant expenditure	£m	-	-	-	-	2.84
governance	£m	0.31	0.32	0.33	0.34	0.41
other expenditure	£m	0.39	-	-	-	-
TOTAL EXPENDITURE	£m	54.9	59.6	65.2	71.2	83.7
gains revaluations	£m	2.76	(2.30)	2.04	5.08	0.66
NET INCREASE IN FUNDS	£m	9.58	4.11	8.82	10.4	1.73
land build oth fxd	£m	35.8	40.3	43.9	50.0	51.4
investments	£m	64.4	61.3	66.1	70.9	71.6
stock debtors cash	£m	10.2	12.8	12.5	13.9	14.4
liabilities	£m	5.34	5.19	4.45	6.33	7.27
pension liability	£m					
TOTAL FUNDS	£m	105	109	118	128	130

DOLLOND CHARITABLE TRUST

INC £1.35m **EXP** £2.20m **FUNDS** 505 / £41.5m

AIMS: To or for such charitable purpose or purposes and or for such charitable institution or institutions in the UK or elsewhere as the Trustees in their absolute discretion shall from time to time determine. **GRANT MAKER:** Yes. **EXP ANALYSIS:** (31 Mar 15) Jewish general - 100%.

EXECUTIVES: B Dollond (s). **ADDRESS:** 22 Russell Gardens, London, NW11 9NL. Tel: 020 8346 6446. Fax: 020 8349 3990. **FOUNDED:** 1986. **CONST:** Trust. **CC NO:** 293459.

AUDITORS: FMCB, London; audit fee £6k. **BANKERS:** Barclays. **LEGAL ADVISERS:** Goodman Derrick LLP, London. **INV MANAGERS:** Canaccord Genuity Wealth Management, London; Credit Suisse Asset Management Limited, London.

year ended 31 March		2011	2012	2013	2014	2015
legacies	£m	-	-	-	-	-
other voluntary income	£m	~	0.55	0.02	0.41	-
activities gen funds	£m	-	-	-	-	-
investment income	£m	0.59	0.59	1.05	1.42	1.35
charitable activities	£m	-	-	-	-	-
other incoming	£m	-	-	-	-	-
TOTAL INCOME	£m	0.59	1.13	1.08	1.83	1.35
voluntary costs	£m	-	-	-	-	-
cost generating funds	£m	-	-	-	-	-
investment costs	£m	0.02	0.02	0.10	0.23	0.31
charitable exp	£m	0.04	0.04	0.03	0.03	0.02
grant expenditure	£m	2.28	2.09	1.66	1.90	1.85
governance	£m	0.02	0.02	0.02	0.02	0.02
other expenditure	£m	-	-	-	-	-
TOTAL EXPENDITURE	£m	2.37	2.17	1.81	2.17	2.20
gains revaluations	£m	2.57	(1.91)	3.38	0.39	3.67
NET INCREASE IN FUNDS	£m	0.78	(2.94)	2.65	0.04	2.81
land build oth fxd	£m					
investments	£m	38.2	33.8	36.6	37.9	40.8
stock debtors cash	£m	0.71	2.20	2.05	0.84	0.76
liabilities	£m	0.05	0.02	0.03	0.11	0.11
pension liability	£m					
TOTAL FUNDS	£m	38.9	36.0	38.6	38.6	41.5

DOLPHIN SQUARE CHARITABLE FOUNDATION, THE

INC 821 / £10.9m **EXP** £2.05m **FUNDS** 125 / £149m

GRANT MAKER: No. **EXP ANALYSIS:** (31 Mar 15) Housing and accommodation general - 100%.

EXECUTIVES: J Gooding (ce). **EMPLOYEES:** 8 (10). **PAY:** £0.63m (£0.65m). **ADDRESS:** 4th Floor, 11 Belgrave Road, London, SW1V 1RB. Tel: 020 3667 7870. Fax: 020 3667 7877. **INTERNET:** www.dolphinsquarefoundation.com. **CC NO:** 1110090.

AUDITORS: Crowe Clark Whitehill LLP, London; audit fee £21k. **LEGAL ADVISERS:** Devonshires, London; Nabarro, London; Stone King LLP, London; Wragge Lawrence Graham & Co, Birmingham. **INV MANAGERS:** Cazenove Charities, London.

year ended 31 March		2011	2012	2013	2014	2015
legacies	£m	-	-	-	-	-
other voluntary income	£m	2.00	5.00	0.30	28.8	0.62
activities gen funds	£m	-	-	-	-	-
investment income	£m	2.28	2.78	3.07	3.04	2.27
charitable activities	£m	-	-	-	-	-
other incoming	£m	-	-	-	-	8.02
TOTAL INCOME	£m	4.28	7.78	3.37	31.8	10.9
voluntary costs	£m	-	-	-	-	-
cost generating funds	£m	-	-	-	-	-
investment costs	£m	0.15	0.09	0.06	0.02	0.09
charitable exp	£m	0.64	0.72	1.17	1.33	1.63
grant expenditure	£m	0.03	0.05	0.07	0.03	0.08
governance	£m	0.13	0.16	0.14	0.14	0.14
other expenditure	£m	-	-	0.03	-	0.09
TOTAL EXPENDITURE	£m	0.95	1.02	1.47	1.52	2.05
gains revaluations	£m	(0.46)	(1.20)	(0.54)	(0.31)	(0.36)
NET INCREASE IN FUNDS	£m	2.88	5.56	1.36	30.0	8.51
land build oth fxd	£m	0.01	3.66	6.28	52.4	92.6
investments	£m	99.1	92.0	82.4	54.2	28.9
stock debtors cash	£m	4.78	13.7	22.1	34.8	30.5
liabilities	£m	0.49	0.38	0.39	1.08	3.08
pension liability	£m					
TOTAL FUNDS	£m	103	109	110	140	149

DOMINICAN COUNCIL

INC £2.77m **EXP** £2.53m **FUNDS** 1124 / £17.8m

ALTERNATIVE NAMES: English Province of the Order of Preachers, The. **GRANT MAKER:** No. **EXP ANALYSIS:** (30 Sep 14) Roman Catholics - 100%.

CONNECTED CHARITIES: The Leitch Trust; The Hoper-Dixon Trust. **BRANCHES:** 7.

EMPLOYEES: 23 (22). **PAY:** £0.27m (£0.21m). **ADDRESS:** Blackfriars, St Giles, Oxford, Oxfordshire, OX1 3LY. Tel: 01865 288231. **INTERNET:** english.op.org. **FOUNDED:** 1930. **CONST:** Trust. **CC NO:** 231192. **OSCR NO:** SC039062.

AUDITORS: RSM, London; audit fee £23k. **BANKERS:** Royal Bank of Scotland Group plc, The. **LEGAL ADVISERS:** Farrer & Co LLP, London. **INV MANAGERS:** BlackRock, London.

year ended 30 September		2010	2011	2012	2013	2014
legacies	£m	0.23	0.18	0.04	0.85	0.06
other voluntary income	£m	1.08	0.98	0.91	1.05	1.14
activities gen funds	£m	0.14	0.15	0.17	0.16	0.17
investment income	£m	0.33	0.36	0.36	0.37	0.39
charitable activities	£m	0.95	0.98	1.08	1.13	0.98
other incoming	£m	0.08	~	~	0.01	0.02
TOTAL INCOME	£m	2.82	2.65	2.56	3.57	2.77
voluntary costs	£m	~	0.01	0.01	0.01	0.01
cost generating funds	£m	-	-	-	-	-
investment costs	£m	0.04	0.05	0.06	0.05	0.06
charitable exp	£m	2.14	2.21	2.23	2.48	2.42
grant expenditure	£m	-	-	-	-	-
governance	£m	0.05	0.03	0.03	0.03	0.03
other expenditure	£m	-	-	-	-	-
TOTAL EXPENDITURE	£m	2.23	2.29	2.32	2.56	2.53
gains revaluations	£m	0.40	(0.52)	0.77	0.67	0.45
NET INCREASE IN FUNDS	£m	0.99	(0.17)	1.01	1.69	0.69
land build oth fxd	£m	4.73	5.13	5.72	5.63	5.61
investments	£m	10.0	9.29	9.79	10.9	12.2
stock debtors cash	£m	0.33	0.48	0.44	1.03	0.47
liabilities	£m	0.44	0.46	0.51	0.41	0.42
pension liability	£m					
TOTAL FUNDS	£m	14.6	14.4	15.4	17.1	17.8

INC 723 / £12.2m   EXP 990 / £8.65m   FUNDS 446 / £48.3m

DOMINICAN SISTERS (THIRD ORDER) CONGREGATION OF NEWCASTLE NATAL

ALTERNATIVE NAMES: Sisters of the Third Order of St Dominic, Congregation of St Catherine. **AIMS:** The advancement of the Roman Catholic Religion. **GRANT MAKER:** No. **EXP ANALYSIS:** (31 Dec 14) Roman Catholics - 100%.

EXECUTIVES: R D Bolton (df); Sr M Tuohy. **EMPLOYEES:** 347 (345). **PAY:** £5.16m (£5.47m). **ADDRESS:** Rosary Priory, 93 Elstree Road, Bushey Heath, Bushey, Watford, Bushey, Hertfordshire, WD23 4EE. Tel: 020 8950 6065. Fax: 020 8950 7991. **INTERNET:** www.dominicansisters.org.uk. **CC NO:** 233236.

AUDITORS: BDO LLP, London; audit fee £30k.

year ended 31 December		2010	2011	2012	2013	2014
legacies	£m	0.07	-	-	-	-
other voluntary income	£m	1.10	0.88	0.83	0.74	0.78
activities gen funds	£m	-	-	-	-	-
investment income	£m	1.00	1.13	1.28	1.29	1.28
charitable activities	£m	7.17	7.59	7.37	7.07	6.47
other incoming	£m	1.18	0.35	2.95	0.05	3.69
TOTAL INCOME	£m	10.5	9.95	12.4	9.16	12.2
voluntary costs	£m	-	-	-	-	-
cost generating funds	£m	-	-	-	-	-
investment costs	£m	0.04	0.05	0.05	0.06	0.06
charitable exp	£m	9.88	9.41	9.08	9.00	8.56
grant expenditure	£m	-	-	-	-	-
governance	£m	0.13	0.03	0.03	0.03	0.03
other expenditure	£m	-	-	-	-	-
TOTAL EXPENDITURE	£m	10.1	9.48	9.16	9.09	8.65
gains revaluations	£m	2.20	(1.05)	1.42	2.46	0.46
NET INCREASE IN FUNDS	£m	2.65	(0.59)	4.69	2.53	4.03
land build oth fxd	£m	7.05	6 17	6.23	5.79	4.70
investments	£m	28.3	28.0	33.0	34.8	34.3
stock debtors cash	£m	3.96	4.51	3.91	5.01	10.9
liabilities	£m	1.72	1.63	1.48	1.39	1.69
pension liability	£m	-	-	-	-	-
TOTAL FUNDS	£m	37.6	37.0	41.7	44.2	48.3

INC £1.10m   EXP £0.54m   FUNDS 1175 / £16.8m

DONATING CHARITY LIMITED

AIMS: To foster and assist and to promote the activities of any charitable or educational institutions professing and teaching traditional Judaism and to benefit poor pious people. **GRANT MAKER:** Yes. **EXP ANALYSIS:** (31 Mar 15) Grantmaking to a wide variety of charitable causes - 100%.

ADDRESS: 121 Princes Park Avenue, London, NW11 0JS. **FOUNDED:** 1961. **CONST:** Company. **CO REG NO:** 873763. **CC NO:** 247490.

AUDITORS: Cohen Arnold, London; audit fee £9k.

year ended 31 March		2011	2012	2013	2014	2015
legacies	£m	-	-	-	-	-
other voluntary income	£m	-	-	0.10	-	-
activities gen funds	£m	-	-	-	-	-
investment income	£m	0.97	0.97	1.07	1.01	1.10
charitable activities	£m	-	-	-	-	-
other incoming	£m	-	-	-	-	-
TOTAL INCOME	£m	0.97	0.97	1.17	1.01	1.10
voluntary costs	£m	-	-	-	-	-
cost generating funds	£m	-	-	-	-	-
investment costs	£m	0.04	0.07	0.05	0.31	0.06
charitable exp	£m	-	-	-	-	-
grant expenditure	£m	0.37	0.68	0.52	0.43	0.47
governance	£m	0.01	0.01	0.01	0.01	0.01
other expenditure	£m	-	-	-	-	-
TOTAL EXPENDITURE	£m	0.42	0.76	0.59	0.75	0.54
gains revaluations	£m	0.02	~	1.54	0.06	0.07
NET INCREASE IN FUNDS	£m	0.57	0.21	2.12	0.33	0.62
land build oth fxd	£m	-	-	-	-	-
investments	£m	11.4	11.4	13.0	13.0	13.1
stock debtors cash	£m	2.27	2.49	3.11	3.46	4.07
liabilities	£m	0.22	0.23	0.27	0.35	0.41
pension liability	£m	-	-	-	-	-
TOTAL FUNDS	£m	13.5	13.7	15.8	16.1	16.8

INC £0.96m   EXP £3.28m   FUNDS 1611 / £11.8m

DONCASTER & BASSETLAW HOSPITALS NHS TRUST

AIMS: NHS and Health Authority Trust. **GRANT MAKER:** Yes. **EXP ANALYSIS:** (31 Mar 14) Health Authority trust funds - 100%.
EXECUTIVES: M Pinkerton (ce). **EMPLOYEES:** 1 (1). **PAY:** £0.03m (£0.03m). **ADDRESS:** Armthorpe Road, Doncaster, South Yorkshire, DN2 5LT. Tel: 01302 366666. **INTERNET:** www.dbh.nhs.uk. **FOUNDED:** 1996. **CONST:** Trust. **CC NO:** 1057917.
AUDITORS: PricewaterhouseCoopers LLP, Leeds; audit fee £6k. **BANKERS:** Royal Bank of Scotland Group plc, The. **LEGAL ADVISERS:** DAC Beachcroft LLP, Leeds. **INV MANAGERS:** Investec Wealth & Investment, London.

year ended 31 March		2010	2011	2012	2013	2014
legacies	£m	0.28	0.05	~	0.14	0.28
other voluntary income	£m	0.51	0.52	0.73	0.40	0.26
activities gen funds	£m	0.11	0.09	0.16	0.02	0.05
investment income	£m	0.38	0.44	0.43	0.40	0.38
charitable activities	£m	-	-	-	-	-
other incoming	£m	-	-	-	-	-
TOTAL INCOME	£m	1.29	1.09	1.33	0.95	0.96
voluntary costs	£m	0.07	0.09	0.09	0.04	0.03
cost generating funds	£m	-	-	-	-	-
investment costs	£m	0.03	0.04	0.04	0.04	0.04
charitable exp	£m	-	-	-	-	-
grant expenditure	£m	1.31	1.21	1.62	2.40	3.12
governance	£m	0.09	0.06	0.07	0.09	0.09
other expenditure	£m	-	-	-	-	-
TOTAL EXPENDITURE	£m	1.50	1.40	1.82	2.57	3.28
gains revaluations	£m	3.25	0.63	(0.05)	1.22	0.66
NET INCREASE IN FUNDS	£m	3.04	0.32	(0.54)	(0.40)	(1.66)
land build oth fxd	£m	-	-	-	-	-
investments	£m	13.1	13.7	13.7	13.3	11.9
stock debtors cash	£m	1.23	0.85	0.29	0.72	0.25
liabilities	£m	0.30	0.19	0.09	0.60	0.37
pension liability	£m	-	-	-	-	-
TOTAL FUNDS	£m	14.1	14.4	13.9	13.5	11.8

INC 581 / £14.8m   EXP 544 / £15.0m   FUNDS £(3.29)m

DONCASTER CULTURE AND LEISURE TRUST

AIMS: To manage the leisure and entertainment experience to improve the lives and well-being of our clients and their communities. **GRANT MAKER:** No. **EXP ANALYSIS:** (31 Mar 15) Sport and recreation general - 100%.
EXECUTIVES: M Hart (ce); J Barrett (s). **EMPLOYEES:** 566 (496). **PAY:** £7.07m (£6.83m). **ADDRESS:** The Dome, Doncaster Leisure Park, Bawtry Road, Doncaster, South Yorkshire, DN4 7PD. Tel: 01302 370777. Fax: 01302 532239. **INTERNET:** www.dclt.co.uk. **CC NO:** 1103465.
AUDITORS: BDO LLP, Leeds; audit fee £9k, non-audit fee £7k.

year ended 31 March		2011	2012	2013	2014	2015
legacies	£m	-	-	-	-	-
other voluntary income	£m	1.08	0.47	0.61	0.44	0.69
activities gen funds	£m	1.85	1.94	2.22	2.60	2.29
investment income	£m	-	~	~	0.03	~
charitable activities	£m	2.51	8.86	9.44	11.7	11.8
other incoming	£m	-	-	-	-	-
TOTAL INCOME	£m	5.44	11.3	12.3	14.7	14.8
voluntary costs	£m	-	-	-	-	-
cost generating funds	£m	1.67	1.73	1.92	2.26	2.21
investment costs	£m	-	-	-	-	-
charitable exp	£m	3.99	9.06	10.2	11.9	12.6
grant expenditure	£m	-	-	-	-	-
governance	£m	0.09	0.10	0.13	0.16	0.14
other expenditure	£m	-	1.91	~	-	(0.01)
TOTAL EXPENDITURE	£m	5.75	12.8	12.2	14.3	15.0
gains revaluations	£m	-	(0.04)	(0.42)	(0.27)	(1.31)
NET INCREASE IN FUNDS	£m	(0.31)	(1.57)	(0.36)	0.12	(1.49)
land build oth fxd	£m	0.29	2.41	2.44	2.73	5.29
investments	£m	-	-	-	-	-
stock debtors cash	£m	0.81	1.66	2.97	2.07	2.09
liabilities	£m	1.09	3.64	4.88	3.86	6.63
pension liability	£m	-	2.00	2.46	2.74	4.05
TOTAL FUNDS	£m	~	(1.57)	(1.93)	(1.80)	(3.29)

INC 1317 / £6.70m	**EXP** 1278 / £6.54m	**FUNDS** £1.86m

DONCASTER DEAF TRUST

ALTERNATIVE NAMES: Doncaster College for the Deaf; Doncaster School for the Deaf. **GRANT MAKER:** No. **EXP ANALYSIS:** (31 Aug 14) Primary and secondary education general - 100%.

EXECUTIVES: A W Robinson; J D Weston (cs). **EMPLOYEES:** 162 (189). **PAY:** £4.63m (£5.16m). **ADDRESS:** Leger Way, Doncaster, South Yorkshire, DN2 6AY. Tel: 01302 386700. Fax: 01302 361808. **INTERNET:** www.deaf-trust.co.uk. **FOUNDED:** 1948. **CONST:** Company. **CO REG NO:** 4105045. **CC NO:** 1088060.

AUDITORS: Allotts, Doncaster; audit fee £8k, non-audit fee £4k. **BANKERS:** HSBC. **LEGAL ADVISERS:** Veale Wasbrough Vizards, Bristol.

year ended 31 August		2010	2011	2012	2013	2014
legacies	£m	-	-	-	-	~
other voluntary income	£m	0.02	0.01	0.01	0.01	0.03
activities gen funds	£m	0.10	0.11	0.15	0.16	0.16
investment income	£m	0.13	0.11	0.09	0.09	0.07
charitable activities	£m	8.00	7.82	6.40	5.89	6.41
other incoming	£m	0.06	0.07	0.07	0.02	0.02
TOTAL INCOME	£m	8.32	8.12	6.73	6.17	6.70
voluntary costs	£m	-	-	-	-	-
cost generating funds	£m	-	-	-	-	-
investment costs	£m	-	-	-	-	-
charitable exp	£m	8.89	8.78	7.56	6.72	6.47
grant expenditure	£m	-	-	-	-	-
governance	£m	0.07	0.07	0.07	0.07	0.07
other expenditure	£m	-	-	-	-	-
TOTAL EXPENDITURE	£m	8.96	8.85	7.64	6.79	6.54
gains revaluations	£m	0.65	1.03	(0.44)	0.66	(0.59)
NET INCREASE IN FUNDS	£m	0.01	0.30	(1.35)	0.04	(0.43)
land build oth fxd	£m	3.43	3.17	2.98	2.96	2.91
investments	£m	2.64	2.68	2.33	1.71	1.39
stock debtors cash	£m	1.10	1.40	0.90	0.32	1.12
liabilities	£m	1.01	1.66	1.37	0.57	0.81
pension liability	£m	2.86	1.99	2.59	2.12	2.74
TOTAL FUNDS	£m	3.30	3.60	2.25	2.29	1.86

INC 1328 / £6.63m	**EXP** 1228 / £6.88m	**FUNDS** £8.46m

DONISTHORPE HALL

AIMS: The operation of a residential nursing home for the Jewish elderly. **GRANT MAKER:** No. **EXP ANALYSIS:** (31 Dec 14) Welfare of Jews - 100%.

EXECUTIVES: Ms C Holworth (df); Candice Trant (hr). **EMPLOYEES:** 232 (229). **PAY:** £4.41m (£4.10m). **ADDRESS:** Shadwell Lane, Leeds, West Yorkshire, LS17 6AW. Tel: 0113 268 4248. Fax: 0113 237 0502. **INTERNET:** www.donisthorpehall.org. **FOUNDED:** 1991. **CONST:** Company. **CO REG NO:** 3847954. **CC NO:** 1077573.

AUDITORS: KPMG LLP, Leeds; audit fee £10k, non-audit fee £4k. **BANKERS:** Bank of Scotland Corporate. **LEGAL ADVISERS:** Wrigleys Solicitors LLP, Leeds.

year ended 31 December		2010	2011	2012	2013	2014
legacies	£m	0.25	0.02	0.07	0.06	0.26
other voluntary income	£m	0.15	0.13	0.11	0.35	0.25
activities gen funds	£m	-	-	-	-	-
investment income	£m	0.09	0.08	~	0.04	~
charitable activities	£m	6.05	5.71	5.43	5.84	6.00
other incoming	£m	0.26	0.41	0.06	0.08	0.13
TOTAL INCOME	£m	6.79	6.36	5.67	6.37	6.63
voluntary costs	£m	0.01	0.01	0.01	0.01	0.01
cost generating funds	£m	-	-	-	-	-
investment costs	£m	-	-	-	-	-
charitable exp	£m	6.60	6.02	5.91	6.37	6.86
grant expenditure	£m	-	-	-	-	-
governance	£m	0.01	0.02	0.01	0.01	0.01
other expenditure	£m	-	-	-	-	-
TOTAL EXPENDITURE	£m	6.62	6.04	5.93	6.40	6.88
gains revaluations	£m	-	(0.31)	0.02	-	-
NET INCREASE IN FUNDS	£m	0.17	0.01	(0.24)	(0.03)	(0.25)
land build oth fxd	£m	7.37	7.39	7.41	7.10	7.63
investments	£m	0.91	0.60	-	-	-
stock debtors cash	£m	1.83	1.99	2.31	2.72	2.01
liabilities	£m	1.15	1.00	0.98	1.11	1.17
pension liability	£m	-	-	-	-	-
TOTAL FUNDS	£m	8.96	8.97	8.74	8.71	8.46

DONKEY SANCTUARY, THE

THE DONKEY SANCTUARY

AIMS: The provision of care, protection and/or permanent security anywhere in the world for donkeys and mules which are in need of attention by reason of sickness, maltreatment, poor circumstances, ill-usage or other like causes and the prevention of cruelty and suffering among donkeys and mules. To provide Donkey Assisted Therapy for children and adults with additional needs. **GRANT MAKER:** Yes. **EXP ANALYSIS:** (31 Dec 14) Animal life - 100%. **BENEFICIAL AREA:** UK; International; Europe. **GRANTS AVAILABLE:** Not known.

CONNECTED CHARITIES: The Elisabeth Svendsen Trust for Children and Donkeys;. **TRADING SUBS:** Donkey World Limited; The Hayloft (Donkey Sanctuary) Limited.

EXECUTIVES: D A Cook (ceo); G Minns (hr); J Akers (leg); S Blakeway (int); A Foxcroft (welf); M Steele (fr & mkd); C Young (cfo); Dawn Vincent. **EMPLOYEES:** 538 (520). **PAY:** £13.4m (£12.8m). **ADDRESS:** Slade House Farm, Sidmouth, Devon, EX10 0NU. Tel: 01395 578222. Fax: 01395 579266. **INTERNET:** www.thedonkeysanctuary.org.uk. **FOUNDED:** 1969. **CONST:** Trust. CC NO: 264818.

TRUSTEES: Prof S Reid (ch); Natalie Cook; R Crawford; Prof J L Duncan; Dr R Gillespie; Susan Griffin; D Howarth; Christine Purdy; J S Sewell-Rutter; W Tetlow.

AUDITORS: KPMG LLP, Plymouth; audit fee £25k. **BANKERS:** Barclays. **LEGAL ADVISERS:** Bircham Dyson Bell LLP, London; Freeths LLP (Trading as Henmans Freeth), Oxford; Gilbert Stephens, Ottery St. Mary; Stone King LLP, London; Wilsons Solicitors LLP, London; Wrigleys Solicitors LLP, Leeds. **INV MANAGERS:** Investec Wealth & Investment, London.

INC 251 / £32.4m   **EXP** 262 / £29.5m   **FUNDS** 331 / £65.0m

year ended 31 December source of figures		2010[15] Aud	2011 Aud	2012 Aud	2013 Aud	2014 Aud
legacies	£m	18.5	16.5	18.0	20.0	20.8
public grants	£m	-	-	-	-	-
lottery, arts council	£m	-	-	-	-	-
gifts in kind	£m	-	-	5.11	-	-
donations	£m	5.78	4.75	6.74	7.62	8.77
donated goods	£m	0.04	~	~	~	~
other trading	£m	1.63	1.14	1.13	1.11	1.28
other inc generating	£m	-	-	0.01	0.03	0.03
interest, dividends, rent	£m	0.66	0.56	0.54	0.57	0.50
charitable activities	£m	-	-	-	-	-
other income	£m	0.35	0.70	0.71	1.44	1.09
TOTAL INCOME		26.9	23.6	32.2	30.7	32.4
GAINS, REVALUATIONS	£m	1.90	(1.54)	0.33	0.98	(0.49)
voluntary costs	£m	2.10	2.96	3.26	4.21	5.13
cost generating fnds	£m	1.28	0.91	0.87	0.86	0.99
investment costs	£m	0.09	0.07	0.08	0.08	0.08
grant expenditure	£m	1.51	0.80	0.64	0.87	0.83
direct charitable exp	£m	22.2	18.0	20.2	21.1	22.1
governance	£m	0.37	0.32	0.34	0.35	0.37
other costs	£m	-	-	-	-	-
TOTAL EXPENDITURE		27.5	23.1	25.4	27.4	29.5
NET INCREASE IN FUNDS	£m	1.32	(0.97)	7.13	4.28	2.48
land & buildings	£m	17.4	17.4	20.3	20.3	20.2
other fixed assets	£m	2.17	2.26	2.56	2.62	2.69
fxd investments	£m	17.5	15.3	17.1	19.4	20.9
stocks, debtors	£m	10.4	12.2	12.3	12.1	12.8
cur investments	£m	-	-	-	-	-
cash deposits	£m	6.94	5.53	7.56	10.2	10.6
creditors	£m	2.26	1.49	1.59	2.05	2.13
borrowings	£m	-	-	-	-	-
pension liability	£m	-	0.10	-	-	-
endowment funds	£m	0.05	0.05	-	-	-
other restricted funds	£m	0.95	0.92	2.58	2.55	2.46
unrestricted funds	£m	51.1	50.2	55.7	60.0	62.6
pension fund	£m					
TOTAL FUNDS	£m	52.1	51.2	58.3	62.6	65.0

INC 1441 / £6.02m EXP 1416 / £5.84m FUNDS £8.86m
DONMAR WAREHOUSE PROJECTS LTD

ALTERNATIVE NAMES: Omega Projects Ltd. **AIMS:** To promote, maintain, improve and advance education particularly by the encouragement of the arts including the arts of drama, ballet, music, singing, literature, sculpture and painting. **GRANT MAKER:** No. **EXP ANALYSIS:** (31 Mar 15) Drama and theatre - 100%.

EXECUTIVES: S Meadon (s). **EMPLOYEES:** 29 (23). **PAY:** £2.10m (£1.78m). **ADDRESS:** 3 Dryden Street, London, EC2E 9NA. **INTERNET:** www.donmarwarehouse.com. **FOUNDED:** 1981. **CONST:** Company. **CO REG NO:** 1611861. **CC NO:** 284262.

AUDITORS: Saffery Champness, London; audit fee £18k, non-audit fee £10k. **BANKERS:** Coutts & Co. **LEGAL ADVISERS:** Bates Wells Braithwaite (London), London.

year ended 31 March		2011	2012	2013	2014	2015
legacies	£m	-	-	-	-	-
other voluntary income	£m	1.31	3.01	3.13	3.73	4.57
activities gen funds	£m	0.54	0.93	0.98	0.95	0.28
investment income	£m	0.01	0.01	0.01	~	~
charitable activities	£m	3.62	2.15	1.67	1.74	1.17
other incoming	£m	-	-	-	-	-
TOTAL INCOME	£m	5.48	6.10	5.79	6.42	6.02
voluntary costs	£m	0.24	0.34	0.34	0.41	0.49
cost generating funds	£m	-	-	-	-	-
investment costs	£m	-	-	-	-	-
charitable exp	£m	5.39	5.02	4.65	4.55	5.33
grant expenditure	£m	-	-	-	-	-
governance	£m	0.08	0.03	0.02	0.02	0.02
other expenditure	£m	-	-	-	-	-
TOTAL EXPENDITURE	£m	5.72	5.39	5.01	4.99	5.84
gains revaluations	£m	(0.07)	-	-	-	-
NET INCREASE IN FUNDS	£m	(0.31)	0.71	0.77	1.43	0.18
land build oth fxd	£m	1.80	3.11	3.61	6.96	6.97
investments	£m	-	-	-	-	-
stock debtors cash	£m	4.36	4.07	4.68	3.09	3.16
liabilities	£m	0.40	0.71	1.05	1.37	1.27
pension liability	£m	-	-	-	-	-
TOTAL FUNDS	£m	5.76	6.47	7.25	8.68	8.86

INC £0.92m EXP £0.81m FUNDS 925 / £22.4m
DONNINGTON HOSPITAL TRUST

AIMS: The provision and management of almshouses. **GRANT MAKER:** No. **EXP ANALYSIS:** (31 Dec 14) Almshouses - 100%.

EMPLOYEES: 7 (7). **PAY:** £0.07m (£0.07m). **ADDRESS:** Trust Office, 1 Groombridge Place, Donnington, Newbury, Berkshire, RG14 2JQ. Tel: 01635 551530. **INTERNET:** www.donningtonhospital.com. **FOUNDED:** 1353. **CONST:** Trust. **CC NO:** 226021.

AUDITORS: Griffins, Newbury; audit fee £13k. **LEGAL ADVISERS:** Clifton Ingram LLP, Wokingham.

year ended 31 December		2010	2011	2012	2013	2014
legacies	£m	-	-	-	-	-
other voluntary income	£m	0.09	0.11	0.12	0.14	0.15
activities gen funds	£m	-	-	-	-	-
investment income	£m	0.74	0.66	0.59	0.71	0.77
charitable activities	£m	-	-	-	-	-
other incoming	£m	-	-	-	-	-
TOTAL INCOME	£m	0.83	0.77	0.71	0.85	0.92
voluntary costs	£m	-	-	-	-	-
cost generating funds	£m	-	-	-	-	-
investment costs	£m	0.14	0.16	0.20	0.19	0.23
charitable exp	£m	0.30	0.31	0.28	0.39	0.36
grant expenditure	£m	-	-	-	-	-
governance	£m	-	-	-	-	-
other expenditure	£m	0.17	0.14	0.22	0.20	0.22
TOTAL EXPENDITURE	£m	0.60	0.61	0.69	0.78	0.81
gains revaluations	£m	-	-	(0.82)	-	-
NET INCREASE IN FUNDS	£m	0.23	0.17	(0.81)	0.07	0.11
land build oth fxd	£m	1.75	1.74	1.70	1.72	1.76
investments	£m	22.8	22.8	23.4	23.2	23.2
stock debtors cash	£m	0.34	0.52	0.58	0.66	0.92
liabilities	£m	2.04	2.03	3.50	3.29	3.49
pension liability	£m	-	-	-	-	-
TOTAL FUNDS	£m	22.9	23.0	22.2	22.3	22.4

INC £(1.57)m EXP FUNDS 646 / £33.0m
DONTCHEV FOUNDATION

AIMS: To advance education and relieve poverty and to promote such other purposes as are now or may hereafter be deemed by English law to be charitable. **GRANT MAKER:** Yes. **EXP ANALYSIS:** (31 Oct 14) Grantmaking to a wide variety of charitable causes - 100%.

EXECUTIVES: A Tulloch (s). **ADDRESS:** 4 Hill Street, London, W1J 5NE. Tel: 0207 318 1180. **FOUNDED:** 2004. **CONST:** Company. **CO REG NO:** 4946116. **CC NO:** 1103251.

AUDITORS: Mackenzie Field, London.

year ended 31 October		2010	2011	2012	2013	2014
legacies	£m	-	-	-	-	-
other voluntary income	£m	1.32	0.06	~	30.1	-
activities gen funds	£m	0.05	-	-	0.41	(1.57)
investment income	£m	-	-	-	-	-
charitable activities	£m	-	-	-	-	-
other incoming	£m	-	-	-	-	-
TOTAL INCOME	£m	1.37	0.06	~	30.5	(1.57)
voluntary costs	£m	-	-	-	-	-
cost generating funds	£m	-	-	-	-	-
investment costs	£m	-	-	-	-	-
charitable exp	£m	-	-	-	-	-
grant expenditure	£m	0.05	0.06	-	-	-
governance	£m	~	~	~	-	-
other expenditure	£m	-	-	-	-	-
TOTAL EXPENDITURE	£m	0.05	0.06	~	-	-
gains revaluations	£m	-	-	-	-	-
NET INCREASE IN FUNDS	£m	1.32	~	~	30.5	(1.57)
land build oth fxd	£m	-	-	-	-	-
investments	£m	-	4.01	4.01	4.02	4.01
stock debtors cash	£m	4.02	~	~	30.5	29.0
liabilities	£m	-	-	-	-	-
pension liability	£m	-	-	-	-	-
TOTAL FUNDS	£m	4.02	4.02	4.02	34.6	33.0

INC £0.48m EXP £0.50m FUNDS 1729 / £10.9m
DORIS FIELD CHARITABLE TRUST

AIMS: General charitable purposes at the trustees discretion. **GRANT MAKER:** Yes. **EXP ANALYSIS:** (15 Aug 15) Grantmaking to a wide variety of charitable causes - 100%. **NO OF GRANTS:** 212 (195).

ADDRESS: Blake Morgan LLP, Seacourt Tower, West Way, Oxford, Oxfordshire, OX2 0FB. Tel: 01865 262183. **FOUNDED:** 1990. **CONST:** Trust. **CC NO:** 328687.

AUDITORS: Wenn Townsend, Oxford; audit fee £4k, non-audit fee £4k. **BANKERS:** NatWest. **LEGAL ADVISERS:** Blake Morgan, Oxford. **INV MANAGERS:** Barclays Wealth, London; Rathbone Investment Management, London. **PROP ADVISERS:** Carter Jonas LLP, Oxford.

year ended 15 August		2011	2012	2013	2014	2015
legacies	£m	-	-	-	-	-
other voluntary income	£m	-	-	-	-	-
activities gen funds	£m	-	-	-	-	-
investment income	£m	0.34	0.35	0.39	0.47	0.48
charitable activities	£m	-	-	-	-	-
other incoming	£m	-	-	-	-	-
TOTAL INCOME	£m	0.34	0.35	0.39	0.47	0.48
voluntary costs	£m	-	-	-	-	-
cost generating funds	£m	0.06	0.06	0.12	0.07	0.06
investment costs	£m	0.06	0.10	0.06	0.07	0.04
charitable exp	£m	-	-	-	-	-
grant expenditure	£m	0.29	0.24	0.29	0.27	0.38
governance	£m	0.03	0.04	0.07	0.03	0.03
other expenditure	£m	-	-	-	-	-
TOTAL EXPENDITURE	£m	0.44	0.44	0.54	0.43	0.50
gains revaluations	£m	0.26	0.09	2.43	0.06	0.59
NET INCREASE IN FUNDS	£m	0.15	~	2.28	0.10	0.57
land build oth fxd	£m	-	-	-	-	-
investments	£m	7.93	5.15	10.2	10.3	10.9
stock debtors cash	£m	0.11	2.88	0.17	0.21	0.17
liabilities	£m	0.13	0.12	0.18	0.18	0.22
pension liability	£m	-	-	-	-	-
TOTAL FUNDS	£m	7.91	7.92	10.2	10.3	10.9

INC £0.59m EXP £0.43m FUNDS 1866 / £9.82m
DORNEYWOOD THOMSON ENDOWMENT TRUST FUND B

AIMS: The maintenance and improvement of the Dorneywood estate, the mansion house, and other buildings thereon. **GRANT MAKER:** No. **EXP ANALYSIS:** (31 Dec 14) Historic buildings and structures - 100%.

EXECUTIVES: T Price (s). **EMPLOYEES:** 7 (7). **PAY:** £0.20m (£0.20m). **ADDRESS:** Dorneywood, Burnham, Buckinghamshire, SL1 8PY. Tel: 01628 665 361. Fax: 01628 665 361. **CC NO:** 213166.

AUDITORS: Wenn Townsend, Oxford; audit fee £3k, non-audit fee £7k. **LEGAL ADVISERS:** Charles Russell Speechlys LLP, London.

year ended 31 December		2010	2011	2012	2013	2014
legacies	£m	-	-	-	-	-
other voluntary income	£m	-	-	-	-	-
activities gen funds	£m	-	-	-	-	-
investment income	£m	0.29	0.31	0.30	0.41	0.49
charitable activities	£m	0.04	0.02	0.03	0.03	0.11
other incoming	£m	-	-	-	-	-
TOTAL INCOME	£m	0.33	0.34	0.34	0.43	0.59
voluntary costs	£m	0.06	0.05	0.06	0.08	0.08
cost generating funds	£m	-	-	-	-	-
investment costs	£m	-	-	-	-	-
charitable exp	£m	0.35	0.51	0.33	0.36	0.34
grant expenditure	£m	-	-	-	-	-
governance	£m	0.01	0.01	0.01	0.01	0.01
other expenditure	£m	-	-	-	-	-
TOTAL EXPENDITURE	£m	0.41	0.57	0.39	0.45	0.43
gains revaluations	£m	0.60	(0.66)	1.08	1.11	0.07
NET INCREASE IN FUNDS	£m	0.52	(0.89)	1.03	1.09	0.23
land build oth fxd	£m	0.04	0.03	0.03	0.03	0.03
investments	£m	8.28	7.40	8.42	9.54	9.74
stock debtors cash	£m	0.12	0.09	0.07	0.05	0.09
liabilities	£m	0.07	0.05	0.02	0.03	0.04
pension liability	£m	-	-	-	-	-
TOTAL FUNDS	£m	8.36	7.47	8.50	9.59	9.82

INC 835 / £10.8m EXP 731 / £11.5m FUNDS 1271 / £15.5m
DOROTHY HOUSE FOUNDATION LTD, THE

ALTERNATIVE NAMES: Dorothy House Hospice Care. **GRANT MAKER:** No. **EXP ANALYSIS:** (31 Mar 15) Home nursing and assistance - 100%.

EXECUTIVES: Gill Cannon (dfr); J Davies (ce); Tony De Jaeger (df); J McDonald. **EMPLOYEES:** 231 (214). **PAY:** £8.00m (£7.36m). **ADDRESS:** Winsley, Bradford-on-Avon, Wiltshire, BA15 2LE. Tel: 01225 722988. Fax: 01225 721478. **INTERNET:** www.dorothyhouse.co.uk. **FOUNDED:** 1976. **CONST:** Company. **CO REG NO:** 1360961. **CC NO:** 275745.

AUDITORS: Bishop Fleming, Bristol; audit fee £11k. **BANKERS:** NatWest. **LEGAL ADVISERS:** Thrings LLP, Swindon. **INV MANAGERS:** Rathbone Investment Management, London.

year ended 31 March		2011	2012	2013	2014	2015
legacies	£m	1.82	1.03	0.83	1.66	2.29
other voluntary income	£m	1.61	1.76	1.89	1.97	1.82
activities gen funds	£m	2.53	2.91	3.37	3.94	4.02
investment income	£m	0.22	0.26	0.26	0.23	0.23
charitable activities	£m	2.32	1.99	2.04	2.57	2.42
other incoming	£m	-	-	-	-	-
TOTAL INCOME	£m	8.50	7.94	8.39	10.4	10.8
voluntary costs	£m	0.45	0.46	0.47	0.60	0.65
cost generating funds	£m	1.84	2.04	2.44	3.10	3.53
investment costs	£m	0.03	0.05	0.04	0.05	0.04
charitable exp	£m	5.52	5.74	6.12	6.66	7.28
grant expenditure	£m	-	-	-	-	-
governance	£m	0.04	0.04	0.04	0.04	0.03
other expenditure	£m	-	-	-	-	-
TOTAL EXPENDITURE	£m	7.88	8.33	9.12	10.4	11.5
gains revaluations	£m	0.41	(0.12)	0.78	0.13	0.45
NET INCREASE IN FUNDS	£m	1.04	(0.51)	0.05	0.06	(0.30)
land build oth fxd	£m	6.16	6.73	7.20	7.49	7.33
investments	£m	9.33	9.24	7.64	6.91	7.16
stock debtors cash	£m	1.85	0.83	1.96	2.53	2.41
liabilities	£m	1.12	1.09	1.04	1.11	1.39
pension liability	£m	-	-	-	-	-
TOTAL FUNDS	£m	16.2	15.7	15.8	15.8	15.5

INC 1942 / £3.99m EXP 1819 / £4.25m FUNDS £6.92m
DOROTHY KERIN TRUST, THE

AIMS: For the charitable purpose of carrying on and furthering by every means which is legally charitable (but in no other way) the work of spiritual and medical healing formerly carried out by Dorothy Kerin and continued since her death by the trustees. **GRANT MAKER:** No. **EXP ANALYSIS:** (31 Dec 14) Christian general - 100%.

EXECUTIVES: James Archer; John Ashelford. **EMPLOYEES:** 115 (116). **PAY:** £2.90m (£2.78m). **ADDRESS:** Burrswood, Groombridge, Tunbridge Wells, Kent, TN3 9PY. Tel: 01892 863623. **INTERNET:** www.burrswood.org.uk. **CC NO:** 1095940.

AUDITORS: Saffery Champness, London; audit fee £15k.

year ended 31 December		2010	2011	2012	2013	2014
legacies	£m	0.71	0.05	0.28	0.21	0.35
other voluntary income	£m	0.40	0.45	0.43	0.47	0.32
activities gen funds	£m	0.16	0.17	0.15	0.18	0.28
investment income	£m	0.02	0.02	0.02	0.03	0.02
charitable activities	£m	2.59	2.85	3.15	3.24	3.03
other incoming	£m	-	-	0.01	-	-
TOTAL INCOME	£m	3.88	3.53	4.04	4.13	3.99
voluntary costs	£m	0.17	0.18	0.21	0.17	0.18
cost generating funds	£m	0.15	0.16	0.17	0.30	0.30
investment costs	£m	-	-	-	-	-
charitable exp	£m	3.64	3.61	4.30	3.80	3.77
grant expenditure	£m	-	-	-	-	-
governance	£m	0.07	0.09	0.02	0.01	0.01
other expenditure	£m	-	-	-	-	-
TOTAL EXPENDITURE	£m	4.03	4.04	4.70	4.28	4.25
gains revaluations	£m	(0.06)	-	(0.08)	0.30	0.03
NET INCREASE IN FUNDS	£m	(0.22)	(0.51)	(0.75)	0.14	(0.24)
land build oth fxd	£m	9.11	8.94	8.19	7.41	7.26
investments	£m	-	-	-	-	-
stock debtors cash	£m	1.40	0.51	0.51	1.14	0.64
liabilities	£m	2.24	1.70	1.69	1.40	0.98
pension liability	£m	-	-	-	-	-
TOTAL FUNDS	£m	8.26	7.76	7.01	7.15	6.92

INC 1243 / £7.13m EXP £3.26m FUNDS 1176 / £16.7m
DORSET & SOMERSET AIR AMBULANCE CHARITY, THE

AIMS: The relief of sickness and injury and the protection of human life by the provision or support of air ambulance service for the benefit of the population of the counties of Dorset and Somerset. **GRANT MAKER:** No. **EXP ANALYSIS:** (31 Mar 15) Ambulance services - 100%.

EXECUTIVES: W Sivewright (ce); C Launchbury (s). **EMPLOYEES:** 15 (17). **PAY:** £0.48m (£0.48m). **ADDRESS:** Landacre House, Castle Road, Chelston Business Park, Wellington, Somerset, TA21 9JQ. Tel: 01823 669604. **INTERNET:** www.dorsetandsomersetairambulance.co.uk. **CONST:** Company. **CO REG NO:** 3893356. **CC NO:** 1078685.

year ended 31 March		2011	2012	2013	2014	2015
legacies	£m	0.17	0.15	0.23	1.08	1.29
other voluntary income	£m	1.16	1.22	1.35	1.54	1.53
activities gen funds	£m	2.06	2.56	3.07	3.64	4.14
investment income	£m	0.09	0.18	0.19	0.18	0.17
charitable activities	£m	-	-	-	-	-
other incoming	£m	-	-	-	-	-
TOTAL INCOME	£m	3.49	4.10	4.84	6.43	7.13
voluntary costs	£m	~	~	~	~	~
cost generating funds	£m	0.55	0.70	0.81	0.95	0.81
investment costs	£m	0.02	0.02	0.02	0.03	0.05
charitable exp	£m	1.66	1.77	1.72	2.41	2.37
grant expenditure	£m	-	-	-	-	-
governance	£m	0.31	0.28	0.34	0.04	0.04
other expenditure	£m	-	-	-	-	-
TOTAL EXPENDITURE	£m	2.55	2.76	2.90	3.43	3.26
gains revaluations	£m	0.04	0.01	0.15	0.06	0.27
NET INCREASE IN FUNDS	£m	0.98	1.35	2.09	3.07	4.14
land build oth fxd	£m	0.01	0.01	0.01	0.08	0.06
investments	£m	1.83	1.87	2.06	4.16	4.50
stock debtors cash	£m	4.70	6.01	7.86	8.96	12.8
liabilities	£m	0.45	0.45	0.40	0.61	0.59
pension liability	£m	-	-	-	-	-
TOTAL FUNDS	£m	6.10	7.44	9.53	12.6	16.7

INC 1924 / £4.04m   EXP £3.54m   FUNDS 1699 / £11.0m
DORSET WILDLIFE TRUST

ALTERNATIVE NAMES: Dorset Trust for Nature Conservation. **AIMS:** To conserve and enhance Dorset's rich and varied wildlife; to safeguard Dorset's wildlife areas for the future, and actively encourage sympathetic management of the countryside and coast as a whole. **GRANT MAKER:** No. **EXP ANALYSIS:** (31 Mar 15) Conservation and protection general - 100%.

EXECUTIVES: Dr S Cripps (ce). **EMPLOYEES:** 68 (79). **PAY:** £1.72m (£1.72m). **ADDRESS:** Brooklands Farm, Forston, Dorchester, Dorset, DT2 7AA. Tel: 01305 264620. Fax: 01305 251120. **INTERNET:** www.dorsetwildlifetrust.org.uk. **CC NO:** 200222.

AUDITORS: Smith & Williamson, Southampton; audit fee £13k, non-audit fee £2k. **LEGAL ADVISERS:** Battens, Yeovil.

year ended 31 March		2011	2012	2013	2014	2015
legacies	£m	-	-	-	-	-
other voluntary income	£m	1.72	2.67	2.74	2.02	2.04
activities gen funds	£m	0.26	0.32	0.24	0.19	0.24
investment income	£m	0.04	0.05	0.07	0.07	0.07
charitable activities	£m	0.93	1.15	1.66	2.46	1.62
other incoming	£m	0.16	0.01	0.02	0.06	0.07
TOTAL INCOME	£m	3.11	4.21	4.73	4.80	4.04
voluntary costs	£m	0.35	0.57	0.50	0.55	0.54
cost generating funds	£m	0.39	0.36	0.29	0.12	0.12
investment costs	£m	~	0.01	0.01	0.01	0.01
charitable exp	£m	1.88	2.20	2.38	3.07	2.76
grant expenditure	£m	-	-	-	-	-
governance	£m	0.06	0.06	0.06	0.07	0.06
other expenditure	£m	0.03	0.05	0.05	0.04	0.05
TOTAL EXPENDITURE	£m	2.71	3.25	3.29	3.85	3.54
gains revaluations	£m	0.42	0.01	0.17	0.07	0.08
NET INCREASE IN FUNDS	£m	0.82	0.97	1.61	1.02	0.58
land build oth fxd	£m	4.05	4.17	5.02	6.45	6.99
investments	£m	0.59	1.60	1.89	1.93	1.90
stock debtors cash	£m	2.56	2.33	2.89	2.43	2.60
liabilities	£m	0.35	0.27	0.37	0.35	0.45
pension liability	£m	-	-	-	-	-
TOTAL FUNDS	£m	6.86	7.83	9.44	10.5	11.0

INC £0.96m   EXP £0.96m   FUNDS 1439 / £13.5m
DOUAI ABBEY

ALTERNATIVE NAMES: Community of St Edmund; Trustees of Douai Abbey. **AIMS:** Education, the advancement of Roman Catholic religion and the relief of poverty. **GRANT MAKER:** No. **EXP ANALYSIS:** (31 Aug 14) Roman Catholics - 100%.

AFFILIATIONS: English Benedictine Congregation.

EMPLOYEES: 15 (13). **PAY:** £0.23m (£0.19m). **ADDRESS:** Upper Woolhampton, Reading, Berkshire, RG7 5TQ. Tel: 0118 971 5300. Fax: 0118 971 5305. **INTERNET:** www.douaiabbey.org.uk. **FOUNDED:** 1934. **CONST:** Trust. **CC NO:** 236962.

AUDITORS: Buzzacott LLP, London; audit fee £11k. **BANKERS:** NatWest. **LEGAL ADVISERS:** Charles Lucas & Marshall, Hungerford. **INV MANAGERS:** SG Hambros Bank Limited, London.

year ended 31 August		2010	2011	2012	2013	2014
legacies	£m	0.11	~	0.07	~	0.25
other voluntary income	£m	0.23	0.18	0.18	0.32	0.24
activities gen funds	£m	0.01	0.02	0.04	0.04	0.03
investment income	£m	0.16	0.16	0.18	0.18	0.21
charitable activities	£m	0.21	0.20	0.19	0.19	0.21
other incoming	£m	0.04	0.03	0.05	0.03	0.02
TOTAL INCOME	£m	0.76	0.59	0.71	0.76	0.96
voluntary costs	£m	-	-	-	-	-
cost generating funds	£m	~	~	~	~	~
investment costs	£m	0.03	0.03	0.03	0.08	0.10
charitable exp	£m	0.78	0.83	0.81	0.80	0.85
grant expenditure	£m	-	-	-	-	-
governance	£m	0.02	0.01	0.01	0.01	0.01
other expenditure	£m	-	-	-	-	-
TOTAL EXPENDITURE	£m	0.84	0.87	0.86	0.89	0.96
gains revaluations	£m	0.29	0.09	0.11	(0.05)	0.24
NET INCREASE IN FUNDS	£m	0.21	(0.19)	(0.04)	(0.18)	0.24
land build oth fxd	£m	8.31	8.16	8.03	7.84	7.76
investments	£m	5.17	5.14	5.36	5.76	5.90
stock debtors cash	£m	0.26	0.21	0.14	0.20	0.37
liabilities	£m	0.10	0.06	0.11	0.58	0.56
pension liability	£m	-	-	-	-	-
TOTAL FUNDS	£m	13.6	13.4	13.4	13.2	13.5

INC £3.67m   EXP 183 / £40.4m   FUNDS ~
DOUGLAS HAIG MEMORIAL HOMES

ALTERNATIVE NAMES: Haig Homes. **AIMS:** Providing housing for ex-service families of HM Forces and their dependants in financial need. **GRANT MAKER:** No. **EXP ANALYSIS:** (31 Mar 14) Welfare of service and ex-service personnel - 100%.

EXECUTIVES: J Richardson; Amy Rodwell. **EMPLOYEES:** 21 (43). **PAY:** £0.97m (£1.90m). **ADDRESS:** Alban Dobson House, Green Lane, Morden, Surrey, SM4 5NS. Tel: 020 8685 5777. Fax: 020 8685 5778. **INTERNET:** www.haighomes.org.uk. **FOUNDED:** 1929. **CONST:** Trust. **CC NO:** 207318. **OSCR NO:** SC038321.

AUDITORS: Crowe Clark Whitehill LLP, London; audit fee £2k. **LEGAL ADVISERS:** Batchelors, Bromley; Bates Wells Braithwaite (London), London; Trowers & Hamlins LLP, London.

year ended 31 March		2010	2011	2012	2013	2014
legacies	£m	-	-	-	-	-
other voluntary income	£m	0.09	0.18	0.10	0.09	~
activities gen funds	£m	-	-	-	-	-
investment income	£m	0.09	0.06	0.05	0.07	0.01
charitable activities	£m	6.23	6.37	6.68	7.03	3.66
other incoming	£m	0.01	-	-	0.01	-
TOTAL INCOME	£m	6.42	6.61	6.83	7.20	3.67
voluntary costs	£m	0.02	0.02	0.02	0.01	~
cost generating funds	£m	-	-	-	-	-
investment costs	£m	-	-	-	-	-
charitable exp	£m	5.20	6.00	6.18	6.66	3.83
grant expenditure	£m	1.73	0.15	0.79	0.15	36.5
governance	£m	0.14	0.02	0.02	0.02	~
other expenditure	£m	0.26	-	-	-	-
TOTAL EXPENDITURE	£m	7.35	6.18	7.01	6.84	40.4
gains revaluations	£m	0.38	5.83	0.06	0.25	0.03
NET INCREASE IN FUNDS	£m	(0.54)	6.25	(0.12)	0.62	(36.7)
land build oth fxd	£m	27.4	33.3	33.0	32.5	-
investments	£m	1.80	1.89	1.95	2.33	-
stock debtors cash	£m	3.81	4.00	4.01	5.00	~
liabilities	£m	3.10	3.02	2.92	3.17	-
pension liability	£m	-	-	-	-	-
TOTAL FUNDS	£m	29.9	36.2	36.0	36.7	~

INC 783 / £11.5m   EXP 803 / £10.6m   FUNDS 1686 / £11.1m
DOUGLAS MACMILLAN HOSPICE

AIMS: To provide comprehensive care for patients with progressive, advanced, terminal and degenerative disease in order that they may achieve the best possible quality of life and holistic support for families and carers. **GRANT MAKER:** No. **EXP ANALYSIS:** (31 Mar 15) Hospices - 100%.

EXECUTIVES: Michelle J Roberts (ce & cs); Dr C Hookey; Chris Ekin. **EMPLOYEES:** 256 (245). **PAY:** £8.07m (£7.43m). **ADDRESS:** Barlaston Road, Stoke-on-Trent, ST3 3NZ. Tel: 01782 344300. Fax: 01782 344301. **INTERNET:** www.dmhospice.org.uk. **CONST:** Company. **CO REG NO:** 3615904. **CC NO:** 1071613.

AUDITORS: Geens, Stoke-on-Trent; audit fee £14k. **LEGAL ADVISERS:** Grindeys, Stoke-on-Trent.

year ended 31 March		2011	2012	2013	2014	2015
legacies	£m	1.36	1.21	2.74	1.17	2.09
other voluntary income	£m	1.42	0.84	1.04	0.96	0.60
activities gen funds	£m	3.67	3.96	4.30	5.24	5.69
investment income	£m	0.19	0.20	0.21	0.25	0.36
charitable activities	£m	2.41	2.40	2.51	3.05	2.84
other incoming	£m	-	-	-	(0.02)	(0.10)
TOTAL INCOME	£m	9.06	8.60	10.8	10.6	11.5
voluntary costs	£m	0.49	0.45	0.44	0.55	0.60
cost generating funds	£m	1.34	1.63	1.99	2.33	2.60
investment costs	£m	-	-	-	-	-
charitable exp	£m	6.03	6.58	6.63	7.13	7.36
grant expenditure	£m	-	-	-	-	-
governance	£m	0.07	0.08	0.08	0.07	0.07
other expenditure	£m	-	-	-	-	-
TOTAL EXPENDITURE	£m	7.93	8.74	9.14	10.1	10.6
gains revaluations	£m	0.50	(1.27)	(0.23)	0.89	0.06
NET INCREASE IN FUNDS	£m	1.62	(1.42)	1.42	1.46	0.90
land build oth fxd	£m	4.32	4.92	4.69	4.80	5.78
investments	£m	3.15	3.07	4.63	5.09	6.22
stock debtors cash	£m	2.70	2.13	2.46	2.57	1.71
liabilities	£m	0.74	0.57	0.54	0.56	0.59
pension liability	£m	0.65	2.19	2.45	1.67	1.97
TOTAL FUNDS	£m	8.78	7.36	8.78	10.2	11.1

INC £0.45m EXP £0.55m FUNDS 1188 / £16.5m
DOUGLAS TURNER TRUST, THE

AIMS: General charitable purposes at the trustees' discretion. **GRANT MAKER:** Yes. **EXP ANALYSIS:** (31 Dec 14) People with physical disabilities general - 22.37%; Housing and community affairs general - 20.49%; Welfare of the young general - 19.09%; Hospices - 10.77%; Environment general - 8.2%; Welfare of the aged general - 7.85%; Culture and arts general - 7.49%; International activities general - 3.51%; Medical research and specific conditions general - 0.23%.

EXECUTIVES: T J T Patrickson. **ADDRESS:** 3 Poplar Piece, Inkberrow, Worcester, Worcestershire, WR7 4JD. Tel: 01386 792014. **CC NO:** 227892.

AUDITORS: RSM, Birmingham; audit fee £6k.

year ended 31 December		2011	2012	2012[9]	2013	2014
legacies	£m	-	-	-	-	-
other voluntary income	£m	-	-	-	-	-
activities gen funds	£m	-	-	-	-	-
investment income	£m	0.36	0.39	0.31	0.45	0.45
charitable activities	£m	-	-	-	-	-
other incoming	£m	-	-	-	-	-
TOTAL INCOME	£m	0.36	0.39	0.31	0.45	0.45
voluntary costs	£m	-	-	-	-	-
cost generating funds	£m	-	-	-	-	-
investment costs	£m	0.06	0.06	0.05	0.07	0.07
charitable exp	£m	0.03	0.02	0.02	0.03	0.04
grant expenditure	£m	0.44	0.38	0.28	0.39	0.43
governance	£m	0.01	0.01	0.01	~	0.01
other expenditure	£m	-	-	-	-	-
TOTAL EXPENDITURE	£m	0.54	0.48	0.36	0.49	0.55
gains revaluations	£m	0.86	0.08	0.19	1.41	0.36
NET INCREASE IN FUNDS	£m	0.67	~	0.14	1.37	0.26
land build oth fxd	£m	-	-	-	-	~
investments	£m	14.6	14.6	14.7	16.1	16.4
stock debtors cash	£m	0.23	0.21	0.21	0.24	0.16
liabilities	£m	0.03	0.03	0.03	0.03	0.04
pension liability	£m	-	-	-	-	-
TOTAL FUNDS	£m	14.8	14.8	14.9	16.3	16.5

INC 1057 / £8.56m EXP £1.12m FUNDS 1718 / £10.9m
DOVECOT FOUNDATION

AIMS: To advance and support visual arts, craft and design at a national and international level in Scotland. **GRANT MAKER:** No. **EXP ANALYSIS:** (30 Jun 14) Culture and arts general - 100%.

EMPLOYEES: 27 (25). **PAY:** £0.33m (£0.37m). **ADDRESS:** 10 Infirmary Street, Edinburgh, EH1 1LT. **DOMICILE:** Scotland. **CONST:** Company. **CO REG NO:** SC 375263. **OSCR NO:** SC041370.

AUDITORS: Saffery Champness, Edinburgh; audit fee £18k. **BANKERS:** Bank of Scotland Corporate. **LEGAL ADVISERS:** Murray Beith Murray, Edinburgh.

year ended 30 June		2013	2014
legacies	£m	-	-
other voluntary income	£m	1.05	7.84
activities gen funds	£m	0.24	0.56
investment income	£m	0.11	0.10
charitable activities	£m	0.16	0.05
other incoming	£m	-	-
TOTAL INCOME	£m	1.55	8.56
voluntary costs	£m	-	-
cost generating funds	£m	0.28	0.28
investment costs	£m	-	-
charitable exp	£m	0.87	0.82
grant expenditure	£m	-	-
governance	£m	0.02	0.02
other expenditure	£m	~	~
TOTAL EXPENDITURE	£m	1.16	1.12
gains revaluations	£m	(0.27)	0.03
NET INCREASE IN FUNDS	£m	3.47	7.47
land build oth fxd	£m	1.81	9.23
investments	£m	1.32	1.45
stock debtors cash	£m	0.46	0.45
liabilities	£m	0.12	0.18
pension liability	£m	-	-
TOTAL FUNDS	£m	3.47	10.9

INC £0.61m EXP £0.62m FUNDS 1127 / £17.8m
DOWAGER COUNTESS ELEANOR PEEL TRUST, THE

AIMS: For the benefit of charitable bodies particularly medical charities, those for old people and those who have fallen on evil days through no fault of their own. **GRANT MAKER:** Yes. **EXP ANALYSIS:** (05 Apr 15) Grantmaking to a wide variety of charitable causes - 54.54%; Medical research and specific conditions general - 44.64%; Welfare of the aged general - 0.82%.

EMPLOYEES: 6 (6). **ADDRESS:** 50 Foundation Street, Manchester, Greater Manchester, M2 2AS. Tel: 020 7423 8000. Fax: 020 7423 8001. **INTERNET:** www.peeltrust.com. **CC NO:** 214684.

AUDITORS: Saffery Champness, London; audit fee £8k.

year ended 5 April		2011	2012	2013	2014	2015
legacies	£m	-	-	-	-	-
other voluntary income	£m	-	-	-	-	-
activities gen funds	£m	-	-	-	-	-
investment income	£m	0.52	0.58	0.59	0.60	0.61
charitable activities	£m	-	-	-	-	-
other incoming	£m	-	-	-	-	~
TOTAL INCOME	£m	0.52	0.58	0.59	0.60	0.61
voluntary costs	£m	-	-	-	-	-
cost generating funds	£m	-	-	-	-	-
investment costs	£m	0.04	0.04	0.04	0.04	0.04
charitable exp	£m	0.08	0.08	0.07	0.08	0.08
grant expenditure	£m	0.34	0.37	0.64	0.80	0.49
governance	£m	0.01	0.01	0.01	0.01	0.01
other expenditure	£m	-	-	-	-	-
TOTAL EXPENDITURE	£m	0.46	0.50	0.76	0.93	0.62
gains revaluations	£m	0.65	(0.43)	1.42	1.47	0.30
NET INCREASE IN FUNDS	£m	0.71	(0.35)	1.25	1.14	0.28
land build oth fxd	£m	-	-	-	-	-
investments	£m	15.6	15.2	16.4	17.8	18.1
stock debtors cash	£m	0.21	0.18	0.53	0.38	0.35
liabilities	£m	0.39	0.27	0.55	0.72	0.68
pension liability	£m	-	-	-	-	-
TOTAL FUNDS	£m	15.5	15.1	16.4	17.5	17.8

INC 997 / £9.03m EXP 860 / £9.80m FUNDS 1235 / £15.9m
DOWNSIDE ABBEY GENERAL TRUST

AIMS: Any such charitable purpose or purposes approved by the Controller as in the opinion of the Trustees is or are conducive to the advancement or maintenance of the Roman Catholic religion. **GRANT MAKER:** No. **EXP ANALYSIS:** (31 Aug 14) Roman Catholics - 100%.

EXECUTIVES: S D Treloar. **EMPLOYEES:** 171 (172). **PAY:** £5.84m (£5.31m). **ADDRESS:** Downside Abbey, Stratton-on-the-Fosse, Radstock, Bath & North East Somerset, BA3 4RH. Tel: 01761 235 161. **INTERNET:** www.downside.co.uk. **CC NO:** 1158507.

AUDITORS: Old Mill Audit LLP, Wells; audit fee £15k, non-audit fee £4k. **LEGAL ADVISERS:** Stone King LLP, Bath. **INV MANAGERS:** BNY Mellon, London.

year ended 31 August		2010	2011	2012	2013	2014[13]
legacies	£m	-	-	-	-	-
other voluntary income	£m	0.77	0.38	0.54	0.78	0.62
activities gen funds	£m	0.32	0.41	0.43	0.36	0.27
investment income	£m	0.06	0.06	0.06	0.06	0.33
charitable activities	£m	7.72	8.18	8.30	7.74	7.45
other incoming	£m	0.07	~	0.01	0.01	0.36
TOTAL INCOME	£m	8.93	9.02	9.34	8.94	9.03
voluntary costs	£m	0.15	0.14	0.16	0.14	0.19
cost generating funds	£m	0.38	0.36	0.40	0.40	0.41
investment costs	£m	-	-	-	-	-
charitable exp	£m	7.51	7.42	7.81	8.13	9.15
grant expenditure	£m	-	-	-	-	-
governance	£m	0.04	0.04	0.04	0.04	0.05
other expenditure	£m	-	-	-	-	-
TOTAL EXPENDITURE	£m	8.08	7.95	8.41	8.71	9.80
gains revaluations	£m	0.20	0.15	0.30	2.99	0.84
NET INCREASE IN FUNDS	£m	1.04	1.22	1.22	3.21	0.07
land build oth fxd	£m	11.0	11.0	11.5	10.9	11.3
investments	£m	2.19	2.34	2.64	6.46	7.64
stock debtors cash	£m	4.47	5.14	5.05	4.76	3.61
liabilities	£m	7.49	7.13	6.57	6.29	6.65
pension liability	£m	-	-	-	-	-
TOTAL FUNDS	£m	10.2	11.4	12.6	15.8	15.9

DR EDWARDS & BISHOP KING'S FULHAM CHARITY

| **INC** | £0.45m | **EXP** | £0.44m | **FUNDS** | 1884 / £9.67m |

AIMS: Charitable help either generally or individually to people in need resident in the old Metropolitan Borough of Fulham. **GRANT MAKER:** No. **EXP ANALYSIS:** (31 Mar 15) Grantmaking to a variety of local charitable causes - 100%.

EXECUTIVES: J Martin (cs); Marianne Harper. **EMPLOYEES:** 3 (3). **PAY:** £0.06m (£0.12m). **ADDRESS:** Percy Barton House, 33-35 Dawes Road, London, SW6 7DT. Tel: 020 7386 9387. Fax: 020 7610 2856. **INTERNET:** www.debk.org.uk. **CC NO:** 1113490.

AUDITORS: Buzzacott LLP, London; audit fee £4k, non-audit fee £4k. **LEGAL ADVISERS:** Russell-Cooke, London.

year ended 31 March		2011	2012	2013	2014	2015
legacies	£m	-	-	-	-	-
other voluntary income	£m	-	-	-	-	-
activities gen funds	£m	-	-	-	-	-
investment income	£m	0.35	0.24	0.38	0.44	0.45
charitable activities	£m	-	-	-	-	-
other incoming	£m	-	-	-	-	-
TOTAL INCOME	£m	0.35	0.24	0.38	0.44	0.45
voluntary costs	£m	-	-	-	-	-
cost generating funds	£m	-	-	-	-	-
investment costs	£m	-	-	-	-	-
charitable exp	£m	0.02	0.02	0.02	0.04	0.09
grant expenditure	£m	0.31	0.32	0.29	0.36	0.33
governance	£m	0.01	0.01	0.02	0.02	0.02
other expenditure	£m	-	-	-	-	-
TOTAL EXPENDITURE	£m	0.35	0.36	0.33	0.42	0.44
gains revaluations	£m	0.05	(0.02)	0.64	0.23	0.37
NET INCREASE IN FUNDS	£m	0.06	(0.14)	0.69	0.25	0.39
land build oth fxd	£m	0.35	0.34	0.33	0.32	0.31
investments	£m	7.36	7.34	7.98	8.21	8.58
stock debtors cash	£m	0.81	0.73	0.79	0.86	0.84
liabilities	£m	0.03	0.06	0.05	0.10	0.06
pension liability	£m	-	-	-	-	-
TOTAL FUNDS	£m	8.49	8.35	9.04	9.28	9.67

DR MORTIMER AND THERESA SACKLER FOUNDATION

| **INC** | 962 / £9.34m | **EXP** | 782 / £10.9m | **FUNDS** | 809 / £26.3m |

AIMS: The advancement of education of the public in the UK and elsewhere in the fields of art, science and medical research. **GRANT MAKER:** Yes. **EXP ANALYSIS:** (31 Dec 14) Grantmaking to a wide variety of charitable causes - 100%.

EXECUTIVES: M D Sackler; Tiercel Services Limited (s). **ADDRESS:** New Zealand House, 9th Floor, 80 Haymarket, London, SW1Y 4TQ. Tel: 020 79304944. **CONST:** Company. **CC NO:** 1128926.

AUDITORS: Ernst & Young LLP, London; audit fee £1k. **LEGAL ADVISERS:** Christopher B Mitchell, London; Wiggin Osborne Fullerlove, Cheltenham.

year ended 31 December		2010	2011	2012	2013	2014
legacies	£m	-	-	-	-	-
other voluntary income	£m	16.6	15.2	8.51	28.6	8.67
activities gen funds	£m	-	-	-	-	-
investment income	£m	0.09	0.46	(0.08)	(0.36)	0.67
charitable activities	£m	-	-	-	-	-
other incoming	£m	-	-	-	-	-
TOTAL INCOME	£m	16.7	15.6	8.43	28.3	9.34
voluntary costs	£m	-	-	-	-	-
cost generating funds	£m	-	-	-	-	-
investment costs	£m	-	-	-	-	-
charitable exp	£m	-	-	-	-	-
grant expenditure	£m	6.87	12.6	25.9	7.26	10.9
governance	£m	~	~	0.01	0.03	0.02
other expenditure	£m	-	-	-	-	-
TOTAL EXPENDITURE	£m	6.87	12.6	25.9	7.28	10.9
gains revaluations	£m	-	-	(0.90)	(0.12)	1.07
NET INCREASE IN FUNDS	£m	9.83	2.98	(18.4)	20.9	(0.47)
land build oth fxd	£m	-	-	-	-	-
investments	£m	-	-	-	-	-
stock debtors cash	£m	28.2	36.3	32.7	44.0	41.9
liabilities	£m	6.85	12.0	26.8	17.2	15.6
pension liability	£m	-	-	-	-	-
TOTAL FUNDS	£m	21.3	24.3	5.91	26.8	26.3

DRAPERS' CHARITABLE FUND, THE

| **INC** | £2.05m | **EXP** | £1.73m | **FUNDS** | 434 / £49.4m |

ALTERNATIVE NAMES: D C F. **AIMS:** To support charitable causes at the trustees' discretion. **GRANT MAKER:** Yes. **EXP ANALYSIS:** (31 Jul 14) Grantmaking to a wide variety of charitable causes - 100%. **NO OF GRANTS:** 191 (208).

ADDRESS: Drapers' Hall, Throgmorton Avenue, London, EC2N 2DQ. Tel: 020 7588 5001. Fax: 020 7628 1988. **INTERNET:** www.thedrapers.co.uk. **FOUNDED:** 1959. **CONST:** Trust. **CC NO:** 251403.

AUDITORS: Saffery Champness, London; audit fee £2k.

year ended 31 July		2010	2011	2012	2013	2014
legacies	£m	-	-	-	-	-
other voluntary income	£m	5.45	0.47	8.02	0.69	0.99
activities gen funds	£m	-	-	-	-	-
investment income	£m	0.66	0.74	1.03	1.05	1.06
charitable activities	£m	-	-	-	-	-
other incoming	£m	-	1.00	1.00	-	-
TOTAL INCOME	£m	6.11	2.21	10.1	1.74	2.05
voluntary costs	£m	-	-	-	-	-
cost generating funds	£m	-	-	-	-	-
investment costs	£m	-	-	-	-	-
charitable exp	£m	0.07	0.09	0.07	0.07	0.06
grant expenditure	£m	0.86	0.97	1.47	1.33	1.65
governance	£m	0.02	0.03	0.05	0.03	0.02
other expenditure	£m	-	-	-	-	-
TOTAL EXPENDITURE	£m	0.96	1.09	1.59	1.42	1.73
gains revaluations	£m	2.29	3.11	0.28	3.75	2.08
NET INCREASE IN FUNDS	£m	7.44	4.23	8.75	4.07	2.39
land build oth fxd	£m	-	-	-	-	-
investments	£m	28.2	32.9	41.5	45.6	48.3
stock debtors cash	£m	1.79	1.37	1.53	1.49	1.14
liabilities	£m	0.03	0.09	0.13	0.09	0.09
pension liability	£m	-	-	-	-	-
TOTAL FUNDS	£m	29.9	34.2	42.9	47.0	49.4

DRAPERS' CHARITIES POOLING SCHEME, THE

| **INC** | 1980 / £3.85m | **EXP** | £1.97m | **FUNDS** | 271 / £80.9m |

AIMS: To provide two pooled investment funds which meet, as nearly as possible, the requirements of the various charities eligible to participate in the pools. **GRANT MAKER:** No. **EXP ANALYSIS:** (31 Jul 14) Services for philanthropic organisations general - 100%.

EXECUTIVES: A Mellows; R Winstanley. **ADDRESS:** Drapers' Hall, Throgmorton Avenue, London, EC2N 2DQ. Tel: 020 7588 5001. Fax: 020 7628 1988. **INTERNET:** www.thedrapers.co.uk. **FOUNDED:** 1997. **CONST:** Trust. **CC NO:** 1061675.

AUDITORS: Saffery Champness, London; audit fee £10k.

year ended 31 July		2010	2011	2012	2013	2014
legacies	£m	-	-	-	-	-
other voluntary income	£m	0.15	7.40	1.13	0.35	1.08
activities gen funds	£m	-	-	-	-	-
investment income	£m	1.59	1.87	2.46	2.68	2.77
charitable activities	£m	-	-	-	-	-
other incoming	£m	-	-	-	-	-
TOTAL INCOME	£m	1.74	9.27	3.59	3.03	3.85
voluntary costs	£m	-	-	-	-	-
cost generating funds	£m	-	-	-	-	-
investment costs	£m	0.30	0.24	0.22	0.21	0.21
charitable exp	£m	1.60	1.58	1.72	1.74	1.75
grant expenditure	£m	-	-	-	-	-
governance	£m	0.01	0.01	0.01	0.01	0.01
other expenditure	£m	-	-	-	-	-
TOTAL EXPENDITURE	£m	1.91	1.82	1.95	1.96	1.97
gains revaluations	£m	5.75	3.94	0.03	5.57	2.68
NET INCREASE IN FUNDS	£m	5.57	11.4	1.67	6.64	4.56
land build oth fxd	£m	-	-	-	-	-
investments	£m	56.4	66.8	67.9	73.9	77.6
stock debtors cash	£m	0.81	1.65	2.48	3.00	3.82
liabilities	£m	0.54	0.40	0.72	0.52	0.54
pension liability	£m	-	-	-	-	-
TOTAL FUNDS	£m	56.6	68.0	69.7	76.3	80.9

INC 1506 / £5.75m   EXP 1502 / £5.44m   FUNDS £0.95m

DRINKAWARE TRUST, THE

AIMS: The preservation, protection and promotion of public health through the provision of evidence based education programmes and research on alochol related matters. **GRANT MAKER:** No. **EXP ANALYSIS:** (31 Dec 14) Other education and training general - 100%.
EXECUTIVES: Elaine Hindal (ce); Vishal Goswami (cs). **EMPLOYEES:** 18 (16). **PAY:** £0.97m (£0.83m). **ADDRESS:** 3rd Floor, Salisbury House, London Wall, London, EC2M 5QQ. Tel: 020 7669 9900. Fax: 020 7504 8217. **INTERNET:** www.drinkaware.co.uk. **CC NO:** 1094586. **OSCR NO:** SC043163.

AUDITORS: Kingston Smith LLP, London; audit fee £11k, non-audit fee £1k.

year ended 31 December		2010	2011	2012	2013	2014
legacies	£m	-	-	-	-	-
other voluntary income	£m	5.16	5.25	5.01	5.10	5.55
activities gen funds	£m	-	-	-	-	-
investment income	£m	~	0.01	0.02	0.02	0.01
charitable activities	£m	0.13	0.07	0.05	0.05	0.06
other incoming	£m	~	0.06	0.02	0.01	0.13
TOTAL INCOME	£m	5.30	5.39	5.11	5.17	5.75
voluntary costs	£m	0.02	0.04	0.03	0.02	0.13
cost generating funds	£m	-	-	-	-	-
investment costs	£m	-	-	-	-	-
charitable exp	£m	5.33	5.04	4.66	4.97	5.21
grant expenditure	£m	-	-	-	-	-
governance	£m	0.14	0.11	0.16	0.26	0.10
other expenditure	£m	-	-	-	-	-
TOTAL EXPENDITURE	£m	5.49	5.19	4.85	5.25	5.44
gains revaluations	£m	-	-	-	-	-
NET INCREASE IN FUNDS	£m	(0.20)	0.20	0.26	(0.08)	0.31
land build oth fxd	£m	0.14	0.08	0.40	0.29	0.13
investments	£m	-	-	-	-	-
stock debtors cash	£m	0.96	0.91	1.72	1.85	2.21
liabilities	£m	0.84	0.53	1.40	1.50	1.38
pension liability	£m	-	-	-	-	-
TOTAL FUNDS	£m	0.26	0.46	0.72	0.64	0.95

INC 787 / £11.4m   EXP 748 / £11.3m   FUNDS £3.84m

DRIVE LIMITED

AIMS: To enable people with disabilities to have valued lives. **GRANT MAKER:** No. **EXP ANALYSIS:** (31 Mar 15) Care and training of people with mental disabilities - 100%.
EXECUTIVES: B Gallagher (ce & cs). **EMPLOYEES:** 452 (451). **PAY:** £9.31m (£9.19m). **ADDRESS:** Unit 8, Cefn Coed, Parc Nantgarw, Nantgarw, Cardiff, CF15 7QQ. Tel: 01443 224205. Fax: 01443 224105. **INTERNET:** www.driveltd.org.uk. **FOUNDED:** 1990. **CONST:** Company. **CO REG NO:** 2506147. **CC NO:** 703002.

AUDITORS: Broomfield & Alexander, Cardiff; audit fee £8k. **BANKERS:** Barclays. **LEGAL ADVISERS:** Hugh James, Cardiff; Passmores, Barry.

year ended 31 March		2011	2012	2013	2014	2015
legacies	£m	-	-	-	-	-
other voluntary income	£m	-	-	-	-	-
activities gen funds	£m	-	-	-	-	-
investment income	£m	~	0.02	0.01	0.01	0.02
charitable activities	£m	10.3	10.4	11.0	11.4	11.4
other incoming	£m	0.19	0.17	0.36	-	-
TOTAL INCOME	£m	10.5	10.6	11.3	11.4	11.4
voluntary costs	£m	-	-	-	-	-
cost generating funds	£m	-	-	-	-	-
investment costs	£m	-	-	-	-	-
charitable exp	£m	10.3	10.4	11.1	11.1	11.3
grant expenditure	£m	-	-	-	-	-
governance	£m	0.04	0.04	0.04	0.04	0.04
other expenditure	£m	-	-	-	-	-
TOTAL EXPENDITURE	£m	10.4	10.4	11.1	11.1	11.3
gains revaluations	£m	-	-	-	-	-
NET INCREASE IN FUNDS	£m	0.17	0.15	0.23	0.27	0.07
land build oth fxd	£m	1.23	1.23	1.29	1.31	1.27
investments	£m	-	-	-	-	-
stock debtors cash	£m	2.97	3.20	3.32	3.56	3.56
liabilities	£m	1.08	1.16	1.10	1.11	0.98
pension liability	£m	-	-	-	-	-
TOTAL FUNDS	£m	3.13	3.27	3.50	3.77	3.84

INC 1781 / £4.53m   EXP £2.69m   FUNDS £7.06m

DRUG SAFETY RESEARCH TRUST, THE

AIMS: To monitor, study and communicate the safety of medicines by providing education and training in pharmacovigilance and related subjects. **GRANT MAKER:** No. **EXP ANALYSIS:** (31 Dec 14) Drug addiction - 100%.
EXECUTIVES: Prof S A W Shakir. **EMPLOYEES:** 34 (37). **PAY:** £1.26m (£1.31m). **ADDRESS:** Bursledon Hall, Blundell Lane, Southampton, Hampshire, SO31 1AA. Tel: 023 8040 8600. Fax: 023 8040 8609. **INTERNET:** www.dsru.org. **FOUNDED:** 1986. **CONST:** Trust. **CC NO:** 327206.

AUDITORS: Cartwrights, Barnet; audit fee £11k. **BANKERS:** Lloyds Bank Corporate Markets. **LEGAL ADVISERS:** Paris Smith LLP, Southampton.

year ended 31 December		2010	2011	2012	2013	2014
legacies	£m	-	-	-	-	-
other voluntary income	£m	1.60	1.70	2.94	2.98	4.32
activities gen funds	£m	-	-	-	-	-
investment income	£m	0.05	0.04	0.06	0.05	0.07
charitable activities	£m	-	-	-	-	-
other incoming	£m	0.20	0.21	0.19	0.14	0.14
TOTAL INCOME	£m	1.86	1.95	3.19	3.17	4.53
voluntary costs	£m	-	-	-	-	-
cost generating funds	£m	-	-	-	-	-
investment costs	£m	0.01	0.01	0.01	0.01	0.01
charitable exp	£m	1.28	1.33	1.21	1.42	1.95
grant expenditure	£m	-	-	-	-	-
governance	£m	0.67	0.69	0.79	0.71	0.73
other expenditure	£m	-	-	-	-	-
TOTAL EXPENDITURE	£m	1.97	2.03	2.00	2.14	2.69
gains revaluations	£m	0.11	(0.09)	0.08	0.09	0.01
NET INCREASE IN FUNDS	£m	~	(0.17)	1.27	1.13	1.85
land build oth fxd	£m	0.74	0.73	0.70	0.66	0.67
investments	£m	1.66	1.39	1.50	1.62	1.71
stock debtors cash	£m	0.73	0.86	2.01	3.03	4.76
liabilities	£m	0.16	0.17	0.12	0.09	0.08
pension liability	£m	-	-	-	-	-
TOTAL FUNDS	£m	2.98	2.81	4.08	5.21	7.06

INC £3.42m   EXP £1.98m   FUNDS 365 / £59.1m

DUCHESNE TRUST

AIMS: To promote the charitable work carried out or supported by the members of the Roman Catholic Religious Order, the Society of the Sacred Heart. **GRANT MAKER:** No. **EXP ANALYSIS:** (31 Mar 15) Roman Catholics - 100%.
ADDRESS: Sacred Heart Provincial Admin, 9 Bute Gardens, Hammersmith, London, W6 7DR. Tel: 020 8741 4688. Fax: 020 8834 7380. **INTERNET:** www.societysacredheart.org.uk. **CC NO:** 288467.

AUDITORS: Haines Watts, Swindon; audit fee £6k.

NOTES: 31 December 2015 figures expressed in £ sterling from underlying accounts in Euros at the rate of £1 = 1.382 (2014 = 1.210; 2013 = 1.203; 2012 = 1.233; 2011 = 1.198).

year ended 31 March		2011[9]	2012	2013	2014	2015
legacies	£m	-	-	0.20	-	-
other voluntary income	£m	0.31	27.7	6.81	1.82	2.48
activities gen funds	£m	-	-	-	-	-
investment income	£m	0.24	1.08	1.39	1.58	0.92
charitable activities	£m	-	-	-	-	-
other incoming	£m	-	-	-	-	0.03
TOTAL INCOME	£m	0.56	28.8	8.40	3.40	3.42
voluntary costs	£m	-	-	-	-	-
cost generating funds	£m	-	-	-	-	-
investment costs	£m	-	-	-	-	-
charitable exp	£m	-	-	-	-	-
grant expenditure	£m	0.40	1.06	1.52	1.84	1.81
governance	£m	0.04	0.05	0.09	0.14	0.17
other expenditure	£m	-	-	-	-	-
TOTAL EXPENDITURE	£m	0.44	1.11	1.61	1.97	1.98
gains revaluations	£m	1.41	(1.44)	3.88	(0.61)	2.76
NET INCREASE IN FUNDS	£m	1.53	26.2	10.7	0.83	4.21
land build oth fxd	£m	-	-	-	-	-
investments	£m	15.7	42.6	53.9	51.8	60.5
stock debtors cash	£m	1.53	0.86	0.78	5.04	1.73
liabilities	£m	~	~	0.59	1.95	3.08
pension liability	£m	-	-	-	-	-
TOTAL FUNDS	£m	17.2	43.4	54.1	54.9	59.1

INC £0.38m   EXP £0.57m   FUNDS 1540 / £12.5m

DUCHY OF LANCASTER BENEVOLENT FUND

AIMS: Supports charitable causes in the County Palatine of Lancaster (Lancashire, Greater Manchester and Merseyside) and elsewhere in the country where the Duchy of Lancaster has historical links such as land interests and church livings). **GRANT MAKER:** Yes. **EXP ANALYSIS:** (31 Mar 15) Education, training and research general - 37.08%; Social services and relief general - 26.98%; Welfare of people with disabilities and their families - 21.51%; Religion general - 8.41%; Grantmaking to a wide variety of charitable causes - 6.02%.

ADDRESS: Duchy of Lancaster Office, 1 Lancaster Place, Strand, London, WC2E 7ED. Tel: 020 7269 1707. **CC NO:** 1026752.

year ended 31 March		2011	2012	2013	2014	2015
legacies	£m	-	-	-	-	-
other voluntary income	£m	-	-	-	-	-
activities gen funds	£m	-	-	-	-	-
investment income	£m	0.10	0.39	0.36	0.37	0.38
charitable activities	£m	-	-	-	-	-
other incoming	£m	-	-	-	-	-
TOTAL INCOME	£m	0.10	0.39	0.36	0.37	0.38
voluntary costs	£m	-	-	-	-	-
cost generating funds	£m	-	-	-	-	-
investment costs	£m	-	-	-	-	-
charitable exp	£m	0.02	0.02	0.02	0.02	0.02
grant expenditure	£m	0.38	0.36	0.37	0.39	0.54
governance	£m	0.01	0.01	0.01	0.02	0.01
other expenditure	£m	-	-	-	-	-
TOTAL EXPENDITURE	£m	0.40	0.38	0.40	0.42	0.57
gains revaluations	£m	0.47	0.09	1.17	(0.01)	0.97
NET INCREASE IN FUNDS	£m	0.17	0.10	1.14	(0.06)	0.78
land build oth fxd	£m	-	-	-	-	-
investments	£m	10.5	10.5	11.7	11.6	12.5
stock debtors cash	£m	~	0.12	0.11	0.08	0.19
liabilities	£m	0.03	~	0.02	0.01	0.19
pension liability	£m	-	-	-	-	-
TOTAL FUNDS	£m	10.5	10.6	11.7	11.7	12.5

INC £2.72m   EXP £0.24m   FUNDS 1129 / £17.8m

DUCHY OF LANCASTER JUBILEE TRUST, THE

AIMS: The maintenance and preservation of historical or architectural interest in the Duchy; to support the Queen's Chapel of the Savoy and other charitable purposes. **GRANT MAKER:** Yes. **EXP ANALYSIS:** (31 Mar 15) Welfare of the clergy - 100%.

EXECUTIVES: T Crow (s); M Hudson (ch). **ADDRESS:** Duchy of Lancaster, 1 Lancaster Place, London, WC2E 7ED. Tel: 020 7269 1707. **CONST:** Trust. **CC NO:** 1085881.

AUDITORS: Saffery Champness, London; audit fee £20k. **LEGAL ADVISERS:** Farrer & Co LLP, London. **INV MANAGERS:** Newton Investment Management, London.

year ended 31 March		2011	2012	2013	2014	2015
legacies	£m	-	-	-	-	-
other voluntary income	£m	-	-	1.25	0.84	2.47
activities gen funds	£m	-	-	-	-	-
investment income	£m	0.18	0.29	0.25	0.25	0.25
charitable activities	£m	-	-	-	-	-
other incoming	£m	-	-	-	-	-
TOTAL INCOME	£m	0.18	0.29	1.49	1.09	2.72
voluntary costs	£m	-	-	-	-	-
cost generating funds	£m	-	-	-	-	-
investment costs	£m	~	-	-	-	-
charitable exp	£m	-	-	-	-	-
grant expenditure	£m	0.17	0.28	0.24	0.24	0.23
governance	£m	-	~	~	~	~
other expenditure	£m	-	-	-	-	-
TOTAL EXPENDITURE	£m	0.17	0.28	0.24	0.25	0.24
gains revaluations	£m	0.27	(0.14)	1.30	0.26	1.17
NET INCREASE IN FUNDS	£m	0.28	(0.13)	2.55	1.11	3.66
land build oth fxd	£m	-	-	-	-	-
investments	£m	10.5	10.4	11.7	13.2	14.4
stock debtors cash	£m	0.10	0.10	1.35	0.95	3.41
liabilities	£m	-	~	~	~	~
pension liability	£m	-	-	-	-	-
TOTAL FUNDS	£m	10.6	10.5	13.0	14.1	17.8

INC 1721 / £4.79m   EXP 1904 / £3.93m   FUNDS £2.32m

DUDLEY AND WEST MIDLANDS ZOOLOGICAL SOCIETY LIMITED

ALTERNATIVE NAMES: Dudley Zoological Gardens. **AIMS:** The collection, preservation, care and exhibition of living animals and the promotion and advancement of the sciences of zoology, horticulture and botany. **GRANT MAKER:** No. **EXP ANALYSIS:** (31 Dec 14) Zoological research - 100%.

EXECUTIVES: P Suddock (ce). **EMPLOYEES:** 97 (94). **PAY:** £1.54m (£1.37m). **ADDRESS:** Castle Hill, Dudley, West Midlands, DY1 4QF. Tel: 0844 474 2272. Fax: 01384 456048. **INTERNET:** www.dudleyzoo.org.uk. **CONST:** Company. **CC NO:** 507221.

AUDITORS: RSM, Birmingham; audit fee £14k, non-audit fee £4k.

year ended 31 December		2010	2011	2012	2013	2014
legacies	£m	-	-	-	-	-
other voluntary income	£m	0.11	0.15	0.17	0.79	0.93
activities gen funds	£m	0.81	0.91	0.94	1.08	1.17
investment income	£m	0.01	0.01	0.01	0.06	0.06
charitable activities	£m	1.55	1.81	1.94	2.40	2.62
other incoming	£m	-	0.06	-	0.05	-
TOTAL INCOME	£m	2.48	2.93	3.05	4.39	4.79
voluntary costs	£m	-	-	-	-	-
cost generating funds	£m	0.54	0.59	0.64	0.79	0.91
investment costs	£m	-	-	-	-	-
charitable exp	£m	1.92	2.02	2.17	2.48	2.63
grant expenditure	£m	-	-	-	-	-
governance	£m	0.10	0.10	0.13	0.14	0.14
other expenditure	£m	-	0.09	0.05	0.51	0.26
TOTAL EXPENDITURE	£m	2.56	2.81	2.98	3.92	3.93
gains revaluations	£m	-	-	-	-	-
NET INCREASE IN FUNDS	£m	(0.08)	0.13	0.07	0.47	0.86
land build oth fxd	£m	1.03	1.02	1.37	1.54	2.60
investments	£m	-	-	-	-	-
stock debtors cash	£m	0.36	0.62	0.44	0.83	0.85
liabilities	£m	0.60	0.72	0.82	0.90	1.13
pension liability	£m	-	-	-	-	-
TOTAL FUNDS	£m	0.79	0.92	0.99	1.46	2.32

INC £0.22m   EXP £0.32m   FUNDS 1494 / £12.9m

DUKE OF DEVONSHIRE'S CHARITABLE TRUST

AIMS: General charitable purposes at the Trustees' discretion including medicine, religion, hospices, housing associations, and libraries. **GRANT MAKER:** Yes. **EXP ANALYSIS:** (05 Apr 15) Grantmaking to a wide variety of charitable causes - 100%.

ADDRESS: 30 Queen Anne Street 21 Buckingham Gate, London, W1G 9HY. Tel: 01246 565437. **INTERNET:** ddct.org.uk. **CONST:** Trust. **CC NO:** 213519.

AUDITORS: Saffery Champness, London; audit fee £2k. **LEGAL ADVISERS:** Currey & Co, London. **INV MANAGERS:** Smith & Williamson, London.

year ended 5 April		2011	2012	2013	2014	2015
legacies	£m	-	-	-	-	-
other voluntary income	£m	0.03	-	-	-	-
activities gen funds	£m	-	-	-	-	-
investment income	£m	0.21	0.24	0.24	0.25	0.22
charitable activities	£m	-	-	-	-	-
other incoming	£m	-	-	-	-	-
TOTAL INCOME	£m	0.24	0.24	0.24	0.25	0.22
voluntary costs	£m	-	-	-	-	-
cost generating funds	£m	-	-	-	-	-
investment costs	£m	-	-	-	-	-
charitable exp	£m	-	-	-	-	-
grant expenditure	£m	2.20	0.16	1.20	0.23	0.31
governance	£m	0.01	0.01	0.01	0.01	0.01
other expenditure	£m	-	-	-	-	-
TOTAL EXPENDITURE	£m	2.21	0.17	1.21	0.24	0.32
gains revaluations	£m	0.77	(0.05)	1.03	0.46	1.19
NET INCREASE IN FUNDS	£m	(1.21)	0.02	0.06	0.46	1.09
land build oth fxd	£m	-	-	-	-	-
investments	£m	11.2	11.2	11.2	11.6	12.8
stock debtors cash	£m	0.09	0.17	0.21	0.21	0.12
liabilities	£m	~	0.01	0.01	~	0.01
pension liability	£m	-	-	-	-	-
TOTAL FUNDS	£m	11.3	11.3	11.4	11.8	12.9

INC 1760 / £4.62m EXP 1692 / £4.69m FUNDS 1363 / £14.3m
DUKE OF EDINBURGH'S AWARD INTERNATIONAL FOUNDATION, THE

AIMS: To provide or assist in the provision of facilities for recreation or other voluntary time occupation in the interests of social welfare for young people anywhere in the world. **GRANT MAKER:** No. **EXP ANALYSIS:** (31 Mar 15) International welfare of the young - 100%.

EXECUTIVES: John May (s). **EMPLOYEES:** 38 (34). **PAY:** £2.06m (£1.80m). **ADDRESS:** Award House, 7-11 St Matthew Street, London, SW1P 2JT. Tel: 020 7222 4242. Fax: 020 7222 4141. **INTERNET:** www.intaward.org. **CC NO:** 1072453.

AUDITORS: PricewaterhouseCoopers LLP, London; audit fee £25k.

year ended 31 March		2011	2012	2013	2014	2015
legacies	£m	-	-	-	-	-
other voluntary income	£m	2.77	2.26	2.90	2.43	3.27
activities gen funds	£m	0.73	0.28	0.41	0.96	1.35
investment income	£m	0.38	0.36	0.12	0.08	~
charitable activities	£m	-	-	-	-	-
other incoming	£m	-	-	-	-	-
TOTAL INCOME	£m	3.87	2.89	3.43	3.46	4.62
voluntary costs	£m	1.26	0.87	1.01	1.35	1.25
cost generating funds	£m	-	-	-	-	-
investment costs	£m	0.09	0.08	0.01	-	-
charitable exp	£m	2.45	2.62	3.37	3.16	3.28
grant expenditure	£m	-	-	-	-	-
governance	£m	0.24	0.29	0.26	0.20	0.19
other expenditure	£m	-	-	-	0.75	(0.03)
TOTAL EXPENDITURE	£m	4.05	3.86	4.65	5.46	4.69
gains revaluations	£m	0.75	(0.31)	0.47	0.19	1.19
NET INCREASE IN FUNDS	£m	0.58	(1.28)	(0.74)	(1.81)	1.12
land build oth fxd	£m	0.33	0.40	0.35	0.42	0.39
investments	£m	16.1	14.1	13.4	12.1	12.9
stock debtors cash	£m	1.06	1.74	1.66	1.75	1.49
liabilities	£m	0.46	0.50	0.42	1.08	0.43
pension liability	£m	-	-	-	-	-
TOTAL FUNDS	£m	17.1	15.8	15.0	13.2	14.3

INC 778 / £11.5m EXP 733 / £11.5m FUNDS 1285 / £15.3m
DUKE OF EDINBURGH'S AWARD, THE

AIMS: To establish and administer a scheme of awards for young people in the United Kingdom and elsewhere and thereby, through the development of their character, to promote good citizenship for the public benefit. **GRANT MAKER:** No. **EXP ANALYSIS:** (31 Mar 15) Youth recreational organisations - 100%.

EXECUTIVES: P Westgarth (ce); Jacqui Larcombe (dfr); G Jenkins (df). **EMPLOYEES:** 160 (139). **PAY:** £6.38m (£5.74m). **ADDRESS:** Gulliver House, Madeira Walk, Windsor, Berkshire, SL4 1EU. Tel: 01753 727450. Fax: 01753 810666. **INTERNET:** www.dofe.org. **CC NO:** 1072490. **OSCR NO:** SC038254.

AUDITORS: PricewaterhouseCoopers LLP, London; audit fee £46k, non-audit fee £43k.

year ended 31 March		2011	2012	2013	2014	2015
legacies	£m	-	-	-	-	-
other voluntary income	£m	3.33	4.57	3.57	3.80	3.78
activities gen funds	£m	4.95	4.90	5.55	6.46	7.33
investment income	£m	0.24	0.20	0.06	0.01	0.02
charitable activities	£m	0.39	0.38	0.48	0.45	0.39
other incoming	£m	-	-	-	-	-
TOTAL INCOME	£m	8.90	10.0	9.66	10.7	11.5
voluntary costs	£m	1.47	0.95	1.41	1.39	1.93
cost generating funds	£m	0.94	0.98	0.82	1.04	1.02
investment costs	£m	0.05	0.04	~	-	~
charitable exp	£m	6.24	6.63	6.25	7.62	8.39
grant expenditure	£m	-	-	-	-	-
governance	£m	0.69	0.24	0.26	0.28	0.31
other expenditure	£m	-	-	-	2.37	(0.13)
TOTAL EXPENDITURE	£m	9.38	8.84	8.74	12.7	11.5
gains revaluations	£m	0.36	(0.22)	0.44	0.19	1.54
NET INCREASE IN FUNDS	£m	(0.12)	0.99	1.36	(1.80)	1.56
land build oth fxd	£m	2.38	2.09	2.07	3.89	4.61
investments	£m	9.13	8.94	11.8	10.6	9.06
stock debtors cash	£m	2.82	4.24	2.54	2.89	3.13
liabilities	£m	1.14	1.09	0.92	3.60	1.49
pension liability	£m	-	-	*	-	-
TOTAL FUNDS	£m	13.2	14.2	15.5	13.7	15.3

INC £3.65m EXP £3.46m FUNDS 230 / £91.4m
DULVERTON TRUST, THE

AIMS: To support charitable causes concerned with youth and education, conservation and general welfare, religion, industrial relations, peace and security and preservation. **GRANT MAKER:** Yes.

EXECUTIVES: A Stafford (ce); Karon Cook (df); Anna De Pulford; Kate Wilson. **EMPLOYEES:** 3 (4). **PAY:** £0.23m (£0.22m). **ADDRESS:** 5 St James's Place, London, SW1A 1NP. Tel: 020 7495 7852. Fax: 020 7495 6201. **INTERNET:** www.dulverton.org. **CC NO:** 1146484.

AUDITORS: Smith & Williamson, London; audit fee £8k. **LEGAL ADVISERS:** Farrer & Co LLP, London; Freeths LLP (Trading as Henmans Freeth), Oxford; Wrigleys Solicitors LLP, Leeds.

year ended 31 March		2011	2012	2013	2014	2015
legacies	£m	-	-	-	-	-
other voluntary income	£m	-	-	-	-	-
activities gen funds	£m	-	-	-	-	-
investment income	£m	2.58	3.24	3.21	3.54	3.65
charitable activities	£m	-	-	-	-	-
other incoming	£m	-	-	-	-	-
TOTAL INCOME	£m	2.58	3.24	3.21	3.54	3.65
voluntary costs	£m	-	-	-	-	-
cost generating funds	£m	-	-	-	-	-
investment costs	£m	(0.01)	0.52	0.53	0.67	0.60
charitable exp	£m	0.36	0.33	0.33	0.31	0.34
grant expenditure	£m	2.80	3.49	2.83	3.05	2.48
governance	£m	0.03	0.05	0.05	0.03	0.04
other expenditure	£m	-	-	-	-	-
TOTAL EXPENDITURE	£m	3.17	4.38	3.73	4.06	3.46
gains revaluations	£m	2.14	3.28	8.95	2.34	2.83
NET INCREASE IN FUNDS	£m	1.55	2.14	8.43	1.82	3.03
land build oth fxd	£m	2.17	7.13	7.13	8.12	8.11
investments	£m	73.6	71.9	81.0	81.1	84.4
stock debtors cash	£m	1.00	0.94	0.34	1.35	0.70
liabilities	£m	0.80	1.83	1.92	2.17	1.82
pension liability	£m	-	-	-	-	-
TOTAL FUNDS	£m	76.0	78.2	86.6	88.4	91.4

INC 917 / £9.69m EXP 529 / £15.4m FUNDS 64 / £263m
DULWICH ESTATE, THE

AIMS: Management of lands and estate to generate funds for the benefit of education and the poor. **GRANT MAKER:** Yes. **EXP ANALYSIS:** (31 Mar 15) Social services and relief general - 100%.

EXECUTIVES: H Bratter; J E Major (ce). **EMPLOYEES:** 26 (25). **PAY:** £1.35m (£1.22m). **ADDRESS:** The Old College, Gallery Road, Dulwich Village, London, SE21 7AE. Tel: 020 8299 1000. Fax: 020 8693 2456. **INTERNET:** www.thedulwichestate.org.uk. **FOUNDED:** 1619. **CONST:** Trust. **CC NO:** 312751.

AUDITORS: BDO LLP, London; audit fee £24k. **LEGAL ADVISERS:** Charles Russell Speechlys LLP, London; Reed Smith, London; Thackray Williams LLP, Bromley; Wilsons Solicitors LLP, London. **INV MANAGERS:** Sarasin & Partners LLP, London.

year ended 31 March		2011	2012	2013	2014	2015
legacies	£m	-	-	-	-	-
other voluntary income	£m	-	-	-	-	-
activities gen funds	£m	0.28	0.25	0.13	0.20	0.22
investment income	£m	8.83	8.98	9.37	9.77	9.47
charitable activities	£m	-	-	-	-	-
other incoming	£m	-	-	-	-	-
TOTAL INCOME	£m	9.11	9.24	9.49	10.0	9.69
voluntary costs	£m	-	-	-	-	-
cost generating funds	£m	0.24	0.21	0.21	0.20	0.21
investment costs	£m	2.90	2.61	2.68	3.35	3.39
charitable exp	£m	-	-	-	-	-
grant expenditure	£m	5.65	15.9	11.0	6.26	11.8
governance	£m	0.07	0.07	0.09	0.08	0.08
other expenditure	£m	-	-	-	-	-
TOTAL EXPENDITURE	£m	8.86	18.8	13.9	9.89	15.4
gains revaluations	£m	10.6	3.99	18.8	10.9	32.4
NET INCREASE IN FUNDS	£m	10.9	(5.61)	14.4	11.0	26.6
land build oth fxd	£m	156	154	162	166	182
investments	£m	55.3	53.2	60.6	62.7	73.7
stock debtors cash	£m	8.14	7.12	6.34	10.9	10.7
liabilities	£m	4.54	4.17	4.95	4.43	4.95
pension liability	£m	(0.86)	(0.81)	(0.70)	(0.55)	(0.58)
TOTAL FUNDS	£m	216	211	225	236	263

INC £3.33m | EXP 1790 / £4.36m | FUNDS 836 / £25.5m

DULWICH PICTURE GALLERY

GRANT MAKER: No. **EXP ANALYSIS:** (31 Mar 15) Art and art galleries - 100%.

TRADING OUTLETS: 1.

EXECUTIVES: Ian Dejardin; Lily Harriss; James Murly-Gotto; Radhika Radhakrishnan (cha). **EMPLOYEES:** 80 (70). **PAY:** £1.85m (£1.55m). **ADDRESS:** Gallery Road, London, SE21 7AD. Tel: 020 8693 5254. Fax: 020 8299 8700. **INTERNET:** www.dulwichpicturegallery.org.uk. **FOUNDED:** 1811. **CONST:** Trust. **CC NO:** 1040942.

AUDITORS: BDO LLP, Norwich; audit fee £7k. **BANKERS:** Barclays. **LEGAL ADVISERS:** Farrer & Co LLP, London; Michelmores, Exeter. **INV MANAGERS:** Rathbone Investment Management, London.

year ended 31 March		2011	2012	2013	2014	2015
legacies	£m	1.84	-	-	0.09	0.02
other voluntary income	£m	3.27	3.22	2.45	2.59	1.24
activities gen funds	£m	0.50	0.48	0.31	0.46	0.66
investment income	£m	0.48	0.61	0.65	0.58	0.68
charitable activities	£m	0.65	0.66	0.47	0.91	0.72
other incoming	£m	-	-	-	-	-
TOTAL INCOME	£m	6.73	4.97	3.87	4.62	3.33
voluntary costs	£m	0.37	0.43	0.38	0.33	0.32
cost generating funds	£m	0.31	0.33	0.23	0.30	0.35
investment costs	£m	0.03	0.04	0.07	0.07	0.09
charitable exp	£m	2.78	3.50	2.85	2.61	3.18
grant expenditure	£m	-	-	-	-	-
governance	£m	0.05	0.04	0.06	0.06	0.11
other expenditure	£m	-	-	-	-	0.30
TOTAL EXPENDITURE	£m	3.53	4.34	3.59	3.38	4.36
gains revaluations	£m	1.41	(0.53)	0.91	(0.18)	1.71
NET INCREASE IN FUNDS	£m	4.61	0.10	1.19	1.07	0.68
land build oth fxd	£m	2.96	3.08	3.06	3.06	2.91
investments	£m	17.9	18.6	18.7	22.3	23.3
stock debtors cash	£m	2.45	1.83	3.05	0.56	0.83
liabilities	£m	0.61	0.60	0.63	0.55	1.51
pension liability	£m	0.21	0.38	0.40	0.53	-
TOTAL FUNDS	£m	22.4	22.5	23.7	24.8	25.5

INC 1755 / £4.63m | EXP £2.17m | FUNDS 855 / £24.8m

DUNARD FUND

GRANT MAKER: Yes. **EXP ANALYSIS:** (31 Mar 15) Dance, music and opera - 86.37%; Culture and arts general - 8.59%; Environment general - 5.04%. **NO OF GRANTS:** 20 (34).

EXECUTIVES: Carol C Grigor. **ADDRESS:** 4 Royal Terrace, Edinburgh, EH7 5AB. Tel: 0131 556 4043. **FOUNDED:** 1986. **DOMICILE:** Scotland. **CONST:** Trust. **OSCR NO:** SC039685.

AUDITORS: Grant Thornton UK LLP, Edinburgh; audit fee £3k. **BANKERS:** Adam & Co. **LEGAL ADVISERS:** J & H Mitchell, Pitlochry.

year ended 31 March		2011	2012	2013	2014	2015[11]
legacies	£m	-	-	-	-	-
other voluntary income	£m	1.00	2.20	3.50	18.5	4.50
activities gen funds	£m	-	-	-	-	-
investment income	£m	0.04	0.07	0.11	0.08	0.13
charitable activities	£m	-	-	-	-	-
other incoming	£m	-	-	-	-	-
TOTAL INCOME	£m	1.04	2.27	3.61	18.6	4.63
voluntary costs	£m	-	-	-	-	-
cost generating funds	£m	-	-	-	-	-
investment costs	£m	-	-	-	-	-
charitable exp	£m	-	~	~	~	0.03
grant expenditure	£m	1.44	2.42	1.99	2.59	2.13
governance	£m	0.01	0.01	0.01	0.01	0.01
other expenditure	£m	-	-	-	-	-
TOTAL EXPENDITURE	£m	1.45	2.44	2.00	2.60	2.17
gains revaluations	£m	(0.07)	-	-	-	-
NET INCREASE IN FUNDS	£m	(0.48)	(0.17)	1.61	16.0	2.47
land build oth fxd	£m	0.29	0.29	0.29	0.49	0.49
investments	£m	-	0.30	0.30	0.05	-
stock debtors cash	£m	5.56	6.60	7.15	23.1	25.7
liabilities	£m	0.95	2.47	1.40	1.35	1.40
pension liability	£m	-	-	-	-	-
TOTAL FUNDS	£m	4.89	4.72	6.34	22.3	24.8

INC 1751 / £4.65m | EXP 1672 / £4.79m | FUNDS £3.24m

DUNDEE REPERTORY THEATRE LTD

ALTERNATIVE NAMES: Dundee REP. **AIMS:** Repertory productions of contemporary local work and work from the classical repertoire in translation. **GRANT MAKER:** No. **EXP ANALYSIS:** (31 Mar 15) Drama and theatre - 100%.

TRADING SUBS: Dundee Repertory Theatre Trading Limited.

EXECUTIVES: Nicholas Parr (ce). **EMPLOYEES:** 126 (118). **PAY:** £2.22m (£2.16m). **ADDRESS:** Tay Square, Dundee, DD1 1PB. Tel: 01382 227684. Fax: 01382 228609. **INTERNET:** www.dundeereptheatre.co.uk. **DOMICILE:** Scotland. **CONST:** Company. **CO REG NO:** SC 021201. **OSCR NO:** SC017315.

AUDITORS: Henderson Loggie, Dundee; audit fee £9k. **LEGAL ADVISERS:** Blackadders, Dundee.

year ended 31 March		2011	2012	2013	2014	2015
legacies	£m	-	-	-	-	-
other voluntary income	£m	2.61	0.12	0.11	0.15	0.13
activities gen funds	£m	1.04	0.42	0.32	0.41	0.43
investment income	£m	~	-	~	-	-
charitable activities	£m	0.92	3.29	3.44	3.81	4.08
other incoming	£m	-	-	-	-	-
TOTAL INCOME	£m	4.57	3.83	3.88	4.37	4.65
voluntary costs	£m	0.02	0.04	0.07	0.07	0.05
cost generating funds	£m	1.22	0.40	0.33	0.35	0.38
investment costs	£m	-	-	-	-	-
charitable exp	£m	3.67	3.56	3.67	4.03	4.30
grant expenditure	£m	-	-	-	-	-
governance	£m	0.04	0.04	0.03	0.03	0.05
other expenditure	£m	-	-	-	-	-
TOTAL EXPENDITURE	£m	4.95	4.03	4.09	4.48	4.79
gains revaluations	£m	-	-	-	-	-
NET INCREASE IN FUNDS	£m	(0.38)	(0.20)	(0.22)	(0.11)	(0.13)
land build oth fxd	£m	4.00	3.84	3.68	3.54	3.35
investments	£m	-	-	-	-	-
stock debtors cash	£m	0.40	0.30	0.20	0.56	0.68
liabilities	£m	0.51	0.44	0.40	0.72	0.78
pension liability	£m	-	-	-	-	-
TOTAL FUNDS	£m	3.89	3.70	3.48	3.38	3.24

INC 1364 / £6.46m | EXP 1194 / £7.13m | FUNDS £(11.4)m

DUNDEE STUDENT VILLAGES

AIMS: To develop new housing accommodation and amenities and better managing of the existing accommodation facilities of the University of Dundee. **GRANT MAKER:** No. **EXP ANALYSIS:** (31 Jul 14) Student accommodation and welfare - 100%.

EXECUTIVES: Chiene & Tait (s). **ADDRESS:** 61 Dublin Street, Edinburgh, EH3 6NL. **DOMICILE:** Scotland. **CONST:** Company. **CO REG NO:** SC 245981. **OSCR NO:** SC035072.

AUDITORS: Grant Thornton UK LLP, Glasgow; audit fee £20k. **BANKERS:** Bank of Scotland Corporate.

year ended 31 July		2010	2011	2012	2013	2014
legacies	£m	-	-	-	-	-
other voluntary income	£m	-	-	-	-	-
activities gen funds	£m	1.23	0.99	0.94	0.97	1.09
investment income	£m	0.17	0.19	0.22	0.27	0.33
charitable activities	£m	4.49	4.43	4.63	5.07	5.03
other incoming	£m	-	-	-	-	-
TOTAL INCOME	£m	5.89	5.60	5.79	6.31	6.46
voluntary costs	£m	-	-	-	-	-
cost generating funds	£m	1.19	0.80	0.90	0.88	0.99
investment costs	£m	-	-	-	-	-
charitable exp	£m	6.54	6.26	5.52	5.65	6.02
grant expenditure	£m	-	-	-	-	-
governance	£m	0.07	0.12	0.10	0.08	0.12
other expenditure	£m	-	-	-	-	-
TOTAL EXPENDITURE	£m	7.80	7.19	6.52	6.62	7.13
gains revaluations	£m	-	-	-	-	-
NET INCREASE IN FUNDS	£m	(1.91)	(1.59)	(0.73)	(0.31)	(0.67)
land build oth fxd	£m	44.6	43.0	41.3	40.0	38.3
investments	£m	-	-	-	-	-
stock debtors cash	£m	4.95	4.91	5.15	6.50	8.23
liabilities	£m	57.7	57.6	56.9	57.3	57.9
pension liability	£m	-	-	-	-	-
TOTAL FUNDS	£m	(8.14)	(9.73)	(10.5)	(10.8)	(11.4)